*The* HELLENISTIC WORLD
*and the Coming of* ROME

VOLUME II

*The*
# HELLENISTIC
## WORLD *and*

Erich S. Gruen

*the Coming of* ROME
VOLUME · II

UNIVERSITY OF CALIFORNIA PRESS

*Berkeley   Los Angeles   London*

University of California Press
Berkeley and Los Angeles, California
University of California Press, Ltd.
London, England
© 1984 by
The Regents of the University of California
Printed in the United States of America
1  2  3  4  5  6  7  8  9

Library of Congress Cataloging in Publication Data

Gruen, Erich S.
  The Hellenistic world and the coming of Rome.

  Bibliography: p.
  Includes index.
    1. Rome—History—Republic, 265–30 B.C.
2. Greece—History—281–146 B.C.   3. Hellenism.
4. Imperialism.   I. Title.
DG241.2.G78   1984      937'.02      82–8581
ISBN 0–520–04569–6 (2 vols.)      AACR2

# Contents

· *Part* III ·

# The Patterns of Behavior

# Chapter 11

# Rome, Macedonia, and Illyria (I)

Rome crossed the Adriatic in arms for the first time in 229 B.C. Polybius declared the event a milestone: no mere sidelight but central for comprehending the rise and march of Roman rule.[1] Central, to be sure, for Polybius' own conception, as he affirms. In retrospect, this initial expedition seemed crucial, generating the long series of campaigns that ultimately brought Hellas under Roman sway. The Dalmatian coast and northwest Greece could serve as a foothold and a staging-ground for Rome's armed might in the East. Roman involvement with Illyria later gave way to conflict with her greater neighbor, the kingdom of Macedonia. Contests and interchange with Illyria and Macedonia brought the Republic ever increasingly to the fore in the eyes of Hellenes. Interventions in the third century climaxed in domination during the second. The process seemed single-minded—from the perspective of one writing at its conclusion. More careful scrutiny affords a different perspective. The course of Rome's relations with Illyria and Macedonia followed an unsteady and broken path. It needs to be charted with some care.

## The Crossing of the Adriatic

Rome's first venture against Illyria came with stunning force. Both consuls of 229 were dispatched by the senate, heading an armada

1. Polyb. 2.2.1–2: κατὰ δὲ τοὺς καιροὺς τούτους Ῥωμαῖοι τὴν πρώτην διάβασιν εἰς τὴν Ἰλλυρίδα καὶ ταῦτα τὰ μέρη τῆς Εὐρώπης ἐπεβάλοντο ποιεῖσθαι μετὰ δυνάμεως · ἅπερ οὐ παρέργως, ἀλλὰ μετ' ἐπιστάσεως θεωρητέον τοῖς βουλομένοις ἀληθινῶς τήν τε πρόθεσιν τὴν ἡμετέραν συνθεάσασθαι καὶ τὴν αὔξησιν καὶ κατασκευὴν τῆς Ῥωμαίων δυναστείας.

of two hundred ships, an infantry that numbered twenty thousand, and a cavalry of two thousand.[2] The figures are suspiciously proportional, but the enormity of the expedition need not be doubted. It made short work of the First Illyrian War. A single campaigning season, or rather less, sufficed to overawe resistance and force capitulation.[3] Clearly a formidable display of power against what proved to be a feeble foe: but why?

Our sources conflict. Polybius refers to Illyrian marauders long in the habit of harassing traders from Italy. Rome was wont to ignore complaints against them. When Illyrians took Phoenice in 230, however, some of their corsairs conducted especially frightful raids, plundering, murdering, or taking captive numerous merchantmen. The senate at last took action: two envoys went to the Illyrian queen Teuta, now investing Issa, and registered their outrage. The interview degenerated into harsh exchanges, and Teuta arranged the murder of one of the envoys on his trip home. That provocation spurred Rome to mobilize.[4] Appian, writing nearly four centuries later, undertook inquiries and researched the matter, but professed himself unable to explain origins or motives with precision.[5] In his version the principal aggressor is Agron, king of the Illyrians, engaged in imperial expansion from Corcyra to Pharus. Rome answered an appeal from the island of Issa, presently under threat from Agron. But her envoys never got there. They were attacked en route by Illyrian vessels and one of them killed, together with an Issaean ambassador. Rome thereupon undertook military intervention against Agron's wife Teuta, Agron having died in the interim.[6] The account of Dio-Zonaras combines elements of both versions, with further complications. The people of Issa, in conflict with Agron, freely put themselves under Roman authority. For Rome this was a convenient opportunity not only to take up the cause of the Issaeans but to complain of offenses committed against ships sailing from Brundisium. Senatorial representatives arrived in Issa to find Agron already dead and Teuta in charge. The volatile queen imprisoned some envoys and executed others, thus prompting Roman retaliation. Out of fear, she repented and disclaimed responsibility, but she would accept no terms and the Romans proceeded with force.[7] The Latin tradition—what remains of

---

2. Polyb. 2.11.1, 2.11.7.

3. Surrender and a treaty came early the next spring: Polyb. 2.12.3.

4. Polyb. 2.8.

5. Appian, *Ill.* 6: ὅπως δὲ αὐτοὺς [the Illyrians] ὑπηγάγοντο Ῥωμαῖοι, ὡμολό-γησα μὲν . . . οὐκ εὑρεῖν τὰς ἀκριβεῖς τῶν πολέμων ἀρχάς τε καὶ προφάσεις.

6. Appian, *Ill.* 7.

7. Dio, 12.49 = Zon. 8.19.

it—stresses the murder of Roman envoys and the recklessness of Teuta, hence a justifiable reaction from Rome.[8]

In this welter of discordant testimony, how best to assess motives? *Ex eventu* justifications plague the tradition. To lay blame on Teuta is insufficient. The portrait of the explosive, unreasoning woman who yielded to her emotions and threw a female tantrum is plainly rhetorical, exaggerated for literary effect.[9] As for the murder of a Roman envoy, that tale is supplied in various irreconcilable versions: one or more ambassadors killed, either before reaching Issa or while there or after departure.[10] Clearly, the story lacked firm basis. That a member of the mission perished before returning home may well be true. The imputation of responsibility to Teuta, however, is transparent invention after the fact.[11] The alleged appeal from Issa stands on no firmer ground. Polybius has not a hint of it. Appian makes the Issaeans ask for Roman aid; Dio has them perform an act of *deditio*. The muddle has been explained in sharply contrasting ways, depending on one's view of the facts: either Polybius' silence derives from Fabius Pictor, who omitted an episode that might suggest unwarranted intervention by Rome, or "annalistic" sources invented the appeal to help justify intervention.[12] A simpler solution is at hand. Roman envoys went to Issa to deliver their complaint for an obvious reason: the Illyrian ruler happened to be there at the time, conducting a siege of

8. Florus, 1.21; Orosius, 4.13.1–2; Livy, *Per.* 20.

9. Polyb. 2.8.7–12: ἡ δὲ γυναικοθύμως κἀλογίστως δεξαμένη τὴν παρρησίαν; Dio, 12.49.3–7; Zon. 8.19; Florus, 1.21; cf. G. Walser, *Historia* 2 (1954): 311; Petzold, *Historia* 20 (1971): 204. Holleaux, *Rome, la Grèce*, 100–101, takes the Polybian portrait at face value.

10. Polyb. 2.8.12: one envoy killed after setting sail from Issa; cf. Livy, *Per.* 20. Dio, 12.49.3 = Zon. 8.19: several envoys killed and imprisoned in Issa. Appian, *Ill.* 7: one Roman and one Issaean killed before reaching Issa. Florus, 1.21: several envoys and ship captains axed and burned in Issa; cf. Orosius, 4.13.1–2. Pliny, *NH*, 34.24: two Romans killed on Teuta's orders.

11. Derow, *Phoenix* 27 (1973): 127–128, argues for the historicity of Appian's account partly on the ground that he includes a circumstantial detail omitted by all others: murder of the Issaean representative Cleemporus, a name known—from one other example—to be in use among Illyrians. The detail may be accurate. But it hardly follows that Illyrians did murder the envoys (what reason did they have for it?), let alone that this murder determined Rome on war.

12. For the first view, see Gelzer, *Kleine Schriften*, 3, 67–68; Walser, *Historia* 2 (1954): 317–318; Petzold, *Historia* 20 (1971): 222–223. A variation in Derow, *Phoenix* 27 (1973): 128–132, who has Polybius follow an account deriving from Roman ambassadors to Greece in 228, who allegedly suppressed the appeal from Issa as superfluous or damaging. For the second view, see Holleaux, *Rome, la Grèce*, 23, n. 6; Walbank, *Commentary* I: 159; Hammond, *JRS* 58 (1968): 5, n. 16; Harris, *War and Imperialism*, 195–196, n. 4; adumbrated already by G. Zippel, *Die römische Herrschaft in Illyrien bis auf Augustus* (Leipzig, 1877), 47–50.

the island. Nothing more is implied by Polybius and nothing more needed. Later sources misread the circumstances and assumed that Rome had come at the request of Issa.[13]

The grievances of Italian merchants offer a better alternative. Yet they cannot tell the whole story. Rome had paid them no heed in the past, says Polybius, despite depredations by Illyrian marauders.[14] It is quite implausible that stepped-up terrorism by a few Illyrians who detached themselves from the main body at Phoenice would suddenly prod Rome into action.[15] What then accounts for the *volte-face*? An imperialist endeavor, as many have regarded it, a deliberate effort to establish Roman control across the Adriatic?[16] Fear of Illyrian power, whether legitimate fear or one based on misapprehension?[17] Concern about the even greater power looming behind Illyria, the kingdom of Macedonia?[18] Or were more direct and immediate concerns behind the senate's decision?

Maritime trade between the cities of Magna Graecia and the mainland of Greece had a long history by this date. Hellenic towns on the Ionian Gulf and across the straits of Otranto played a central role in the commerce. Their location guaranteed it. That Rome had a direct stake in these enterprises is unattested and unlikely. But she was certainly aware of them. The extension of Roman authority over southern Italy in the first half of the third century gave her ties to the cities of Magna Graecia. The story of envoys from Apollonia in Rome ca. 266, whatever their purpose and whatever the outcome, has plausi-

---

13. That Issa did send an envoy to Rome while under threat from Illyrians is, of course, possible, and would explain Appian's reference to Cleemporus. But this is quite inadequate to account for Roman interest. The senate brought no aid to Issa which was still under siege a year or more later. The island entered into Rome's *fides* only near the end of the campaigning season in 229, after the Republic's forces gained control of Corcyra, Apollonia, Epidamnus, the Parthini, and the Atintanes: Polyb. 2.11.1–2. Appian's chronology is, in any case, badly confused; he has Agron take part of Epirus, Corcyra, Epidamnus, and Pharus *before* the Issaean appeal: *Ill.* 7. In fact, those conquests belong to Teuta, *after* the Roman mission: Polyb. 2.8–9.

14. Polyb. 2.8.1–3. How far back this raiding goes is beyond knowing. Dell, *Historia* 16 (1967): 344–358, reduces the time span perhaps too sharply.

15. Polyb. 2.8.2. The view of Badian, *Studies*, 3–4, that the Illyrians attacked Italian "blockade-runners" lacks evidence; see Hammond, *JRS* 58 (1968): 4, n. 15; Petzold, *Historia* 20 (1971): 203–204, n. 16.

16. E.g., Niese, *Geschichte* II:281; G. Colin, *Rome et la Grèce* (Paris, 1905), 24; more recently, Larsen, *Greek Federal States*, 359–361; Hammond, *JRS* 58 (1968): 20; J. L. Ferrary, in C. Nicolet, *Rome et la conquête du monde méditerranéen* (Paris, 1978) 2:732–733; Harris, *War and Imperialism*, 195–197.

17. Badian, *Studies*, 4–5; Hammond, *JRS* 58 (1968): 5–6—not entirely in accord with what he says on p. 20.

18. Holleaux, *Rome, la Grèce*, 102, n. 3; 107–112.

bility.[19] Apollonia would have an interest in making contact with the power who held sway over Hellenic towns in southern Italy. Further, the establishment of a Latin colony at Brundisium in 244, directly across the straits from Apollonia, put Rome in close touch with merchants who used that waterway.[20] It was natural enough that complaints by Italian shippers about Illyrian raids should be heard in Rome. The senate, however, had ignored them—until 230. Suddenly they received a favorable hearing. How to account for it?

The reason lies not in increased intensity of piratical harassment. More to the point is a marked change in the political and military position of the Ardiaean kingdom of Illyria. In 231 Illyrian forces, in the pay of Demetrius II of Macedonia, sailed with one hundred ships and five thousand men to relieve the siege of Medion in Acarnania. The expedition delivered a stunning blow to the mighty Aetolian League, whose armies abandoned Medion and fled in a state of shock.[21] The victors contented themselves with carrying off plunder and returning home.[22] Ease of victory, however, stimulated Illyrian ambitions. Agron controlled forces larger and more powerful than any Illyrian king before him had commanded. A new expedition was soon mounted by his widow Teuta in 230.[23] She had more in mind than a mere pillaging raid. The Illyrians planned an assault on Elis and Messene and captured the important city of Phoenice, routing an Epirote army in the process.[24] The shock-waves reverberated through Greece. Contingents from both the Aetolian and Achaean leagues arrived to assist Epirus. No further battle took place, for Teuta recalled her troops to deal with an internal rebellion. Illyrian power had nonetheless left a profound impression. The Epirotes and Acarnanians reversed their allegiances on the spot. Both concluded treaties of alliance with the Ardiaean monarchy and promised future cooperation

19. Livy, *Per.* 15; Dio, 10.42 = Zon. 8.7; Val. Max. 6.6.5; see above pp. 63–64.

20. Vell. Pat. 1.14.8; cf. Livy, *Per.* 19.

21. Polyb. 2.2.4–2.4.5. On the date, see De Sanctis, *Storia dei Romani* III: 1, 285, n. 73. The arguments of Derow, *Phoenix* 27 (1973): 133–134, for 230 are unpersuasive. That this period constitutes a new phase in Illyrian history is rightly stressed by Dell, *Historia* 16 (1967): 344–358; Cabanes, *L'Épire*, 202–208. The earlier history, however, is woefully ill-documented; see the discussion of F. Papazoglou, *Historia* 14 (1965): 143–179, and Hammond, *BSA* 61 (1966): 239–253.

22. Polyb. 2.3.8.

23. Polyb. 2.2.4, 2.4.6–9.

24. Polyb. 2.5. Illyrians had previously made a practise of raiding the Peloponnese: Polyb. 2.5.1–2; Plut. *Cleom.* 10.6; Paus. 4.35.5–7. But this new expedition was plainly on a different level altogether; cf. Polyb. 2.6.8. Petzold, *Historia* 20 (1971): 203, n. 16, unduly minimizes the taking of Phoenice as "improvisation" and "a piece of piracy."

against Aetolia and Achaea.[25] The implications of this diplomatic revolution need emphasis. A treaty that made Epirus and Acarnania allies of the Illyrians meant that those lands were now ruled out as objects of plunder. Piracy would henceforth take a back seat. The terms of the pact, which envisaged future operations against Achaeans and Aetolians, reinforce that conclusion. The Illyrians were transforming themselves from disreputable buccaneers to respectable imperialists. The spoils of Phoenice fired Teuta with greater ambitions. She put down the insurrection in Illyria and undertook the siege of Issa to gain a firm grip on her northern holdings. The effort had as its goal a renewed invasion of Greece.[26] The Ardiaeans were now intent upon becoming a major power in Hellas.

At this juncture the Romans elected to send an embassy to Teuta. Italian traders prompted it but they alone do not explain it. The whole pattern of commercial and diplomatic relations between Greek cities on both shores of the Adriatic now seemed under threat. It was one thing to suffer harassment from Illyrian marauders, an annoyance but not a disaster, quite another to face organized forces which had already whipped Aetolians and Epirotes and a state which now had established foothold in Epirus and Acarnania. No wonder that the Greeks along the Adriatic coast were in a state of panic.[27] We need not hypothesize that *Rome* feared the Illyrians, a power she disposed of quite handily once she put her mind to it. Nor that she was concerned for the security of her own trading interests, which can hardly have been very large in the Adriatic.[28] But the interests of Greek states from Epidamnus to Corcyra were closely linked to the cities of southern Italy; and the latter in turn had now come within the orbit of Rome.[29] The senate could at least go so far as to send an embassy and register complaint.

What follows, however, is most revealing for the Roman attitude —and for the Illyrian. Far from showing a zeal for empire, the senate acted with circumspection and caution. Neither Rome nor Teuta

25. Polyb. 2.6.1–10. The Epirotes may also have ceded Atintania to Illyria at this time as well: Polyb. 2.5.6, 2.5.8, 2.11.11; Appian, *Ill.* 7; Holleaux, *Rome, la Grèce*, 110, n. 1; Walbank, *Commentary* I: 156–157.

26. Polyb. 2.8.4–5.

27. Polyb. 2.6.7–8; cf. 2.12.6.

28. They are exaggerated by M. A. Levi, *PP*, 28 (1973): 324–325, and by those who regard relations with Issa as paramount in Roman thinking; Walser, *Historia* 2 (1954): 316–317; Derow, *Phoenix* 27 (1973): 125–127. That there was Italian commerce with states across the Adriatic is verifiable; cf. M. Fluss, *RE* Suppl. 5: 347–348, "Issa;" Cabanes, *L'Épire*, 217–218; Crawford, *Essays for H. Sutherland* (London, 1978), 1–11. This is not identical with *Roman* commerce.

29. Cf. Oost, *Roman Policy in Epirus and Acarnania*, 10–11.

looked for war with the other, and neither expected it. The *patres* sent envoys simply to "investigate."[30] What transpired in their interview with Teuta is past knowing. The dramatic interchange given by Polybius rests on no first-hand information, is polluted by anti-feminine invective, and cannot be used to support any reconstruction.[31] Nothing shows that Teuta or Rome considered themselves at war after the mission returned. One of the envoys perished before return, but his death, as we have seen, only became transformed into a *casus belli* by later apologists. Teuta went ahead with plans that she had already formulated to extend Illyrian power over the Greeks on the Ionian Gulf. In spring of 229, her forces attacked Epidamnus, Corcyra, and Apollonia.[32] It is difficult in the extreme to believe that she did so in knowledge of a coming war with Rome.[33] When once the Romans did come, the Illyrians turned tail and fled.[34] But they had not yet come, nor, apparently, had they given any indication that they would. The beleaguered people of Corcyra, Epidamnus, and Apollonia appealed for aid to Aetolia and Achaea. Apparently no one considered the possibility of Roman intervention.[35] The Illyrians, reinforced by ships from Acarnania, true to her treaty, delivered a smashing defeat to the Achaean-Aetolian fleet off the island of Paxos. Corcyra, despairing of assistance, surrendered to Teuta. The Illyrians proceeded again to besiege Epidamnus.[36] Their campaign had met with astonishing success. The Greek fears of Illyrian dominance of the Adriatic now seemed close to reality. There had been no prospect of a check from Rome.

30. Polyb. 2.8.3: κατέστησαν πρεσβευτὰς εἰς τὴν Ἰλλυρίδα τοὺς ἐπίσκεψιν ποιησομένους.

31. Holleaux, *Rome, la Grèce*, 99, believes the envoys delivered a *rerum repetitio*; so also Badian, *Studies*, 5. The idea is at variance with their instructions simply to "investigate;" so, rightly, Walbank, *Commentary* I:159–160; cf. S. Albert, *Bellum Iustum* (Kallmünz, 1980), 56. In the view of P. Treves, *Athenaeum* 22 (1934):388, Teuta gave a friendly reply, equivalent to an offer of *asylia*: Polyb. 2.8.8. But that is unwarranted by the text and not even Polybius' own opinion; cf. Walbank, *Commentary*, I:159. Badian, *Studies*, 4–5, goes so far as to have the Roman envoys decide upon war on their own, deliver an insulting reply to Teuta, and render the conflict inevitable. Rightly criticized by Petzold, *Historia* 20 (1971): 205, who points out that Teuta continued the siege of Issa during this time: Polyb. 2.11.11.

32. Polyb. 2.9.1–7.

33. As, e.g., Treves, *Athenaeum* 22 (1934): 391; Badian, *Studies*, 5. Similarly, Errington, *Dawn of Empire*, 37: "a virtual declaration of war."

34. Polyb. 2.11.9: οἱ δ' Ἰλλυριοὶ συνέντες τὴν ἔφοδον τῶν Ῥωμαίων, οὐδενὶ κόσμῳ λύσαντες τὴν πολιορκίαν ἔφυγον; cf. Appian, *Ill.* 7; Dio, 12.49.5–7, has Teuta alternate between panic and irrational courage.

35. Polyb. 2.9.8. Correctly insisted on by Holleaux, *Rome, la Grèce*, 24–27, 101; cf. Hammond, *JRS* 58 (1968), 5; Albert, *Bellum Iustum*, 58–59.

36. Polyb. 2.9.9–2.10.9.

The campaigning season of 229 was well advanced. Only then, when the forces of Teuta had resumed the investment of Epidamnus, did the Romans set sail with an army and a fleet.[37] Just when they declared war is a matter of guesswork. The time of their mobilization, however, demolishes the idea that a decision was taken in wake of the embassy to Teuta or the alleged assassination of an envoy, perhaps as much as a year earlier. The events that transpired in the interim take on the greater importance: Illyrian humbling of the Aetolian and Achaean navies, the occupation of Corcyra, and the live menace to all the Hellenic cities of the coastline.

Rome had looked with indifference upon Italian complaints about piratical activity. She had gone no further than to send an investigatory commission in 230, although that activity had taken on a more military cast. Indeed, Rome seemed content to bide her time even after representatives had conversed with Teuta. But when the queen engaged in still more major expeditions and no Hellenic resistance seemed capable of thwarting her, the Republic at last mobilized. Rome had nothing to fear from Illyria, still less from Macedonia, which makes not a solitary appearance in the story.[38] The Romans sprang into action when Hellenic towns across the Ionian Gulf had succumbed or were about to succumb to the barbarian, and when other champions had failed to prevent the surrender. The route to south Italy via northwest Greece was crucial for the people of Magna Graecia—and they did have claims on Rome. The thrust and goal of Roman intervention emerges from the treaty that followed it: a restriction on Illyrian vessels, only two of which could sail south of Lissus,

---

37. Polyb. 2.10.9–2.11.1. The Romans, according to Polybius, originally expected to find Corcyra still under siege, which might imply a somewhat earlier time in the season: 2.11.2; cf. 2.9.1–7. But it is clear that the Republic's forces did not depart until after communications came from Demetrius of Pharus, when he was already in charge of Corcyra—and after its surrender: Polyb. 2.11.3–4. The Pharian dynast, an ally or client of Teuta, had been appointed by her to hold Corcyra, but now angled for the favor of Rome. Treves' view, *Athenaeum* 22 (1934): 389–390, that Demetrius had earlier contacted the Roman envoys at Issa in 230 is false; see Badian, *Studies*, 27, n. 19. That Rome did not intervene until after the series of Illyrian successes is suggested also by Appian, *Ill.* 7, though he wrongly attributes the successes to Agron.

38. Illyrians had been hired by Demetrius II to relieve the siege of Medion in 231: Polyb. 2.2.5. But that was no more than the engaging of mercenaries, certainly not an "alliance" between Macedonia and Illyria. And it shows only that Demetrius was not himself capable of relieving Medion. By 229, no one in Rome would have reckoned Macedonia a threat. Demetrius died in that year and his son was too young to take over: Polyb. 2.44.2; Plut. *Arat.* 34.3–4; Justin, 28.3.9–16. Macedonia lost control of Argos and Athens, and the new ruler Antigonus Doson had his hands full with the Dardanians: Plut. *Arat.* 34–35; Polyb. 2.44.3–6.

and those unarmed.[39] Rome had acted to keep the shipping lanes open, and to maintain the loyalty of her allies in southern Italy. A limited war, only indirectly touching Roman interests, and one that could swiftly be disposed of.

The size of the expedition assured its rapid success. The Romans evidently did not intend to linger across the Adriatic. Corcyra and Apollonia immediately entered into *amicitia* with the western power. Illyrian forces abandoned Epidamnus in a panic directly upon hearing of Roman arrival, thus making plain that Teuta had never expected it. The Parthini and Atintanes yielded next. And the Romans encountered no serious resistance in lifting the siege of Issa, a task they could certainly have accomplished a year before, had they wished. Teuta was ready to accept terms by the spring of 228.[40]

A continued Roman presence in Illyria was neither required nor desired. The treaty of 228 imposed an indemnity upon the Ardiaean monarchy, reduced its holdings, and delivered control of certain places to Demetrius of Pharus, who had cooperated with Rome. Just how much territory was retained under the nominal suzerainty of young Pinnes, son of Agron, and how much came into the hands of Demetrius is disputed in the testimony and beyond knowing. Nor does it matter much.[41] The sources concur on one clause of the treaty: that Illyrians could send no armed vessels south of Lissus. That mattered to the Greeks of the Ionian Gulf, and to the traders of south Italy across the straits.[42] It misleads to speak of a Roman "protectorate" covering the area south of Lissus, designed to erect a bulwark against Macedonia or establish a foothold for further expansion.[43] The Republic had entered into *amicitia* with Corcyra, Epidamnus,

39. Polyb. 2.12.3; Appian, *Ill.* 7.
40. Polyb. 2.11.4–2.12.3; cf. Appian, *Ill.* 7–8.
41. Polybius, 2.12.3, has Teuta yield up "all of Illyria except a few places," with most of the area put under Demetrius' authority: 2.11.17; cf. Dio, 12.49.7. By contrast, Appian, *Ill.* 7–8, has Pinnes retain everything but areas that surrendered to Rome, i.e. Corcyra, Pharus, Issa, Epidamnus, and the Atintanes, while Demetrius got only temporary control of some strongholds. For various conjectures, see Holleaux, *Rome, la Grèce*, 104–106; Badian, *Studies*, 8–9; Hammond, *JRS* 58 (1968): 7–9; Petzold, *Historia* 20 (1971), 206–214. Demetrius subsequently married Triteuta, mother of Pinnes, thus effectively gaining trusteeship of the Ardiaean holdings: Dio, 12.53. That may explain Polybius' statement about the extent of his dominions. Harris, *War and Imperialism*, 64, believes that Rome levied tribute on the Illyrians, for which there is no evidence and little likelihood. Livy, 22.33.5, refers to an installment payment on the indemnity.
42. Polyb. 2.12.3: καὶ τὸ συνέχον ὃ μάλιστα πρὸς τοὺς Ἕλληνας διέτεινε; Appian, *Ill.* 7; cf. Dio, 12.49.2.
43. Roman concern about Macedonia is nowhere attested, and decisively refuted by Dell, *CP* 62 (1967): 94–103.

Apollonia, Issa, the Parthini, and the Atintanes. The peace treaty made Pinnes a "friend" also, as was Demetrius. Rome made no territorial acquisitions and no claims of suzerainty. She explicitly released control and left her *amici* free.[44] The Greeks of the coast may have hoped for continued protection against Illyrian aggrandizement, a hegemony in accord with Hellenistic practice.[45] Rome, however, disavowed hegemonial aspiration. She sent legates to Aetolia and Achaea, and, shortly afterwards, to Corinth and Athens, explaining the reasons for the war and communicating the terms of the treaty. The legates announced that Greeks could abandon fear of Illyria—and, by implication, that they had nothing to fear from Rome.[46]

## A Reassertion of Authority

The senate evinced no further interest in Illyria for nearly a decade. Internal affairs in that land concerned them not at all. Demetrius of Pharus consolidated and expanded his power during the 220s. His wedding to Triteuta made him guardian of the young Pinnes, still a minor, and gave him effective control of lands belonging to the Ardiaean monarchy.[47] The extent and form of his authority remain nebulous. The tribal structure of Illyria made for a complex and fluid situation, not readily dominated by a single ruler. Scerdilaidas, for example, probably a brother of Agron and uncle of Pinnes, exercised independent authority, controlled his own forces, and conducted his own diplomacy.[48] The Illyrian dynasts felt free to develop their foreign policies with neighboring realms and powers. Demetrius by 222 had

44. Appian, *Ill.* 8, who refers explicitly to Corcyra and Apollonia, but the freedom was certainly not restricted to them alone.

45. Cf. Polyb. 2.11.5: ἔδωκαν [the Corcyraeans] παρακληθέντες εἰς τὴν τῶν Ῥωμαίων πίστιν, μίαν ταύτην ὑπολαβόντες ἀσφάλειαν αὐτοῖς ὑπάρχειν εἰς τὸν μέλλοντα χρόνον πρὸς τὴν Ἰλληριῶν παρανομίαν.

46. Polyb. 2.12.4–8: ἱκανοῦ τινος ἀπολελυκότες φόβου τοὺς Ἕλληνας διὰ τὰς προειρημένας συνθήκας; cf. Zon. 8.19. Harris' assertion, *War and Imperialism*, 138, that the "target of this policy" was Macedonia, lacks any basis. The existence of a "protectorate" is rightly questioned by Petzold, *Historia* 20 (1971): 206, 220–221. Polybius' later reference to πόλεις τὰς ὑπὸ Ῥωμαίους ταττομένας derives from propaganda against Demetrius and justification for the Second Illyrian War: Polyb. 3.16.3. And Philip's treaty with Hannibal which specifies states over which Romans are κύριοι is, of course, anti-Roman propaganda: Polyb. 7.9.13–14.

47. Dio, 12.53.

48. Cf. Polyb. 4.16.9–10, 4.29.2–7. Scerdilaidas' relationship with Agron is suggested by the name of his son Pleuratus: Polyb. 2.2.4; Livy, 31.28.1; cf. Zippel, *Die römische Herrschaft*, 57.

agreed to cooperate with Antigonus Doson of Macedonia and contributed forces to his victory at Sellasia.[49] Rome showed not a trace of
alarm at this development, any more than she did at Scerdilaidas'
marriage alliance with the king of Athamania.[50] And why should she?
Tribal loyalties and political divisions fragmented Illyria. Though Demetrius linked himself to Doson, other Illyrian peoples invaded the
kingdom of Macedonia.[51] Rome was remote and uninterested.

The Illyrian dynasts had felt no restraint from the western
power, and had no reason to expect any.[52] In 220 Demetrius and Scerdilaidas made a joint naval expedition down the Adriatic coast to the
Peloponnese where they assaulted Pylos, without success. Their cooperation then ended and each went his separate way: Demetrius
with fifty ships sailed on a raiding expedition in the Aegean; Scerdilaidas with forty vessels agreed to support the Aetolians in an invasion of the Achaean League.[53] That each acted as a free and independent agent is plain enough. While Scerdilaidas collaborated with the
Aetolians, Demetrius was persuaded to assist the Macedonian cause
against Aetolia on his return via the Isthmus of Corinth.[54] From the
vantage point of Rome—if she took any notice at all—Illyrian activities on both sides of the Social War promised to keep Hellas embroiled in strife and offered not the slightest menace to the West. Demetrius, emboldened by his ventures into distant places, returned to
expand his authority in Illyria, sacking some cities and winning the
allegiance of the Atintanes.[55] Given Rome's aloofness to this point,
Demetrius had reason to believe that he could conduct his operations

49. Polyb. 2.65.4, 3.16.3. That there was a formal alliance is questionable. In 220
Demetrius hoped for Macedonian support on the basis of his collaboration at Sellasia—
not on any alliance: Polyb. 3.16.3; Dell, CP 62 (1967): 101; contra: Hammond, JRS 58
(1968): 10, n. 37; Cabanes, L'Épire, 225 and n. 191.

50. Polyb. 4.16.9.

51. Polyb. 2.70.1; Plut. Cleom. 30.1.

52. Appian's assertion, Ill. 8, that Rome suspected Demetrius right from the start
in 228, is plainly post eventum; correctly noted by Badian, Studies, 8.

53. The joint expedition: Polyb. 4.16.6–8; cf. 4.25.4, 9.38.8; Demetrius' activities:
Polyb. 3.16.3, 4.16.8; Scerdilaidas' activities: Polyb. 4.16.9–11, 4.29.5.

54. Polyb. 4.19.7–9.

55. Polyb. 3.16.3. The tenses of the infinitives show clearly that the activities in
Illyria followed the return from the Aegean; Walbank, Commentary I:325, with bibliography. Those activities should be connected with the notice in Appian, Ill. 8, that
Demetrius won over the Atintanes; cf. Dio, 12.53 = Zon. 8.20. Appian's telescoped
chronology, imbedded in an exaggerated and hostile account of Demetrius, does not
bear the weight placed on it by Hammond, JRS 58 (1968): 10–11, n. 38, and accepted by
Petzold, Historia 20 (1971): 212, n. 55. Strictly speaking, in any case, Appian puts the
adherence of the Atintanes to Demetrius after the Istrian uprising—which comes in
221 and 220; see below p. 372.

with impunity.[56] Yet in the following spring of 219, the Romans moved in force: an army crossed the Adriatic, with the intent of crushing Demetrius.[57] What provoked this Second Illyrian War?

Roman apologists went to work after the fact. Demetrius was depicted as an ungrateful beneficiary, bent on an anti-Roman path. For Polybius, the Illyrian dynast took courage from Rome's fear of the Gauls and of Carthage, and counted on the backing of the Macedonian monarchy. Hence, he made bold to sail beyond Lissus, thus violating the treaty of 228, to carry on raids against southern Greece and the Cyclades, and to plunder Illyrian cities tied to Rome. The Romans, apprehensive about a coming war with Hannibal and fearful of the rising fortunes of Macedonia, decided to protect their eastern flank by knocking out the Illyrian menace.[58] The tradition in Appian adds further transgressions: Demetrius, untrustworthy and faithless from the start, seeing that Rome had her hands full with the Gauls, stirred the Istrians into piratical enterprises and brought the Antintanes from the Roman side to his own, thus prompting retaliation.[59]

These explanations will not do. The contamination of hindsight and apologia taint the evidence. Rome had concluded the Gallic wars with triumphant success in 222.[60] A contest with Carthage was anything but certain in 220; Hannibal did not even begin the siege of Saguntum until Rome sent her armies to Illyria in the spring of 219.[61] As for Macedonia, Demetrius could hardly have banked on her support in 220. Doson had perished the year before, in the course of a war against Illyrians; the untested, seventeen-year old Philip now sat on the throne; and the kingdom was mobilizing resources and allies for the Social War.[62] This of all times seems about the worst for Demetrius to have provoked a conflict with Rome.[63]

Nor do his actions betoken any such provocation. An assault on Pylos and a raiding expedition in the Cyclades took him far indeed from any conceivable Roman sphere of interest. Moreover, this venture shows how loose were his connections with Macedonia. De-

56. Holleaux, *Rome, la Grèce*, 131–135, who, however, wrongly takes Demetrius' association with Doson as an anti-Roman move. Similarly, Treves, *Athenaeum* 23 (1935): 45–46; M. T. Piraino, *AttiAccadPalermo* 13 (1952–53): 345–353. A better analysis in Badian, *Studies*, 11.

57. Polyb. 3.16.7; cf. Zon. 8.20; Appian, *Ill.* 8.

58. Polyb. 3.16.1–4; cf. 4.16.6.

59. Appian, *Ill.* 8; cf. Dio, 12.53 = Zon. 8.20.

60. Polyb. 2.34.2–2.35.2; Zon. 8.20; Plut. *Marc.* 6.2–7.5, 8.1; Eutrop. 3.6; Orosius, 4.13.15; Livy, *Per.* 20.

61. Polyb. 3.16.7–3.17.1, 4.37.4; Walbank, *Commentary* I: 327–328.

62. Polyb. 2.70.6–8, 4.3.1–3, 4.5.3, 4.13.6, 4.22.5, 4.25–27; Plut. *Cleom.* 30.1–2.

63. See the forceful and persuasive arguments of Badian, *Studies*, 12–14.

metrius had to be bribed into cooperation against the Aetolians when he landed unexpectedly at the Isthmus; and the cooperation was brief, as well as abortive.[64] Roman concern about Macedonia is plainly a red herring. As for violation of the treaty by sailing past Lissus, that too fails to give sufficient cause. The charge may well have been brought against Demetrius in retrospect, but surely not at the time. Whether the treaty of 228, concluded with the Ardiaean monarchy and prohibiting armed voyages below the Lissus line, even applied to Demetrius is questionable. Demetrius certainly does not seem to have thought so, and with good reason. In 222 he had transported sixteen hundred troops to join Doson at Sellasia. Unless they had made an arduous overland journey all the way to the Peloponnese (a most doubtful proposition), they must have gone by sea and passed the line of Lissus—engendering no objection from Rome.[65] Demetrius could feel confident of similar impunity in 220. More to the point, his fellow Illyrian dynast Scerdilaidas took fifty ships past Lissus as well in that year, yet never received rebuke or retaliation from Rome. The purpose of the boundary was to protect Greeks on the coast and traders of south Italy from the assaults of Illyrian marauders. It can be no accident that neither Demetrius nor Scerdilaidas touched Rome's *amici* at Epidamnus, Apollonia, or Corcyra. Provocation of the Republic was not their aim. Demetrius, to be sure, proceeded to extend his influence over the Atintanes, *amici* of Rome since 229.[66] Yet he too was an *amicus* and the connection need not be objectionable to Rome. She held no brief for Atintania.[67] In view of all this, the charge that Demetrius plundered and destroyed Illyrian cities "subject to Rome" can safely be adjudged as *post eventum*.[68] A different approach is needed.

Rome had brought her forces across the Adriatic in 229 in order

64. Polyb. 4.19.7–9. Note also that, when Demetrius eventually fled to the court of Philip V after the Roman victory in 219, his arrival was unexpected; Polyb. 3.19.8: παρα-δόξως. The implications of these passages are overlooked by J. V. A. Fine, *JRS* 26 (1936): 30–39, who argues—rightly—that Philip did not instigate Demetrius' raids in 220.

65. Polyb. 2.65.4.

66. Appian, *Ill.* 8.

67. In 205 they readily yielded it up to Philip: Livy, 29.12.13.

68. Polyb. 3.16.3. The evidence of Dio, 12.53 = Zon. 8.20, speaks only of ravaging neighboring tribes —a "misuse of Roman friendship." Badian's perceptive analysis, *Studies*, 14–16, is fundamental. But his conclusion, that Rome wished to punish an ungrateful client and needed to rid herself of a powerful neighbor in the East with war looming against Carthage, is inadequate—though repeated in exaggerated form by Errington, *Dawn of Empire*, 107–108. The account of Holleaux, *Rome, la Grèce*, 130–146, valuable in many ways, is marred by his conviction that the Romans feared Macedonia. Hammond, *JRS* 58 (1968): 10–11, accepts the tainted evidence against Demetrius without criticism; so also Petzold, *Historia* 20 (1971): 211–214.

to guarantee the free access of Italian vessels to that sea. Her motives a decade later may have been no different. The appropriate context in which to view the Second Illyrian War is that of Roman operations against the Istri in the northern Adriatic. Our sources are fragmentary and sparse, with the loss of Livy. Nonetheless, the Livian tradition preserves some important facts. Roman grain ships had been preyed upon by pirates based in Istria. The senate determined to wipe out that lair. A campaign conducted by both consuls of 221 brought the Istrians to heel; and then a second one, again involving two consular armies, consolidated Rome's position in the Alpine area.[69] Why the grain ships had been sailing near Istria is unknown. Perhaps they had supplied Rome's forces in the Gallic wars of 225–222.[70] Or perhaps they signal a greater maritime activity in north Adriatic waters than is otherwise attested. In either case, Rome plainly determined to eliminate any menace to the shipping. Now, it is precisely in connection with the Istrian campaigns that one strand of the apologetic tradition associates Demetrius of Pharus: he engaged in piracy and took the Istri as partners in crime.[71] The charge need not be believed. Demetrius, as we have seen, had every reason to avoid rousing Roman anger.[72] But Rome took a dim view of marauders in the Adriatic. Once the Istri had been subdued in 220, she decided upon a show of power in Illyria. Demetrius' assaults on the Peloponnese and in the Aegean revived among the Greeks memories of Illyrian depredations a decade before. Rome mobilized against Demetrius not because of what he had done but because of what he might do. The Second Illyrian War was a logical corollary of the Istrian campaigns.[73]

The forces of the Republic made as short work of the Illyrians

69. The clearest statement in Eutrop. 3.7: *M. Minucio Rufo, P. Cornelio consulibus* (221 B.C.), *Histris bellum inlatum est, quia latrocinati navibus Romanorum fuerant, quae frumenta exhibebant, perdomitique sunt omnes.* The campaign is mentioned also by Livy, *Per.* 20; Orosius, 4.13.16; Appian, *Ill.* 8; Zon. 8.20; cf. Livy, 21.16.4. Zonaras, 8.20, records a follow-up campaign in 220, which went up to the Alps and brought about the submission of many peoples without need for warfare. The possible relationships between these two operations are explored in detail by G. Bandinelli, *Athenaeum* 69 (1981): 3–28, who ignores any connection with the Illyrian war.

70. A plausible suggestion by Dell, *Historia* 19 (1970): 34–35.

71. Appian, *Ill.* 8: τὴν θάλασσαν ἐλῄξετο καὶ Ἴστρους, ἔθνος ἔτερον Ἰλλυριῶν ἐς τοῦτο προσελάμβανε.

72. Dell, *Historia* 19 (1970): 36, accepts the accusation without question. Holleaux, *Rome, la Grèce,* 134, n. 1, arbitrarily denies the very existence of an Istrian war.

73. Appian, *Ill.* 8: οἱ δὲ ἐπεὶ τὰ Κελτῶν διετέθειτο, εὐθὺς μὲν ἐπιπλεύσαντες, αἱροῦσι τοὺς λῃστάς, ἐς νεώτα δὲ ἐστράτευον ἐπὶ Δημήτριον καὶ Ἰλλυριῶν τοὺς συναμαρτόντας αὐτῷ; cf. Livy, 21.16.4: *Sardos Corsosque et Histros atque Illyrios lacessisse magis quam exercuisse Romana arma.* See Cassola, *I gruppi politici,* 232–233.

the second time as they had the first. Both consuls crossed the sea in the spring of 219.[74] Demetrius, evidently unprepared and surprised, swiftly placed garrisons in Dimale and Pharus and established supporters in charge of various other cities.[75] These last-minute efforts were to no avail. Roman forces took Dimale in a week, breaking the back of any resistance and prompting Illyrian towns to rush into submission. Pharus fell some time in the summer and Demetrius' cause was lost. He slipped away by boat and found refuge at the court of Philip V. By late summer the consuls were already back in Rome to celebrate triumphs.[76] No troops remained, no hegemony ensued. Rome added but one *amicus*, Dimale, to those already among her friends since 228.[77] Scerdilaidas, who still controlled parts of Illyria, was left alone—despite the fact that he had made an accord with Philip V.[78] Pinnes stayed on his throne as monarch of the Ardiaeans, in payment of a token indemnity.[79] There was hardly anything that could be termed a "settlement."[80] Rome had made a demonstration of her massive power. She need not and did not intend to do more. The Adriatic was safe.[81]

## The First Confrontation with Philip V

In another year Rome became engaged in the struggle with Hannibal, her attention riveted on Italy and Spain. To the East she could pay little heed, even had she a mind to. The affairs of Illyria and Macedonia were remote indeed to a Republic pushed to the limit against the Carthaginian invader. The Social War raged in Hellas, with no resonance across the water. There is but a single notice of continued Roman interest in the East. Report has it that the *patres* sent a delegation to Philip V demanding surrender of the fugitive Demetrius of Pharus, and a concurrent mission to Pinnes reminding him

74. Polyb. 3.16.7 gives only Aemilius Paullus. But there is no doubt that Livius Salinator accompanied him; evidence in Münzer, *RE* XIII:1, 892, "Livius," n. 33; cf. Walbank, *Commentary* I:327.

75. Polyb. 3.18.1–2.

76. Polyb. 3.18–19, 4.66.4; Zon. 8.20; Appian, *Ill.* 8.

77. Cf. Polyb. 7.9.13.

78. Polyb. 4.29.1–7, 5.4.3.

79. Appian, *Ill.* 8; Livy, 22.33.5.

80. Polybius' allusion to an "arrangement" of Illyrian affairs refers only to the actions of the consul, not any senatorial settlement; 3.19.12: πάντα διατάξας κατὰ τὴν αὐτοῦ προαίρεσιν.

81. Rome's subsequent lack of interest in Illyria is plain from Polyb. 29.4.2, 32.13.5.

of delinquency in payment of his indemnity.[82] If the embassies be authentic, however—which some have doubted—they signal only a public relations move: an effort to show that Rome still carried international authority, even after the disaster at Trasimene.[83] Philip certainly ignored the request, and, for all we know, Pinnes never paid up. Eastern matters simply could not occupy the thoughts of the Roman senate. Scerdilaidas was now the principal dynast of Illyria, and the principal thorn in the side of young Philip V. He had framed a temporary alliance with Philip in 220/19 and brought assistance during the Social War, but then broke with him in 217, claiming that the Macedonian had reneged on promises of pay. Scerdilaidas then reverted to form as a piratical raider, harassing the vessels of Philip's allies and plundering luckless merchantmen. A counterattack by the king was too slow and missed its targets. Scerdilaidas went on to march into Dassaretis, taking several towns and overrunning parts of western Macedonia.[84] In all this there is no mention of Rome; and the modern idea that she prodded Scerdilaidas into activity is entirely baseless.[85]

The Social War came to an end in the late summer of 217. Philip had taken the initiative, eager to free his hands for other ventures. Polybius, with hindsight to the fore, has him act on the counsel of Demetrius of Pharus. The news of Trasimene had arrived and Demetrius urged an invasion of Illyria, to be followed by an expedition to Italy, the time now ripe as Rome was about to go under. For Polybius, that advice kindled the young monarch's ambitions, even haunted his sleep, as he dreamed of world conquest.[86] It is all retrojection. Philip could hardly contemplate an invasion of Italy with not a single harbor in his hands and his own kingdom under assault. A neglected passage in Livy—who was unlikely to minimize the king's grand designs—puts the lie to this notion: Philip did not consider Rome's fortunes to be sinking until after the battle of Cannae.[87] He

82. Livy, 22.33.3, 22.33.5.

83. Holleaux, *Rome, la Grèce*, 143, n. 6, dismisses the demand for Demetrius as "annalistic fiction." Many other scholars pass over it altogether. Polybius' reference to Roman embassies to the Greeks, 5.105.8, is plainly anticipatory: Walbank, *Commentary*, I:629–630.

84. The alliance with Macedonia: Polyb. 4.29.1–7, 5.4.3; the break over pay: Polyb. 5.95.1; Philip's abortive counterattack: Polyb. 5.101.1–3; Scerdilaidas' invasion: Polyb. 5.108.1–2.

85. That idea may be found in Holleaux, *Rome, la Grèce*, 165–166; Fine, *JRS* 26 (1936): 39; Walbank, *Philip V*, 68; Oost, *Roman Policy in Epirus and Acarnania*, 113, n. 96; Cabanes, *L'Épire*, 250. Rightly rejected by Badian, *Studies*, 18, and Hammond, *JRS* 58 (1968): 15–16, n. 54.

86. Polyb. 5.101.6–5.102.1, 5.105.1, 5.105.5, 5.108.4–7.

87. Livy, 23.33.1–4.

had good reasons to conclude the Social War in 217, and they had nothing to do with Rome. Scerdilaidas had invaded Dassaretis and was conducting raids into Macedonia itself. Philip had to extricate himself from Hellas, lest his own kingdom begin to totter. Insofar as he took the advice of Demetrius, it directed him to halt the advance of Scerdilaidas and to gain control of Illyria, thus allowing the Pharian, of course, to recover his possessions.[88] It is no accident that Philip's first moves, after the peace of Naupactus, drove Scerdilaidas from Dassaretis and Pelagonia and occupied territory around Lake Lychnitis.[89] Philip now had a foothold in southern Illyria, with the prospect of installing Demetrius as his loyal surrogate. Rome, without ties formal or informal to Scerdilaidas, seemed fully occupied elsewhere.

As the sequel shows, Philip never bargained on the intervention of Rome. Scerdilaidas was the immediate object, as well as the coastal cities, control of which could extend Macedonian dominions to the shores of the Adriatic. A fleet of one hundred *lembi* was built to that end in the winter of 217/16, a force woefully inadequate to cope with the Roman navy, as Philip well knew. He did not expect the Roman navy.[90] Scerdilaidas, on the run and with nowhere else to turn, appealed for assistance to the Republic. The response was swift but minimal. A mere ten ships, detached from the fleet at Lilybaeum, sailed across the Ionian Sea. They could hardly have done more than investigate the situation, a token display to reassure Apollonia and other cities on the coast which were probably as apprehensive of Scerdilaidas as of Macedonian power. Their approach, however, changed everything. Once Roman quinqueremes were sighted, Philip abandoned his project on the spot. Panic gripped the fleet and the king. Philip beat a hasty retreat and soon found his way back to Macedonia. It is plain that the appearance of Roman vessels caught him completely by surprise.[91] Neither Rome nor Philip V looked for confrontation with one another.[92]

The senate had shied away from obligations and commitments. At most the *patres* would keep an eye on events in the southern Adriatic, thus maintaining faith with allies in southern Italy and their Greek friends across the water. For the next five years the initiative stayed with Philip. It was he who framed alliance with Hannibal in

88. Cf. Polyb. 5.101.8, 5.108.5–7: μόνως γὰρ οὕτως ἐπέπειστο [Demetrius] τὴν ἐν τῷ Φάρῳ δυναστείαν κατακτήσασθαι πάλιν.

89. Polyb. 5.108.8.

90. Polyb. 5.109.1–4: τοῦτο μὲν γὰρ οὐδ᾽ ἂν ἤλπισε δυνατὸς εἶναι, 'Ρωμαίοις διαναυμαχεῖν.

91. Polyb. 5.110.

92. As Livy, 23.33.6–8 shows, many Romans even in 215 were prepared to believe that Philip would make alliance with them.

215, an alliance which promised removal of Roman influence from Corcyra, Epidamnus, Apollonia, Pharus, Dimale, the Parthini and Atintanes, and the restoration of the friends of Demetrius the Pharian.[93] It was he who marched an army through Epirus and sailed a fleet up the Aous to attack Apollonia and Oricum in 214.[94] It was he who took a firm grip on Dassaretis, won over the Parthini and Atintanes, occupied Dimale, and finally broke through to the coast, capturing Lissus and its fortress of Acrolissus, in 213 and 212. Illyrian tribes and towns fell under his sway; Scerdilaidas lost hold even of the Ardiaei.[95] A striking series of campaigns, with a consistent object: to knock out Scerdilaidas, take control of Illyria, and push Macedonian hegemony to the Adriatic. On those goals Philip had trained his aim throughout, not on direct engagement against Rome, let alone an invasion of Italy. The limits are spelled out clearly enough in the pact with Hannibal: Philip's assistance would be used if and when the Carthaginian called for it. He never did.[96] Hannibal was pleased to have an ally who (from the Carthaginian point of view) could open a second front against Rome and might divert some of the senate's attention from Italy. Philip in turn expected that Hannibal would keep the Romans distracted while he operated against his neighbors. Further, he received guarantees of Punic recognition for his authority in Illyria once the war was over. That the king anticipated no Roman resistance to his designs emerges plainly in his assaults on Apollonia and Oricum in 214. When Rome did detach a squadron to defend those cities, Philip was caught quite off guard. He barely saved his own skin by a last minute escape, abandoning camp half-nude, burned his ships, and made an ignominious retreat to Macedonia.[97] Thereafter he operated in the interior—where he would not have to encounter any Roman forces.

93. Polyb. 7.9.13–14; cf. Zon. 9.4; Eutrop. 3.12.2. For Philip's initiative, see Livy, 23.33.1–4; Zon. 9.4; Appian, *Mac.* 1—who affirms that the king had hitherto suffered no harm from the Romans.

94. Livy, 24.40.2–3; Plut. *Arat.* 5.1; cf. Zon. 9.4.

95. Dassaretis: Polyb. 8.14b; the Atintanes: Livy, 27.30.13, 29.12.13; the Parthini and Dimale: Livy, 29.12.3, 29.12.13; Lissus: Polyb. 8.13–14; Illyrian towns and the Ardiaei: Polyb. 8.14.10–11; Livy, 27.30.13.

96. Polyb. 7.9.11: βοηθήσετε δὲ ἡμῖν, ὡς ἂν χρεία ᾖ καὶ ὡς ἂν συμφωνήσωμεν; see Bickermann, *AJP* 73 (1952): 15; Walbank, *Commentary* II:55. This decisively refutes the tradition that the treaty provided for a Macedonian expedition to Italy: Livy, 23.33.9–12, 24.13.5; Appian, *Mac.* 1; Zon. 9.4. Hannibal captured Tarentum in 213: Polyb. 8.24–34; Livy, 25.7–11. But he did not offer it as landing place for Macedonian forces. Indeed, Philip had already burned his fleet: Livy, 24.40.17; Zon. 9.4; Plut. *Arat.* 51.2. The year before, when Philip still had his ships, Hannibal made no serious effort to take Tarentum; cf. Livy, 24.13, 24.20.

97. Livy, 24.40; Zon. 9.4; Plut. *Arat.* 51.2. On Hannibal's motives, cf. Polyb. 9.22.5.

Through all this Rome severely limited her involvement. It is uncertain even that she considered herself formally at war with Philip.[98] When the pact between Hannibal and Macedonia came to light, the senate stationed a fleet at Tarentum to protect the coast and to receive information about Philip's movements.[99] The *patres* did not intend to prosecute a Macedonian war, but had a simpler and more restricted purpose: to make sure Philip did not cross to Italy.[100] The one Roman venture across the straits in these years came in 214, on an appeal from Oricum, after Philip's forces had already attacked Apollonia and taken Oricum; the Romans did not even know of his invasion until then.[101] The praetor M. Valerius Laevinus took his ships across the water, regaining Oricum and driving Philip from Apollonia; it was this expedition which caused the king to flee in surprise and terror.[102] Laevinus wintered in Oricum in 214/13 rather than return to Brundisium, thereby the better to deter future aggression in the area.[103] As in the Illyrian wars, the security of the southern Adriatic exercised Roman concern. The presence of the fleet reassured the coastal cities. That was as far as it went. No offensive operations were conducted or contemplated, despite the fact that Laevinus continued to be prorogued with "Greece and Macedonia" as his *provincia*. Philip's string of successes in inland Illyria during 213 and 212, which even deprived Scerdilaidas of much of his dominion, stirred not a sign of activity in the Roman camp.[104]

In autumn 212 or 211 Rome adopted at last a more vigorous plan, a plan which, however, others would have the burden of implementing. She concluded an alliance with Aetolia for joint cooperation against Philip, the Aetolians to face him on land, the Romans to supply naval support.[105] Rome had initiated the contact and Rome had persuaded the Aetolians to concur.[106] But why only now, why not any time in the previous five or six years when Philip's westward aggressions were taking place? The reason surely lies in his most recent successes, in particular the occupation of Lissus. For here the

98. No evidence for a declaration of war in Livy, 23.38.4–11.

99. Livy, 23.38.5–10.

100. Livy, 23.38.11: *daretque operam ut Philippum in regno contineret*; cf. 23.48.3, 26.28.2: *classem satis esse ad arcendum Italia regem*; 31.7.4. The fleet was shortly thereafter transferred to Brundisium: Livy, 24.11.3, 24.40.2.

101. Livy, 24.40.1–4.

102. See above, n. 97.

103. Livy, 24.40.17; cf. Polyb. 8.1.6: καὶ μὴν τοῖς κατὰ τὴν Ἑλλάδα τόποις ἐφώρμει καὶ ταῖς ἐπιβολαῖς τοῦ Φιλίππου στόλος.

104. For Laevinus' province, see Livy, 24.44.5.

105. SEG, XIII, 382 = IG, IX, 1², 241 = Schmitt, *Staatsverträge*, no. 536; Livy, 26.24.11. On the date, probably autumn, 211, see Walbank, *Commentary* II: 11–13.

106. Livy, 25.23.9, 26.24.1–8. See above p. 19.

Macedonians had, for the first time, achieved a station on the coast. Hard pressed though it was, the Republic could not view with equanimity Philip's presence on the Adriatic shore, any more than it had tolerated Illyrian and Istrian marauders when they had become a menace to the sea lanes. Atintanes, Parthini, even Ardiaei were nothing to Rome. But a major power, operating from Lissus and controlling the hinterland, could have the southern Adriatic at its mercy. That called for more determined measures. Roman interests in the area, limited but firm, had remained consistent since the mid-third century.

The treaty signals no increased Roman designs on foreign territory: on the contrary. Aetolia was in the driver's seat, for Rome needed her cooperation, and the agreement largely followed her prescriptions.[107] Whatever conquests were to be made, Rome would receive the movable booty or a share thereof; Aetolia took rights to all cities and land.[108] The agreement imposed geographic limits on this distribution, according to Livy: "from Aetolia to Corcyra."[109] That restriction does not appear on the stone recording the compact, which implies a broader range of operations, as indeed do the subsequent events of the war.[110] Livy may report a preliminary draft of the document, later modified in course of ratification, or else he supplies a loose paraphrase referring to immediate objectives, which concentrated in the area of northwest Greece.[111] Nevertheless, there is every reason to believe that Roman negotiators insisted on Corcyra as an upper limit for territory subject to occupation. The senate would find Aetolian presence on the Straits of Otranto and the Ionian Gulf no more welcome than Illyrian or Macedonian. In this matter, senatorial policy maintained unflagging consistency. Elsewhere Aetolia could keep what she could take. Rome was uninterested in occupying foreign lands.

Indeed, Rome's interest in the eastern conflict itself never rose beyond the marginal, at best. So long as Aetolia kept Philip busy and diverted his ambitions away from the Adriatic, that sufficed. The ill-named "First Macedonian War" was primarily a Hellenic-Macedonian contest, a revival, for the most part, of the Social War. The Roman

---

107. See above pp. 18–20.

108. *SEG*, XIII, 382 = Schmitt, *Staatsverträge*, no. 536, lines 4–15; Livy, 26.24.11. The differences between the inscription and Livy's account on rights to the booty are irrelevant. They agree that all territory captured by force will go to Aetolia; cf. Polyb. 9.39.2–3, 11.5.5, 18.38.7; Livy, 26.26.3, 33.13.10.

109. Livy, 26.24.11: *urbium Corcyrae tenus ab Aetolia incipienti solum tectaque et muri cum agris Aetolorum, alia omnis praeda populi Romani esset.*

110. *SEG* XIII, 382 = Schmitt, *Staatsverträge*, no. 536, line 2: τούτους πάντας, i.e. all allies of Philip; confirmed by Polyb. 11.5.4–5; cf. 9.39.2, 22.8.9–10; Livy, 26.26.3.

111. Livy, 26.24.10–11: *bellum ut extemplo Aetoli cum Philippo terra gererent . . . darentque operam Romani ut Acarnaniam Aetoli haberent*; cf. McDonald, *JRS* 46 (1956): 154.

navy acted in support of and as encouragement to the enemies of Philip V.[112]

The course of the war can be passed over, except to observe how peripheral was the Roman involvement.[113] Near the end of 211 Laevinus' fleet captured Zacynthus and took some towns in Acarnania, which were promptly handed over to Aetolia.[114] The next spring Laevinus cooperated in the seizure of Anticyra in Phocis, once again turning the city over to his allies.[115] From Laevinus' point of view, Rome had little more to do. Philip had made a brief sortie against Oricum and Apollonia in winter 211/10, but had abandoned that sector and was now fully engaged elsewhere.[116] When Laevinus returned home in 210 he reported that Rome no longer needed a legion there: the fleet was enough to keep Philip from Italy.[117] This statement speaks directly to the limits of Rome's concern. The senate was swift to agree. It issued instructions to Laevinus' successor in Greece, the proconsul Sulpicius Galba, to dismiss his entire army, retaining only the *socii navales*.[118] The Roman commitment was already slackening. Galba's ships were active during the next three years but their successes were indecisive and their conquests duly resigned to Aetolia. Galba acquired a reputation for savagery, well earned; his atrocities were more conspicuous than his military prowess.[119] Rome confined her objectives primarily to keeping her allies in the fight. As a Macedonian spokesman justly observed, Aetolians and Peloponnesians face danger in the forefront, Romans hang back and wait on events.[120] When a peace parley in 209 seemed on the point of bringing hostilities to an end, the Roman fleet appeared at Naupactus to stiffen

112. Livy, 26.24.10; cf. 27.30.2, 29.12.4; Appian, *Mac.* 3.1.

113. A full discussion in Holleaux, *Rome, la Grèce*, 213–257, Walbank, *Philip V*, 84–107.

114. Livy, 26.24.15; cf. Polyb. 9.39.2.

115. Livy, 26.26.1–3; cf. Polyb. 9.39.2.

116. Livy, 26.25.2–3; cf. Zon. 9.6.

117. Livy, 26.28.1–2.

118. Livy, 26.28.9. The reliability of that notice is not above reproach. In the following year, Galba's command was prorogued *eadem legione eademque classe*: Livy, 27.7.15; and he certainly had some troops with him in 209: Livy, 27.32.2. Yet in 208 the prorogation is described simply as *ut eadem classe Macedoniam Graeciamque provinciam haberet*: Livy, 27.22.10. Whatever the truth of the matter, there is no reason to doubt that Rome reduced her involvement already in 210.

119. Failure to lift siege of Echinus: Polyb. 9.42.1–3. Capture of Aegina, then transferred to the Aetolians: Polyb. 9.42.5–8, 11.5.8, 22.8.9. An indecisive engagement in Elis: Livy, 27.32.2–7. Mixed success and failure in Euboea: Livy, 28.5.18–28.6.12. Capture of Dyme: Paus. 7.17.5; cf. Livy, 32.21.8, 32.22.10. Brutality and Galba's reputation: Polyb. 9.42.5–8, 11.5.6–8; Livy, 28.7.4, 32.22.10; Paus. 7.17.5; and, especially, Appian, *Mac.* 3.1, 7.

120. Polyb. 10.25.3: προκινδεύουσι μὲν Αἰτωλοὶ καὶ Πελοποννησίων οἱ τούτοις συμμαχοῦντες, ἐφεδρεύουσι δὲ Ῥωμαῖοι.

Aetolian resolve. The Aetolians then drove a hard bargain, demanding among other things that Philip yield up the Atintanes to Rome and the Ardiaei to Scerdilaidas and his son Pleuratus. The terms obviously issued from Roman suggestion and, being quite unacceptable to Philip, they promptly broke up the peace conference.[121] Rome had achieved her end. The Aetolians fought on, and the event stirred up rebellion in Dassaretis and even encouraged an offensive by Scerdilaidas and Pleuratus.[122]

The *patres* could now happily reduce Roman involvement still further. In the years 207 and 206 the Republic's forces were altogether inactive in the East. Galba retained a command in "Macedonia and Greece," but his forces contributed nothing to the war effort.[123] The proconsul appears once more in the record of these years, again to undermine peace efforts and to keep Philip's enemies in the field. He communicated privately to the senate what it already knew: that it was to Rome's advantage for Aetolians to continue the fight against Philip.[124] The *patres* sent no further aid, even ignoring an Aetolian plea, though after the battle of the Metaurus they were in a better position to do so. The East remained a tangential concern.[125] Only in spring 205, after Aetolia, battered and frustrated, had at last come to terms with Philip, did a new Roman army cross the Adriatic, eleven thousand men and thirty-five ships under P. Sempronius Tuditanus. Finding the Aetolians already at peace, they landed at Epidamnus, urged the Parthini and other tribes to rebellion, and began a siege of Dimale.[126] It was the most vigorous Roman offensive of the war. But what does it amount to? Certainly not an imperialist design on the territories of Illyria and Macedonia. Rome could have sent such a force in previous years, had she been so inclined. There had been no need or desire to do so, as long as Greeks carried the burden of fighting against Philip. The timing of this expedition discloses its purpose unambiguously. Rome made a show of force and determination in

121. Livy, 27.30.4–15.

122. Livy, 27.32.9; Polyb. 10.41.4 = Livy, 28.5.7.

123. Livy, 29.12.1, 31.31.19. Balsdon's brusque dismissal of this, *JRS* 44 (1954): 31, has no force.

124. Appian, *Mac.* 3.1: ὅτι Ῥωμαίοις συμφέρει πολεμεῖν Αἰτωλοὺς Φιλίππῳ. This clearly refers to the peace negotiations of 207, not to 208; Polyb. 11.4.1; cf. Meloni, *Il valore storico e le fonti del libro macedonico di Appiano* (Rome, 1955), 9–13.

125. The Aetolian plea: Livy, 32.21.17: *ut Philippus Aetolos nequiquam opem Romanorum implorantes depopularetur.* Appian, *Mac.* 3.1, has the senate send ten thousand infantry and one thousand horses to buttress the Aetolians in 207 or 206. But this is plainly a confusion with the expedition of 205, for which we have the identical figures: Livy, 29.12.2; cf. Meloni, *Il valore storico,* 14–16.

126. Livy, 29.12.1–4.

order to disrupt peace and induce the Aetolians back into the fray.[127] That goal coincided with all her previous policy in the area. She had not the slightest intention of waging her own war with Macedonia. When Philip marched to Apollonia, ravaged the surrounding fields, and offered battle, the Romans stayed inside the walls, waiting for Aetolia to move.[128] But the Aetolians had had enough. They stuck to their agreement with the king, and Rome had no option but to conclude peace herself.

The peace of Phoenice in 205 brought an amicable settlement. Philip, in a strong bargaining position, received Roman recognition of his authority in Atintania. The king, in turn, released claims on the Parthini, on Dimallum, and on two other Illyrian towns.[129] Nothing more is known of territorial arrangements under the peace—or of any other arrangements. The two principal signatories were presumably otherwise content with what they had. Rome's demand of four years before, that Philip surrender Atintania and the territory of the Ardiaei, had now apparently been given up. The king certainly retained Atintania, almost certainly Dassaretis, and probably some control over the Ardiaei.[130] That gave him a position in Illyria and afforded security for the borders of western Macedonia. The Adriatic coast seemed now to hold less attraction for him. He made no claims upon the Greek cities of the Ionian Gulf. Such demands would perpetuate hostilities with Rome, hostilities he preferred to rid himself of. Philip's ambitions would now turn to the East.

For the Republic, the peace terms were more than satisfactory. The southern Adriatic was free of menace, the one goal that had motivated Rome throughout. Rome could happily sacrifice the Atintanes, as well as other portions of south Illyria where Philip held sway, and redirect her attention to the West. She lacked aspirations in Hellas.[131]

127. Livy, 29.12.5: *pacemque, si posset, turbandam.*
128. Livy, 29.12.5–6.
129. Livy, 29.12.13.
130. The Roman tradition would certainly not have *omitted* any concessions on Philip's part. Hence, the omission of Lissus is especially troublesome. Holleaux, *Rome, la Grèce*, 278–279, n. 2, regards it as improbable that Rome would have left it in Philip's hands. But was it still in Philip's hands? J. M. F. May, *JRS* 36 (1946): 48–52, argues that Philip had already abandoned it ca. 208 when he saw no further hope of collaborating with the Carthaginian fleet. Yet the hope of such collaboration is itself pure conjecture. The absence of Lissus from Livy's account of the peace must rule out the possibility of Philip's yielding it at that time. It can be argued, of course, that Rome was not in a position to insist. But, more to the point, Lissus was not among the places demanded of Philip in 197, when Rome *was* in a position to insist: Polyb. 18.47.12; Livy, 33.34.11. In all likelihood, he had lost interest in it when his ambitions were diverted away from the Adriatic, and by 205 it was no longer at issue.
131. The presence of *adscripti* to the peace of Phoenice was good Hellenistic

## The Origins of the Second Macedonian War

The origins of the Second Macedonian War remain among the most controversial and the most important subjects of classical history. After that conflict Rome found it increasingly difficult and ultimately impossible to extricate herself from the circumstances of the Hellenistic world. The consequences for Mediterranean history and culture were vast. Hence, a plethora of scholarly analyses have been devoted to the topic, a multitude of answers provided, disagreement on points small and large, constituting an ongoing and ever more convoluted discussion. It would be superfluous and tedious to rehearse the protracted modern debate.[132] But the issue must be joined. If Rome evaded embroilment in the East down to the end of the third century, what tempted her to engage in fateful struggle with Philip V of Macedonia?

The annalists who fashioned Roman history into the tradition known to and further elaborated by Livy had a variety of answers, not all of them consonant with one another, but all in justification of the Republic's action.

A war in defense of allies, injured and threatened by Macedonian aggrandizement, allegedly supplied ground for the motion presented to the *comitia* in the spring of 200.[133] The theme appears several

---

practice: Livy, 29.12.14; see above p. 21. Those states, whether or not all of them are authentic, had good reason to seek inclusion in a treaty between major powers. They by no means imply anything about Roman ambitions in the East. The notion that Rome regarded the peace of Phoenice as a "makeshift peace" and saw it as a future "convenient *casus belli* against Philip" (Balsdon, *JRS* 44 [1954]: 32–33; similarly, Ferro, *Le origini*, 117–119), thus creating "conditions which led almost inevitably to an appeal for military help" (Harris, *War and Imperialism*, 207–208) is unwarranted. A better appreciation by Holleaux, *Rome, la Grèce*, 284–305, who, however, wrongly believes that Rome was in a position to dictate the terms of the treaty in 205; *op. cit.*, 177–179. In retrospect, it was natural enough to reckon the peace of Phoenice as a mere stop-gap. The idea appears in late authorities: Appian, *Mac.* 3.2; Justin, 29.4.11; Zon. 9.15.1. But nothing shows that it prevailed at the time. Nor that it was to be found in Polybius: as Bickermann, *CP* 40 (1945): 147–148; rightly criticized by Walbank, *JRS* 53 (1963): 7. Livy, 29.12.16, may well be Polybian, as argued by Derow, *JRS* 69 (1979): 6–7. But the passage need not imply that Romans intended (or that Polybius believed they intended) to resume hostilities with Philip once the Hannibalic war was over.

132. For recent bibliographical summaries, see Will, *Histoire politique* II: 125–128; Dahlheim, *Struktur und Entwicklung*, 239–241, n. 20; Werner, *ANRW* I:1, 540–548; L. Raditsa, *ANRW* I:1, 564–576; Briscoe, *Commentary*, 39–40; Ferrary, in Nicolet, *Rome et la conquête* 2:738–740.

133. Livy, 31.6.1: *rogationem promulgavit, vellent iuberent Philippo regi Macedonibusque qui sub regno eius essent, ob iniurias armaque inlata sociis populi Romani bellum indici.* Cf. Justin, 30.3.6: *titulo ferendi sociis auxilii bellum adversus Philippum decernitur.*

times in Livy's text.[134] Some particulars are filled in by a tale of envoys from *sociae urbes* in Greece who arrived at Rome in 203 to complain of fields ravaged by Philip's troops. The senate dispatched an embassy and three quinqueremes to assert that Philip had violated his treaty.[135] Their report came back more than a year later in 201: Philip had indeed been harassing Roman allies and the senate's envoy had nobly organized resistance to protect them against his aggressions. The *patres* now repeated their charge that Philip had transgressed the treaty and wronged the *socii* of the *populus Romanus*.[136]

It requires faith to believe this tale. Who were the *sociae urbes*? Of all the Greek cities and states attacked by Philip in the years after Phoenice, none was a *socius* of Rome and only one, Attalus, an *amicus*—and he was not menaced in 203. The absence of reference to any specific place sows suspicion right away. And these "allies" play no further role in the story. The apologists evidently created a grievance to show that Rome was alert and resistant to Philip's depredations well before she declared war.[137] In their zeal to justify the war some even alleged that Rome acted in defense of her "ally" Aetolia![138] That is enough to discredit the tradition. Polybius delivers the final blow: the Romans demanded of Philip that he make war on none of the Greeks. Polybius has not a word about defense of *socii*.[139]

Alarm over the growing power of Philip served also as annalistic justification. A Roman legate in "Macedonia," it was averred, reported a massive military build-up in 201. The king was equipping armies and navies on a huge scale, to stir up not only cities on the mainland but the islands of the sea. He was the new Pyrrhus, and a mightier Pyrrhus.[140] The same danger, painted in bolder colors, appears in the speech of Sulpicius Galba urging the *comitia* to declare

134. Cf. Livy, 31.1.9: *infensos Philippo cum ob infidam adversus Aetolos aliosque regionis eiusdem socios pacem.* The argument of Ferro, *Le origini*, 12–19, that the *socii* are allies of Aetolia, specifically Echinus, Phthiotic Thebes, Pharsalus, and Larisa (Polyb. 18.3.12, 18.38.3–6; Livy, 32.33.16, 33.13.6) is invalid. In the context, the *socii* must be allies of Rome; McDonald, *JRS* 53 (1963): 188. Other examples of the theme in Livy, 31.3.1, 31.5.8–9, 31.9.4, 31.11.9, 31.31.2, 34.22.8–9.

135. Livy, 30.26.2–4.

136. Livy, 30.42.1–10.

137. Bredehorn, *Senatsakten*, 105, remarkably asserts that the absence of specifics is an argument for the authenticity of the tradition! The discussion of Petzold, *Die Eröffnung*, 44–47, remains unrefuted. See above, Chapter 1, n. 42.

138. Livy, 31.1.9; Paus. 7.7.7; cf. Livy, 34.23.7. For Rome's true feelings about Aetolia at this time, see Appian, *Mac.* 4; Livy, 31.29.4. And, on Aetolia's attitude, Livy, 31.15.9–11, 31.46.4.

139. Polyb. 16.27.2, 16.34.3.

140. Livy, 31.3.4–6; cf. Justin, 30.3.2; Zon. 9.15.

war: Philip far exceeds Pyrrhus in strength of resources, Rome is now much weaker from the demands of the Hannibalic conflict; the Republic must fight Philip in Macedonia or she will face him in Italy.[141] In short, the pretext legitimizes a preventive war. That, however, is patent exaggeration and hardly serves to explain the Roman decision. Philip's power, to be sure, had grown and his aggressions increased. The direction of his endeavors, however, was decidedly eastwards, well away from any Roman sphere of interest. From 204 to 201, he engaged his forces in Crete, the Propontis, Thasos, the Cyclades, Samos, Ionia, Pergamum, and Caria.[142] Rome had no stake in any of these areas and no cause to feel apprehension. The king had indeed built a fleet. More than fifty warships and one hundred fifty *lembi* were available to him by 201.[143] But the Romans remembered well their previous naval encounters with him. The mere appearance of Roman vessels had been enough to plunge Philip into flight in 217/16 and again in 214.[144] Romans who knew their recent history could have felt nothing but scorn for the king who raced in terror rather than face the foe. If word reached the *patres* of Philip's new fleet, they must also have heard of his devastating losses at the battle of Chios: nearly half his ships sunk or captured, the heaviest cost in lives he had ever suffered in a single contest.[145] By the beginning of winter 201/0, the king was blockaded at Bargylia by the fleets of Rhodes and Pergamum.[146] That the senate could have feared a naval invasion of Italy is manifestly absurd.[147]

141. Livy, 31.7.2–13: *ignorare, inquit, mihi videmini, Quirites, non utrum bellum an pacem habeatis vos consuli—neque enim liberum id vobis Philippus permittet, qui terra marique ingens bellum molitur—sed utrum in Macedoniam legiones transportetis an hostes in Italiam accipiatis.*

142. Crete: Polyb. 13.3–5, 18.54.8; Diod. 28.1–2; Polyaen. 5.17; the Propontis: Polyb. 15.21–23, 18.2.4, 18.3.11–12, 18.4.7, 18.5.4; Livy, 32.33.15, 32.34.6; Strabo, 12.4.3 (C 564); Thasos: Polyb. 15.24.1–3; the Cyclades: Livy, 31.15.8; Samos: Polyb. 16.2.4, 16.2.9, 16.7.6; Appian, *Mac.* 4.1; Livy, 31.31.4; Habicht, *AthMitt* 72 (1957): 233–241; Ionia: Polyb. 16.2–10, 16.14–15; Pergamum: Polyb. 16.1; Appian, *Mac.* 4; Diod. 28.5; Caria: Polyb. 16.11.1–16.12.1, 16.24, 18.2.3, 18.8.9, 18.44.4; Appian, *Mac.* 4; Livy, 33.18.1, 33.18.19–20, 34.32.5. In general on Philip's campaigns, see Walbank, *Philip V,* 108–127.

143. Polyb. 16.2.9.

144. Polyb. 5.110; Livy, 24.40; Zon. 9.4; Plut. *Arat.* 51.2.

145. Polyb. 16.7.1–2, 16.7.5, 16.8.6. Polybius' Rhodian sources may have exaggerated the losses; cf. Walbank, *Commentary* II: 509–510. But to reckon this a "strategic victory" (as G. T. Griffith, *CHJ* 5 [1935]: 8) is special pleading; see Harris, *War and Imperialism,* 214.

146. Polyb. 16.24.1–2. On Philip's naval campaigns in these years, see Walbank, in W. L. Adams and E. N. Borza, *Philip II, Alexander the Great, and the Macedonian Heritage* (Washington, D.C., 1982), 228–233.

147. Equally far-fetched is the theory of Passerini, *Athenaeum* 9 (1931): 542–562,

A related but different theme is the "stab-in-the-back" theory.
Philip had supported Hannibal in the Second Punic War and Rome
would now have her just revenge.[148] This idea is bound up with the
suggestion that Rome reckoned the peace of Phoenice a mere respite
until her hands were free to deal with Philip.[149] The annalists were
swift to add that Philip had sent troops and money to aid Hannibal in
Africa, even a *legio Macedonum* which served at Zama.[150] The notices
warrant little credence. Macedonian soldiers are not listed in the battle array at Zama given by Polybius and Appian, nor do they appear
in the fighting even as given by Livy.[151] The treaty between Hannibal
and Philip in 215, as we have seen, provided for Macedonian assistance only if Hannibal should summon it. The pact, however, was
manifestly otiose once Philip came to terms with Rome in 205. The
king never gave aid to his ally while the treaty remained in effect. And
it would be folly indeed for him to supply troops and resources for
Carthage at a time when Rome's victory was imminent and his own
efforts fully engaged in the East.[152] Resentment against Philip is part
of the later apologetic tradition. It obviously weighed little with the
*comitia* which overwhelmingly rejected war in 200 B.C.

One other pretext for intervention shows itself in the annalistic
accounts: Rome had come to the defense of the once great and now
beleaguered and helpless cultural capital of Hellas, Athens.[153] Livy
records no fewer than three Athenian embassies dispatched to seek
aid from the Republic. The first came ostensibly in late 201, complaining of fields plundered and the citizenry driven behind their walls.[154]

---

that Rome feared a renewed African war to be stirred up by Philip. The hypothesis is in
no way supported by the texts which Passerini cites: Appian, *Mac.* 4; Livy, 31.11.4–7.

148. Livy, 31.11.9, 34.22.8, 45.22.6; cf. Florus, 1.23.4.

149. Cf. Livy, 31.1.9–10; Appian, *Mac.* 3.2; Justin, 29.4.11; Zon. 9.15.1.

150. Livy, 30.26.3, 30.33.5–6, 30.42.4, 30.42.6, 31.1.10, 31.11.9; cf. Frontin. *Strat.*
2.3.16; Sil. Ital. 17.418ff.

151. Polyb. 15.11; Appian, *Lib.* 40; Livy, 30.34.5, 30.35.9. It does not help much to
suggest that some Macedonian mercenaries fought for Hannibal; as Bickermann, *CP* 40
(1945): 143, n. 17; Balsdon, *JRS* 44 (1954): 34; Dorey, *AJP* 78 (1957): 185–187; Ferro, *Le
origini*, 19–20; Bredehorn, *Senatsakten*, 120–121. Even had they done so, this could not
be held against Philip. Livy, 30.42.4, may suggest mercenaries, but the thrust of his
narrative is to regard them as an official Macedonian force; cf. Livy, 30.42.6. The whole
tradition is more than suspect; cf. especially Petzold, *Die Eröffnung*, 50–57.

152. Carthage allegedly did request Macedonian aid, for the first and only time,
in 205: Livy, 29.4.4; Zon. 9.11. But Philip's response is clear: he made peace with Rome
instead.

153. Livy, 31.1.10: *preces Atheniensium, quos agro pervastato in urbem compulerat, excitaverunt ad renovandum bellum*; 45.22.6; *Per.* 31; cf. 31.7.6, 31.9.1–4; Paus. 7.7.7–8.

154. Livy, 31.1.9–31.2.1; so also Appian, *Mac.* 4. Philip's assault, in response to
an Acarnanian appeal, is described in Livy, 31.14.6–10.

Then a second, at the beginning of the consular year 200, announced that the king approached their borders and would soon have the city at his mercy.[155] Finally, a third mission, begging for relief of the siege of Athens, applied to Sulpicius Galba upon his arrival across the Adriatic in autumn, 200.[156] How many of these embassies are authentic—and which ones—has generated reams of copy that can mercifully be passed over here.[157] What matters is the Polybian testimony. It demonstrates unequivocally that the Athenians themselves only decided on war against Philip after Roman envoys reached Athens and after Attalus and the Rhodians had persuaded them of Rome's commitment to check the Macedonian.[158] When Rome's legates delivered their demands to Philip's general and to Philip himself, the claims of Athens are conspicuously absent.[159] So, whatever one makes of Athenian embassies to the senate, they cannot explain the Roman decision for war.

Subsequent apologia proves suspect and, on any analysis, insufficient. The annalists largely ignored or soft-pedaled the complex events that entwined Hellenistic states in conflict. By focusing their attention on Rome and Philip, they oversimplified the circumstances, exaggerated or fabricated the king's transgressions against Rome and her *socii*, and even saw the war as a logical outcome of previous hostilities.[160] The fragments of Polybius provide an invaluable corrective. Unhappily, however, they do not include his views on the motives for

155. Livy, 31.5.2, 31.5.5–8. Ferro's effort, *Le origini*, 75, to interpret *finibus suis* as referring to *Philip's* borders ignores the plain context of the statement; so, rightly, McDonald, *JRS* 53 (1963): 188.

156. Livy, 31.14.3; the date in Livy, 31.22.4.

157. There was one at least, conducted by Cephisodorus: Paus. 1.36.6; cf. *Hesperia* 5 (1936): 419–428 = *ISE*, no. 33. The first and second legations recorded by Livy, with much the same complaint, may perhaps be amalgamated, and identified with Cephisodorus' mission. Whether or not the third embassy is historical makes little difference in understanding Roman motives, for a consular army was already in Illyria. Among many discussions of the chronology and authenticity of the Athenian legations, see Walbank, *Philip V*, 311–313, with bibliography; Petzold, *Die Eröffnung*, 66–81; Balsdon, *JRS* 44 (1954): 35–37; Ferro, *Le origini*, 74–90; Briscoe, *Commentary*, 42–45; Habicht, *Studien*, 150–158.

158. Polyb. 16.25.4–6, 16.26.6–8. The same in Livy, 31.15.1–5, who, however, leaves out the Roman embassy. It would not fit with his description of the embassy's purpose: Livy, 31.2.3–4. Nor would it suit the annalistic version that Rome's decision was influenced by Athenian importuning.

159. Polyb. 16.27.2, 16.34.3. Lepidus does mention aggression against the Athenians, but only among various grievances and only as an afterthought, not as part of the formal demands: Polyb. 16.34.5.

160. Cf. Livy, 31.1.6: *pacem Punicam bellum Macedonicum excepit*; 31.1.10: *excitaverunt ad renovandum bellum*; 32.21.16–18. See the brilliant paper of Bickermann, *CP* 40 (1945): 137–148; cf. Raditsa, *ANRW* I:1, 571–573.

Roman intervention. Nor can we be confident that they would have provided much enlightenment anyway.[161] Hence, other reasons have been excogitated by moderns, argued at length, and ultimately proved inconclusive.

One hypothesis held the field longest. The "secret pact" between Philip and Antiochus the Great, concluded ca. 203/2, proposed to carve up the realm of the Ptolemies between them. The agreement, so it was argued, threatened to shatter the balance of the Hellenistic world and unite the massive power of the Antigonids and Seleucids. Once it came to light in Rome, it stimulated the senate to take action lest Italy become prey to this fearsome coalition.[162] A multitude of difficulties arise from this thesis, which do not here require rehearsal. The authenticity of the pact has itself been denied.[163] One need not go that far: Polybius believed it was genuine, and it appears in a number of other sources, including Appian, whose account seems independent of the Polybian tradition.[164] But its terms, character, and duration alike are obscure. Even contemporaries, if they knew anything of it, must have been baffled. Appian reports it only as a rumor, and the provisions he records do not march with the actions of Philip given by Polybius as consequences of the pact.[165] What is Rome likely to have known and how much did she care? Appian has

161. Notice the schematic and simplistic design that has the Antiochene war follow from the Macedonian, the Macedonian from the Hannibalic, and the Hannibalic from the First Punic War; Polyb. 3.32.7.

162. This is the classic thesis of Holleaux, *Rome, la Grèce*, 306–322; followed, e.g., by Griffith, *CHJ* 5 (1935):1–6; McDonald and Walbank, *JRS* 27 (1937): 182–187, 205–207; Walbank, *Philip V*, 127–128; H. Stier, *Roms Aufstieg zur Weltmacht und die griechische Welt* (Köln and Opladen, 1952), 101–104; Albert, *Bellum Iustum*, 104–106.

163. See Magie, *JRS* 29 (1939): 32–44, who sees it as a fabrication of the Rhodians. Cf. also Errington, *Athenaeum* 49 (1971): 336–354, who holds that it was a mere private agreement between Philip and Antiochus' *strategos* in Asia Minor, Zeuxis—an unlikely solution; cf. R. M. Berthold, *CJ* 71 (1975–76): 100–101.

164. Polyb. 3.2.8, 15.20.2, 16.1.8; cf. 16.10.1, 16.24.6; Appian, *Mac.* 4; Livy, 31.14.5; Justin, 30.2.8; Porphyry, *FGH*, 260 F 44; John Antioch. fr. 54. On the independence of Appian's account, see Meloni, *Il valore storico*, 37–42. Strongest argument on behalf of authenticity by Schmitt, *Untersuchungen*, 237–261, though his efforts to reconcile the testimony of Polybius and Appian are strained and unconvincing. Bibliography on the subject in Dahlheim, *Struktur und Entwicklung*, 235–236, n. 6.

165. Appian, *Mac.* 4: λόγος τε ἦν . . . τήνδε τὴν δόξαν. For Appian, the agreement gave Egypt and Cyprus to Antiochus, Cyrene, the Cyclades, and Ionia to Philip. Polybius has Philip attack Egypt, Caria, and Samos, while Antiochus moved against Coele Syria and Phoenicia, after the arrangement was made: Polyb. 3.2.8. Most have emended Αἴγυπτον to Αἴγαιον. But Polybius evidently believed that Philip did intend an assault on Egypt: 16.10.1; see Pedech, *REG* 67 (1954): 391–393; Schmitt, *Untersuchungen*, 252; Walbank, *Commentary* II:471–472; *contra*: Errington, *Athenaeum* 49 (1971): 339–340.

the news brought to the senate by Rhodians, Justin by Alexandrians.[166] So there is confusion even here. Whatever the provisions of the pact, its effectiveness was virtually nil. Philip's assaults in Asia Minor in 201 impinged on territories claimed as a Seleucid sphere of influence.[167] Antiochus' agent Zeuxis offered the Macedonian little help and that most reluctantly.[168] More rivals than partners, the two monarchs, as Polybius affirms, while they carved up the holdings of Egypt, violated their own arrangements and broke faith with one another.[169] By the time news of the compact reached Rome, Philip was being blockaded at Bargylia and getting only minimal assistance from Zeuxis. Rhodians or Alexandrians, if they did report the agreement to the senate, would not only have to exaggerate its aims but also conceal its ineffectiveness! That the senate paid any attention is unlikely in the extreme.[170]

Was there concern over aggression in Illyria and a threat to the Adriatic? Such worries had prodded Rome before. And they have been hypothesized as providing a reason for her action on this occasion as well.[171] Yet direct evidence is lacking, a notable omission, for a menace to those areas would supply an appropriate motive or pretext: there could be no reason for the tradition to suppress them. During negotiations at Nicaea in winter 198/7, Flamininus demanded that Philip hand over to the Romans certain (unspecified) places in Illyria of which he had secured control since the peace of Phoenice. That, however, constituted but one amid a series of demands, including evacuation of Greece and restoration of cities to Ptolemy. Nothing suggests or implies that occupation of these Illyrian places had endangered Roman interests, let alone that they had provoked the Republic to war.[172] When Rome at last imposed territorial arrangements

166. Appian, *Mac.* 4; Justin, 30.2.8.

167. Cf. Polyb. 16.24.8; *OGIS*, 234 = *FDelphes*, III, 4, 163.

168. Polyb. 16.1.8, 16.24.6.

169. Polyb. 15.20.6: αὐτῶν παρασπονδούντων μὲν ἀλλήλους.

170. Even in Appian there is no suggestion that news of the pact determined Rome on war; ἐκταράσσουσαν ἅπαντας refers to Greeks. Only Justin makes the connection: 30.2.8–30.3.6—an account imbedded in his questionable narrative of Rome's tutelage of the young Egyptian king; see Errington, *Athenaeum* 49 (1971): 343–345, 353–354.

171. Cf. Badian, *Studies*, 22–23; *Foreign Clientelae*, 63–66; Errington, *Dawn of Empire*, 131–134.

172. Polyb. 18.1.14: τοὺς δὲ κατὰ τὴν Ἰλλυρίδα τόπους παραδοῦναι Ῥωμαίοις, ὧν γέγονε κύριος μετὰ τὰς ἐν Ἠπείρῳ διαλύσεις. Livy, 32.33.3, mistranslates παραδοῦναι with *restituenda*, thus delivering the erroneous impression that Rome had a prior claim on the sites. The view of Zippel, *Die römische Herrschaft*, 73, and Holleaux, *Rome, la Grèce*, 278, n. 1, that μετὰ τὰς ἐν Ἠπείρῳ διαλύσεις means "after and in accordance with the peace of Phoenice" is plainly wrong and adequately refuted by Badian, *Stud-*

after the Second Macedonian War in 196, the only Illyrian places yielded up by Philip were two sites, Lychnis and Parthus, to be handed over to Pleuratus, a clear indication that Roman interests in the area remained quite limited.[173] Had Philip interfered with the Greek cities of the Ionian Gulf, whom Rome had defended more than once in the past, we should certainly have heard of it. The ultimata delivered to the king make no mention of that sector and breathe not a word about Illyria. The issue is without relevance.

Did Rome act to discharge obligations contracted in the past? One will be hard pressed to discern any such obligations. As already observed, Rome had scrupulously avoided framing permanent treaties of alliance with eastern states prior to the second century.[174] Of all the legations that came to Italy in the months before declaration of war, from Athens, Rhodes, Pergamum, Aetolia, and Egypt, none alluded to a formal pact and none even made reference (though some could have) to an *amicitia*. The senate was untrammeled by previous commitments, as they all knew. Did Rome then take up a posture as guarantor of the peace of Phoenice, a *koine eirene* which she had moral, if not legal, obligation to uphold? An attractive idea at first glance, and one that has had a powerful advocate.[175] Yet the very existence of a *koine eirene* under the treaty of 205 is itself questionable. Livy's phrase *pax communis* probably lacks technical significance and, in any case, applies to the aspirations of the Epirotes, rather than to the conclusion of the treaty.[176] The agreement was one between Rome and Philip, to which some *adscripti* were added on one side or the

---

ies, 33, n. 102, and Balsdon, *CQ* 47 (1953): 163–164. That tiresome debate was renewed, to no good effect, by Oost, *CP* 54 (1959): 158–164, and by Dorey, Oost, and Badian in *CP*, 55 (1960) 180–186. But, though the phrase cannot signify that Philip's gains in Illyria were authorized by Phoenice, neither does it suggest that they *violated* the terms of Phoenice. Briscoe's assertion, *Commentary*, 55, that "the places involved were part of the Roman protectorate" is unfounded. Some have endeavored to connect Philip's acquisitions in Illyria with the annalistic reports of appeals to Rome from *sociae urbes*: Livy, 30.26.2, 30.42.2, 30.42.5, 30.42.8, 31.1.9; Badian, *Studies*, 22–23; *Foreign Clientelae*, 61–62; Bredehorn, *Senatsakten*, 100–113; Briscoe, *Commentary*, 54–55. Quite apart from the dubious character of these reports, the *sociae urbes* are described as *ex Graecia*, not from Illyria: Livy, 30.26.2. And the *socii* who are *eiusdem regionis* as Aetolia (Livy, 31.1.9) can hardly be Illyrians. On all this, see the sensible and economical remarks of Walbank, *Commentary* II:551.

173. Polyb. 18.47.12. Livy, 33.34.11, wrongly infers *Parthini* from Πάρθος; cf. Walbank, *Commentary*, II:618–619; and see now Hammond, *A History of Macedonia* I (Oxford, 1972), 96, n. 4.

174. See above pp. 17–25.

175. Bickermann, *RevPhilol* 61 (1935): 59–81, 170; cf. Piraino, *RivFilol* 33 (1955): 62–65; Ferro, *Le origini*, 118; Raditsa, *ANRW* I:1, 569–571.

176. Livy, 29.12.8: *Epirotae . . . legatos de pace communi ad Philippum misere.*

other, not a general peace applying to all Greeks.[177] Even the annalistic tradition, which accuses Philip of violating the pact, alleges his attacks on Roman *socii* and omits mention of disturbing a common peace.[178] The demands made of the king by Roman envoys in 200 do indeed require him to abjure war on all Greeks, but the peace of Phoenice is nowhere cited as justification. On the contrary, it is Philip who insists that if Rome should press her demands to the point of war *she* would be in violation of the treaty—an assertion that goes uncontradicted in the record.[179] The senate had avoided formal or moral commitments. And it claimed no authority under the peace of Phoenice.

Other modern suggestions can be passed over briefly. Nothing in the ancient testimony implies commercial or economic considerations. Rome was as yet without financial interests in the Aegean or further East and could hardly have worried about Philip's ambitions there. Indeed, Roman creditors who had lent funds to the state during the Hannibalic war objected to the new venture as postponing repayment and complained of wars following wars. They had to be mollified into compliance by a compromise arrangement.[180] Philhellenism, "sentimental politics," a noble desire to liberate Greeks from the Macedonian yoke are similarly undemonstrable motives.[181] Even the slogans of "Greek freedom" did not enter Roman propaganda until the war was well underway, and then they were suggested by Hellenic allies; they cannot explain the Republic's initial intervention.[182] Roman politics has also been invoked as a cause: a party of the senate with special interests in the East, "Fulvians" or "Claudians," eager to earn military distinctions and to eclipse the glories of Scipio Africanus.[183] It is all pure hypothesis. The existence of an "eastern lobby" can safely be rejected.[184]

177. Livy, 29.12.14; Appian, *Mac.* 3.2: καὶ ἐγένοντο συνθῆκαι Ῥωμαίοις καὶ Φιλίππῳ, μηδετέρους ἀδικεῖν τοὺς ἑκατέρωθεν φίλους. Cf. Dahlheim, *Struktur und Entwicklung*, 207–221.

178. Livy, 30.26.2–4, 30.42.8–10, 31.1.9.

179. Polyb. 16.34.7; Appian, *Mac.* 4; Diod. 28.6; Livy, 31.18.4; cf. 30.42.3. The ultimatum at Abydus included the claims of Ptolemy and the Rhodians, neither of whom was signatory to the peace of Phoenice: Polyb. 16.34.3. Even Bickermann has to admit "c'est une intervention de Rome pure et simple, sans que rien l'y oblige, dictée donc par les raisons d'ordre politique;" *RevPhilol* 61 (1935): 166.

180. Livy, 31.13: *aliis ex aliis orientibus bellis*; cf. Passerini, *Athenaeum* 9 (1931): 559–561. The economic motive is advocated by Colin, *Rome et la Grèce*, 89–95.

181. For the "philhellenic" view, see Mommsen, *Römische Geschichte*, I[10], 698–700; Frank, *Roman Imperialism*, 150–151; Stier, *Roms Aufstieg*, 103–119.

182. See above pp. 145–146.

183. Dorey, *AJP*, 80 (1959), 288–295; Briscoe, *Commentary*, 31, 45–46; Bruzzi, *I sistemi informativi*, 170–173; more cautiously expressed by Harris, *War and Imperialism*, 217–218.

184. See above pp. 204–207.

That some men looked forward to conquest, spoils, and honor may well be true. But their aspirations define no particular faction of the senate. Nor do the sources identify any individual warmonger in that body.[185] Was it then simply a matter of aggressive imperialism?[186] The idea does not correspond to Rome's previous behavior in the East. Her actions had been brief, limited, or half-hearted, confined to keeping the Adriatic clear and encouraging other powers to curtail the ambitions of Macedonia. Indeed, after Philip's defeat, conquered lands were set free or bestowed upon other states. The Roman empire was no larger after the Second Macedonian War than before. The Greeks may have expected overlordship by a western hegemony, but they did not get it. Withdrawal of troops and garrisons, abjuration of territory and tribute, belie imperialistic intent.

The motives for war proffered by ancients and hypothesized by moderns prove unsatisfactory. A fundamental question needs to be asked. Did Rome want war? Certainly the bulk of men voting in the *comitia centuriata* did not. They rejected the motion presented to them in overwhelming numbers. They were weary of war, chafed at its length and burdens, decried its dangers and hardships.[187] The monied classes also registered protest, as we have seen. They predicted that repayment of their loans would be indefinitely postponed; use of funds for one war that had been loaned for another they likened to confiscation of property.[188] The state offered concessions: a property settlement for the creditors, and a promise to the *comitia* that only volunteers would be recruited, no one to be impressed into service against his will.[189] Yet hostile attitudes persisted. When Villius took over the army in Macedonia in 199, he found it in a state of mutiny. Soldiers complained that they had been forced into service without their

185. Sulpicius Galba, of course, presented the war motion to the *comitia* and argued vigorously in its behalf: Livy, 31.6.1, 31.7. But this was in his capacity as consul, representing the senate's will, not as leader of a faction. The tribune Baebius, who opposed the war, accused all the *patres* of seeking it, and, if Livy is to be believed, each of them encouraged Galba to press the motion: Livy, 31.6.4–6.

186. So, e.g., De Sanctis, *Storia dei Romani* IV:1, 23–26; J. Carcopino, *Les Étapes de l'imperialisme romain* (Paris, 1934), 68–105; Petzold, *Die Eröffnung, passim*; Will, *Histoire politique*, II:116–125; Harris, *War and Imperialism*, 212–218.

187. Livy, 31.6.3: *Rogatio de bello Macedonico primis comitiis ab omnibus ferme centuriis antiquata est. Id cum fessi diurnitate et gravitate belli sua sponte homines taedio periculorum laborumque fecerant*. Briscoe, *Commentary*, 71, rightly points out that *omnibus* is an exaggeration since voting stopped once a majority was reached. But it was doubtless more than a narrow rejection.

188. Livy, 31.13.4: *si in Punicum bellum pecunia data in Macedonicum quoque bellum uti res publica vellet, aliis ex aliis orientibus bellis, quid aliud quam publicatam pro beneficio tamquam noxia suam pecuniam fore?*

189. Livy, 31.8.6, 31.13.5–9, 31.14.2.

consent: they had grown old through endless campaigns in Sicily, Africa, and Macedonia without a glimpse of Italy, exhausted with toil, and drained of blood from the many wounds sustained in conflict.[190] Eagerness for war plainly did not run through the Roman populace. The Republic, it appears, was also hard pressed by continued demands from its creditors. In order to make repayment in 196, money had to be extorted from priests and augurs, leading to severe political conflict.[191] Patriotic acceptance of this eastern adventure was far from thorough. The *comitia*, of course, reversed the initial negative vote and sanctioned a declaration of war. The reason can hardly be that they suddenly welcomed a military contest in the East.

Nor did the senate hasten into this war. Far from it. If the annalistic tradition be reliable, Rome had grievances against Philip as early as 203. Yet she contented herself with sending an embassy, an embassy still abroad two years later, confirming all of Philip's misdeeds and defending Rome's allies. The senate dispatched a propraetor with some ships across the Adriatic in late 201, whence came news of even greater Macedonian plans of aggression. Only then could the *patres* begin to turn Roman minds to war.[192] Even were one to dismiss this whole narrative as fiction—as well it might be—the Polybian evidence also demonstrates a long delay in the coming of war. Delegations from Rhodes and Pergamum reached Rome in 201 with reports of Philip's activities in Asia Minor and rumors of his agreement with Antiochus III. Since Philip knew of hostile embassies to Rome by the time he was blockaded in Bargylia in winter of 201, those embassies must have harangued the senate during the autumn, if not before.[193] The subsequent chronology is unclear and much disputed. But we know when Roman forces first arrived in Illyria: the autumn of 200, at least a year later and with loss of a full campaigning season.[194] There was no haste for mobilization.

More telling still are the activities of the Roman embassy sent abroad prior to the outbreak of hostilities. Livy sets its appointment in autumn, 201, before the consular elections for 200. The purpose, in his narrative, was to go to Ptolemy, announce the defeat of Hannibal,

190. Livy, 32.3.2–5.

191. Livy, 33.42.2–4.

192. Livy, 30.26.1–4, 30.42.1–10, 31.3, 31.5.5: *opportune irritandis et bellum animis.*

193. Polyb. 16.25.3. Rhodian and Pergamene envoys are registered by Livy, 31.2.1, and Justin, 30.3.5. Appian, *Mac.* 4, mentions only the Rhodians and the report of the Syro-Macedonian pact. Whether or not an Athenian mission was also there, as Livy, 31.1.10 and Appian, *Mac.* 4, is irrelevant.

194. Livy, 31.22.4 (from Polybius); *autumno ferme exacto.* For the meaning of the phrase, see Holleaux, *Études* IV: 338–340; Walbank, *Philip V*, 317; Pédech, *La méthode*, 462; Briscoe, *Commentary*, 115–116: mid-September or October.

and ask the king to maintain his loyalty in the event of war against Philip.[195] The details of annalistic chronology seldom justify confidence. Yet no warrant exists for wrenching the embassy's appointment out of the year in which it is placed.[196] It should come some time before the consular year 200, i.e. before March 15 according to the Roman calendar—and, in fact, before January or February according to the Julian year.[197] The purpose is another matter. As Polybius' fragments demonstrate, the envoys' commission had much wider scope. They visited various states in Hellas: Epirus, Athamania, Aetolia, Achaea, Athens, and Rhodes. Not until late summer or autumn, 200 did one of their number sail to Abydus, under siege by Philip, and deliver to the king the demands authorized at Rome, failure to comply with which would bring war.[198] So here too, a long time elapsed between the ambassadors' departure and the completion of their task.

The delegation requires closer scrutiny. Its members' conduct in Hellas was remarkable indeed. The senate had armed them with a message stating that Philip must make war on none of the Greeks and should submit his differences with Attalus to arbitration.[199] Yet the envoys were in no hurry to deliver that message to the king. Instead they announced its contents to the Epirotes at Phoenice, to Amynander in Athamania, to the Aetolians at Naupactus, and to the Achaeans at Aegium. Then, with similar intent, they arrived in the Piraeus where they met Attalus and were welcomed by the Athenians. Attalus,

195. Livy, 31.2.2–4.

196. Modern treatments often put it in late winter 201/0 or spring, 200, after entry of the new consuls into office—without sound reason; Holleaux, Études IV: 290–291; Bickermann, RevPhilol 61 (1935): 165; McDonald and Walbank, JRS 27 (1937): 189; Walbank, Philip V, 314; Commentary II:534. Luce, Livy, 53–67, argues that annalists often did not know when particular events occurred within a consular year and distributed them arbitrarily. Even if true, this does not allow transference of the embassy's appointment from 201 to 200. Ferro, Le origini, 90–94, shifts it from before the consular elections to after, on the illegitimate assumption that Rome must first have reckoned war a probability.

197. That the Roman calendar ran ahead of the Julian at this time is well known, probably one or two months ahead: see P. Marchetti, AntCl 42 (1973): 473–496; Derow, Phoenix 30 (1976): 265–281.

198. Polyb. 16.25.2, 16.25.6, 16.27, 16.34.1–7. The approximate date is clear enough. Polybius implies that Lepidus, the Roman envoy, reached Abydus near the end of the siege: 16.33.1–16.34.1, 16.34.7; cf. Livy, 31.18.1: ante deditionem. Philip learned of the arrival of Galba in Greece shortly after Abydus fell: Livy, 31.18.9 (from Polybius). Since Galba's crossing came in September or October (Livy, 31.22.4), the parley between Philip and Lepidus cannot have been much earlier. According to Appian, Mac. 4, the embassy's purpose was to warn Antiochus off Egypt and Philip off the "friends" of Rome; cf. Justin, 30.3.3.

199. Polyb. 16.27.2.

encouraged by their presence, persuaded the Athenians to declare war, suggesting among other things that they could expect the support of Rome.[200] As it happened, Macedonian forces under Nicanor chose that moment to launch an assault on Attica, ravaging her fields up to the Academy. The attack was not and could hardly have been anticipated by the Roman legates. Under the circumstances, they improvised. They delivered their message to Nicanor and asked him to transmit it to his king.[201] How Philip took the news we cannot say. His subsequent actions, however, show plainly enough that he ignored it. If Livy is to be believed, Philip immediately dispatched a force to Attica under Philocles to ravage the terrain once again, a clear act of defiance.[202] Whether that report be true or not, the king certainly proceeded to reduce towns in Thrace that had been Ptolemaic possessions and to advance on the Hellespont, thus paying no attention to any demands that he refrain from war on Greeks.[203] He obviously did not consider the Roman message an immediate threat of war.

The senatorial legates meanwhile continued on their way. Their next stop (so far as is known; there may have been others enroute) was Rhodes. Their length of stay is uncertain, but considerable time passed while Philip was campaigning in Thrace and heading for Abydus. The envoys next expected to sail for Alexandria, there to bring about reconciliation between Antiochus and Ptolemy.[204] Months had passed with not a move toward Philip. The legates had a message for him in their pockets for the better part of a year, with instructions to deliver it in person, yet had scrupulously avoided confronting him. It was only during their stay on Rhodes, when news arrived of the siege of Abydus, that they decided to postpone the rest of their journey and bring the demands to Philip himself: improvisation once more.[205] But the demands were unchanged: Philip must war on no

200. Polyb. 16.25–26, 16.27.4; cf. Livy, 31.14–15—without mention of the Roman envoys.

201. Polyb. 16.27.1–3.

202. Livy, 31.16.1–2. But Livy does not mention the attack by Nicanor; and some have seen Philocles' assault as a doublet; e.g., Balsdon, *JRS* 44 (1954): 39; *contra*: Ferro, *Le origini*, 101–102; Walbank, *Commentary* II:537; Briscoe, *Commentary*, 44.

203. Livy, 31.16.3–5.

204. Polyb. 16.27.5, 16.34.2; cf. Livy, 31.18.1.

205. Polyb. 16.34.2: οἱ γὰρ Ῥωμαῖοι τὸ σαφὲς ἀκούσαντες ἐν τῇ Ῥόδῳ περὶ τῆς τῶν Ἀβυδηνῶν πολιορκίας καὶ βουλόμενοι πρὸς αὐτὸν τὸν Φίλιππον ποιήσασθαι τοὺς λόγους κατὰ τὰς ἐντολάς, ἐπιστήσαντες τὴν πρὸς τοὺς βασιλέας ὁρμὴν. There is no reason at all to take κατὰ τὰς ἐντολάς as referring to *new* instructions recently arrived from the senate. Polybius' statement clearly asserts that it was the report of Abydus under siege that determined the mission, not any directive from Rome. The envoys would otherwise have gone on to Alexandria: see, most recently, Rich, *Declaring War*, 84–86.

Greeks and submit differences to arbitration, else he could expect conflict with Rome.[206] It had been a peculiar and interesting journey: long in duration, conducted by legates who kept postponing the final accomplishment of their mission. How does one explain it?

The relationship between this legation and the declaration of war by the *comitia* in Rome enfuriatingly eludes discovery. We can establish neither an absolute nor a relative chronology. All reconstructions based on hypothetical fittings-together of annalistic and Polybian material stand on shaky ground.[207] Best not to rest any findings on such reconstructions. We cling to what is known. The war motion was presented to the *comitia* by Sulpicius Galba, consul in 200, rejected by the assembly, later resubmitted and then accepted.[208] How much time elapsed between these two votes simply cannot be established and it is useless to guess.[209] Nor is there any clear connection between the comitial decisions and the movements and delivery of messages by the legates abroad. They were acting on directives of the senate.[210] Whether their declarations to Nicanor and to Philip should be described as *rerum repetitio, denuntiatio belli,* or *indictio belli,* depending on what the assembly had or had not voted, is quite beyond recovery, despite much scholarly discussion.[211] Just one precious

206. Polyb. 16.34.3–4. The complaints of Ptolemy and Rhodes are here added to the message previously transmitted to Nicanor. This obviously reflects events of the interim: Philip's gains in Thrace at Ptolemy's expense and the envoys' stay in Rhodes. It required no new directives from Rome.

207. So, rightly, Luce, *Livy*, 53–73.

208. Livy, 31.6.1–31.8.1.

209. Some have hypothesized a long gap of some months between decisions; e.g., Holleaux, *Études* V:16, n. 1; McDonald and Walbank, *JRS* 27 (1937): 189–197; Walbank, *Philip V,* 314–315. Others see only a short space: Balsdon, *JRS* 44 (1954): 37–39; Rich, *Declaring War,* 79–81.

210. Observe Polyb. 16.34.3: διεσάφει τῷ βασιλεῖ διότι δέδοκται τῇ συγκλήτῳ παρακαλεῖν, etc.; noted by Dahlheim, *Struktur und Entwicklung,* 247–248. It does not follow, however, that there had been no comitial decision on war before the colloquy at Abydus.

211. The major contributions by Bickermann, *RevPhilol* 61 (1935): 172–174; McDonald and Walbank, *JRS* 27 (1937): 192–197; Bickermann, *CP* 40 (1945): 139; Walbank, *CP* 44 (1949): 15–19; Balsdon, *JRS* 44 (1954): 41; a summary of the debate in Rich, *Declaring War,* 76–78. Rich argues persuasively, *op. cit. passim,* that the senate had no fixed procedures on declaring war in this period. Arbitrarily dismissed by Albert, *Bellum Iustum,* 13–14, n. 17. Galba consulted the *fetiales* as to proper procedure and received for answer that an *indictio belli* could be delivered to Philip in person or announced on the frontiers of his territory, as the consul wished. The *patres* then gave him authority to select a non-senator as legate to transmit the *indictio belli*: Livy, 31.8.3–4. This looks like *ad hoc* maneuvering. An obvious temptation arises to associate this "non-senator" with M. Lepidus, the young legate who actually reported Roman demands to Philip at Abydus. Lepidus, however, was selected by his colleagues on the embassy, not by a

chronological link exists, deriving from Polybius. And to that we must hold fast. Roman terms for maintenance of peace were delivered by the legate Lepidus to Philip at Abydus and rejected by the king. Once the city fell and Philip departed for Macedonia, word reached him of the crossing of Roman forces to Illyria.[212] The association of those events can hardly be accidental. Rome's representatives had been a very long time before presenting their conditions to Philip. But when he found them unacceptable, the forces of the Republic at last made their move. Hostilities began. The fall of Abydus finally turned Roman minds to war.[213]

The Polybian evidence represents our one firm foundation. It also allows for answer to the main problem. The senatorial legates made the rounds of Greek states, great and small, announcing the conditions they would ask Philip to fulfill. And conditions they were, not an ultimatum demanding abject surrender or an irrevocable commitment to war. By taking their time, they could hope to win widespread support in Hellas and give Philip plenty of opportunity to contemplate the consequences.[214] The plan seemed sound enough.

---

directive from Galba, and his trip was occasioned by news of the siege, not by consular order: Polyb. 16.34.2; Livy, 31.18.1. A formal *indictio belli*, for all we know, may simply have been pronounced by a subordinate of Galba upon reaching Illyria; so, Bickermann, *CP* 40 (1945): 139; Rich, *Declaring War*, 79, 86–87.

212. Livy, 31.18 (from Polybius); cf. Zon. 9.15.

213. Livy, 31.18.9: *Philippo Abydenorum clades ad Romanum bellum animos fecisset.* Rich's view, *Declaring War*, 86, that this timing was "mere coincidence" is most implausible. He operates on the peculiar assumption that the embassy was abroad for months with the senate unaware, unconcerned, and uninformed of its activities and whereabouts. Bickermann's argument, *RevPhil* 61 (1935): 173–174, that the actual declaration of war in Rome did not come until after Philip's rejection of terms requires much too tight a chronological sequence, as was correctly pointed out by McDonald and Walbank, *JRS* 27 (1937): 194, n. 92. Bickermann himself retreated somewhat from his earlier position in *CP* 40 (1945): 139. But it is still adopted, without resolution of the chronological problems, by Dahlheim, *Struktur und Entwicklung*, 247–248, and Werner, *ANRW* I:1, 546–547. As Polybius, 16.35.1–2, makes clear, the Roman envoys on Rhodes after the fall of Abydus considered their state at war with Philip.

214. It is noteworthy that among the states visited was Aetolia: Polyb. 16.27.4. This is not easy to square with the report of an Aetolian mission to Rome in late 201, seeking aid, a mission that was rudely rebuffed by the senate (Appian, *Mac.* 4; Livy, 31.29.4)—especially as Rome actively sought an Aetolian alliance in winter, 200/199, after hostilities had begun: Livy, 31.28.3. Hence, the Aetolian request is sometimes rejected as fabrication; e.g., Passerini, *Athenaeum* 9 (1931): 266, n. 1; Badian, *Latomus* 17 (1958): 208–211. Or else it has been taken out of the chronological context in which Appian places it and put into 202, before Rome seriously considered war with Philip; Holleaux, *Rome, la Grèce*, 293 n. 1; Walbank, *Philip V*, 36; Oost, *Roman Policy*, 41; McDonald, *JRS* 53 (1963): 188. Others defend the authenticity of the mission: Dorey, *CR* 10 (1960): 9; and, indeed, Appian's date: Meloni, *Il valore storico*, 45–49; Ferro, *Le origini*, 46–47; Derow, *JRS* 69 (1979): 7–8. Polybius' remarks in 16.24.3 need not imply an

Delivery of conditions to the king would be delayed as long as possible until Rome had the backing of Greece and could intimidate him into compliance, which they had good reason to expect would be forthcoming.[215] The terms did not require Philip to dismantle Macedonian territory, yield up his gains, or abdicate his throne. Rather, they asked him to cease making war and to let impartial arbitrators, in conventional Greek fashion, decide the disputes at stake. Otherwise, he would have to face a hostile Greece, backed by the power of Rome. When war-weary Romans adopted the senatorial decree for mobilization, after first rejecting it, these considerations must have been foremost. From the vantage-point of Italy, it was hard to imagine that the king who had twice before fled at the very sight or report of Roman ships, who had been an ineffective ally of Hannibal, who had been fought to a standstill by Aetolians when the Republic had given but minimal support, would now be willing to defy conditions endorsed by Greeks and brought by the victor of the Second Punic War.[216] It was a miscalculation, of course—on both sides. Philip rejected the terms at Abydus, as he had ignored them when forwarded by Nicanor, disbelieving that the dilatory Republic would actually resort to invasion. Neither party backed down, and hostilities commenced. Miscalculations are no small factors in the creation of war.[217]

And why had the senate been willing to make demands of Philip in the first place? Not out of fear or resentment, not from imperialist greed or philhellenism, not for the defense of allies or the discharge of commitments. Rather, a matter of pride. The Republic's previous engagement in the "First Macedonian War" had left a tarnished image—and a bad taste in the mouths of Greeks. Her armies had been brutal, giving rise to charges of barbarism.[218] In addition, she proved

---

Aetolian embassy in 201; cf. Walbank, *Commentary* II:530. A more significant statement, also stemming from Polybius and unduly neglected in this debate, is Livy, 31.46.4: Attalus had asked for Aetolian support against Philip in summer, 201, and was turned down. He asked again in 200, receiving the same negative response: Livy, 31.15.9–10. That Aetolia went to Rome in the meantime is hardly likely. It still seems best to set the mission in 202, after Philip had seized Aetolian dependencies in the Propontis: Polyb. 15.23.7–9. The Roman rebuff explains Aetolia's subsequent reluctance to enter the war.

215. The announcement of terms to Nicanor, as we have seen, was an unexpected improvisation. Since Attica was being ravaged, the envoys needed to make some representation to show the Athenians—and Attalus and the Rhodians—that Rome meant business.

216. As Polybius observes, Philip feared a coalition of Romans and Aetolians: 16.24.2.

217. See the sound remarks of Bickermann, *RevPhilol* 61 (1935): 173–176.

218. Cf. Polyb. 9.37.5–8, 9.39.1–3, 11.5.4–8; Livy, 31.29.12–15, 32.22.10; Appian, *Mac.* 7.

to be a broken reed, her support weak and withdrawn, after she had encouraged others into the fight. That was a past she had to live down.[219] When appeals came from Attalus and Rhodes—perhaps even from Athens—in 201, they presented a golden opportunity. The senate could now put on show its vigor and integrity, and erase its prior reputation in Hellas. Rome's representatives carried a proud message abroad: the Republic stood for an end to Macedonian aggression and for the peaceful resolution of disputes. The Roman envoys made sure to advertise that stance in state after state, among Philip's friends as well as his enemies; they would bring it even to Alexandria to effect concord between Antiochus and Ptolemy and to deprive the Macedonian of hope from that quarter. Steps were soon taken to mobilize an army, in the event that Greeks proved sceptical and Philip failed to see reason. The risks seemed small. Philip would surely yield. If not, Rome could expect a host of Hellenic allies to help bring him to submission.[220] In the meanwhile, the Republic was polishing its image and restoring its repute as a power of magnitude and magnanimity.

219. Polyb. 10.25.2; Livy, 29.12.1, 31.29.3: *inutili societate Romana*; 31.31.19, 32.21.17.

220. Note the vigorous efforts to solicit as much Greek participation in the war as possible; Livy, 31.28.3–4, 31.31, 31.40.7–10, 32.14.4–8, 32.19–23, 33.16–17; cf. 31.2.3–4.

# Chapter 12

# Rome, Macedonia, and Illyria (II)

Rome had sought no foothold in Macedonia. And the results of the Second Macedonian War gave her none. Indeed another eventful half-century was to pass before she took the decision to exercise direct authority in the lands of Macedonia and Illyria. That gap of time is both remarkable and symptomatic.

## The Last Years of Philip V

Philip, in consequence of his defeat, had to withdraw from all Greek cities that had come under his control.[1] Nothing less could have satisfied the propaganda with which Rome entered the conflict and which developed during it. Macedonia would now contract to its own bounds. Rome did not carve up the land or dismantle it, let alone acquire any portion for herself. She detached just a single tribe, the Orestae, from the Macedonian realm. They had revolted earlier and now received autonomy.[2] In Illyria only two sites were reclaimed from Philip, and both were bestowed upon Pleuratus.[3] Rome imposed neither troops nor tribute. Philip kept his throne, despite Aetolian objections; indeed, he became an *amicus* of the Republic, in time-honored Hellenic fashion.[4]

1. Polyb. 18.44.2–4; Livy, 33.30.2–3.
2. Polyb. 18.47.6; Livy, 33.34.6; cf. 31.40.1–3, 39.23.6, 39.28.2; Walbank, *Commentary* II:616; Hammond, *Epirus*, 620–621.
3. Polyb. 18.47.12; Livy, 33.34.11; see above pp. 388–389.
4. See above, Chapter 2, n. 149; for Aetolian objections, cf. Polyb. 18.36.5–9, 18.37.11, 18.48.8–9; Livy, 33.12.3–4, 33.12.12, 35.35.2–8.

*Amicitia*, as we have seen, was a presumption of cordiality, rather than an instrument of hegemony. Philip remained an independent agent, Macedonia remained outside the Roman sphere. When the king cooperated with Rome during the later 190s, it was in his own interests (his indemnity still outstanding and his son a hostage in Italy) and of his own volition. Philip provided a force of fifteen hundred Macedonians for Rome's war against Nabis in 195.[5] The loyalty soon gained him a promise of remission of his indemnity and restoration of his son.[6] In 193 the Aetolians sent feelers to Philip, to sound him out on a prospective invasion by Antiochus. They got nowhere. We need not hypothesize Roman pressure. In fact, it was the Romans who were careful to avoid alienating Philip.[7] For good reason. In winter 192/1 Antiochus, on the advice of Hannibal, sought Philip's aid in a grand coalition with Aetolia for dominance in Greece. The Macedonian, hitherto aloof, rejected the advances and offered cooperation to Rome. The decision was his.[8]

Far from commandeering Philip's services, Rome paid a price for them. The king received promises that any Thessalian cities he recaptured from the Aetolians could be incorporated into his own kingdom. Further, he had free rein to operate against Athamania, even to extend his sway over that land.[9] So much for the "freedom of the Greeks" and the sloganeering of the Second Macedonian War. Macedonia was extending her frontiers once more—this time with Roman sanction.

Some concern arose in the Roman camp lest Philip's gains become too large. The Romans hastened their siege of Heraclea, so as to be able to turn to Lamia before that city fell to Philip in summer, 191.[10] Later in the year they made truce with Aetolia, on the advice of Flamininus, thereby to deprive Philip of excuse for conquest of still further territory.[11] His conquests, however, were already substantial: Dolopia, Aperantia, and Perrhaebia, in addition to Athamania, and the key city of Demetrias, all with Roman acquiescence.[12] The senate

5. Livy, 34.26.10.

6. Diod. 28.15.1; Livy, 35.31.5.

7. Livy, 35.12.2, 35.12.5–6, 35.12.10–14. Flamininus held back from denying a rumor that the city of Demetrias would be returned to Philip; Livy, 35.31.5–11: *ne timorem vanum iis demendo spes incisa Philippum abalienaret.*

8. Livy, 36.7–8; Appian, *Syr.* 16; Zon. 9.19. See, especially, Livy, 36.8.6: *qui ad id tempus fortunam esset habiturus in consilio.* Livy, 36.4.1–4, is inaccurate.

9. Livy, 36.10.10, 36.13–14, 38.1.2, 39.23.10, 39.25.5; cf. Zon. 9.19; see, especially, Livy, 36.14.9: *ita Athamania omnis in ius dicionemque Philippi concessit.*

10. Livy, 36.25, 39.23.9, 39.28.3; Zon. 9.19.

11. Livy, 36.34.1–36.35.6; Plut. *Flam.* 15.4–5.

12. Livy, 36.33, 36.34.9, 39.23.11–12, 39.28.4.

would not take them from him, despite the fact that those areas had been "liberated" in the settlement of 196.[13] Indeed Rome was more eager than ever to retain the king's good will, restoring his son Demetrius to him and promising cancellation of his indemnity.[14] Philip's cooperation would be essential for the invasion of Asia. The Scipios acted with utmost caution in soliciting it, sending out an envoy in 190 to test his sentiments. The independence of Macedonia from Roman dictation can hardly be plainer. Philip, in fact, collaborated once more, gave the Romans safe passage through his territory, escorted them to the Hellespont, provided resources and men, and showed conspicuous *bona fides*. Termination of the indemnity came as his reward.[15]

While the Romans concentrated on Antiochus, Philip was largely on his own. A resurgence by the Aetolians and revolts in Athamania, Amphilochia, Aperantia, and Dolopia cost the king many of his acquisitions of the past two years.[16] How much of this territory was restored to him in the peace settlement after the Aetolian war in 189, and how much retained by Aetolia or Thessaly is unspecified in the evidence.[17] The treaty affirmed only that Aetolia must yield claim to all cities taken by or surrendered to the Romans since 192.[18] Philip had reason to be less than fully satisfied with the vagueness of that clause. And he cannot have been pleased by the action of the Roman praetor Q. Fabius Labeo, who fixed an eastern boundary to the Macedonian realm that excluded Aenus and Maronea from its control.[19] In practice, however, Philip wore few shackles. A settlement once effected, Rome retreated to apathy. Within the next three years the king had redrawn the Thracian frontiers and reoccupied Aenus and Maronea; he controlled cities in Thessaly and Perrhaebia, as well as Magnesia and Dolopia, and he exercised authority, so it was claimed, over all Athamania.[20]

The testimony allows some notable conclusions. Rome had not made Macedonia a dependency or Philip a client.[21] During the decade

13. Polyb. 18.47.6; Livy, 33.34.6.

14. Polyb. 21.3.1–3; Livy, 36.35.12–13; Appian, *Mac.* 9.5; *Syr.* 20; Plut. *Flam.* 14.2.

15. The Scipios' envoys to Philip: Livy, 37.7.8–14; Philip's cooperation: Livy, 37.7.13, 37.7.15–16, 37.39.12, 39.28.8–9; Appian, *Mac.* 9.5; *Syr.* 23; Zon. 9.20; termination of indemnity: Polyb. 21.11.9; Livy, 37.25.11–12; Appian, *Syr.* 23.

16. Polyb. 21.25, 21.31.4; Livy, 38.1–3, 38.5.10, 38.7.1, 38.10.3.

17. Philip sent envoys to Rome complaining of these losses in 189, but we are not told whether he got them back at that time: Polyb. 21.31.3–4; Livy, 38.10.3.

18. Polyb. 21.32.13; Livy, 38.11.9.

19. Livy, 37.60.7, 39.27.10. The king's dissatisfaction is reflected in rumors that he had a hand in the Thracian ambush of Manlius' troops in 188: Livy, 38.40.7–8. ·

20. Polyb. 22.6.1–3; Livy, 39.23.13, 39.24.6–12, 39.25.3–9, 39.25.16–17, 39.28.4.

21. Livy's statement, 33.30.6, 42.25.4, that the treaty of 196 forbade Philip to

after the closing of the Second Macedonian War the Republic treated Philip with circumspection and welcomed his assistance. She never issued him directives or commandeered his support. The king was an *amicus* and an independent agent. Rome backed off even from strict enforcement of the treaty of 196. In the Aetolian war of 191–189 Philip's gains were his to keep, the losses his to recover. The same held for the aftermath of that conflict. Philip rebuilt the resources of his kingdom, expanded his territory, and extended his influence. The realm of Macedonia was, in fact, considerably more powerful in 186 than it had been a decade before. Rome was unworried and uninterested.

This is not the place for a résumé of the final years of Philip V. The tale has been told more fully elsewhere.[22] What needs to be underscored is the passivity of Roman policy during those years.[23] Complaints and protestations against the king's aggrandizements came in flocks to Rome in the mid-180s. The senate dragged its feet, uttered some disapproving noises, sent envoys who were uninformed, evasive, or ineffectual, and generally allowed its rulings to be skirted. In the end an amicable compromise brought resolution. Withdrawal of Macedonian garrisons from Aenus and Maronea and extension of Roman favor to the younger prince Demetrius silenced Greek critics and permitted Philip to proceed unhampered.[24] The king's transgressions against Thessalians and others, even his responsibility for a massacre at Maronea, went unpunished. Polybius' portrait of a vengeful monarch, nursing resentment and plotting retaliation, derives from suspect sources and contains its own refutation. And the idea that Rome meddled in Macedonian affairs, promoting her own candidate for the throne in order to make the nation subservient, is a modern invention. Philip's last years, in fact, were plagued by tragic dissension within his own house, an embittered rivalry between his sons that issued in Demetrius' execution, Philip's agonizing remorse and death, and the accession of Perseus. Rome had kept out of it.

make war without Roman consent is plainly false—and refuted by Polyb. 18.44. The weak arguments of L. Bivona, *Kokalos* 2 (1956): 50–57, fail to make a case for the authenticity of that tradition. See Walbank, *Commentary* II:609–610, with bibliography.

22. Gruen, *GRBS* 15 (1974): 221–246, with references to the evidence and to modern literature.

23. The passivity is denied again by Ferrary, in Nicolet, *Rome et la conquête* 2:753–754, without new arguments. Similarly, M. Greco, *Miscellanea Manni* (1980), IV:1157–1171, who argues that Rome promoted Philip's son Demetrius in an effort to extend her influence in Macedonia, but then dropped him when he became an embarrassment. Roman intrigue, as well as machinations in the Macedonian court, are emphasized by Brizzi, *I sistemi informativi*, 199–221.

24. Cf. especially Polyb. 23.2.6–9; Livy, 39.47.5–11; Appian, *Mac.* 9.6.

## The Policies of Perseus

What notice did the senate take of Macedonia in the early years of Perseus' reign? The fact of the Third Macedonian War in 171–168 engendered speculation and hypotheses as to its roots. The enemies of Perseus, both Greek and Roman, and those eager to dissociate themselves from him reinterpreted the events of his early years to find reason for hostility and pretext for resistance. Polybius went further still: the origins of conflict belonged to the reign of Philip; Perseus simply brought to fruition anti-Roman schemes already hatched by his father.[25] Questionable motives and hindsight infect the tradition. Perseus' actions, when examined dispassionately, show no sinister objectives and created no distress in Rome.

The king, upon accession in 179, renewed his father's *amicitia* with the Republic. An exchange of embassies occurred in Pella and Rome, with courteous receptions and friendly formalities. The *patres* gave official recognition to Perseus' legitimacy.[26] Even Polybius transmits a flattering portrait of the new ruler at the outset of his reign.[27] Few had reason to expect trouble. Perseus defended his frontiers with vigor, expelling the Thracian princeling Abrupolis who had seized the occasion of Philip's death to overrun the area around Mt. Pangaeus and to threaten even Amphipolis.[28] It was later asserted that removal of Abrupolis, a *socius et amicus* of Rome, gave grounds for Roman retaliation.[29] That was certainly not the senate's view at the time. The *patres* paid no attention to the affair and renewed their arrangement with Perseus, leaving the unhappy Abrupolis to his fate.[30]

25. Polyb. 22.18; Livy, 39.23–24; Plut. *Aem. Paull.* 8.4–6; Diod. 29.30; cf. Welwei, *Könige und Königtum im Urteil des Polybios* (Cologne, 1963), 53–54; Pédech, *La méthode*, 125–134, 180–182; Gruen, *GRBS* 15 (1974): 221–225; Werner, *Grazer Beiträge*, 6 (1977), 149–216; Derow, *JRS* 69 (1979): 12–13.

26. Polyb. 25.3.1; Livy, 40.58.8, 41.24.6, 45.9.3; Diod. 29.30; Zon. 9.22; cf. Appian, *Mac.* 11.5.

27. Polyb. 25.3.4–8.

28. Polyb. 22.18.2–3; Livy, 42.41.10–12; Appian, *Mac.* 11.6; Diod. 29.33. Perseus' campaigns in Thrace are referred to in a new inscription from Amphipolis; C. Koukouli-Chrysanthaki, in H. Dell, ed., *Ancient Macedonian Studies in Honor of Charles F. Edson* (Thessaloniki, 1981), 229–241.

29. Livy, 42.13.5, 42.40.5, 42.41.10; Appian, *Mac.* 11.2; Paus. 7.10.6.

30. Appian, *Mac.* 11.6. That Abrupolis was not an ally of Rome anyway, but simply a signatory to the peace of 196 is indicated by *Syll.*³ 643 = *FDelphes*, III, 4, 75 = Sherk, *RDGE*, no. 40, lines 15–17 (with Colin's restorations): [κ]αὶ Θρᾶικας μὲν, ὄντας ἡμετέ[ρους συμμάχους, ἐκράτησε · Ἀβρούπ]ολιν δὲ, ὃν ἡμεῖς περιελάβομεν [ταῖς πρὸς Φίλιππον συνθήκαις, ἐξέβ]αλεν ἐκ τῆς βασιλείας. Accuracy of the restorations apart, the contrast affirmed by the μὲν . . . δὲ is plain and vitiates the insertions of Pomtow: Sherk, *loc. cit.*

Perseus went on to frame marriage alliances with the royal houses of Syria and Bithynia in 178 or 177, a standard Hellenistic move. Moderns see it as foreboding; but nothing in the evidence reveals the slightest dismay in Rome.[31] Eumenes may have been upset and unhappy. The senate refrained from comment.

Perseus courted popularity among his subjects and among Hellenes. He gave amnesty to Macedonians who had fled the country under sentence for debts or crimes against the state and pardoned those still held in custody for like offenses. The generosity was advertised in Greek shrines and won Hellenic favor. Perseus would set his kingdom on a new course and erase the hostility engendered in Greece by his father.[32] The policy bore fruit. Macedonia enjoyed good relations with Thessaly, Epirus, and even Aetolia.[33] She retained her two seats on the Amphictyonic council.[34] The Aetolians appealed to Perseus in the mid-170s to help settle civil strife growing out of the problems of the indebted, and Thessaly may have made a similar appeal.[35] The king had friends in Achaea;[36] he brought military aid to Byzantium;[37] in 174 or 173 he concluded an alliance with Boeotia.[38] Subsequent propaganda by Eumenes set these acts in the worst possible light, and, when relations became strained and pretexts sought, they were bound to be reinterpreted as anti-Roman moves. But they were not so viewed in the mid-170s. The Aetolians in their plight quite ingenuously called on both Rome and Perseus for succor.[39] The Rhodians maintained cordial relations with both powers down to the eve of

31. Polyb. 25.4.8–10; Livy, 42.12.3–4; Appian, *Mithr.* 2; *Mac.* 11.2; perhaps reflected in *IG*, XI, 1074. Scholars have interpreted it as formation of an anti-Roman coalition, encompassing even the island of Rhodes; e.g., Niese, *Geschichte* III:82–83, 100; Meloni, *Perseo*, 122–125; Schmitt, *Rom und Rhodos*, 134–137; Hopp, *Untersuchungen*, 35—wrongly; see Giovannini, *BCH* 93 (1969): 855; Gruen, *CQ* 25 (1975): 66–67. A cautious formulation in Walbank, *Commentary* III:280: "perhaps unwelcome to Rome." The connection between the Antigonid and Seleucid houses may have earlier roots; see J. M. Helliesen in H. Dell, *Ancient Macedonian Studies in Honor of Charles F. Edson* (Thessaloniki, 1981), 219–228.

32. Polyb. 25.3.1–4; cf. Livy, 41.22.7, 41.24.12, 42.5.1; Appian, *Mac.* 11.1.

33. Livy, 41.24.10.

34. *Syll.*³ 636, lines 5–7; cf. Giovannini, *Ancient Macedonia* 1 (1970), 147–154.

35. Aetolia: Livy, 42.12.7, 42.40.7, 42.42.4; Appian, *Mac.* 11.1, 11.7; Thessaly: Livy, 42.13.9; Appian, *Mac.* 11.1; Diod. 29.33.

36. Livy, 41.23.4, 41.24.19, 42.12.6.

37. Livy, 42.13.8, 42.40.6, 42.42.4; Appian, *Mac.* 11.1, 11.7.

38. Polyb. 27.1.8; Livy, 42.12.5, 42.38.5, 42.40.6, 42.42.4, 42.43.5, 42.46.7, 45.31.15; Appian, *Mac.* 11.7. On the date, see Meloni, *Perseo*, 146, n. 1; Deininger, *Widerstand*, 153, n. 1.

39. Livy, 41.25.2, 42.12.7, 42.42.4; Appian, *Mac.* 11.7.

war.[40] Perseus felt free to broadcast his alliance with Boeotia all over Greece and even confidently to announce it to the Roman senate.[41] An Achaean spokesman could assert in 174 that to patch up relations with Macedonia would not bring the wrath of Rome; it would indeed only implement Rome's own policy of concord.[42] Perseus had made concerted efforts to undo the damage perpetrated by his predecessor and to clean up the soiled image of the Antigonids in Hellas. The Romans seemed quite complacent.[43]

A different sort of protest did reach the senate. Some time in 176 envoys from the Dardanians arrived in Rome with tales of an invasion by the Bastarnae, warriors massive in size and numbers, and allegations that they were in league with Perseus and the Gauls. Representatives from Thessaly appeared also in order to confirm the story. The *patres* made their customary response: they would send an embassy to investigate.[44] Livy records the return of that embassy in 175. In his account, they reported only that a Dardanian war was underway. Appian adds that they had observed a major military build-up in Macedonia. Perseus, in the meantime, dispatched his own envoys to Rome with denials that he had any part in the activities of the Bastarnae.[45] It matters little whether one believes the king's protestations. The policy of egging on the Bastarnae goes back to Philip, an effort to root out the Dardanians and secure the northern borders of Macedonia. Perseus was, at most, pursuing his father's scheme.[46] The senate washed its hands of the affair in typical fashion: it would neither

40. Polyb. 25.4.9–10, 27.3–4; Livy, 42.45–46; cf. Gruen, CQ 25 (1975): 66–69.

41. Livy, 42.12.5–6, 42.42.4; Appian, Mac. 11.7. There was obviously no secret about it, despite Livy, 42.40.6.

42. Livy, 41.24; especially, 41.24.7: *haec omnia pacis equidem signa esse iudico non belli; nec Romanos offendi posse si ut bellum gerentes eos secuti sumus, nunc quoque pacis auctores sequamur.* The allegation of Livy, 42.6.2, about Roman hatred of Perseus, is anachronistic inference. Note that it is associated with Eumenes' visit to the senate which did not come until 172: Livy, 42.6.3

43. The conventional view that Perseus catered to the Greek masses, thus undermining the propertied classes who relied on Rome, lacks foundation. Note, e.g., his offer to Achaea to restore fugitive slaves, a proposal heartily endorsed by the Achaean slave owners: Livy, 41.23.2–4. And, on the subject in general, see Gruen, AJAH 1 (1976): 29–60; D. Mendels, *Ancient Society* 9 (1978): 55–73—who overlooks the Achaean episode.

44. Polyb. 25.6.2–6.

45. Livy, 41.19.4–5; Appian, Mac. 11.1. Meloni, *Il valore storico*, 121–123, needlessly postulates two separate Roman embassies and two separate sets of envoys from Perseus. Other discussions noted by Walbank, *Commentary* III: 282.

46. Livy, 40.57.4–9, 41.23.12, 45.4.3. The notion that Philip planned to use this as a means for invading Italy is, of course, absurd: Livy, 39.35.4, 40.57.7, 42.11.4.

censure nor absolve Perseus, but simply directed that he take care to *give the appearance* of observing his treaty with Rome.[47] A decade earlier they had given the same advice to Philip.[48] The purpose at that time corresponded exactly: outward cordiality would discourage protesters and relieve the senate of vexing missions from Greece. And outward cordiality there was.[49]

Perseus justifiably felt at liberty to tighten control of his realm and enhance his image among the Greeks. When the Dolopians executed Perseus' governor in 174 and rebelled against Macedonian authority, hoping to gain Roman sanction for their independence, the king swiftly crushed the revolt and reestablished his sway.[50] This too later served as a charge against him. But Perseus argued, with good reason, that Dolopia formed part of his own kingdom, awarded to his father with Rome's approval during the Aetolian war. He had merely crushed an internal insurrection. At the time Rome had issued no complaint.[51] Nor did the senate object when Perseus made a trip to Delphi in 174 to consult the oracle and returned via Thessaly with his army but without inflicting any damage on lands through which he passed. It was clearly a publicity move, calculated to advertise his adherence to Hellenic traditions and to demonstrate his pacific posture. Perseus took the occasion to send envoys and communications to various states of Greece announcing his good will and expressing a desire to end quarrels with all Hellenes, including the Achaeans.[52] The march itself caused alarm in some quarters. Yet a noteworthy fact needs to be observed. Those who felt threatened sent hasty appeals to Eumenes. No one delivered a message to Rome.[53]

Throughout this period of the early and mid-170s the senators expressed but a modicum of interest in Macedonia. As in the last decade of Philip's reign, they appeased appellants by sending investiga-

47. Livy, 41.19.6: *senatus nec liberavit eius culpae regem neque arguit; moneri eum tantum modo iussit, ut etiam atque etiam curaret ut sanctum habere foedus quod ei cum Romanis esset, videri posset.*

48. Polyb. 23.9.7: ἐπὶ μὲν τοῖς γεγονόσιν ἐπῄνει τὸν Φίλιππον, εἰς δὲ τὸ λοιπὸν ᾤετο δεῖν προσέχειν αὐτὸν ἵνα μηδὲν ὑπεναντίον φαίνηται πράττων Ῥωμαίοις.

49. Cf. Livy, 41.24.6: *audimus legatos Romanos venisse ad regem Persea et eos benigne exceptos*—which may refer to the embassy sent to inquire about Dardania; so Bickermann, *REG* 66 (1953): 505, n. 5.

50. Livy, 41.22.4, 41.23.13, 41.24.8, 42.13.8.

51. The accusation was first made by Eumenes in 172: Livy, 42.13.8, and later echoed by Philippus: Livy, 42.40.8. Perseus' response: Livy, 42.41.13; Appian, *Mac.* 11.6.

52. Livy, 41.22.5–8, 42.23.13–16, 42.5.1, 42.42.1–3.

53. Livy, 41.22.5. Of course, these actions of Perseus too were later distorted and turned into an accusation against him: Livy, 42.13.8, 42.40.6; cf. *Syll.*³ 643 = *FDelphes*, III, 4, 75 = Sherk, *RDGE*, no. 40, lines 7–8.

tory missions, they asked for compromise and a show of good will, but they evinced no interest in taking action.[54] The embassy to Dardania, as we have seen, demonstrates this with welcome clarity. Other missions too are recorded in the annalistic accounts, some of them dubious accretions, perhaps inventions or doublets, designed to provide a diplomatic background for the opening of hostilities. Roman legates returned from Africa in 174 with a rumor promoted by Massinissa that there had been an exchange of ambassadors between Perseus and Carthage. The senate dispatched a mission to Macedonia to inquire.[55] What did it discover? The notice is suspicious and the evidence tangled. No further mention is made anywhere of Perseus' supposed contact with Carthage. Livy later records the return of a Roman embassy that had been sent to both Aetolia and Macedonia; its members reported on unchecked civil strife among the Aetolians; as for Perseus, they had not even been allowed to see him, but had observed great war preparations in his kingdom.[56] Only the most foolhardy will attach weight to that testimony. Massinissa's allegations— if he ever made them—were self-serving and never substantiated. And the idea that a Roman embassy would be denied an interview with Perseus but permitted to observe military preparations is quite incredible.[57] Under the year 173 Livy places a legation from Thessaly bringing news of events in Macedonia. Just what the news was is unrecorded.[58] Not long thereafter the *patres* appointed still another set of envoys, with the by now familiar commission: to "look into" the Macedonian situation.[59] One wonders how often the *patres* needed to go through this ritual. Which and how many embassies actually went provokes unnecessary guesswork. There is no reason to doubt that some complaints about Perseus from Massinissa, Thessalians, and others reached Rome. Perseus himself had more than once sent

54. Note, for example, the response of the senate to Perseus' representatives, perhaps in 173: they were willing to ignore all charges against him, requesting only restoration of Abrupolis: Diod. 29.33. Obviously this asks for a mere gesture.

55. Livy, 41.22.1–3.

56. Livy, 42.2.1–3.

57. There may be confusion too between this Roman mission and another appointed to settle debt disputes in Aetolia: Livy, 41.25.5–6, 41.27.4, 42.2.1–2, 42.4.5; cf. Nissen, *Untersuchungen*, 241–242. Bickermann, *REG* 66 (1953): 506, reckons it a doublet of the legation sent to Dardania. Meloni, *Perseo*, 127–129, 142–143, doubts Massinissa's information but accepts the report on Rome's mission to Macedonia. Bredehorn, *Senatsakten*, 178–182, accepts it all.

58. Livy, 42.4.5: *Thessali legati nuntiantes quae in Macedonia gererentur.* Cf. Appian, *Mac.* 11.1.

59. Livy, 42.6.4: *qui res in Macedonia aspicerent.* The embassy's task also included a trip to Alexandria to renew *amicitia* with Ptolemy. So, Macedonia may not have been the prime item on the agenda.

envoys to the senate to present his case against accusers, finding a mixed reception in the *curia*.[60] The senate's reaction, however, had been limited to noncommittal statements and investigatory embassies. The repetitive pattern prevailed through the year 173. Rome kept herself at a cool distance from the affairs of Macedonia.[61]

## The Background of the Third Macedonian War

The reasons for the Third Macedonian War thereby become the more difficult to assess. The origins of this conflict are as complex and almost as often discussed as those of the war with Philip. We can forego extended analyses of modern opinions.[62] Polybius, as already observed, stressed Philip's passion for revenge, the son simply inheriting an inevitable contest from the father. That notion does not withstand examination and commands no support. Avowed reasons given at the time in justification of Rome's hostility carry even less conviction. The war proposal passed by the *populus* resorted to general statements about sweeping but nonspecific offenses: Perseus had attacked Roman *socii*, ravaged fields and taken cities, and he was preparing war on Rome.[63] When specifics receive mention, in Philippus' colloquy with Perseus and in a Roman letter to Delphi, they rake up old charges or manufacture new ones, most of them drawn from Eumenes' rag-bag of accusations. Perseus' every controversial action was claimed as violation of his treaty with Rome: the expulsion of Abrupolis, oppression of the Dolopians, the march through Thessaly, the appearance at Delphi, the assistance to Byzantium, involvement in Aetolia, and the alliance with Boeotia. Not one of these deeds, however, engendered Roman complaint at the time of perpetration.

60. Livy, 41.19.5, 42.42.4; Appian, *Mac.* 11.1; cf. 11.5; Diod. 29.33.

61. Callicrates' supposed speech in 174, claiming that war between Rome and Perseus is inevitable (Livy, 41.23), may be disregarded. It echoes Polybius' conviction that the conflict was already set in motion by Philip and retails accusations that did not surface before 172. Even if Callicrates delivered some such oration, this reflects only his policy of preventing a rapprochement between Macedonia and Achaea and claiming Roman support for his own political purposes. The companion speech of Archon correctly refutes the allegations against Philip and Perseus and affirms the existence of concord: Livy, 41.24.1–7. Cf. on these years in general, Bickermann, *REG* 66 (1953): 486–495; Meloni, *Perseo*, 61–150; Will, *Histoire politique* II: 215–222; Giovannini, *BCH* 93 (1969): 853–858.

62. For the most important discussions, see U. Kahrstedt, *Klio* 11 (1911), 415–430; De Sanctis, *Storia dei Romani* IV: 1.262–278; Bickermann, *REG* 66 (1953): 492–506; Meloni, *Perseo*, 150–209; Giovannini, *BCH* 93 (1969): 853–861. A summary of opinions in Raditsa, *ANRW* I: 1 (1972), 576–589; and see below pp. 417–418, n. 106.

63. Livy, 42.30.10–11; cf. Diod. 31.8.2.

And not one of them infringed any known clause of the Roman-Macedonian treaty. Other allegations bordered on the comic or the absurd: that Perseus gave refuge to the assassins of an Illyrian prince, that he planned the murder of two Theban envoys, that he arranged an avalanche to crush Eumenes at Delphi, and that he bribed a citizen of Brundisium to poison Roman generals and envoys who passed his way![64] Recourse to far-fetched and fabricated offenses discloses the weakness of Rome's case. The very quantity of alleged misdeeds undermines their credibility. The senate had not a legal leg to stand on.

The analogy of the Second Macedonian War affords a better route to understanding. Some striking parallels impress themselves upon attention: long hesitation before Rome took any irrevocable steps, the use of envoys to whip up Greek public opinion and isolate the Macedonian, the conditional demands which, if complied with, could bring a settlement short of war. Here, as with the contest against Philip, framing the right question is essential. Not why did Rome seek war, but did she seek it?

The possibility of armed conflict was raised in early 172. The consuls of that year hoped for allocation of Macedonia as a province, in the event that hostilities might erupt. A senatorial majority would have none of it, and assigned Liguria to both consuls. The *patres* eschewed provocative action.[65] The real provocateur was Eumenes. He presented himself to the senate in spring, 172, and produced a long list of charges against Perseus, ranging from his marriage alliances with Hellenistic kings to his execution of two Thebans. Further, he laid special stress upon the strength and resources of the Macedonian kingdom, its vast manpower, grain supplies, and an arsenal clogged with weapons, all in readiness for an invasion of Italy.[66] The senate was moved by this oration, says Livy.[67] How far and to do what? Our sources do not know, though they claim knowledge. Eumenes' address was delivered behind closed doors. Outsiders were left to guess, and guess they did. It was natural to assume that the senate passed a resolution in secrecy, still more natural to infer after the fact that the

64. Livy, 42.40.3–9; *Syll.*³ 643 = *FDelphes*, III, 4, 75 = Sherk, *RDGE*, no. 40; cf. Livy, 42.15–17; Appian, *Mac.* 11.4–7; Polyb. 22.18.2–5. All these charges are taken seriously by Brizzi, *I sistemi informativi*, 231–236! Rightly questioned by Albert, *Bellum Iustum*, 123–125. The notion that Perseus was violating the treaty depends on belief in a clause forbidding the Macedonian to wage any war outside his borders without Roman authorization: Livy, 33.30.6, 42.25.4—which is pure invention; see above, n. 21.

65. Livy, 42.10.11–12.

66. Livy, 42.11–13; Appian, *Mac.* 11.1–2. Livy even has him mouth the theory that Perseus' planned invasion was a legacy from Philip; 42.11.4–5—a theory which, according to Errington, *Dawn of Empire*, 207–208, Polybius took from Eumenes.

67. Livy, 42.14.1: *haec oratio movit patres conscriptos.*

resolution authorized a war against Perseus. But that is pure inference and not evidence. Reports about that senatorial meeting were
first leaked after the war was over—when Romans were eager to em-
phasize that they had been resolved from the beginning.[68] The allegations of Eumenes, in fact, had little substance, some of them referring
to events of six or seven years earlier to which senators had already
turned a blind eye.[69] It is unlikely that the *curia* would suddenly find
them menacing now. Nor did Eumenes have things all his own way.
Perseus had representatives in Rome to refute the Pergamene's assertions. Rhodes too sent a legation to denounce Eumenes and undermine his credibility. Indeed, there were a good many senators who
regarded the king's speech as a piece of self-interested and tendentious hyperbole.[70]

What actions did the *patres* take in the spring and summer of
172? From what we can tell, few or none. The annalistic tradition preserved in Livy embraces the idea that war was now inevitable and fil-
ters every event through that prism. Its material is suspect, illogical,
and refutable. Perseus' representative appears as obstinate and arrogant, claiming that the king is ready for war if Rome wants it, and
his report back to Macedonia makes Perseus the more zealous for
confrontation.[71] This is at sharp variance with the king's own behavior
which, as we shall see, remained conciliatory for long thereafter.[72] The
Roman legation, so the annalists record, which had gone to "investigate" in 173, now returned to confirm Eumenes' charges and even introduced the man from Brundisium who alleged that Perseus paid
him to poison Roman visitors—a fantastic tale that can hardly have
been bought by any sober senator.[73] The legates evidently had no specific information of their own to deliver. Annalists even invented still
another Roman mission which actually delivered a *rerum repetitio* to
Perseus, adding the details that Perseus exploded at them in a fit of

68. Livy, 42.14.1: *in praesentia nihil, praeterquam fuisse in curia regem, scire quisquam
potuit: eo silentio clausa curia erat. Bello denique perfecto, quaeque dicta ab rege quaeque res-
ponsa essent emanavere*; Appian, *Mac.* 11.3; Val. Max. 2.2.1: *non ante sciri potuit quid aut ille
(Eumenes) locutus esset aut patres respondissent quam captum Persen cognitum est.*

69. Cf. Livy, 42.13.10: *haec cum vobis quiescentibus et patientibus fecerit.*

70. Appian, *Mac.* 11.3: τῶν δὲ βουλευτῶν πολλοὶ τὸν Εὐμένη δι᾽ αἰτίας εἶχον ὑπὸ
φθόνου καὶ δέους αἴτιον τοσοῦδε πολέμου γεγόμενον. Cf. Cato's denunciation of Eumenes' acquisitiveness; Plut. *Cato*, 8.7–8. The Rhodian embassy is noted also, in exaggerated fashion, by Livy, 42.14.6–9. Perseus' envoys: Livy, 42.14.3–4; Appian, *Mac.*
11.3.

71. Livy, 42.14.3–4, 42.15.1–2.

72. See below pp. 416–417. Note that, according to Diodorus, 29.34, the king's
envoy made no reply at all.

73. Livy, 42.17.

ire, insisted that he was not bound by any treaty made by Philip, and unceremoniously ejected them from his kingdom.[74] That narrative is a fiction rightly discarded by almost all scholars. It suits nothing else that is known of either Rome's or Perseus' demeanor in these months, and is refuted by Livy himself. The senate did not pass even a conditional motion against Perseus until 171—prior to which there could hardly have been any *rerum repetitio*.[75] The *patres*, in fact, postponed any firm decision. They would not hurry into a Macedonian war and the whole question was shelved until the consuls of 171 could take office, a time still several months in the future.[76]

The first move came only in the autumn of 172. And then it took the form of extensive diplomatic activity. The parallel of 200 B.C. is pertinent and revealing. At that time a senatorial legation had visited numerous Greek sites, enlisted Hellenic sympathies, and avoided Philip as long as possible, in order to present him with a formidable coalition that could induce compliance. The method employed in 172 was identical. Only now the diplomacy would be even more widespread, thereby the better to intimidate Perseus. A whole battery of envoys scattered themselves around the Greek world, some to central and northern Greece, some to the Peloponnese, some to Illyria. Others had instructions to visit Asian cities, the Aegean islands, Crete, and Rhodes; and still others to sound out a number of Hellenistic kings, Eumenes, Antiochus, Ariarathes, Massinissa, and Ptolemy. An impressive array of diplomats.[77] The nature of their task is clear. The Lentuli solicited expressions of loyalty from various cities of the Peloponnese. Philippus tested the sympathies of Epirotes, Aetolians, and Thessalians, receiving welcome affirmations from all; he took advantage of internal conflict in Boeotia to encourage fragmentation of her confederacy and effectively render it useless to Perseus; and at a

74. Livy, 42.25.1–13.

75. Livy, 42.30.10–11. Only Bredehorn, *Senatsakten*, 195–200, is prepared to defend the story. It is correctly demolished by Nissen, *Untersuchungen*, 246–247; followed by almost all; cf. Meloni, *Perseo*, 177–179; Rich, *Declaring War*, 89–90.

76. Livy, 42.18.2, 42.18.6.

77. Central and northern Greece, the Peloponnese, and Illyria: Livy, 42.37.2–4; Appian, *Mac.* 11.4. Asian cities, the Aegean, Crete, and Rhodes: Polyb. 27.3.1; Livy, 42.19.7–8, 42.45.1. Hellenistic kings: Appian, *Mac.* 11.4; Livy, 42.26.7. On the date of departure, at least for the missions sent to Greece, see Livy, 42.37.3: envoys hoped to sail around the Peloponnesian coast *ante hiemem*. Thus, they left probably in September or October; cf. Walbank, *JRS* 31 (1941): 84–85; Meloni, *Perseo*, 179–180; Pedech, *La Méthode*, 462; Rich, *Declaring War*, 93–94. A different chronology in V. M. Warrior, *AJAH* 6 (1981):9–11, 24–26. They operated κατὰ χειμῶνα and returned: Polyb. 27.2.12; cf. Livy, 42.44.8: *principio hiemis*, i.e. sometime from December to February: Pédech, *La méthode*, 463–464.

meeting of the Achaean League he requested a troop of one thousand men to garrison Chalcis—a demonstration that Perseus could make no headway there. Ti. Claudius and his colleagues touched at various Aegean and Asian sites, with special attention to Rhodes, where they were promised forty ships in readiness should they be needed. Decimius sought out the Illyrian ruler Genthius in hope of finding him true to his *amicitia* with Rome.[78] In all this flurry of activity, the important fact remains that no one had instructions to meet with Perseus. There was no ultimatum to be delivered, no *rerum repetitio*, no terms or demands on the king, let alone any declaration of war. The legates busied themselves in rounding up a maximum of Greek support, in order to establish Hellenic solidarity and to demonstrate the isolation of Macedonia.

It was Perseus who had to seek out the envoys for an interview. He took the initiative in dispatching a letter to them shortly after their arrival in Corcyra, asking the reason for their mission. The legates, however, plainly had no desire to encounter him or even to engage in formal correspondence at the outset of their trip. They gave only an evasive oral reply to the king's messenger—and went off to their several destinations.[79] Perseus subsequently tried again, this time with a personal appeal to Philippus for a meeting. The Roman consented, though only after he had completed successful trips to Epirus, Aetolia, and Thessaly and had made contact with Acarnanians and Boeotians, all of whom gave avowals of fidelity in the event of war.[80] The narrative of events, drawn here by Livy from Polybius, affords a clear picture. Philippus' goal was to assure the adherence of Hellas. He dodged a meeting with Perseus when the Greek reaction was untested and agreed to it when he had strong cards to play. The speech of Philippus at the Peneus river, however, is another matter. A Polybian or Livian construct, it repeats all the charges voiced by Eumenes, it distorts Perseus' actions into violations of the treaty, and adds even the ludicrous claims that Perseus was responsible for hiring a poisoner at Brundisium and for planning the attempted murder of Eumenes.[81] How much of this was actually said and how much believed

78. The Lentuli in the Peloponnese: Livy, 42.37.7–9. Philippus in central and northern Greece: Livy, 42.38.1–4, 42.38.6–7. Philippus and Boeotia: Polyb. 27.1.1–27.2.10; Livy, 42.38.5, 42.43.4–42.44.6; cf. Gruen, *AJAH* 1 (1976): 44–46. Philippus in Achaea: Polyb. 27.2.11–12; Livy, 42.44.6–7. Ti. Claudius in Rhodes and elsewhere: Polyb. 27.3; Livy, 42.45.1–7; the annalistic version of this is worthless: Livy, 42.26.8–9; cf. Gruen, *CQ* 25 (1975): 59, n. 2, with literature cited there. Decimius in Illyria, where his efforts came to naught: Livy, 42.37.2, 42.45.8.

79. Livy, 42.37.5–6.

80. Livy, 42.38.

81. Livy, 42.40.

by Philippus is unworthy of speculation. Such allegations, in any case, did not determine Roman policy. The senate had issued Philippus no instructions to deliver to Perseus, for they had not contemplated such a meeting. At most, the Roman legate may have outlined the sorts of charges that Eumenes and others had been leveling against Perseus—charges which Perseus' own speech more than adequately disposes of.[82] What matters is the outcome of the colloquy. Philippus suggested that the king send envoys to Rome and he accepted Perseus' proposition that there be no hostilities until that mission be complete. Livy adds that Philippus welcomed the proposal for it would give Rome needed respite to prepare for war.[83] We can accept the fact, without endorsing the interpretation. Philippus lacked orders to make peace or war. The advice to send representatives to Rome followed logically from his position. Only the senate could decide whether further action was needed, and Philippus was eager to get on with his task in Greece. When he returned to Italy in the winter of 172/1, there was still no war.

Several months had elapsed, the better part of a year at least, since Eumenes had called on Rome to take up arms and forestall the supposedly inevitable invasion of Italy. Other appeals had come too, from Thracian peoples, from Thessaly, from Aetolia, and even from the inhabitants of Issa warning of a coalition between Perseus and Illyria.[84] Yet the *patres* had dragged their feet. They had waited until autumn before sending Philippus and the other delegates. And they showed no sign of mobilization until near the end of the consular year 172. At that time the praetor Cn. Sicinius received a commission to conduct forces to Brundisium and take them across to Apollonia, where they could protect the coastal cities and secure landing places for a consular army the next year, if it should be needed.[85] They had

82. Livy, 40.41–42. A similar speech in Appian, *Mac.* 11.5–8, though he has it delivered in Rome by an envoy of the king.

83. Livy, 42.43.1–4; cf. 42.46.10, 42.47.1, 42.47.3, 42.47.10. The establishment of a "truce" (*indutiae*) is inaccurate language. There was as yet no war, hence there could be no cessation of hostilities. And Philippus, as an envoy rather than an *imperator*, could not call a truce anyway; cf. Bickermann, *REG* 66 (1953): 497. This was simply an agreement to refrain from hostilities until the king's ambassadors could bring their case to the senate—which is all that Polybius implies with διὰ τὰς ἀνοχάς; 27.5.7.

84. Livy, 42.19.6, 42.25.14, 42.26.2.

85. As is notorious, Livy's chronology is badly confused on this, the result of combining and repeating evidence of the annalists and the narrative of Polybius. Sicinius' commission is given three separate times: Livy, 42.18.2–3, 42.27.3–6, 42.36.8–9. On the first occasion, Livy places it not long after the embassies that had come to Rome, evidently in the spring or early summer of 172, which is patently false: 42.18.2–3. Later, he has the missions of Philippus and others depart "a few days" after Sicinius' arrival in Apollonia: Livy, 42.36.8–42.37.1. Though some have accepted that order of

waited a long time to take this step, perhaps even until the return of Philippus' embassy.[86] In any event, it constituted only a holding operation to reassure Greeks and to show that Rome was prepared to use force, if it came to that. But it need not have come to that.

The declaration of war, according to the annalists, occurred at the beginning of the consular year, 171.[87] The complaints against Perseus were couched in general terms: he had violated the treaty, attacked Rome's allies, and prepared war against the *populus Romanus*. This step, however, was still by no means irrevocable. The *rogatio* possessed a clearly conditional character: Rome would begin war only if the king failed to give satisfaction.[88] Similar instructions went to the consul to whom Macedonia would be allotted as a *provincia*. He had a commission to undertake war if Perseus and his supporters did not meet the terms of the Roman people.[89] Perseus still had time to comply. Two more months passed, and a consular army had not yet crossed the Adriatic.

In the meantime, Philippus and his colleagues had returned to Rome to announce the success of their mission. The Polybian version has him boast of deceiving Perseus, the king lulled into a false sense

---

events, it is difficult to maintain. As scholars were swift to point out, no such forces had crossed the straits by the time of Philippus' interview with Perseus; Livy, 42.43.3, 42.47.2; see Kahrstedt, *Klio* 11 (1911): 415–430; Walbank, *JRS* 31 (1941): 82–86; Meloni, *Perseo*, 179–181; *contra*: Luce, *Livy*, 123–129; Warrior, *AJAH* 6 (1981):8–14, 23. One may add two passages in Polybius; 27.2.11: Philippus asks the Achaeans to garrison Chalcis until the crossing of the Romans; and 27.4.3–5: Perseus requests the Rhodians to maintain neutrality and, if Rome should attack Macedonia, to attempt mediation. Both imply that any Roman mobilization still lay in the future. Cf. also Polyb. 27.5.7–8: Perseus replies to Boeotian appeals that he cannot give aid because of his truce with Rome. Sicinius' forces, in fact, did not gather at Brundisium until the Ides of February, and, by the time of his crossing, his *imperium* had to be prorogued, thus demonstrating that the new consular year had opened: Livy, 42.27.5–6; cf. 42.28.4. Rich's effort, *Declaring War*, 96–97, to get around this testimony is singularly ineffective. Cf. also Oost, *CP* 48 (1953): 217–230. On Livy's combination of the Polybian and Roman material, see Luce, *Livy*, 129–135.

86. This may be implied by Livy, 42.47.1–3; cf. Zon. 9.22. The relative timing cannot be fixed with certainty. The Roman calendar was well out of joint with the Julian at this time, perhaps three and a half months, according to the recent calculation of Derow, *Phoenix* 27 (1973): 345–356. If so, the gathering of forces at Brundisium on the Ides of February would in fact have come in the end of October. Philippus can hardly have returned by that time. But other calculations are possible. A date in mid-December cannot be ruled out and would allow for Philippus' prior return; cf. Rich, *Declaring War*, 93.

87. Livy, 42.30.8–11.

88. Livy, 42.30.10–11: *nisi de iis rebus satisfecisset, bellum cum eo iniretur*. The arguments of Warrior, *AJAH* 6 (1981):5–6, against a conditional war vote fail to shake this explicit testimony.

89. Livy, 42.31.1: *nisi populo Romano satisfecissent, bello persequeretur*.

of security through a truce and the empty hope of peace, thus giving Rome time to make her military preparations. Its substance has gone unquestioned by almost all scholars.[90] Yet the analysis is set in a moralizing context: the older men disapproved of this *nova sapientia* and argued that Rome had waged her wars in the past with courage rather than trickery; but a majority paid greater heed to advantage than to integrity and approved Philippus' machinations.[91] Polybian interpretation has here crept into the narrative. Elsewhere he identifies the Third Macedonian War as a time when Roman morality began to go downhill.[92] Polybius also had personal experience with Philippus, a man who had once placed him in an embarrassing and difficult position and a man whom he persistently sees as engaging in deceit and duplicity.[93] Philippus no doubt had to defend his actions before the *patres*; he had not had instructions for a parley with Perseus and needed to explain that interruption of and temporary deflection from his task. But the idea of a grand design to mislead the king and allow Rome opportunity to mobilize against him is more than suspect. Philippus only agreed to a meeting on Perseus' appeal, an event unforeseen when the legation was appointed. Perseus, be it noted, found no reason for urgency. His envoys to Rome, sent as result of his meeting with Philippus, did not arrive until spring of 171.[94]

The senate gave them hearing but expected capitulation. Rome had now gathered a solid Hellenic coalition and had an advance force at Apollonia. The Macedonian envoys, however, spoke in generalities, their one specific point being denial of Perseus' culpability in an attempt on Eumenes' life. That was inadequate. Negotiations were broken off and the envoys ordered out of Italy. Now and only now, in June of 171, did the senate at last direct the consul to assemble his army and prepare to cross the Adriatic. If Perseus wished to give satisfaction he would have to send legates to the consul in Macedonia, not to the senate in Rome.[95] Yet even this did not exclude the

---

90. E.g., Walbank, *JRS* 31 (1941): 91–93; Meloni, *Perseo*, 202–203; Briscoe, *JRS* 54 (1964): 68; Errington, *Dawn of Empire*, 210–212.

91. Livy, 42.47.1–9; Diod. 30.7.1—both obviously deriving from Polybius.

92. Polyb. 31.25.4–6.

93. Polyb. 28.13, 28.17; Livy, 42.43.1–3; cf. Frank, *CP* 5 (1910): 358–361; Gruen, *CQ* 25 (1975): 71–74.

94. Livy, 42.35.3, 42.36.1. Walbank's theory, *JRS* 31 (1941): 93, that they had come four months earlier and were kept waiting while the Romans geared up their war machine, postulates extraordinary naiveté on Perseus' part and is refuted by Livy, 42.36.1: *per idem tempus legati ab rege Perseo venerunt*.

95. Polyb. 27.6.1–4; Diod. 30.1; Appian, *Mac.* 9. Livy records the embassy and its hearing twice, once following Polybius and once from an annalistic version: 42.36.1–7, 42.48.1–4. The doublet is plain, acknowledged even by Bredehorn, *Senatsakten*, 210–214.

possibility of a solution short of war. When Perseus' envoys returned to Pella, a royal council debated the posture to assume and some voices urged the wisdom of making whatever concessions were needed to avert conflict with Rome. A majority overbore that view. Perseus finally prepared to confront the legions of the Republic.[96]

The recapitulation of the evidence brings an important conclusion into focus. As in the preliminaries to the war against Philip, Rome procrastinated and held back, waiting for concessions rather than hastening into conflict. More than a year elapsed between the urgent pleas of Eumenes and the forwarding of a consular army to Hellas. The senate relied on the pressures of diplomacy and the gathering of Greek public opinion to intimidate Perseus without recourse to arms. Was this not, it might be asked, a naive and empty hope? Ought not the Republic to have known better after the failure of similar tactics with Philip three decades earlier? Rhetorical questions are easily framed in retrospect. At the time, however, Romans can hardly be blamed for expecting Perseus to yield to pressure. The king had shown anything but belligerency to Rome. Cordial relations had marked the opening of his reign, an exchange of ambassadors and renewal of *amicitia*. He had taken the trouble to inform the *patres* and explain his relationships with Aetolia, Byzantium, and Boeotia.[97] He met the accusations of his enemies with embassies to Italy reaffirming nonhostile intent.[98] Acting on a communication from Rome, he had even expelled from his kingdom the alleged assassins of an Illyrian prince.[99] When Philippus was in Greece, Perseus sought him out, appealed to their *hospitium*, and offered to make amends for any wrongdoing, affirming that he had not knowingly committed any offense.[100] He turned down a request from certain Boeotian cities for military aid in order not to break the peace with Rome.[101] He called on the Rhodians to maintain neutrality and to mediate a settlement in the event that Romans should invade Macedonia.[102] As late as June, 171, the king's representatives in Rome expressed his willingness to submit to

96. Livy, 42.50.1–42.51.1.

97. Livy, 42.42.4.

98. Livy, 41.19.5, 42.14.3–4; Appian, *Mac.* 11.1, 11.3; Diod. 29.33. Appian, *Mac.* 11.5, gives still another Macedonian embassy between that which was present at the time of Eumenes' accusations and the mission of June, 171; cf. Livy, 42.40.9. Its authenticity is defended by Meloni, *Perseo*, 176–177; *Il valore storico*, 148–149; *contra*: Rich, *Declaring War*, 97–98.

99. Livy, 42.41.8; Appian, *Mac.* 11.6.

100. Livy, 42.38.8–9, 42.42.4, 42.42.8: *conscius mihi sum nihil me scientem deliquisse, et, si quid fecerim imprudentia lapsus, corrigi me et emendari castigatione hac posse.*

101. Polyb. 27.5.5–8; Livy, 42.46.9–10.

102. Polyb. 27.4.4–5; Livy, 42.46.3–4.

the senate's judgment any claims that Roman allies had against him.[103] And, as noted above, even after the dismissal of his last embassy, Perseus called a council to consider his next move and at least entertained the proposition of paying tribute, surrendering territory, or yielding to any other demand that might prevent war.[104] It was therefore entirely in character that he should offer generous peace terms after his initial victory of the war, indeed an offer to pay indemnity and evacuate holdings, as if he were the vanquished instead of the victor.[105] Perseus clearly did not want this war. The senate had every reason to expect that he would bow to bullying.

In the end, that bullying went too far. Perseus drew the line at abject humiliation, and, with a Roman army already in Greece, the momentum of war could no longer be halted.

We need not search for deep and hidden motives for the Republic's intervention. A multitude of suggestions have been tendered by scholars: fear of Perseus, anxiety about Macedonian-Syrian coalition, desire to prevent a lower-class revolution promoted by Perseus against the friends of Rome in Greece, the influence of warmongering "new men" in Rome, the need to teach Perseus the proper behavior of a "dutiful client." All of them depend on the unfounded assumption that Rome actively desired war, whether for her own aggrandizement or to prevent that of Macedonia.[106] More properly assessed, Roman

103. Livy, 42.36.3. The assertion that Perseus had already invaded Perrhaebia and captured towns in Thessaly (Livy, 42.36.4) is false. Those actions took place later: Livy, 42.47.10, 42.53.5–8.

104. Livy, 42.50.2.

105. Polyb. 27.8; Livy, 42.62.3–15; Appian, *Mac.* 12; cf. Livy, 44.25.3: *Persea iam inde ab initio belli omni modo spem pacis temptasse.* For a sober account of Perseus' attitude generally, see W. L. Adams, in Adams and Borza, *Philip II, etc.*, 237–256.

106. Roman fear of Macedonia: Mommsen, *Römische Geschichte* I:754–763; De Sanctis, *Storia dei Romani* IV:1, 262–274; Meloni, *Perseo*, 148–149, 158–159, 444–451; Walbank, *Ancient Macedonia* 2 (1977): 81–94. In fact, Perseus lacked a navy and could not possibly have contemplated an invasion of Italy. And none of his actions, as we have seen, show belligerency towards the Republic. Anxiety about a Macedonian-Syrian alliance: Bickermann, *REG* 66 (1953): 501–505. But Perseus had been linked in marriage to Seleucus IV, an association now otiose since Antiochus IV had ascended the Syrian throne as ally of Eumenes: *OGIS* 248; Appian, *Syr.* 45. For chronological arguments against Bickermann's view, see Walbank, *Ancient Macedonia* 2 (1977): 82–86. Desire to prevent a lower-class revolution prompted by Perseus: Giovannini, *BCH* 93 (1969): 858–861. That notion does not conform to the evidence; see Gruen, *AJAH* 1 (1976): 29–60; Mendels, *Ancient Society* 9 (1978): 55–73—unknown to Giovannini, *Rome et la circulation monetaire*, 88–94. The influence of "new men": Scullard, *Roman Politics*, 194–200; Bickermann, *REG* 66 (1953): 500–501; cf. Briscoe, *JRS* 54 (1964): 73–77; Adams, in Adams and Borza, *Philip II, etc.*, 249–250. No evidence buttresses the view that any particular faction steered Rome into war; so, rightly, Harris, *War and Imperialism*, 232, n. 6. Even the complaints about *nova sapientia* referred to the means of waging war, not an

behavior and attitudes approximate closely those discerned prior to
the Second Macedonian War. Eumenes had pointed out to the senate
that as Perseus' popularity waxed, Rome's waned.[107] The Macedonian
had acquired the good will of Hellenes everywhere, a man who had
revived the fortunes of the Antigonid house and claimed the role of
benefactor of Greece.[108] In the analysis conveyed by Appian, Rome
was vexed by the thought that Greeks revered Perseus as a philhellene while they despised the Republic for the deeds of her generals.[109] This calls to mind the Roman eagerness in 200 to eradicate the
negative impression left by her commanders in the First Macedonian
War. One ought not to infer that the Greeks chafed under the oppression of Rome and welcomed Perseus as liberator. The evidence points
in a very different direction. It was precisely Rome's withdrawal from
Hellenic affairs that gave an opening to Perseus and the opportunity
to resuscitate Macedonia as patron of Hellas. The Greeks saw diminished value in appealing to an uninterested senate and found the
Antigonid a more promising hegemon. The advantages brought by
earlier Roman victory were fading into oblivion; Perseus was creating
a new image at Rome's expense.[110] Eumenes expressed it accurately:
while Rome sits back in passivity and indifference, Greece is falling
into Perseus' lap.[111]

The Republic had little reason to fear Perseus' power. But Romans were sensitive, as always, to their reputation. Eumenes met resistance from those in the *curia* who rejected the plunge into a war for
the advantage of Pergamum. A majority, however, saw the value of
demonstrating that Rome was not a helpless, pitiful giant. The Romans sent deputations throughout Hellas and they rattled sabers to

objection to war: Livy, 42.47.4–8. The need to enforce Perseus' clientship: Errington,
*Dawn of Empire*, 212—a strictly modern concept which ignores Perseus' consistent conciliatory gestures. Sheer aggrandizement and desire for a new theater of war to collect
booty: Harris, *War and Imperialism*, 227–233; this overlooks all the diplomatic preliminaries and the lengthy delays before Rome committed herself to the war.

107. Livy, 42.12.2: *invidia adversus Romanos favorem illi conciliet.*

108. Cf. Polyb. 25.3.1–7: πολλοὺς ἐμετεώρισε, δοκῶν καλὰς ἐλπίδας ὑποδεικ-
νύναι πᾶσι τοῖς Ἕλλησιν ἐν αὐτῷ; Livy, 42.12.1, 42.14.8–9.

109. Appian, *Mac.* 11.1: καὶ μάλιστα αὐτοὺς ἠρέθιζεν ἡ τῶν Ἑλλήνων φιλία καὶ
γειτνίασις, οἷς ἔχθος ἐς Ῥωμαίους ἐπεποιήκεσαν οἱ Ῥωμαίων στρατηγοί; cf. Appian,
*Mac.* 11.3, 11.4, 11.7. The sentiments derive from an anti-Roman Greek source, according to Meloni, *Il valore storico*, 119–121, and *passim*. For A. Mastrocinque, *AttiIstVeneto*
84 (1975–76): 31–40, Appian used two divergent annalistic sources, one of them reflecting "Catonian" hostility to Eumenes.

110. Cf. Polyb. 27.10.3: εἰ δὲ καὶ βραχέα τις ὑπέμνησε τῶν γεγονότων ἐκ μὲν τῆς
Μακεδόνων οἰκίας δυσκόλων τοῖς Ἕλλησιν ἐκ δὲ τῆς Ῥωμαίων ἀρχῆς συμφερόντων,
καὶ λίαν ἂν παρὰ πόδας αὐτοὺς ὑπολαμβάνω μεταμεληθῆναι; Livy, 42.30, 45.31.

111. Livy, 42.13.10: *haec cum vobis quiescentibus et patientibus fecerit et concessam sibi
Graeciam esse a vobis videat.*

wrench concessions from Perseus. The majesty of Rome would be put on display again, sufficient to dazzle the Greeks and cast Macedonia in the shade. So it was thought. Yet when Perseus, hitherto compliant, was forced to choose, he chose resistance. And Rome had gone too far to retreat.

## Illyria in the Early Second Century

The kingdom of Macedonia had occupied the center of Hellenic concerns, an obsession to Aetolians, Thessalians, Pergamenes, Rhodians, and Achaeans. Roman attention had been diverted there only sporadically and briefly, and under prodding from others. The same holds for Illyria. Two short wars in the later third century to keep the Adriatic free of marauding incursions and resistance to those who threatened cities on the Ionian Gulf constituted the limit of Roman activity. Thereafter, affairs in Illyria went largely unnoticed.

Pleuratus, son of Scerdilaidas, ruled the Ardiaei at the end of the third century, a signatory to the Peace of Phoenice and an ally of Rome in the Second Macedonian War.[112] This cooperation gained him some territory in the settlement after Philip's defeat, and he supported Rome once more in the Aetolian war in 189.[113] Scipio could affirm that the Romans had transformed Pleuratus from a petty dynast to an acknowledged monarch, an assertion echoed by Eumenes—who claimed that Pleuratus had done little to deserve the elevation.[114]

What importance did Rome attach to this relationship? The immediately subsequent years give the answer: virtually none. Pleuratus' successor Genthius, who took over some time in the 180s, felt no obligations to the senate and had none imposed on him. Relations deteriorated, or—better—barely existed. By 180 complaints reached Rome about Genthius' hostile activities. Roman representatives had been to see him but failed to obtain an interview. His own ambassadors denied all the charges. The Romans had no firm information and took no steps against the king.[115] Eight years later, envoys from Issa protested Genthius' attacks and tried to persuade the *patres* that he was in league with Perseus. The Illyrian's messengers were denounced as spies. Rome sent still another mission.[116] Genthius played

---

112. Peace of Phoenice: Livy, 29.12.14; cf. 26.24.9, 27.30.13. Actions in Second Macedonian War: Livy, 31.28.1–2, 31.34.6, 31.38.7, 31.40.10.

113. Territory acquired in 196: Polyb. 18.47.2; Livy, 33.34.11; see above pp. 388–389. Support in 189: Livy, 38.7.2—the only mention of him in the war.

114. Polyb. 21.11.7–8, 21.21.3.

115. Livy, 40.42.1–5.

116. Livy, 42.26.2–7.

his cards close to the vest, a man unattached and uncommitted, an object of suspicion to some Romans but independent also of Macedonia.[117] When the Republic endeavored to confirm loyalties in the Greek world and to overawe Perseus in 172/1, a cautious approach was made to Genthius, a hope that he might respect his *amicitia* with Rome. The legate who approached him got nowhere at all.[118] As is plain, the Romans had paid little heed to maintaining influence with the Ardiaean monarchy. The area under Genthius' authority, far from being a matter of priority, had faded almost altogether from Roman attention. Genthius maintained an unhelpful neutrality in the opening years of the Third Macedonian War and eventually became persuaded to join the cause of Perseus. The argument that convinced him deserves special notice: that Rome was entirely unprepared for a war on the coasts of Illyria and Epirus. That is telling testimony on the absence of Roman concern for the area during the first third of the second century.[119]

Illyria, as we have had occasion to observe more than once, was a divided land, fragmented by tribal loyalties, an arena for dynasts, chieftains, and princelings.[120] Some looked for Roman assistance in their rivalries against one another, though they got little profit from it. An otherwise unknown dynast Arthetaurus is described as a Roman *socius et amicus*. His murder at the hands of assassins later became a charge leveled at Perseus, who had provided refuge for the killers. The senate went so far as to register a protest, inducing Perseus to expel the assassins from his kingdom. Small comfort for Arthetaurus.[121] Other Illyrians had complained to the senate about

117. Livy, 42.29.11: *Gentius rex Illyriorum fecerat potius cur suspectus esset Romanis quam satis statuerat, utram foveret partem impetuque magis quam consilio his aut illis se adiuncturus videbatur.* Cf. May, *JRS* 36 (1946): 52–54, who exaggerates Macedonian influence in Genthius' realm.

118. Livy, 42.37.2: *L. Decimius missus est ad Gentium regem Illyriorum, quem si aliquem respectum amicitiae cum populo Romano habere cerneret, temptare ut etiam ad belli societatem perliceret iussus; 42.45.8: Decimius unus sine ullo effectu . . . Romam redit.*

119. Polyb. 29.4.2: τῶν γὰρ Ῥωμαίων εἰς τέλος ἀπαρασκεύων ὄντων πρὸς τοῦτο τὸ μέρος κατά τε τοὺς περὶ τὴν Ἤπειρον καὶ τοὺς περὶ τὴν Ἰλλυρίδα τόπους. A Roman officer took over fifty-four *lembi* of Genthius in 171, claiming that they had been dispatched for Rome's use: Livy, 42.48.8. But that was done without Genthius' knowledge and consent. Rome could certainly not rely on his support: Livy, 43.9.4. Perseus at last won him over in 168, after lengthy and, for a time, abortive negotiations: Polyb. 28.8–9, 29.3–4, 29.9.13, 29.11; Appian, *Mac.* 18.1; *Ill.* 9; Livy, 43.18.3–43.20.4, 43.23.7–8, 44.23, 44.26.2, 44.27.8–12, 44.29.6–8; Plut. *Aem. Paull.* 13.1–2; Diod. 30.9.1–2.

120. Note, e.g., a certain Aeropus who seized Lychnidus and occupied certain places in Dassaretis in 208, raising opposition to Philip V: Livy, 27.32.9.

121. Livy, 42.13.6, 42.40.5, 42.41.5–8; Appian, *Ill.* 11.2, 11.6. One may note that Arthetaurus receives no mention in the Delphic inscription giving a list of Perseus' offenses: *Syll.*³ 643 = *FDelphes*, III, 4, 75 = Sherk, *RDGE*, no. 40.

depredations by Philip in 184/3, but there is no evidence that they got any satisfaction.[122] Divisions continued to dominate, Genthius himself was plagued with internal dissension in the royal house, even executing a brother for fear he would range the Dardanians against the Ardiaeans.[123] Genthius had already lost control of the Dalmatians, who revolted from his authority early in the reign, subdued other tribes on their borders, and made them tributary.[124] On the eve of the Third Macedonian War, the Dassareti and some Illyrians requested Roman garrisons as protection against Perseus; other Illyrian chieftains remained impervious to Roman requests for a display of loyalty.[125] Perseus took advantage of these divisions in campaigns against the Penestae, in order to put pressure on Genthius and gain his adherence for the war.[126] With this sort of fragmentation it is hardly surprising that Illyrian matters played so small a role on the Roman agenda.

One item could rouse curiosity and even engage action. Piracy in the Adriatic had brought the Romans out in force during the late third century. Its revival in the second century made an impression that Illyrian internal rivalries could not make. Word came from Brundisium and Tarentum in 181 that Italian coastal areas had fallen prey to piratical raids from across the Adriatic. The effect was immediate. L. Duronius, the praetor assigned to Apulia, received the added responsibility of dealing with the Istrians. An interesting combination: obviously his task was to protect the entire Adriatic coastline.[127] Duronius sailed to Illyria in the course of his duty and returned in 180 with some alarming reports: Genthius had organized the marauders, all the raiding parties had embarked from his realm, Romans and Latins alike had been victims of Genthius, and Romans were even said to be held at Corcyra.[128] How much of this was true or even believed is

122. Polyb. 23.1.10; cf. 23.2.9.
123. Polyb. 29.13; Livy, 44.30.2–4. Observe also a certain Pleuratus, exile at Perseus' court: Polyb. 28.8.1, 28.8.8–9; Livy, 43.19.13, 44.11.7.
124. Polyb. 32.9.3–4.
125. Livy, 42.36.9, 42.45.8, 43.9.4–7. Dell, *Ancient Macedonia* 2 (1977): 310–314, fails to establish that Rome maintained a persistent interest in Dassaretis and the high lake country between 200 and 168.
126. Livy, 43.18.3, 43.19.2–3; cf. 44.11.7. On the geography of the campaign, see Hammond, *Macedonia* I:44–45; Dell, *Ancient Macedonia* 2 (1977): 311–313.
127. Livy, 40.18.4: *L. Duronio Apulia; et Histri adiecti, quod Tarentini Brundisinique nuntiabant maritimos agros infestos transmarinarum navium latrociniis esse.* Zippel, *Die römische Herrschaft*, 81, needlessly questions Livy's account here on grounds that Duronius went to Illyria and Q. Fabius Buteo fought in Istria: Livy, 40.26.2, 40.42.1. He fails to observe the close connection, at least in the Roman mind, between Istrians and Illyrians, so far as protecting the Adriatic shore from brigandage is concerned.
128. Livy, 40.42.1–5: *haud dubie in regem Illyriorum Gentium latrocinii omnis ma-*

uncertain. Genthius' envoys denied everything, and Rome withheld any moves against him. But the *patres* certainly took sharp notice of brigandage in the Adriatic. In 178 the *duumviri navales* were both assigned to that sea, their operations to center upon Ancona, one to defend the coastline from Ancona to Aquileia, the other from Ancona to Tarentum. The enemy, it is stated, was the "Illyrian fleet." Romans here evidently lumped Istrians and Illyrians together in an unspecific reference to piratical depredations on Italian shipping. In fact, Istria was the real object, with a standing garrison established in the vicinity.[129]

The senate had recognized the need for some action in that area a few years earlier. Plans were laid for a Latin colony at Aquileia in 183 and there were calls for an Istrian war, temporarily postponed.[130] After the complaints from Tarentum and Brundisium in 181 and reports that the Istrians interfered with the colonizing of Aquileia, the Roman praetor in Gaul undertook a campaign against them.[131] Duronius, as mentioned, received the Istrians as part of his responsibility in defending the Adriatic in 180. Operations began in earnest two years later: not just the assignment of *duumviri navales*, but a Roman consul went against Istria, subsequently joined by his colleague after initial defeats at the hands of the enemy.[132] Both men were prorogued for 177 and still another consular army was dispatched under the new consul of that year. This time, despite bitter feuding among the commanders, the war was pressed to a conclusion and Istria brought under firm Roman control.[133] The reasons for all this are quite unambiguous. Romans cared little for Illyria, for Genthius, Arthetaurus, or other petty princelings. They mobilized when marauders prowled the Adriatic. "Illyrians" and Istrians were of a piece for the *patres* in this regard; it was pirates they were after, their bases and their locus of support. Istria seemed the principal menace, and Istria was subjugated.[134] Roman policy, its direction and its limits, shows remarkable continuity—from the time of Teuta through that of Genthius.

---

*ritimi causam avertit; ex regno eius omnes naves esse, quae superi maris oram depopulatae essent . . . ad ea Duronius adiecit multis civibus Romanis et sociis Latini nominis iniurias factas in regno eius, et cives Romanos dici Corcyrae retineri.*

129. Livy, 41.1.3–6.
130. Livy, 39.55.4–6.
131. Livy, 40.18.4, 40.26.2–3; cf. 40.34.2.
132. Livy, 41.1–5. The senate had not officially decreed the war, evidently expecting that naval operations might be sufficient. The consul in Gaul, A. Manlius Vulso, felt the need to act swiftly, before consultation of the *patres*, for which he subsequently received sharp criticism—especially as his opening campaign was a fiasco: Livy, 41.1.1–2, 41.7.4–10. On some topographical problems connected with the fighting, see A. Grilli, *RendIstLomb* 110 (1976): 142–151.
133. Livy, 41.8.4–5, 41.9.1–3, 41.10.11, 41.12.3, 41.13.6, 41.14.6; Polyb. 25.4.1.
134. Istrians and Illyrians, as we have seen, seem almost interchangeable in our

Once the danger from Istria had been dispelled, the senate lapsed back into languor. As we have seen, they had no installations and no guarantees of loyalty in Illyria when war erupted with Perseus. The Republic had to make *ad hoc* preparations in 172/1. Allies were found among the Dassareti, the Parthini, and the Penestae, who had reason to fear Perseus, and in Issa which felt threatened by Genthius.[135] Elsewhere, the Ardiaei and other Illyrians rejected Rome's advances. The senate's forces faced hard fighting and some embarrassing reverses in the lands of the Penestae in 170 and 169.[136] By 168 they were in desperate straits and on the point of disaster.[137] All this decided Genthius to throw in his lot with the Macedonians. It seemed a good decision at the time; in the event it proved calamitous. The Roman praetor, L. Anicius Gallus, attacked his territory in 168, assaulted the citadel at Scodra, and brought the hapless Genthius to his knees in tearful surrender within a single month's campaign. The news of victory reached Rome before anyone even knew the fighting had begun.[138]

The swiftness with which Rome destroyed Ardiaean resistance, once she put her mind to it, bears emphasis. In retrospect, the defeat of Genthius seemed a mere sideshow.[139] And so it was. The fact that Rome took so long to make serious headway in Illyria during the Third Macedonian War demonstrates how little regard she had paid to that theater in the past generation.

## The Settlement After Pydna

The conflict with Perseus was lengthy and arduous, a far sterner test than Rome had anticipated or bargained for. It had proved no easy matter to display the *maiestas populi Romani*.[140] When victory came at last, the senate resolved not to have to face such a challenge again.

---

sources for this purpose: Livy, 40.18.4, 40.42.1, 41.1.3–6. And note that in 171 Aquileia is said to be threatened by Istrians and Illyrians: Livy, 43.1.5–6. The remark of Florus, 1.26, that Rome warred on the Istrians because they had "recently" supported Aetolia, is absurd. The Aetolian war had ended eight years before the first operations in Istria.

135. Livy, 42.36.9, 43.9.4–7, 43.21.1–3, 43.23.6; cf. 42.26.2–3.

136. Livy, 43.10, 43.18.3–43.21.1.

137. Livy, 44.20.5: *in summo periculo*; cf. Polyb. 28.13.7.

138. Livy, 44.30.6–44.32.5, 45.3.1, 45.16.7, 45.43.4; Appian, *Ill.* 9; Plut. *Aem. Paull.* 13.2; Florus, 1.29; Zon. 9.24.

139. Livy, 45.7.2: *Syphax . . . tantum accessio Punici belli fuerat, sicut Gentius Macedonici; 45.39.3.*

140. Cf. Livy, 44.22.2–3 (the speech of Aemilius Paullus): *consul sum creatus . . . neque id ob aliam causam, quam quia bello in Macedonia, quod diu trahitur, existimastis dignum maiestate populi Romani exitum per me imponi posse.* Cf. Diod. 30.8.1.

The Republic imposed stiff terms on Macedonia and Illyria in 167, much stiffer and more far-reaching, on the surface at least, than any inflicted on eastern foes in the past. Polybius, one of the victims of the settlement in Greece, looked back upon this year as the culmination of Roman conquest and extension of authority over the Hellenic world.[141] In earlier wars, vanquished monarchs had retained their thrones: Pinnes, Philip, Nabis, Antiochus. This time Perseus was led in chains to Rome before the triumphal chariot of his conqueror.[142] The senate decreed abolition of the Macedonian monarchy. Henceforth the land would be divided into four separate republics, each with its own governing body. *Decem legati* went forth to consult with the victorious proconsul L. Aemilius Paullus and to administer the details of the settlement. Together they delineated the new frontiers and established the four districts. Intercourse among the regions was to be sharply restricted, no marriage contracts and no ownership of property permitted outside one's own district. The senate had determined to minimize the likelihood that Macedonia could ever congeal into a unity again.[143]

A limitation on Macedonian resources accompanied these measures. The mines had been a major source of revenue. Under senatorial directive, contracts for those revenues were to be abolished. The *decem legati* closed the gold and silver mines altogether, though they permitted the working of iron and copper mines.[144] Half the taxes that Macedonians had paid to the king would now go to Rome.[145] A ban was imposed on commerce in salt and on the cutting of ship timber.[146] Romans had been deeply impressed by the wealth that Macedonia had accumulated in the three decades since Philip's defeat.[147] The new measures would make economic recovery on that scale forever impossible.

Illyria suffered a like fate. Genthius was hauled off to Italy to grace a triumphal procession.[148] The Ardiaean monarchy came to an abrupt end, Illyria carved up instead into three independent regions by a senatorial commission.[149] Genthius' former subjects would now also contribute half their usual taxes to Roman coffers, while those Illyrians who had prudently sided with Rome were relieved of financial obligations.[150]

141. Polyb. 3.4.2–3; cf. 1.1.5, 6.2.3. It was an opinion which he subsequently, however, modified; see above pp. 344–345.

142. Livy, 45.40.6; Plut. *Aem. Paull.* 34.1–2.

143. Livy, 45.17.1–3, 45.18.6–8, 45.29.1–10, 45.32.1–2; Diod. 31.8.1, 31.8.6–9.

144. Livy, 45.18.3, 45.29.11; Diod. 31.8.7.

145. Livy, 45.18.7, 45.29.4; Diod. 31.8.3; Plut. *Aem. Paull.* 28.3.

146. Livy, 45.29.11, 45.29.14.          147. Livy, 45.40.1–3.

148. Livy, 45.43.6.

149. Livy, 45.17.1, 45.17.4, 45.18.1, 45.18.7, 45.26.15; Diod. 31.8.6.

150. Livy, 45.18.7, 45.26.13–14; Diod. 31.8.3, 31.8.5.

The sum of these moves forms a clear pattern. Rome had determined to eradicate the possibility that Macedonia or Illyria could ever again become major powers. Their economic resources were curtailed and their military potential all but eliminated. The Illyrians had yielded up their entire fleet, thus ridding the Adriatic of that menace. And, though the Macedonian regions bordering on barbarian peoples could retain some garrisons at their frontiers, the national army of Macedonia was no more.[151]

That much is plain enough. Can one go further into a more significant conclusion: that Rome now stepped into a new role? No longer content with victory, did she now intend to rule? The eastern world henceforth to be an appendage of the western power?[152] Such a conclusion, even for 167, would be hasty and erroneous.

The Romans withdrew their forces from Hellas after the Third Macedonian War, as they had after all previous wars. They were no more inclined now for administration in the East than they had been before. The senate proclaimed that Macedonians and Illyrians were to be autonomous, self-governing, free of garrisons, and at liberty to live under their own laws.[153] It was propaganda, of course, propaganda of a familiar kind to both Greeks and Romans. Macedonians could hardly greet with equanimity and seriousness the concept of "living under their own laws"—but without a monarchy. Nevertheless, the propaganda was more than empty gesturing. The settlement effected by Paullus and the *decem legati* took care to provide a genuine governmental machinery in the four Macedonian republics, a machinery to be run by the Macedonians. Each district would possess its own ruling council or assembly and its own capital, would collect its own revenues, and elect its own officials.[154] One may justifiably decline to

151. Livy, 45.29.14, 45.43.10; Diod. 31.8.9.

152. Cf., e.g., Errington, *Dawn of Empire*, 222: "From now on, Rome was not only the acknowledged mistress of the Mediterranean world, but she was also prepared to act the part . . . the Senate now intended to rule." Similarly and most recently, Dahlheim, *Gewalt und Herrschaft*, 117–120. The proposition, with regard to Macedonia, is criticized by Gruen, in Adams and Borza, *Philip II, etc.*, 257–267.

153. Livy, 45.18.1, 45.22.3, 45.26.12, 45.29.4, 45.32.3–4; Diod. 31.8.1–6; Plut. *Aem. Paull.* 28.3, 29.1; cf. Polyb. 36.17.13.

154. Existence of separate governing bodies in each region is affirmed in Livy, 45.18.7 and 45.29.9. Whether these are primary assemblies [as M. Feyel, *BCH* 70 (1946): 187–198] or representative assemblies [as Larsen, *CP* 44 (1949): 73–90; cf. Frank, *CP* 9 (1914): 49–59] cannot be determined with certainty; see Aymard, *CP* 45 (1950): 96–107; Walbank, *Commentary* III:467. Livy elsewhere speaks of *senatores quos synhedros vocant*: 45.32.2; cf. Polyb. 31.2.12: δημοκρατικῆς καὶ συνεδριακῆς πολιτείας; 31.17.2. But that is not enough to establish the existence of a federal body administering all four republics, as argued by Feyel, *loc. cit.* Capitals of each district: Livy, 45.29.9; Diod. 31.8.8. Collection of revenues and election of officials: Livy, 45.29.9: *eo concilia suae cuiusque regionis indici, pecuniam conferri, ibi magistratus creari*; Diod. 31.8.9: ἐν ταύταις ἀρχηγοὶ

ascribe altruism or a zeal for Macedonian liberty to those who arranged the settlement in 167. Different motives prevailed, in particular a desire to establish effective institutions administered and staffed by Macedonians, institutions that would allow Rome to withdraw and that would obviate the need for subsequent involvement. Aemilius Paullus evacuated his forces with a final exhortation: Macedonians should remember that Rome has brought them freedom and that its maintenance through stability and concord is now their responsibility.[155] The words echo those expressed by Flamininus a generation before, upon his departure from Hellas: Rome has bestowed liberty; the Greeks must preserve and protect it.[156] Rome's attitude toward supervision of Hellenic affairs remained unchanged. She abjured it.

The economic exactions seem at first sight more telling. Rome shut down the Macedonian gold and silver mines. Further, she fixed a tribute for both Illyrians and Macedonians. Half of what they had been paying to their kings would go to the Roman treasury. Does this imply a new relationship of permanent dependency?

The issue of the mines warrants examination. According to Livy, the senate's initial decision was not to close down the mines, but rather to abolish the farming out of their revenues, as well as the farming out of revenues from the (presumably royal) landed estates.[157] That sets matters in a somewhat different light. Livy gives double reason for the decision: revenue contracts would involve *publicani* who will violate the rights and liberty of the *socii*, and, if managed by the Macedonians themselves, would give rise to sedition and upheaval.[158] What lurks behind this is easy to imagine. The *publicani*

---

τέσσαρες κατεστάθησαν καὶ οἱ φόροι ἠθροίζοντο. These officials are perhaps to be distinguished from the annual magistrates elected by individual communities: Livy, 45.29.4; Justin, 33.2.7. The latter are identified by C. Schuler, *CP* 55 (1960): 90–100, with politarchs, known from subsequent inscriptions. But the office, as a new find reveals, existed before 167, and thus was not a Roman creation; C. Koukouli-Chrysanthaki, in Dell, *Ancient Macedonian Studies in Honor of Charles F. Edson* (Thessaloniki, 1981), 229–241. See B. Helly, *Ancient Macedonia* 2 (1977): 531–544; cf. F. Gschnitzer, *RE* Suppl. 13, "Politarches," 483–500.

155. Plut. *Aem. Paull.* 29.1: παρακαλέσας τοὺς Μακεδόνας μεμνῆσθαι τῆς δεδομένης ὑπὸ 'Ρωμαίων ἐλευθερίας σώζοντας αὐτὴν δι' εὐνομίας καὶ ὁμονοίας.

156. Livy, 34.49.11: *redditam libertatem sua cura custodirent servarentque.*

157. Livy, 45.18.3: *metalli quoque Macedonici, quod ingens vectigal erat, locationes praediorumque rusticorum tolli placebat.* Crawford, *Economic History Review* 30 (1977): 44, wrongly infers that "the senate originally wished to close the mines in Macedonia." Larsen, *Greek Federal States*, 299, has no warrant for the assertion that "the mines and royal estates were confiscated and became the property of the Roman state."

158. Livy, 45.18.4–5: *nam neque sine publicano exerceri posse et, ubi publicanus esset, ibi aut ius publicum vanum aut libertatem sociis nullam esse.* A similar explanation appears in Diod. 31.8.7—though without explicit mention of *publicani*: κατέλυσαν δὲ καὶ τὰς ἐκ τῶν μετάλλων ἀργύρου καὶ χρυσοῦ προσόδους διά τε τὸ τῶν ἐνοικούντων ἀνεπηρέασ-

lobbied for the system of letting contracts for mines and public estates, a system already in force in Spain. To extend it to Macedonia seemed logical. Resistance arose in the senate. It cannot be coincidence that only two years earlier a fierce quarrel had erupted between the censors and certain groups of *publicani* over the letting of contracts, a quarrel in which one censor barely escaped conviction on a capital charge.[159] The episode was still fresh in the minds of *patres* who had opposed the tax gatherers at that time. Hence, resistance to *locationes* in Macedonia is explicable. The struggle behind the scenes is not disclosed to us. But the outcome reflects it. The gold and silver mines were simply shut down, thus foreclosing any opportunities for the *publicani*. The iron and copper mines were to be managed by Macedonians who would pay to the Roman government half the tax they had previously paid to the king.[160] In short, a political contest in Rome underlay this decision, rather than an effort to extend control over Macedonia. A mere decade later, with the contest no longer at issue, the mines were quietly reopened.[161]

The collection of tribute stands in a different category. Was this fixed as a sign of Macedonian and Illyrian subjection to Rome's power? Indemnity payments imposed upon a defeated foe represented standard practice. Yet here the vanquished people were compelled to send to the Roman treasury half of what had customarily been due to their monarchs.[162] That looks like a permanent and regular levy, and so it is almost always understood.[163] Must it be so? No

---

τον καὶ ὅπως μή τινες μετὰ ταῦτα νεωτερίζοιεν διὰ τῶν χρημάτων ἀνακτώμενοι τὴν Μακεδόνων ἀρχήν.

159. Livy, 43.16; cf. 44.16.8. The connection is rightly made by Badian, *Publicans and Sinners: Private Enterprise in the Service of the Roman Republic* (Ithaca, N.Y., 1972), 39–42. Reaffirmed now by Calboli, *Marci Porci Catonis Oratio Pro Rhodiensibus*, 150–181, who notes also that the censor under heavy fire in 169, C. Claudius Pulcher, was one of the *decem legati* in Macedonia in 167: Livy, 43.16, 45.17.2. L. Perelli's conjecture, *RivFilol* 103 (1975): 410–412, that the mines were closed because an oversupply of metal depressed its value and fed inflation, lacks any evidence.

160. Livy, 45.29.11.

161. Cassiodorus, *Chron.* s.v. 158 B.C. Crawford, *Economic History Review* 30 (1977): 45, suggests a connection with the resumption of silver coinage at Rome in 157; cf. Crawford, *Roman Republican Coinage* I:47–48, 74; II:635—a possible, but unverifiable, conjecture. Whether the mines were now to be operated by *publicani* or by the Macedonians is simply unknown. Perelli, *RivFilol* 103 (1975): 408–409, argues that the Macedonians must have run them, on the grounds that Roman *publicani* could only be engaged in a Roman province. A fallacious argument: see Diod. 36.3.

162. Livy, 45.18.7, 45.26.13–14, 45.29.4; Diod. 31.8.3; Plut. *Aem. Paull.* 28.3.

163. Rightly questioned by Frank, *CP* 9 (1914): 58, who, however, needlessly sees the hand of an "anti-imperialistic party." Note also Badian, *Roman Imperialism*, 18–19; Dahlheim, *Gewalt und Herrschaft*, 255–261. In the most recent discussion, Harris, *War and Imperialism*, 73–74, again finds Rome's purpose to be that of enriching herself, the taxation "set at the maximum level possible."

source affirms that the tax was established in perpetuity. The Macedonians, of course, expected heavy exactions. Some had urged Perseus to consent to them as early as 171, as a means of averting war.[164] Perseus himself, following victory, offered to indemnify the Romans on the same terms accepted by his father, following defeat.[165] Rome had long been in the habit of making her defeated enemies pay the expenses of war. She naturally applied the principle again. This time, however, there was a difference, easily overlooked but obvious when pointed out. Conquered kings in the past had kept their thrones and paid their indemnities. Perseus, by contrast, had been removed, the Antigonid monarchy terminated. Rome made a sharp distinction between the royal house, her defeated foe, and the people of Macedonia, her "liberated" beneficiaries.[166] Who then would defray the Roman war costs? The senate hit upon a useful idea consonant with both its *dignitas* and its propaganda. The Macedonians would pay the same taxes they had always paid, but half the money would stay at home to support their own administration and the other half would revert to Rome. The people were "free," it could be asserted, for they were no longer contributing their resources to an autocratic regime.[167] How long these payments remained in effect is unknown; they receive no later mention in our evidence.[168] Once they sufficed to reimburse Rome, they may, for all we know, have been allowed to lapse. It is illegitimate and rash to conclude that Macedonia and Illyria had become tributary vassal-states of Rome.[169]

164. Livy, 42.50.2.

165. Polyb. 27.8.2; Livy, 42.62.10.

166. Cf., especially, Diod. 31.8.1–4; Livy, 45.18.1–2, 45.32.3–7.

167. Polyb. 36.17.13: κοινῇ μὲν πάντες ἀπολυθέντες μοναρχικῶν ἐπιταγμάτων καὶ φόρων καὶ μεταλαβόντες ἀπὸ δουλείας ὁμολογουμένως ἐλευθερίαν. Cf. 30.31.9. It is noteworthy that the payment of half their taxes is directly associated with the "freeing" of Macedonians and Illyrians: Livy, 45.29.4; Diod. 31.8.3, 31.8.5. In fact, some of the Illyrians were tax-exempt, others required to pay half to Rome, but all were "free"; Livy, 45.26.12–14. Cf. Robert, *Hellenica* 11–12 (1960): 509–514.

168. One may observe that the author of 1 Maccabees 8:4 refers to annual tribute paid to Rome by the "kings." In all likelihood, this refers to indemnity exactions. It cannot, in any case, apply to Macedonia after 167, which no longer had a monarchy. The *tributum* collected periodically from Italians was suspended in 167, not to be revived for more than a century. It is natural to connect this with an annual income derived from Macedonia; so, most recently, Crawford, *Economic History Review* 30 (1977): 44; Ferrary, in Nicolet, *Rome et la conquête*, 760. Yet the connection nowhere appears in the evidence. Rather, the release of Romans and Italians from *tributum* is explicitly associated with the windfall of booty from the East: Cic. *De Off.* 2.76; Pliny, *NH*, 33.56; Plut. *Aem. Paull.* 38.1; Val. Max. 4.3.8.

169. Interesting, though late, information ignored by most scholars in this context, should be brought into the reckoning. Eusebius, *Chron.* 424C (Helm), in referring to the Roman settlement of 148, states Μακέδονας . . . ὑποφόρους ἐποίησαν. The same

The Romans would neither occupy nor administer those lands. They carried back captured booty, as always after conquest. They requisitioned payments to cover their costs and to punish their foes. They eliminated the monarchies, broke up the territory, and reduced the economic resources of Macedonia and Illyria to render them militarily harmless. But they fostered new governments that could run themselves without Roman supervision and that could maintain concord without (it was hoped) Roman intervention. The Republic, its martial supremacy and reputation restored, could turn its back once again. The alternative was a burdensome and unwelcome occupation. In 167, as before, that alternative was rejected. Some may have considered it. The *publicani* certainly hoped for a share of the profits it could bring. But Cato spoke for the majority: since the Macedonians cannot be defended, best to leave them free.[170]

## The Fate of Macedonia

For the Romans, "leaving them free" meant leaving them alone. For the next two decades that is precisely what they did. Polybius claims that the Roman settlement of 167 rid the Macedonians of civil strife and internal disorders.[171] The picture is too rosy, as his own account elsewhere reveals. Within four years of the settlement Macedonians were already quarreling among themselves; a group of their officials had been assassinated, and their murderers had fled the country to take up service with Ptolemy. The people had not yet adjusted to democratic and republican institutions.[172] Rome stayed her hand. The senate sent the customary "investigative" commission; it was a minor item among many on the agenda of diplomatic activities—and no outcome of the mission survives on record.[173] Another dozen years later, in 151, internal stasis still plagued the land, but Macedonian leaders had ceased to appeal to the senate. Instead, they made private application to Scipio Aemilianus, son of Aemilius Paullus who had implemented the settlement of 167. Scipio turned down

in Porphyry, *FGH* 260, F 3.19; Jerome, *Chron.* 143 C (Helm): *Romani interfecto Pseudofilippo Macedonas tributarios faciunt.* If this evidence has any value, it indicates that Macedonia had not previously been tributary.

170. *SHA,* "Hadrian," 5.3: *Macedonas liberos pronuntiavit, quia tueri non poterant;* cf. Harris, *War and Imperialism,* 144–146.

171. Polyb. 36.17.13.

172. Polyb. 31.2.12: συνέβαινε γὰρ τοὺς Μακεδόνας ἀήθεις ὄντας δημοκρατικῆς καὶ συνεδριακῆς πολιτείας στασιάζειν πρὸς αὑτούς; 31.17.2.

173. Polyb. 31.2.12: καὶ τὰ κατὰ τὴν Μακεδονίαν ἐπισκέψασθαι.

the request; he had better things to do.[174] The Macedonians could be left to their own devices.

If anything can be inferred from these few scraps of information, it appears that the former realm of the Antigonids did not take easily to republican forms of government, especially with the once united nation divided arbitrarily into four separate principalities. The new regimes had failed to eradicate ancient sentiments for monarchy. That fact may lurk behind Polybius' statement about the Macedonians as still unaccustomed to democratic institutions. It is reflected also in the appeal to Scipio Aemilianus, presumably from men who owed their positions to the new machinery established by his father and who faced opposition from those who undermined the machinery. It would soon explode to the surface in the revolt of Andriscus. Rome, however, remained resolutely aloof.[175]

A threat to the Adriatic would receive a more interested hearing in the senate. The division of "Illyria" into three parts in 167 involved only southern Illyria. For the rest no arrangements seemed necessary.[176] The Dalmatians, who had earlier shaken off the yoke of Genthius, stood outside this settlement and, in its aftermath, engaged in raids and aggrandizement against their neighbors. Appeals came to Rome from the island of Issa and from the Daorsi, both of whom had supported the Republic against Genthius and had received tax-exempt status as a consequence.[177] The pattern that formed prior to the First Illyrian War, three-quarters of a century earlier, repeated itself here. Appeals went unheard for some time; at last, in 158, the senate sent a mission to the Dalmatians; the envoys were mistreated and abused; Rome then took military action to punish the offenders.[178] Polybius suggests a discreditable motive on the part of the Romans: their troops had been idle for a dozen years, they needed some campaigns to strengthen their sinews, and they seized on the pretext of Dalmatian rudeness to send a force.[179] How far he is to be trusted on this

174. Polyb. 35.4.10–12.

175. The only known Roman action in this period is the reopening of Macedonia's gold and silver mines in 158: Cassiodorus, *Chron.* s.v. 158 B.C. It is possible that the senate took that decision in order to ease economic pressures and relieve civil strife in Macedonia. But the *patres* would not themselves interfere directly.

176. Livy, 45.26.15. The northernmost site named here is Rhizon. Zippel, *Die römische Herrschaft*, 96, puts the northern frontier at the Naro river.

177. Polyb. 32.9; cf. Livy, 45.26.13–14.

178. Polyb. 32.9, 32.13; Appian, *Ill.* 11; Zon. 9.25; Livy, *Per.* 47. Insult to Roman ambassadors is given as the stated reason for war by Polybius and Appian, attacks on Roman "allies" by Livy; both appear in Zonaras. Background and bibliography in Walbank, *Commentary* III: 528–529.

179. Polyb. 32.13.5–9.

point is uncertain. Polybius finds almost none but discreditable motives for Roman foreign policy in the years after Pydna.[180] Insofar as
the Dalmatians conducted their raids inland, the Romans had little
reason to trouble themselves. But the Issaeans complained of assaults
on their territory and of attacks on Epetium and Tragyrium, two
coastal towns. These imply a Dalmatian push to the Adriatic.[181] The
senate overlooked the charges on several occasions but, when their
own investigatory commission got a rough reception, they decided to
demonstrate that the sea was exempt from Dalmatian depredations.
More devious intent need not be imputed. Even if one were to accept
Polybius' cynical analysis, however, it shows only how little the Illyrian
situation concerned the Romans: they used it as a mere training
ground to keep soldiers from getting soft. The fighting itself proved
a bit stiffer than expected. It required two campaigning seasons, in
156 and 155, before the Dalmatians submitted and a Roman consul
could celebrate his triumph.[182] The result sufficed for Rome's purposes. It brought nothing in the way of occupation or even enduring
pacification.[183]

Roman inattention to Macedonia soon produced dramatic consequences. Sentiments for the Antigonid monarchy still seethed below the surface, nearly two decades after the removal of Perseus. A
certain Andriscus, of unknown origins, took advantage of his resemblance to the Antigonid physiognomy and claimed to be Philip, son of
Perseus, reared in secrecy by a foster family. Demetrius of Syria, to
whom Andriscus had applied for assistance in regaining his inheritance, would have none of him and shipped him off to Rome for internment.[184] The *patres*, as might be expected, were altogether indifferent. They turned not a hair when Andriscus escaped from Italy
and won converts for his cause in Miletus and Byzantium.[185] The

180. His analysis is accepted without question by Harris, *War and Imperialism*,
233–234. Walbank, *Commentary* III:535, finds Polybius' statement "generally acceptable." Some proper skepticism in J. J. Wilkes, *Dalmatia* (London, 1969), 30–31.

181. Polyb. 32.9.1–2.

182. C. Marcius Figulus' campaign in 156: Polyb. 32.14.2; Appian, *Ill.* 11; Livy,
*Per.* 47; Florus, 2.25; Obseq. 16. P. Scipio Nasica's campaign in 155: Zon. 9.25; Livy, *Per.*
47; Strabo, 7.5.5 (C 315); Frontin. *Strat.* 3.6.2; *Vir. Ill.* 44.

183. Polybius includes among Roman motives a desire to "compel Illyrians to
obey their commands"; 32.13.8: καταπληξάμενοι τοὺς Ἰλλυριοὺς ἀναγκάσαι πειθαρχεῖν τοῖς ὑπ' αὐτῶν παραγγελλομένοις. Yet the recalcitrance of Illyrian tribes and the
absence of any Roman installations created more occasions for fighting twenty years
later and in subsequent years: Appian, *Ill.* 10, 11; Livy, *Per.* 56, 59; cf. Zippel, *Die
römische Herrschaft*, 132–139.

184. Livy, *Per.* 48–49; Zon. 9.28; Diod. 31.40a, 32.15.1.

185. Diod. 32.15; Livy, *Per.* 49; Zon. 9.28. According to Diodorus, 32.15.3, the
Milesians temporarily arrested him and asked advice of certain envoys as to his fate.

adventurer now took heart and gathered forces from Thracian chieftains—including one who was related by marriage to the Antigonid
house.[186] Suddenly and shockingly he descended upon Macedonia in
150. Two battles are recorded around the Thracian border. Then the
nation fell into his hands without resistance. Before the outside world
knew what had happened, Andriscus was already threatening Thessaly, like the Antigonid kings of old.[187]

Who could explain it? Polybius found the events incredible: the
pseudo-Philip had, as it were, dropped out of the sky to sweep all
before him, while men stood paralyzed in amazement and disbelief.[188]
The absence of armed forces in the interior of Macedonia helps to account for the swiftness of Andriscus' success. But there is more to it
than that. The welcome for this putative prince should not be ac-
counted as a display of anti-Romanism or an effort to throw off the
western yoke. There had been no yoke, no Roman presence, indeed
hardly any Roman interest since the fall of Perseus. Nothing in the
evidence suggests a surge of anti-Roman feeling in Macedonia.[189] Andriscus tapped deep-rooted sentiments in the nation: an attachment
to the Antigonid royal house, a commitment to monarchy.[190] The people of Macedonia had developed little fondness for the petty republics, cut off from one another, immersed in factional strife, and ignored by Rome.

It is remarkable and revealing that, when Andriscus' attention
turned to Thessaly, the Thessalians hastened to seek aid not from
Rome, but from Achaea.[191] The Romans, as was by now well known,
were slow to act, slower to take decisive action. The same held true at
this juncture. A single legate was sent by the patres in 150, P. Scipio
Nasica, his purpose to negotiate a peaceful settlement.[192] That Rome

---

The envoys refused to take him seriously and advised his release. If these are Roman
envoys, as normally assumed, it is further evidence for the Republic's total lack of
concern.

186. Diod. 32.15.5–7; Zon. 9.28.

187. Polyb. 36.10.4–5; Livy, Oxyr. Per. 49; Zon. 9.28; Diod. 32.15.7; cf. Florus,
1.30.3. A full account of events in G. Cardinali, RivFilol 39 (1911): 1–14; De Sanctis,
Storia dei Romani IV:3.120–123. Further literature noted in Walbank, Commentary
III:668–670.

188. Polyb. 36.10; cf. 36.9.1.

189. The nearest we have to it is a statement of Zon. 9.28 that several Thracian
princes backed Andriscus because of their dislike of Rome. But this does not imply
Macedonian dislike. And the Thracian motive is differently explained by Diod.
32.15.5–7: connection with the Antigonid monarchy.

190. Cf. Florus, 1.30.3: regiam formam, regium nomen, animum quoque regis implevit.

191. Polyb. 36.10.5.

192. Zon. 9.28: τὸν Σκιπίωνα τὸν Νασικᾶν ἔπεμψαν εἰρηνηκῶς πως τὰ ἐκεῖ
διοικήσοντα.

could contemplate a pacific solution is itself noteworthy. It suggests either that she was quite uninformed on the circumstances or that she had no deep commitment to the settlement of 167—or both. Nasica, however, found Macedonian forces pressing Thessaly. He took impromptu steps to round up Hellenic troops, especially Achaeans, already mobilized at Thessalian request, and prevented further advance by Andriscus.[193] Only in 149 did Rome send out a legion, under the praetor P. Iuventius Thalna, who suffered total defeat and lost his own life. The willingness of Macedonians to fight for the newly revived crown, even in the hands of a dubious pretender, is impressive.[194]

Thalna's disaster, of course, sealed Macedonia's fate. Rome could not accept the disgrace with equanimity. The fear that Rome now meant business caused defection in Andriscus' ranks for the first time, requiring him to take cruel measures against the defectors.[195] In 148 the senate dispatched a major force, under the praetor Q. Metellus, armed with proconsular *imperium* and two legions, and assisted by a fleet from Pergamum, always alert to any resurgence of Macedonian power. The result was swift and decisive. In a single campaigning season, the Macedonians were crushed and Andriscus fled to Thrace where he was betrayed and taken.[196] Even so, another pretender, claiming to be the son of Perseus, collected supporters and had to be put to rout by Metellus.[197] Still another sprang up five years later, producing an army before he too was suppressed.[198] The depth of Macedonian feeling for the monarchical past can hardly be plainer.

That past was now gone forever. And Macedonian liberty, in any meaningful sense, came to an abrupt end. What steps the Romans took to organize the land after the fall of Andriscus remain strangely obscure. Scholarly unanimity asserts without discussion or argument that a *lex provinciae* followed, that Macedonia became a Roman province, that annual governors were appointed by the senate to

193. Zon. 9.28; Livy, *Per.* 50.

194. Zon. 9.28; Livy, *Per.* 50; Florus, 1.30.4; Diod. 32.9a; Eutrop. 4.13; and, especially, Polyb. 36.17.14: ἀνδρὶ δὲ στυγνῷ συναγωνιζόμενοι καὶ περὶ τῆς τούτου βασιλείας ἀνδραγαθήσαντες ἐνίκησαν Ῥωμαίους.

195. Polyb. 36.17.13; Diod. 32.9a–b. P. A. Mackay, *ANSMN* 14 (1968): 36–37, oddly takes this as evidence for "republican" sympathies among Andriscus' victims.

196. Sources in Broughton, *MRR* I:461. On Metellus' rank and authority, see M. G. Morgan, *Historia* 18 (1969): 423–425. The campaign was over by the end of 148: Livy, *Oxyr. Per.* 50; Obseq. 19. The Pergamene fleet: Zon. 9.28; Strabo, 13.4.2 (C 624). In general on Adriscus, see Cardinali, *RivFilol* 39 (1911): 14–20; De Sanctis, *Storia dei Romani* IV:3.123–127.

197. Zon. 9.28.

198. Livy, *Per.* 53; Eutrop. 4.15; Varro, *De Re Rust.* 2.4.1–2. Not a doublet of the preceding pretender; see Morgan, *Historia* 18 (1969): 430–431.

supervise and administer its affairs from 148 or 146 on.[199] Yet we need to be reminded how thin the evidence is for such a superstructure. No source anywhere makes reference to a *lex provinciae* for Macedonia. Nor even to any organization of the land as a province.[200] As for the list of Roman governors, carefully compiled by scholars, the large majority are men who fought barbarian tribes on the Macedonian borders or settled quarrels in their environs—and for many of the years of the late Republic no governor of Macedonia is known at all.[201] It is not certain even that the senate appointed "governors" annually to the area, let alone that any regular administrative machinery was erected.[202] The four Macedonian republics, in fact, continued in

199. There is no need to append a bibliography, since every work that touches on this subject makes the above assumptions, explicitly or implicitly. See, most recently, Dahlheim, *Gewalt und Herrschaft*, 121; Ferrary, in Nicolet, *Rome et la conquête* 2:770–771. Morgan, *Historia* 18 (1969): 422–446, argues at length that the organization of Macedonia was the work of Mummius and the *decem legati* after the Achaean war, rather than of Q. Metellus. But he takes for granted the existence of a *lex provinciae* for Macedonia. F. Papazoglou, *ANRW* II:7.1 (1979), 304–307, believes that the arrangements of 167 made a new *lex provinciae* unnecessary, that Macedonian institutions were largely left intact, but that Rome nevertheless formally created a province in 146.

200. Florus' statement, 1.32.3, *Metello ordinanti tum maxime Macedoniam*, means no more than that Metellus was bringing order to the land; cf. Morgan, *Historia* 18 (1969): 441–442.

201. A recent list appears in Θ. Χ. Σαρικακη, Ῥωμαῖοι ἄρχοντες τῆς ἐπαρχίας Μακεδονίας (Thessalonica, 1971), 27–151, 189–201. He counts forty-six known governors in the 120 years between 148 and 27 B.C., with another seventeen *incerti*. The list is slightly revised by Papazoglou, *ANRW* II:7.1 (1979), 309–311, with a different calculation. The period of civil wars is excluded, leaving one hundred years for which approximately forty governors are known, their tours of duty accounting for nearly three-quarters of the relevant years.

202. An inscription found at Thebes refers to [Μακεδονίαι] τῆ Ῥωμαίων ἐπαρχείαι καὶ ἧς ἐπάρχουσ[ιν τῆς Ἑλλάδος]: *IG*, VII, 2413–2414 = Sherk, *RDGE*, no. 44, lines 2–3. That has been taken as definitive both for a Macedonian province and for the attribution of part of Greece to it: Accame, *Il dominio romano*, 2–7. Yet the analysis depends on restorations in the text. And even if they be accepted, this need not imply a formal provincial organization in 148 or 146. Accame dates the document to 112 or 111 B.C., a generation after the fall of Andriscus. Others put it in 146, while Mummius and the *decem legati* were still in Greece; so, recently, Sherk, *op. cit.*, 250–252. If that be so, there could hardly yet have been a "province of Macedonia," for that would require senatorial ratification of the commissioners' settlement. Other evidence is equally inconclusive. Q. Fabius Maximus, who imposed penalties after an uprising at Dyme ca. 115, is not described as governor of Macedonia, but simply as ἀνθύπατος Ῥωμαίων; *Syll.*[3] 684 = Sherk, *RDGE*, no. 43, line 3. Elsewhere we hear of Romans who served as στρατηγὸς or στρατηγὸς ἀνθύπατος ἐν Μακεδονίᾳ during the later second century; e.g., *IGRR*, IV, 134, lines 9–11 (M. Cosconius in 135); *Syll.*[3] 704, I[1] = *FDelphes*, III, 2, 70, line 1; *Syll.*[3] 704, I[3] and I[4] = *FDelphes*, III, 2, 70b, lines 3–4; *Syll.*[3] 704K = *FDelphes*, III, 2, 248a, lines 1–2; *Syll.*[3] 705B = *FDelphes*, III, 2, 70a = Sherk, *RDGE*, no. 15, lines 32–33, 59–60 (Cn. Cornelius Sisenna ca. 118). Or as *praetor in Macedonia*; e.g., Varro, *De Re Rust.* 2.4.1–2 (Licinius Nerva in 143 or 142); Cic. *De Fin.* 1.24; Livy, *Per.* 54; *Oxyr. Per.* 54;

existence and are attested even in the period of the early Roman Empire.[203] Regulations set down by Aemilius Paullus in 167 remained in effect at least to the end of the Republic.[204] It does not appear that the senate made any major organizational changes after the elimination of Andriscus. Roman reluctance to undertake administration is remarkable.

Nevertheless, the conclusion of this war marks a clear dividing line. The very fact that praetors and proconsuls engaged frequently, if not annually, after 146 to protect the Macedonian borders, confront barbarian tribes, and settle disputes sets off the subsequent age from all that had gone before. The "Macedonian era" was ever after reckoned to have begun in 148—the date of Metellus' victory, not the installation of a province.[205] The senate at this time, apparently, imposed a regular and permanent tribute upon the land.[206] Since Roman forces would now take over the task of discouraging barbarian incursions, it was appropriate to guarantee a steady income to pay expenses. The Republic accepted responsibility for the defense of Macedonia and of Illyria, even without a formal administrative structure.[207] Her generals would enforce order whenever necessary—and would find excuses for hunting triumphs even when not necessary.[208] A

---

Val. Max. 5.8.3. (D. Junius Silanus in 141). On other occasions, however, a commander could be described as operating in Thrace or Macedonia interchangeably; e.g., Livy, *Per.* 56; *IGRR*, IV, 134, lines 9–11 (M. Cosconius in 135); Livy, *Per.* 63; Vell. Pat. 2.7.8–2.8.1; Florus, 1.39.1–5 (C. Porcius Cato in 114); Sallust, *Iug.* 35.4; Livy, *Per.* 65; Eutrop. 4.27.5 (M. Minucius Rufus, 109–106). By 100 B.C. a governor for the ἐπαρχεία of Macedonia is noted as a customary matter: *FDelphes*, III, 4, 37B, lines 28–29; III, 4, 37C, line 8; *JRS* 64 (1974): 201, lines 13–15, 26–27, 204, lines 6–8, 12–13, 26–27, 32–33, 41–42. But we cannot be sure that this was an annual occurrence; nor does this evidence suggest anything regarding a permanent administration. Even as late as the 50s B.C., there were no hard and fast frontiers that defined a province of Macedonia; cf. Cic. *In Pis.* 38: *ut semper Macedonicis imperatoribus idem fines provinciae fuerint qui gladiorum atque pilorum.*

203. Acts 16:12; *AE* (1900), no. 130; Edson, *CP* 41 (1946): 107.

204. Livy, 45.32.7; Justin, 33.2.7.

205. See Tod, *BSA* 23 (1918–1919): 206–217; *BSA* 24 (1919–1921): 54–67; *Studies Presented to D. M. Robinson* (1953), II: 382–397. After Augustus the date of Actium is more common on official documents than the beginning of the "Macedonian era," but that does not affect the issue; cf. Papazoglou, *BCH* 87 (1963): 517–526.

206. Euseb. *Chron.* 424c (Helm); Porphyry, *FGH*, 260, F 3.19; Jerome, *Chron.* 143c (Helm). Regular revenues from Macedonia are attested in 100 B.C.; *JRS* 64 (1974): 204, lines 11–18.

207. Certainly Illyria did not receive provincial status. But Roman commanders periodically fought wars in the area: Appian, *Ill.* 10, 11; Livy, *Per.* 56, 59; cf. Zippel, *Die römische Herrschaft*, 132–139. Promagistrates sent to Macedonia presumably also had jurisdiction over Illyria: cf. Cic. *In Pis.* 83, 86, 96.

208. Cf. Appian, *Ill.* 11: Καικίλιος Μέτελλος ὑπατεύων οὐδὲν ἀδικοῦσι τοῖς Δαλμάταις ἐψηφίσατο πολεμεῖν ἐπιθυμίᾳ θριάμβου.

logical step soon followed: construction of the via Egnatia, stretching from Apollonia to Byzantium, which allowed for ready movement of troops and for effective military dominance.[209] Independence for Macedonia and Illyria had vanished.[210]

**V**

The outcome was sudden rather than gradual, the product of *ad hoc* decisions rather than a steady development. Nothing had been more unsteady than Roman policy on Illyria and Macedonia, if policy it can be termed at all. Over eighty years passed after the time of the First Illyrian War before Rome determined to assume a more direct supervision of affairs in that area. The Republic occasionally intervened to keep faith with allies in southern Italy and to clear the Adriatic of piracy. Twice the Romans entered major wars with the Antigonid house when their reputation was at stake and when the kings refused to be overawed by diplomatic pressure and threats. But Rome maintained no persistent interest in the area, preferring to shun commitments, occupation, or administration. She was obsessed neither by fear of Macedonians and Illyrians nor by desire to control them. She elected to regard defeated foes as *amici*, keeping kings on their thrones or creating institutions that would be self-perpetuating without need for recurrent intervention. She fostered the image of benefactor and liberator, in traditional Hellenistic fashion, not out of philhellenism or for aggrandizement but to keep herself at a distance. Only when the fragility of the system installed after Pydna was rudely exposed by Andriscus and when Rome suffered unwonted humiliation did she resolve to assume a burden evaded for three-quarters of a century: responsibility for the maintenance of order across the Adriatic.

209. The *via Egnatia* was built before the death of Polybius, who made reference to it: Strabo, 7.7.4 (C 322); *Epitome*, 7.57; cf. Cic. *De Prov. Cons.* 4; *In Pis.* 40. See also the recently published milestone from the vicinity of Thessalonica, attesting the name of the proconsul Cn. Egnatius, C.f., from whom the road doubtless derived its designation; C. Romiopoulou, *BCH* 98 (1974): 813–816; cf. P. Collart, *BCH* 100 (1976): 177–200; Daux, *Journal des Savants* (1977): 145–147; Walbank, *LCM* 2 (1977): 73–74.

210. Cf. Florus, 1.30.5: *Metellus . . . Macedoniam servitute multavit*; Festus, *Brev.* 7: *Macedonia quoque populo Romano adiuncta est.*

# Chapter 13

# Rome and Greece (I)

The ancient glory of Greece proper had long since faded in the larger world of Hellenistic politics. Philip II and Alexander the Great had forced the once proud city-states into the background. In the great struggles of the Antigonid, Seleucid, and Ptolemaic monarchies, the *poleis* of the mainland and of the Aegean had become political playthings, bounced around by the major powers and reduced to second-class status. Yet they had not lost a sense of their own identity and a longing for independence, however shaky or restricted that independence might be. The city-states could still take advantage of the changed circumstances that prevailed in the world after Alexander. They utilized the protection of Hellenistic kings, even played them off against one another, they created leagues and experimented with new institutions, they framed and reframed new alliances with an eye to holding some control over the political and military contests of the third century. Some states, like the Aetolian and Achaean confederacies, rose to the level of significant powers, others, like Sparta, Athens, and Boeotia, clung to old traditions, and played roles, far from nugatory, in the complex rivalries of the Hellenistic age.

They never, of course, congealed into a united front, as much engaged in struggles with one another as manipulating or being manipulated by greater powers. That was the curse of Hellas from the beginning. It was also the very life-blood of her history. No genuine understanding of Roman-Greek relations can come without acknowledging the preeminence of this feature. Conventional phrases like "the Illyrian wars" or "the Macedonian wars" derive from Roman sources and from the Roman vantage-point. They serve more to distort than to clarify. What lay in the background to such events, as we have seen, were the aspirations of Illyrians to become a Hellenic power, Philip V's ambitions to strengthen his frontiers and extend his sway over the East, Perseus' desire to rebuild his state's influence in Hellas, the longings of the Macedonians to recover their monarchy and to reunify their nation after 167. Similarly, the Greeks had their own interests to the fore, engaged with or against one another throughout the third century and well into the second. Even after the initial Roman interventions across the Adriatic, the Greeks remained absorbed in their own affairs. The Social War of 220–217 was an exclusively Hellenic conflict, and the "First Macedonian War" almost exclusively so. Rome's intrusions after 200 were welcomed, encouraged, and prodded by some, frightened others, and puzzled most. They expected the Western state to behave like a Hellenistic power, took advantage of Rome when she did so, and were frustrated when she did not. But they viewed her always, whether as beneficent or barbaric, in the context of their own rivalries and in the light of their own history.

## Greek Aspirations in the War with Philip

From the standpoint of Rome, the Greeks of the mainland and the islands were for a very long time barely noticeable. The sole exceptions, in any meaningful sense, down to 200 were the Greek cities on the Gulf of Ionia. Here, as we have already observed, close connections prevailed between those *poleis* and the cities of southern Italy which, since the mid-third century, had come under the supervision of Rome. Insofar as the Republic took any positive actions in the East during the last third of the third century, they were all tied in one way or another to the interests of those states and to the protection of the Adriatic waterway.[1]

The First Illyrian War created *amicitiae* with Corcyra, Apollonia, and Epidamnus.[2] Roman legates went on, after the war, to make representations in Achaea and Aetolia, which had previously fought the Illyrians, and in Corinth and Athens, which may also have had interests in the commercial lanes to Magna Graecia.[3] But these were mere explanatory missions and resulted in no formal relationships. The Adriatic interested Rome, not Hellas. When the coastal cities seemed

---

1. Connections between Greeks on both sides of the Straits of Otranto will explain the mission of Apollonia to Rome in the mid-third century, if that visit be authentic: Val. Max. 6.6.5; Dio, fr. 42; Zon. 8.7; Livy, *Per.* 15. See above pp. 63–64. No formal association resulted anyway.

2. Polyb. 2.11.5–10; Appian, *Ill.* 7; cf. Polyb. 7.9.13.

3. Polyb. 2.12.4–8; cf. Zon. 8.19.

under threat from Philip—and possibly from Scerdilaidas—in the winter of 217/16, the senate detached ten vessels and sent them on an exploratory voyage to the Ionian Sea. That sufficed to dispel any danger.[4] Similarly in 214, a Roman squadron went into action when Philip attacked Apollonia and Oricum, and once again put the Macedonian to rout.[5] The fleet then stationed itself at Oricum to keep closer watch on the security of the area.[6] The timing of Rome's alliance with Aetolia in 212 or 211 must be explained, in part at least, by Philip's capture of Lissus, which put him once more on the Adriatic; and the clause of the alliance which restricted territorial acquisitions to areas south of Corcyra plainly aimed to protect those coastal cities from Aetolia's grasp as from Macedonia's.[7] At the peace of Phoenice Rome willingly resigned the Atintanes to Philip, as well as other Illyrian areas that had come under his control, so long as the towns on the Ionian Gulf remained inviolate. They alone mattered.

Rome had not bothered even with the nearest neighbors of her *amici* on the coast, Epirus and Acarnania. Her legations to Greece after the First Illyrian War bypassed them altogether. Those two principalities, recently allies of Illyria, but ineffective and unimportant, could safely be ignored. Their interests and hostilities were directed more toward Aetolia against whom they fought in the Social War on the side of Macedonia. Greek cities on the straits of Otranto, despite their proximity, were outside the effective sphere of Epirus and certainly of Acarnania. When the Romans wooed the Aetolians in 212, control of Acarnania was held out as the most tempting prize; their assistance would help deliver it to the Aetolians, and Epirus too, for all the Romans cared. Aetolia was free to subjugate all the area south of Corcyra—but not beyond.[8] Rivalry with Aetolia dominated the concerns of Epirus and Acarnania, now as before, old Hellenic concerns. In the peace of Phoenice, the two states appear among the signatories on Philip's side. Rome had paid them no heed.[9]

4. Polyb. 5.110.
5. Livy, 24.40; Zon. 9.4; Plut. *Arat.* 51.2.
6. Livy, 24.40.17; cf. Polyb. 8.1.6.
7. Livy, 26.24.11.
8. Livy, 26.24.6, 26.24.8, 26.24.11. The Romans duly cooperated against Acarnania, captured Acarnanian towns and turned them over to Aetolia: Livy, 26.24.15; cf. Polyb. 9.39.2. Epirus, in the event, stayed out of the war for the most part, though she remained a nominal ally of Philip: Polyb. 9.38.5, 11.5.4; Livy, 29.12.14. The conjecture that Epirus entered a private accord with Rome (as Oost, *Roman Policy*, 32; Cabanes, *L'Épire*, 257–258) lacks any evidence. Rome simply ignored the area and Aetolia was occupied elsewhere. That the Epirotes feared Aetolian attacks is clear from Polyb. 10.41.3–4. For the events, see Oost, *op. cit.*, 30–39; Cabanes, *op. cit.*, 252–264.
9. Livy, 29.12.14. No need to assume that the treaty made them *amici* of Rome, as

The one Greek state whose alliance Rome actively sought was Aetolia. The reasons have already been outlined. At a time when the Republic had her hands full with Hannibal, Aetolia could provide valuable service in drawing Philip's attention away from the Adriatic. The alliance constituted a temporary arrangement, with specific aims, and all territorial gains would go to Aetolia. Rome's contribution to the fighting was minimal, and became the more so as it progressed. The "First Macedonian War" misnamed what was basically a contest among Hellenes and Macedonians, a revival of the Social War, a reflection of Hellenistic politics.[10] In the course of it Rome contracted temporary alliances with Sparta, Messenia, and Elis as well. The objectives here were the same: not an extension of Roman influence, but a move to occupy Philip's chief ally in the Peloponnese, the Achaean League. Those three states, in fact, entered the war because of their ties to Aetolia rather than because of any connection with Rome.[11] Longstanding Peloponnesian rivalries played themselves out in that area, rivalries that on one occasion even saw the Spartans attack their nominal ally Elis. Roman involvement in the sector was small and insignificant. The major battle took place at Mantinea in 207, a smashing victory by Achaean forces over Sparta. Sparta then effectively withdrew from the war, as did Elis and Messenia. Romans were nowhere in evidence.[12] The peace of Phoenice included Sparta, Elis, and Messenia among the adscripti. And they subsequently retained their amicitiae with Rome—as with Aetolia. Conventional Hellenistic practices underlay those associations. They entailed no lasting commitments and guaranteed no cooperation. Indeed, the Peloponnese quickly became embroiled again in internal strife. In the final years of

Oost, *Roman Policy*, 37–38. That status, attested only in 191, probably followed the Second Macedonian War: Livy, 36.12.1–2, 36.35.9. Epirotes leaned toward Philip in that war as well, though they preferred neutrality: Livy, 31.7.9, 32.10.1, 32.14.5–6. The Acarnanians, out of fear of Aetolia, stayed on the Macedonian side: Livy, 33.16.

10. See above pp. 377–381.

11. Polyb. 9.30.6, 9.31.1–4, 10.25.3, 16.3.3. See above pp. 20–21.

12. Roman operations confined themselves to brief ravaging in the area around Sicyon and Corinth and the installation of some forces in Elis in 209: Livy, 27.31.1–3, 27.32.2–6. This was no doubt designed to keep the Aetolians in the war, for they had only recently been on the point of negotiating a settlement with Philip: Livy, 27.30.9–15. Sulpicius Galba subsequently destroyed Dyme as an object lesson, but without any enduring effect. He immediately withdrew, and the town was soon restored by Philip: Paus. 7.17.5; Livy, 32.21.28, 32.22.10. For the Spartan attack on Elis, see Livy, 28.7.14. The battle of Mantinea: Polyb. 11.11–18; Plut. *Phil.* 10.1–8. Sparta withdrew from the war thereafter; cf. Polyb. 13.6.1. Nor is there any evidence for continued fighting by Elis and Messenia. On the Peloponnesian contest in general, see Errington, *Philopoemen*, 49–69, who misleadingly entitles his chapter "War with Rome." Achaean forces never engaged the Romans.

the third century Achaean expansionism revived, the League absorbed Megara, relations between Achaea and Macedonia cooled, a
new war erupted with Sparta, and the Spartan ruler Nabis even conducted an assault on his own—and Rome's—"ally" Messenia. It need
hardly be added that no one gave a thought to the Republic across the
sea—and vice-versa.[13] It was Hellenistic politics as usual.

Down to 200 B.C. Rome had refrained from any enduring en-
tanglements with mainland Greeks, apart from a few cities on the Ionian Gulf. The temporary alliance with Aetolia had already been severed in 206 when the League came to terms with Philip—and her
envoys got rude treatment when they came to Rome in 202 or 201.[14]
*Amicitiae* with Peloponnesian states were mere formalities, and those
states were left to fight their own battles. Rome may have entered into
friendly relations with Athens, but certainly none that imposed any
obligations upon her.[15] A shallow involvement heretofore.

A Roman legation moved around the Greek world in 200, sounding out opinion, announcing the senate's demands on Philip, and
endeavoring to gather a consensus which could intimidate the Macedonian. The mainland states which that legation visited provoke surprise and interest—both for those that are included and for those that
are not. Sparta, Elis, and Messenia, allies in the previous conflict and
*amici* now, were bypassed. Instead, the Roman envoys went to Aetolia which had broken with Rome in 206, to Achaea which had been
Philip's principal ally, to Epirus a neutral but on Philip's side, to Athamania and to Athens both of whom had acted as mediators in the

13. Sparta, Elis, and Messenia as *adscripti* at Phoenice: Livy, 29.12.14. Their inclusion in the peace—and Aetolia's absence from it—implies, though some have thought
the contrary, that they had not framed separate peace treaties with Philip in 206 as
Aetolia had done. Continued *amicitiae* with Rome: Polyb. 18.42.7; Livy, 34.31.5,
34.32.16. And with Aetolia: Polyb. 16.13.3. Achaean absorption of Megara: Plut. *Phil.*
12.3; Polyb. 20.6.7–12; Paus. 8.50.5. Coolness with Macedonia: Polyb. 13.3–5, 13.8.2,
18.54.8; Plut. *Phil.* 12.2; Paus. 8.50.4; Justin, 29.4.11; cf. Livy, 28.8.1–6, 32.5.4; Errington, *Philopoemen*, 66–67, 70–77. Conflict between Achaea and Sparta: Polyb.
13.8.2–7, 16.36–37; Plut. *Phil.* 12.4–5; Livy, 31.25.3–4; Paus. 8.50.5; cf. Errington, *op.
cit.*, 77–81; J.-G. Texier, *Nabis* (Paris, 1975), 37–40, with some inaccurate references.
Nabis' attack on Messene: Polyb. 16.13.3, 16.16.1–16.17.7; Livy, 34.32.16; Paus. 8.50.5.
In general, see Aymard, *Premiers rapports*, 38–50.

14. Livy, 31.29.4; Appian, *Mac.* 4.2; see above pp. 396–397, n. 214.

15. Roman legates had visited Athens after the First Illyrian War; Polyb. 2.12.8;
cf. Zon. 8.19. And Athens appears among the *adscripti* at Phoenice; Livy, 29.12.14. But
the authenticity of that notice is more than questionable and cannot be used to support
any reconstruction; bibliography on this in Dahlheim, *Struktur und Entwicklung*,
219–221, n. 99. Most decisive against it is the fact that Philip, after ravaging the land of
Attica, could still warn the Romans not to violate the peace of Phoenice: Polyb.
16.34.5–7.

First Macedonian War.[16] Reasons can readily be excogitated for each of these diplomatic calls: Epirus and Athamania bordered Macedonia; Aetolia and Achaea were Greece's most powerful leagues; Athens had been the site of Philip's recent depredations. The important fact, however, is that Rome did not summon up loyalties or associations garnered in the prior war and saw no continuity between it and the present circumstances. Only hindsight can find here a logical and natural step in the development of Roman imperialism. The senate sought to project a more positive image and to overawe Philip, not to capitalize upon or expand earlier connections.

Once Philip chose to resist, the pragmatic requirements of warfare dictated Rome's diplomatic dealings with mainland Greeks. She naturally endeavored to bring over as many important states as possible to her side, to dislodge allies from Philip, and to parcel out the burdens of fighting. Past relations with those states, whether friendly, hostile, or nonexistent, were simply irrelevant. Sulpicius Galba, through Athamanian and Athenian intermediaries, attempted to win Aetolia's adherence to the Roman cause in winter 200/199 and spring 199.[17] When Flamininus took over in 198, one of the demands he made of Philip was the liberation of Thessaly, a demand designed no doubt in part to spark hope of rebellion in that land.[18] Flamininus' stay in Epirus was marked by notable restraint, a conspicuous avoidance of plunder and rapine, thus assuring that Philip could not count on its support and also winning many Epirotes to his own camp.[19] There followed a vigorous effort to put pressure on Achaea, encouraged by internal political developments, and to bring the League over to Rome's side. Achaea had wavered hitherto, inactive one way or the other in the war, her leaders and her cities deeply divided, but the combination of Roman threats and promises decided the issue.[20] The Republic's generals had no objections to negotiating with any power which might be serviceable in the fight against Philip, regardless of its previous behavior and sympathies. Flamininus quickly consented to talks with Nabis of Sparta in winter 198/7, despite the fact that this

16. Polyb. 16.27. 'On mediating efforts by Athamania and Athens, see Livy, 27.30.4, 29.12.12, 36.31.11; Appian, *Mac.* 3.1.

17. Livy, 31.28.3, 31.29.1–2, 31.30–31.

18. Livy, 32.10.7; cf. 32.13.4–8, 32.14.4; Plut. *Flam.* 5.2.

19. Plut. *Flam.* 5.1–2; Livy, 32.14.5–8. There had been some Epirote sympathizers for Rome before Flamininus' arrival: Polyb. 27.15.2; Livy, 32.6.1, 32.11.1–5; Plut. *Flam.* 4.3. But most had previously leaned toward Philip: Livy, 32.10.1, 32.14.5; cf. Diod. 28.11. This is not to deny that Flamininus could use terror and savagery to cow the Greeks, as well as diplomacy; cf. Eckstein, *Phoenix* 30 (1976): 134–138.

20. Livy, 32.19.1–32.23.3; Appian, *Mac.* 7. Achaea had previously maintained her official alliance with Macedonia but had held back from participation in the war: Polyb. 16.35; Livy, 31.25, 32.5.4–6, 32.19.1.

ruler had recently made an arrangement with Philip. A mutual agreement for the duration of the war was concluded without difficulty.[21] Not long thereafter, Flamininus, assisted by a display of force and by speeches from Attalus and from the Achaean leader Aristaenus, persuaded the Boeotians, whose loyalties too had wavered, to abandon Philip and join a Roman alliance.[22] At about the same time, his brother, L. Flamininus, attempted to detach the Acarnanians by persuasion and use of sympathizers. Opinion here also was divided, but the assembly, after various machinations, voted to keep faith with Macedonia. Only then did the Roman commander use force, and, when the news of Cynoscephalae arrived, Acarnania capitulated, the last holdout among Philip's allies.[23]

An important element in all this needs emphasis. Just as prior associations had no bearing on Rome's casting about for allies in the Second Macedonian War, so these new alliances had no weight in determining Rome's actions in the future. They were wartime associations and nothing more, recalled when it seemed useful, ignored when not. So, for example, Flamininus in 195 chose to forget the agreement made with Nabis two years earlier and stressed instead the Spartan's violation of their earlier pact, even condemning him for the assault on Messenia in 201, though Rome had cared not a whit about that at the time.[24] The Epirotes in 192/1 did not regard their *amicitia* with Rome as precluding negotiations with Antiochus; indeed they offered him welcome if he could promise protection—and the Epirote negotiator was none other than Charops, a man who had conspicuously supported the Roman cause against Philip.[25] The same was true in Chalcis where debates ensued about policy toward Antiochus and it was argued with plausibility that relations with Rome did not rule out cooperation with the Syrian.[26] One state, the Achaean League, actively sought a formal written alliance with the Republic, thereby to guarantee security and collaboration. The senate postponed the request indefinitely.[27] The *patres* had no intention of binding their hands for the future.

21. Livy, 32.39; Zon. 9.16. The prior agreement between Philip and Nabis: Livy, 32.38.2–5, 34.12.16–19.

22. Livy, 33.1–2; Plut. *Flam.* 6; Zon. 9.16. Some Boeotians, however, still fought in Philip's ranks: Polyb. 18.1.2, 18.43.1; Livy, 33.14.5, 33.27.5, 33.27.8.

23. Livy, 32.40.7, 32.16–17.

24. Livy, 34.32.16–20: *parce, sis, fidem ac iura societatis iactare.* Nabis' appeal to this arrangement of 197 (Livy, 34.31.5, 34.31.8, 34.31.10, 34.31.15, 34.31.19) is simply ignored by Flamininus.

25. Polyb. 20.3; Livy, 36.5, 36.35.8–9.

26. Livy, 35.46.5–7, 35.46.12. Cf. the Aetolian speech in Achaea: Livy, 35.48.8–9.

27. Livy, 32.23.1–2; Polyb. 18.42.6–7.

More significant still are Greek attitudes. The circumstances of the Second Macedonian War compelled some hard decisions. But the decisions they reached depended not so much on allegiance to one or the other of the major protagonists as to special interests, claims, fears, or aspirations. The struggle between Rome and Philip, which dominates the sources, should not close our eyes to the fact that Hellenic states had individual concerns, long antedating the coming of Rome, which remained uppermost even in the course of that mighty struggle.

The Aetolians, for example, held off for a time, hesitating to commit themselves. Rival speeches by Macedonians and Romans were of no account. Aetolia entered the war in 199 when it appeared that Rome had the upper hand. She could as easily have moved the other way.[28] Aetolia cared naught for Macedonia or Rome. Her aims were specific and undisguised: to recover cities that had fallen under Philip's sway and to reunite them with the Aetolian Confederacy.[29] The power struggles of central Greece were in the forefront of Aetolian calculations. The Acarnanians held out longest among Philip's allies. A national habit of loyalty is given as reason, but not the only reason: fear and hatred of Aetolia kept them in line.[30] Once again the rivalry of Hellene against Hellene prevailed.

In Achaea matters were more complex (or, rather, our evidence is somewhat fuller). The League had remained faithful to Philip in the First Macedonian War, but confined its attention to the Peloponnese and never confronted Roman forces. Cracks soon began to show in the alliance. Philip had promised to withdraw his garrisons and restore certain Peloponnesian towns to Achaea in 208, but failed to make good on the promise. Revival of the Achaeans' military fortunes under Philopoemen and their successes at the end of the third century may have made Philip wary of too much Achaean independence. Rumors circulated that the king even attempted to arrange Philopoemen's assassination.[31] The League became increasingly divided. It held to Philip at the outset of the war, though without par-

28. Livy, 31.29–32, 31.40.9–31.41.1; especially 31.32.5: *utrius partis melior fortuna belli esset, ad eius societatem inclinaturos.*

29. Polyb. 18.2.6, 18.3.11–12, 18.8.9, 18.38.3–7, 18.47.7–9; Livy, 32.13.9–15, 32.33.8, 32.33.15–16, 32.35.11, 33.13.6, 33.34.7–8.

30. Livy, 33.16.2: *duae autem maxime causae eos tenuerant in amicitia regis, una fides insita genti, altera metus odiumque Aetolorum.*

31. For Achaean activities in the late third century, see above pp. 440–441. Philip promised to restore the towns in 208, but did not do so for a decade: Livy, 28.8.1–6, 32.5.4; see the discussion of Aymard, *Premiers rapports*, 59–61, n. 53; cf. Briscoe, *Commentary*, 174–175. Rumors of an assassination plot: Plut. *Phil.* 12.2; Paus. 8.50.4; Justin, 29.4.11.

ticipating.[32] The king appeared in person at a meeting of the League in 200, offering assistance in the fight against Nabis in return for Achaean troops to garrison Oreus, Chalcis, and Corinth. The Achaeans were tempted but declined, unwilling to commit soldiers to a cause that was Philip's, not their own.[33] A year later he tried again, this time handing over the cities that he had promised in 208; he got a mutual exchange of oaths but no practical assistance.[34] In the meantime Achaea had exiled the man most identified with Philip's cause, Cycliades, and had elected to the *strategia* Aristaenus, who became a strong advocate of joining the war on Rome's side.[35] The circumstances encouraged Flamininus to seek the adherence of Achaea in 198, an act which provoked heated debate, bitter recriminations, the defection of Megalopolis, Dyme, and some Argives, before a rump assembly agreed to join Rome.[36] A number of tangled and conflicting issues affected that debate. Loyalty to Macedonia ran deep in certain circles, especially at Megalopolis, Dyme, and Argos, a loyalty that induced them to break with the Confederacy over this matter.[37] Others suspected Philip's motives, distrusted him, and feared an outcome in which he would be victor.[38] Then there was the looming presence of the Roman fleet, docked at Cenchreae and about to attack Corinth. Aristaenus argued, with vigor and logic, about the discrepancy between Roman and Macedonian power, about the naïveté of relying on Philip's promises, about the necessity of opting for Rome before it was too late to save the state.[39]

But that is not the whole story. Achaean attention had been focused for the past decade upon an intermittent war with Nabis, a struggle for supremacy within the Peloponnese. The League had rejoiced in 200 when Philip offered assistance in that struggle, but balked

32. Polyb. 16.35.

33. Livy, 31.25, 32.21.10–11; cf. Polyb. 16.38: ὁ δὲ Φίλιππος ὁρῶν τοὺς ᾿Αχαιοὺς εὐλαβῶς διακειμένους πρὸς τὸν κατὰ ῾Ρωμαίων πόλεμον, ἐσπούδαζε κατὰ πάντα τρόπον ἐμβιβάσαι αὐτοὺς εἰς ἀπέχθειαν.

34. Livy, 32.5.4–6.

35. Livy, 32.19.2; cf. Aymard, *Premiers rapports*, 66–69, 78–79. The sharp distinction made by moderns between "pro-Macedonian" and "pro-Roman" parties (as e.g. Errington, *Philopoemen*, 72–75, 81–87), however, is overdrawn. It is well to remember that Philip's request for Achaean troops was rebuffed in the *strategia* of Cycliades, 200/199: Livy, 31.25. And the renewal of oaths between Philip and Achaea came in the *strategia* of Aristaenus, 199/198: Livy, 32.5.4–6.

36. Livy, 32.19.1–32.23.3; Zon. 9.16; Appian, *Mac.* 7. An exhaustive analysis in Aymard, *Premiers rapports*, 79–102.

37. Livy, 32.19.7, 32.22.10–12.

38. Livy, 32.19.7–8, 32.21.21–25.

39. Polyb. 18.13.8–10; Livy, 32.21.4–20, 32.21.26–37: *hos si socios aspernamini, vix mentis sanae estis; sed aut socios aut hostes habeatis oportet*; cf. 32.22.6.

when he wanted Achaean manpower for his war on Rome. The Achaeans sought to crush Nabis, not to fight Philip's war.[40] They welcomed the Macedonian's restoration of Peloponnesian towns in 199/8, but still would not join him against Rome.[41] The aim of Achaea was what it had always been: to unite the Peloponnese under her authority, a project that required the humbling of Sparta and the evacuation of Macedonian garrisons, especially the garrison at Corinth. In 198 these issues still took precedence. Nabis remained a powerful and persistent menace.[42] And the Romans held out a seductive inducement: the reuniting of Corinth with the Achaean Confederacy.[43] It is no accident that Aristaenus, in arguing for the Roman alliance, stressed Philip's past uselessness in supporting Achaea against Nabis and the present danger from Sparta.[44] He also alluded to something equally important: a longstanding desire among Achaeans to free themselves from dependency upon Philip.[45] Nationalistic aspirations predominated. Rome would be a more valuable ally in disposing of Nabis, regaining Corinth, and eliminating Macedonian influence in the Peloponnese.[46]

Similarly, Nabis' own tergiversations underline the centrality of Hellenic concerns. His eye was fixed on Argos. The city had recently defected to Philip, who now in 197 offered it to Nabis, at least on a temporary basis, with other promises perhaps lurking behind the agreement.[47] The Spartan swiftly took control and just as swiftly turned about and initiated negotiations with Flamininus. Not that he had any more interest in the Roman cause than in the Macedonian. Nabis' object, unquestionably, was a firmer guarantee for his hold on Argos. Flamininus insisted on a peace between Sparta and Achaea, thereby to have both powers collaborate against Philip. The Spartan

40. Livy, 31.25.3–11.

41. Livy, 32.5.4–6.

42. Livy, 32.19.6: *terrebat Nabis Lacedaemonius, gravis et adsiduus hostis.* Appian, *Mac.* 7: οἱ δὲ ἐνοχλούμενοι μὲν οἰκείῳ καὶ γείτονι πολέμῳ Νάβιδος τοῦ Λακεδαιμονίων τυράννου.

43. Livy, 32.19.4: *legatos ad gentem Achaeorum mitti pollicentes, si ab rege ad Romanos defecissent, Corinthum contributuros in antiquum gentis concilium.* The fact that Corinth, and not the Acrocorinth, is specifically mentioned need not be significant. Aymard, *Premiers rapports*, 85–86, unduly minimizes the importance of the offer. And he overlooks Aristaenus' remarks in Livy, 32.21.30 and 32.21.35: *nolite si quod omnibus votis petendum erat, ultro offertur, fastidire.* The promise of Corinth is clear from Polyb. 18.2.5, 18.45.12.

44. Livy, 32.21.9–13, 32.21.28.

45. Livy, 32.21.36: *liberare vos a Philippo iam diu magis vultis quam audetis.*

46. These issues are ignored altogether by Deininger, *Widerstand*, 42–46, who sees only conflict between pro and anti-Roman factions.

47. Livy, 32.25, 32.38.2–4; cf. Aymard, *Premiers rapports*, 133–134, n. 9; Texier, *Nabis*, 50–51.

ruler consented, but only up to a point. There would be armistice rather than peace, a truce to last till the end of the Macedonian war. Nabis hoped to have his hands free for a future contest with Achaea.[48] An imperialistic policy in the Peloponnese motivated the Lacedaemonian. War between Rome and Macedonia was a sideshow that he could exploit to his own advantage.

These examples clearly demonstrate that the goals of individual Greek states—goals of territory, power, and ascendancy over other Greek rivals—held chief priority. Attachments to Rome were transitory and pragmatic, the "Second Macedonian War" an opportunity for Hellenes to achieve their private ends.

The Greek demands crop up again and again in the course of the war and its aftermath, bedeviling negotiations and requiring Flamininus to perform delicate balancing acts in order to accomplish his personal aim of *gloria*, to bring Philip to terms, and to satisfy the claims of the allies. So, at the conference of Nicaea in winter 198/7, the Achaeans insisted on recovery of Corinth and Argos, the Aetolians on reacquisition of various cities for their league, tantamount to Philip's total evacuation of Greece.[49] The demands caused considerable perplexity and wrangling. Philip made a few concessions but not many. Matters got referred back to the Roman senate where the allies' stipulations that Macedonian garrisons be removed from the "Three Fetters" broke off the parley.[50] The machinations of Flamininus play a central role in the Polybian evidence and are endlessly discussed by moderns, but here it needs to be stressed that Greek claims had their own impact both on Flamininus and on the senate, not merely minor items to be manipulated by Rome.[51]

48. Livy, 32.38.5–32.40.4; cf. Zon. 9.16; Justin, 30.4.5. Nabis also undertook social and institutional changes in Argos: Polyb. 18.17; Livy, 32.38.7–9, 32.40.10–11. In general on this affair, see Aymard, *Premiers rapports*, 132–154; Texier, *Nabis*, 45–66.

49. Polyb. 18.2.5–6, 18.3.10–12, 18.4.5–7, 18.5.4–5; Livy, 32.33.7–8, 32.33.15–16, 32.34.5–6. The Achaeans surely expected to get both the Acrocorinth and Corinth, not just the latter: cf. Polyb. 18.6.8; Livy, 32.34.13. See Holleaux, *Études* V:54, n. 2; Briscoe, *Commentary*, 233; *contra*: Aymard, *Premiers rapports*, 118–120; Walbank, *Commentary* II:553. Philip, of course, was willing to yield only Corinth: Polyb. 18.8.9, 18.11.13; Livy, 32.35.11, 32.37.3–5, 33.14.1–2.

50. Polyb. 18.6–12; Livy, 32.34.7–32.37.6; Appian, *Mac.* 8; Plut. *Flam.* 5.6, 7.1–2; Justin, 30.3.8–10; Zon. 9.16.

51. Cf. Polyb. 18.7.5, 18.8.2–6, 18.9.1, 18.9.6–18.10.1–2, 18.11.2–13; Livy, 32.35.4–6, 32.35.12, 32.36.5–8, 32.37.1–4: *moverunt eo maxime senatum, demonstrando maris terrarumque regionis eius situm*, etc.; Appian, *Mac.* 8. On Flamininus' machinations, see Holleaux, *Études*, V:29–79; Walbank, *Commentary* II:548–564, with bibliography. More recently: Balsdon, *Phoenix* 21 (1967): 179–185; Lehmann, *Untersuchungen*, 170–174; Badian, *Flamininus*, 40–48; Schlag, *Regnum in Senatu*, 85–88; Briscoe, *Commentary*, 24–26.

## Postwar Ambitions

After Cynoscephalae, conflicting expectations became the more entangled. Overt friction arose between Flamininus and the Aetolians, especially on the issue of Philip's retaining his throne and of Roman forces in the "Fetters." The Aetolians had even more direct concerns: it appeared that they might not receive the cities of Larisa Chremaste, Pharsalus, and Echinus, for which they had been angling since the outset of their participation.[52] But this conflict ought not to be exaggerated. Polybius emphasized it, perhaps magnified it, as partial explanation for the future war between Aetolia and Rome.[53] Flamininus could not yield on the matter of Philip remaining monarch, a policy decided by the senate. And the issue of Roman troops in the "Fetters" still hung suspended so long as the Romans were uncertain about the aims of Antiochus the Great. Flamininus nonetheless paid due heed to the goals for which individual Greek states had entered the war. He solicited from each its specific expectations and desires of the peace.[54] Philip consented to accept the terms that had been demanded by Flamininus and the Greeks at Nicaea; on that basis the senate agreed to peace and sent *legati* to implement details.[55] Their application shows the effect of Hellenic opinion. The "freedom of the Greeks," as directed by senatorial decree and advertised by Flamininus at the Isthmian Games, took its cue from sloganeering long prevalent in the Hellenistic world.[56] But the territorial ambitions of particular Greek states were not thereby shut off, any more than they had been when the slogans were mouthed by Greeks. Achaea acquired control of Corinth, as long promised, and of Triphylia and Heraea as well, a fair start on the way to reviving her former days of glory.[57] The

52. Friction began already over the right to booty at Cynoscephalae: Polyb. 18.27.3–4, 18.34.1. On the issue of Philip's retaining his throne, for which the Romans were resolved, see Polyb. 18.36.6–7, 18.37.8–9; Livy, 33.12.3–4, 33.12.10; Appian, *Mac.* 9.1–2. Other Greeks too seem to have complained: Polyb. 18.37.5; cf. K. S. Sacks, *JHS* 95 (1975): 103. Complaints about Roman troops in the "Fetters": Polyb. 18.45.1–6; Livy, 33.31.1–3. Dispute over towns desired by the Aetolians: Polyb. 18.38.3–9; Livy, 33.13.6–13; bibliography on this in Schmitt, *Staatsverträge* III:265–266; Briscoe, *Commentary*, 273. Bitterness between Flamininus and the Aetolians appears also in Polyb. 18.34.1–8; Livy, 33.11.4–9; Plut. *Flam.* 9; on the problems raised by these passages, see Holleaux, *Études* V:86–103; Sacks, *JHS* 95 (1975): 98–102.

53. See the acute analysis of Sacks, *JHS* 95 (1975): 92–106.

54. Polyb. 18.36.2; Livy, 33.12.1.

55. Polyb. 18.38.2, 18.42.1, 18.42.4–5; Livy, 33.13.4, 33.24.3–7, 33.25.7–8; cf. Appian, *Mac.* 9.3.

56. See above pp. 133–147.

57. Polyb. 18.42.7, 18.45.12, 18.47.10; Livy, 33.31.11, 33.34.9. The Romans at this time, of course, still held the citadel.

Thessalians got their independence from Macedonia, and also got Phthiotic Achaea.[58] Amynander too obtained his reward: control of all the strongholds he had wrested from Philip in the war—including the important strategic site of Gomphi.[59] Even the Aetolians, despite their grumblings and discontent, came away anything but empty-handed. All of Phocis and Locris became theirs, with Roman approval.[60] They receive Phthiotic Thebes and their claim to Pharsalus was at least referred to the senate for adjudication.[61] The "freedom" of individual cities was entirely consistent with the hegemony of larger states, a thoroughgoing Greek concept happily embraced by Flamininus.[62] Rome certainly did not intend to stay and supervise them.

Even the celebrated Boeotian affair, often read in the opposite sense, supports this conclusion. Flamininus granted without hesitation Boeotia's request to spare and restore her forces, which had fought on Philip's side.[63] The result, however, backfired. Boeotians expressed gratitude to Philip rather than to the Roman, recalled and elevated to high office those who had served in Philip's ranks. As a consequence, politicians identified with the Roman alliance felt their position threatened, planned to assassinate the rival leader Brachylles, and sought Flamininus' sanction. He avoided personal involvement but did not discourage the deed.[64] A fierce reaction ensued, including clandestine murders of Roman soldiers, before Flamininus mobilized forces, war being averted only by the intervention of Achaean and Athenian mediators.[65] The episode does not show Roman interference in the internal affairs of Boeotia. Flamininus permitted the recall of pro-Macedonian soldiers, looked the other way but neither initiated nor implemented

58. Polyb. 18.47.7; Livy, 33.34.7.

59. Polyb. 18.47.13; Livy, 33.34.11. On Amynander, see Oost, *CP* 52 (1957): 1–8; Welwei, *Historia* 14 (1965): 252–256.

60. Polyb. 18.47.9; Livy, 33.34.8; cf. Walbank, *Commentary* II:617–618.

61. Polyb. 18.47.7–9, 18.48.9; Livy, 33.34.7, 33.35.12; cf. Livy, 33.49.8, 34.23.7–8, 36.10.9, 39.25.8–9. Note also the senate's instructions that Flamininus write to Prusias about the freeing of Cius, a city on which Aetolia had claims: Polyb. 18.44.5; Livy, 33.30.4; cf. Polyb. 15.23.6–10, 18.3.12, 18.4.7; Livy, 32.33.16, 32.34.6. Aetolian control of Dolopia was probably sanctioned as well; cf. Livy, 32.13.9–15, 36.14.12–15; R. Flacelière, *Les Aetoliens à Delphes* (Paris, 1937), 348–349; Walbank, *Commentary* II:616–617. But see Livy, 38.3.4.

62. Note, e.g., that the Isthmian declaration begins with the Corinthians, Phocians, and Locrians, peoples whom Rome was about to hand over to Achaea and Aetolia: Polyb. 18.46.5; Livy, 33.32.5.

63. Polyb. 18.43.1–2; Livy, 33.27.5–6.

64. Polyb. 18.43.3–12. Livy, 33.27.6–33.28.3, leaves Flamininus out. It is noteworthy that he asked the Boeotians to apply to the Aetolian *strategos*, an indication that his relations with Aetolia were not as hostile as Polybius otherwise suggests.

65. Livy, 33.28.4–33.29.12; cf. Polyb. 20.7.3; Livy, 35.47.3, 36.6.1. Deininger, *Widerstand*, 54–58, sees a class struggle here, unattested by the sources; see Livy, 33.29.1.

the murder of Brachylles, mobilized troops only when Roman *milites* had been killed, and then dropped the matter when other Greeks intervened. Boeotia was then left alone.[66]

The Peloponnese, as usual, presented greater complexity. The duplicitous Nabis had cooperated with the allied cause against Macedonia but had agreed only to a temporary truce with the Achaeans. A struggle for Peloponnesian supremacy could readily be foreseen.[67] The "tyrant," as his enemies branded him, had accumulated large forces, a mobilized citizenry, Argives, ephebes, and numerous mercenaries; he built or fortified the walls, he possessed connections as far away as Crete, and he had developed a Spartan navy.[68] The expansionist aims of Nabis were clear. Now he held control of Argos, a matter of special interest to Achaea and a genuine menace to the League. The wartime agreement between Flamininus and the Spartan gave *de facto* recognition of his right to Argos, but no juridical sanction, the dispute over his claim having been left in abeyance.[69] The Isthmian proclamation was pointedly silent about Argos, her fate evidently still undecided.[70] Yet a year later Roman forces, in collaboration with a host of Greek allies, made war on Nabis. How does one explain what appears to be blatant Roman involvement in an internal Peloponnesian dispute? No parallel to it exists for another half-century—if then.

Conjectures are easy to offer. Rome, it is suggested, feared a coming war with Antiochus, a war in which the Syrian might find sympathy both in Aetolia and in Sparta. Roman troops needed to be kept in Greece to prevent that danger, and hostilities against Nabis could provide the excuse for keeping them there.[71] Concern about Antiochus may indeed have troubled the senate, a reason for the retention of armies and for the prorogation of Flamininus in 195.[72] The report of the *decem legati* in Rome drew a magnified picture of Antiochus' ambitions, warned of Aetolian restlessness, and pointed out the tyranny of Nabis, which, if undisturbed, would soon dominate Greece.[73] Nevertheless, as motive for Roman behavior, this is singu-

66. Observe that Zeuxippus who had applied to Flamininus and then fled from Boeotia was allowed to languish in exile. Flamininus took no steps for his recall until several years later: Livy, 33.28.14–15; Polyb. 22.4.4.

67. Livy, 32.39.10–11, 32.40.4.

68. Nabis' forces: Livy, 34.27.2, 34.29.4, 34.29.14; *Syll.*³ 594. The walls: Livy, 34.38.2, 39.37.2, 39.37.5. Cretan connections: Polyb. 13.8.2; Livy, 32.40.4, 34.27.2, 34.35.9. The navy: Livy, 34.29.3, 34.35.5, 35.12.7. Cf. also the Delian decree honoring Nabis: *Syll.*³ 584.

69. Livy, 32.40.1–3.

70. Cf. Polyb. 18.47.10; Livy, 33.34.9.

71. So Aymard, *Premiers rapports*, 194–203, 206.

72. Polyb. 18.45.10–11; Livy, 33.31.4–6, 33.31.10, 33.43.6.

73. Livy, 33.44.6–9.

larly unsatisfactory. Nothing attests to any association among Nabis, Aetolia, and Syria at this time. The Aetolians indeed were soon to assert that they would take responsibility for coercing Nabis.[74] If Rome wished to retain her garrisons in the "Fetters," a potential menace from Antiochus would supply reason or pretext. It does not explain a war on Nabis. The tyrant's "left-wing" revolutionary activities in Sparta and Argos have also been cited as grounds for Roman intervention.[75] But, though Flamininus made mention of these activities among his many charges against Nabis, they played no role in the initial decision for war, and their importance is refuted by the eventual settlement—which kept Nabis on his throne and did not even recall the Spartan exiles.[76] Nor does it make any sense to imagine that Rome feared the danger of Nabis' ships for her naval power and her maritime commerce.[77] Nabis' "piratical" activities are mentioned only at the conclusion of Flamininus' speech and in connection with the Spartan's alliance with Philip—which lasted no time at all.[78] One might invoke Flamininus' "desire to gain yet greater *gloria*."[79] True enough, but inadequate. There is much more evidence which this explanation fails to take account of.

One must ask a basic question. To what extent was this a Roman war, in any significant sense? When the *decem legati* raised the spectre of Nabis at Rome in winter 196/5, the *patres* debated as to whether there were grounds for war or whether the matter should simply be left for Flamininus to decide. They chose the second alternative.[80]

74. Livy, 34.23.11. Nabis' later claim (Livy, 34.37.5), that he could expect support from Antiochus and the Aetolians, was a desperate rallying cry to his people, faced with threat of a Roman siege, and altogether empty of content. Even the report of the *decem legati*, while portraying Nabis as a menace, did not suggest any ties to Aetolia or to Syria: Livy, 33.44.8–9.

75. Cf. Larsen, *Greek Federal States*, 400. On Nabis' social reforms, see B. Shimron, *Late Sparta: The Spartan Revolution, 243–146 B.C.* (Buffalo, 1972), 79–90, 95–99; Texier, *Nabis*, 28–36, 54–61; D. Mendels, *Athenaeum* 57 (1979): 311–333.

76. Charges of revolutionary activity: Livy, 34.31.14, 34.32.9—plainly minor in the context. The initial decision for war does not mention them: Livy, 34.24.6–7, 34.26.5–7. Nabis kept on his throne: Livy, 34.41.4–7; Plut. *Flam.* 13.1. Exiles not recalled: Livy, 34.36.2.

77. For Texier, *Nabis*, 82, 88–89, that is the principal reason for Roman intervention. He stresses Rome's fear of Nabis' power again in *REA* 78–79 (1976–1977): 147–148, 153–154.

78. Livy, 34.32.17–19. Reference here is to raids on supply ships—not to maritime commerce. The brevity of the alliance: Livy, 32.38.2–32.39.1.

79. So Harris, *War and Imperialism*, 218–219.

80. Livy, 33.45.2–3: *cum diu disceptatum esset, utrum satis iam causae videretur, cur decerneretur bellum, an permitterent T. Quinctio, quod ad Nabim Lacedaemonium attineret, faceret, quod e re publica censeret esse, permiserunt.* Livy later, in a Polybian passage, 34.22.5, states that there was a *senatus consultum* which decreed war. Aymard, *Premiers rapports*, 198–202, seeks to salvage the latter by arguing that it expressed the intention if not the

There was no *rerum repetitio*, no *indictio belli*, no formalities at all. The senate declined to give official sanction: let Flamininus determine if it seems worthwhile. For the *patres*, a war on Nabis, whether hastened or delayed, was a matter of no great importance.[81] Nor indeed did Flamininus undertake the war on his own responsibility. Instead he summoned a panhellenic congress to Corinth and pointed out the anomaly of Nabis tyrannizing over Argos while the rest of Greece was free. It was a matter of complete indifference to the Romans, he said, but, if the Greeks wished, they could have his support in liberating Argos.[82] Disingenuous, one might assume. Surely the Greeks knew what Flamininus wanted and simply followed suit. Perhaps. Yet the formalities have their own significance. This was to be a panhellenic war, declared by Greeks, not by Rome. The Aetolians certainly felt free to quarrel with the proposal, denouncing Rome for retention of the "Fetters" and for employing Nabis as a pretext. They called for Roman withdrawal and promised to see to it that Nabis yielded Argos, whether by force or by persuasion.[83] Other Greeks, however, supported action against Sparta, most prominently, of course, the Achaeans. They stood most to gain from the humbling of Nabis and they would certainly not want to see Aetolians in the Peloponnese.[84] War was declared by the Hellenic congress, all assenting, save perhaps Aetolia. In an official sense, it was not a Roman war.[85]

Flamininus maintained that posture throughout the conflict. He called a council at its outset to determine whether Argos or Sparta should be the initial target.[86] After parley with Nabis, Flamininus inclined to frame terms of peace; the Greek allies urged that the war be pressed on. Another council was summoned and Flamininus got his

---

action of the senate: it gave Flamininus a blank check to wage war when he saw fit. Nevertheless, there can be no doubt that the senate and people refrained from any declaration of war.

81. Livy, 33.45.4: *eam rem esse rati, quae maturata dilatave non ita magni momenti ad summam rem publicam esset*; cf. Justin, 31.1.6: *senatus . . . scripsit Flaminino, si ei videatur, sicuti Macedoniam a Philippo, ita et Graeciam a Nabide liberet*.

82. Livy, 34.22.6–13: *haec consultatio, ut videtis, tota de re pertinente ad vos est; Romanos nihil contingit*.

83. Livy, 34.23.5–11.

84. Livy, 34.23.1–3, 34.24.1–5.

85. Livy, 34.24.6–7. Its participants included Rhodians, Macedonians, Thessalians, and even Eumenes himself; Livy, 34.26.10–11. Note the Athenian speech stating that the Romans *non rogatos ultro adversus tyrannum Nabim offerre auxilium*: Livy, 34.23.3.

86. Livy, 34.26.4–8. Here he chose to follow the advice of Aristaenus, the Achaean *strategos*, against that of all the others. Decisions, of course, were not made by head count. But the fact of consultation remains important. Texier, *REA* 78–79 (1976–1977): 150, is inaccurate.

way—but only through persuasion and by temporarily agreeing with the majority until they changed their minds.[87] When he offered a truce to Nabis, it was a truce that involved only Rome, Pergamum, and Rhodes.[88] The omission of Achaeans and other mainland Greeks indicates that he respected their dissent and would not claim to treat in their name. In fact, the final peace terms did not fully satisfy the Achaeans, let alone the Aetolians, who had hoped for the deposition of Nabis.[89] Flamininus had carried out the expressed will of the panhellenic congress: the liberation of Argos.[90] The congress had given no authorization for the removal of Nabis, nor could Flamininus expect Roman approval for such a move. The *patres* had kept Philip on his throne. Flamininus knew the limits imposed on his actions.

The war was, strictly speaking, a Hellenic war, undeclared by Rome, and proclaimed by a gathering of Hellenes. In this regard, it resembles crusades announced by Philip II and Alexander against the Persians, by Antigonus Doson against Sparta, by Philip V against Aetolia in the Social War, all sanctioned by a general congress of Greek allies. Nothing like it had happened prior to the Second Macedonian War. In the crusade against Nabis, Flamininus followed Hellenic models and (officially) carried out the will of the Greeks.

This does not mean, of course, that the Roman proconsul was a disinterested servant of Hellenic opinion. He called the meeting and he urged the war. And the *patres* in Rome, while they did not decree hostilities, left that option open by allowing Flamininus to make his own decision. What lay behind it? Personal glory for Flamininus, yes. But the direction of his propaganda is significant. The image of Rome abroad is referred to over and again. The *decem legati* had put the matter in those terms before the senate: what good was it to rid Greece of the Macedonian tyrant while leaving her prey to the Spartan tyrant at Argos?[91] Flamininus dwelled on the same theme at the congress in Corinth: so long as Nabis has a stranglehold on Argos, Greek liberty is incomplete and Rome's reputation as liberator flawed.[92] He reiterated it in his speech to Nabis: Rome cannot set Greece free while Argos and Sparta remain in slavery.[93] In fact, the proconsul never did insist on the deposition of Nabis from Sparta. The "liberation" of

87. Livy, 34.33–34.
88. Livy, 34.35.2. Briscoe, *Commentary* II:106, implausibly suggests that Livy, for some reason, omitted mention of the mainland Greeks.
89. Livy, 34.41.4–7.
90. Livy, 34.24.6–7, 34.26.5–7, 34.41.1–3.
91. Livy, 33.44.8–9.
92. Livy, 34.22.12: *Romanos nihil contingit, nisi quatenus liberatae Graeciae unius civitatis servitus non plenam nec integram gloriam esse sinit.*
93. Livy, 34.32.4–5.

Argos was enough, and, be it noted, that liberation is reckoned throughout, by Flamininus and the Greeks, as equivalent to Argos' absorption by Achaea.[94] The Hellenistic concept prevailed. The freeing of Argos (and its reunification with the Achaean Confederacy) was the first item on the list of terms presented to Nabis, and the first act after his capitulation—thus giving Flamininus another opportunity for propaganda display at the Nemean Games.[95]

Rome did not have a legal leg to stand on in this conflict. Neither senate nor people gave it overt authorization. Flamininus' speech to Nabis fails to meet any of the Spartan's points.[96] Juridical considerations, however, were irrelevant. Reputation mattered to the *patres*, though they were unpersuaded that it really was involved in an intra-Peloponnesian contest. A senatorial majority contented itself with allowing Flamininus to make the determination. And he was particularly sensitive to the issue. Flamininus' personal repute and integrity had come under fire by the Aetolians. Already in the previous year he had sought to persuade Roman commissioners to evacuate all troops from Greece, lest Rome's image be tainted by insincerity.[97] Now, with the "Fetters" still occupied and the Aetolians still alleging Roman deceit, he took the opportunity to vindicate Rome's—and his own—honor. It is unnecessary to ascribe to him an elaborate "balance of power" policy,[98] nor even to urge that he planned a careful settlement that would bring stability to the Peloponnese.[99] The proconsul did attempt to satisfy a number of Hellenic interests in that troubled area, without imposing any extreme solution. Argos was recovered by the

94. Livy, 34.22.11, 34.23.6, 34.24.6. Cf. Aymard, *Premiers rapports*, 205.

95. Livy, 34.35.3, 34.41.1–3; Plut. *Flam.* 12.2; Diod. 28.13. Observe that as soon as Nabis offered to evacuate Argos Flamininus began to incline to peace: Livy, 34.33.3–9. That the proconsul also worried about being superseded before the war ended had its effect on his calculations as well: Livy, 34.33.14. Aymard, *Premiers rapports*, 235–237, plays down the latter consideration, without acknowledging the former.

96. All the proconsul's charges were refuted in advance by Nabis. He pointed out that the "transgressions" preceded his own alliance with Flamininus, who had ignored them at that time: Livy, 34.31.8–15. On the speeches, see, most recently, Mendels, *Scripta Classica Israelica* 4 (1978): 38–44, with bibliography; Briscoe, *Commentary* II: 97–104. Mendels' argument that the speech of Flamininus got most of the facts right is irrelevant to the question of the strength or weakness of the Roman case.

97. Polyb. 18.45.8–9: διδάσκων ὡς εἴπερ βούλονται καὶ τὴν τῶν Ἑλλήνων εὔκλειαν ὁλόκληρον περιποιήσασθαι, καὶ καθόλου πιστευθῆναι παρὰ πᾶσι διότι καὶ τὴν ἐξ ἀρχῆς ἐποιήσαντο διάβασιν οὐ τοῦ συμφέροντος ἕνεκεν, ἀλλὰ τῆς τῶν Ἑλλήνων ἐλευθερίας, ἐκχωρητέον εἴη πάντων τῶν τόπων καὶ πάσας ἐλευθερωτέον τὰς πόλεις τὰς νῦν ὑπὸ Φιλίππου φρουρουμένας; Livy, 33.31.8.

98. As, e.g., Colin, *Rome et la Grèce*, 166; Briscoe, *Past and Present* 36 (1967): 9; Errington, *Philopoemen*, 89.

99. See the lengthy and hypothetical argumentation of Aymard, *Premiers rapports*, 238–247.

Achaean League and the towns of the Laconian coast placed under its supervision, but Nabis retained his throne and Sparta her independence; the king's military power would be dismantled, his external holdings yielded, and an indemnity paid, but the men he exiled would remain so, to be settled in the maritime communities.[100] Equilibrium, however, was not the main goal. The settlement, in fact, brought little stability and contained the seeds of turmoil, as we shall see. Flamininus' purposes had been more limited: to reinforce his esteem and justify his propaganda. The senate at home remained content and largely without interest. Establishment of the Republic's hold on Hellas was neither an aim nor an outcome of this affair.

The following spring of 194 saw evacuation of all Roman forces from Greece. The *patres* dismissed arguments about a potential menace from Antiochus and found no further reason for the stationing of soldiers in the East.[101] Flamininus seized the occasion for yet another Hellenic gathering at Corinth and yet another display of rhetoric. Criticism had been voiced by Achaeans and Aetolians about Nabis' retention of power in Sparta. The proconsul met it by a response consistent with his propaganda line: Nabis could be removed only by crushing Sparta, and thereby robbing her of the fruits of liberty.[102] That the city remained independent of Achaean authority, unlike Argos, distressed some Achaeans but coincided properly with the Roman posture. Argos had been part of the League before the Second Macedonian War, Sparta free of it, indeed antagonistic to it. Rome would strip Nabis of much of his military power, but she did not intend an arbitrary and radical rearrangement of Hellenic political geography.[103] Flamininus now announced removal of Roman garrisons from the "Fetters" and withdrawal of all troops back to Italy. He emphasized unabashedly the value of the move in terms of Rome's

---

100. The terms imposed by Flamininus: Livy, 34.35.3–11. Achaean supervision of the Laconian coastal towns: Livy, 35.13.2, 38.31.2. Nabis' retention of his throne: Livy, 34.41.4–7; Plut. *Flam.* 13.1; Justin, 31.3.1. The exiles: Livy, 34.35.7, 38.30.6.

101. Livy, 34.43.3–8.

102. Livy, 34.41.4–7, 34.48.5–34.49.3; Plut. *Flam.* 13.3; Diod. 28.13.

103. Achaea now reacquired control of the Acrocorinth as well: Livy, 34.49.5. Flamininus did hear disputes on appeal from some Greek states while wintering at Elatea in 195/4 and backed the claims of those politicians ousted from power by Philip's supporters; Livy, 34.48.2. Similar circumstances apparently prompted his actions in Thessaly in spring 194, where "liberating" the cities required cleansing them of the turmoil created by Philip's policies and henchmen, and introducing, at least temporarily, a census qualification for senate and officials: Livy, 34.51.3–6; cf. *Syll.*³ 593 = Sherk, *RDGE*, no. 33; Gruen, *AJAH* 1 (1976): 39. These, however, constituted the finishing touches on the settlement of the Second Macedonian War, the rooting out of Philip's influence in Hellas, as promised from the outset. That he subsequently reintroduced influence in certain areas did not much concern the Romans; see above pp. 400–401.

image and reputation: it gave the lie to Aetolian denunciations of the Republic's insincerity.[104] Liberty, achieved by Rome, was now Greece's to protect.[105] Propaganda and posturing, to be sure: but the propaganda and posturing coincided with policy.

## Rome, Aetolia, and Antiochus III

Polybius' explanation of Rome's momentous clash with Aetolia and Antiochus the Great from 191 to 189 places the ire of the Aeto-lians squarely in the center. Their resentment and fury at slights received at Rome's hands induced them to summon Antiochus to Greece and to go to any lengths to satisfy their anger.[106] Such is the Polybian conception, and it pervades his narrative of events, as they can be reconstructed from Livy. Hence, scholars repeatedly present a picture of Aetolia forcing a war to release Hellas from the Roman yoke and to eliminate the "protectorate" of the western power.[107] Polybius' perspective is the large one: that of Roman expansion in Hellas, a process in which the Aetolian-Antiochene war was but a step in the ongoing development.[108] As such it simplifies and distorts. Aetolia had her own designs on power and dominion in Greece. Not all her statesmen—if any—were blinded by rage at Roman behavior, past and present.[109] Aetolia's ambitions required her to reckon on the pos-

104. Livy, 34.49.5–6: *ut omnes scirent utrum Romanis an Aetolis mentiri mos esset, qui male commissam libertatem populo Romano sermonibus distulerint et mutatos pro Macedonibus Romanos dominos.*

105. Livy, 34.49.11: *alienis armis partam, externa fide redditam libertatem sua cura custodirent servarentque.*

106. Polyb. 3.3.3: μνησθησόμεθα τῆς Αἰτωλῶν ὀργῆς, καθ' ἣν 'Αντίοχον ἐπι-σπασάμενοι τὸν ἀπὸ τῆς 'Ασίας 'Αχαιοῖς καὶ 'Ρωμαίοις ἐξέκαυσαν πόλεμον; 3.7.1–2: καὶ μὴν τοῦ κατ' 'Αντίοχον καὶ 'Ρωμαίους δῆλον ὡς αἰτίαν μὲν τὴν Αἰτωλῶν ὀργὴν θε-τέον · ἐκεῖνοι γὰρ δόξαντες ὑπὸ 'Ρωμαίων ὠλιγωρῆσθαι κατὰ πολλὰ περὶ τὴν ἔκβασιν τὴν ἐκ τοῦ Φιλίππου πολέμου, καθάπερ ἐπάνω προεῖπον, οὐ μόνον 'Αντίοχον ἐπεσπά-σαντο, πᾶν δὲ καὶ πρᾶξαι καὶ παθεῖν ὑπέστησαν διὰ τὴν ἐπιγενομένην ὀργὴν ἐκ τῶν προειρημένων καιρῶν.

107. E.g. Larsen, *Greek Federal States*, 406–407; Deininger, *Widerstand*, 68; Golan, *RivStorAnt* 6–7 (1977): 316–320.

108. See Sacks, *JHS* 95 (1975):92–106. Cf. Derow, *JRS* 69 (1979): 11–12.

109. A different kind of distortion may stem from Polybius' informants on Aetolian affairs, most notably Nicander of Trichonium. An exile in Italy because of allegations during the Third Macedonian War, Nicander had reason to blacken his political opponents, among whom was Thoas, a man who had turned on him, despite owing a debt of gratitude: Polyb. 20.11.10, 27.15.14, 28.4.6–12, 28.6.7. Not surprisingly, Thoas appears in the evidence as a principal instigator of conflict and a hard-liner; cf. Polyb. 21.31.12–13; Livy, 35.45, 37.45.17, 38.10.6. That Polybius got direct testimony from Ni-cander seems clear from Polyb. 20.11; cf. 21.25.7. Pédech's doubts, *La méthode*, 361, based on Polyb. 21.27.9, are unpersuasive; cf. Walbank, *Commentary* I:34, III:126.

sibility of a war with Rome and to make her calculations accordingly. The ambitions, however, were traditional Hellenic ones, neither aimed at a Roman war nor rendering one inevitable. The evidence allows for a different perspective.

A meeting at Naupactus in 193 set the chain of events in motion. The Aetolian gathering authorized a trio of missions, to Sparta, Philip, and Antiochus. To what end? If Livy (and presumably Polybius) is to be believed, the goal was to form a coalition against Rome.[110] A most inept scheme, when analyzed in that fashion. Only Nabis moved, to recover control of the maritime towns of Laconia: hardly a preparation for war on Rome. No response came from Philip or Antiochus.[111] If ever there was an unlikely time to speak of casting off a Roman yoke, it was surely now. The senate had removed all garrisons and withdrawn all soldiers only a few months before. Visible signs of control were gone. Opportunity, not oppression, motivated the Aetolians. The evacuation of Greece stirred them to hope.[112] On Nabis they pressed the argument (with reason) that Rome would never bring back her legions to protect Laconian coastal cities.[113] Aetolian leaders, like Thoas, disappointed by the settlement of 196, looked to increase the League's territory and to recover places they felt they had earned for contribution to victory.[114] Arousing Nabis made good sense; an assault on the coastal towns was an assault on Achaea, under whose authority they had been placed. Hostilities in the Peloponnese would occupy the Achaeans and redound to the advantage of Aetolia.[115] Representations to Antiochus and to Philip had the value of sounding out potential allies in the event that Rome might interfere with Aetolian aggrandizement. Mobilization against the western power was neither necessary nor desirable.

Several months passed before Rome took any notice. Nothing had occurred but the actions of Nabis, which were directed at Achaea rather than at the Republic.[116] Senatorial discussions with regard to

110. Livy, 35.12. Note 35.12.5: *qui . . . suis quemque stimulis moverent ad Romanum bellum;* 35.12.18: *per totum simul orbem terrarum Aetoli Romanis concitabant bellum.* The date of the meeting cannot be fixed with any degree of probability. It could have come any time from winter 194/3 to autumn 193; cf. Aymard, *Premiers rapports,* 296; Badian, *Studies,* 138, n. 84; Larsen, *Greek Federal States,* 407–408.

111. Livy, 35.13.1.

112. Livy, 35.12.2: *ii post deportatos ex Graecia exercitus primo in spe fuerant.*

113. Livy, 35.12.8: *nullum exercitum Romanum in Graecia esse, nec Gytheum aut maritimos alios Laconas dignam causam existimaturos Romanos, cur legiones rursus in Graeciam transmittant.*

114. Livy, 35.12.4: *conquestus iniurias Romanorum statumque Aetoliae, quod omnium Graeciae gentium civitatiumque inhonoratissimi post eam victoriam essent, cuius causa ipsi fuissent.*

115. Cf. Livy, 34.24.1–5.

116. See below, p. 463.

the East focused primarily upon Antiochus. In winter 193/2 the *patres* took the precautionary steps that are now familiar, following the same pattern which can be discerned prior to conflict with Philip, and which would be followed again prior to conflict with Perseus. No eastern province was assigned to the consuls of 192 and no consular army prepared for the East. Instead, two praetors, one with infantry forces, one with a fleet, received instructions to assist Achaea against Nabis, if necessary. In the meantime, diplomatic action was taken. A legation headed by Flamininus went to Greece to reconfirm sympathies, should Antiochus make any move.[117]

The envoys made their rounds in early 192, visiting Achaea, Athens, Chalcis, Thessaly, and Demetrias.[118] Aetolian propaganda had already begun to have some effect. A rumor surfaced in Demetrias that the city, recently relieved of foreign garrisons, was to be annexed by Philip, with Roman approval. The issue caused sharp dissension in Demetrias, especially when Flamininus failed to deny the rumor, unwilling to alienate Philip. Eurylochus, head of the Magnesian Confederacy, openly denounced Roman intentions, calling forth an impassioned speech from Flamininus, and resulting in Eurylochus' own banishment.[119] It is no accident that Eurylochus took refuge in Aetolia, nor that much of the dispute revolved around the possibility of Demetrias attaching herself to Aetolia and to Antiochus.[120] Antiochus was not yet in evidence, but Aetolian machinations certainly were. Using the exile Eurylochus as a front and capitalizing on the support of his partisans within the city, Aetolian forces restored him to Demetrias, probably in early summer 192. Leaders who opposed Eurylochus were promptly executed. The result met all expectations: Demetrias now became an Aetolian dependency.[121] Not a word here about war against Rome. Aetolian hegemonial schemes stood in the forefront.[122]

In the meantime, an envoy of Antiochus appeared before the Aetolian assembly in spring, 192. The king's representative boasted of his wealth, power, and armaments, and reiterated his sloganeering: Antiochus was champion of Greek liberty, a liberty compromised so

117. Livy, 35.20.1: *Romae destinabant quidem sermonibus hostem Antiochum, sed nihildum ad id bellum praeter animos parabant*; 35.20.13–14, 35.22.1–3, 35.23.5, 35.25.1–5, 35.31.1.

118. Livy, 35.31.2–3.

119. Livy, 35.31.3–35.32.1.

120. Livy, 35.31.4–6, 35.31.10, 35.32.1–2.

121. Livy, 35.34.5–12: *ita Demetrias Aetolorum facta est*; cf. 35.42.4.

122. Discussion purely in terms of pro- and anti-Roman factions, as Deininger, *Widerstand*, 76–78, is oversimplification. Livy speaks of Eurylochus' faction and an opposing faction: 35.31.6, 35.34.7, 35.34.11.

long as it depended on the will of Rome.[123] Athenian spokesmen and then Flamininus himself addressed the gathering, admonishing the Aetolians not to break relations and hasten into conflict.[124] Livy's account delivers the impression that peace or war was here being debated. That misconceives the circumstances, in line with Polybius' retrospective interpretation. Antiochus' message did not require war, any more than the Aetolians sought it.[125] Antiochus proposed to substitute himself for Rome as patron of Hellenic freedom; the Romans were false patrons. Aetolia, unable to achieve her aims as ally of Rome, had greater hopes in the Seleucid. The subject of debate was the subject that had long tried Aetolia's patience, recovery of the cities for which she had fought in the Second Macedonian War.[126] Flamininus proposed a legation to Rome which could ask for arbitration or a senatorial judgment.[127] The Aetolians would have none of it. They had tried that route before and had gotten nowhere.[128] The assembly passed a formal vote with unanimous consent and in a significant formulation: Antiochus was invited to liberate Greece and to *arbitrate between Aetolia and Rome*.[129] The meaning is not to be explained away by hindsight. This is no declaration of war, rather a summons to Antiochus as patron and judge. The Romans had forfeited their claims as impartial arbiters; they were a party to the dispute. In Antiochus the Aetolians would find a more responsible guardian of "liberty," i.e. a more favorable judge of their territorial claims.[130]

123. Livy, 35.32.2–4, 35.32.8–11: *ea autem in libertate posita est, quae suis stat viribus, non ex alieno arbitrio pendet.*

124. Livy, 35.32.12–14, 35.33.4–6.

125. Some even spoke of Antiochus' wealth buying off the Romans! Livy, 35.32.4: *tantum advehi auri, ut ipsos emere Romanos posset.*

126. Livy, 35.33.4: *de iure civitatium de quibus ambigeretur.*

127. Livy, 35.32.5–6.

128. Polyb. 18.47.8–9, 18.48.9; Livy, 33.34.7, 33.35.12, 33.49.8, 34.23.7–8.

129. Livy, 35.33.8: *accerseretur Antiochus ad liberandam Graeciam disceptandumque inter Aetolos et Romanos.* Briscoe, *Commentary* II:33, 194, wrongly makes this "tantamount to a declaration of war."

130. Livy, 35.33.9–11, has the Aetolian *strategos* Damocritus go further, insult Flamininus, and boast that he would deliver the decree in person from a camp pitched on the banks of the Tiber. The story, though accepted by almost all scholars, is out of tune with Aetolia's official posture and is probably inserted to drive home a moral lesson. Damocritus' *hybris* duly provokes his *nemesis* when, instead of invading Italy, he is captured and imprisoned in Italy; Livy, 36.24.12. The story of his boastful remarks is recorded only in the context of his capture in Appian, *Syr.* 21 and Zon. 9.19. And it is surely no coincidence that he perished after escape from prison, when cut down on the banks of the Tiber! Livy, 37.46.5. Rightly skeptical about the tale is De Sanctis, *Storia dei romani* IV:1, 134. Livy's general claim that the lower classes inclined to Antiochus and the upper to Rome (35.33.1, 35.34.3) is more questionable still. Not only are there aristocrats in various cities who advocated the cause of Aetolia and Antiochus, e.g. Livy,

The Aetolians now made bold to further their schemes of aggrandizement. At Demetrias, as we have seen, they succeeded in bringing the city under their authority by installing Eurylochus and his faction in power. A parallel effort at Chalcis fell short. The Aetolians had promoted the party of another exile, Euthymidas, bringing in troops for his restoration. This time, however, support within the city failed to materialize and the Aetolian claim of liberating Chalcis met with cold response. The Chalcidians knew why they had come: to turn the city into an Aetolian dependency like Demetrias. They rejected the proposition.[131] The Confederacy withdrew its troops, leaving Euthymidas high and dry.[132] In Sparta a similar attempt came to naught. On pretense of sending a squadron to assist Nabis against Achaea, Aetolians in fact assassinated the Spartan ruler and seized his palace. But the assassins bungled their opportunity, provoked a popular rising, and were butchered or fled.[133] A potential war with Rome dictated none of these ventures. It is especially noteworthy, though never noted, that the man chosen to eliminate Nabis and take control of Sparta was Alexamenus, the same Alexamenus who enjoyed the trust of Flamininus.[134] To characterize Aetolian policy as an anti-Roman movement is erroneous. Aetolia pursued her own ends.

A compliant Demetrias gave Antiochus the opportunity to cross to Greece in the autumn of 192. Aetolia could now look forward to further gains in Hellas with the Seleucid's authority behind her.[135] The forces he brought with him had a moral and psychological impact, rather than a military one. They were pitifully small, remarks Livy, with some surprise in view of his own interpretation, hardly enough to occupy an undefended Greece, let alone to sustain a war with Rome.[136] The fact is, despite his interpretation, the Aetolians were as yet unpersuaded that they would have to sustain a war with Rome.

35.31.6, 35.31.11, 35.37.4–5; there was also support for Rome to be found among the *multitudo*: Livy, 35.31.12–13, 35.32.1, 35.43.5, 35.50.4; cf. 35.39.6. The analysis is far too schematic to engender trust.

131. Livy, 35.37–38. See 35.38.5: *ne sinerent Aetolorum Chalcidem fieri; Euboeam habituros, si Chalcidem habuissent; graves fuisse Macedonas dominos; multo minus tolerabiles futuros Aetolos.*

132. Livy, 35.38.11–14.

133. Livy, 35.35–36.

134. Cf. Polyb. 18.43.11; Livy, 35.34.5.

135. Livy, 35.42.4–5, 35.43.2–5; Appian, *Syr.* 12; cf. Zon. 9.19: ὁ Ἀντίοχος . . . πρὸς τὰς τῶν Αἰτωλῶν ἐλπίδας ἔσπευσε; Livy, 35.44.6 (Antiochus' speech): *liberam vere Graeciam atque in ea principes Aetolos fecisset.* The people of Demetrias, who welcomed Antiochus, had recently rebuffed a Roman delegation—but at the same time could say, without inconsistency, that they remained friends of Rome: Livy, 35.39.3–7.

136. Livy, 35.43.6: *vix ad Graeciam nudam occupandam satis copiarum, nedum ad sustinendum Romanum bellum*; cf. 35.44.3, 35.49.9–11.

They had recently elected Phaeneas to the *strategia*, a man who certainly hoped to avoid such a conflict. Their first act upon learning of Antiochus' arrival in Demetrias was to reconfirm the decree by which they had invited him.[137] The significance of that needs emphasis—a reminder to the king that he had been summoned as arbiter, not as warlord. But a split developed in Aetolian counsels once Antiochus appeared in their territory and spoke of vast forces which he could transport to Hellas the following spring. Phaeneas reasserted the interests of Aetolia as hitherto defined: Antiochus would be arbitrator of differences and bringer of peace, the majesty of his presence would keep Rome in line without resort to violence.[138] Others, however, felt that matters had gone too far for pacific gestures. Thoas argued that Rome only understood the language of force, that justice was unobtainable from the senate, that Romans would see reason only if Antiochus showed the sword.[139] The latter opinion prevailed. An Aetolian vote named the king as commander-in-chief of the Confederacy.[140]

Does this mean that Aetolia had now committed herself to war on the Republic, thereby rendering such a war inescapable?[141] Certainly she had committed herself to Antiochus, thus assuring a powerful ally in the event of war. That was a pragmatic and prudent step. Aetolian attitudes, however, are not to be summed up as a driving ambition to confront Rome. Quite apart from Phaeneas' opinion, surely not an isolated one in view of his recent election, Thoas' position—and the state's—was more nuanced than mere militancy. One might observe, for instance, a neglected fact. It was Thoas who persuaded Antiochus to cancel his scheme of sending Hannibal with a fleet to Africa.[142] Nothing could have been better calculated to stir up Roman resistance than Hannibalic intrigues in his homeland. Thoas deflected that purpose. And his argument that Antiochus be enjoined to bring his troops to Greece in impressive numbers fell short of a declaration of war. The aim was to overawe Rome and wring concessions from her, concessions for the benefit of Aetolia—in other words, implementation of those same territorial demands that the state had

137. Livy, 35.43.7.

138. Livy, 35.45.3–4: *Phaeneas reconciliatore pacis et disceptatore de iis quae in controversia cum populo Romano essent utendum potius Antiocho censebat quam duce belli: adventum eius et maiestatem ad verecundiam faciendam Romanis vim maiorem habituram quam arma.*

139. Livy, 35.45.5–8.

140. Livy, 35.45.9; Appian, *Syr.* 12: αὐτοκράτορά τε στρατηγὸν Αἰτωλῶν Ἀντίο-χον ἀποφαίνοντες.

141. So scholars have almost invariably taken it; e.g. Deininger, *Widerstand*, 75: "womit der militärische Zusammenstoss mit Rom praktisch unabwendbar geworden war."

142. Livy, 35.42.2–35.43.1; cf. Nepos, *Hann.* 8.1.

been making since 196. Antiochus needed to come armed to the bargaining table, else Rome would not listen.[143] Even election of the king as commander-in-chief of the League is a symbolic gesture of union rather than a declaration of war. Aetolia had awarded the same honor to Attalus for 209 but had gone on to conduct her own policy.[144] One may go further. Aetolian ambassadors proceeded in late 192 to make representations in Chalcis, Achaea, Boeotia, and Athamania. To the Chalcidians and Achaeans they could still assert that entering into *amicitia* with Antiochus involved no breach of relations with Rome; to Amynander of Athamania they promised the throne of Macedonia for his brother-in-law! A war against the Republic had not even yet become a reality.[145] And when it did come in 191, the Aetolians proved noticeably reluctant to contribute their manpower. Their leaders faced serious recruitment problems in supplying troops for Antiochus at Thermopylae.[146] Aetolia had hoped to gain her ends without facing Roman might.[147]

## Contention for Ascendancy in the Peloponnese

If one turns to the Peloponnese, the same analysis applies. Hellenic rivalries prevailed there, not a clash of pro- and anti-Roman elements.

143. Livy, 35.45.8: *armatum regem aliquid impetraturum; inermem non pro Aetolis modo, sed ne pro se quidem ipso momenti ullius futurum apud Romanos.* That the old territorial demands were still fundamental for Aetolia is clear from Livy, 35.45.6.

144. Livy, 27.29.10, 27.30.1. Cf. also the naming of Ptolemy III as commander in chief by the Achaean League in 243: Plut. *Arat.* 24.4. And Philip V's honorific position as προστάτης of the Cretan *koinon* in 220: Polyb. 7.11.9.

145. Livy, 35.46–50. For Chalcis, see especially Livy, 35.46.5–7: *Aetoli magnopere suadere ut salva Romanorum amicitia regem quoque adsumerent socium atque amicum: neque enim eum inferendi belli, sed liberandae Graeciae causa in Europam traiecisse, et liberandae re, non verbis et simulatione quod fecissent Romani.* The Chalcidians did not spurn *amicitia* with Antiochus and the Aetolians, but were unwilling to compromise themselves in the eyes of the Romans: Livy, 35.46.12–13. For Achaea: Livy, 35.48.8–10. For Amynander: Livy, 35.47.5–8; Appian, *Syr.* 13: Oost, *CP* 52 (1957): 8–9, questions the story but fails to refute it and ends by accepting something like it. The arguments used in Boeotia are not recorded, but probably similar: Livy, 35.50.5. Note Antiochus' later request there; Livy, 36.6.4: *ut amicitiam secum institui, non bellum indici Romanis postularet.*

146. Livy, 36.15.2–5; cf. 36.16.3–4, 36.16.6–11, 36.17.9; Appian, *Syr.* 18. They were, of course, more vigorous later in the war, when Antiochus was back in Asia, and when opportunity arose for territorial annexations: Polyb. 21.25.3–7; Livy, 38.3.3–6.

147. Note that when Demetrias had come under her sway, she evidently refrained from installing a garrison there: Livy, 35.39.3–8, 36.33.1–7. A garrison might have provoked Rome, who had removed her own.

When Nabis attacked Gytheum and other cities on the Laconian coast in 193, it was the interests of the Achaean League that were directly affected. Those towns had been placed under Achaean hegemony by Flamininus in 195.[148] Nabis, we may be sure, did not intend to spark a war with Rome. His recent experience in such a war was too fresh. But Roman troops had been evacuated and unlikely to return, so the Aetolians argued. By turning the cities over to Achaea Rome had signalled a denial of direct interest. With Aetolian encouragement, Nabis ventured to recover his old holdings.[149] The Spartan sought outlets to the sea, a counterweight to Achaea, revived influence in the Peloponnese. As in Aetolia, so in Sparta, the withdrawal of Roman forces gave rise to new militancy and particularist aspirations.[150]

Achaea reacted firmly but cautiously. Reinforcements went to Gytheum, now under siege by Nabis in the autumn of 193. Nabis was warned that his actions violated the Roman treaty. A mission also sailed to Rome to report the state of affairs. The League, however, refrained from full mobilization against Sparta. They would await the return of their envoys from Rome.[151] The restraint is often ascribed to an Achaean recognition of dependency on Rome.[152] That conclusion goes well beyond the evidence and is refuted by subsequent events. It was only logical for the League to inform Rome of Nabis' actions. Appeal to the Roman treaty might give the Spartan second thoughts, and the prospect of Roman backing for Achaea might discourage him altogether. As for delay, it was only temporary. Achaea did not hesitate to throw a garrison into Gytheum. Any further action may have been stalled in view of the winter season.

Rome took steps toward partial mobilization in early 192, as we have seen. One of those steps involved instructions to the praetor

---

148. Livy, 35.13.2, 38.31.2.

149. Livy, 35.12.6–10, 35.13.1; cf. 35.18.5.

150. Cf. Justin, 31.3.2: *cum Romanus exercitus in Italiam reportatus esset, velut vacua rursus possessione sollicitatus multas civitates repentino bello invasit;* Texier, *Nabis,* 94–96.

151. Livy, 35.13.2–3, 35.25.2–4.

152. Cf. Aymard, *Premiers rapports,* 299–300; Texier, *Nabis,* 96–97. The Achaean *strategos* of 194/3 is unknown. Hence, it is tempting to assume that he "belonged to the party which favored deferring to Rome and avoiding independent action": Larsen, *Greek Federal States,* 408. The election of Philopoemen for 193/2 then suggests a turning to a more vigorous and autonomous line: Aymard, *op. cit.,* 303–304; A. M. Castellani, *ContIstFilClass* (1963), 78. By contrast, Errington, *Philopoemen,* 93, sees Philopoemen, already *strategos,* as behind the steps taken in autumn 193, including the embassy to Rome. The fact is, however, that we do not know precisely when the embassy went, nor whether it came before or after the Achaean elections for 193/2. Errington's assertion on this is no more plausible than Aymard's.

A. Atilius Serranus to take a fleet to Greece, in response to reports of Nabis' activities.[153] A show of force, but no more. The principal Roman move was diplomatic: Flamininus' mission.[154] The senate's reply to Achaea's ambassadors reached the League by spring, 192, a most interesting reply. It apparently requested the Achaeans to consult with and take the advice of Flamininus.[155] The implications of that message recall nothing more clearly than senatorial attitudes of three years earlier when a war with Nabis was in prospect. The *patres* left the matter to Flamininus. Far from taking an active role, they still looked on the affairs of the Peloponnese with relative indifference. The point, overlooked in modern discussions, bears stress.

Flamininus in fact counseled delay: the Achaeans should wait until arrival of the Roman fleet under Atilius.[156] Flamininus had something of a proprietary interest in the Peloponnesian settlement, which he had himself engineered in 195, an interest reinforced by the senate's continued willingness to give him a free hand in the area. An Achaean meeting in spring, 192, however, overrode his advice. The Achaeans would conduct war unilaterally, without waiting for Roman assistance. The *strategos* Philopoemen professed neutrality on the issue, but his sentiments for direct action were clear. And his pretext, that the situation did not permit further delay, was no more than pretext.[157] The Achaeans acted to forestall Roman intervention and reap the benefits for themselves. The haste of their preparations proves it. Philopoemen dragged out an ancient captured vessel (eighty years old!) as his flagship—a vessel that fell apart upon first contact, causing defeat and total humiliation in the naval encounter against Nabis.[158] Much of the humiliation was wiped out by an infantry campaign into Spartan territory which inflicted a defeat upon Nabis and enabled Philopoemen to ravage Laconia. Gytheum, however, the main object of his war, had fallen to the Spartan. The League had enjoyed but mixed success, or worse. Haste was largely responsible, an unwillingness to share credit for victory. Achaean pride manifested itself here, as well as a desire to claim exclusive rights on territory acquired.[159] And pride surged in the aftermath: Philopoemen, despite the incon-

153. Livy, 35.20.13–14, 35.22.1–2, 35.23.4.
154. Livy, 35.23.5: *quia non copiis modo sed etiam auctoritate opus erat ad tenendos sociorum animos.*
155. Though not stated explicitly by Livy, it is clearly implied in Livy, 35.25.3–4; cf. Aymard, *Premiers rapports*, 300–301.
156. Livy, 35.25.5.
157. Livy, 35.25.5–12; cf. Justin, 31.3.3.
158. Livy, 35.26; Plut. *Phil.* 14.1–3; Paus. 8.50.7.
159. The campaign is described in Livy, 35.27–30; Plut. *Phil.* 14.4–7; Paus. 8.50.8; see the discussions of Aymard, *Premiers rapports*, 306–309; Texier, *Nabis*, 97–98.

clusiveness of the campaign, the defeat at sea, the loss of Gytheum, and the inability to take Sparta, returned to a tumultuous welcome in Achaea, honored for his victories, and hailed as a commander the equal of or even superior to Flamininus.[160] The meaning of those demonstrations is unmistakable. Achaea celebrated a national triumph, achieved without the assistance of foreign troops.

Flamininus was understandably vexed. His advice had been ignored and he had been powerless to enforce it.[161] Atilius' fleet had not yet made an appearance and—more to the point—was not under Flamininus' authority anyway.[162] We may well believe our sources when they report the personal friction between Flamininus and Philopoemen that arose out of this series of events.[163] But there is nothing to show or even suggest that the senate in Rome was in any way distressed.

The decisive development in Sparta in summer, 192, came neither from Rome nor from Achaea. It was the treacherous assassination of Nabis at the hands of the Aetolians.[164] Aetolian aspirations in the Peloponnese, however, were frustrated by the ineptitude of their own agents. The Spartan populace rose to expel and eliminate the invaders. The city itself, leaderless and in a state of chaos, was now a ready prey to outside forces. Philopoemen leaped to the opportunity. He marched troops directly to Sparta, met with no resistance, and

160. Livy, 35.30.12–13; Plut. *Phil.* 15.1; *Flam.* 13.2; Justin, 31.3–4.

161. There is some evidence that Flamininus concluded a truce with Nabis after Philopoemen's campaign: Plut. *Phil.* 15.2; Paus. 8.50.10—accepted now almost unanimously by scholars as a move to prevent Philopoemen's capture of Sparta and restore Roman influence; see Aymard, *Premiers rapports*, 311–312; Lehmann, *Untersuchungen*, 236; Larsen, *Greek Federal States*, 411; Errington, *Philopoemen*, 105–106; Deininger, *Widerstand*, 110; Texier, *Nabis*, 98; Briscoe, *Commentary* II: 189–190. It was long ago placed in doubt by Nissen, *Kritische Untersuchungen*, 172, who did not argue the case in detail. The report is quite unreliable. No mention of such a truce exists in Livy, an omission not easily explained away, for his narrative of the campaign is unusually full. Plutarch's account is demonstrably inaccurate. He has confused the Roman war on Nabis of 195 with the Achaean war of 192, combining both and mixing up their details, as is plain from Plut. *Phil.* 14.1 and *Flam.* 13.1–3. The truce is undoubtedly that of 195; cf. Livy, 34.35.1–3. Pausanias is probably guilty of the same confusion. In 192 Flamininus was an envoy, not an *imperator*, and without authority to impose a truce. And Rome was not officially at war with Sparta anyway. The fact that Philopoemen returned to Achaea instead of besieging Sparta hardly requires the assumption of a truce. A siege of Sparta would be lengthy, difficult, and probably unprofitable; cf. Castellani, *op. cit.*, 79, n. 55.

162. Aymard's conjecture, *Premiers rapports*, 309–311, that Flamininus was responsible for Atilius' delay, hoping that the Achaeans would see the folly of their ways and seek Roman succor, is arbitrary and unfounded.

163. Plut. *Phil.* 15.1; *Flam.* 13.2, 17.1; Livy, 35.47.4. The information clearly stems from Polybius: cf. Polyb. 23.5.2.

164. See above p. 460.

swiftly accomplished the most coveted and longstanding of Achaean goals: the absorption of Lacedaemon into the Confederacy.[165] Philopoemen abjured radical changes within the city, for which there was neither time nor immediate need at this juncture, content with cultivating the support of Spartan leaders and factions.[166] He had achieved the principal end, extension of Achaean authority over Sparta. Flamininus can hardly have been pleased. His settlement of 195 had explicitly provided for Lacedaemonian independence. Yet official Roman policy remained aloof. Indeed, if Livy is right, the fortuitous appearance at last of Atilius' ships off Gytheum helped smooth the path for Philopoemen's usurpation.[167]

Roman policy at this point had but one overriding interest: the consolidation of Hellenic opinion against Antiochus. Of this policy Flamininus was servant, not master. Aetolians had hoped to exploit the strained relations between Philopoemen and Flamininus, thus to persuade Achaea to a position of neutrality. The hope proved empty. Flamininus' speech at the Achaean assembly of autumn, 192, reminded them of the advantages of cooperation with Rome in a major war.[168] Philopoemen was, in any case, out of office, replaced by Diophanes as *strategos* for 192/1.[169] The Achaeans voted without hesitation or debate: they would have the same friends and enemies as Rome and would order a declaration of war on Antiochus and the Aetolians.[170] Here unanimity prevailed. If Rome and the Aetolians were to come to blows, there could be no question where Achaea stood.[171] On the affairs of the Peloponnese, however, the League had

165. Livy, 35.37.1–2; Plut. *Phil.* 15.2; Paus. 8.50.10–8.51.1; cf. Zon. 9.19.

166. Polyb. 20.12; Plut. *Phil.* 15.2–6; Livy, 35.37.1–2; Paus. 8.51.2; cf. Aymard, *Premiers rapports*, 318–322; Errington, *Philopoemen*, 110–112. Walbank, *Commentary* III:2, 85–87, dates the episode of Philopoemen's refusal of a Spartan bribe to 191.

167. Livy, 35.37.3: *eo etiam facilius quod ad idem forte tempus A. Atilius cum quattuor et viginti quinqueremibus ad Gytheum accessit.*

168. Livy, 35.47.4, 35.48–49.

169. His *strategia* explicitly noted by Livy, 36.31.6. At the time of the meeting in 192 Philopoemen is referred to as *princeps* rather than *praetor*: Livy, 35.47.4. Hence, his term had evidently expired. It does not follow that Diophanes' election represents a changed Achaean attitude toward Rome; as Aymard, *Premiers rapports*, 323–324; Castellani, *op. cit.*, 79. Nor need one adopt the reverse position, that Diophanes secured election through Philopoemen's influence; as Lehmann, *Untersuchungen*, 266; Errington, *Philopoemen*, 112–113; Walbank, *Commentary* III:93. But the presence of Diophanes as presiding officer no doubt softened any tension that might have existed between Flamininus and Philopoemen.

170. Livy, 35.50.1–2. Polybius later claimed, long after Philopoemen's death, that he had taken a share in the passage of the decree: Polyb. 39.3.8; cf. 24.13.9. Nothing of this in Livy's account of the meeting which stems from Polybius.

171. That the official Achaean commitment need not have carried the hearts of all the League's citizens is indicated by Cato's trip in early 191 to assure the loyalty of Corinth, Patrae, and Aegium: Plut. *Cato*, 12.3.

made its own arrangements in violation of Flamininus' wishes and settlement—and had gone undisturbed by Rome.

The principal attention of Achaea to the Peloponnese never wavered. She had agreed to take up arms against Antiochus and fulfilled the commitment, but did hardly more than the minimum. Five hundred soldiers went to Chalcis and another five hundred to the Piraeus as garrison forces in autumn, 192. At Chalcis they proved quite ineffectual and soon had to evacuate the city; at Athens there was little fighting to be done anyway.[172] No Achaean forces participated in the battle of Thermopylae. In winter 191/90 Achaean ships ravaged the Aetolian coastline, notably that part of it that stood opposite the Peloponnese, an opportunity to harass the old rival.[173] Slightly more venturesome was the contribution of one thousand infantry and one hundred cavalry to assist Eumenes in Asia, the consequence of a Pergamene alliance, in spring, 190.[174] The following year saw another raiding mission on Aetolian shores, together with the Illyrians, and a token number of slingers recruited from Achaean cities to assist at the siege of Same.[175] That is the sum of Achaean activity in the larger conflict—a war which was not their own and for which they showed little enthusiasm. In the counsels of the League Antiochus and Aetolia took a distant second place to the issues of the Peloponnese. Opportunity existed for consolidation and expansion there, and the Achaeans seized it. Internal political rivalries among Philopoemen, Diophanes, and others revolved around it. And Flamininus, his *dignitas* wounded but his Hellenic connections still widespread, also had a personal stake in the Peloponnese. Local issues dominated the Achaean scene; the Roman war on Antiochus constituted a mere diversion.

The *strategia* of Diophanes in 192/1 demonstrates the fact with all desired clarity. A new outburst of trouble in Sparta threatened to undermine Achaean control in early 191. Its precise nature is unknown and speculation may be suspended. Dissatisfaction with Sparta's subordinate status, at least among certain elements of the population, is readily understandable. A secessionist movement provoked the crisis.[176] Diophanes immediately sprang into action and invaded Laconia,

172. Livy, 35.50.3–4, 35.51.8; cf. Plut. *Phil.* 17.1.

173. Livy, 37.4.6.

174. Polyb. 21.3b; Livy, 37.20.1–2; Appian, *Syr.* 26; *Syll.*[3] 606. Cf. Walbank, *Commentary* III, 92.

175. Livy, 38.7.2–3, 38.29.3–8.

176. Plut. *Phil.* 16.1–2; Paus. 8.51.1. Aymard, *Premiers rapports*, 333–334, may be right in saying that there was no official secession, but an effort in that direction is clear from the result; Plut. *Phil.* 16.2: κατέστησε τοὺς Λακεδαιμονίους πάλιν εἰς τὸ κοινόν, ὥσπερ ἐξ ἀρχῆς ἦσαν. Flamininus may have reproached the Spartans for planning some anti-Roman action, as Paus. 8.51.1, but that is hardly evidence for such a plan. The Spartans had no immediate grievance against Rome. For speculation on the inter-

accompanied by Flamininus. The Roman here saw an occasion to revive his faltering influence, especially in concert with a political rival of Philopoemen. The effort foundered. Philopoemen outraced them to the city and put an end to the disturbances himself. The gates were shut on Diophanes and Flamininus.[177] No policy differences existed here. It was a matter of prestige and patronage. Philopoemen would not countenance others either upsetting or reimposing the settlement he had made. Diophanes would have to find other outlets for his energy. Flamininus again had to swallow frustration; as he knew, no backing for private schemes in Sparta could be expected from the Roman senate.

Diophanes' object was to achieve Peloponnesian unity under Achaean domination, an object he proudly claimed to have accomplished on a subsequent dedication.[178] His goal coincided with that of Philopoemen, but the question of who should receive credit divided Achaean politics. Polybius later gave the credit to Philopoemen.[179] That disagreement reflects a contemporary rivalry between the two men who had once been master and pupil in the art of war.[180] On the main issue, however, there was unanimity: Achaean ascendancy in the Peloponnese. Diophanes pursued it with vigor. The *strategos* mobilized against Messene, on the grounds of her sympathies toward Aetolia. It was a pretext at best. Forcible incorporation into the Confederacy was the real motive.[181] The Messenians resisted but were overmatched. They appealed for rescue to Flamininus, offering to surrender their city to him rather than have it fall into the hands of the Achaeans.[182] There was some basis for hope: Messene had once been allied to Rome in the First Macedonian War, had supported Flamininus in the war on Nabis in 195, and had received certain concessions from him after that contest.[183] The Roman jumped at the opportunity to reassert his *auctoritas* in the Peloponnese. He ordered Diophanes to halt the invasion, even rebuking him for undertaking it without his consent, and proceeded to suggest a settlement of his

---

nal Spartan situation, see Errington, *Philopoemen*, 118–119; Shimron, *Late Sparta*, 102–104, 138–139. Shimron's dating of the affair to autumn or winter of 191 is refuted by Plut. *Phil.* 16.1.

177. Plut. *Phil.* 16.2; Paus. 8.51.1.

178. Paus. 8.30.5.

179. Polyb. 2.40.2.

180. Polyb. 21.9.1, 22.10.4; Livy, 37.20.2, 38.32.6.

181. Livy, 36.31.1–2: *Messene in Peloponneso ab Achaeis, quod concilii eorum recusaret esse, oppugnari coepta est.*

182. Livy, 36.31.4–5.

183. For the alliance, see above p. 20. The Messenian Deinocrates had fought on Flamininus' side against Nabis: Polyb. 23.5.2; cf. Aymard, *Premiers rapports*, 219. For concessions to Messene, see Livy, 34.35.6.

own.[184] But what was the nub of the settlement? That Messene must enter the Confederacy of the Achaeans! A remarkable decision and a most revealing one. Flamininus had accepted Messenian submission and then denied them the very object for which they had submitted, their independence. Diophanes had suffered rebuke, and then achieved his goal. There can be but one explanation for this paradoxical turn of events. Flamininus had no authorization and could anticipate no sanction from Rome in enforcing his own policy on the Peloponnese. His mission had not much longer to run. It was easy to predict that Achaea would soon coerce the Messenians if they remained outside the League, a coercion that could only bring more embarrassment to Flamininus: better to endorse the incorporation that was inevitable anyway.[185] Flamininus bolstered his own prestige, so far as possible within those bounds. He issued haughty directives to Diophanes, he instructed the Messenians to recall their exiles, and he proposed himself as arbiter for any temporary disputes that might arise out of the settlement.[186] But Achaea was the real gainer. Senatorial indifference set limits to Flamininus' intrigues.

The conclusion is reinforced by the experience of Elis. When Achaea declared for Rome in the war against Antiochus, the Eleans knew precisely what that meant for them: an Achaean invasion of their territory.[187] They asked for and got a garrison from Antiochus.[188] The Eleans were under no misapprehension that Achaea would be deflected from her main purpose by commitment to a Roman war. Rather, the Roman war served as cover for Achaean aggrandizement. In the summer of 191, Diophanes duly demanded Elis' annexation to the League. The Eleans expelled their Syrian garrison and temporized, hoping for favorable terms.[189] Flamininus again sought to take advantage, raising the Elean issue at the autumn meeting of the League. The representatives of Elis cut the ground out from under

184. Livy, 36.31.6–9.

185. Aymard, *Premiers rapports*, 343–345, misconceives the situation in identifying Flamininus' policy with Rome's and interpreting his action as enforcing Achaean deference to the western power.

186. Livy, 36.31.8–9. That this would be temporary arbitration and not enduring patronage is clear from the fact that Flamininus asked disputants to bring their cases to him at Corinth. He was not to be there for long. So, rightly, Aymard, *Premiers rapports*, 346, n. 14. The suggestion that exiles be recalled has been seen as an effort to bring stability: Aymard, *op. cit.*, 346; or a cynical move to promote instability: Errington, *Philopoemen*, 127. Neither hypothesis is necessary. Flamininus, hampered by circumstances outside his control, desired some display of personal influence.

187. Polyb. 20.3.5: ἐψηφισμένων γὰρ τῶν Ἀχαιῶν τὸν πόλεμον εὐλαβεῖσθαι τὴν τούτων ἔφοδον; Livy, 36.5.2.

188. Polyb. 20.3.7; Livy, 36.5.3.

189. Livy, 36.36.2–3.

him. With the example of Messene before them, they announced willingness to join the Confederacy but on their own terms, not through Roman intermediacy.[190] The annexation followed. Flamininus could do nothing to prevent it.[191]

On one issue only did Flamininus feel free to impose his will against Achaean aggrandizement. Diophanes, as representative of the League, had purchased the island of Zacynthus, sold by an appointee of Amynander after the defeat of Antiochus at the battle of Thermopylae and Amynander's own expulsion from his kingdom.[192] Flamininus denounced the proceeding, spoke sharply at an Achaean meeting, and insisted that the island belonged to Rome by right of war. A defense by Diophanes was unavailing. The Achaeans overbore him and ceded the island to Rome.[193] On this matter Flamininus meant business, as the Achaeans obviously realized since they declined to support Diophanes and meekly submitted. Zacynthus belonged in a category very different from that of Sparta, Elis, and Messene. It was not a mere matter of bullying the League, though Flamininus no doubt welcomed the opportunity to throw his weight around. He could evidently count on senatorial backing on this issue, as on none of the others. For good reason. Roman forces had occupied the island once before, in 211, at the outset of the First Macedonian War. At that time Rome intended no permanent control. Zacynthus soon fell into the hands of Philip who ceded it in 207 or 206 to Amynander, under whose authority it had remained for fifteen years without Roman objection.[194] But now the Republic took a keener interest. As we have seen, its one continuous interest in the East had been the security of Greek cities on the Ionian Gulf. Illyria and Macedonia no longer threatened them. Aetolia, however, was the new foe; several cities in Acarnania had embraced the cause of Antiochus; and Epirote "neutrality" was anything but reliable. Rome determined to guarantee the security of islands in the southern part of the Ionian Sea. This attitude had been demonstrated already in the Second Macedonian War when L. Flamininus coerced Leucas into capitulation.[195] The island was coveted by Aetolia but denied to her.[196] In the Aetolian war Rome paid

190. Livy, 36.35.7: *Elei per se ipsi quam per Romanos maluerunt Achaico contribui concilio.*

191. That the annexation came before the end of Diophanes' *strategia* is perhaps implied by his claim of unifying the Peloponnese: Paus. 8.30.5. Elis was certainly in the League by 189; Livy, 38.32.3. The presence of the consul Glabrio with Flamininus at the Achaean meeting does not imply any endorsement from Rome on the matter of Elis; Livy, 36.35.7.

192. Livy, 36.31.10–36.32.1.      193. Livy, 36.31.10, 36.32.2–9.
194. Livy, 26.24.15, 36.31.10–11.      195. Livy, 33.16–17.
196. Polyb. 18.47.8–9; Livy, 33.34.7, 33.49.8.

special attention to Cephallenia, kept it separate from any treaty arrangements, and assured that Aetolia could have no later claims to it.[197] The insistence upon Zacynthus makes sense only within that context. Flamininus felt justifiable confidence in blustering here. Achaean expansion in the Peloponnese would not bother the senate; but the islands of the Ionian Sea were off limits to any major Greek power.[198]

The exception of Zacynthus neatly proves the rule. Within the Peloponnese Flamininus failed to curb Achaean expansionism for the simple reason that he could not carry the backing of the senate. The Spartan question, raised again in autumn, 191, confirms the fact once more. Flamininus brought it before the Achaean gathering, requesting jointly with the consul Glabrio that Spartan exiles be restored to their native city.[199] Philopoemen, evidently now *strategos* for 191/90, stepped in to block the request: the exiles would be restored eventually, but by the Achaeans, not by the Romans.[200] That forceful response, so dramatically different from Achaea's submission on the issue of Zacynthus, points the moral with decisiveness. The Peloponnese was Achaea's bailiwick. Flamininus lacked authority to press the matter—and dropped it. This time the senate's viewpoint can be discerned by something more than an argument from silence. Spartan representatives had come to Rome perhaps in summer or early autumn, 191, asking for return of the hostages held in Italy since Nabis' defeat in 195 and for recovery of the perioecic towns. Lacedaemonian patriotic pride had not abated.[201] The senate promised nothing,

197. Polyb. 21.30.5, 21.32.12; Livy, 37.50.5, 38.9.10, 38.11.7, 38.28.5–38.30.1. Note the piratical activity around Cephallenia in 190, which the Romans certainly took seriously: Livy, 37.13.11–12.

198. Cf. Livy, 36.32.5–8. One may observe also that the Epirotes and Acarnanians were allies of Achaea: Livy, 35.27.11—which may have played a role in Rome's prohibiting of Achaean expansion into the Ionian Sea.

199. Livy, 36.35.7; Plut. *Phil.* 17.4. These are presumably men exiled by Nabis and still settled in the perioecic and maritime towns.

200. Plut. *Phil.* 17.4: βουλόμενος δι' αὐτοῦ καὶ τῶν Ἀχαιῶν, ἀλλὰ μὴ Τίτου μηδὲ Ῥωμαίων χάριτι τοῦτο πραχθῆναι; Livy, 36.35.7: *quia suae gratiae reservari exulum causam Achaei . . . maluerunt*; Paus. 8.51.4. On Philopoemen's *strategia* for 191/0, see Aymard, *Études*, 4–11; Errington, *Philopoemen*, 251–255.

201. Polyb. 21.1.1–2. On the chronology, see Aymard, *Premiers rapports*, 356–360. Placement of the mission in 191/0 by Lehmann, *Untersuchungen*, 239, n. 193, and Errington, *Philopoemen*, 286–287, ignores the fact that Polybius' text refers to the embassy's return to Sparta. It does not follow, as Aymard believes, that Flamininus and Glabrio, in addressing the League in autumn 191, were acting on senatorial instructions. The *patres'* response to the Spartans refers to senatorial envoys being sent to deal with some of these questions; Polyb. 21.1.3: ἔφησεν ἐντολὰς δώσειν τοῖς παρ' αὐτῶν ἀποστελλομένοις πρέσβεσιν. This can hardly refer to Flamininus and Glabrio who were already in Greece and had long been there. Errington's elaborate reconstruction of

postponed all, and disappointed expectations. On the outlying towns, senators would give some directives to envoys; on the hostages, they would deliberate further.[202] The issue of restoring exiles also came up. A brusque pronouncement came from the *patres*: they were surprised, they said, that the Spartans had not recalled them home, since the city was "free."[203] The import of that statement is commonly misunderstood. It does not express senatorial interest in restoring the exiles, let alone senatorial initiative on the matter then transmitted to Flamininus. Spartans clearly raised the question, after failing to get satisfaction at Achaea. The senate brushed them off with irony and sarcasm: recall them yourselves, since you are "free."[204]

Philopoemen's resistance had drawn no Roman fire. Flamininus returned home empty-handed. The senate did send back Spartan hostages in early 190, a token gesture only. There were but five of them anyway, Nabis was already dead, and the one hostage of potential importance, Nabis' son, was retained.[205] The senate restored neither the maritime cities nor the exiles.[206] Flamininus had endeavored in vain to utilize his influence. The senate did not care.

The dramatic sequel suitably extends this pattern. Spartan citizens, frustrated by the unfulfillment of their aims, hard pressed by loss of an outlet to the sea, and harassed by or fearful of the exiles settled in the maritime towns, took matters into their own hands. They made a strike on the coastal town of Las in autumn, 189, capturing it temporarily and spreading panic all along the coast.[207] Philopoemen, *strategos* again for 189/8, reacted swiftly, denouncing Spartan violation of the pact of 195 which had put the maritime cities under

---

Spartan events, including the hypothesis of an unattested internal coup, *Philopoemen*, 133–136, is altogether speculative; cf. Shimron, *Late Sparta*, 142–143.

202. Polyb. 21.1.1–3.

203. Polyb. 21.1.4: περὶ δὲ τῶν φυγάδων τῶν ἀρχαίων θαυμάζειν ἔφησαν, πῶς οὐ κατάγουσιν αὐτοὺς εἰς τὴν οἰκείαν, ἠλευθερωμένης τῆς Σπάρτης.

204. That this is a senatorial response, not a senatorial initiative, appears from the parallelism in Polybius' language on the issues of hostages, villages, and exiles: περὶ μὲν . . . περὶ δὲ . . . περὶ δὲ. Aymard, who believes that Flamininus "cannot have had an opinion different from that of the senate on the matter of Spartan exiles," *Premiers rapports*, 360, then lands himself in immense difficulty in trying to explain why the senate failed to back him when Philopoemen successfully blocked the proposal: *op. cit.*, 368–372. Errington, *Philopoemen*, 133–136, 286, suggests unconvincingly and without evidence that the senate's response followed Flamininus' return to Rome and was dictated by him: "Flamininus' policy then showed itself, in its new senatorial guise."

205. Polyb. 21.3.4; cf. Livy, 34.35.11, 34.52.9.

206. On the maritime cities, see Livy, 38.30.6. Plut. *Phil.* 17.4 says Philopoemen restored the exiles, but this is plainly confusion with the events of 189/8. See below p. 474.

207. Livy, 38.30.6–9.

Achaean control and grasping the occasion to implement a long desired goal, repatriation of the Lacedaemonian exiles.[208] He had simply
postponed the matter in 191, lest any credit for such repatriation go to
Flamininus. The Achaean *strategos* wished to guarantee that the beneficiaries of a new Spartan settlement would be his—and Achaea's—
beneficiaries.[209] By order of the League, the Spartans were now instructed to give up the men responsible for the raid on Las for trial in
Achaea. Terror seized the government in Sparta—and desperation.
They rejected the command, indeed executed those who approved it,
and forthwith appealed to the Roman consul M. Fulvius Nobilior,
making full *deditio* to the Romans.[210]

The reaction, both by Achaea and by Fulvius, bears particular
notice. The League, having drawn the proper lesson from its successful withstanding of Flamininus' machinations, simply disregarded the
Lacedaemonian *deditio* to Rome. An Achaean council unanimously
declared war on Sparta and, though the winter prevented an invasion, raids and harassment began almost immediately.[211] Fulvius had
learned the same lesson. He completed the siege of Same in late winter 188, now free to intervene and armed with the Spartan *deditio*. Yet
he elected to make no unilateral pronouncement; instead he brought
the matter to an Achaean meeting.[212] Fulvius himself refrained from
taking sides in the quarrel, despite the fact that Sparta had put herself
entirely under his authority. That authority, as Flamininus had discovered, carried severe limits so long as the senate remained uninterested. When heated debate broke out and no resolution seemed
possible, Fulvius took the only position open to him consonant both
with his *dignitas* and with the political restrictions he faced: a recom-
mendation that parties to the dispute send ambassadors to Rome.[213]
Achaean leaders consented readily enough. It would not do to offend

208. Livy, 38.30.9–38.31.2, 38.31.4: *quod iam diu moliretur*. Despite the apparent
implication of Livy, 38.32.10, Philopoemen was surely not elected to two successive
generalships; cf. Aymard, *Études*, 11–18; Errington, *Philopoemen*, 251–253.

209. Plut. *Phil.* 17.4; Livy, 36.35.7.

210. Livy, 38.31.2–6.

211. Livy, 38.32.1–2.

212. Livy, 38.32.3. Fulvius' inability to sway Achaean opinion had recently been
demonstrated on another matter: the question of whether Achaean meetings should
continue to be held at Aegium or should rotate among various League cities. Fulvius
preferred the former, but gave up any effort to persuade when it became clear that the
majority of Achaeans followed Philopoemen in support of the latter: Livy, 38.30.1–5.
On this issue and Livy's confused chronology, see the rival reconstructions of Aymard,
*Melanges Glotz* I (1932), 49–73; Badian and Errington, *Historia* 14 (1965): 13–17; Lehmann, *Untersuchungen*, 251–253; and Walbank, *Commentary* III: 137, 412–413.

213. Livy, 38.32.4.

the consul needlessly. And the winter season prevented serious operations anyway.

In Rome the *patres* took no more notice of the Lacedaemonian
*deditio* than Fulvius had. Two men, with separate viewpoints, headed
the Achaean delegation, representatives from Sparta brought their arguments, and envoys from the exiles arrived as well, a confusing
assemblage. Lycortas presented the case for Philopoemen: Achaea
should have free rein to carry out her own decisions, in conformity
with the treaty and her statutes. Diophanes, stung by Philopoemen's
opposition in 191, proposed that senatorial adjudication decide all the
controversies at stake.[214] How deeply committed he was to this policy
in principle may be questioned. The man who boasted of unifying the
Peloponnese can hardly be labeled a Roman toady. On this issue,
however, political rivalry had greater weight. A settlement, if left to
the Achaeans, would redound to Philopoemen's credit and push Diophanes further into the background. Better to let Rome decide it. But
Rome pointedly did not decide it. The senate offered a mere hedge:
that there be no change in Spartan circumstances.[215] The enigmatic
statement allowed for broad and conflicting interpretations. Sparta
took it as a concession to her autonomy, Achaea as a blank check for
aggression.[216] Whether the ambiguity was deliberate or inadvertent,
the *patres* had washed their hands of the affair.

The result was disaster for Sparta. Philopoemen mobilized in
the spring of 188. The Spartans, despairing now of Roman intervention, surrendered the alleged miscreants for trial. Violence broke out
when embittered exiles attacked their tormentors, a massacre at Compasium, followed by swift justice and execution of those still alive.[217]
Sparta was now wholly at the League's mercy. On Philopoemen's orders, her walls were torn down, foreign mercenaries were expelled,
the freed helots banished on pain of reenslavement, the exiles returned, and the Spartan social and political system abolished to bring
it into conformity with League institutions.[218] It was a high point of
Achaean aggrandizement. Far from knuckling under to Roman pressure—or indeed even receiving Roman pressure—the Achaeans had
exploited a Roman war to gather their own benefits. While hostilities
raged between Rome and Antiochus, Achaea supplied token assis-

214. Livy, 38.32.5–8.
215. Livy, 38.32.9: *novari tamen nihil de Lacedaemoniis placebat.*
216. Livy, 38.32.10.
217. Livy, 38.33, 39.36.9–16; Plut. *Phil.* 16.3.
218. Livy, 38.34, 39.37.1–8; Plut. *Phil.* 16.4–5, 17.4; cf. Polyb. 21.32c.3, 22.11.7.
Discussion in Errington, *Philopoemen*, 144–147; Shimron, *Late Sparta*, 106–107, 112–
113; Walbank, *Commentary* III:138–139.

tance but kept her eye trained firmly on the Peloponnese wherefrom she richly benefited in prestige and power.

## The Lesser States

Of the lesser states in Hellas less is known. For them the Aetolian and Antiochene wars constituted a grievous burden, unwelcome and potentially disastrous. To characterize them in terms of pro- or anti-Roman sympathies badly misjudges the circumstances.[219] They neither precipitated nor desired the war, though some suffered heavily during it. Expediency or force directed their loyalties during the conflict, not any deep attachment to one side or the other.

An embassy of Epirotes, sent to Antiochus in winter 192/1, expressed the anxiety of smaller powers with eloquence. They pleaded with him not to involve them in a war against Rome. If the king could promise protection and guarantee safety, they would welcome him into their cities and harbors. If not, he should understand their reluctance to compromise themselves in Roman eyes and to invite Roman retaliation.[220] The case could not be better put, and it was put by Charops, a man who had been most active in Rome's cause during the Second Macedonian War. For states like Epirus, and for good reason, loyalty was bounded by security. The battle of Thermopylae showed in what direction security lay. Epirote envoys went to the Roman consul and to the senate in Rome, apologizing for their failure to support the winning side and claiming that, at least, they had done little to support the loser. They entered a plea to be restored to Roman *amicitia*. The senate responded coolly, though without hostility.[221] An opportunity to make amends came in 189, when the consul Fulvius arrived in Apollonia. The Epirotes were swift to consult with him and offer advice: best to attack Ambracia, which might draw the Aetolians out or would, at least, wrest the city from their control. The nation was now officially at war with Aetolia and only too happy to assist in the siege of Ambracia. One may venture without audacity to suggest that Epirus' interest in the Roman cause was secondary or tertiary. But she could have hopes of Ambracia as a prize of war.[222] The Epirotes looked to their own concerns—as they had to.

219. That is the fundamental failing of Deininger's analysis; *Widerstand*, 76–96.
220. Polyb. 20.3.1–4; Livy, 36.5.1, 36.5.3–7.
221. Livy, 36.35.8–11; cf. Zon. 9.19. It does not follow that Epirus thereafter lost all power to conduct an independent foreign policy; as Cabanes, *L'Épire*, 282–284.
222. Polyb. 21.26.1–8; Livy, 38.3.9–38.4.10. The suggestion appears in Oost, *Roman Policy*, 64–65. She never did get Ambracia, however. The city was awarded its freedom in 187: Livy, 38.43.3–4.

Acarnania faced still heavier pressure. Antiochus made a concerted effort to win over the land in early spring, 191. Bribery, guile, and a show of force gained him Medion and several other Acarnanian cities. Leucas, however, he made no attempt on; the Roman fleet was too close. The Thyrreans shut their gates to the king's envoys.[223] There is nothing here to indicate sentiment for Antiochus or Rome. The people of Leucas feared the Roman navy in their vicinity, those of Thyrreum were on their guard against the machinations that had taken Medion.[224] Each city made its calculations accordingly. Thermopylae decided the issue for Acarnania as for Epirus. Thereafter the Acarnanians were at war with Aetolia, a belated but intelligible decision.[225] They gained something from the peace, recovery of the city of Oeniadae, a welcome acquisition; but Rome harbored no illusions about the quality of Acarnanian enthusiasm for her cause.[226]

A similar pattern of behavior is discernible in Athamania. Amynander, ruler of the minor but strategically important kingdom that bordered Epirus, Thessaly, and Macedonia, opted for the side of Antiochus. A prize dangled before him supposedly determined his decision: promise of the Macedonian throne for his wife's brother, Philip of Megalopolis.[227] However little value one places on that tale, it indicates—what could be assumed anyway—that private ambitions motivated Amynander, not zeal for the cause of Antiochus. Athamanian forces engaged on the Aetolian and Syrian side in 191, but their operations, significantly, concentrated on western Thessaly, and the results gave them control of several towns across the Athamanian border into Thessaly.[228] The successes proved to be shortlived and Amynander's choice an imprudent one. Philip V elected to join the Roman cause; he had eyes for Thessaly and Athamania above all. The Macedonian, in concert with Roman troops, overwhelmed Amynander's garrisons in Thessaly, forced the king to abandon his realm, and took full control of Athamania.[229] A counterattack in 189, backed by the Aetolians, enabled Amynander to regain his sovereignty and beat back Macedonian resistance.[230] But he knew where the future lay. Gratitude to Aetolia notwithstanding, Amynander immediately en-

223. Livy, 36.11.8–36.12.11, 42.38.3; Appian, *Syr.* 16.

224. Livy, 36.11.9, 36.12.7.

225. Cf. Polyb. 21.29.4; Livy, 38.4.10, 38.5.6, 38.9.2.

226. Recovery of Oeniadae: Polyb. 21.32.14; Livy, 38.11.9. On the Roman attitude, see Livy, 42.38.4.

227. Livy, 35.47.5–8; Appian, *Syr.* 13. Doubts on the efficacy of this motive in Oost, *CP* 52 (1957): 8–9.

228. Livy, 36.9.1, 36.10.5, 36.13.5–6.

229. Livy, 36.13.5–36.14.9, 36.34.9, 38.1.2, 39.23.10–11; Appian, *Syr.* 17.

230. Livy, 38.1–2.

tered into negotiations with Rome, apologizing for his earlier indiscretions and blaming others for his behavior.[231] Whether the belated *volte-face* gained him anything or even salvaged his position is unknown, as Amynander shortly thereafter drops from the record.[232] His tergiversations, determined by hope for advantage rather than commitment to the major combatants, exemplify attitudes among the smaller Greek powers.

Athens, without the means to play a significant role, got caught in the vise of conflicting pressures. A Roman embassy appeared in the city in 192, as did Eumenes of Pergamum, to confirm Athens' allegiance. Yet the pro-Aetolian Euthymidas also found refuge there.[233] The wealth of Antiochus attracted many Athenians and prompted a strong movement in his favor, but others, relying on Flamininus and Roman power, expelled adherents of the king and stayed with Rome. An Achaean garrison was needed to enforce their loyalty.[234] Though Athens nominally remained in the Roman camp, her allegiance was no better than lukewarm, her interests both before and during the conflict primarily directed toward peace.[235]

Boeotia found herself in the same vise. She gave evasive replies to Aetolian envoys in late 192. A detachment of Roman soldiers at Delium may have enforced caution.[236] The troop was subsequently cut to pieces by Antiochus' forces, and when the king approached Thebes he received welcome from Boeotian leaders.[237] The Confederacy, now driven to comply, passed a resolution in favor of Antiochus—in mild language, so as not to lay itself open to reprisals.[238] After Thermopylae, of course, Boeotia stood exposed to Roman retaliation and, like so many other lesser powers, immediately took on the position of suppliant, begging forgiveness for errors of judgment.[239] The new posture contained no more sincerity than the previous one. Boeotia simply struggled to survive.

Chalcis supplies another example. Aetolia made two attempts

231. Polyb. 21.25.1–2; Livy, 38.3.1–2.

232. The last mention in Polyb. at 21.29; Livy, at 38.9.4–7.

233. Livy, 35.31.3, 35.37.4–6, 35.38.13, 35.39.2.

234. Livy, 35.50.3–4.

235. Athens as nominal ally: Livy, 36.20.8, 37.14.2. Cato in 191 delivered a speech there to hold her loyalty: Plut. *Cato*, 12.4–5; Cato, *ORF*, fr. 20. The peace-making efforts: Livy, 35.32.6–7, 35.32.12–14, 37.6.4–7, 37.7.4–5, 38.9.3, 38.10.2–6; Polyb. 21.29.9, 21.30.7, 21.31.5–16.

236. Livy, 35.47.2–3, 35.50.5, 35.50.9.

237. Polyb. 20.7.5; Livy, 35.51.1–4, 36.6.1–3; Appian, *Syr.* 12–13.

238. Livy, 36.6.4–5: *neminem quid ageretur fallebat; decretum tamen sub leni verborum praetextu pro rege adversus Romanos factum est.*

239. Livy, 36.20.1–4.

upon her in 192 through support of an internal faction and threat of force. Reliance upon strong walls, plus fear of Aetolian domination, steeled the Chalcidian will to resist.[240] It was steeled further by garrison troops from Pergamum and Achaea.[241] Anything was better than admitting the Aetolians into the citadel.[242] The resistance collapsed before long, for Antiochus temporarily had the bigger battalions. When his army moved up, the Chalcidians forgot their earlier defiance and opened the gates. The whole of Euboea then fell into the king's hands.[243] That situation too lasted but a short time. Thermopylae proved decisive for Euboea as elsewhere. Antiochus fled to Asia; Chalcis and other Euboean cities now threw open their gates to Rome.[244] The consul Glabrio, unconcerned about Chalcis' prior loyalty and mindful only of her recent collaboration with Antiochus, prepared to take grim revenge on the city. He was deterred at the last moment through the intercession of Flamininus, honored thereafter as Chalcis' savior.[245] Flamininus saw rightly that the city had been coerced and had no real love for Antiochus; but Glabrio was right too: Chalcis had no real love for Rome either.

In northern Greece other painful and unwelcome decisions had to be made. At Demetrias, as we have seen, internal turmoil tore apart the citizenry. The circumstances which persuaded her for attachment to Aetolia in 192 were not so much pro-Aetolian sentiments or even anti-Roman sympathies, but the fear that Demetrias would once again be placed under the hegemony of Philip.[246] Her fear had a sound basis. Abandoned by Antiochus and the Aetolians after Thermopylae, Demetrias had to capitulate to Macedonian forces and fell once more into Philip's hands.[247] Most vulnerable of all were the Thessalians. Much of the fighting would take place on their territory, regardless of which side they chose. At the outset Flamininus counted on their loyalty and he got it. The Thessalian cities rejected Antiochus' overtures.[248] As the king well knew, however, a successful assault on one principal Thessalian town would cause the rest to collapse.[249] He was right: when Pherae was brought to surrender in early 191, a number of Thessalian communities swiftly fell into line, only Larisa hold-

240. Livy, 35.37.4–35.38.14, 35.46.2–35.47.1.
241. Livy, 35.39.2, 35.50.3, 35.50.6.
242. Livy, 35.38.5: *graves fuisse Macedonas dominos; multo minus tolerabiles futuros Aetolos.*
243. Livy, 35.51.6–10.
244. Polyb. 20.8.5; Livy, 36.21.1–3; Plut. *Flam.* 16.2; Appian, *Syr.* 20–21.
245. Plut. *Flam.* 16.1–4; *IG*, XII, 9, 931.
246. See above p. 458.                    247. Livy, 36.33, 39.23.12.
248. Livy, 35.31.3, 35.39.4, 36.8.2, 36.9.1–8.
249. Livy, 36.9.9–10.

ing out, bolstered by arrival of Roman forces together with Philip.[250] A counteroffensive by Romans and Macedonians wrecked Antiochus' position in Thessaly.[251] Yet the Thessalians can hardly have been overjoyed with the course of events. Their land had again been turned into a battleground, an object of ambition on various sides by Athamanians, Aetolians, and Macedonians. The struggle between Rome and Antiochus had been just a temporary one in that area; the ambitions of other Greek powers were enduring. To secure Philip's assistance, in fact, the Romans had granted him the right to occupy Thessalian cities taken from Aetolia.[252] That concession, a source of so much grievance later, showed the Roman attitude clearly enough. It underlines the meaning of the war to the Thessalians: whichever side won, they stood to lose.

**V**

Rome, having once engaged actively in the war, fought it through, as usual, to conclusion. She accepted nothing but total surrender from the Aetolians, so she could dictate terms without restriction.[253] The terms included Aetolia's renunciation of sovereignty over all cities which had been taken by or had surrendered to the Romans since 192.[254] Rome again eschewed occupation or annexation. Where testimony exists, it points to the customary declarations of freedom, as for Delphi and for Ambracia.[255] Even in the cases of Cephallenia and Zacynthus, firmly excluded from the grasp of Aetolia and Achaea, nothing suggests the establishment of any Roman troops.[256] Elsewhere, disputed places were left to be quarreled over by Philip, Aetolia, and the Thessalians. Aetolia was stripped of (some) conquests, but her confederacy, like Philip's kingdom in 196, remained intact. The Romans showed a decided lack of interest in making territorial arrangements in 189.[257]

Instead, treaties locked in the settlement. The alliance with Aetolia, punctuated by the notorious "*maiestas*-clause," mandated the promises of lasting Aetolian quiescence. The *foedus* with Achaea,

250. Livy, 36.9.11–36.10.14.
251. Livy, 36.13–14.
252. Livy, 39.23.10, 39.25.3–5, 39.28.4; see above p. 400.
253. On the various negotiations, see above pp. 26–30.
254. Polyb. 21.32.13; Livy, 38.11.9.
255. Delphi: *Syll.*[3] 609 = Sherk, *RDGE*, no. 37A, lines 9–10; *Syll.*[3] 611 = Sherk, *RDGE*, no. 38, lines 17–20. Ambracia: Livy, 38.44.4.
256. See above pp. 470–471.
257. The only item specified is the detachment of Oeneadae from Aetolia and its transference to Acarnania: Polyb. 21.32.14; Livy, 38.11.9.

probably concluded about this time, and the permanent φιλία with Antiochus had similar purposes. They advertised the enduring character of concord now established in Hellas. They neither entrenched Rome's control nor facilitated her intervention. To the contrary: by publicizing the permanence of this settlement the Romans meant to eliminate the circumstances that could invoke their reentry.[258]

The Republic's presence and actions over the past quarter-century had, of course, made a profound impact on Greece. But observation from the Roman vantage point conceals the most important facts. Internal rivalries within Hellas played themselves out on the stages provided by Rome's wars against Macedonia and Syria. The Republic took but minor part in the conflicts of the late third century, which were dominated by clashes between Aetolia and Macedonia and by a struggle for Peloponnesian ascendancy waged among various Greek states. Private and public concern for reputation helped stimulate Roman intervention against Philip in 200 and against Nabis in 195. For the Hellenes, however, their own quarrels and ambitions held first place. Aetolians, Achaeans, Spartans, Thessalians, Athamanians, and others engaged to satisfy territorial aims and gain advantages for themselves.

Aetolia bears a heavy responsibility for provoking the fateful clash between Rome and Antiochus the Great. Yet that had not been her intention or expectation. The League simply pursued conventional ends of aggrandizement in Hellas, capitalizing on Roman withdrawal and brandishing the support of the Seleucid to extend influence and suzerainty. When war did come, Aetolia gave little help to Antiochus but fought tenaciously for her own aspirations in Greece. The same held true for Achaea on the other side. Ineffectual in her contributions to the Roman cause, she proved most energetic in expanding her hegemony over the Peloponnese. Flamininus attempted to curb that expansion, but Rome allowed it to run its course. Minor states were swept up in the turmoil, hoping to avoid dismemberment and gain some measure of security, compelled to take a stand and swift to change sides when expediency and circumstances dictated. They lacked both reason and desire for commitment to the great powers.

Local affairs remained paramount, particularist considerations still occupied the center. To concentrate upon conflict between Rome and Macedonia or between Rome and Syria misses what was most significant to the Greeks. They exploited those larger conflicts—or suffered from them—in struggles for local power with their own neighbors.

258. On these treaties and their interpretation, see above pp. 25–38.

· *Chapter 14* ·

# Rome and Greece (II)

$R$oman involvement with mainland Greece over the next four decades, from 188 to 146 B.C., has left very imperfect traces. A few rays of
light emanate from the sources; most is left in darkness. Polybius survives only in fragments, Livy's interest in the East glows only during
the wars. Testimony on Roman-Greek relations resolves itself primarily into testimony on Roman-Achaean relations—and even there
the picture is far from complete. Nonetheless, it illuminates the subject in important and indispensable ways. Conventional assumptions
hold that Rome became ever more densely engaged in the affairs of
Hellas, her interests entrenched and augmented, her envoys manipulating, her senate deciding. A close study will cast grave doubts on
those assumptions and give cause for a different understanding. Circumstances in Achaea were, of course, not altogether typical. What
can be gleaned from them, however, coheres with other information
and supplies a touchstone for analysis.

## Rome and the Peloponnesian Imbroglio

The massacre of Spartans in the mêlée at Compasium in 188
had opened the way for forcible absorption of Lacedaemon into the
Achaean Confederacy. It had also given Philopoemen the pretext for
wiping out the Spartan constitution and restoring exiles, with all
the disruption and turmoil that entailed.[1] An embassy of Spartans
soon made its way to Rome with harsh words for the measures of

1. See above p. 474.

Philopoemen and with request for some Roman action to remedy the situation. The embassy made sure to play up to the senate, alleging that Philopoemen's settlement undermined the power and hegemony of Rome.[2] Philopoemen, near the end of his *strategia* in 189/8, caught wind of the Spartan mission and forthwith sent his own envoys to explain matters to the *patres*.[3] The delegations waited for some time. Roman senators were in no hurry to reply. As we have seen on several occasions, they could not easily be persuaded that the Republic's "power and hegemony" were compromised by events in the Peloponnese.[4] At last the Spartans wrested a message from Rome, a letter from the consul of 187, M. Lepidus, which offered a mild rebuke to Achaea: she had not acted properly with regard to Sparta.[5] The Achaean envoys reported that same reaction: senatorial displeasure at the pulling down of Sparta's walls and the murders of Compasium. What action would the *patres* take? None at all. They announced unwillingness to undo any arrangements already made.[6] The expression of displeasure constituted a sop to Spartan complainants. But the senate would not bestir itself to interfere.

The message from Rome reached Achaea during the *strategia* of Aristaenus in 188/7. It was not acted upon and did not need to be acted upon. The *strategos* simply shelved it.[7] Aristaenus, of course,

2. Polyb. 22.3.1: νομίσαντες ὑπὸ τοῦ Φιλοποίμενος ἅμα τὴν δύναμιν καὶ τὴν προστασίαν καταλελύσθαι τὴν Ῥωμαίων. No reason to emend the Ῥωμαίων to Λακεδαιμονίων. Precisely which Spartan group is here represented Polybius does not say. Perhaps the survivors of Compasium? So Errington, *Philopoemen*, 148–149. Or some of the restored exiles still dissatisfied with the new arrangements? So Shimron, *Late Sparta*, 107, 145–146. It is all guesswork and unprofitable to pursue.

3. That is the natural reading of Polyb. 22.3.4: ὧν πρεσβευόντων, εὐθέως ὁ Φιλοποίμην πρεσβευτὰς καταστήσας τοὺς περὶ Νικόδημον τὸν Ἠλεῖον ἐξέπεμψεν εἰς τὴν Ῥώμην; cf. 22.7.1. The chronology followed here is that cogently argued by Errington, *Philopoemen*, 255–261. The alternative reconstruction has Philopoemen dispatch his envoys in a *strategia* of 187/6 after return of the Spartan mission to the Peloponnese: Aymard, *Études*, 18–30; followed by most scholars; e.g. Castellani, *ContIstFilClass*, 1 (1963): 90; Lehmann, *Untersuchungen*, 262–263; Larsen, *Greek Federal States*, 449; Walbank, *Commentary* III:9, 177–178. This is difficult to square with Polybius' language. Division on the chronology, however, does not affect the main issues.

4. Delay in responding to the Spartans is clear from Polyb. 22.3.2: καὶ τέλος ἐξεπορίσαντο γράμματα. And Philopoemen's envoys did not return to Achaea until the following *strategia*, that of Aristaenus: Polyb. 22.7.1, 22.7.5.

5. Polyb. 22.3.3: φάσκων οὐχ ὀρθῶς αὐτοὺς κεχειρικέναι τὰ κατὰ τοὺς Λακεδαιμονίους.

6. Polyb. 22.7.6: ὅτι δυσαρεστοῦνται μὲν καὶ τῇ τῶν τειχῶν συντελέσει * καὶ τῇ καταλύσει * * * τῶν ἐν τῷ Κομπασίῳ διαφθαρέντων, οὐ μὴν ἄκυρόν τι ποιεῖν; Diod. 29.17. The letter of Lepidus and the message of the senate are normally taken as two separate acts. They may well be identical, the *patres*' official communiqué delivered under the name of its presiding consul.

7. Polyb. 22.7.7: οὐθενὸς δ' οὔτ' ἀντειπόντος οὔτε συνηγορήσαντος, οὕτω πως παρεπέμφθη.

had his differences with Philopoemen, especially on the issue of relations with Rome, the latter advocating a more independent Achaean
posture, the former a greater willingness to yield to Roman pressure.[8]
The senate, however, eschewed the application of pressure here.
Aristaenus was no less an Achaean patriot than Philopoemen, and no
less eager to advance the prestige and authority of the League.[9] The
strategos refrained from exploiting Rome's annoyance with Philopoemen's Spartan settlement. A readjustment of Lacedaemonian interests might weaken the League's control, a result that Aristaenus
would have found as unwelcome as would his rival.

Achaea, in fact, pursued a most vigorous and autonomous foreign policy in the strategia of Aristaenus, of which the Polybian fragments afford a rare glimpse. Representatives from no fewer than three
Hellenistic monarchs, Ptolemy, Eumenes, and Seleucus IV, appeared
before the League to renew alliance or φιλία, each with promise of
elaborate gifts. Hellenistic diplomacy is here in full swing, without the
merest hint that the western power even existed. The Achaeans conducted their deliberations in complete autonomy, with varying responses corresponding to various circumstances, both internal and
external. Φιλία with the Seleucid was renewed, though his offer of
ships was spurned, at least temporarily.[10] In the case of Egypt, negotiations had been undertaken the previous year by Philopoemen and
his appointees. When they returned to Achaea with Ptolemy's envoys, Aristaenus embarrassed them by pointing out that they had
not done their homework: a number of alliances existed between
the League and Egypt, negotiators had failed to observe their differences or to consider which alliance they were proposing to renew.
The strategos scored a point over his political rivals, though without
damaging relations to the Ptolemaic kingdom. The issue of renewing
the alliance was postponed until researchers could consult the ar-
chives.[11] A far harsher position was taken with regard to Eumenes.
His proposed gift of a handsome sum to be used in paying Achaeans
for attendance at their assemblies received a rude rejection. Achaeans
refused to be beholden to the Pergamene for an endowment that

---

8. The famous contrast appears in Polyb. 24.11–13, much discussed and debated; cf. Aymard, *Premiers rapports*, 391–394; Pédech, *La méthode*, 299–300; Lehmann,
*Untersuchungen*, 240–250; Errington, *Philopoemen*, 218–220; Deininger, *Widerstand*, 111–
115; Walbank, *Commentary* III:264–265. And see above pp. 331–333.

9. As Polybius makes clear, 24.13.8–9: ὅμως ἀμφότεροι διετήρησαν ἀκέραια τὰ
δίκαια τοῖς Ἀχαιοῖς πρὸς Ῥωμαίους. Cf. Aristaenus' remark in 198: Livy, 32.21.36; see
above pp. 445–446. The modern idea that each election of Aristaenus represents a defeat for Philopoemen and vice versa ignores Achaea's propensity for alternating her
leaders, thereby to maintain a balance of viewpoints.

10. Polyb. 22.7.4, 22.9.13; cf. Diod. 29.17.

11. Polyb. 22.3.5–6, 22.7.1–2, 22.9.1–12.

might place them in his dependence. Instead they turned the tables and asked him to relinquish his claims to the island of Aegina.[12] The League's fierce commitment to independence stands out boldly. Aristaenus might discomfit his political opponents by showing up their sloppy diplomacy, but he had as firm a stake as they in his nation's international position. Roman interests are conspicuous by their absence. The Achaeans had no compunction even about delivering a sharp insult to Eumenes, who had been Rome's chief ally and principal beneficiary in the recent war on Antiochus. Achaea flaunted her prestige in the world of Hellenistic diplomacy, a prestige acknowledged by the monarchs of the East.

The conclusion is reinforced when one examines an occasion on which Rome did exert some pressure. Flamininus, back in Rome since early 190, endeavored to keep his hand in the affairs of Hellas. His previous efforts in the Peloponnese having been thwarted by senatorial indifference, he could hope to apply a little more direct influence in Rome itself. Flamininus attempted now to maneuver the restoration to Boeotia of Zeuxippus, a man in exile since 196 for murder of a pro-Macedonian leader and a man for whose cause the Roman had expressed some interest at that juncture.[13] His efforts on Zeuxippus' behalf had borne no fruit for some time. The *patres* at last consented to write to Boeotia for recall of Zeuxippus and the exiled members of his party. Boeotia, interestingly and revealingly, balked at the request, feeling no obligation to accede to Roman wishes. Indeed, she reiterated the condemnation of Zeuxippus and dispatched a mission to Rome declaring that the judgments of her courts were binding.[14] The prospect of senatorial retaliation did not occur to the Boeotians— nor, for that matter, to the senate. Zeuxippus pleaded his cause in person before the *patres*, but they declined to take direct action. Instead, letters went out to the Achaeans and Aetolians, bidding them see to the exiles' restoration.[15] Aetolia's reaction is not recorded, but Achaea's is —and it tells a fascinating tale. The request came during the *strategia* of Philopoemen, whether in 189/8 or 187/6.[16] The *strategos*

12. Polyb. 22.7.3, 22.7.8–9, 22.8.1–13; Diod. 29.17. Whether the alliance was renewed is uncertain. The hostile Achaean reply would seem to be against it. But Polybius' language points in the other direction; 22.7.8: οἱ παρ᾽ Εὐμένους πρέσβεις καὶ τήν τε συμμαχίαν τὴν πατρικὴν ἀνενεώσαντο.

13. Polyb. 18.43; Livy, 33.27–29; see above pp. 449–450.

14. Polyb. 22.4.4–8. Note, especially, 22.4.8: ταῦτα δὲ διοικήσαντες οὐκέτι προσεῖχον τοῖς γραφομένοις.

15. Polyb. 22.4.9.

16. Polybius, 22.4.1, puts it after the treaty of Apamea, which occurred in spring, 188. Hence, a suggestion that the events took place in the Achaean year 189/8. And the fragment sits between one which refers to Compasium in 189/8 and a later one which

behaved shrewdly and with circumspection. A request from Flamininus was one thing, a letter from the senate quite another. Philopoemen made a show of formal compliance as courtesy to Achaea's western ally. League representatives went to Boeotia to ask for Zeuxippus' recall. They deliberately refrained from carrying out the recall themselves. Instead, Philopoemen seized the occasion to further his own state's aims and demand settlement of property disputes outstanding between citizens of the two leagues. When Boeotia proved recalcitrant, Philopoemen forced the issue by having Achaean claimants appropriate property in Boeotia, an action that led to violence and hostility, until arbitration, evidently by the Megarians, brought a resolution.[17] In the course of all this, a request to restore Zeuxippus simply got lost in the shuffle. The senate did not care enough to follow up its own letter. Boeotia got away with defiance, Achaea with a token gesture swiftly converted into a maneuver that advanced her private interests. The *patres* were willing to indulge Flamininus' whims, but stopped short of enforcing them: they were not a matter of state policy.[18]

Sparta, however, remained an open sore in the Confederacy. The senate had announced its dissatisfaction with the situation two years before, upon importuning by Spartan envoys. There the matter rested, since Rome asked for no changes and Achaea made none. Social and political divisions within Sparta became increasingly troublesome as a consequence. In summer, 185, a Roman embassy to Macedonia, headed by Q. Metellus, stopped in Achaea on its way home. A meeting of League magistrates was called by Aristaenus, *strategos* in 186/5, as courtesy to the Romans. Metellus repeated the senatorial line, by now a worn refrain. He criticized Achaea for excessive severity and harshness toward the Lacedaemonians, and added further remarks calling upon Achaea to remedy her previous misbehavior.[19] Does that reflect sharpening of the senate's position, or impromptu blustering by the legate? The latter is almost certainly right. Metellus

alludes to Aristaenus' *strategia*, evidently in 188/7: Polyb. 22.3, 22.7. But the order of the fragments is not secure. The first, in any case, records not just the Spartan embassy of 189/8 but also the letter of Lepidus which came in 187. Moreover, though Polybius puts the affair after Apamea, his account indicates that much had transpired since then: 22.4.1–9. Hence, a date in 187/6 remains possible.

17. Polyb. 22.4.10–17. *Lacunae* in Polybius' text make the role of the Megarians unclear, whether as parties to the dispute or as arbiters. The latter, however, seems more probable, in view of *IG*, VII, 21; cf. Asheri, *StudClassOrient* 18 (1969): 61–62.

18. Philopoemen no doubt took special pleasure in again frustrating one of Flamininus' designs. It was probably in this *strategia* also that he altered arrangements involved in Messenia's incorporation into the League, arrangements that had been made by Flamininus in 191: Polyb. 22.10.6; cf. Livy, 36.31.1–9.

19. Polyb. 22.10.1–2: παρεκάλει διὰ πλειόνων διορθώσασθαι τὴν προγεγενημένην ἄγνοιαν.

carried no senatorial instructions on Achaea, his visit a mere stopover after his main business in Macedonia.[20] He placed his own interpretation upon the *patres'* previous stance and extended it.

The remarks produced consternation and sparked political wrangling. Aristaenus kept silence. Although twice *strategos* since Rome's initial expression of rebuke, he had made not a move toward altering the Spartan arrangements.[21] Diophanes, however, saw an opening for political advantage. Much as he had done in 188, he sought to capitalize on the Roman position by discrediting Philopoemen, criticizing not only his Spartan settlement but his tampering with Flamininus' arrangements on Messene.[22] Metellus, hitherto engaged in an unofficial parley, now felt emboldened to ask for a formal Achaean assembly before which the whole issue could be protested. The League's magistrates drew the line at that request. Philopoemen and others of his faction defended their activities with vigor and refused to call an assembly, since Metellus had no written mandate from the senate. That bold front terminated proceedings. The Roman legate withdrew in a huff.[23]

Here, if ever, there were grounds for Roman retaliation, should the senate desire retaliation. Metellus returned home with acrimonious complaints about his treatment in Achaea. A delegation of Spartans appeared in Rome as well, headed by Areus and Alcibiades, representatives of the old exiles who had been restored by Philopoemen but disappointed in their hopes of reviving prestige for the city. They denounced the Achaean settlement for its emasculation of Sparta, its expulsion of much of the populace, and its authoritarian control. Those accusations made a mockery of the Achaean. claim, also expressed to the *patres* in winter 185/4, that Philopoemen's arrangements for Sparta were the best things that ever happened to the city.[24] Rome had ample pretexts for intervention. But intervention found no advocates among the *patres*. Their reply indeed was remarkably mod-

20. Polyb. 22.10.1, 22.10.11; cf. Paus. 7.9.1.

21. Polybius, 22.10.3, interprets Aristaenus' silence as assent to the statements of Metellus, a questionable interpretation. Rightly doubted by Errington, *Philopoemen*, 167–171, though he goes too far in his condemnation of Polybius for swallowing Philopoemenist propaganda. Suspicions about Aristaenus' real feelings were current at the time, however unfounded they may have been: cf. Polyb. 22.10.14–15, 24.13.10. The Polybian interpretation is accepted unhesitatingly by Castellani, *op. cit.*, 91–93, Lehmann, *Untersuchungen*, 263–265, and Deininger, *Widerstand*, 121–122.

22. Polyb. 22.10.4–6.

23. Polyb. 22.10.7–13; Paus. 7.9.1; Livy, 39.33.5.

24. Polyb. 22.11.1, 22.11.4–22.12.3; Paus. 7.9.1–2; Livy, 39.33.6–7. Shimron, *Late Sparta*, 107–108, 139–140, argues that the mission of Areus and Alcibiades represents the official Spartan government and thus implies an upheaval in 185 which put them in power; accepted by Walbank, *Commentary* III: 196.

erate and noncommittal. Another embassy would be sent to look into
Lacedaemonian affairs; as for the Achaeans, they should be polite to
Roman envoys, giving them the same courtesies that Rome extends
to foreign diplomats.[25] Metellus had got little satisfaction, his feathers
no doubt still ruffled. The senate was not bound by the behavior and
reports of its legates.

Achaean leadership had thus far felt itself in no important way
circumscribed by Roman opinion. In fact, Philopoemen's lieutenant
Lycortas, now *strategos* in 185/4, mobilized the League's machinery to
exact vengeance against the ungrateful Spartans Areus and Alcibiades. A motion of Lycortas, adopted by the Confederacy, condemned
them to death, a decision taken despite—indeed because of—their
mission to Rome. The Achaeans' trust in Roman indifference could
hardly receive clearer expression.[26] This time, however, patriotic passion had exceeded prudence. The Roman delegation, with Ap. Claudius Pulcher at its head, soon arrived in Achaea in 184. Its primary
purpose, like that of its predecessor under Metellus, had been to investigate the situation in Macedonia. The Achaean trip was again only a
side issue. But the senate had made certain to give Appius written
instructions, to avoid the previous embarrassment. Appius further
had in tow the two Spartan complainants Areus and Alcibiades, convicted traitors but now sheltered under the legate's authority.[27]

Ap. Claudius delivered the senate's communiqué. Its character
demands notice: not a jot different from the stance taken by the *patres*
for the past four years. They deplored the slaughter at Compasium
and criticized the measures taken by Achaea in coercing the Spartans and obliterating the Lacedaemonian constitution.[28] Lycortas responded in a long and rhetorical speech. The authenticity of its ver-
biage as given by Livy must, of course, remain in doubt. In essence,
according to the Livian version, Lycortas challenged all allegations,
blamed Spartan exiles for Compasium, justified the institutional
changes, and questioned Rome's *locus standi* in the dispute.[29] Re-
sounding applause greeted the discourse, a noble reaffirmation of

---

25. Polyb. 22.12.4, 22.12.9–10: τοῖς δὲ πρεσβευταῖς τοῖς αἰεὶ παρ᾽ ἑαυτῶν ἐκπεμ-
πομένοις παρῄνει προσέχειν τὸν νοῦν καὶ καταδοχὴν, ποιεῖσθαι τὴν ἁρμόζουσαν, καθάπερ καὶ Ῥωμαῖοι ποιοῦνται τῶν παραγινομένων πρὸς αὐτοὺς πρεσβευτῶν. The pronouncement is enlarged and distorted by Livy, 39.33.8: *ostendit senatus curae iis esse
debere, ut legatis Romanis semper adeundi concilium gentis potestas fieret, quem ad modum et
illis quotiens vellent senatus daretur.*

26. Polyb. 22.11.8; Livy, 39.35.5–8; Paus. 7.9.2.

27. Livy, 39.35.8–39.36.2; Paus. 7.9.3.

28. Livy, 39.36.3–4.

29. Livy, 39.36.6–39.37.17. Authenticity of the speech defended by Lehmann,
*Untersuchungen,* 278–279; questioned by Errington, *Philopoemen,* 177.

Achaean autonomy. Appius then struck back with firmness: he counseled the Achaeans to respond to Roman wishes voluntarily, lest they be compelled to do so against their will.[30] The assembly now feared the consequences of refusal, lifted the condemnation on Areus and Alcibiades, and begged only that the Romans not involve them in violation of their own oaths.[31]

Does the episode disclose a hardening of Roman attitude and a determination to force compliance upon the League? On the surface Livy's account might imply it. Yet, quite apart from the question of how far his language preserves accurate detail, a closer look leads to a different conclusion. The behavior of legates and the sentiments of the senate, as we have seen on many occasions, do not necessarily coincide. This instance is exemplary. Appius' conveyance of the senate's message shows it to be unchanged from resolutions uttered during the past four years. The *patres* complained of Achaean actions but insisted on no remedy. Indeed Appius did not go so far even as his predecessor Metellus, who had asked Achaea to rectify the situation. It was only after Lycortas delivered an unbending speech, admitting no errors and challenging Rome's right to exercise judgment, that Appius retorted with sudden vigor. The scion of the noble Claudii held his *dignitas* no less dear than Q. Metellus. A supposition of senatorial instructions behind his response is entirely unnecessary and implausible. Livy himself makes clear that the response was impromptu, provoked by the immediate situation: Lycortas' speech had been hailed by the Achaeans; Appius could save face only by a stiff reply.[32] Further, although the assembly rescinded its capital conviction of Areus and Alcibiades and consented to have the Spartan situation adjudicated in Rome, it entered a critical proviso: that no action be taken in violation of Achaean oaths. If that proviso was adhered to, the main props of the League's settlement stood firm. For all the arrangements made in the incorporation of Sparta had been enshrined on written records and sanctified by sacred oaths.[33] The Achaeans wisely refrained from any further provocation of Ap. Claudius. But they had created a large loophole with which to defend their case in Rome. As they knew from repeated experience, the badgering of Roman legates and the attitude of the Roman senate were two quite different things.

30. Livy, 39.37.18–19: *ut, dum liceret voluntate sua facere, gratiam inirent, ne mox inviti et coacti facerent*; Paus. 7.9.4.

31. Livy, 39.37.20–21; cf. Paus. 7.9.4.

32. Livy, 39.37.18: *cum adsensu maximae partis est auditus, et locutum omnes pro maiestate magistratus censebant, ut facile appareret molliter agendo dignitatem suam tenere Romanos non posse.* Nothing here supports the contention of Errington, *Philopoemen*, 177–178, that Appius expressed the dictates of a patron to his clients.

33. Livy, 39.37.16, 39.37.21.

Appius' bullying and Achaea's ostensible compliance gave heart to Spartans of every political background and faction. It appeared that Rome might at last render a decision that could take matters out of the hands of the Acheans. A veritable flood of Spartan delegations poured into Rome in winter 184/3, four separate groups with four separate and conflicting goals. Achaea had sent her own representatives to observe events and protect the League's interest. A certain Lysis headed one Lacedaemonian embassy, expounding the claims of old exiles to full restoration of their property. Areus and Alcibiades were there as well, "old exiles" too, but seeking restitution only to the value of a talent, the rest of the property to be distributed to those "worthy of citizenship." The demand recalls a scheme of Cleomenes III, an equitable division of *kleroi* designed to revive Spartan nationalist aspirations, consonant with the aims expressed by Areus and Alcibiades in the previous year. A third group had as spokesman Serippus, content with circumstances as they were when Sparta entered the Confederacy, either in 192 or in 188, the beneficiaries of Philopoemen's measures. A last faction, that of Chaeron, representing those banished or condemned to death after Achaea's forcible annexation of the city in 188, insisted on recall of the exiles and reenactment of the old Spartan system.[34] The *patres*, who had paid but scant attention to the intricacies of Peloponnesian politics, must have found their patience strained to the breaking point. Indeed, they would not even consider passing judgments on issues outside their interests and unworthy of detailed scrutiny. The whole matter was dropped in the lap of the three Romans who had been to the Peloponnese in recent years: Flamininus, Metellus, and Ap. Claudius. The move, as we have seen earlier, does not imply senatorial reliance on a panel of "experts." Flamininus' prior meddlings in the Peloponnese had made little impact on the *patres*; Metellus' sole visit to the area had earned only a rebuff; and Appius had contributed no new ideas or policy on the issues at stake. In turning the dispute over to these three, the senate merely expressed its own detachment. If Flamininus, Metellus, and Appius had any axes to grind, let them hear the clamorous disputants themselves.[35]

The three commissioners labored mightily to reach a compromise solution. All parties could not, of course, be satisfied. But an effort was made, it seems, to effect some balance between the Spartan

---

34. Polyb. 23.1.6, 23.4.1–6, 23.4.11–12; Paus. 7.9.4–5; Livy, 39.48.2–3. A sensible presentation in Errington, *Philopoemen*, 179–181. Shimron's complicated analysis of Spartan parties, distributed in various parts of his book, renders understanding difficult; *Late Sparta*, 108–109, 113–116, 138–139, 146–150. Cf. now Walbank, *Commentary* III:216–219.

35. Polyb. 23.4.7. Pausanias, 7.9.5, erroneously has the Roman commissioners sent to Greece.

desire for self-esteem and Achaea's claims on hegemony. The arbiters decreed recall of those exiled and convicted in 188, thus increasing the citizenry, and the reconstruction of the walls which would cater to Lacedaemonian civic pride. On the other hand, the city was to remain part of the Achaean Confederacy. To ease concern about actions like the Achaean condemnation of Areus and Alcibiades, capital cases were henceforth to be heard by outside arbiters, though all other jurisdiction would remain in the League's hands. The property issue proved to be the stickiest of all, the commissioners unable to agree on a formula.[36] Rather than prolong the wrangling, they preferred to have the disputants sign their approval to the clauses agreed upon. The Achaean representatives also added their signatures. Displeased with the recall of exiles which, among other things, was at variance with the oaths they had sworn, the Achaeans nevertheless felt most relieved on the main point: that Sparta would remain under federal authority.[37]

None of this marks any notable change in Roman attitude toward the Peloponnese. The senate had declined responsibility as a body, resigning matters to its appointees. The compromise they reached, while equitable on the surface, was awkward and cumbersome, leaving ample grounds for further quarrels. Recall of exiles could heighten rather than resolve factional struggles, especially as property claims remained unsettled. Tension continued between the Spartan pull for independence and the recognition of Achaean suzerainty. Rome had established no interests in the Peloponnese and had staked out no claims as a patron state. She had consented to arbitrate, in a fashion familiar to Hellenistic diplomacy. Implementation of the agreement would be left to the Peloponnesians themselves.

No decision by a judicial board could hope to dissolve the complex factional and social strife in Sparta, bedeviled further by the city's tumultuous relationship with Achaea. It is unlikely that any Romans, even the three commissioners, expected that it might. The stubborn Lacedaemonian problem simply would not go away. In the immediately subsequent years it arose again in various bewildering ways unfathomable in detail because of the fragmentary character of our

36. Recall of exiles, retention of Sparta within the League, and an impasse on the property dispute given by Polyb. 23.4.8–9; cf. Livy, 39.48.4. Pausanias, 7.9.5, adds the rebuilding of Spartan walls and the measures on jurisdiction. Errington, *Philopoemen*, 181–182, sees these decisions as largely the work of Flamininus. In fact, the Spartans who had hopes in Flamininus were the "old exiles"; Polyb. 23.5.18. Yet their representatives, Areus and Alcibiades on the one hand and Lysis on the other, got nothing concrete out of the settlement. It was precisely their demands, on the issue of property, which found the commissioners at odds with one another.

37. Polyb. 23.4.10–15.

evidence. Spartan parties resumed their quarrels, groups were exiled or reexiled, embassies came and went, Achaean politicians clashed with one another over the Lacedaemonian question. Through it all, Romans were irritated, baffled, embarrassed, and frustrated. Nowhere, however, can one discern even the outlines of a Roman "policy" on the Peloponnese: one was never formulated.

After the arbitral judgment of 184/3, the senate dispatched Q. Marcius Philippus as legate to Macedonia, with a request that he also look in on the Peloponnese.[38] If anything was said there about the Spartan issue we do not hear of it. Polybius' narrative of the embassy is missing and Livy did not care to record it.[39] Dissatisfaction in Sparta, however, was still rife. Serippus' party held authority in the city and Chaeron's group may have been restored in accordance with the commissioners' ruling. But the "old exiles" found themselves out in the cold. They hoped for backing from Flamininus, who stopped in Naupactus in the course of his journey to Bithynia in 183. Flamininus, however, lacked a mandate from the senate to interfere in the Peloponnese. When he asked the Achaeans to call an assembly, he received a direct rebuff, engineered by Philopoemen, *strategos* for 183/2: the League would not obey the behests of individual Romans without official standing. Flamininus dropped the matter, having been burned too often before. The "old exiles" suffered disappointment. Flamininus tacitly acknowledged that, on this issue, as on others, he could not rely on senatorial enforcement of his private meddling.[40]

The "old exiles," with little hope of persuading Achaea to their view, tried Rome once again. Their representatives appeared before the senate in winter, 183/2. In opposition came an embassy from Sparta, headed by Serippus.[41] The exasperation of the *patres*, who felt that they had washed their hands of these vexatious envoys, rings forth in their reply: they had done all they could for the Spartans; the matter is no longer of interest to them.[42] The envoys themselves were

38. Polyb. 23.4.16; Livy, 39.48.5.

39. The main item of discussion, in any case, was the Messenian revolt; see below p. 494.

40. Polyb. 23.5.14–18. It is normally assumed that the "old exiles" had recently been exiled again by the new parties in power at Sparta, some time between the commissioners' decision in winter 184/3 and Flamininus' arrival in Greece ca. autumn 183; e.g. Lehmann, *Untersuchungen*, 280–281, n. 285; Larsen, *Greek Federal States*, 454; Errington, *Philopoemen*, 187–188, 288–289; Walbank, *Commentary* III:223. Shimron, *Late Sparta*, 146–148, offers the more economical interpretation that they had been in exile for some time and were so when they conducted embassies to Rome in 184/3.

41. Polyb. 23.6.1–3, 23.9.1, 23.9.11.

42. Polyb. 23.9.11: διότι πάντα πεποιήκασιν αὐτοῖς τὰ δυνατά, κατὰ δὲ τὸ παρὸν οὐ νομίζουσιν εἶναι τοῦτο τὸ πρᾶγμα πρὸς αὐτούς. The additional phrase, βουλόμενοι μετέωρον ἐᾶσαι τὴν πόλιν, is Polybius' editorializing.

temporarily detained in Rome, as the senate wished to await the outcome of the Messenian revolt.[43] Lack of interest in Spartan affairs,
however, had been unambiguously declared.[44]

That attitude reinforced and reconfirmed the position of Achaean
patriots, in particular the Philopoemenist party. Its implications, when
once recognized, are quite striking. The judgments of the three Roman
commissioners in 184/3 had supplied guidelines for a Spartan settlement. How far would the senate itself go in implementing those
guidelines? Nowhere at all. That was its message to the Spartan delegations of 183/2—and that is how the message was read in Achaea.
Once the League had stamped out Messenia's rebellion in 182, attention turned to the Spartan issue once more. The *strategos* Lycortas
brandished before an assemblage at Sicyon the Roman disclaimer of
interest in Spartan affairs. He now felt free to propose incorporation
of the city on new terms.[45] This may or may not imply that Sparta had
seceded in the interim, perhaps during the Messenian revolt.[46] More
to the point, Lycortas urged a settlement in complete disregard of the
Roman commission's pronouncement of two years earlier. Dispute
arose between Lycortas and Diophanes, a typical wrangle among the
League's leadership. But neither one made reference to the Roman
decision. Lycortas insisted on retention of the party presently in
power at Sparta and exclusion of the "old exiles" who had dishonored
themselves by their ingratitude toward the Confederacy. Diophanes
took the part of the exiles, arguing for their recall as a sign of conciliation and concord. A compromise ultimately took effect: some but not
all the exiles would be restored, those unsoiled by the stain of ingratitude. On that basis a fresh document was drawn up, inscribed on
stone and marking the conditions of Sparta's membership in the federal union.[47] The meaning of this deserves reiteration. However con-
scientious Flamininus, Metellus, and Ap. Claudius had been in seek-

43. Polyb. 23.9.14; see below pp. 494–496.

44. Castellani, *op. cit.*, 101, finds the senate's reply "assolutamente priva di lo-
gicità," which means simply that she cannot reconcile it with her own reconstruction of senatorial attitudes. In fact, as we have seen, it is quite consistent with prior
pronouncements.

45. Polyb. 23.17.5–9. This occurred either near the end of the Achaean year
183/2, during which Lycortas had succeeded Philopoemen after the latter's death: Plut.
*Phil.* 21.1; or early in 182/1 when Lycortas had perhaps been elected for a full year;
cf. Polyb. 24.6.3–5. For discussions of the chronology, see Aymard, *Études*, 39–42; Errington, *Philopoemen*, 263.

46. So Errington, in a speculative discussion; *Philopoemen*, 196, 288–291; accepted by Walbank, *Commentary* III:251; questioned by Derow, *Essays Presented to C. M.
Bowra* (Oxford, 1970), 15, n. 1.

47. Polyb. 23.17.5–23.18.2.

ing a solution for the manifold Peloponnesian problems in 184/3, the *patres* showed not the slightest intention of seeing to its implementation. Achaean envoys had affixed their seals to the protocols produced by the commission, a prudent move at the time, but the League could wait on events. Now, armed with attestation of senatorial indifference, the Achaeans ignored that prior settlement, imposed their own, and displayed it for all to see.

The senate reacted with perfect consistency. Achaea took the precaution of sending an envoy, Bippus of Argos, to inform the Romans of her decision.[48] Representatives also went from the Spartans in power; and still another from the exiles, a last hope that they might yet get some expression of Roman favor.[49] That much they did get, in a familiar and well-worn form. The senate promised a letter to the Achaeans asking for restoration of the exiles.[50] It was a standard formality. A similar letter had been sent in 187, ignored with impunity, and reiteration of the message by Roman legates in the meanwhile had produced little effect. On those previous occasions the requests had been coupled with rebuke of Achaea for maltreatment of the Spartans. This time the *patres* avoided the unnecessary embarrassment of having their criticism as well as their suggestions disregarded. They simply voiced no criticism. All the envoys of whatever faction received courteous welcome and departed without any censure.[51] The envoys made what they could of the senate's letter, bringing it to the attention of the League and asking for its implementation. When Achaea's own delegate Bippus returned from Rome, however, he reminded his fellow citizens of the realities: the letter derived not from any senatorial interest in the exiles but merely from desire to quiet their pleas.[52] The lesson was well learned. Achaea held to her own settlement without change.[53]

The rebellion of Messenia occurred during these same years. The struggle between federalism and particularism in the Peloponnese supplies a fundamental element of continuity, characteristic of

48. Polyb. 23.18.3. Note the phrase διασαφήσοντας τῇ συγκλήτῳ περὶ πάντων: the mission would inform the senate, not ask its approval.

49. Polyb. 23.18.4–5.

50. Polyb. 24.1.5; Livy, 40.20.2.

51. Polyb. 24.1.4–7: οὐδὲν ἐπετίμησε περὶ τῶν γεγονότων . . . οὐθενὶ δυσαρεστήσασα περὶ τῶν οἰκονουμένων ἡ σύγκλητος ἀπεδέξατο φιλανθρώπως τοὺς πρεσβευτάς.

52. Polyb. 24.2.1, 24.2.4: οὐ διὰ τὴν τῆς συγκλήτου σπουδήν, ἀλλὰ διὰ τὴν τῶν φυγάδων φιλοτιμίαν. Errington, *Philopoemen*, 200, remarkably, considers this as "Achaean misrepresentation of the senate's attitude."

53. Polyb. 24.2.5.

the Hellenistic age and unaltered by the Republic across the water. Evidence on the rebellion further demonstrates and substantiates the pattern already discerned.

The Messenian leader Deinocrates traveled to Rome in 183 in hopes of garnering senatorial support for a proposed secession. Upon learning that Flamininus had been appointed a legate to Asia, Deinocrates abandoned his plan of visiting the senate and pinned his hopes on the legate, with whom he had earlier established a close association. It was largely on Deinocrates' importuning that Flamininus ventured to call an Achaean assembly. But, as noted above, the absence of official instructions deprived him of any standing. The League refused him, and Flamininus went off to Asia.[54] Failure to obtain Roman endorsement notwithstanding, the Messenians burst into revolt some time in 183.[55] In the course of it, Rome's envoy to Macedonia, Q. Marcius Philippus, arrived in the Peloponnese. Nothing suggests that he had specific orders from home to intervene in the dispute. In the tradition of Roman legates in the Peloponnese, Philippus issued some impromptu advice: the Achaeans should not take action against Messene without first consulting Rome.[56] His advice received no consideration at all. The League regarded itself sovereign over constituent members, overrode Philippus' suggestion, and declared war on Messene.[57]

The sequel is enlightening. Philippus' indignant complaints upon his return to Rome get most attention from scholars. More interesting, however, is the Achaean mission to Italy, probably in late 183. Far from offering apologies for their rudeness to Philippus, they came to request Roman assistance against the Messenians, in accordance with their treaty, or, at least, a guarantee that no arms or supplies reach the rebels from Italy.[58] Experience had already taught them some facts of Roman political life. Ignoring the requests of a legate required no apology. Only the senate counted. Achaea could unashamedly seek military aid without a word about Philippus. A plethora of embassies had crowded into Rome at this time, two of them from Sparta, as well as envoys from Eumenes, Pharnaces, Philip, and Rhodes. The senate was besieged with requests.[59] Philippus delivered his report, laced with ire: the Achaeans were overblown with self-importance, heeded no Roman advice, and wished to handle all mat-

---

54. Polyb. 23.5.1–3, 23.5.13–18; cf. Plut. *Flam.* 17.3.
55. Plut. *Phil.* 18.3; Livy, 39.48.5.
56. Polyb. 24.9.12; cf. 23.9.8.
57. Polyb. 24.9.13.        58. Polyb. 23.9.12.
59. Polyb. 23.9.1–2.

ters themselves. He recommended that the senate turn down their application and let matters take their course. Sparta, he predicted, would soon join Messene in revolt, and then the Achaeans would truly come begging to Rome.[60] The senate took his advice and gave brusque reply to the League's envoys: no help would be applied and, so far as the *patres* were concerned, they did not care if Sparta, Corinth, or Argos abandoned the Confederacy.[61] To take this as open invitation, indeed encouragement, of rebellion is a serious misreading. The pronouncement must be viewed in context. The senators had just delivered their impatient reply to Sparta's envoys, declaring that the Spartan situation was of no concern to them. Their outburst to the Achaeans has the identical quality. They were fed up with Peloponnesian requests and would take no action even if every state in the League seceded.[62]

Achaea proceeded to take on the rebels herself. The campaign issued in the capture and death of Philopoemen, but Lycortas secured command in his stead and brought the Messenians to surrender in summer, 182.[63] Messene was once again annexed to the League and certain towns detached from her authority, though she was granted a three-year exemption from taxes to help economic recovery. Achaean suzerainty had been dramatically reasserted.[64] Characteristically enough, the senate had stayed entirely aloof. It had kept the Peloponnesian envoys in Rome, awaiting the outcome of the conflict, so as to strike the correct posture when it was over. And find it the *patres* did. Once news came of the Achaean victory, they proclaimed that they had lived up to their treaty and had permitted no materials to go to the rebels. It was a face-saving device. Had results gone the other way, they would no doubt have stressed their refusal to aid Achaea.[65] When Bippus arrived in Rome to announce the

60. Polyb. 23.9.8–10.

61. Polyb. 23.9.13.

62. Polybius' assertion, 23.9.14, that the senate gave full publicity to this reply is questionable. In fact, they detained the envoys, thus leaving open an opportunity to backtrack later. Briscoe, *JRS* 54 (1964): 66–67, overinterprets in finding here a senatorial "policy of ambiguity and deception."

63. Polyb. 23.12.1–3, 23.16; Plut. *Phil.* 18–21; Livy, 39.49–50; Paus. 4.29.11–12, 8.51.5–8; Justin, 32.1.4–10. On the chronology, see Aymard, *Études*, 31–39; Errington, *Philopoemen*, 241–245; Walbank, *Commentary* III:235–239; *contra*: Hoffman, *Hermes* 73 (1938): 244–248; Lehmann, *Untersuchungen*, 184–185, n. 77.

64. Polyb. 23.17.1–2, 24.2.3; cf. 24.9.13.

65. Polyb. 23.17.3. Polybius' addition, 23.17.4, that this pronouncement showed Rome's displeasure if all foreign matters did not proceed according to her wishes, is quite irrelevant in the context. Even if it is an accurate reading of private feelings, it corresponds to none of her public actions.

Messenian as well as the Spartan settlement, he received every courtesy.[66] Achaea had established firm control in the Peloponnese. The senate raised no objections.

## Politics and Policies in Achaea

Subsequent change came not through Roman initiative but through the vagaries of Achaean politics. The successes of the Philopoemenist faction, as represented now by Lycortas, the young Polybius, and others, caused discomfort to their internal opponents for whom there was little room left to maneuver. They clutched at what opportunities they could to embarrass their rivals and stake out a position of their own. The clamor of those Spartan exiles who were still excluded offered a possibility for patronage of persons shunned by the Philopoemenists, as did the plight of Messenians banished from their homeland in consequence of the revolt. Diophanes had taken up the cause of the former with only mixed results, and the issue could still be exploited. Rome's ambiguity, a source of continual frustration and bewilderment, also left an opening for politicians who struggled to make it work for their own advantage.

The senate's letter of 182/1, requesting recall of Lacedaemonian exiles, had been recognized by Lycortas' party for what it was: a gesture to satisfy appellants rather than an insistence upon implementation. Nonetheless, that letter provided ammunition for political foes of Lycortas. One of them, Hyperbatus, gained election to the *strategia* of 181/0, in accord with typical Achaean practice of rotating rival leaders in the highest office. In the course of his year Hyperbatus raised once more the matter of Spartan exiles, pointing to the Roman communiqué as justification.[67] Lycortas, of course, objected. He plumped for the status quo, which meant, in short, continuation of his own Lacedaemonian settlement, and argued with legitimacy that the senate was in the habit of endorsing requests while declining to enforce them upon its friends.[68] That statement, however self-serving, was

66. Polyb. 24.1.6–7.

67. Polyb. 24.8.1; cf. 24.1.5, 24.2.1. There is no good reason to suppose that this refers to a second senatorial message in response to another Spartan mission in the meantime. The νῦν δὲ πάλιν of Polyb. 24.9.14 simply picks up the πρῴην μὲν of 24.9.12; *contra*: Walbank, *Commentary* III:18–19, 260–261. Nor should Hyperbatus' election be adjudged a triumph for the "pro-Roman" party in Achaea. The electorate made a habit of alternating leaders with differing viewpoints, as we have seen. And Hyperbatus seized on the Roman letter primarily to institute a new Spartan settlement for which his group would gain the credit.

68. Polyb. 24.8.2–5.

an accurate characterization of Roman behavior. But behavior did not settle the matter. The contrast between pronouncement and performance that had confused Greeks for so long still allowed contending leaders to fasten on what suited them best. Lycortas stood on the Republic's action (or inaction), Hyperbatus on its words. The internal struggle in Achaea both foundered on the contrast and capitalized upon it.

A new Achaean embassy headed for Rome in 180, perhaps the most notorious of all her embassies. Callicrates was its spokesman, a political associate of Hyperbatus. The mission, so much discussed and debated in modern works, needs no lengthy rehearsal here. Polybius reckoned it a watershed in the history of Roman-Greek relations. Callicrates berated the Romans for turning a blind eye to Hellenic intransigence: so long as the senate stood idle while Greeks treated communications with disdain and flouted recommendations, the friends of Rome would continue to be scorned by the populace and her enemies to enjoy power and prestige. The party of Hyperbatus and Callicrates, so Polybius avers, advocated the subordination of Achaean oaths, laws, compacts, and all else to the will of Rome. The historian then delivers a withering analysis: Rome at last woke up to reality, gave Callicrates a ringing endorsement, and thereafter promoted sycophants while undermining those who might have been her true friends.[69] Does this, in fact, mark the critical turning point toward Roman dictation of Hellenic affairs?[70]

Polybius' reconstruction is far from definitive. Callicrates was the prime opponent of his father Lycortas and the man responsible for Polybius' own banishment in 167. The historian's account, hardly a detached one, contains incongruities and contradictions not readily resolvable. To take but the most glaring: the assertion that anti-Roman politicians rule the roost in Achaea while Rome's friends are humiliated and disgraced. That is flatly contradicted by Hyperbatus' own *strategia* and by Callicrates' very presence as spokesman for the legation.[71] Polybius peered through spectacles ground after 167, or, indeed, after 146. The lamentable fate of Greece he viewed in a broad

69. Polyb. 24.8.6–24.10.10.

70. So it is almost always understood; e.g., Stier, *Roms Aufstieg*, 179–184; Badian, *Foreign Clientelae*, 89–91; Castellani, *op. cit.*, 105–108; Lehmann, *Untersuchungen*, 289–296; Errington, *Philopoemen*, 200–205; Derow, *Essays to Bowra*, 18–23; Deininger, *Widerstand*, 136–143, 199–202. Laudably more cautious is Larsen, *Greek Federal States*, 459–460; cf. Walbank, *Commentary* III: 262–263.

71. Polybius' effort to wriggle out of this by claiming that the mission was sent to propound Lycortas' view and that Callicrates betrayed his instructions only shows the historian's discomfiture: Polyb. 24.8.7–9. For other contradictions and distortions, see Gruen, *AJAH* 1 (1976): 32–33.

perspective. And he found it equally attractive to fix a large responsibility upon his enemy Callicrates. The result is a twisted portrait, not only of Callicrates but of the circumstances that prevailed in 180. Modern arguments about the meaning of the embassy largely miss the point. They debate the merits of Callicrates' motives and achievements: either a traitor to Achaean nationalist aspirations and a Roman toady or a far-sighted statesman who recognized the inevitability of the Republic's hegemony in Greece.[72] It is not the future, however, but the past that needs emphasis. The embassy of 180 can be understood only in the context of contemporary Achaean politics and in the light of Rome's record of ambiguity.

Callicrates' endeavors are little different from those occasionally attempted before by men like Diophanes and Aristaenus—to seize on Roman pronouncements for a sanction of policies that could outmaneuver political rivals at home. However tendentious his speech to the senate (or Polybius' report of it), the substance contained some important truths. Roman advice, suggestions, requests, and directives had been regularly set aside by Achaean leaders, and the Republic had been singularly lax in seeing to the fulfillment of its wishes. Callicrates asked only that Rome close that enfuriating gap between words and actions that had so long confused and befuddled Peloponnesian affairs.[73] The appeal is couched in the most general terms, but Callicrates had some specific objectives in mind: restoration of Spartan and Messenian exiles, grievances of a conventional sort, which, if set right, would be sore embarrassment for the Philopoemenists.[74] Here was Achaean politics as usual.

The response of Rome and its consequences deserve closer scrutiny than they have usually received. The *patres* gave Callicrates an enthusiastic send off, wrote once more to Achaea asking for recall of exiles, advocated their cause in letters to other Greek peoples as well, the Aetolians, Epirotes, Athenians, Boeotians, and Acarnanians, and expressed a desire to see more men like Callicrates in Hellas. Callicrates himself subsequently won election to the *strategia* and duly reinstated the exiles to Sparta and Messenia.[75] How sharp a break did

72. See works cited above, n. 70, and further bibliography contained therein.

73. Cf. especially Polyb. 24.9.9–10: εἰ μὲν οὖν «ἀ»διαφόρως ἔχουσιν ὑπὲρ τοῦ πειθαρχεῖν αὐτοῖς τοὺς Ἕλληνας καὶ συνυπακούειν τοῖς γραφομένοις, ἄγειν αὐτοὺς ἐκέλευε τὴν ἀγωγήν, ἣν καὶ νῦν ἄγουσιν · εἰ δὲ βούλονται γίνεσθαι σφίσι τὰ παραγγελλόμενα καὶ μηθένα καταφρονεῖν τῶν γραφομένων, ἐπιστροφὴν ποιήσασθαι παρεκάλει τοῦ μέρους τούτου τὴν ἐνδεχομένην.

74. Polyb. 24.9.11–14. Representatives of the Spartan exiles, as so often, were in Rome as well: Polyb. 24.10.2.

75. Polyb. 24.10.6–7, 24.10.13–15. Cf. Paus. 7.9.6–7—who does not even men-

this really represent with prior Roman policy? And how far did the senate really dictate the turn of events? No doubt some senators took personal pleasure in heaping praise on Callicrates, thus to disconcert the Philopoemenists—men like Ap. Claudius who had exchanged harsh words with Lycortas, and Q. Metellus and Q. Philippus who had been rebuffed by the Achaeans.[76] But senatorial policy, as we have seen so often, does not derive from the wounded pride of individual members. Courtesies accorded to Greek envoys and praise for their comportment were conventional.[77] The letter requesting installation of the Spartan exiles simply repeated sentiments in a similar missive sent in 182/1. The senate had cared little about the matter then and had no reason to be more enthusiastic now. As for the Messenians, Polybius himself affirms that the *patres* had not even paid attention to them.[78] Letters to various other Greek states to promote the exiles' cause have a clear precedent, overlooked in modern accounts. The senate had taken precisely the same action in the early 180s, writing to Achaeans and Aetolians to effect the restoration of Zeuxippus and his party to Boeotia.[79] Not a new policy, in short: if the banished were to be reinstated, Greeks rather than Romans would have to see to it. Callicrates, in fact, did see to it. But that he owed his election to Roman interference is by no means a necessary—or even plausible— conclusion. His party already wielded extensive influence in Achaea, as witness Hyperbatus' *strategia* in 181/0 and Callicrates' own role in the embassy. His year as *strategos* is customarily dated to 180/79, but a reasonable case can be made for 179/8.[80] If so, another held office in 180/79, perhaps of Lycortas' persuasion, and the Achaean electorate may have performed with customary consistency, alternating its leadership, a practice unaffected by Rome. The exiles recovered their homeland and their status. Callicrates was their patron and Callicrates the man whom they honored in an inscription set up at Olympia. The Romans get no mention.[81]

---

tion Callicrates! For Pausanias, Callicrates' betrayal of Greek interests dates only to the Third Macedonian War: Paus. 7.10.5–8.

76. Pausanias, 7.9.6, gives a principal role to Ap. Claudius. And Callicrates made explicit mention of Philippus: Polyb. 24.9.12; cf. 29.25.1–2. Derow, *Essays to Bowra*, 18–19, goes too far, however, in seeing here the triumph of a particular Roman faction.

77. Cf., e.g., *Syll.*[3] 601 = Sherk, *RDGE*, no. 34, lines 4–11.

78. Polyb. 24.10.13.

79. Polyb. 22.4.9.

80. See Errington, *Philopoemen*, 263–265, who does not recognize the implications. The more conventional chronology in Walbank, *Commentary* III: 19, 264.

81. *Syll.*[3] 634: Λακεδαιμονίων οἱ φυγόντες ὑπὸ τῶν τύρανν[ων] Καλλικράτη Θεοξένου Λεοντήσιον, καταγαγόντα εἰς τὰν πατρίδα καὶ διαλύσαντα ποτὶ τοὺς πολίτας καὶ εἰς τὰν ἐξ ἀρχᾶς ἐ[οῦσαν] φιλ[ίαν ἀποκ]αταστάσαντα.

The conventional wisdom that the Republic now pulled all the strings on her Achaean puppet misconceives the truth. Senatorial engagement in the internal affairs of the Peloponnese was no more vigorous or direct than before. The League conducted an independent foreign policy. Polybius attests to diplomatic interchanges between Achaea and Alexandria in the *strategia* of Hyperbatus.[82] In the same *strategia* apparently the revolutionary activities of Chaeron of Sparta were suppressed, Chaeron himself prosecuted and imprisoned by the Achaean *strategos*.[83] The success of Callicrates was a temporary triumph for his faction, not a delivery of Achaea into the hands of Rome.[84]

The Polybian notion that pro-Roman sycophants controlled the League after 180 is decisively refuted by the facts. Only sparse evidence survives for the next decade of Achaean history, but enough to demonstrate that men connected with Philopoemen and Lycortas retained their prominence and influence. Indeed, the only four Achaean *strategoi* known for the period between 179 and 168 are opponents of Callicrates.[85] The electorate plainly did not take orders from Rome.

The decision-making process continued as before, with the interests of Achaea uppermost. Perseus in 175/4 endeavored to establish relations with the Confederacy, relations that had been severed since 198. Achaean territory was forbidden ground to any Macedonian. The king proposed a renewal of their former φιλία and repeal of that ban, offering in return the restoration of fugitive slaves.[86] Objection came from Callicrates who employed once more the strategy that had served him well in 180: he claimed that an accord with Perseus would violate the Achaean treaty with Rome, denounced the inten-

---

82. Polyb. 24.6.

83. Polyb. 24.7. Derow, *Essays to Bowra*, 15, n. 1, prefers to put this in 183/2. But note that the *strategos* (unnamed) acted to preserve the property of Spartan exiles: Polyb. 24.7.8. This coincides with Hyperbatus' advocacy of the exiles' recall.

84. Just what sort of settlement was made in Sparta is beyond knowing. For some speculation, see Shimron, *Late Sparta*, 117–118. Polybius speaks of a harmonious unity in the Peloponnese, but the achievement is ascribed solely to the Achaeans: Polyb. 2.38.1–9.

85. Namely, Xenarchus in 175/4 (Livy, 41.23.4, 41.24.1; cf. Polyb. 23.4.11–14); Archon in 172/1 (Polyb. 27.2.11; cf. 22.10.8; Livy, 41.24); Archon again in 170/169, with Polybius as hipparch (Polyb. 28.6.9; cf. 28.3.7–8, 28.6.7, 29.23.1–3); and Xenon some time before 167 (Paus. 7.10.9; cf. Polyb. 28.6.2). The claim of Castellani, *op. cit.*, 109, that all the *strategoi* between 179 and 175 must have been of Callicrates' party is altogether without basis. Cf. Paus. 7.10.9.

86. Livy, 41.22.7–41.23.3. The ban was probably instituted in 198 when the League broke with Philip; cf. Livy, 41.24.11; Aymard, *Premiers rapports*, 112, n. 4, 219, n. 24. Errington's hypothesis, *Philopoemen*, 206, n. 2, that it was recent and effected by Callicrates, is unconvincing. Note Livy, 42.6.2: *vetus decretum*.

tions of the king, and averred that a Roman-Macedonian war was inevitable.[87] The arguments, of course, were specious and easily rebutted by another Achaean spokesman, Archon, brother of the *strategos* Xenarchus. As Archon pointed out, relations with Rome were not at issue, Perseus himself was at peace with the Republic, and Achaea's prior quarrels with Philip were irrelevant for the reign of his son.[88] A majority seemed inclined to go along with Archon, but Callicrates carried the day. The issue was at first postponed, and later, when Perseus' envoys came to an Achaean meeting, they were turned away. According to Livy, men who feared a negative Roman reaction achieved that result.[89] Perhaps so. The scare tactics of Callicrates should be given due weight. It does not follow, however, that instructions from Rome ordered the decision.[90] Callicrates suggests none, and Rome gave none. Other matters came into play here, old wounds, and the question of how far they had healed. Archon argued that the sins of Perseus' father should not be visited upon the son and recalled the former *beneficia* which Macedonia had bestowed on Achaeans. The debate raised issues aired a quarter-century earlier when the League was deeply divided between loyalty to the Antigonids and a desire to rid itself of Macedonian hegemony. Archon made explicit reference to that distant discussion, urging that the time had come to resolve bygone quarrels, at least to the extent of cordiality.[91] Achaea's position in the Hellenic world forms a focus for consideration: she should not deny herself the diplomatic connections that other states felt free to establish.[92] Not Roman wishes but Achaean pride overlays the debate. The Achaeans had, after all, kept a hostile distance from Macedonia through all the years while Philip and then Perseus had been *amici* of the Republic. Achaean pride played its part in the decision of 175/4 as well. Despite Achaea's plea and the support of many in the

87. Livy, 41.23.6–18.

88. Livy, 41.24.1–18.

89. Livy, 41.24.19–20; cf. 41.23.4–5.

90. The Roman envoy M. Marcellus, according to Livy, 42.6.1–3, called upon the Achaeans a year later to express approval of the decision. This implies nothing, however, about Roman pressure in 175/4. Marcellus' principal mission was to Aetolia, his crossing to the Peloponnese only a stop-over; Livy, 42.5.10–12. And his endorsement of the League's action is set in the suspicious and anachronistic context of Eumenes' charges against Perseus which did not come until 172. In all likelihood, Marcellus simply made a friendly gesture, praising the Achaeans for their independent posture in staying free of Macedonian influence.

91. Livy, 41.24.11–15: *erat vetusta coniunctio cum Macedonibus, vetera et magna in nos regum merita; valeant et nunc eadem illa, non ut praecipue amici, sed ne praecipue inimici simus.*

92. Livy, 41.24.10: *Quod Aetolis, quod Thessalis, quod Epirotis, omni denique Graeciae cum Macedonibus iuris est, idem et nobis sit.*

Confederacy, indignation shelved Perseus' offer: the king had not even sent a delegation, just a brief missive.[93] When he did at last dispatch envoys it was too late; the League refused to hear them. Memories of former subordination to the Antigonids haunted Achaea.

That League policy followed its own path can be further confirmed. At some time during this period, the Achaeans canceled decrees and inscriptions set up for Eumenes and removed statues erected in his honor, outraged at the Pergamene's request that he should receive still higher distinctions.[94] The occasion is unspecified, clearly before 172 and probably ca. 174.[95] Achaean ire recalls similar action taken in 188/7 when Eumenes offered cash gifts to extend his patronage over the Confederacy and was peremptorily refused.[96] The unwavering commitment to autonomy held firm. No dividing line is discernible in 180. Though Eumenes could claim a special relationship with Rome, the Achaeans felt as free to degrade him in the 170s as they had in the previous decade. The dignity of the League retained its paramount place in the calculations of the leadership.

## Continuities

For no other Greek state does testimony survive to permit a reconstruction even approximating that for Achaea. Only fragments remain down to the period of the Third Macedonian War, when our sources suddenly take on some fullness. What evidence does exist, however, suggests that the Republic had few occasions and little incentive for interference.

The complaints that came to Rome in the mid-180s about Philip V's encroachments in Hellas may be taken as symptomatic. Thessalians, Perrhaebians, and Athamanians were among those who registered grievances in 186/5. The senate duly lent an ear and appointed a commission. Charges and countercharges were hurled between Philip and representatives of the Greek states, especially the Thessalians, regarding a host of disputed cities. Pronouncements issued forth from Roman legates and from the senate, instructing the Macedonians to evacuate them. But Philip bided his time, his influence in northern Greece largely undiminished. As Livy admits, the senate had little in-

93. Livy, 41.24.19: *indignatione principum, quod, quam rem ne legatione quidem dignam iudicasset Perseus, litteris paucorum versuum impetraret, decretum differtur.*

94. Polyb. 27.18.1–2, 28.7.3–5, 28.7.8–15.

95. Cf. Livy, 42.12.6–7.

96. Polyb. 22.7.3, 22.7.8–9, 22.8.1–13; Diod. 29.17.

terest in the claims of Thessaly.[97] A new round of complaints gained voice in 184/3, the Epirotes this time joining Thessalians, Perrhaebians, and Athamanians, to lament territorial losses, theft of slaves and cattle, and Philip's control of judicial procedures. None of them got any satisfaction. The senate accepted Philip's explanations, delivered by his son Demetrius, and thus let the matter drop.[98]

Given that record of indifference, it hardly surprises that the states of northern and northwest Greece rarely appealed again to Rome. Thessaly did send a delegation ca. 176/5 to back the story of the Dardanians about a military buildup among the Bastarnae engineered by Perseus. The *patres*, however, after a decision to send the usual investigatory embassy, did nothing, not even rebuking the Macedonian.[99] Thessalian matters still found the *curia* distinctly uninterested. The most that Rome would trouble to do was to commission an arbiter to resolve debt disputes in Thessaly and Perrhaebia in 173, when those disputes had escalated into internal violence.[100] In this, of course, she simply followed Hellenic precedent, like the mediator from Crete also summoned to arbitrate debt quarrels in Perrhaebia.[101] Epirus, Acarnania, and Athamania disappear from the record, so far as relations with Rome are concerned. That they conducted their own affairs, domestic and foreign, without Roman supervision can be taken as certain. In the cases of Thessaly and Epirus, at least, we know that they established cordial diplomatic associations with the Macedonian royal house by the mid-170s.[102] The senate betrayed no concern.

Aetolia theoretically labored under a restrictive pact that put her in Rome's shadow after 189. In practice, however, one finds not a sign of Roman dictation or direction. The Aetolians too entered into relations with Perseus and held several seats once again in the Delphian Amphictyony.[103] When the League became embroiled in civil strife and brutal violence in the mid-170s, it is noteworthy that warring factions appealed first to Perseus for mediation, only later to Rome. The king delivered a garrison, in efforts to halt the fighting.[104] This evi-

---

97. Livy, 39.24.7: *minus Thessalos curabant*. Sources and discussion on these matters in Gruen, *GRBS* 15 (1974): 227–230.

98. See, especially, Polyb. 23.2.6–9; cf. Gruen, *GRBS* 15 (1974): 232–234.

99. See above pp. 405–406.

100. Livy, 42.5.7–10; cf. 42.13.9; Appian, *Mac.* 11.1; Diod. 29.33.

101. *IG*, IX, 2, 1230; cf. Asheri, *StudClassOrient* 18 (1969): 67–68.

102. Livy, 41.24.10. Note also the Epirote award of citizenship to an Achaean, probably in this period; *SGDI*, 1338; cf. Cabanes, *L'Épire*, 290–291.

103. Livy, 41.24.10; *Syll.*[3] 636.

104. Livy, 42.12.7, 42.42.4; Appian, *Mac.* 11.1, 11.7; cf. Livy, 42.40.7; Diod. 29.33.

dently proved unavailing, and desperate Aetolian leaders, enmeshed in a struggle in which political murders supervened on economic upheaval, turned to Rome. The senate characteristically abjured military intervention. Instead, the customary ambassadorial mission went in 174, its attempts at resolution to no effect. A second embassy the next year, again on Aetolian importuning, got better results, a compromise settlement that at least put a temporary end to the slaughter.[105] As is plain, the Aetolians did not regard themselves and were not regarded as a Roman appendage. They carried on their own diplomacy and, when racked with internal turmoil, looked to Rome only as an afterthought. The Republic at no time initiated intervention and, as arbiter, took no sides.

To Boeotia, as we have seen, the *patres* paid scant attention. They indulged Flamininus' request for restoration of Zeuxippus' faction in the early 180s, but only to the extent of asking other Hellenic states to bring it about. When no help was forthcoming, they abandoned the project.[106] Boeotia went on to establish close ties with Perseus, a revival of longstanding connections to the Macedonian monarchy. Although the alliance was bound to be reinterpreted later, in light of the Third Macedonian War, as an anti-Roman act, it carried no such connotation at the time. Perseus announced it openly to the senate and advertised it widely in Greece.[107] Boeotia was as free to engage in standard Hellenistic diplomacy as was Thessaly or Aetolia or Achaea. The hand of Rome is indiscernible.[108]

The slender evidence yields only a dim outline. Such evidence as there is, however, shows consistency with the circumstances detected in the Peloponnese. Despite dramatic Roman triumphs in the early years of the second century, the Republic forebore to direct, arrange, or supervise the affairs of Hellas. Down to the eve of the Third Macedonian War, Hellenic states pursued their own ambitions and fought their own battles, internal and external. Individuals and communities endeavored periodically to enlist Roman assistance for their causes and purposes, only to find the Republic inconsistent, erratic, and unreliable. The actions of Roman legates were often at variance with the attitude of the senate, and the senate's own actions at variance with its pronouncements. Embassies raised hopes only to frus-

---

105. The evidence in Livy, 41.25.1–6, 41.27.4, 42.2.2, 42.4.5, 42.5.7, 42.5.10–12; cf. Polyb. 30.11.1–6; discussion in Gruen, *AJAH* 1 (1976): 35–36.

106. Polyb. 22.4; see above pp. 484–485.

107. See discussion, with full references, in Gruen, *AJAH* 1 (1976): 43–44.

108. Deininger's persistent ascription of pro- and anti-Roman labels to politicians in each of these states distorts the evidence: *Widerstand*, 146–159.

trate them, answered appeals but neglected to implement them. The confusion derived not from design but from lack of sustained interest. Under such conditions, Hellenic leaders, left to their own devices, manipulated Roman directives or exploited Roman indifference.

## Hellenic Self-Interest and the Third Macedonian War

The Third Macedonian War itself altered the situation suddenly and dramatically. Rome's vacillation gave way to mobilization. The legions of the Republic reentered Hellenic soil with much more devastating impact than before. The Greeks, caught between the appeal of Perseus and the power of Rome, faced unwelcome but unavoidable choices which could determine the future and fate of every community.

Material on the war is relatively abundant—testimony to the interests of our sources who preserve little on interwar periods. The drama of the conflict thrust attitudes and motives into relief. The war throws a flood of light on the aspirations, fears, and compulsions that guided the behavior of Hellenic leaders and their states. Exhaustive discussion is unnecessary, for the material has been treated in detail elsewhere. The highlighting of relevant matters, however, can provide important illumination.

First, it is instructive to remind ourselves of the character of senatorial embassies to Hellas in late 172, embassies which sought a united front to cow Perseus into submission. Nowhere did they cite treaties, nowhere did they demand obedience or subservience, nowhere did they issue directives or commands. Greek states were approached as autonomous powers, their assistance solicited rather than requisitioned. The courtesy, it might be argued, was a feature of prudence and perspicacity. Nevertheless, it underscores the fact that Rome had not fashioned an iron ring of dependencies and had to cajole Hellenic support afresh. The dispatch of her legates repeats the procedure followed in 200 and indicates that the Republic could call on no more certain obligations in 172 than she could a generation before.

Two Roman envoys toured the Peloponnese summoning various cities to show the same zeal for Rome's cause that they had showed in previous wars against Philip and Antiochus. The Achaeans professed their loyalty, but not without a display of petulance. They were annoyed to have been set on a plane with Eleans and Messenians. Achaean pride here raised its head again: by traveling around to individual communities Rome's legates had given insufficient recognition to the League's preeminence in the Peloponnese.[109] The omission was repaired a little later when Philippus arrived and addressed a gathering of the Confederacy, asking for a troop of fifteen hundred men to garrison Chalcis. The *strategos* complied, an official act of voluntary assistance that acknowledged Achaean sensibilities.[110] Perhaps about this time too the League expelled a Spartan of royal blood for communications with Perseus, through a formal decision of the assembly.[111] The Achaeans would cooperate with Rome but would make their own decisions.

In Aetolia Rome's representatives acted with particular circumspection. They awaited the results of an Aetolian election before feeling secure about the League's attitude. Only when the voters returned Lyciscus, a man whose sympathies could be relied on, did the envoys take confidence in Aetolia's support.[112] In view of the official and ostensibly restrictive alliance imposed in 189, Roman restraint is here especially remarkable. Elsewhere, the envoys got varied receptions. A formal meeting of the Thessalians voted full support, after mutual courtesies were exchanged.[113] Thessaly, however, needed little prodding: she stood to benefit from an emasculation of Macedonia. The Epirotes too gave unanimous approval to the Roman cause in a gathering of their council.[114] But beneath that official unanimity lay grave misgivings. Epirus, as always, vulnerable, weak, and exposed, had to give thought first to her own security. Prominent citizens in that land preferred a peaceful resolution and avoidance of conflict. They went along with a Roman alliance but without enthusiasm and with a hope that they could avoid subservience.[115] The one tangible act of the state was to send four hundred men to garrison the Orestes, a people earlier under Epirote authority.[116] Epirus evidently kept her own interests foremost. So also did the Acarnanians. They hastened to express fidelity to Roman envoys, hoping thereby to make amends for past misdemeanors and not to find themselves again on the wrong side.[117] But, so far as our evidence goes, they played no active

109. Livy, 42.37.7–9.

110. Polyb. 27.2.11–12; Livy, 42.44.7–8; cf. Livy, 42.55.10.

111. Livy, 42.51.8.

112. Livy, 42.38.2. Lyciscus is not to be reckoned merely as a Roman creature. He had already exercised positions of leadership in the state; *SGDI*, 2051; 2135.

113. Livy, 42.38.2, 42.38.6–7.

114. Livy, 42.38.1.

115. Polyb. 27.15.10–12; cf. Appian, *Ill.* 11.4.

116. Livy, 42.38.1; cf. *SEG*, XXIII, 471; XXIV, 446; Cabanes, *L'Épire*, 536–539.

117. Livy, 42.38.3–4.

role in the war. Boeotia was engulfed in civil strife. Political turmoil paralyzed the state, aggravated by a separatist movement within the Boeotian Confederacy and intense rivalries among the several cities. The origins preceded any conflict between Rome and Macedonia, but that conflict was fastened on by various parties and communities to make headway against opponents through offering services to one side or the other. Philippus and the Roman legation were the fortunate beneficiaries of this ruinous upheaval, cultivating exiles and dissenting communities to break up the Confederacy and sever most of its ties with Perseus. Rome capitalized on the circumstances, but those circumstances were of Boeotia's own making, a feature of her calamitous internal divisions.[118]

The preliminaries of war thus allow some useful conclusions. Rome did not peremptorily impose or insist upon obligations due from Hellenic states, an index of the loose and distant ties that hitherto prevailed. She needed to enlist aid anew and on an *ad hoc* basis.[119] The Greek states themselves made calculations accordingly, dictated by individual considerations rather than feelings for or against the Republic. Anxiety, pride, need for security, hope of territorial gain, or internal dissension produced the several decisions.

Perseus' initial victory at Callinicus in 171 sent spasms of joy through Greece. Rome had at last found a worthy adversary, and sentiments for the underdog erupted with spontaneous enthusiasm. So says Polybius, who regards this as but a temporary and irrational outburst.[120] Be that as it may, the expressions of jubilance disclose just how shallow was the formal adherence of various states to the Republic in this conflict. But zeal for Perseus did not outrun attention to self-interest. When his fortunes dimmed, his would-be friends drifted or stampeded to the stronger power. Pragmatic rather than ideological or sentimental reasons predominated. The fact may be detected in every state for which information survives.

As usual, information is most plentiful on Achaea. The League had given official endorsement to Rome's side but contributed little to the war effort.[121] Rumor had it that many Achaean leaders were less than wholehearted in their commitment to the cause. There was talk

118. For sources, literature, and interpretation, see Gruen, *AJAH* 1 (1976): 44–45. Cf. now also Walbank's notes: *Commentary* III: 290–292.

119. Cf. the appeal to Greeks in the Roman message to Delphi, probably in 171; *FDelphes* III: 4, 367; cf. J. Bousquet, *BCH* 105 (1981): 407–416.

120. Polyb. 27.9–10; Livy, 42.63.1–2; Diod. 30.8.

121. Apart from the garrison at Chalcis, only a contribution of fifteen hundred light-armed men is recorded: Livy, 42.55.10. Certainly there was no mobilization of the Achaean levy.

also of Roman displeasure and of the possibility that Roman legates might make open accusation of those whom they distrusted, primarily the party of Lycortas. The accusations, in fact, were withheld, if indeed they were ever even contemplated.[122] But the suspicions had a solid basis. Lycortas' friends engaged in a private parley in late 170, a parley of which Polybius, who took part, gives a remarkably candid account. The participants considered the appropriate posture to assume. Some, like Lycortas himself, urged strict neutrality in the war, others went further and advocated opposition to those who curried favor with Rome against the public interest, and still others, including Archon and Polybius, propounded a policy of waiting on events and acting as each circumstance seemed to dictate. The last view prevailed.[123] None, of course, proposed overt defection from the Roman alliance. More striking, however, none counseled support for the Republic, unless it be in Achaea's interest. Nor was this simply a splinter group surreptitiously voicing its grudges outside the springs of power. Archon gained election to the *strategia* for 170/69 and Polybius to the hipparchy.[124] The choice decisively rebuts any notion that Callicrates manipulated affairs in Achaea. His opponents, in fact, held more weight.[125] The policy outlined by Archon and Polybius, to act as Achaean interests directed, is precisely what took effect.

The League committed no forces of any substance to the war until the summer of 169. At that time, the Roman consul, Philippus, was in Thessaly and preparing an invasion of Macedonia. It seemed prudent to make the show of support that had hitherto been withheld. Archon sponsored a decree to call out the full League levy and Polybius was sent to Philippus to announce Achaean preparations for engagement.[126] The hipparch joined Philippus, but even then deferred the announcement until it was clear that Roman forces controlled the approaches to Macedonia and were on the brink of a breakthrough. Only then did Polybius convey to the consul Achaea's readiness to

122. Polyb. 28.3.4–10; cf. 28.12.1. Livy, 43.17.4, omits this from his account. The Roman delegation at Aegium made only cordial noises: Polyb. 28.3.10. Cf. the Argive decree for Cn. Octavius, one of the members of the delegation: *SEG*, XVI, 255 = *ISE*, no. 42. The hypothesis of E. Lanzillotta, *Sesta Miscellanea Greca e Romana* (1978), 233–247, that the absence of a decree for C. Popillius Laenas, head of the mission, indicates genuine Achaean gratitude to the philhellene Octavius and a slight to Popillius, is most dubious. There quite probably was a parallel decree for Popillius; cf. P. Charneux, *BCH* 81 (1957): 181–202.

123. Polyb. 28.6. Errington's depiction of this colloquy is misleading; *Philopoemen*, 210–211. More accurately, Castellani, *op. cit.*, 118–119; Larsen, *Greek Federal States*, 470.

124. Polyb. 28.6.9.

125. Cf. Paus. 7.10.9.          126. Polyb. 28.12.1–5.

join in the conflict. No better example could be desired of the policy of waiting on events.[127] Philippus saw through it well enough. He declined Achaean aid with feigned courtesy and the pretext that, as it was no longer necessary, the League could forego the expense. Further, he advised Polybius to have his state decline a request for assistance from Ap. Claudius Centho, at that time commanding forces in Illyria and Epirus. The historian snidely adds that it was uncertain whether Philippus' counsel derived from regard for the Achaeans or from desire to thwart Appius.[128] Philippus may well have had other motives too. His advice, if followed, would compromise Polybius, prevent the Achaeans later from claiming a share in the victory, and subject the party of Lycortas to subsequent recriminations. Philippus had no love for that party, with whom he had earlier had harsh exchanges.[129] Polybius himself made the best of a bad situation. Upon his return home, he did indeed urge refusal of Appius' petition, but on grounds of the senate's own decree that such requests had to come from the *patres*. Then he referred the whole matter to Philippus, thus shifting onto him the unwelcome burden of dealing with Ap. Claudius. That maneuver shrewdly turned the tables and left Achaea officially blameless. The entire episode demonstrates both the suspicions of Philippus and the determination of Achaea to place her own interests above any loyalty to the protagonists.[130]

The League continued to debate matters of foreign policy, even in the midst of war, without recourse to Rome. In 169, upon appeal from Attalus, the assembly discussed at length the restoration of honors to Eumenes. The decision eventually agreed upon was to revive some of them but not the excessive and objectionable ones, thus

127. Polyb. 28.13.1–4. On the policy, see Polyb. 28.3.8, 30.7.5. Cf. De Sanctis, *Storia dei Romani* IV: 1.291–292; Meloni, *Perseo*, 311–313; Castellani, *op. cit.*, 119–121; Pedech, *LEC* 37 (1969): 256–257; Walbank, *Commentary* III: 344–345.

128. Polyb. 28.13.5–8: πότερα δὲ τοῦτ' ἐποίει κηδόμενος τῶν Ἀχαιῶν ἢ τὸν Ἄππιον ἀπραγεῖν βουλόμενος χαλεπὸν εἰπεῖν.

129. Polyb. 23.9.8, 24.9.12–13. The compromising of Polybius and his friends is clear from Polyb. 28.13.14.

130. Polyb. 28.13.9–13. No need arises to regard Polybius' account as tendentious self-justification for Roman readers, let alone to hypothesize that the refusal of troops to Appius was Polybius' own idea, falsely imputed to Philippus; as, e.g., De Sanctis, *Storia dei Romani* IV: 1. 298–299; Meloni, *Perseo*, 315; Castellani, *op. cit.*, 121–123; *contra*: Briscoe, *JRS* 54 (1964): 70–71; Deininger, *Widerstand*, 181–182; Walbank, *Commentary* III: 346–347. The narrative by no means reads as a cover-up. Polybius quite candidly gives Archon's motives for mobilization as desire to remove suspicion rather than authentic zeal for Rome: 28.12.1. And he admits without compunction that he himself delayed his message until Philippus' success seemed assured: 28.13.1–3. Polybius' faction had no reason of its own to turn down Claudius' request, at a time when Roman prospects looked good.

reestablishing cordial relations with Pergamum. No reference in the debate was made to Rome.[131] Achaean envoys also went to Alexandria to honor young Ptolemy's coming of age and to renew accords with Egypt.[132] In winter 169/8, representatives from Alexandria came with pleas for military assistance in the war against Antiochus IV. The appeal addressed itself especially to Lycortas, Polybius, and their faction, which had a record of particular attachment to Egypt. Contentious arguments ensued at Achaean meetings, with Lycortas and others urging the shipment of forces and carrying a majority with them, while Callicrates, Diophanes, and Hyperbatus blocked the efforts with equal vigor. The latter took their customary posture, invoking the name of Rome: the League should not divide its efforts, but hold its forces in readiness to contribute to Rome's cause against Perseus.[133] The claim was, of course, specious, for Achaean troops had already been judged unnecessary by Philippus, as Lycortas and Polybius were swift to point out. Callicrates, as usual, cloaked himself in pro-Roman garb in order to get the better of his political rivals. An Egyptian expedition would redound to the glory of Lycortas' friends, who were explicitly requested to head the forces.[134] One observes with interest that Achaean sentiment expressed itself clearly for Lycortas and Polybius, a sign of continued commitment to an independent foreign policy.[135] Only the intervention of a letter from Philippus stemmed the tide. The consul asked Achaea to send a peace mission which might reconcile differences between Antiochus and the Ptolemies, instead of engaging her armies and escalating the conflict. Once again Philippus may have been as eager to undermine Lycortas' party as to promote senatorial policy. The letter, in any case, had its effect. Polybius backed down and the League dispatched an embassy to resolve conflict in the Near East. This was no time to give further offense to Philippus when Rome appeared to have the upper hand in Macedonia.[136] The composition of that embassy, however, should not pass without notice. It consisted of Archon, Arcesilaus, and Ariston, all adherents of Lycortas' faction.[137] Prudence and the exigencies of circumstances induced Achaea to abandon her plan of military intervention in Alexandria. Yet she pointedly deprived Callicrates of satis-

---

131. Polyb. 28.7, 28.12.7.
132. Polyb. 28.12.8–9.
133. Polyb. 29.23–24.
134. Polyb. 29.23.5–7, 29.25.7. So, rightly, Lehmann, *Untersuchungen*, 301, 304; oddly denied by Deininger, *Widerstand*, 182–183, n. 34.
135. Polyb. 29.23.8, 29.24.5, 29.24.9, 29.24.11, 29.24.15, 29.25.1.
136. Polyb. 29.25.
137. Polyb. 29.25.6; cf. 28.6.2.

faction by designating his foes to represent the state. The demands of the time dictated compromise and flexibility. The League nonetheless had showed decided favor to those who stood for national pride.

Aetolia too behaved in ways very different from that of a Roman satellite. She took the Republic's part officially, supplied some troops in 171, but also allowed her citizens to enroll as foreign auxiliaries in Perseus' army.[138] Certain political figures, in Aetolia as elsewhere, profited from the war by identifying rivals as Macedonian sympathizers in efforts to rid themselves of troublesome opponents. Lyciscus played that game with vigor and some success.[139] But the Aetolians generally had not surrendered their claims to self-determination. When Roman envoys in 170 arrived to take hostages from those suspected of activities inimical to their cause, a stormy session of the assembly rejected that demand without equivocation and assaulted their own leaders who advocated it. Aetolia might fight on Rome's side but would not subject herself to humiliation.[140] Politicians and people made up their own minds in this war. While Lyciscus attached himself to Rome's coattails, other notable figures collaborated with Macedonia.[141] Firm conviction and loyalty to foreign powers, however, played little part. The fact emerges plainly in Perseus' attempt on Stratus in 169. The city's inhabitants wavered, in consultation of their own security. Perseus' arrival was anticipated by a Roman force. The inhabitants of Stratus who had at first invited the Macedonian now welcomed the Romans. Aetolia's own hipparch, bringing a force ostensibly to support Perseus, made a quick calculation and joined Rome. Ad hoc conditions proved decisive; there is no suggestion that the Aetolians were influenced by commitments or obligations to any but themselves.[142]

The same drive to combine security with national integrity manifested itself in Acarnania. Her people rushed to show allegiance to Rome in 172 lest their state suffer reprisals for previous activities.[143] When some of her leaders carried sycophancy to excess, however, and asked for installation of Roman garrisons to suppress dissent in 170, the assembly stiffened. They threw out the idea of a Roman military

138. Livy, 42.51.9, 42.55.9.

139. He got five of his principal enemies shipped off to Italy after the battle of Callinicus: Polyb. 27.15.14; Livy, 42.60.8–9; Appian, *Mac.* 12; cf. Polyb. 20.11.10, 28.4.6, 28.6.7. See Deininger, *Widerstand*, 168–170.

140. Polyb. 28.4; Livy, 43.17.5–6; cf. Gruen, *AJAH* 1 (1976): 37–38.

141. Livy, 43.21.9–43.22.1, 44.43.6, 45.31.15; Plut. *Aem. Paul.* 23.3.

142. Livy, 43.21.5–43.22.8. The Roman garrison commander knew very well how shallow was the fidelity of those in Stratus: Livy, 43.22.6–7.

143. Livy, 42.38.3–4.

presence, declaring that their support would come in voluntary fashion and not under constraint. Rome's legates in Acarnania, as in Aetolia, declined to press the issue, out of respect for public opinion.[144] Hellenic pride and self-interest still counted, even in the smaller states.

The Thessalians, under the shadow of Macedonia, had good reason to associate themselves with the Roman enterprise. And so they did.[145] Yet even here Thessaly's contribution to the fighting, much of it on her own soil, was far from significant. A full levy of the Thessalian cavalry had been expected in 171; in fact, only three or four hundred horsemen showed up.[146] After the battle of Callinicus we hear of no further participation by that state's forces in the war. One city, at least, that of Aeginium, had declared for Perseus and was sacked in consequence.[147] The news of Pydna, of course, found the Thessalians hastening to offer congratulations to L. Paullus.[148] But reports circulated, probably not altogether without foundation, that many leaders in Thessaly and Perrhaebia, as in Achaea, had withheld their services to the war effort, "waiting on events."[149] The suspicions carry plausibility. Thessalians had shown little favor for this contest.

Epirus faced particularly agonizing decisions. A pledge of cooperation with Rome came in 172.[150] The Epirotes could soon expect Roman troops in or near their territory, while Perseus was far away. Reasons of security prompted the decision. Statesmen like Cephalus and Antinous hoped to keep their nation out of war, indeed hoped to avert war altogether. They would abide by the Roman alliance so long as Epirus' interests were served, but not to the point of subservience or servility.[151] The war itself, however, promoted the ambitions of less scrupulous men. Charops had spent his formative years in Rome, now back in his homeland to resuscitate his career by traducing other politicians and branding them with the label of anti-Romanism. Insinuations and accusations drove some men to the side of Perseus and split the Epirote leadership.[152] Divisions then spread well beyond that leadership. Rome's defeat at Callinicus must have brought second thoughts to many in Epirus, raising the question of just where her security lay. Temptations pulled in diverse directions, since neutrality

144. Polyb. 28.5; Livy, 43.17.7–9.

145. Livy, 42.38.6–7.

146. Livy, 42.55.10, 42.58.14. The Thessalians who fought at Callinicus, however, fought bravely: Livy, 42.60.10. And a new inscription from Larisa honors two officers of Eumenes II who had shared in the battle, together with the Thessalians and the Roman consul P. Crassus: *AthAnnArch* 13 (1981): 246–248.

147. Livy, 44.46.3, 45.27.1–3.      148. Livy, 44.46.9.

149. Polyb. 30.7.5.      150. Livy, 42.38.1.

151. Polyb. 27.15.7, 27.15.10–12.

152. Polyb. 27.15, 30.7.2; Livy, 43.18.2; Diod. 30.5.

was no longer possible. A Roman consul narrowly escaped kidnapping in Epirus in 170, a sign that the League's solidarity was about to crack.[153] And crack it did. The Molossians followed Cephalus, Antinous, and others over to the Macedonian side, as did some places outside that area. Most of Thesprotia and Chaonia held to the Roman alliance, led by Charops who had staked his political future on that choice.[154] The League had now split itself asunder, partially through quarrels in the leadership, partially perhaps through regional rivalries, but primarily through a scramble by individuals and communities to elect the best course for survival.[155] Genuine sentiments for one or the other of the major protagonists ran no more deeply in Epirus than elsewhere in Greece. When confronting victorious Roman legions in late 168, the people of towns that had committed themselves to Perseus ignored the pleas of their compromised leaders and hurried into surrender.[156] Bitter choices had driven a fatal cleavage into Epirus. The nation was to suffer heavily for a war it had not made.

In Boeotia, as we have seen, the cleavages preceded war.[157] The conflict then intensified them shatteringly. Civil strife in Thebes tore apart the city. Her decision to go with Rome came only after internal violence and upheaval.[158] Boeotia had longstanding connections with the royal house of the Antigonids. She did not break them lightly —and certainly not for reasons of sentiment or with pleasure and ease.[159] Expediency tipped the scales. As it was, some Boeotian cities, notably Coronea, Haliartus, and Thisbae, held fast to their ancient allegiance and stood by Perseus.[160] Hostility to Thebes was as potent a force as fidelity to Macedonia in that decision. Even within the pro-Macedonian cities there were elements who worked against official policy in order to save themselves in the event of Roman victory.[161]

153. Polyb. 27.16; Diod. 30.50.
154. Polyb. 30.7.2, 30.15; Livy, 43.18.2, 43.21.4–5, 43.22.9, 43.23.3, 43.23.6, 44.16.2, 45.26.3–5; cf. Cabanes, L'Épire, 293–297.
155. Regional rivalries are stressed by Scullard, *JRS* 35 (1945): 58, 62, and Oost, *Roman Policy*, 74–75; political quarrels by Cabanes, L'Épire, 295–296. Deininger, as usual, sees only a struggle between "radical pro-Romans" and those who opposed dependency on Rome: *Widerstand*, 173–174.
156. Livy, 45.26.3–10.
157. Cf. Livy, 42.43.5: *ibi motus coeperat esse discedentibus a societate communis concilii Boeotorum quibusdam populis.* See above p. 507.
158. Polyb. 27.1–2; Livy, 42.44.1–6.
159. Cf. Polyb. 27.2.7.
160. Polyb. 27.5; Livy, 42.46.7–10.
161. This is clear for Thisbae at least; see Livy, 42.63.12; *Syll.*³ 646 = Sherk, *RDGE*, no. 2. And for Coronea, see Livy 43.4.11; Robert, *Études épigraphiques et philologiques* (Paris, 1938), 287–292 = Sherk, *RDGE*, no. 3; cf. Errington, *RivFilol* 102 (1974):

The Boeotian Confederacy broke into pieces. The several choices of its people tellingly reflect that instinct for self-preservation which crisis brings to the fore.[162]

The Third Macedonian War had driven harsh options upon the Hellenes. None had desired it, but none could easily stay out of it. A faulty decision might have fatal consequences. Pragmatic judgments, in the interests of advantage or survival, were demanded by the times. What stands out most remarkably, however, is the extent to which the Greeks steered their own course within those toilsome circumstances. Even when making formal declaration for Rome, they refrained from or put severe limits on active engagement, keeping their hands free to capitalize on subsequent developments. Achaea held back her forces until she could detect the tide of war. Aetolians, Epirotes, and Thessalians contributed but minimally to the Roman effort, Acarnanians and Boeotians not at all. Rome had to wage this war largely on her own. National pride still held sway among Hellenes. The Achaeans showed it in their elevation of Lycortas' party and their conduct of foreign policy, the Aetolians in resisting the surrender of hostages, the Acarnanians in refusing the imposition of Roman garrisons. The major disasters suffered by Greek states stemmed from internal causes, exacerbated but not initiated by the war: the factional contests that drove out leaders from Aetolia, Epirus, and Boeotia, the regional rivalries and intercity antagonisms that wrecked the Epirote and Boeotian confederacies. Struggles within Hellas had a dynamic of their own, independent of machinations by Rome.

## Greece After Pydna

Internal struggles in Greece also were largely responsible for the consequences that flowed from Roman victory. Political factions in state after state rushed to capitalize on the new state of affairs, heaping abuse on their adversaries, blackening them with imputations of anti-Roman activities or—when evidence was lacking—anti-Roman intentions. Charges that got little hearing from a distant and uninterested senate had more impact with a proconsul and *decem legati* in

---

79–86; Walbank, *Commentary* III:298. Only Haliartus held out with some unanimity—provoking disastrous results: Livy, 42.56.3–5, 42.63.3–12; cf. Polyb. 30.20; Strabo, 9.2.30 (C 411); Paus. 9.32.5, 9.35.2; Meloni, *Perseo*, 245, n. 2.

162. The evidence does not establish that class divisions had any significant impact in Boeotia; cf. Gruen, *AJAH* 1 (1976): 45–46. G. E. M. de Ste. Croix, *The Class Struggle in the Ancient Greek World* (London, 1981), 659, n. 2, oddly prefers Livy's recast terminology to the extant Polybian originals.

Hellas. The Romans, fresh from a bloody and difficult war, for which Greek support had been negligible, were now ready to listen. Reports of fifth-column enterprises and of clandestine sympathies for Perseus among those who had been lukewarm and uncooperative took on plausibility.

Greek politicians, it needs emphasis, seized the initiative. Lyciscus and his party in Aetolia did not await formal hearings and a postwar settlement. The sharp antagonisms, both economic and political, that had tormented Aetolia in the 170s culminated in savagery. Lyciscus ordered the execution of no fewer than five hundred and fifty *principes*, drove others into exile and expropriated the property of his enemies, while a Roman prefect stood by with soldiers to cow any opposition.[163] The survivors rendered desperate pleas to L. Aemilius Paullus, victor of Pydna, in 167, who consented to hear them at Amphipolis in the presence of the *decem legati* recently arrived from Rome. The proconsul delivered a rebuke to A. Baebius, prefect in charge of the garrison which had looked on and even assisted in the Aetolian slaughter—a gesture to disassociate official policy from that deed. Otherwise, however, Paullus had no fault to find with the assassins. The justice of the massacre was of secondary consideration; what mattered was whether the victims had backed Rome or Perseus. Paullus pronounced the steps taken as proper, thus endorsing both the murders and the expulsion.[164]

The decision gave heart to a multitude of embassies from Greek parties which had gathered at Amphipolis to arraign their political enemies for alleged Macedonian leanings. Lyciscus himself was there with a list of foes to be implicated, as were Callicrates and his partisans from Achaea, Charops from Epirus, and their opportunistic counterparts from Boeotia and Acarnania. Reports arrived also of dissenters in Thessaly and Perrhaebia. Roman commissioners were besieged with petitions which they had not prompted but which they did nothing to discourage.[165] Letters were dispatched, under the names of the Roman commanders, to the several states, directing deportation to Rome of the men named in each of the indictments.[166] Two of the *decem legati* went in person to Achaea thereby, according to Polybius, to strengthen the hand of Callicrates. No written testimony

163. Livy, 45.28.7; cf. Polyb. 30.11.5.

164. Livy, 45.28.6–8, 45.31.1–2: *noxa liberati interfectores; exilium pulsis aeque ratum fuit ac mors interfectis.*

165. Polyb. 30.13.1–5, 30.13.11; Livy, 45.31.5–9: *hi cum frequentes et ex Peloponneso et ex Boeotia et ex aliis Graeciae conciliis adessent, implevere aures decem legatorum.* On Thessalians and Perrhaebians, see Polyb. 30.7.5.

166. Polyb. 30.13.6–7; Livy, 45.31.9.

from the captured Macedonian correspondence implicated any Achaeans.[167] Precisely what transpired there is unclear, for Polybius' account is missing and Pausanias' is embellished and not altogether trustworthy. Hearings of some sort took place, with charges hurled about, and the Achaean statesman Xenon defending himself and others against the accusation of friendship with Macedonia. The forthright address of Xenon, in any case, rings true: an insistence that his behavior constituted neither treachery nor defection, and that he was willing to stand trial in Achaea or Rome. The outcome, however, was foreordained: Achaeans named by Callicrates would be shipped to Italy, to accompany victims of like-minded politicians elsewhere in Greece.[168] More than one thousand Achaeans, we are told, suffered internment in Italy and unspecified numbers from Aetolia, Boeotia, Epirus, Acarnania, Thessaly, and Perrhaebia.[169]

Hellenic politics clearly provoked these developments. But Rome does not thereby escape responsibility. Paullus and the ten commissioners concurred readily in the proposition to remove numerous Greek leaders from their homeland and thus effectively terminate their careers. It was their decision too to execute two prominent statesmen who had overtly benefited Perseus, an Aetolian and a Theban.[170] Instructions from the senate lay behind Paullus' brutal retaliation in Epirus: seventy Epirote towns were demolished and 150 thousand men sold into slavery, with vast booty accumulated by Roman soldiers. The Republic had determined to make an example of Epirus, whose statesmen had nearly kidnapped a Roman consul and whose defection had endangered the Roman line of communications.[171] Out-

167. Polyb. 30.13.8–11; Livy, 45.31.9–11; cf. Polyb. 30.7.5–8. Polybius' addition, that Paullus personally disapproved of these proceedings, does not sound convincing; cf. Badian, Foreign Clientelae, 98, n. 1.

168. Paus. 7.10.7–10. Pausanias' assertion that the Roman commissioners bullied the Achaeans and insisted on a blanket death sentence even before revealing the names of the accused is implausible; cf. Larsen, Greek Federal States, 479. Lehmann, Untersuchungen, 306, n. 342, is too credulous; cf. Deininger, Widerstand, 197–198. The sharply anti-Roman tone of this account must come from a source other than Polybius.

169. The Achaean figure is given only by Paus. 7.10.11; other evidence in Polyb. 30.7.5–7, 32.5.6; Livy, 45.31.9, 45.34.9, 45.35.1; Zon. 9.31.1. Justin's reference to Aetolian deportees, 33.2.8, appears to be a mistake for Achaeans.

170. Livy, 45.31.15. Cf. also Roman letters sent to root out Greek dissenters who had sought refuge at Hellenistic courts: Livy, 45.35.2; cf. Polyb. 30.9.

171. Polyb. 30.15; Livy, 45.34.1–6; Plut. Aem. Paul. 29.1–3; cf. Pliny, NH, 4.39. The senate had issued the orders; Livy, 45.34.1; Plut. Aem. Paul. 29.1—though Paullus' alleged reluctance to carry them out is questionable; Plut. Aem. Paul. 30.1. No reason to hypothesize that Charops suggested this brutality to Rome; as Scullard, JRS 35 (1945): 58–64; followed by Cabanes, L'Épire, 304–305. See the criticisms of Oost, Roman Policy, 134–135, n. 112. Larsen, Greek Federal States, 481–482, more plausibly suggests indignation at interference with the route from Italy to the Balkans.

rage and exasperation here exploded in ferocity. Rome had fought a lengthy and burdensome war, a more difficult task than anticipated—and a more perilous one. She was only too ready to give ear to Greeks indicting their countrymen for subverting Rome's enterprise either by lack of cooperation or by hostility. Suspicious personages would now be held in Italy, open enemies done away with. Hellas needed to be taught a lesson. The Republic exercised its power as victor. Yet the men who benefited from—and, to a large extent, occasioned—this retaliation were Hellenes themselves, following an old pattern of ingratiating themselves with the conqueror in order to entrench their position at home.

The ire of Rome in the immediate aftermath of the Third Macedonian War is plain. Once the dust settled, however, how much significant change had really taken place in mainland Greece? It is easy to assume that the era of Hellenic independence was now forever at an end, but far harder to document. What evidence there is points in a different direction. Nothing suggests that Rome took steps toward or had any intention of converting Greeks into satellite states of the western power. The Republic withdrew its troops after the defeat of Perseus, as it had after all previous eastern wars. Further, there was a remarkable dearth (outside of Macedonia and Illyria) of territorial arrangements, a fact that warrants notice. Only a very few changes occurred in the political geography of Greece. The *decem legati* detached Leucas from the authority of Acarnania.[172] Reasons spring easily to mind: not a novel departure, but pursuit of an old policy to keep the islands of the Ionian Sea free of interference from the mainland and thus guarantee security of the sea lanes to southern Italy.[173] The same motive may have come into play in the savage actions in Epirus. Rome would not tolerate actual or potential threat to the coasts of northwest Greece.[174] Elsewhere we hear only that Aetolia lost control of Amphilochia as result of a decision by the ten commissioners.[175] Not long thereafter, the senate, upon Athenian request, granted to Athens suzerainty over the town of Haliartus—which had provided fierce resistance to the Republic.[176] Apart from that, nothing. The

---

172. Livy, 45.31.12.

173. See above pp. 470–471.

174. Note also the award of 220 captured Illyrian *lembi* to Corcyra, Apollonia, and Epidamnus: Livy, 45.43.10.

175. Diod. 31.8.6. In an inscription of ca. 165 the *koinon* of the Aetolians is listed separately from those of the Dorians, Aenians, Oetaeans, and East Locrians: *Syll.*[3] 653 = *FDelphes* III, 1, 218; cf. Daux, *BCH* 89 (1965): 498–502. But there is no evidence that Rome removed these areas from Aetolian authority. Note that Dorians, Aenians, and Locrians also had individual representatives to the Delphian Amphictyony in 178, when they were under Aetolian control: *Syll.*[3] 636.

176. Polyb. 30.20; Strabo, 9.2.30 (C 411).

Boeotian League, in fact, seems to have been reconstituted some time after the war, and Epirus also soon regained her federal union.[177] Rome obviously forebore to carve up the map of Greece in any substantial way—let alone to govern or administer the land.

To be sure, one can argue, Rome had seen to it that troublesome or independent-minded politicians were safely removed to Italy and under observation. Parties who now exercised power in Hellenic states were those who had shown due deference to the Republic and could be counted on to execute Rome's will. To what extent did Roman will determine the events of Hellas after 167?

The senate held on to Greek hostages in Italy. At least five embassies from Achaea visited Rome between 166 and 154 to seek release of the detainees, but came back empty-handed.[178] For Polybius, the *patres* were motivated by desire to keep Callicrates in power, to silence his enemies, and to give an example to other Greeks who might chafe under the regimes of Rome's friends.[179] Polybius, of course, is no impartial witness, himself a victim of Callicrates, and brimming with resentment at the circumstances which kept him in Italy. His account is replete with difficulties and exaggerations; it does not bear the force of objective reportage.[180] Rome had intelligible motives for retaining the deported Hellenes. Their release could only trigger factional and property disputes of a more serious sort, provoking the inevitable, irksome appeals that the *patres* wished to rid themselves of. That is very different from a desire to control the affairs of Greece. The notion that Callicrates in Achaea, Charops in Epirus, Lyciscus in Aetolia, and others of their stamp had things their own way and acted as Roman surrogates in Hellas does not suit the facts as we know them. The very persistence with which embassies from Achaea returned to the senate to request restoration of the detainees demonstrates that Callicrates lacked a monopoly in League politics. Prominent men stood in opposition to him, including Thearidas, the brother of Polybius himself.[181] Callicrates' popularity with the Achaean people reached low ebb; he was regularly ridiculed at public gatherings and insulted by children in the streets.[182] Rome took no positive action to shore up his position. Charops instituted a reign of terror in

177. Boeotia: Paus. 7.14.6, 7.16.9; cf. Accame, *Il dominio romano*, 193–196; P. Roesch, *Thespies et la confédération béotienne* (Paris, 1965), 69–71. Epirus: *Syll.*³ 653 = *FDelphes*, III, 1, 218; *Syll.*³ 654 = *FDelphes* III, 2, 135; cf. Cabanes, *L'Épire*, 306–307.

178. Polyb. 30.29.1, 30.30.1, 30.32.1–9, 32.3.14–17, 33.1.3–8, 33.3.1–2, 33.3.14.

179. Polyb. 30.32.8.

180. Gruen, *JHS* 96 (1976): 48–49.

181. Polyb. 32.7.1; cf. *Syll.*³ 626.

182. Polyb. 30.29.

ROME AND GREECE (II) • 519

Epirus during the postwar years, but when he sought to obtain Roman sanction for his policy ca. 158, he found the doors of L. Paullus and M. Lepidus firmly shut to him and the senate cool and noncommittal.[183] Charops perished not long thereafter at Brundisium, perhaps in exile from his country.[184] Rome had ignored him. And she cared little more for the Epirote quarrels that followed his demise.[185] The same fate awaited Lyciscus, assassinated during civil strife in Aetolia ca. 159, whereby power fell into the hands of his foes, with not a move by Rome.[186] Change of leadership, natural or violent, occurred in Boeotia and Acarnania as well. New regimes took authority, replacing those installed in power as consequence of the Third Macedonian War.[187] The Roman Republic paid not the slightest attention.

Evidence on the history of mainland Greece after 167 is so slim as to be virtually negligible. Where fragments do exist they disclose striking continuities with the past. The internal and external affairs of Hellenic states appear to have proceeded with little detectable interference from Rome. We have had occasion to note already instances in which interstate arbitration by and for Greeks continued to prevail, indeed reached a heyday, in and around this period.[188] When Rome was called upon to arbitrate, her normal practice was to delegate matters to Greek tribunals.[189] Cities and states persisted in carrying on their own diplomacy, showering honors and distinctions upon Hellenistic kings.[190] In the case of Achaea, where a little more information survives, disputes and controversies involving members of the League or other communities found Rome consistently upholding the authority of the Confederacy.[191] Representatives from both Rhodes and Crete

183. Polyb. 32.5.5–32.6.9.

184. Polyb. 32.5.4.

185. Polyb. 32.14. The Epirote Confederacy, it seems, was reunited at some time during this period; cf. *Syll.*³ 653 = *FDelphes* III, 1, 218; *Syll.*³ 654 = *FDelphes* III, 2, 135; Cabanes, *L'Épire*, 306–307.

186. Polyb. 30.11.6, 32.4.1, 32.5.1.

187. Polyb. 32.5.1–3.

188. Among cases involving states of the Greek mainland, see, e.g., *Syll.*³ 668; cf. Daux, *Delphes*, 329–335, 679–681; *SEG*, XI, 377 = *ISE*, no. 43; *SGDI*, 4546, 4547 = Tod, *International Arbitration*, no. 3; *IG*, IX, 2, 7 = Tod, *op. cit.*, no. 30; *IG*, IX, 2, 488 = Tod, *op. cit.*, no. 31; *IG*, IX, 2, p. x = Tod, *op. cit.*, no. 40; *Syll.*³ 675; cf. Paus. 7.11.7–8; Gruen, *JHS* 96 (1976): 51–53; *FDelphes* III, 4, 169; *IG*, IX, 2, 1106; see above pp. 109–110.

189. Examples collected in Chapter III, n. 52.

190. E.g. *Syll.*³ 670–672; *FDelphes* III, 3, 121; III, 3, 237–239; *IG*, II², 953 (for Eumenes); *OGIS*, 352 (for Ariarathes); *IdeDélos*, 1525 = Dürrbach, *Choix*, no. 90 (for Ptolemy). And on Eumenes' policy of cultivating Greek supporters, see Polyb. 32.8.5, 38.14.2.

191. Evidence and discussion, with bibliographical references, in Gruen, *JHS* 96 (1976): 50–53.

sought military alliances with Achaea ca. 154, and when Andriscus' occupation of Macedonia threatened Thessaly in 150, the Thessalians also applied to Achaea for help.[192] The League retained its political integrity and its status within the Hellenistic world. That world did not yet march to the orders of Rome.

Events that led to the climactic and catastrophic Achaean war of 146 can pass without narration here. That story has been told in full elsewhere.[193] A remarkable characteristic stands out: the signal repetition of previous Roman behavior, the unmistakable sense of déja vu. Two decades after Pydna and a half-century after Cynoscephalae one finds a stunning sameness in the issues that beset the Peloponnese and the actions taken to resolve them, most particularly in the conflict between Achaea and Sparta, in the efforts by the Lacedaemonians to wriggle out of the embrace of the Achaean Confederacy. A separatist movement took hold once again in Laconia, challenging the jurisdiction of the League. At least three times, around the middle of the century, appeals went to Rome from the Spartan government or from Spartan exiles, their claims countered by representatives of Achaea. Debates before the patres by contending Lacedaemonian and Achaean spokesmen sounded old refrains, reviving the arguments of nearly forty years before, as if nothing had occurred in the meantime.[194] Senatorial reaction was cast in the traditional mold: evasive and noncommittal answers which each party read in accord to its own wishes and employed to justify steps already determined upon. The scenario of the 180s played itself out all over again.[195]

The aura of recurrence pervades this atmosphere at every turn. The senate promised embassies but dallied in sending them. Rome's commander in Macedonia, Q. Metellus, advised the League to refrain

192. Rhodes and Crete: Polyb. 33.16.1–8. Callicrates successfully opposed Achaean intervention in their war, invoking, as usual, the claim that Rome ought to be consulted first. But there is nothing to suggest that Rome directed his stance here. Achaea had ties to both states and good reason for neutrality. On the Thessalian appeal in 150, see Polyb. 36.10.5.

193. Gruen, JHS 96 (1976): 53–66. Harris, War and Imperialism, 240–244, unfortunately returns to the old view that Rome, with malice aforethought, deliberately provoked Achaea into war. This entails, among other things, his dismissal of Polyb. 38.9.3–8. So also Walbank, Commentary III:700. A somewhat middle position taken by Ferrary, in Nicolet, Rome et la conquête 2:769–770.

194. Paus. 7.12.2–8.

195. Paus. 7.12.4–5, 7.12.9: τοὺς μὲν δὴ παρῆγεν ὁ Δίαιος ὡς τὰ πάντα ἔπεσθαι Λακεδαιμόνιοί σφισιν ὑπὸ τῆς Ῥωμαίων βουλῆς εἰσιν ἐγνωσμένοι, Λακεδαιμονίους δὲ ὁ Μεναλκίδας ἠπάτα παντελῶς τοῦ συνεδρεύειν ἐς τὸ Ἀχαϊκὸν ὑπὸ Ῥωμαίων αὐτοὺς ἀπηλλάχθαι. Note the almost identical language of Livy, 38.32.9–10—with regard to 188!

from war on Sparta, just as another Roman legate, thirty-five years earlier, had advised it to halt preparations against Messenia—with precisely the same results: the messages were ignored or sidestepped, and Achaea proceeded with force against Sparta.[196] The senate's ambassador in 147, L. Aurelius Orestes, endeavored to make the Achaeans see reason, even threatening them with a dissolution of the Confederacy, a prospect aired once before in Rome—also more than three decades ago. A tumultuous assembly refused to countenance the bluster, causing Orestes to storm home in a rage and spread tales of insult and abuse, once again a replay of Philippus' mission of 183.[197] The sequel too had the familiar overtones of past history: Orestes made noisy complaint of his treatment, Achaea instructed a delegation to apologize for any unintended offense, and the *patres* sent a new mission which offered only gentle rebuke and asked for more courtesy in the future. The episode parallels closely a similar train of events that occurred forty years earlier.[198] The dilatoriness and reserve of the *patres'* demeanor, the contrast between the assertiveness of Roman legates and the restraint of senatorial attitude, the inconsistency of words and action all demonstrate how little had changed over the course of a half-century.[199]

The conflict was touched off for reasons identical to those that had operated so many times before: Sparta's secession from the League and Achaea's determination to force her back into compliance. Intra-Peloponnesian quarrels formed the centerpiece, an ancient Hellenic dispute neither fashioned nor fostered by Rome. Given the long record of senatorial indifference, Achaea's behavior makes perfect sense. She would not tolerate defection and expected to mete out harsh discipline to recalcitrant members of the Confederacy without interference from the Republic. Rome might send her customary missives or envoys, might express faint displeasure, but would surely not intervene in force. This was a Greek contest, to be fought by Greeks.

196. The Roman embassy arrived in Corinth a year and a half after it was promised: Paus. 7.12.9, 7.14.1. Metellus' messages and the Achaean response: Paus. 7.13.2–7. Cf. Philippus' experience in seeking vainly to prevent the League's war on Messenia in 183: Polyb. 23.9.8, 24.9.12–13.

197. Polyb. 38.9.1–2, 38.9.6–8; Paus. 7.14.2–3; cf. Cic. *Imp. Pomp.* 11; Strabo, 8.6.23 (C 381); Livy, *Per.* 51; Florus, 1.32.3; Dio, 21.72.2; Justin, 34.1.9.

198. Polyb. 38.9.3–5, 38.10.1–5; Dio, 21.72.2; cf. Paus. 7.14.3. For the affair of 186/5, see Polyb. 22.10, 22.12.5–10; Paus. 7.8.6, 7.9.1; Livy, 39.33.3–8.

199. Dilatoriness continued into 146. Even when the second Roman embassy returned without accomplishment, the senate made no move. The next message to Achaea came from Metellus, with the same mild and amicable language as before: Polyb. 38.12.1–3; cf. Paus. 7.15.1.

To coerce Heraclea, which had also thrown off the League's yoke, Achaea had enlisted the aid of Thebans and Chalcidians, peoples with independent though undiscernible motives for participation.[200] None had reckoned on actual resistance from Rome, a telling indicator of the absence of serious Roman involvement during the preceding decades. This time, however, the Achaeans had miscalculated. Roman requests to stay mobilization had been spurned once too often. When Metellus' envoys got a rude reception in spring, 146, harassed and mocked by a jingoist gathering at Corinth, the *patres* determined that Rome's *dignitas* would not be further compromised.[201] A Roman army was already in Macedonia, having recently crushed Andriscus and making preliminary arrangements for a new settlement. Conflagration in Greece caused sore embarrassment for the Republic, now about to announce imposition of a lasting peace in the north. Rome determined to snuff it out swiftly and definitively.

The astonishment and shock of the Achaeans—as of other Greeks—tells the tale most eloquently. Rome's forcible intrusion took them all by surprise.[202] Achaea, to her credit, resolved to see the fight through. Pride in her position of leadership in the Peloponnese and passion for the maintenance of unity in the League had motivated her throughout the past century. Despite rivalries among politicians and nuanced differences in policy, those fundamental propositions held firm. The majority of Achaeans determined to sustain them whatever the cost and however unequal the struggle.[203] Unequal, of course, it was. Metellus smashed Achaean contingents with his army from Macedonia. Then L. Mummius, leading the Republic's forces from Italy, wiped out the last resistance and delivered his stern and unforgettable lesson: the city of Corinth, where Roman envoys had been jeered and ridiculed, was ruthlessly sacked.[204]

The clash with Rome had been unforeseen by Achaea, the calamitous results unexpected and unplanned. The episode began as an

200. Paus. 7.14.6–7, 7.15.9; Livy, *Per.* 52; cf. Polyb. 39.6.5.

201. Polyb. 38.12.1–4; Paus. 7.15.1.

202. Paus. 7.15.3–6, 7.15.10–11; Polyb. 38.16.11–12.

203. That determination emerges with clarity, despite Polybius' savage denunciation of League leaders and his disparagement of their motives: Polyb. 38.16–18; cf. *IG*, IV, 757 = F. G. Maier, *Griechische Mauerinschriften* (Heidelberg, 1959), I, no. 32; *IG*, IV, 894. See De Sanctis, *Storia dei Romani*, IV:3, 153; A. Fuks, *JHS* 90 (1970): 87–88.

204. Metellus' victories: Paus. 7.15.2–11; Zon. 9.31; Florus, 1.32.3–4; Oros. 5.3.3; Val. Max. 7.5.4; *Vir. Ill.* 60.2, 61.2; Livy, *Per.* 52; cf. Polyb. 38.16.4–12, 39.1.11. Mummius' campaign: Paus. 7.15.1, 7.16; Zon. 9.31; cf. Polyb. 39.2; Livy, *Per.* 52; *Oxyr. Per.* 52; Florus, 1.32.4–7; *Vir. Ill.* 60.1–3; Oros. 5.3.5–7. Discussion and bibliography in Gruen, *JHS* 96 (1976): 65–69.

internal Hellenic struggle, a resurrection of old disputes, aspirations, and hostilities. Issues that divided Greeks among themselves, not conflict between East and West, still held sway.[205] The Republic intervened out of exasperation and ire, its decision made *ad hoc* after long foot-dragging, certainly not a calculated design to bring Hellas into subjection. Error and miscalculation, rather than a considered project, determined the events that unfolded in the Achaean war. A classic case of ἀτυχία.[206]

## The Settlement

The nature of Rome's settlement in Greece in 146 defies secure reconstruction. Conflicting and intractable evidence baffles inquiry. That should be enough to suggest that efforts to discern a neat overall pattern may be misdirected. The *patres* certainly did not enter this conflict with any deliberate scheme for uniform application. And there is every indication that they imposed no such scheme.

*Decem legati*, of course, went out in 146 to assist Mummius in enforcing a peace settlement upon the vanquished. That was customary, even indispensable, procedure after every foreign war. Their task was completed in six months.[207] What precisely did they accomplish? The fragmentary text of Polybius reports nothing more specific than sale of property confiscated from those who had led the fight against Rome.[208] As disposal of war booty from the defeated foe, this was legitimate enough. It affords a clue that the commissioners' activity directed itself primarily against those who had taken up arms, rather than toward an overall settlement of Greece. Cicero reinforces that impression, though his rhetorical statement need not be taken at face value: Mummius destroyed Corinth and placed many cities of Achaea and Boeotia *sub imperium populi Romani dicionemque*.[209] There was more than this, however. Polybius refers to a πολιτεία and νόμοι instituted

205. Cf. Polyb. 3.5.6: Λακεδαιμονίων δὲ τῆς τῶν ᾿Αχαιῶν συμπολιτείας ἀποστάντων, ἅμα τὴν ἀρχὴν καὶ τὸ τέλος ἔσχε τὸ κοινὸν ἀτύχημα πάσης τῆς ῾Ελλάδος.

206. Cf. Polyb. 38.1. Polybius' view, modified and distorted so as to pin blame on Greek demagogues, is analyzed in Gruen, *JHS* 96 (1976): 46–48.

207. Polyb. 39.4.1, 39.5.1; Paus. 7.16.9. The commission's personnel is not fully recoverable; cf. *OGIS*, 321–324; and see Broughton, *MRR* I:467–468; Walbank, *Commentary* III:731. Inscriptions dedicated by and honoring Mummius or the *decem legati* are collected conveniently by Schwertfeger, *Der Achaiische Bund*, 19–20, n. 4.

208. Polyb. 39.4.

209. Cic. *Verr.* 2.1.55. The sweeping statements of later sources do not provide elucidation: Diod. 33.26.2; Strabo, 8.6.23 (C 381); Tac. *Ann.* 14.21.

by the Roman *legati* and left to Polybius himself to help implement in various communities.²¹⁰ A subsequent inscription of ca. 115 confirms the existence of some sort of πολιτεία accorded to Achaea by the Romans.²¹¹ Pausanias alone among literary sources offers some particulars: Mummius abolished democracies and established new governments based on a census qualification, Hellas was made subject to tribute, individuals were forbidden to hold property abroad, ethnic leagues everywhere were dissolved.²¹²

At first sight, this looks like substantial restructuring indeed. Yet the limits of Rome's settlement need to be emphasized. She certainly did not convert Greece into a province. A full century passed before Julius Caesar took that step at last in 46 B.C., and then the chaos of the triumviral period disrupted it once more until Augustus made a final disposition in 27 B.C.²¹³ *Communis opinio* among moderns holds that parts of Greece, primarily those states that had taken up arms against Rome, were made subject to the Roman governor in Macedonia, the rest in some sense left free.²¹⁴ The fundamental premise of this conjecture—that Macedonia received annual Roman governors after 146— rests on shaky evidentiary ground.²¹⁵ It is difficult in the extreme, moreover, to conceive how such a system, with Greek communities scattered in various areas subject to the authority of a proconsul off in Macedonia while most of their neighbors were exempt, would have worked: better not to imagine a "system" at all. If any state ought to have suffered subjection after 146, on this theory, it was surely Achaea. Yet it is precisely in an Achaean context that Rome described her Greek settlement as one which brought ἐλευθερία.²¹⁶

210. Polyb. 39.5.

211. *Syll.*³ 684 = Sherk, *RDGE*, no. 43, lines 9–10: τῆι ἀποδοθείσηι τοῖς ['Α]-χαιοῖς ὑπὸ 'Ρωμαίων πολιτ[εία]ι; cf. lines 19–20: τῆς ἀποδοθείσης πολιτεί[ας]; cf. *Hesperia* 35 (1966): 327, no. 7, line 12 (with regard to Mummius and the *decem legati*): [το]ὺς νόμους γεγονότα[ς].

212. Paus. 7.16.9.

213. For Caesar, see Cic. *Ad Fam.* 6.6.10; cf. 13.17–28. For Augustus, Dio, 53.12; Strabo, 17.3.25 (C 840); Suet. *Aug.* 47. Pausanias' implication, 7.16.10, that governors of Greece began to be appointed ca. 145 is plainly erroneous. See Plut. *Cim.* 2.1: ἡ δὲ κρίσις ἦν ἐπὶ τοῦ στρατηγοῦ τῆς Μακεδονίας, οὔπω γὰρ εἰς τὴν Ἑλλάδα 'Ρωμαῖοι στρατηγοὺς διεπέμποντο (with reference to the late 70s or 60s B.C.).

214. So, Accame, *Il dominio romano*, 2–7, and *passim*. Though some of his details have been challenged, the general theory has gone unquestioned; see, most recently, Schwertfeger, *Der Achaiische Bund*, 19; Bernhardt, *Historia* 26 (1977): 62–73; Ferrary, in Nicolet, *Rome et la conquête* 2:772–773; Dahlheim, *Gewalt und Herrschaft*, 124. But Dahlheim hedges his own view later; *op. cit.* 129–130.

215. See above pp. 433–435.

216. *Syll.*³ 684 = Sherk, *RDGE*, no. 43, lines 15–16: [τ]ῆς ἀποδεδομένης κατὰ [κ]οινὸν τοῖς Ἕλλη[σιν ἐ]λευθερίας; cf. Zon. 9.31.6; *SEG*, I, 152.

The details provided by Pausanias are less than satisfactory. All Greek confederacies were broken up, he says, with specific mention of Achaea, Boeotia, and Phocis. The evidence fails to stand up. Pausanias himself backtracks and adds that a few years later Rome permitted the reestablishment of those leagues, a signal that he did not fully comprehend the situation.[217] Epigraphic testimony, in fact, guarantees the continued existence of Hellenic confederacies.[218] That Achaea was stripped of some of her holdings, including certain major cities of her league, as a result of the war can readily be assumed. But the κοινὸν τῶν Ἀχαιῶν, in some attenuated form, endured.[219] Rome had no ideo logical objection to federal organizations.

As for suppression of democracies and establishment of property qualifications for office, we have only Pausanias' testimony. Mummius may indeed have toppled regimes in states that fought openly against Rome. But Hellenic institutions, once the Romans retired, had a way of slipping back into place. Nothing, even in the Achaean documents, indicates the existence of census requirements, and the democratic character of governmental forms seems to have remained in force.[220]

Imposition of tribute is a more serious matter. Pausanias affirms it—and he alone. No epigraphic testimony backs the statement.[221] To be sure, Rome occasionally declared communities "free and immune from tribute," but this conventional formula, taken from Hellenistic practice, merely expresses the senate's good will and in no way es-

---

217. Paus. 7.16.10.

218. E.g. for Boeotia, see the evidence in Accame, *Il dominio romano*, 195–196; Roesch, *Thespies*, 71–72; for Phocis, Accame, *op. cit.*, 201–202; for Achaea, Accame, *op. cit.*, 147–151; Schwertfeger, *Der Achaiische Bund*, 19–26.

219. The phrase appears in a document of ca. 71; *IvOlympia*, 328. For De Sanctis, *Storia dei Romani* IV:3. 174–176 and Accame, *Il dominio romano*, 148–149, the League was reduced to Achaea proper. Schwertfeger, *Der Achaiische Bund*, 27–63, correctly adds a number of cities in northern and western Arcadia, on the basis of *SEG*, XV, 254 = *ISE*, no. 60. It does not follow that the League fell into the category of states under the control of the Roman governor of Macedonia. The intervention of a Roman proconsul, Q. Fabius Maximus, ca. 115, to suppress upheaval at Dyme seems to constitute *ad hoc* action. He had been summoned by a party in the city; *Syll.*[3] 684 = Sherk, *RDGE*, no. 43, lines 4–6. And he is not described as governor of Macedonia anyway.

220. See Touloumakos, *Der Einfluss Roms*, 11–32; *contra*: Schwertfeger, *Der Achaiische Bund*, 65–67.

221. Evidence from the Sullan period is inadmissible. Accame, *Il dominio romano*, 18, cites *Syll.*[3] 747 = Sherk, *RDGE*, no. 23 to show imposition of tribute on Oropus before 86. But senatorial regulations for the *publicani*, lines 35–38, are hardly likely to go back to 146. The need for occasional *ad hoc* exactions, as at Messenia, Gytheum, and Tegea, implies the absence of regular contributions; *IG*, V, 1, 1432–1433 (Messenia); *IvOlympia*, 328 (Gytheum); *IG*, V, 2, 20 (Tegea).

tablishes that other communities paid a regular tax. One may recall that the *patres* affirmed "immunity" for Teos as early as 193—when certainly no Hellenes were liable to Roman taxation.[222] Corinth, of course, suffered heavily for her obstinacy and insolence, an object lesson to the Greeks. Part of her territory became Roman *ager publicus* and contributory to the *vectigalia* of the Roman people. As Cicero makes clear, however, no other state suffered such treatment.[223] It is particularly noteworthy that the only specific financial levies which Pausanias himself ascribes to Mummius were fines imposed upon Boeotia and Achaea—and these were to go to Heracleans, Euboeans, and Spartans![224] In all likelihood, fixed and regular exactions in Greece began only with the establishment of the province under Augustus.[225]

The Roman settlement of 146 does not seem unduly harsh or restrictive. Honorary decrees for L. Mummius sprang up in various places, and the commander left a number of dedications of his own to show favor to the Hellenes. Mere formalities, no doubt. Yet Polybius, who was there, attests that Mummius' behavior had been exemplary and that the Greeks felt genuine joy at his unexpected leniency.[226] On one matter we get specifics: Mummius and the *decem legati*, after Polybius' plea, left standing the statues and inscriptions set up in honor of Philopoemen. The symbolic gesture represented no mean concession to the pride of Achaea.[227] Although the commissioners did make some constitutional arrangements for Hellas, just as commissioners had done for Macedonia in 167, an important fact needs notice: they did not stay around to enforce them, but turned the matter over to a Greek, Polybius himself, to see to their implementation.[228] Romans even now still shrank from the administering or organizing of Greeks.

One will not thereby minimize the impact of the war. Polybius recognized it as an event of the first magnitude, a turning point in

---

222. *Syll.*[3] 601 = Sherk, *RDGE*, no. 34, lines 20–21. The same gesture was made for Delphi in 189; *Syll.*[3] 612 = Sherk, *RDGE*, nos. 1A and B, lines 5–6 = *FDelphes* III:4, 353. For similar proclamations after 146, see, e.g., *IG*, VII, 2413–2414 = Sherk, *RDGE*, no. 44, lines 5–6 (the Dionysiac guilds); Cic. *Ad Att.* 1.19.9 (Sicyon); Paus. 10.34.2 (Elateia). On *civitates liberae* generally, see Accame, *Il dominio romano,* 46–74; Bernhardt, *Imperium und Eleutheria*, 88–176.

223. Cic. *De Leg. Agrar.* 1.5; *FIRA*, I, no. 8, lines 96–101; cf. Strabo, 8.6.23 (C 381); Zon. 9.31.

224. Paus. 7.16.10.

225. So, H. Hill, *CP* 41 (1946): 35–42. Observe that, according to Zon. 9.31, Greeks suffered monetary requisitions in the immediate aftermath of the war, but were subsequently exempt.

226. Polyb. 39.6.                    227. Polyb. 39.3.

228. Polyb. 39.5.

Hellenic history, the culmination of calamity for Greece.[229] Subsequent documents employ dating by an "Achaean era," its beginning fixed in 146/5 or 145/4, thus acknowledging a milestone, after which the fortunes of Hellas could never be the same.[230] The Romans declined to exercise overlordship and continued to speak of "freedom and autonomy," but the emasculation of Greece, for all practical purposes, was complete.

**V**

A clearer picture has now taken shape. The notion of a slow and ineluctable fate overtaking Greece during the first half of the second century must give way. Only misdirected hindsight can find Rome engaged in ever-increasing encroachment leading to Hellenic subjection. Continuities and repetition prevail, rather than gradual disintegration and submissiveness. The centrality of Greek concerns takes precedence throughout. A struggle for power within the Peloponnese, internal upheaval in Aetolia, Thessaly, and Boeotia, relations of states and leagues with the Macedonian monarchy—these were the matters that occupied most attention in the 180s and 170s. Rome was dragged into the maelstrom by contending Greek politicians, exiles, or oppressed communities with special axes to grind. Inter-Hellenic competitions generated appeals and endeavored to mobilize Roman opinion for their several causes. Interventions by the western power, half-hearted and inconsistent, rarely got results. Little coordination existed between the behavior of legates and the attitudes of the senate, and a large gap separated the expressed will of the *curia* from any action to enforce it. Appellants found frustration, determined leaders and communities framed their own policies. Indifference predominated in Rome.

Space for maneuvering received sudden restriction in the Third Macedonian War. But even under those trying conditions Greek states marked out their paths in calculation of national interests, not in subservience to Rome. Consequences of the war were harsh. Roman fury vented itself on offenders, while ambitious Hellenes grasped the

---

229. Polyb. 38.1.1: τὴν συντέλειαν τῆς τῶν Ἑλλήνων ἀτυχίας; 38.11.1: τὸ δὲ τέλος τῆς ἀπωλείας; 38.16.9: ἠτύχησαν ἀτυχίαν ὁμολογουμένην; cf. 3.5.6: ἅμα τὴν ἀρχὴν καὶ τὸ τέλος ἔσχε τὸ κοινὸν ἀτύχημα πάσης τῆς Ἑλλάδος; 38.18.7–12; and, in general, 38.1–4.

230. E.g., *IG*, V, 1, 30; V, 2, 265; V, 2, 266; V, 2, 354; V, 2, 439; V, 2, 441; V, 2, 443; V, 2, 445; see W. B. Dinsmoor, *The Archons of Athens in the Hellenistic Age* (Cambridge, Mass., 1931), 234–236; Accame, *Il dominio romano*, 11–14.

occasion to rid themselves of rivals and entrench their regimes. The explosion, however, proved to be temporary rather than enduring. Old patterns soon came back into force. Rome retreated to indifference, the war's beneficiaries slipped or were pushed from power, a vigorous Hellenistic diplomacy revived, in which the Republic played but a marginal role. The events which led to disaster in 146, far from exposing a changed world, demonstrate just how unchanged it was. Familiar scenes replayed themselves, with eery reminiscences of the past: Spartan defection from Achaea, rival disputants before the *patres*, ambiguous Roman response, contrast between envoys' bluster and senatorial restraint, Greek confidence in the absence of the Republic's interference. Only this time error and chance intervened to upset calculations and bring about the disastrous humbling of Hellas. The result derived neither from preconceived plan nor from progressive evolution. Even after 146 Rome established no uniform system and proved reluctant to take in hand the affairs of Greece. Hellenic history in the second century must be read in terms of its internal energy, rather than as gradual crumbling before Roman power.

# Chapter 15

# Rome and Asia Minor (I)

Roman interests across the Aegean developed in halting steps, unsystematically, and late. Asia Minor and the islands stood remote from areas of principal concern to the Republic. Their affairs impinged but little upon Roman consciousness in the third century and the early decades of the second. Why should they? Rome accumulated *amici*, to be sure. The numbers can be estimated and the associations chronicled, but only to miss the point. To treat the Hellenic states of the Aegean and Anatolia as an expanding collection of Roman friends and allies puts the matter back to front. Emphasis again belongs on the Greek perspective. Jealous rivalries and armed contests had carved up Asia Minor long before the arrival of Rome. The area furnished a battleground for the contending ambitions of Seleucids, Ptolemies, and Attalids, an explosive mix that included principalities ruled by Iranian or semi-Iranian dynasties, the hated and menacing Galatians, and a host of Greek cities groping for autonomy or longing for protection, caught in the crossfire of greater powers. Tempestuous Asia and the islands off its shores slowly drew Rome into the vortex. Initiative and occasion repeatedly came from the East. The cities and states of the area prodded the Republic to advance their own causes, sheltered themselves behind her might, or exploited her prestige to tip the balance in their quarrels. Hellenic circumstances generated the involvement of Rome—and Hellenic ingenuity endeavored to sustain it.

529

## The Resistance to Philip V

Attalus I of Pergamum entered into *amicitia* with Rome ca. 210, the first Asiatic prince to do so.[1] What did it amount to? The event constituted rather less than a milestone on the road to Roman absorption of the East. The association, in fact came about in indirect fashion, and through an intermediary. Attalus was ally of Aetolia. The Roman-Aetolian pact of 212 or 211 against Philip V of Macedonia allowed for participation on equal footing of *amicitia* by the *amici* of both partners.[2] When Attalus joined the fray, he came on solicitation of the Aetolian League. The so-called First Macedonian War provided the occasion, a contest which concerned the Pergamene prince only when opportunity presented itself for his own advantage. The Aetolians accorded Attalus the signal honor of election to their highest office, the *strategia*, in 210. They also offered more tangible benefits: for the token sum of 30 talents the Aetolians sold to Attalus the island of Aegina, recently captured by Roman forces and turned over to the League.[3] Not until 209 did the Pergamene fleet sail into the Aegean, and the king headed straight for his new acquisition, where he spent the winter.[4] Active participation by his land and naval forces confined itself to just part of the campaigning season of 208.[5] Debate over Attalus' aims in the Aegean (whether desire for territorial aggrandizement and a maritime empire or access to a northern Aegean trade route) can be set aside as speculation. Aegina was offered him; Aegina he took and kept.[6] Elsewhere he helped himself to spoils when victory offered them. But the situation in Asia Minor took precedence over all else. When word came that Pergamene territory had been violated by Prusias I of Bithynia, Attalus collected his troops forthwith and sailed for home. He dropped his partnership with Rome and the Aetolians on the spot.[7]

---

1. Polyb. 21.20.3: πρῶτος μετασχὼν τῆς ὑμετέρας φιλίας καὶ συμμαχίας; Livy, 26.24.9, 29.11.2, 37.53.7.

2. Livy, 26.24.9, 31.46.3.

3. Election to the *strategia*: Livy, 27.29.10, 27.30.1. Acquisition of Aegina: Polyb. 9.42.5, 11.5.8, 22.8.9–10. Association of some form between Pergamum and Aetolia dates back at least to 219; Polyb. 4.65.6; cf. *Syll.*³ 523. The Aetolians were confident of Pergamene participation in 210—or so at least they told the Spartans; Polyb. 9.30.7.

4. Livy, 27.29.10, 27.30.7, 27.30.11, 27.33.5, 28.5.1.

5. References and discussion in E. V. Hansen, *The Attalids of Pergamum* (2nd ed., Ithaca, 1971), 47–49; R. B. McShane, *The Foreign Policy of the Attalids of Pergamum* (Urbana, 1964), 105–110.

6. Debate on Attalus' aims in Holleaux, *Rome, la Grèce*, 204–208; McShane, *Foreign Policy*, 100–109. For Attalid rule in Aegina, see R. E. Allen, *BSA* 66 (1971): 1–12.

7. Livy, 28.7.10: *omissis Romanis rebus atque Aetolico bello in Asiam traiecit*: Dio,

The collaboration had been shortlived and relatively inconsequential. Attalus showed relish for the war when territorial advantage presented itself and abandoned it hastily when his homeland came under threat. The king took his place among *adscripti* to the peace of Phoenice in 205, appropriately enough, as a former participant in the contest against Philip and on the same side as Rome. The *amicitia* held. But each state kept its own concerns foremost, Rome engrossed in deadly combat with Hannibal, Attalus struggling to protect his own holdings. The Romans staked no claim in the Aegean and Anatolia. Apart from the now ceremonial association with Attalus and perhaps a sentimental attachment to Ilium, they were still strangers to the area.[8]

If previous rapport had existed between Rome and the island of Rhodes, there was no longer any sign of it. Rhodian representatives more than once had pressed mediation upon the combatants in the First Macedonian War—at times when Rome preferred to keep her allies in the fight. Other islanders too joined in the peace efforts, Chians, Byzantines, and Mytilenaeans. Fear that Greece might fall victim to one or more of the major powers (whether Philip, Attalus, or Rome) motivated the mediators, so we are told. Polybius puts harsh words in the mouth of a Greek orator, probably a Rhodian, who, among other things, brands the Romans as barbarians and delivers dire warnings about their imperialist ambitions. Authenticity of the speech lies outside demonstration. In any case, Rhodians and other islanders focused on the security of the Aegean, a security they reckoned as menaced by continuing warfare among the larger states. Those concerns did not march with the aims of Rome.[9]

---

17.58. It can be claimed that Prusias acted on behalf of Philip V, his relative by marriage; cf. Polyb. 15.22.1–3; Livy, 27.30.16. But the Bithynian king had his own differences with Attalus; cf. Polyb. 4.49.1–3. He took the opportunity for aggrandizement afforded by Attalus' absence.

8. The *adscripti* to Phoenice: Livy, 29.12.14. Ilium is included there as well—whether or not an authentic inclusion has been too much debated to too little effect; most of the long bibliography given by Dahlheim, *Struktur und Entwicklung*, 210–211, n. 75; 219–220, n. 99. Whatever the truth, Ilium carries no implications for Roman interests in the East. Nor does the mission to obtain the sacred stone, emblematic of the *mater Idaea*, from Pessinus, a mission accomplished through the good offices of Attalus in 205. The Sibylline Books had advised it, Delphi allegedly confirmed it. The object, however, was to rid Italy of Hannibal, not to expand contacts in Asia: Livy, 29.10.4–29.11.7, 29.14.5–14; Ovid, *Fasti*, 4.247–349.

9. Mediation efforts: Polyb. 11.4.1–2; Livy, 27.30.4–5; *cura erat . . . ne Philippus regnumque eius rebus Graeciae, grave libertati futurum, immisceretur*; 27.30.10: *ne causa aut Romanis aut Attalo intrandi Graeciam esset*; 28.7.13–15; Appian, *Mac.* 3.1. The speech: Polyb. 11.4–6. Speaker is identified only in the margin as Thrasycrates, quite possibly a Rhodian; cf. Walbank, *Commentary* II:274–275. It goes too far to consider mediation

The Republic withdrew attention from the East after the peace of Phoenice, indeed had largely done so more than two years earlier. Greek affairs reverted to form. The final years of the third century customarily call forth discussions of the preliminaries of Rome's "Second Macedonian War." Yet the contests which ultimately turned into that war were well under way before anyone anticipated or considered Roman intervention. Those years witnessed the convulsive realignments that had characterized Hellenistic history since the age of the *diadochoi*.

Attalus had pulled out of the previous war to halt the aggrandizements of Bithynia. The king had his hands full in protecting his own dominions. Prusias, it appears, could count some notable gains at Pergamene expense.[10] More ominous still, Antiochus III made a sudden appearance in western Asia Minor in 204 or 203, fresh from his spectacular *anabasis* into Iranian lands. The Great King detached Teos from Attalid control, as an inscription happens to reveal. He made additional inroads in Caria, encroachment near the Rhodian sphere of influence.[11] Rhodes herself faced direct challenge in a Cretan war, the war sparked and then fanned into activity by agents of Philip V. The Rhodians held their own, if one may judge from epigraphical treaties with individual Cretan cities, treaties in which Rhodes plainly has the upper hand.[12] The expansionism of Philip,

---

efforts as directed explicitly against Rome, as Holleaux, *Rome, la Grèce*, 35–38. See the discussion of Schmitt, *Rom und Rhodos*, 54–58, 193–211. But Schmitt fails to observe that attempts at a peaceful resolution can hardly have been welcome to Rome, whose principal purpose was to keep Aetolia in the war in order to distract the energies of Philip V; cf. Appian, *Mac.* 3.1: Ῥωμαίοις συμφέρει πολεμεῖν Αἰτωλοὺς Φιλίππῳ; Livy, 29.12.4–8. Whether an agreement between Rome and Rhodes dates back to 306 B.C., as implied by Polyb. 30.5.6–8, remains indeterminable; see above p. 68, n. 74. The alleged agreement, in any case, had no apparent effect on Rhodian policy and attitudes in the late third century.

10. "Mysia" was in his hands before 188, seized from Pergamum: Polyb. 21.46.9–10; Livy, 38.39.15. Perhaps as consequence of this war; so G. Vitucci, *Il regno di Bitinia* (Rome, 1953), 45–46; *contra*: Habicht, *Hermes* 84 (1956): 91–96; Walbank, *Commentary* III:172.

11. Teos: Herrmann, *Anatolia* 9 (1965): 34–35, lines 18–20, 33–34. Caria: *OGIS*, 234 = *FDelphes* III:4, 163; Welles, *RC*, nos. 38, 40; cf. Schmitt, *Untersuchungen*, 245–246. A newly published inscription from Athens honors two envoys from Alabanda, perhaps about this time; R. Pounder, *Hesperia* 47 (1978): 49–57. Whether the mission of the envoys had been prompted by fear of Antiochus, as suspected by the editor, is quite uncertain. The stone alludes only to a grant of *asylia*.

12. The Cretan war and Philip's encouragement of it: Polyb. 13.4–5, 18.54.8; Diod. 27.3, 28.1–2; Polyaenus, 5.17. Rhodian treaties with Hierapytna and Olus, probably near or after the conclusion of the war: *Syll.*³ 581 = *IC*, III, 3, 3A = Schmitt, *Staatsverträge*, nos. 551, 552a; cf. Holleaux, *Études* IV:124–145, 163–177; van Effentere, *La Crète*, 221–234; Spyridakis, in Burstein and Okin, *Panhellenica*, 119–128.

however, persisted. A pact between the Macedonian and Antiochus III menaced the equilibrium of the East—whether or not either one ever intended active cooperation with the other.[13] Philip, in any case, swept into the Propontic area in 202, taking Lysimacheia, Chalcedon, and Cius. Attalus had reason to feel anxiety, especially as Philip turned Cius over to Prusias, the Pergamene's old foe. Threat to her Pontic trade alienated Rhodes altogether, and the island now determined to resist. Philip's ambition appeared insatiable. Perinthus fell into his hands, then Thasos, then various Cyclades, then Samos.[14] A coalition of maritime states gathered to meet the threat: Rhodes, Byzantium, Cyzicus, Cos, and Chios. Most important, Attalus declared his readiness to join the struggle. There was no love lost between Pergamum and Rhodes, and relations between the states had hardly run a smooth course in recent years. Common interests and common danger drove them together.[15] The diplomatic reshuffling, the temporary shelving of old enmities, and the formation of convenient alliances follow the worn track of Hellenistic experience.

The campaigning season of 201 furnished stern tests for the combatants. Philip's fleet engaged the combined navies of Rhodes, Pergamum, and Byzantium in a destructive battle at Chios. The Macedonian claimed victory, but he had sustained damaging losses and declined further engagement there. At Lade, however, Philip faced only Rhodian ships and carried the day. Miletus, intimidated by the outcome, hastened to offer submission, and the king now controlled part of the Ionian coastline. Philip even aimed a knockout blow at Pergamum herself, tearing up the countryside, though failing to take the city. Rhodes suffered equal humiliation. Macedonian forces overran the Peraea, pushed into Caria, installed garrisons at Iasus, Bargylia, Euromus, and elsewhere. Smaller cities scrambled for allies. By the end of the season Philip had ensconced himself at Bargylia.[16] The

13. On the pact, with references, bibliography, and discussion, see above pp. 387–388.

14. For a narrative of events, with references, see Walbank, *Philip V*, 114–118. On Samos, see further Habicht, *AthMitt* 72 (1957): 233–241.

15. Byzantium: Polyb. 16.2.10; Cyzicus: Polyb. 16.31.3; Cos: *Syll.*³ 569; Polyb. 16.15.4; Chios: Polyb. 16.2.1; Appian, *Mac.* 4.1. The extant text of Polybius does not record formation of the Rhodian and Pergamene alliance. They were united by the time of the battle of Chios; Polyb. 16.2.5, 16.19.4; cf. 18.6.2. Prior relations between the states had been, at best, strained; cf. Polyb. 4.47.1–4.48.2; Livy, 27.30.4, 27.30.10.

16. Battle of Chios: Polyb. 16.2–9. Battle of Lade and submission of Miletus: Polyb. 16.15.1–8; cf. 16.10.1, 16.14.5. Assault on Pergamene territory: Polyb. 16.1.1–9; Appian, *Mac.* 4; Diod. 28.5. Campaigns in Rhodian Peraea and Caria: Polyb. 16.11.1–16.12.1, 18.2.3, 18.8.9, 18.44.4; Appian, *Mac.* 4; Livy, 33.18.1, 33.18.19–20, 34.32.5. Philip at Bargylia: Polyb. 16.24. A full discussion in Holleaux, *Études* IV:211–335.

precise order of these events eludes detection and continues to fuel controversy. The issue need not detain us.[17] What matters is that rivalry and warfare, alignment and realignment, among the Hellenistic powers proceeded almost without interruption after the peace of Phoenice; that western Asia Minor and the eastern and northern Aegean supplied deadly battlefields to settle or aggravate disputes; that cities and territory exchanged suzerains at an accelerated pace; that Philip, Rhodes, Pergamum, Prusias, and, to a lesser extent, Antiochus and Ptolemy embroiled themselves in dizzying quarrels. All this before anyone undertook to solicit the intervention of Rome.

Missions from Rhodes and Pergamum presented themselves to the Roman senate for the first time in the late summer or fall of 201. Ostensibly this was a momentous occasion. The calling in of Rome to rescue the victims of Philip would seem an admission of impotence on the part of the appellants, an invitation to the Republic to become arbiter of Hellenic affairs. The event needs reconsideration.

The ancient testimony, when scrutinized with care, makes surprisingly little of these missions, a fact rarely observed in the scholarship. Livy's text reports no more than the occurrence of the Pergamene and Rhodian embassies: they announced that the cities of Asia were being roused.[18] A single reference in Justin adds nothing: the delegations complained of offenses committed by Philip.[19] Appian remarks that Rhodian envoys disclosed at Rome the existence of the pact between Philip and Antiochus III; no word about a Pergamene embassy. That is the sum of the evidence: a most meager harvest.[20] Though the fact may be readily inferred, we are not told even that the envoys asked for Roman assistance! The possibility arises that these missions possessed much less importance than is customarily ascribed to them.

Given Rome's behavior in the "First Macedonian War," Attalus can hardly have been sanguine about her active involvement this time. The king, in fact, tried elsewhere as well. He put in a personal appearance at Athens in order to steel the resolve of her citizens and

17. Most of the lengthy bibliography, with a useful weighing of the positions, in R. M. Berthold, *Historia* 24 (1975): 150–163. Add now A. Mastrocinque, *La Caria e la Ionia meridionale in epoca ellenistica* (Rome, 1979): 165–173.

18. Livy, 31.2.1: *ab Attalo rege et Rhodiis legati venerunt nuntiantes Asiae quoque civitates sollicitari.*

19. Justin, 30.3.5: *legationes Attali regis et Rhodiorum iniurias Philippi querentes Romam venerunt.*

20. Appian, *Mac.* 4. The extant text of Polybius does not narrate the embassies. They are, in all probability, alluded to in Polyb. 16.24.3: Philip had learned by the time he was in Bargylia in winter 201/0 that his (unnamed) enemies had sent envoys to Rome. This helps to date the missions but provides no further information.

urge them into war. His representatives exerted the same appeal upon Aetolia, though without success. And in Crete, at about this time, he framed alliances with Lato and Malla. Attalus endeavored to build his coalition where he could. From Rome he perhaps expected no more than stern warnings to Philip, enough to intimidate him into yielding up his gains in Asia Minor. It was with surprise and elation that the king encountered Roman envoys at Athens in 200, and found them prepared to take a militant stance against Macedonia.[21] The envoys, supplied with a plausible case, demanded of Philip that he submit his differences with Attalus to arbitration.[22] The Pergamene had obtained the verbal backing he desired. He could now proceed to see to his own holdings, as evidently he did. Abydus, in any case, received but token Pergamene support when she came under siege by Philip in 200. Attalus had more direct concerns to protect. Rome would be serviceable to him primarily by diverting Philip's attention.[23]

Rhodes pursued an independent and cautious line. It was in her interests, as in Attalus', to provoke some Roman action, thereby to deflect Philip from his Aegean ambitions. She held back from a full Roman embrace. Her representatives too reached Athens, together with Attalus, in the spring of 200, where they encountered Roman envoys and made a joint appeal to the Athenians to declare war on Philip.[24] That mission accomplished, the Rhodians returned to matters of first importance: control of the Aegean. During the voyage home, they brought into alliance all the Cycladic islands, save three which were held by Macedonian garrisons.[25] Therein lay the thrust of Rhodes' policy. She had no intention of hitching her wagon to Rome's star. Relations between the two states were loose and undefined. Rome's initial demands on Philip included no reference to Rhodian claims. Only after the senate's legates visited Rhodes and, presumably, were set straight did they insist to Philip that damages suffered

21. Polyb. 16.25.2–4: θεωρῶν δ' αὐτοὺς καὶ τῆς προγεγενημένης κοινοπραγίας μνημονεύοντας καὶ πρὸς τὸν κατὰ τοῦ Φιλίππου πόλεμον ἑτοίμους ὄντας περιχαρὴς ἦν. Attalus' stay in Athens generally: Polyb. 16.25–26; Livy, 31.14.11–31.15.6. The appeals to Aetolia: Livy, 31.15.9–10. The treaties with Lato and Malla: N. Platon, *Kret-Chron* 7 (1953): 436–445; P. Ducrey and H. van Effentere, *KretChron* 21 (1969): 277–300; Ducrey, *BCH* 94 (1970): 637–659.

22. Polyb. 16.27.1–2, 16.34.1–4; Livy, 31.18.1–5; Diod. 28.6.

23. Polybius is critical of Attalus' failure to supply more substantial aid to Abydus: Polyb. 16.28.3, 16.34.1; Livy, 31.15.10–11, 31.16.6–8. C. G. Starr, *CP* 33 (1938): 63–68, ascribes the fact to friction between Rhodes and Pergamum. But the conclusion is a *non sequitur*. And the two powers, even though their interests normally diverged, had only recently operated in collaboration at Bargylia: Polyb. 16.24.1; cf. Hansen, *Attalids*, 60. Abydus was perhaps not a matter of the highest importance to Attalus.

24. Polyb. 16.26.6–10; Livy, 31.14.11, 31.15.4–7.

25. Livy, 31.15.8; cf. Polyb. 16.26.10.

by the island should also come under arbitration.[26] The Rhodians, as so often in their history, preferred to be the wooed rather than the wooer. They offered little assistance to Abydus, electing instead to prod the Romans into action there.[27] Rhodes attended to her own bailiwick. When Abydus fell, Achaean ambassadors showed up in the island and exhorted its citizens to reach an agreement with Philip— evidently not an unthinkable proposition even at that point. It took the importunings of Rome's delegation to derail the effort; only then did the Rhodian assembly resolve to honor a *philia* with Rome.[28] Rhodes' leaders had kept their own counsel, playing off the western power against Philip rather than following a Roman line.[29]

The Second Macedonian War served as vehicle for the territorial ambitions of Rome's eastern allies. Attalus, now a septuagenarian, led his forces in person and conducted his own diplomacy, showing a vigor that belied his years, like the *diadochoi* of old. Neither the liberty of the Greeks nor loyalty to Rome bestirred him into activity, whatever his propagandists asserted, but the increase of his kingdom. Cooperation with Roman forces put the island of Andros into his possession in 199, an island that had been coveted by Rhodes. Shortly thereafter, another joint attack battered the Euboean city of Oreus into submission, and it too was handed over to Attalus. A year later, a greater Euboean city, Eretria, under heavy assault by the combined navies of Rome, Rhodes, and Pergamum, elected to offer surrender to the king. Attalus perished before the conclusion of the war, but his successor Eumenes II claimed his acquisitions for the crown. Request for reparations from Philip had been the initial demand, reiterated during the war. It was no longer enough. Pergamum now unabashedly sought overseas possessions. The *decem legati* in 196 expressed willingness to comply but were overruled by Flamininus who referred matters back to Rome. The senate, in fact, liberated Oreus and Eretria, frustrating the avarice of Eumenes. But Andros, it appears, remained in Pergamene hands, joining Aegina as among the kingdom's dependencies in the Aegean.[30] Attalus had also employed his

26. Polyb. 16.27.2, 16.34.2–4.

27. Polyb. 16.28.3, 16.34.1–2; Livy, 31.15.10–11, 31.16.6–7.

28. Polyb. 16.35.1–2: ἔδοξε προσέχειν τῷ δήμῳ τοῖς Ῥωμαίοις καὶ στοχάζεσθαι τῆς τούτων φιλίας.

29. An oft-repeated conjecture has Theophiliscus, the Rhodian navarch, as prime obstacle to the summoning of Roman aid, an obstacle removed with his death at the battle of Chios; as, e.g., Schmitt, *Rom und Rhodos*, 59–61. No evidence buttresses that suggestion; so, rightly, Berthold, *CJ* 71 (1975–76): 99. But Berthold too exaggerates the importance of Rhodes' appeal to Rome: *op. cit.*, 106–107.

30. Acquisition of Andros: Livy, 31.45.1–8. Rhodes had earlier attempted, in vain, to take the island: Livy, 31.15.8. Subsequent Attalid rule in Andros has epigraphi-

diplomatic skills to expand Pergamene influence in mainland Greece. The king purchased land sacred to Apollo and restored it as gift to Sicyon in 198, and later supplied both cash and grain to the city, for which he received signal honors: a colossal statue, a gilded portrait, and the establishment of annual sacrifices on his behalf.[31] Attalus now had a foothold inside the Achaean League. He ingratiated himself further with members of the League (or endeavored to do so) by objecting to Nabis' questionable methods of acquiring control in Argos.[32] His posturing continued to the end. A speech delivered to the Boeotians in 197 reminded them of his and his forefathers' benefactions to that land. It was Attalus' last speech; he collapsed from the exertion, a prelude to his death not long thereafter.[33] The Pergamene kings, as is evident, exploited the Second Macedonian War to expand hegemony in the Aegean and authority in Greece proper.

Rhodian motives were no different. The island's forces held back from active combat at first. A delegation from Rome in winter 200/199 had to make specific request that the Rhodians involve themselves in the war.[34] The reason was not idleness or cowardice. Rhodes concentrated attention upon the Cyclades, upon Caria, and especially upon the Rhodian Peraea, areas where Philip's encroachments had touched her directly. Efforts to recover the Peraea appear to have occupied much of the war.[35] The peace talks at Nicaea in late 198 found Rhodian spokesmen demanding that Philip evacuate the Peraea and certain key cities of Caria.[36] The Rhodians focused unswervingly on their principal concerns. When the tide of war flowed against Philip,

---

cal attestation; see the evidence collected by Holleaux, *Études* II:169, n. 1; V:42, n. 1; cf. Larsen, *CP* 32 (1937): 17, n. 7. The submission of Oreus: Livy, 31.46.6–16; cf. *OGIS*, 284, 288. Surrender of Eretria: Livy, 32.16.6–17. Eumenes' claims on Oreus and Eretria and their denial by the senate: Polyb. 18.45.4–5, 18.47.10–11; Livy, 33.31.3, 33.34.10. Previous Pergamene petitions confined themselves to seeking reparations for losses suffered at Philip's hands: Polyb. 16.27.2, 16.34.3, 18.2.1–2; Livy, 32.33.5.

31. Polyb. 18.16.1–4; Livy, 32.40.8–9.

32. Livy, 32.40.1–2. McShane, *Foreign Policy*, 128, rather generously sees this as authentic Pergamene championship of autonomy.

33. Polyb. 18.17.6; Livy, 33.2.1–3. 33.21.1; Plut. *Flam.* 6.3. For earlier Pergamene benefactions to Boeotia, see *OGIS*, 310, 311, 749.

34. Livy, 31.28.4: *ad Rhodios quoque missi legati ut capesserent partem belli.*

35. Such may be inferred from the inscriptions of Nicagoras, four times *strategos* during the war and in charge of operations in the Peraea; e.g., *Syll.*[3] 586, lines 3–5: [σ]τραταγήσας ἐ[ς τὸ πέραν κα]τὰ πόλεμον ἐκ πά[ντων τε]τράκις; see Fraser and Bean, *Rhodian Peraea*, 99, n. 1.

36. Polyb. 18.2.3, 18.8.9; Livy, 32.33.6, 32.34.8. They added, for good measure, that Philip must withdraw from Perinthus, Sestus, and Abydus, and all markets and harbors in Asia—a dramatic gesture on behalf of freedom of the seas: Polyb. 18.2.4; Livy, 32.33.7.

they took full advantage in an all-out assault upon the Peraea which, at last, they wrested from Philip.[37] They had already made inroads in the Cyclades in 200. And reestablishment of control over the Nesiotic League belongs in or around these years.[38] The demands voiced at Nicaea now saw fulfillment. A *senatus consultum* on the peace settlement declared that Philip must remove his garrisons from cities in Caria, the Hellespont, and the northern Aegean.[39]

Polybius found fault with Attalus and the Rhodians for dilatoriness and inadequate zeal in prosecuting the war, a criticism echoed by Livy.[40] True enough, insofar as the contest between Rome and Philip is concerned. But that contest, *per se*, from the vantage point of Rhodes and Pergamum, was a diversion, a valuable means to draw Philip away from the Aegean and Asia Minor, where they themselves had staked out their claims. They showed more than adequate zeal in advancing their own interests, including interests which might bring them into conflict with one another.[41] Far from being lackeys of Rome, they had succeeded in maneuvering the western power into a situation from which they could reap the benefits.

## The Resistance to Antiochus the Great

As the shadow of Philip receded from Asia Minor, that of Antiochus the Great crept into its place. The Seleucid king's movements swiftly alerted sensitive antennae in Pergamum and Rhodes. Complex machinations embroiled the three powers during the mid-190s, events which our inadequate documentation supplies only in disjointed fragments. Clues survive, however, to allow some glimpse of attitudes and policies.

As early as 198, if Livy is to be trusted, Attalus' delegates reported to the Roman senate an invasion of Pergamene territory by Antiochus' forces. They requested either a relief expedition from Rome or release of Attalus' own troops to return home and protect his kingdom. The senate would not commit its armies but did appoint envoys to dissuade Antiochus from further encroachment, in the name of their common *amicitia*. Antiochus complied, unwilling at this point to strain relations with the Republic. Attalus placed a weighty golden crown on the Capitoline as token of his gratitude.[42] The tale has been

37. Livy, 33.18.1–20.
38. Livy, 31.15.8; cf. *BCH* 78 (1954): 338–344; Schmitt, *Rom und Rhodos*, 71–72.
39. Polyb. 18.44.4; Livy, 33.30.3.
40. Polyb. 16.28; Livy, 31.15.10–11.
41. E.g. Attalus' acquisition of Andros; see above, n. 30.
42. Livy, 32.8.9–16, 32.27.1.

doubted in whole or in part—unnecessarily so. Neither chronological objections nor appeals to "annalistic falsification" are cogent. Attalus' behavior, in fact, is characteristic. By threatening to withdraw his forces from the war on Philip, he nudged Rome into pulling his chestnuts out of the fire.[43]

Rhodes employed a similar device to check the advance of Antiochus in 197. The king sent an army to Sardis and used his fleet to subdue Ptolemaic cities on the coasts of Cilicia, Lycia, and Caria. No resistance materialized as Antiochus picked off the cities one by one, until forced to put Coracesium to siege. There the Rhodians dispatched envoys with a brave speech, asserting that they would permit him to go no further. The Seleucid backed down—or, at least, took on a friendly posture, pointing to a history of good relations with Rhodes and insisting that his actions had no hostile intent.[44] Rhodian sources lie behind the narrative here, a handsome tribute to the valor and scruples of the state. That bias can be discounted, but there is no reason to question the encounter itself. What rouses interest is the character of the Rhodians' argument. They justified their intervention on the grounds that they could not allow Antiochus to join forces with Philip and thus endanger the liberty of the Greeks. The implicit or explicit threat here is that further advance by Antiochus would bring him in conflict with Rome, who was still fighting a war against Philip.[45] That Antiochus in fact expected to link with Philip—or that Rhodes ever thought he did—is most dubious. The Seleucid made no move even to support Philip's holdings in Caria.[46] Rhodes' anxiety centered upon her own sphere of influence, now menaced by Antiochus' aggrandizement. The invoking of Rome was a contrivance.

43. Holleaux, *Études* III:331–335, rejected the tale altogether; similarly, Magie, *RRAM* II:753–754, n. 48. But the chronological objections were answered by O. Leuze, *Hermes* 58 (1923): 190–201. Livy may have embellished the speech of Attalus' envoys, but there is no good reason to regard the episode as sheer invention; cf. Badian, *Studies*, 114–115; Schmitt, *Untersuchungen*, 269–270; Bredehorn, *Senatsakten*, 140–144. Schmitt's conjecture, *op. cit.*, 271–276, about extensive territorial gains by Antiochus in 198, however, lacks plausibility. The thesis, among other things, requires jettisoning Livy, 32.27.1, without sound reason; see also Livy, 33.20.8–9. Schmitt's arguments are justly criticized by Rawlings, *AJAH* 1 (1976): 4–5.

44. Livy, 33.19.9–33.20.7; Porphyry, *FGH*, 260 F 46.

45. Explicit in Livy, 33.20.2–3: *si eo fine non contineret classem copiasque suas, se obviam ituros, non ab odio ullo, sed ne coniungi eum Philippo paterentur et impedimento esse Romanis liberantibus Graeciam.* Polybius' formulation does not mention Rome, but it is only a fragment, and a reference to Philip suffices to make the implication: 18.41a.1: κωλύειν δὲ τὸν Ἀντίοχον παραπλεῖν, οὐκ ἀπεχθείας χάριν, ἀλλ' ὑφορώμενοι μὴ Φιλίππῳ συνεπισχύσας ἐμπόδιον γένηται τῇ τῶν Ἑλλήνων ἐλευθερίᾳ. The pro-Rhodian flavor of the whole account has long been recognized; see, e.g., Nissen, *Kritische Untersuchungen*, 142; Schmitt, *Rom und Rhodos*, 74–78; Rawlings, *AJAH* 1 (1976): 9–10.

46. Cf. Livy, 33.18.

And it worked. Antiochus, disinclined to alienate the Republic, treated Rhodes gingerly, denied that his actions were directed against her, and affirmed his own *amicitia* with Rome.[47] The immediate sequel reinforces this analysis. News of Cynoscephalae arrived in Rhodes while Antiochus' envoys were there. The Rhodians suddenly abandoned their militant posture against Antiochus. The reason is clear enough: they could no longer shield themselves behind a Roman war on Philip.[48] So Rome (or the name of Rome) had once again been utilized by Rhodes to her own ends.

Closing of the Second Macedonian War dictated a shift in tactics. Rhodes evidently reached a *modus vivendi* with Antiochus. The Seleucid turned over to her the city of Stratonicea which he had evidently occupied after Cynoscephalae. Rhodes maintained the posture of protectress of cities attached to Ptolemy and guarantor of their "freedom," which meant, in fact, that Antiochus evinced no further interest in them. Rhodes would be their patron, a recovery of her position of prestige in southwestern Asia Minor.[49] In recompense,

47. Livy, 33.20.7–9. The supposed desire to collaborate with Philip is found also in Livy, 33.19.11.

48. Livy, 33.20.10.

49. The acquisition of Stratonicea, probably in 197 or not long thereafter: Livy, 33.18.20–22. This arrangement is surely alluded to by Rhodian spokesmen thirty years later; Polyb. 30.31.6: Στρατονίκειαν ἐλάβομεν ἐν μεγάλῃ χάριτι παρ' Ἀντιόχου καὶ Σελεύκου. Identification of the Antiochus and Seleucus has caused much debate, with several scholars opting for a pair some time in the third century as the origins of Rhodian claims on the city, thus giving full force to Livy's *nec recipi nisi aliquanto post per Antiochum potuit.* Principal bibliography in Briscoe, *Commentary*, 283, and Walbank, *Commentary* III:457–458; add Mastrocinque, *La Caria*, 123–125. But *recipere* need not mean "recover," as Livian usage in nearby passages clearly shows: 33.18.6, 33.18.19; so, rightly, Briscoe, *loc. cit.* It is hard not to see the "Antiochus" in Polyb. 30.31.6 as Antiochus III. The addition of Seleucus, with no elucidation, is troublesome on any theory. The old emendation of Niebuhr, Ἀντιόχου τοῦ Σελεύκου, has been unjustly dismissed and ignored. In fact, it causes the fewest difficulties of any solution. The version of Valerius Antias, that *Rome* handed over Stratonicea and other Carian cities to Rhodes, is transparent fiction: Livy, 33.30.10–11. For Rhodes' protection of the "freedom" of Ptolemaic cities, see Livy, 33.20.11–12. The propaganda is accepted at face value by Magie, *RRAM* II:946, n. 49; cf. Will, *Histoire politique* II:156. Others take the opposite position: Rhodes removed Ptolemaic influence and took the cities under her control; Niese, *Geschichte* II:640; Holleaux, *Études* V:364; Rawlings, *AJAH* 1 (1976): 9–13. The practical difference is small. Rhodes certainly kept up appearances. Her acquisition of Caunus, we happen to learn, came through formal purchase from Ptolemy's generals probably in 197 or 196; Polyb. 30.31.6; on the date, see Holleaux, *Études* IV:304–305. Walbank, *Commentary* III:457, prefers 191/0. But there can be little doubt that genuine Ptolemaic influence in these years is a chimera. Rhodian authority had risen in its place. The fact that some of these cities, Myndus, Samos, Halicarnassus, and probably Caunus, acted as mediators in the peace treaty for Miletus and Magnesia in 196 (*Syll.*[3] 588, lines 9–13) by no means shows that they were independent of Rhodian dominance.

Rhodians turned a blind eye to Antiochus' gains in Lycia, Ionia, and Aeolia, and even tolerated his influence in parts of Caria. By the spring of 196, the king held Ephesus and Abydus—and, in the taking of Ephesus, may indeed have received Rhodian support.[50] The *modus vivendi* was of mutual advantage. Attalus' death in 197 doubtless provided a stimulus and opportunity for Antiochus' aggressions. Rhodes can hardly have been ecstatic about the resurgence of Seleucid power in Asia Minor. But so long as the king's ambitions directed themselves largely toward the Pergamene sphere of influence, the Rhodians could feel reasonably content. They had recovered much of their position in the Peraea and parts of Caria, with Antiochus' blessing. The Rhodian fleet, in turn, refrained from interfering with Antiochus' ventures in the Aegean. The two powers, in essence, stayed out of each other's way.[51]

Of Roman interest in Asia Minor there is hardly a trace. The senate's envoys had persuaded Antiochus to leave off his attacks on Pergamene territory in 198. Rome's intervention, however, had nothing to do with Asia Minor as such; her purpose was simply to keep Attalus in the war against Philip. Rhodes had invoked the Republic's power to give Antiochus second thoughts, but got no tangible

50. The occupation of Ephesus and Abydus: Polyb. 18.41a.2; Livy, 33.38.1–4; Porphyry, *FGH*, 260 F 46. Rhodian assistance in the capture of Ephesus is attested by Frontinus, *Strat.* 3.9.10: *Antiochus adversus Ephesios Rhodiis, quos in auxilio habebat, praecepit*—an episode most plausibly assigned to this time; cf. Rawlings, *AJAH* 1 (1976): 13–14. The course of Antiochus' campaigns in 197 can only be conjectured and the gains partly surmised from later holdings; see discussions by Schmitt, *Untersuchungen*, 278–279; Mastrocinque, *PP* 31 (1976): 307–322; *La Caria*, 176–182. Rawlings' assertion, *op. cit.*, 7, 14, 16, that the king gave Rhodes a free hand in Caria, is inaccurate. Iasus, at least, had come under Seleucid suzerainty: *OGIS*, 237; *Annuario*, 45–46 (1967–68), 2, I and II, pp. 445–448; cf. Livy, 37.17.3. A Roman legate removed the Macedonian garrison from Bargylia in 196: Polyb. 18.48.1–2; Livy, 33.35.1–2. Status of the other Carian cities is a matter of guesswork; see Schmitt, *op. cit.*, 280–281; Walbank, *Commentary* II:610–611, 614–615.

51. It goes too far, however, to reckon this relationship as based on a "pact" or issuing in active collaboration; so, most recently, Rawlings, *AJAH* 1 (1976): 2–28. Active collaboration is attested only for the taking of Ephesus—and even that is uncertain. See previous note. A reasonable amount of information survives on Antiochus' movements in the mid- and late 190s, and nowhere does he receive Rhodian assistance. His suggestion to the Romans in 196 that Rhodes might arbitrate their differences implies that the island was regarded as neutral, not in the camp of the Seleucids: Polyb. 18.52.3–4. Nor does the fact that individual Rhodians are described as "friends of the King" or act as his agents indicate any official compact between the two states: *OGIS*, 243; *BCH* 22 (1898):382, no. 23; *IC*, I, 27, 1; *IC*, II, 12, 21; *IC*, II, 16, 3. Observe the mission of Hegesianax on behalf of Antiochus in 196: Polyb. 18.47.4, 18.49.4; cf. Athenaeus, 4.155 AB. He was from Alexandria Troas (*Syll.*[3] 585, n. 18)—not a city friendly to the king; cf. Livy, 35.42.2.

assistance. The "liberation" of Asia from Philip's garrisons was accomplished, in fact, by Rhodians and by Antiochus. To be sure, the *decem legati*, who announced peace terms in summer, 196, declared that Philip should evacuate the occupied towns of Asia, including Euromus, Pedasa, Bargylia, Iasus, and Abydus.[52] The gesture, however, was largely obsolete even before it was made. When a Roman legate went to see to its implementation, he found Macedonian forces remaining only in Bargylia. Abydus had already fallen into Antiochus' hands, so had Iasus, and, very likely, Euromus and Pedasa as well.[53] In direct talks with Antiochus or his representatives, the Roman commissioners urged his withdrawal from all Asian cities formerly under the suzerainty of Ptolemy and Philip and his abstention from autonomous cities. It was all posturing. Antiochus had proper responses to make; he read the Romans a lesson in Hellenistic history at Lysimacheia and broke up the conference. As the king knew or surmised, Rome had no intention of implementing her requests.[54] The affairs of Asia Minor fell back into the old patterns. The fact is underlined by a border war between Miletus and Magnesia, the antagonists themselves, it appears, entirely oblivious of the great powers jockeying for position in western Anatolia. A settlement came in autumn, 196, with a host of Asian cities signing the document, headed by Rhodes who would be chief guarantor of its terms. There is no sign of Antiochus—nor (it need hardly be said) of Rome.[55]

Some cities hoped to shelter themselves under the Roman umbrella. Lampsacus in 197, through direct appeal and through indirect patronage by Massilia, requested inclusion in the peace treaty between Rome and Philip. Such a move could afford protection against greater powers in Asia Minor, perhaps against Antiochus, perhaps indeed against Pergamum. The Lampsacenes got a number of polite responses, but evidently nothing concrete. Rome would not extend her

52. Polyb. 18.44.4; Livy, 33.30.3.

53. Bargylia alone is mentioned as freed by the Roman representative P. Lentulus: Polyb. 18.48.1–2; Livy, 33.35.1–2. On Abydus, see Livy, 33.38.4; Iasus, above n. 50. Cf. the discussions of Schmitt, *Untersuchungen*, 280–281, 284; Walbank, *Commentary* II:610–611.

54. Polyb. 18.47.1, 18.50–51; Livy, 33.34.2–3, 33.39–41; Appian, *Syr.* 3. Similarly, a Roman message was to be sent to Prusias, requesting him to liberate Cius: Polyb. 18.44.5; Livy, 33.30.4. Nothing, so far as we know, ever came of it; cf. Vitucci, *Il regno di Bitinia*, 50–51.

55. *Syll.*³ 588, lines 4–27, 68–69, 92–94. A recently published document discloses a hitherto unknown war involving Temnos and Clazomenae some time in the early second century. Its conclusion produced arbitration of differences by Cnidus and a treaty between the former belligerents. See the publication and commentary by Herrmann, *1st Mitt*, 29 (1979), 249–271.

protection that far.[56] In autumn or winter, 197, Antiochus launched assaults upon Lampsacus and Smyrna. They wanted their liberty; he would force his own version of it upon them.[57] The two cities made appeal to Rome—or to Flamininus. What satisfaction did they get? The *decem legati*, as we have seen, asked Antiochus to keep his hands off the autonomous cities of Asia. At Lysimacheia Roman legates called upon representatives of Smyrna and Lampsacus to present their case against Antiochus. But the king cut them short, denied Rome's *locus standi*, and ended the interview. The legates pursued it no further.[58] Smyrna sought another means whereby to curry Rome's favor: dedication of a temple to the goddess Roma in 195.[59] That move too failed to evoke any significant Roman response. From the senate's perspective, the affairs of Anatolia were too distant to matter.

Our sources leave the years of the mid-190s, so far as Asia Minor is concerned, almost a complete blank. After the furious activity of 197 and 196, a lull evidently set in. The known activities of Pergamum and Rhodes, in any case, are confined to military assistance in the war on Nabis, an event rather far from their direct environs. Their motives are unrecorded, but can be reconstructed. Each of the powers had its own motivation, separate and distinct, repeating patterns already discerned and designs that would hold in the future.

Eumenes endeavored to ingratiate himself with the Republic, a *quid pro quo* already in mind, his domestic circumstances, as ever, paramount. Antiochus' advances in Anatolia during the last months of Attalus' life and the beginnings of Eumenes' tenure cut into the

---

56. *Syll.*³ 591. See the analysis of Bickermann, *Philologus* 87 (1932): 277–299—not refuted by Desideri, *StudClassOrient* 19–20 (1970–71): 501–506. That Rome accepted no formal or informal relationship with Lampsacus at this time seems clear from Polyb. 18.51.1; Livy, 43.6.7. The Lampsacenes perhaps misconstrued the polite responses as consent: *Syll.*³ 591, lines 32–35, 64–67. The appeal is almost always taken in connection with Antiochus' attack on Lampsacus. Yet the decree does not make mention of Antiochus. Indeed, no attack seems yet to have taken place; cf. lines 35–36: καὶ διότι ἐάν τις [παρενοχλεῖν πειρᾶτ]αι οὐκ ἐπιτρέψει ἀλλὰ κωλύσει. Did Eumenes prod Lampsacus into making the appeal? So McShane, *Foreign Policy*, 137; Hansen, *Attalids*, 74–75: without evidence. Friendly relations between Pergamum and Lampsacus in 218 (Polyb. 5.78.6) proves nothing for 197.

57. Livy, 33.38.3–7: *Zmyrna et Lampsacus libertatem usurpabant . . . spem conabatur facere, brevi quod peterent habituros, sed cum satis et ipsis et omnibus aliis appareret, ab rege impetratam eos libertatem, non per occasionem raptam habere;* cf. Appian, *Syr.* 2. For the chronology, see Schmitt, *Untersuchungen*, 289–295.

58. Appeals to Rome: Diod. 29.7; Appian, *Syr.* 2; cf. Polyb. 18.49.1; Walbank, *Commentary* II:620–621. Roman demands for the integrity of free cities in Asia: Polyb. 18.47.1, 18.50.7; Livy, 33.34.3. The summoning of Lampsacenes and Smyrnaeans at Lysimacheia and the result: Polyb. 18.52.1–4.

59. Tac. *Ann.* 4.56.1.

territory and prestige of the Pergamene royal house. Polybius paints a gloomy picture: Eumenes, upon accession, inherited domains limited to a few insignificant little towns.[60] An exaggerated description, perhaps, designed to contrast with Pergamum's later prosperity, but not altogether without foundation.[61] The inroads of Antiochus, whether through force or diplomacy, had seriously damaged Attalid authority. It is no accident that Eumenes commanded Pergamene ships in person, with a show of force in the Cyclades and a demonstration of unity with the Roman cause against Nabis in 195.[62] Prospects of turning Rome's attention to the Pergamene plight in Asia Minor did not seem bright. Eumenes, however, worked patiently toward that end. Greek envoys in large numbers pressed their causes upon the Roman senate in spring, 193, including missions from a large part of Hellenic Asia and from the kings. Eumenes does not receive specific mention but he was certainly pulling some of the strings. A Roman diplomatic mission, authorized to treat with Antiochus, had instructions to stop first at Pergamum. There Eumenes filled their ears with talk of the Seleucid's ambition, rousing all the wit and authority he could muster to propel Rome into war.[63] When Roman legates met with Antiochus' spokesmen at Ephesus, envoys from various cities of Greek Asia came to register complaints, their charges and behavior carefully orchestrated from behind the scenes by Eumenes.[64] The cities of Smyrna, Lampsacus, and Alexandria Troas continued to resist Antiochus' efforts at negotiation and compulsion in 192, doubtless encouraged by promises from the Pergamenes.[65] Eumenes sent his brother Attalus to Rome in spring of that year with reports that Antiochus had crossed the Hellespont in arms.[66] The growing danger of Eumenes' diplomacy impressed itself upon Antiochus. The Seleucid had already formed a set of marriage connections with Egypt and Cappadocia, and now offered a daughter to Eumenes, thereby to secure his quiescence. Eumenes' brothers expected the alliance to be consum-

60. Polyb. 32.8.3: παραλαβὼν παρὰ τοῦ πατρὸς τὴν βασιλείαν συνεσταλμένην τελέως εἰς ὀλίγα καὶ λιτὰ πολισμάτια; cf. 23.11.7; Livy, 40.8.14.

61. Cf. Strabo, 13.4.2 (C 624).

62. Livy, 34.26.11, 34.29.4–5, 34.30.7, 34.35.2, 34.40.7; Zon. 9.18; Syll.³ 595A: [βασιλεὺς Εὐμένης ἀπὸ] τῶ[ν γενομένων ἐκ τ]ῆς στρατείας λαφύρων [ἣν ἐστρατεύσατο μετὰ Ῥωμαί]ων κ[αὶ τῶ]ν ἄ[λλων] σ[υ]μμάχ[ω]ν ἐπὶ Νάβιν τὸν Λάκωνα.

63. Livy, 34.57.2, 35.13.6–10: cupidus belli adversus Antiochum Eumenes erat . . . quantum auctoritate, quantum consilio valebat, incitabat Romanos ad bellum.

64. Livy, 35.17.1: praeparatas iam ante et instructas ab Eumene.

65. Livy, 35.42.2; cf. Polyb. 21.13.3, 21.14.2.

66. Livy, 35.23.10. Whether the report was true or not remains unsettled; cf. Walbank, Philip V, 328. Eumenes evidently participated about this time in the Achaean war on Nabis, earning honors and gratitude from Achaea; Syll.³ 605; cf. Livy, 35.25–30; Plut. Phil. 14–15. The purpose perhaps was to knock out a potential ally of Antiochus.

mated, but the king himself spurned it. Having played his part in maneuvering Rome and Antiochus into confrontation, he would not now reverse direction.[67] To what extent Eumenes' machinations bear responsibility for the outbreak of war is matter for speculation. His objectives, however, follow lines set out by Attalus I: to deploy Roman might for Pergamene ends.

The Rhodians pursued a different path. Involvement in the war on Nabis in 195 can hardly have been for the purpose of enlisting Roman aid against Antiochus. No clash between Rhodes and the Seleucid loomed ahead. They managed to steer clear of one another.[68] Nor should Rhodian participation in the war against Nabis be taken as cultivating the favor of Rome—who had little stake in that contest anyway. The island sent ships to help blockade Gytheum and its representatives took part in the negotiations. Nothing more is known about Rhodian involvement, and there may have been little more.[69] Rhodes, it can be suggested, had her own reasons for seeking the punishment of Nabis. The Spartan king had connections in Crete, associations with piratical raids conducted by Cretans, and had sponsored marauding activities on the high seas.[70] That gave more than adequate stimulus for Rhodian efforts to cut Nabis off from any outlet to the sea. The island's interests guided policy. Cooperation between Rhodes and Pergamum against Nabis, like their cooperation against Philip, derived from expediency, aims that temporarily converged while enduring interests diverged.

The contrast stands out too in their behavior once Rome did come to blows with Antiochus the Great. Eumenes, who had hoped and conspired for just such an outcome, entered the fray at the beginning. Even before Rome declared war, the king deposited a garrison, on Flamininus' advice, at Chalcis to hold the city against any attempts by Antiochus.[71] Pergamene forces played a major role throughout the war, engaged at Thermopylae, then especially active when the scene shifted to the Aegean and Asia Minor.[72] Rhodes, on the other hand, put in no appearance in the early months of the war. A beneficiary

67. Appian, *Syr.* 5; cf. Polyb. 21.20.8–9; Livy, 37.53.13–14. The Polybian passage may imply that the offer came in 191 after war broke out; so Leuze, *Hermes* 58 (1923): 211, n. 2. The language assigned to Eumenes in a speech of 189, however, should probably not be pressed. Antiochus had reason to appease the Pergamene in 192 when he was urging Rome into war.

68. Cf. Appian, *Syr.* 12.

69. Livy, 34.26.11, 34.29.4, 34.30.7, 34.35.2, 34.38.1, 34.40.7; Zon. 9.18.

70. Polyb. 13.8.2; Livy, 34.32.18, 34.35.9, 34.36.3. See van Effentere, *La Crète,* 257–260.

71. Livy, 35.39.1–2; cf. *Syll.*³ 605 B.

72. Discussion and references in McShane, *Foreign Policy,* 143–147; Hansen, *Attalids,* 77–92.

of the *modus vivendi* with Antiochus, she would not automatically reckon him an enemy and join a crusade against him, a crusade which, if successful, would redound to the advantage of Pergamum. Only after the battle of Thermopylae, when Antiochus retreated ignominiously from Greece, only after a Roman navy sailed into the Aegean, indeed after a victory at sea by Pergamene and Roman ships, did vessels sent by Rhodes join the allied forces against Antiochus.[73] No commitment to Rome nor demands from her mobilized the Rhodians. They waited on events. When the course of war seemed to mark out the prospective winner, they swung into action. Rhodes fought vigorously and conspicuously for the remainder of the conflict.[74]

Roman military power, of course, decided the issue. But Rome had not ordered her allies into war nor dictated their behavior during it. This was more Eumenes' war than the senate's. He stood to gain most from it—and he made his wishes felt. When Antiochus extended peace feelers in 190, both the Roman commander and Rhodian diplomats were ready to comply. Eumenes, however, stepped in to object: he would not consent to negotiate while Antiochus had a stranglehold on Pergamum. A good point, and Eumenes carried it.[75] The Rhodians, for their part, kept their sights trained largely on southwestern Asia Minor. Spokesmen from the island managed to divert the Roman fleet from Ephesus, persuading it to operate off Lycia and to recover for Rhodes possessions on the mainland opposite her. Rhodian opinion prevailed also in calling off a Roman attack on Iasus; exiles from that city had pleaded for Rhodes' intercession lest it be destroyed. The intercession proved successful. Pergamum joined in support and Rome left off the siege.[76] Asian Greeks were not fighting a Roman war; if anything, rather the reverse. Eumenes had pushed it, and Eumenes kept his gaze fixed on potential gains available once the Seleucid tide of expansion had been rolled back. Roman strength would be utilized to build Pergamene domains at Antiochus' expense, and allow Eumenes thereafter to dispense with foreign aid.[77]

73. Livy, 36.45.5; see Rawlings, *AJAH* 1 (1976): 20–21. Not that Rhodes awaited the outcome of that naval battle to make up her mind; the Seleucid admiral expected the arrival of Rhodian ships and hoped to force the battle beforehand: Livy, 36.43.4.

74. Sources and narrative in H. van Gelder, *Geschichte der alten Rhodier* (The Hague, 1900), 134–140. The analysis of M. Martina, *Quaderni di filologia classica* 2 (1979): 45–61, who sees growing hostility between Rome and Rhodes in the early second century, is without foundation.

75. Polyb. 21.10; Livy, 37.19.1–6.

76. Livy, 37.14–17.

77. Livy, 35.13.8: *si pax victo daretur, multa illi detracta sibi accessura, ut facile deinde se ab eo sine ullo auxilio Romano tueri posset.* Antiochus knew well enough that negotiations and a settlement depended above all on the attitude of Eumenes: Polyb. 21.16.5–6; Livy, 37.45.6.

Rhodes had not provoked the war, nor especially desired it. She entered when its outcome could already be foreseen, and she steered it in directions from which she could benefit.

Antiochus once beaten, the victors hastened to claim the spoils. The battle of Magnesia decided Antiochus' fate and bestirred a multitude of missions from Asian states which descended upon Rome already in the early summer of 189. Eumenes made the trip in person, thereby to balance or overmatch the application of Rhodian delegates who would be among the claimants for prizes. Wartime collaborations gave way swiftly to competition for territorial gains. Polybius provides speeches for both the Pergamene king and the Rhodian spokesman. Some have questioned their authenticity, though without compelling reason. The setting and circumstances, in any case, are authentic; and the tone of the orations coincides well with the aspirations of the states involved. Rome never doubted that Pergamum and Rhodes entered the war for tangible benefits. When Eumenes affected modesty, Roman senators insisted that he reveal his wishes: he knew best what would suit his own interests in Asia.[78] The king sought to forestall the arguments of Rhodes' representatives. They will mouth fine phrases about liberty, he asserted, but cities freed at their request will only fall under their sway. Eumenes declared without embarrassment that he had come for his due: both he and the Rhodians were there to gain material advantage for their own states.[79] Roman occupation of lands wrested from Antiochus would, of course, be acceptable, even welcome; but if Rome decides to evacuate them, the conquered territory should go to Pergamum. Eumenes took for granted that there would be some division of territorial spoils.[80] The Rhodians themselves, while duly advocating the liberation of cities rescued from Seleucid control, suggested that Eumenes might have his reward too: territory which in its aggregate would boost his holdings to ten times their present size. So, Rhodes could champion the principle of autonomy while conceding the victor's right to annex the prizes of war—a standard Hellenistic conjunction.[81]

Rome understood the principles. Asia Minor was liberated from Seleucid control and Antiochus confined to areas beyond the Taurus,

78. Polyb. 21.18; Livy, 37.52. See Polyb. 21.18.9: καὶ γὰρ εἰδέναι τὰ διαφέροντα τοῖς ἰδίοις πράγμασιν ἐκεῖνον ἀκριβέστερον τὰ κατὰ τὴν 'Ασίαν. Doubts about the reliability of the speeches expressed by Bickermann, *REG* 50 (1937): 233–234; Magie, *RRAM* I: 108; II: 950, n. 59. But see Gelzer, *SBHeid* (1956): 22–25.

79. Polyb. 21.19–21; Livy, 37.53. See Polyb. 21.19.3: ἐκείνους γὰρ παρεῖναι μὲν οὐδὲν ἧττον ὑπὲρ τῆς σφετέρας πατρίδος συμφερόντως σπουδάζοντας ἧπερ αὐτοὺς ὑπὲρ τῆς ἰδίας ἀρχῆς φιλοτιμεῖσθαι κατὰ τὸ παρόν.

80. Polyb. 21.21.7–9; Livy, 37.53.25–27.

81. Polyb. 21.22–23; Livy, 37.54.

but Rome would not step into the vacuum. Her chief allies expected territorial gains, and they would have them. A *senatus consultum* of 189 laid the groundwork for the peace treaty at Apamea in the following year. Eumenes acquired all that the Rhodians had recommended to the senate and much more. The largest portion of cis-Tauric Asia would be his; that included both Phrygias, Lycaonia, Mysia, Milyas, Lydia, Ionia, and the cities of Tralles, Ephesus, and Telmessus, not to mention Chersonesus, Lysimacheia, and neighboring areas in Europe. Cities once tributary to Attalus would now be liable for that tribute to Eumenes; and he could exact from cities which had sided with Antiochus the payments they had previously rendered to the Seleucid. The gains were handsome and substantial.[82] Rhodes may have had misgivings over so extensive an increase of Pergamene holdings. But she had achieved her own primary objectives as well. As Seleucid power vacated southwestern Asia Minor, the area fell under Rhodian suzerainty, with Rome's blessing: Lycia and all of Caria south of the Meander.[83]

Roman senators could hardly make any plainer their desire to keep Asia Minor at a distance and to leave to others the chore of policing it. Generous awards to Pergamum and Rhodes set them in that role and advertised a stable order in Anatolia, just as treaties with Achaea and Aetolia advertised a stable order in mainland Greece. Of course, all this was accompanied by conventional pronouncements guaranteeing the integrity of "autonomous" cities. Numerous cities came under that heading, those which had been ruled by the Seleucids but had joined the Roman alliance prior to Magnesia. Some of them, indeed, like Clazomenae, Miletus, Chios, Smyrna, Erythrae, Phocaea, and perhaps Ilium, enjoyed increase of territory and additional rewards. Roman officials indulged in the sloganeering familiar to Hellenistic states.[84] Other cities too applied to Rome and got pious

82. The *senatus consultum*: Polyb. 21.24.6–8; Livy, 37.55.5–6, 37.56.1–4. The arrangements at Apamea: Polyb. 21.46.2–3, 21.46.9–10; Livy, 38.39.7–8, 38.39.14–16; Diod. 29.11; Appian, *Syr.* 44. Eumenes wanted more still, staking a claim to Pamphylia on the alleged ground that it lay on his side of the Taurus: Polyb. 21.46.11; Livy, 38.39.17. On Eumenes' acquisitions, see the thorough treatment by Magie, *RRAM* II:758–764, n. 56; cf. Walbank, *Commentary* III:171–174.

83. Polyb. 21.24.7–8, 21.46.8; Livy, 37.55.5, 37.56.5–6; Diod. 29.11; Appian, *Syr.* 44. The Rhodians also made conspicuous their patronage of the city of Soli in Cilicia: Polyb. 21.24.10–15; Livy, 37.56.7–10. On the new holdings, see Fraser and Bean, *Rhodian Peraea*, 107–117.

84. Polyb. 21.24.8, 21.46.2–6; Livy, 37.55.6, 37.56.2, 38.39.7–12. Various identifications of the "free cities" by Bickermann, *REG* 50 (1937): 235–239; Magie, *RRAM* II:958–959, n. 75; Schmitt, *Untersuchungen*, 278–290; Bernhardt, *Imperium und Eleutheria*, 52–71; Walbank, *Commentary* III:166–170. For Roman sloganeering, see above pp. 151–153.

promises: Alabanda, Apollonia, Araxa.[85] None of this, however, implied intention or obligation on the part of the Republic to protect the privileges of smaller communities. Pergamum and Rhodes took precedence. Defense of western Asia Minor and the whole Anatolian coastline would devolve upon them, not upon Rome.

To inland areas the senate paid even less heed. After Antiochus' defeat, Cn. Manlius Vulso, the consul of 189, conducted a savage campaign against the Galatians. Pretexts for that war were at hand: the Celts had supplied auxiliaries for Antiochus' forces and constituted a perpetual menace to the Greek states on their borders.[86] Manlius' own ambitions, however, played a bigger part in the motivation: to eclipse the exploits of the Scipios and to reap the financial rewards of victory. There had been no senatorial declaration of war.[87] Manlius fought the war in conjunction with Pergamene troops commanded by the brothers of Eumenes. Attalus was conspicuous both in the fighting and in the negotiations. When time for a settlement came, Manlius even refrained from imposing terms until Eumenes himself could arrive on the scene.[88] Indeed, the agreement reached was characterized as a "peace with Eumenes." Manlius warned the Galatians off Pergamene territory and advised them to stay inside their own borders.[89] That represented the extent of Roman interests. The Republic's forces carried off their loot, content with having softened up the Galatians for Eumenes, and returned home. Eumenes was the prime beneficiary in this, as in much else.[90]

The king moved to extend his influence further into areas now forfeited by Antiochus and unimportant to Rome.[91] Ariarathes IV of

85. Alabanda: *REG* 11 (1898): 258–266. Apollonia: Robert, *La Carie* II:303–312. Araxa: *SEG*, XVIII, 570. Chronology of these visits, however, is not in every case secure.

86. Livy, 37.60.2, 38.12.3–4.

87. On the campaign, see Polyb. 21.33–39; Livy, 38.12–27. For criticisms of Manlius' personal motives, delivered after the campaign by political foes, see above pp. 229–230. The absence of a senatorial declaration of war, however, is not denied by Manlius: Livy, 38.45.4–7, 38.48.9–12.

88. Polyb. 21.41.6: τοῖς δὲ Γαλάταις ἀπεκρίθη διότι προσδεξάμενος Εὐμένη τὸν βασιλέα τότε ποιήσεται τὰς πρὸς αὐτοὺς συνθήκας; Livy, 38.37.6; cf. 38.12.6.

89. Livy, 38.40.1–2: *leges quibus pacem cum Eumene servarent dixit, denuntiavit ut morem vagandi cum armis finirent agrorumque suorum terminis se continerent*; cf. Polyb. 21.46.12.

90. Magie's assertion, *RRAM* I:21, that the campaign stemmed from a desire to show "that the Romans were now masters of Asia Minor" lacks any basis. Similarly, Liebmann-Frankfort, *La frontière orientale*, 56–60.

91. And not only in Anatolia. In 188–7 Eumenes offered a handsome endowment to the Achaean League, to subsidize meetings of the βουλή. It was, of course, a means of augmenting Pergamene influence—as the Achaeans realized in refusing it.

Cappadocia had committed the blunder of linking himself in marriage to the Seleucid house, supporting Antiochus in the Roman war, and even backing the Gauls against Manlius. He now faced the retribution that came with choosing the wrong side. Manlius demanded a heavy cash settlement, 600 talents, to buy Roman friendship. Ariarathes took refuge in a time-honored Hellenistic device: a new marriage alliance and a new patron. He betrothed his daughter to Eumenes, and the Pergamene interceded to reduce his indemnity by one half. Cappadocia entered into Roman *amicitia*, but it was Pergamene prestige and authority which rose in Anatolia.[92] One final illustration drives the point home. Prusias of Bithynia, old rival of Eumenes, had prudently stayed out of the war, resisting the blandishments and arguments of Antiochus the Great. A letter from the Scipios in 190, with its promise of good will, kept him from the Seleucid camp, followed by a personal visit from a senatorial legate. The diplomacy worked.[93] Once the war ended, however, Prusias' expectations came to naught. Among the dispensations at Apamea was removal of that part of Phrygia which Prusias had taken from Eumenes and its restoration to Pergamene dominions.[94] Scipionic promises notwithstanding, the policy of the senate toward Asia Minor stood out with clarity at Apamea. Eumenes' claims overrode other considerations. Responsibility for maintenance of a stable order would rest with Pergamum and Rhodes. The treaty of Apamea was, to Rome, her ticket for withdrawal.[95]

## Eumenes II, Perseus, and Rome

To what extent did Anatolian affairs matter to Rome in the twenty years between Apamea and Pydna? Eumenes, it is often stated, was

They suggested instead that Eumenes give up his claims on Aegina, which, of course, he would not consider: Polyb. 22.7–8; Diod. 29.17.

92. The association between Ariarathes and Antiochus: Appian, *Syr.* 5; Diod. 31.19.7; Zon. 9.18. Ariarathes' role in the war: Livy, 37.31.4, 37.40.10, 38.26.4; Appian, *Syr.* 32. The indemnity: Polyb. 21.41.4–7; Livy, 38.37.5. Marriage alliance with Eumenes and Eumenes' intercession: Livy, 38.39.6; cf. Polyb. 21.45; Strabo, 13.4.2 (C 624); and see Livy, 42.29.4: *ex quo est iunctus Eumeni adfinitate, in omnia belli pacisque se consociaverat consilia.* Acceptance into Roman friendship noted also by Strabo, 12.2.11 (C 540). Hopp, *Attaliden,* 38, oddly sees this as *Roman* influence on Hellenistic marriage politics!

93. Polyb. 21.11; Livy, 37.25; Appian, *Syr.* 23.

94. Polyb. 21.46.10; Livy, 38.39.15. The territory had perhaps been seized by Prusias shortly after Attalus I's death when Pergamene fortunes were at a low ebb; cf. Habicht, *Hermes* 84 (1956): 90–96; Schmitt, *Untersuchungen,* 276–277.

95. Fundamentally misleading is the formulation of Liebmann-Frankfort, *La frontière orientale,* 43: "elle étendait sa sphère d'hégémonie sur le continent asiatique."

Rome's watchdog in Asia Minor, caretaker of her interests, chief instrument of her hegemony. Rhodes, on most analyses, veered away from the Republic, linking her fortunes to anti-Roman powers, while Rome sought to weaken the island's authority and eventually lashed back in retaliation.[96] The analysis needs sharp revision. Behavior of the Pergamene king and of Rhodian leaders follows closely the paths marked out over the previous two decades before Apamea. Eumenes strove to make headway against rivals in Anatolia, exploiting (or rather attempting to exploit) his connection with Rome to advance that cause. The Rhodians, as usual, went their own way, regarding southwestern Asia Minor as a private preserve, building associations with a number of states and maintaining relations with several power blocs, thereby the better to avoid dependence on any one camp. Rome responded to Eumenes and reacted to Rhodes—but both, as we shall see, in minimalist fashion.

Eumenes was not bashful about announcing to the Roman senate his claims on foreign territory. Only two years after Apamea, his envoys to Rome protested Philip V's occupation of Aenus and Maronea on the Thracian coast, towns which the Pergamene coveted. A few months later, at Thessalonica, the envoys used blunter language. They asserted title to the cities, with specious reasoning: acquisition of Chersonesus and Lysimacheia after the defeat of Antiochus surely implied title to Aenus and Maronea, neighboring cities and lesser in importance. Roman adjudicators and then the senate itself dragged out matters with ambiguous or unenforced pronouncements. In winter 184/3, the ministers of the king were still lamenting Philip's control of the cities. Now they injected an extra charge: that the Macedonian was furnishing direct assistance to his relative Prusias of Bithynia in a war on Pergamum. Eumenes, characteristically enough, bent every effort to enlist Roman power on his behalf, thereby to acquire additional holdings in Europe and to retain what he had taken from Prusias under the terms of Apamea.[97] How much Roman power did he get? The senate eventually induced Philip to evacuate Aenus and Maronea, after lengthy procrastination, but, so far as is known, the towns did not come under Pergamene authority.[98]

Conflict with Prusias hit closer to home and could bring greater

96. So, most recently on Eumenes, Hopp, *Attaliden*, 55–56; on Rhodes, Errington, *Dawn of Empire*, 192–194, 248–252.

97. Complaints about Aenus and Maronea: Polyb. 22.6.1, 22.11.1–4, 23.1.4, 23.3.1; Livy, 39.24.6–7, 39.27.1–5, 39.33.1–4, 39.46.9.

98. On the events and on Rome's behavior, see Gruen, *GRBS* 15 (1974): 226–233. According to Polyb. 23.3.3, the senate went on record in insisting that Philip turn over the cities to Eumenes. If so, however, there is no evidence that the pronouncement took effect. Eumenes, in any case, did not have them in 168/7: Polyb. 30.3.3.

menace, especially if Macedonian force stood behind him. Prusias had engaged the assistance of Galatians and harbored no less than Hannibal himself as a principal military adviser. Bithynian troops had already captured Cierus and Tius, and narrowly missed taking Heraclea Pontica.[99] Border warfare now threatened to spill over into an international quarrel. Rome, however, would not be drawn into it. Eumenes waged war on his own against the consortium of his enemies in the mid-180s. His armies gained a notable triumph on land, then suffered setback at sea when (so it is reported) Hannibal hit upon the novel tactic of hurling containers of poisonous snakes onto Eumenes' flagship.[100] Roman intervention came only in the form of a peace mission headed by Flamininus in 183. The fact of Hannibal's presence at the headquarters of Prusias may have helped call it forth. But senatorial embassies, instructed to reconcile warring states, were a standard feature of Rome's eastern diplomacy, well short of armed interference, indeed a means of avoiding it.[101] Hannibal's death followed on the heels of that mission; any other outcome goes unreported. Eumenes and Prusias did reach an accommodation, though there is nothing in the extant evidence to show that Roman representatives arranged the settlement. Eumenes, who fought his own battles, may have made his own peace.[102] Certainly he took conspicuous pride in the results, reorganizing the Nicephoria festival in 182 and issuing invitations to cities and states all over the Hellenic world to join in the celebration.[103] The king eagerly publicized his accomplish-

99. Galatian assistance: Polyb. 3.3.6; Trogus, *Prol.* 32; *RivFilol* 60 (1932): 446, lines 11–13. Hannibal as adviser: Livy, 39.51.1; Appian, *Syr.* 11; Plut. *Flam.* 20.3; Trogus, *Prol.* 32. Bithynian campaigns against northern cities: Memnon, *FGH*, 434 F 19.1–2.

100. Warfare described by Nepos, *Hann.* 10–11; Justin, 32.4.6–7. The Pergamene victory is celebrated in a decree of Telmessus: *RivFilol*, 60 (1932), 446–447; cf. *OGIS*, 298. That Pharnaces was among the allies of Prusias is conjectured by Hopp, *Attaliden*, 41, n. 37, on the basis of Trogus, *Prol.* 32: *in Asia bellum ab rege Eumene gestum adversus Gallum Ortiagontem, Pharnacem Ponticum et Prusian, adiuvante Prusian Hannibale Poeno.* But Trogus may have conflated the Bithynian and Pontic wars here.

101. See above pp. 111–117.

102. References to the settlement are indirect: Polyb. 22.20.8; Strabo, 12.3.11 (C 546), 12.4.3 (C 563). Habicht's association of the peace with Flamininus' mission, even if the chronological argument holds, is conjectural: *Hermes* 84 (1956): 96–100; followed by Hopp, *Attaliden*, 41–42. *Contra*: McShane, *Foreign Policy*, 160–161, perhaps too certain on the other side. Bithynia, it might be noticed, was not Flamininus' only destination on this trip. He was also scheduled to visit Seleucus: Polyb. 23.5.1. On the suicide of Hannibal, see Livy, 39.51.2–12, 39.56.7; Appian, *Syr.* 11; Plut. *Flam.* 20.3–5; Nepos, *Hann.* 12.2–5; Justin, 32.4.8; Paus. 8.11.11; Zon. 9.21.

103. Welles, *RC*, nos. 49, 50; Robert, *BCH* 54 (1930): 332–343: letters of Eumenes to a city in Caria and to Cos. *Syll.*[3] 629 = *FDelphes* III:3, 240: Aetolian decree in response to the invitation. *Syll.*[3] 630 = *FDelphes* III:3, 261: Delphic decree in response to the invitation.

ments. Elevation of his prestige not only in Asia Minor but across the Aegean continued to preoccupy him. To that end, Eumenes emphasized, indeed exaggerated, his association with Rome.[104] The device, to help overawe rivals, remained a central feature of Pergamene diplomatic propaganda—propaganda characterized more by wishful thinking than by solid expectations.

The exertions of Eumenes and the restricted nature of Rome's responses came to light again in the armed conflict between Pergamum and the Pontic monarchy of Pharnaces I in the late 180s, a conflict which sucked in most of the Anatolian states. Triumph over Prusias and the taking of Bithynia into alliance drew Eumenes to the borders of the Pontic sphere of influence. Hostilities erupted in 183. Pharnaces seized control of the city of Sinope, an event which sent Rhodians, as well as Pergamene envoys, scurrying to Rome in winter 183/2, with accusations against the Pontic king, who had his own representatives there to answer them. The senate performed its normal act of courtesy: dispatch of an inquiring mission.[105] Its report branded Pharnaces as aggressor, Eumenes as reasonable and moderate on all counts, but gave no advice on action. Delegates from Pharnaces were in Rome, as from Eumenes, and also from Ariarathes of Cappadocia, in-law and ally of Eumenes. The war had widened in 182, or was about to do so. Before its completion, areas involved in the conflict included Cappadocia, Galatia, Paphlagonia, and Armenia, as well as a number of independent cities. Stability in the whole region seemed on the point of disintegration. Yet the senate only sent another embassy in early 181 to investigate a little more earnestly.[106] They brought back no accomplishments. Pharnaces simply scorned the envoys. Eumenes' brother Attalus had to arrange a truce, then was sent by the king along with others to make renewed pleas in Rome. Attalus arrived to a lavish reception, delivered himself of vituperation against Pharnaces, and urged that Rome mete out the punishment due an aggressor. The senatorial reply promised only an effort to make peace.[107] That effort itself proved far from energetic. A third Roman delegation reached Asia Minor in 180, to find that fighting had broken out again.

104. So it may be inferred from the language of the Delphic Amphictyony, responding to Eumenes' summoning to the Nicephoria: *Syll.*³ 630 = *FDelphes* III:3, 261, lines 3–10, 17–18; cf. Holleaux, *Études* II:69–72.

105. Polyb. 23.9.1–3; Livy, 40.2.6–8; Strabo, 12.3.11 (C 546).

106. Polyb. 24.1.1–3: πέμψει πρεσβευτὰς τοὺς φιλοτιμότερον ἐπισκεψομένους; Livy, 40.20.1. On the involvement of other states, see Polyb. 24.14.1–2, 25.2.3–13; Diod. 29.23. *PP* 27 (1972): 182–185—on Ariarathes of Cappadocia. Even Seleucus IV considered intervention on Pharnaces' behalf, but thought better of it; Diod. 29.24; cf. Polyb. fr. 96.

107. Polyb. 24.5.1–8; Diod. 29.22.

Negotiations went back and forth, Eumenes showing pliability, Pharnaces recalcitrance. The Roman envoys threw up their hands and went home. War could continue (and did), so far as they were concerned.[108] Pharnaces' defiance of the senate's legates indicates that he knew how shallow was Rome's commitment to this region. Moral suasion having failed, Eumenes returned to physical force. He had gathered a formidable coalition that included Ariarathes IV of Cappadocia, Prusias II of Bithynia and Morzius of Paphlagonia. Pharnaces' links to Armenia and the Galatians proved inadequate. The Pergamene alliance coerced him into submission. It was Hellenistic warfare of a classic variety. So was the treaty of peace which followed in 179, extracting territory and indemnity from the conquered, distributing gains to the victors, while permitting a number of other states to associate themselves with the settlement, typically Hellenistic, uninfluenced and unhampered by Rome.[109]

Traditional power politics among Greek states prevailed in Asia Minor during the 180s and 170s, the actions of the Roman Republic only marginal. Eumenes II of Pergamum played the most conspicuous role, at the center of almost every major development, energetic and tireless like his father, a master manipulator of both persons and events. Active collaboration with the Romans during the Antiochene war had earned him handsome rewards, the foundation of his predominance in Anatolia. He expected to tap that source again and again. Efforts to mobilize Roman assistance against first Bithynia and then Pontus, however, ran into the roadblock of senatorial passivity. Nothing daunted, Eumenes forged his own alliances. Ariarathes IV

108. Polyb. 24.14–15. Eumenes put on a show of force for the envoys, probably in order to gain a better bargaining position for the settlement: Polyb. 24.14.11. The envoys insisted on a withdrawal of the king's troops from disputed territory—not in order to coerce Eumenes, but to establish an atmosphere appropriate for negotiations: Polyb. 24.15.4–6. It was to no avail: 24.15.11–12: ταχέως τοῖς Ῥωμαίοις ἐγένετο δῆλον ὅτι ματαιοπονοῦσιν . . . καὶ τῶν Ῥωμαίων ἀπαλλαγέντων ἐκ τοῦ Περγάμου . . . ὁ μὲν πόλεμος ἐγεγένητο κατάμονος.

109. The treaty, with principals on both sides and additional signatories given by Polyb. 25.2. Cf. Dahlheim, Struktur und Entwicklung, 214–216; Olshausen, RE Suppl. 15 (1978), "Pontos," 411–414; Walbank, Commentary III: 271–274. Armed assistance for Eumenes by Ariarathes: Polyb. 24.14.9. There was also cooperation between Pergamum and Rhodes: Polyb. 24.15.13. The Rhodians, however, did not permit Eumenes to block traffic in the Hellespont: Polyb. 27.7.5; nor do they appear among the signatories of the peace. Eumenes' treaty with thirty Cretan cities in 183 greatly strengthened his recruiting opportunities; Syll.³ 627 = IC, IV, 179; cf. Polyb. 24.14.11. Roman orchestration in the making of peace is sometimes hypothesized; e.g. Will, Histoire politique II: 244–245; Hopp, Attaliden, 48, n. 72. But it is in no way proved by IPE, I², 402; so, rightly, Burstein, AJAH 5 (1980): 1–12; and see above p. 180; nor by Justin, 38.6.2; cf. Niese, Geschichte III, 74, n. 5. Moreover, Polybius' account virtually excludes Roman participation.

became a loyal friend and helpmate after 188; Prusias II, succeeding his father in 182, elected (at least temporarily) to tie his fortunes to Eumenes. Pharnaces, humbled and forced to come to terms in 179, no longer posed a threat. The Galatians, still hostile but weakened by defeats, had fallen under Pergamene influence. And the connections of Eumenes outside Asia Minor included not only the islands of Aegina and Andros where he held sway but Aetolia, Delphi, and Athens where he enjoyed close and cordial relations.[110]

The radiation of influence generated predictable counterreaction. Rhodes collaborated briefly with Eumenes, the Pergamene even coming to Rhodian assistance against rebellious Lycians. The association did not last long. Rhodians objected to Eumenes' effort to block the Hellespont during the war against Pharnaces, thus effectively cooling relations again. The king subsequently reversed himself and began to encourage Lycian activity against Rhodes.[111] In Achaea, as already noted, Eumenes' attempts in the 180s to subsidize political activities and cater to the League's citizens absorbed a sharp rebuff. His aggressive style offended the Achaeans. Some time before 172, they voted to rescind some of the honors and distinctions previously conferred on him, a reaction to his excessive grasping after tokens of esteem. The matter came before independent judges who went further still; their decision stripped Eumenes of all the honors and distinctions previously awarded by Achaea. Not surprisingly, those judges were Rhodians.[112] Hostility between Pergamum and Macedonia spilled over from the reign of Philip to that of Perseus. The new ruler gave his sister in wedlock to Prusias II of Bithynia, who had begged for alliance obviously hoping to get out from under the shadow of Pergamum. Perseus himself ca. 178 took to wife Laodice, daughter of Seleucus IV, the bride conducted to him by a convoy of Rhodian ships, whose sailors returned home each with a golden crown, gift of the king.[113] Bonds that linked Macedonia, Bithynia, Rhodes, and the Seleucid kingdom unquestionably alerted and alarmed Eumenes. Reshuffling alliances in this fashion ignited countermeasures, a repeated feature of Hellenistic history.[114] It is no accident that a year or two later

110. See above pp. 188–189. There was diplomatic interchange also with the Thessalians; *IG*, IX, 2, 512.

111. Polyb. 24.15.13, 27.7.5–6; Livy, 42.14.8.

112. Polyb. 27.18, 28.7. On Achaean attitudes, see especially 28.7.11: οὐ γὰρ ὡς ἠδικημένους τι τοὺς Ἀχαιοὺς βουλεύσασθαι τὰς τιμὰς αἴρειν τὰς Εὐμένους, ἀλλὰ μείζους αὐτοῦ ζητοῦντος τῶν εὐεργεσιῶν τούτῳ προσκόψαντας ψηφίσασθαι τὸ πλεονάζον παρελεῖν. Livy, 42.12.7, establishes the *terminus ante quem* as 172.

113. Polyb. 25.4.8–10; Livy, 42.12.3–4; Appian, *Mithr.* 2; *Mac.* 11.2.

114. To reckon this as an anti-Roman alliance misses the point; see above p. 404, n. 31.

Eumenes intruded with force into Seleucid dynastic quarrels. Pergamene troops and cash eliminated a pretender to the throne, assassin of Seleucus IV, and installed Seleucus' brother Antiochus IV as nominee of Pergamum.[115] The new concert of the Attalid and Seleucid houses dashed Perseus' plans for a diplomatic foothold in Syria and tilted the balance of eastern powers still again. In all of this not a whisper is heard of Roman involvement. Conventional Hellenistic power policies held firm.

Eumenes still expected to make use, when necessary, of his ace-in-the-hole: the brandishing of Roman authority against his adversaries. He had tried, without success, to play it against Bithynia and against Pontus. Rome did not cooperate—or not to the extent that Eumenes hoped. In the struggle of the 180s and 170s he was thrown back on his own resources. The king felt abandoned by Rome, who had proved to be an unreliable ally.[116] But he could hardly discard the ace. Despite successes in Asia, Eumenes' repute sank in Greece. Perseus outdid him in promises and personality. As the Macedonian's prestige swelled, Eumenes' contracted. Indeed, in many Hellenic circles, the latter's association with Rome had contributed to his unpopularity.[117] In those circumstances, Eumenes, rather than witness his influence drain away to the advantage of Perseus, resorted once again to the tactic of prodding Rome into activity. The king delivered himself of a long-winded oration in the senate house in 172, detailing and exaggerating out of all proportion the alleged crimes of Perseus. That this speech, full of holes and hyperbole, actually determined the Roman decision for war is, at best, questionable.[118] It nonetheless takes its place in the continuing process of Attalid diplomatic strategy: to employ Roman force for Pergamene goals.

The Third Macedonian War exposed both the strengths and the weaknesses of Attalid diplomacy. Eumenes' past successes brought a measure of solidarity among his allies. His earnest representations to the senate in 172 gained backing the next year when Ariarathes of Cappadocia, related to Eumenes since 188, promised armed assis-

115. A brief account in Appian, *Syr.* 45. The event is commemorated in an Athenian decree honoring Eumenes' whole family for setting Antiochus on his throne: *OGIS*, 248. Cf. Polyb. 30.30.4–7: the subsequent κοινοπραγία between Eumenes and Antiochus.

116. That surely is the import of Appian, *Syr.* 45. Eumenes and Attalus cultivated the favor of Antiochus IV; certain offenses had caused them to look with suspicion upon the Romans: ἑταιριζόμενοι τὸν ἄνδρα [Antiochus] · ἀπὸ γὰρ τινῶν προσκρουμάτων ἤδη καὶ οἴδε ʽΡωμαίους ὑπεβλέποντο. The passage does not state or imply that *Rome* was annoyed at Attalid expansionism.

117. Livy, 42.5.2, 42.5.6, 42.12.1–2; and see above p. 418.

118. See references and discussions above pp. 409–410.

tance to the Roman effort against Perseus, even entrusted a young son to Roman safekeeping, and Antiochus IV of Syria, beneficiary of Eumenes' intervention in 175, made similar promises of support through his envoys to Italy.[119] The backlash against Pergamene influence, however, manifested itself as well. Rhodian spokesmen sharply rebuked Eumenes before the *patres*. The island's leaders showed little enthusiasm for a war on Perseus. Even less enthusiasm came from the ruler of Bithynia. Prusias II, once a recipient of favors from Eumenes, now a brother-in-law of Perseus, refrained from taking sides and waited upon events. A foot in each camp would allow him to survive, whatever the outcome—or so he reasoned.[120] The Pergamene association with Rome was both asset and liability for Eumenes. Ariarathes rushed to capitalize; so did Antiochus who hoped to fan the flames of the Third Macedonian War, thus to have a freer hand in wresting Coele Syria from the Ptolemies. But neither Prusias nor Rhodes welcomed a conflict that would reintroduce Roman power in the Aegean—and would redound to the benefit of Eumenes. Rome's entry into the war against Perseus helped to solidify the Pergamene alliance, but also to increase Hellenic uneasiness about the aspirations of the Attalid king.[121]

Eumenes, as the interests of state dictated, prosecuted the war with vigor. The king conducted forces in person, together with two of his brothers (the other was left behind to protect Pergamum): a fleet, cavalry, and infantry were brought to Chalcis in 171, there to join the Roman consul. The royal family showed a conspicuous commitment. Both Eumenes and Attalus took part in the war council of the Roman commander. Troops furnished by the king fought in the engagements in Thessaly during that first campaigning season, and his advice held sway with the council. At the same time, Eumenes' appointee in the Hellespontine area broke through to Thrace and threatened the domains of Perseus' ally Cotys. The purpose was not simply to open a second front against Perseus. Eumenes pursued that elusive goal of westward expansion, a foothold in Europe that continued to tantalize Pergamene rulers. The Third Macedonian War was still another means to their ends.[122] The drive into Thrace resumed in 170. Eumenes arranged for betrayal of the city of Abdera, undoubtedly with

119. Livy, 42.19.3–6, 42.29.4–6.

120. Rhodian criticism of Eumenes: Appian, *Mac.* 11.3; Livy, 42.14.6–9; and see below n. 159. Prusias' maneuverings: Livy, 42.29.3; Appian, *Mithr.* 2.

121. Cf., especially, on Rhodian suspicions of Eumenes, Polyb. 27.7.4–8.

122. Pergamene forces and their engagements in Greece: Livy, 42.55.7–8, 42.57.9, 42.58.14, 42.59.5. Eumenes as adviser to the consul: Livy, 42.57.4, 42.60.3. Cf. *AthAnn-Arch* 13 (1981): 246–248. Advance into Thrace: Livy, 42.67.4.

expectation of adding it to his domains. The goal eluded him, for a Roman praetor, L. Hortensius, uninterested in Pergamene purposes, stormed the city and looted it. Abderan envoys later addressed pitiable appeals to the senate and got some satisfaction: the *patres* rebuked Hortensius and declared that the city be restored to *libertas*. Eumenes had to abandon plans for annexation. Not that the outcome reflects Roman intention. The senate simply responded to a situation where its *fides*, through the actions of an overzealous officer, had come into question.[123] Eumenes, in any case, concentrated energies on enhancing his repute in Hellas. The importunings of Attalus helped persuade the Achaeans to reverse previous decisions and to reinstate some of the civic honors that the League had bestowed on Eumenes.[124] The king made a display of force also in Crete, where he dispatched troops to brace the city of Cydonia in her struggle with Gortyn. The demonstration of Pergamene power and prestige in the Aegean and in the Peloponnese occupied Eumenes' attention, even as war raged between Rome and Perseus elsewhere.[125] The king had not, however, turned his back on the Roman effort; he had too much to gain from continued cooperation. Pergamene forces went into action again in the following season of 169. Attalus led a contingent that marched with the Roman army under Q. Marcius Philippus when they forced their way into Macedonia. Eumenes himself commanded twenty ships which joined Roman troops in the sieges first of Cassandrea, then of Demetrias. Both assaults came to naught, but Eumenes' commitment to the common cause was unwavering.[126]

Or was it? At this time precisely rumors pointed to the inception of clandestine negotiations between Eumenes and Perseus. An emissary of the Pergamene ruler began the process, with private messages first at Amphipolis, then at Demetrias, a Cretan emissary at that, who served in the ranks of Perseus, thus lending perhaps a more sinister note to the story. Perseus too sent an envoy to the court of Eumenes, with unknown results.[127] The contacts resumed in 168, with some hard bargaining positions on both sides, or so it was alleged. Perseus' ambassadors warned that a Roman victory would not only topple the

---

123. Diod. 30.6; Livy, 43.4.8–13.

124. Polyb. 27.18, 28.7.

125. Pergamene assistance to Cydonia: Polyb. 28.15. Civil war in Crete was, of course, a common occurrence and had erupted once more in recent years: Livy, 41.25.7; Polyb. 28.14. Cretan soldiers fought on both sides in the Third Macedonian War: Livy, 42.51.7, 42.58.6, 43.7.1–4. But nothing suggests that Eumenes' intervention in Crete was related to divisions on the island with regard to Rome and Perseus.

126. Livy, 44.4.11, 44.10.12, 44.11.4, 44.12.4, 44.13.7–10.

127. Eumenes' emissary: Polyb. 29.6.1, 29.7.8; Livy, 44.13.9, 44.24.9; cf. 44.20.7. Perseus' envoy: Polyb. 29.4.8, 29.6.2; Livy, 44.24.10.

Antigonids but would undo the rule of the Attalids and Seleucids: better that Eumenes seek to mediate an end to the war or, failing that, to join the Macedonian side. The Pergamene king was disposed to listen but demanded a cash settlement, 500 talents for withdrawing his support from Rome and another 1,500 talents for bringing the war to negotiated conclusion. Perseus had the cash but no trust in his royal counterpart. He would put the amount on deposit in Samothrace, to be paid only if and when Eumenes' mediating efforts came to fruition. Mistrust was mutual. Eumenes now broke off talks; he would not countenance a policy of deferred payments. This comic ballet terminated negotiations, threw Perseus back on his own resources, and, from the Roman vantage point, cast odium and suspicion upon the Pergamene king.[128] Polybius exploded with moral indignation: the behavior of both kings was beneath contempt. Devious gamblers rather than admirable statesmen, they outwitted themselves by trying to outwit one another. Perseus dangled the prospect of handsome rewards but would not relinquish the cash; Eumenes threw away his chances by demanding advance payment. Coordination of efforts between the two monarchs collapsed. The one was too miserly, the other too avaricious.[129]

A remarkable tale, puzzling, and, on the face of it, inexplicable. Did Eumenes, in fact, jettison an Attalid policy of more than thirty years' standing? Would he run the risk of alienating a powerful partner whom he had cultivated so assiduously for the sake of adding some bullion to his treasury—and then drop the whole proceeding because he preferred cold cash to promissory notes? Would Perseus indeed, with the happy prospect of consolidating Pergamene and Macedonian forces and reversing the momentum of the war, have withheld payment out of miserliness and mistrust? Polybius was dumfounded and incredulous. He excogitated a number of sound reasons for disbelieving the story: given the bitter animosity between Pergamum and the Antigonids, how could Eumenes have promoted the aims of Macedonia? How could he expect a huge monetary bribe without offering guarantees? If the bargain went through, how could he prevent Roman discovery and retaliation? How could Perseus turn down the opportunity either of gaining Eumenes' assistance or of embroiling him with Rome?[130] Those were cogent objections. Polybius

---

128. Polyb. 29.4.8–10, 29.6.2, 29.8.3–9; Livy, 44.24.1–10, 44.25.5–12; Appian, *Mac.* 18.1.

129. Polyb. 29.7.3: λοιπὸν ἦν ἐξαπατᾶν καὶ στρατηγεῖν ἀλλήλους δι᾽ ἀπορρήτων · ὅπερ ἐποίουν ἀμφότεροι; 29.8.1–4, 29.8.8–9: τοῦ μὲν πανουργοτάτου δοκοῦντος εἶναι, τοῦ δὲ φιλαργυρωτάτου; 29.9.12; Livy, 44.25.12–44.26.1.

130. Polyb. 29.7.1–2, 29.9.2–11; Livy, 44.25.1–2.

agonized over the problem, but, in the end, endorsed the story as he had heard it.[131] Modern scholars have divided on the issue, either rejecting the account as implausible and invented or accepting the judgment of the contemporary historian. None, however, has offered a thorough discussion.[132]

What evidence did Polybius have for his opinion—for opinion it was: τό δοκοῦν?[133] In a word, nothing. The historian appeals to surmise, on the basis of subsequent events. Rome's coldness to Eumenes after Pydna convinced him that tales of treasonable negotiations during the war must have some foundation.[134] That is inadequate. Even if there be connection between the story of diplomatic exchanges and Rome's postwar attitude toward Eumenes (itself questionable), this indicates only that the *patres* believed the story, not that it is true. Polybius' postulated reasons for dealings between the kings and their outcome are quite desperate: sheer avarice and a desire to pull the wool over one another's eyes; in short, plain folly.[135] Not a very compelling analysis, especially when one considers the shrewdness and the remarkably successful record heretofore of those two monarchs. Polybius makes one attempt at a rational explanation: Eumenes had observed Perseus' repeated efforts to get a peace settlement and Rome's failure to make any headway against the Macedonians; hence, he reckoned the time ripe for mediation, considered himself the most suited as mediator, and hoped to reap a financial profit for his services.[136] The suggestion, however, will not do. Perseus may have been ready for peace in 169 and 168, but not Rome. Philippus' campaign in 169 had, in fact, pierced the Macedonian frontier and brought Roman troops into the realm of Perseus. One notes with special interest that

131. Polyb. 29.5.1–3: ὑπὲρ ὧν ἔγωγε διηπόρηκα τί δεῖ ποιεῖν.

132. Among the skeptics are Niese, *Geschichte* III:198–199; Magie, *RRAM* I:22; Hansen, *Attalids*, 116–118; McShane, *Foreign Policy*, 181–182; Walbank, *Commentary* III:365–366. Polybius' opinion is followed by Frank, *Roman Imperialism*, 207; Scullard, *Roman Politics*, 214, 286–287; Meloni, *Perseo*, 335–341; Badian, *Foreign Clientelae*, 102–103; Lehmann, *Untersuchungen*, 173, n. 49; Errington, *Dawn of Empire*, 242–243; Hopp, *Attaliden*, 57–58.

133. Polyb. 29.5.3.

134. Polyb. 29.6.2–5: ἐξ ὧν ὅτι μὲν γέγονέ τις ἐπιπλοκὴ τῷ Περσεῖ πρὸς τὸν Εὐμένη, δι᾽ ἣν ἐπὶ τοσοῦτον ἠλλοτριώθησαν πρὸς αὐτὸν Ῥωμαῖοι προφανὲς ἐκ τῶν εἰρημένων. Polybius refers here to a sharp contrast in Rome's subsequent treatment of Eumenes and that of Attalus. But description of the latter as one who had provided no assistance worthy of note either in the war against Perseus or before hardly suits Attalus. The excerptor or copyist has, in all likelihood, erroneously substituted Attalus for Prusias. That possibility is overlooked by Walbank, *Commentary* III:367.

135. Polyb. 29.7.3, quoted above, n. 129; 29.8.1–4, 29.9.12: τίς οὖν αἰτία τῆς οὕτως ἐκφανοῦς ἀλογιστίας; φιλαργυρία · τί γὰρ ἂν ἄλλο τις εἴπειεν;

136. Polyb. 29.7.4–8.

Prusias of Bithynia, a relative of Perseus, who had held aloof from the war waiting upon events, now decided that events dictated a shedding of his neutrality. In 169 Prusias supplied some ships to the Roman cause, a token gesture, but a clear index that the momentum toward victory now seemed to be Rome's.[137] This would be a singularly inauspicious time for Eumenes to erase three decades of advantageous collaboration for a link with the falling fortunes of Macedonia. The Pergamene ruler, who still enjoyed the fruits of the Antiochene war, knew that he had more to gain from the defeat of Perseus than from premature mediation.

How then to explain the story? That Perseus made approach to Eumenes, as he did to Antiochus, Genthius of Illyria, and the Rhodians, urging him to mediate a settlement is eminently plausible. The Macedonian had been looking for a way to get satisfactory peace even before the war began, and he persisted in that hope.[138] A private meeting took place at Eumenes' court, the king closeted with Perseus' emissary. The subject discussed was innocent enough, according to Eumenes who made explanation to the Roman consul: a conversation about exchange of prisoners. That was mere pretext, designed to allay Roman suspicions, says Livy.[139] But who could know the truth? Certainly not Livy. Not even Polybius. The Greek historian acknowledges quite candidly that the kings conducted their bargaining in secret and that any account of what went on is guesswork based on probabilities.[140] Livy, with uncharacteristic circumspection, follows the Polybian narrative for the most part, but emphasizes the fact that unsubstantiated rumors vouch for the initial contacts between the kings, that secrecy prevailed in their talks, and that no one could know what actually transpired.[141] The field was clear for hearsay, innuendo, and insinuation.

137. Livy, 44.10.12; cf. 44.14.6, 44.24.3. For Prusias' attitude in 171, see Livy, 42.29.3: *eventum expectare*.

138. On Perseus' attitude, see above pp. 416–417; cf. Polyb. 29.7.4; Livy, 44.25.3. Perseus encouraged the Pergamene either to mediate or to join his side, but emphasis was clearly on the former; Polyb. 29.4.10: μάλιστα μὲν διαλύων τὸν πόλεμον, εἰ δὲ μή, βοηθῶν; Livy, 44.24.6. And he cannot realistically have expected Eumenes to take up arms against Rome. Appian, *Mac.* 18.1, adds a third proposition, that Eumenes become neutral.

139. Livy, 44.27.13; cf. 44.24.7.

140. Polyb. 29.5.1–3. According to Diod. 31.7.2, correspondence between Eumenes and Perseus came to light, actually detailing a συμμαχία. The item is more than suspect, unknown to Polybius and to the annalistic sources of Livy. Certainly correspondence of that nature, if it ever existed, was not used against Eumenes at the time. Cf. B. Schleussner, *Historia* 22 (1973): 119–123.

141. Livy, 44.13.9: *fama fuit*; 44.20.7, 44.24.11: *quae colloquia occulta et legationes infames quidem erant, sed quid actum esset quidve inter reges convenisset, ignorabatur.*

A variety of motives and sources conspired to blacken the reputation of Eumenes. Polybius' informants were close friends of Perseus, men he had encountered in their common exile in Italy.[142] They had good reason to despise and discredit Eumenes after the war. Perseus himself, having failed to gain cooperation from Eumenes, may well have encouraged rumors that would compromise the Pergamene in Roman eyes, even while the conflict was undecided.[143] After Pydna, the foes of Eumenes in Asia could capitalize on such reports to besmirch the king.[144] Roman writers too found the stories useful in justifying the senate's snub of Eumenes in the immediate postwar period.[145] Valerius Antias even has the king withdraw from the war in 169, reject Roman requests for assistance, and depart from the front after a quarrel with the consul.[146] The tale is malicious fiction. In the campaign of 168 Eumenes contributed warships and troop transports, officers, sailors, and Galatian mercenaries. Two of his brothers, Attalus and Athenaeus, fought at the battle of Pydna, and Athenaeus went on to accompany Aemilius Paullus on his triumphal tour through Greece.[147] Pergamene participation against Macedonia remained solid throughout.[148] The reports that Eumenes entered into furtive dealings with Perseus with an eye to abandoning the Roman alliance should be discarded.[149] Polybius was a victim of his informants. Elsewhere, he knew better. The king whom he described as avaricious and myopic in this connection, Polybius eulogizes in an obituary as preeminent among princes in virtue, quality of mind, and practical intelligence![150] There can be little doubt that a peculiar combination of

142. Polyb. 29.8.10.

143. Polybius indicates that the rumors of negotiation had already emanated before the close of the war: 29.8.10, 30.1.6. Perseus' desire to cast suspicion upon Eumenes is noted by Appian, *Mac.* 18.1—perhaps based on Polyb. 29.9.7–11.

144. Cf. Diod. 31.7.2.

145. Cf. Polyb. 29.6.2–5.

146. Livy, 44.13.12–14; cf. Vell. Pat. 1.9.2.

147. Eumenes' contribution: Livy, 44.28.4–44.29.5, 45.10.2; cf. Polyb. 29.6.4. Attalus at Pydna: Livy, 44.36.8. Athenaeus at Pydna: *Hesperia* 5 (1936): 429–430. Athenaeus and Paullus on tour: Livy, 45.27.6. The Eumenes who shared joint command with Athenagoras of a small garrison at Thessalonica (Livy, 44.32.6) is surely not the king. *Contra*: McShane, *Foreign Policy*, 181, n. 16.

148. Polyb. 30.1.2.

149. Badian, *Foreign Clientelae*, 102–103, hypothesized that Eumenes proved willing to discuss withdrawal from the war because he intended it anyway, in order to confront the Galatians, and hoped to be subsidized by Perseus. But nothing in the evidence connects the Gallic war with the Macedonian negotiations. And Eumenes' withdrawal, if such it be, in no way affected Pergamene commitment to the war against Perseus.

150. Polyb. 32.8.

strands produced this implausible tale. Eumenes, in fact, was never charged openly by the Roman senate for contemplating defection or consorting with the enemy.[151]

The conclusion is important. Pergamene policy had kept to its old paths, maintaining a steady line from the beginnings of Roman involvement in the East through the conclusion of the Third Macedonian War. The policy is ill described as unwavering loyalty to Rome; rather a consistent series of efforts to engage Rome in support of projects that would redound to the benefit of Pergamum. Eumenes could expect to reap the fruits of Pydna as he had of Magnesia.

## Rhodes Between Apamea and Pydna

Rhodian actions and attitudes also held to a discernibly consistent policy between Apamea and Pydna. Notions of pro- and anti-Roman parties, of veering away from Rome and inclining toward Macedonia, are fundamentally misleading. The eastern Mediterranean had not been divided into two major power blocs that required all lesser states to choose sides. Rhodes' experience demonstrates it. We need not here rehearse that experience in detail. The outlines and highlights will suffice.[152]

The island took pride in its independence and self-sufficiency. Collaboration with Rome and Pergamum arose from *ad hoc* circumstances, under severe pressure from Philip V. The temporary commitments then lapsed. The Rhodians went their own way in the aftermath of the Second Macedonian War, having established both a *philia* with Rome and an amicable arrangement with Antiochus the Great. Their entrance into the conflict between those two powers came well after its inception, a move determined by calculation of self interest. They simply backed the right horse.[153] It was a prudent decision, issuing in substantial territorial gains at Apamea. Rhodian posture after that time, however, repeated the pattern followed between the wars against Philip and Antiochus. There was no question of dependency on Rome or slippage into a client status. Rhodes controlled the Peraea, exercised sway in most of Caria and Lycia, and headed the

---

151. Cf. Polyb. 30.1.6, 30.19.1–6.

152. For a fuller treatment, summarized here, see Gruen, *CQ* 25 (1975): 58–77, with references to sources and literature. The more recent discussion by Calboli, M. *Porci Catonis Oratio Pro Rhodiensibus*, 99–113, produces no new arguments. The idea of a fluctuation between pro- and anti-Roman parties in Rhodes is revived again by Martina, *Quaderni di filologia classica* 2 (1979): 45–51.

153. See above pp. 545–546.

Nesiotic League, thus holding a position of predominance in the Aegean.[154] She kept a cordial relationship with Rome, but did not feel hamstrung by it. Indeed, she developed an equally cordial association with Perseus in the 170s, and with Seleucus IV of Syria.[155] It is noteworthy that even after Seleucus was replaced by Antiochus IV through the efforts of the Attalids, thus presumably snapping ties with Perseus, Rhodes had as close a relationship with the new Seleucid ruler as with his predecessor.[156] The multiplication of diplomatic contacts is typically Rhodian. Rome raised no objections. She had bolstered the island's power and prestige at Apamea, with the expectation that this would lend further stability to the eastern Mediterranean.

With that understanding, Rhodes conducted a vigorous and autonomous foreign policy. The islanders exercised patronage of their own. They championed the cause of Soli, interceded for the Aetolians, advertised the plight of Sinope. They would countenance no interference in their direct sphere of influence. The Lycians rebelled more than once, relying hopefully on ambiguous Roman statements, but were firmly coerced by Rhodian force. Rome made verbal pronouncements but stayed out of the area. Even Eumenes, rarely a friend of Rhodes, cooperated in the quelling of Lycian insurgents. Rhodian diplomacy then extended to Perseus and to Seleucus, healing the rifts that had commenced when their predecessors sat on the Macedonian and Syrian thrones. Rhodes played her diplomatic cards deftly, from Italy to Antioch. Her economy flourished, her prestige was at its height. This was the island's heyday.[157]

The specter of war between Rome and Macedonia brought anguish to the Rhodians. They hoped, of course, to avert a conflict that could only play havoc with their commercial prosperity, and they very much preferred not to have to take sides. It was the situation on the eve of the Antiochene war all over again. The islanders gave cordial reception to envoys of Perseus who asked them to stay neutral or, in the event of war, to take the lead in mediating a settlement. At the same time, however, they displayed good will to the Roman mission

154. Cf. Fraser and Bean, *Rhodian Peraea*, 79–94, 138–172.

155. Polyb. 25.4.7–10; cf. Appian, *Mac.* 11.2.

156. Livy, 41.20.7; *Syll.*³ 644/5.

157. Cf. Polyb. 3.3.7: τῆς αὐξήσεως τοῦ Ῥοδίων πολιτεύματος. Observe the treaty between Miletus and Heraclea-by-Latmus, acknowledging the general ascendancy of Rhodes; *Syll.*³ 633, lines 34–35: μηθὲν ὑπεναντίον πρασσόντων τῶν δήμων τῆι πρὸς Ῥοδίους συμμαχίαι. The championing of Soli: Polyb. 21.24.10–15; Livy, 37.56.7–10. Intercession for Aetolia: Polyb. 21.31; Livy, 38.10. Complaints about the misfortunes of Sinope: Polyb. 23.9.2–3; Livy, 40.2.6–8. Lycian rebellions: Polyb. 22.5.1–10, 25.4.2–25.6.1, 30.31.4; Livy, 41.6.8–12, 41.25.8. Eumenes' assistance: Polyb. 24.15.13. Discussion of all this in Gruen, *CQ* 25 (1975): 64–68.

in Asia, which sounded out Greek opinion for the coming conflict, and announced that a fleet of forty ships was in readiness should Rome require them. Rhodes hedged her bets, as she had done when the Antiochene war opened twenty years before.[158] The issue was not simply one of choosing Rome or Perseus. Closer to home, there had recently been a falling out once again with Pergamum. Distrust of Eumenes ran high on the island—and a distrust of any war which he provoked to his own advantage.[159] A major conflagration could be ruinous. Rhodians divided on how best to proceed, arguments raged over diplomatic tactics, but there was little sentiment on the island for any of the principal protagonists. They declared officially for Rome but provided no substantial assistance.[160]

As the war dragged on the Rhodian economy went into a tailspin, and recriminations began. There were cities in Asia Minor, eager to escape the Rhodian yoke, who spread reports of the island's disloyalty to Rome, provoking embassies and denials of disaffection.[161] Insofar as there *was* Rhodian disaffection, it was less with Rome than with the war itself.[162] Financial and economic hardships induced Rhodes to shift policy at last in 168. A slight shift only, and consistent with the island's basic interests: from tepid support for Rome to active efforts to bring about a peaceful settlement. The importunings of Perseus had greater effect this time, especially as he had gained Genthius of Illyria as ally. Rhodes despaired at the prospect of an indefinite

158. Polyb. 27.3–4; Livy, 42.45–46. A false version of the Roman visit in Livy, 42.26.7–9.

159. Friction between Rhodes and Pergamum in the 170s: Polyb. 27.7.5–6; Livy, 42.14.8. There is nothing to support the idea that Eumenes' assistance to Lycian rebels was done in concert with Rome; as Schmitt, *Rom und Rhodos*, 138; Calboli, *M. Porci Catonis Oratio Pro Rhodiensibus*, 102. Rhodian distrust of Eumenes' motives: Livy, 42.14.6–9; Appian, *Mac.* 11.3; Polyb. 27.7.7–8: · θέλοντος αὐτοὺς ἐκείνου κατὰ πάντα τρόπον ἐμβιβάζειν εἰς τὸν πόλεμον καὶ προσάπτειν τῷ δήμῳ δαπάνας καὶ κακοπαθείας οὐκ ἀναγκαίας.

160. Polyb. 27.7, 27.14.

161. Polyb. 28.2, 28.16, 29.19.3; Livy, 42.26.9, 43.6.4–6, 45.3.5–6, 45.25.13. The account in Livy, 44.14.8–44.15.8, is unreliable.

162. Rhodian envoys got friendly receptions from the commanders of Rome's forces in 169; and their efforts to bring about a reconciliation between Antiochus and Ptolemy had Rome's approval; Polyb. 28.17, 28.23. Polybius imputes to Q. Philippus the devious design of persuading Rhodes to mediate the Macedonian war, thus to jeopardize the island in Roman eyes. But the analysis is questionable; see Gruen, *CQ* 25 (1975): 71–74; cf. Walbank, *Commentary* III:350–351. A different view in Calboli, *M. Porci Catonis Oratio Pro Rhodiensibus*, 104–109, with additional bibliography. Calboli oddly finds merit in the remarks of Will, *ANRW* I:1 (1972), 620–621, n. 32, that there were Ptolemaic ties to Macedonia and that Rome therefore would have encouraged rather than discouraged the Sixth Syrian War. No such ties are attested or even hinted at in the ancient evidence.

prolongation of the war. Her leaders now determined to offer their services as emissaries for peace. Better to run the risk of Roman displeasure than to contemplate continuing hostilities which could wreck the island's prosperity for good. The risk, in any case, did not seem great. An accident of fate brought the Rhodian envoys before the senate only after the results of Pydna had been announced. They spoke unabashedly of their purpose: to serve as intermediaries for reconciliation and thus to end a war so costly to Greeks and Romans alike. By then, unfortunately, the peace mission seemed ill-timed and, to many in Rome, offensive.[163]

Rhodian behavior during the course of the war makes eminent good sense. The island's connections with each of the major protagonists and its tradition of autonomy dictated caution from the outset. There was verbal allegiance to Rome but little in the way of substantive support. Communications remained open to Perseus. Rhodes looked to the security of her situation and the maintenance of her ascendancy in the Aegean. The means taken to guarantee them divided her leaders—not any pro- or anti-Roman feelings, nor commitments to other powers. One observes, interestingly enough, that, while engaged in peace efforts at places as far away as Rome and Alexandria, the Rhodians moved to transform their own peaceful relations with Crete into a military alliance.[164] Control of the seas held precedence in Rhodian thinking, as it had throughout. The protracted character of the war reduced her revenues and crippled her commerce. Those developments tipped the political balance from nominal support for Rome to an endeavor to bring the warring parties together. Rhodes' primary aim remained unshaken: to cling to the prosperity and prestige won during the past two decades.

**V**

The development of Roman-Greek relations in the world of Asia Minor and the Aegean must be viewed principally from the Hellenic perspective. Those areas received only intermittent attention from Rome—and then usually when attention was forced upon her. Com-

163. Perseus' urgings and the Rhodian decision to play an active role for peace: Polyb. 29.3.7–9, 29.4.7, 29.10.1–4, 29.11; Livy, 44.23.4–10, 44.29.6–8. The Rhodian embassy to Rome heard after Pydna: Polyb. 29.19.1–4; Livy, 45.3.3–6; Diod. 30.24; cf. Livy, 44.14.8–13. Discussion of these texts in Gruen, *CQ* 25 (1975): 74–77; and see now Calboli, *M. Porci Catonis Oratio Pro Rhodiensibus*, 110–113. Walbank unfortunately persists in speaking of Rhodian factions in terms of pro- and anti-Roman groups; e.g. *Commentary* III: 182, 297, 303, 352.

164. Polyb. 29.10.6. Walbank, *Commentary* III: 372, wrongly takes this as "a rebuff to Rome."

plaints registered by Attalus I and Rhodes helped to draw the Republic into conflict with Philip; Eumenes' presentations played a role in the preliminaries to both the Antiochene and the Third Macedonian War. But the impact even of these applications upon Roman decisions seems slight. Certainly appeals from lesser states were barely noticed in Rome: Lampsacus and Smyrna in the 190s; Alabanda, Apollonia, Araxa, and the Lycians generally at or in the aftermath of the peace of Apamea; Miletus, Alabanda, and Lampsacus in 170. The cult of the goddess Roma was instituted at places like Smyrna, Cibyra, Antiochia on the Maeander, Caunus, and Stratonicea. None of this, however, determined Roman policy in any discernible way. The settlement at Apamea placed responsibility for maintenance of order in the East squarely upon Pergamum and Rhodes. Rome would not take it up. Despite requests to the Roman senate and certain token gestures in response, Eumenes fought his own wars and the Rhodians kept their dependencies in line by persuasion or force.

Pergamene policy, more often than not, set events in motion. Attalus I established a pattern of soliciting Roman participation in Pergamene wars. Once Rome entered the conflict against Philip, Attalus focused his energies on recovering status in Asia Minor and elevating it in the Aegean and Greece, while the Romans brought Philip to his knees. Attalus' successor Eumenes II put the same techniques to use. His machinations contributed to bringing Rome and Antiochus into confrontation, he took prominent part in the war, especially around his own domains, and he hastily laid claim to a lion's share of the territorial spoils that Antiochus was compelled to evacuate. Eumenes resorted to the maneuver on several occasions in the 180s—to wrest Thracian possessions from Philip, to overawe Prusias and the Galatians, to gain the upper hand over Pharnaces—but without much success. Rome was not easily persuaded to reenter the Asian fray. Eumenes built an alliance system of his own, augmented his international prestige, but also engendered a consortium of enemies. In the late 170s he played the Roman card once more. The Third Macedonian War was, in large part, his war, an effort to recover the status and popularity lost to Perseus. Eumenes had once again prepared the ground for a Roman victory which he intended to exploit to his benefit.

Rhodes, by contrast, preferred to keep the western power at a distance. Pride and a passion for autonomy underlay the attitude. Only grave danger, as after the battle of Lade, could induce the islanders to appeal to Rome, and even then, once the Romans moved into action, Rhodes played hard to get. She collaborated in the Second Macedonian War only to the extent of reestablishing control in her own bailiwick. The Rhodians were as ready to reach an accommodation with Antiochus III or to fraternize with Perseus as to maintain an *amicitia* with Rome. Multiple contacts among various Hellenistic powers had allowed Rhodes to survive and flourish in the past. The technique still held good. So long as she kept herself uncommitted, she could take profit in opportunities from all sides.[165] Rhodes showed little zeal for the Antiochene war or the struggle with Perseus, conflicts which brought Rome back into the eastern Mediterranean. The islanders proved shrewd enough to capitalize on the first but they suffered in the second. They clung fiercely to the hegemony obtained at Λpamea, against rebels and appeals to Rome alike. They preferred to control their own sphere of influence by keeping on good terms with a number of the major powers rather than to gain an empire through dependency on Rome.

Eumenes' association with the Republic was a mixed blessing. He enjoyed substantial gains in terms of political geography and perhaps heightened self-esteem. But Rome proved erratic and unreliable in promoting Pergamene causes. Worse still, the partnership, however thin, alienated others in the Greek world, thus diminishing the king's repute and reducing his authority. Rhodes escaped that sort of dilemma but landed in another. Her flexibility relied on a mutual respect among the great powers and a peacetime atmosphere which allowed her to dominate her dependencies without interference. Contests that embroiled the eastern Mediterranean found her caught in the middle, hands tied and initiative flowing elsewhere. In either case, the circumstances were not created or manipulated by Rome. They emerged from Hellenistic quarrels and rivalries, with the Roman Republic more object than subject, a serviceable resource rather than a director of events. The Aegean and Asia simply did not yet command systematic attention in Italy.

165. Polyb. 30.5.8: ἀκέραιοι διαμένοντες κερδαίνειν τὰς ἐξ ἑκάστων ἐλπίδας; Livy, 45.25.9.

# Chapter 16

# Rome and Asia Minor (II)

The wrath of Rome fell heavily upon Hellas in the wake of the Third Macedonian War. Pydna's aftershocks reverberated across the Aegean. The arduous and punishing war had shaken Rome out of her complaisance. A resurgent Macedonia proved astonishingly formidable. The war also gave reminder that certain other eastern states had the potential of becoming equally formidable, states whose allegiance did not extend beyond their self-interest. Rome took cognizance of those circumstances more directly and more dramatically than ever before. The crackdown followed.

## The Consequences of Pydna

Rhodes felt the heavy hand of the western power. The *patres* delivered stern rebuke to Rhodian envoys who had come to mediate and received audience only after Pydna. Their efforts, so the senate charged, aimed less at promoting peace than at rescuing Perseus. The envoys, after a long wait for the interview, got only a curt dismissal. Senatorial spokesmen affected indignation; in fact, as Polybius suggests, they determined to make an example of Rhodes.[1] Rome's public

---

1. Polyb. 29.19.5: βουλομένη παραδειγματίσαι τοὺς 'Ροδίους. Senators asserted that, if Rhodes were really acting in the interests of Hellas, she would have intervened when Perseus seemed to have the Greeks at his mercy, not when he was on the brink of defeat by Rome: Polyb. 29.19.6–10; Livy, 45.3.6–8. The statement has gone unquestioned as reflecting genuine Roman outrage. Yet it is surely more pretext than reason. Rome would hardly have welcomed Rhodian mediation before she held the upper hand in the war and at a time when Perseus could have driven a hard bargain.

posture was harsh and unyielding. The legate C. Popillius Laenas, warming up for his severe treatment of Antiochus IV at Alexandria, stopped in at Rhodes, at Rhodian request, and proceeded to bully the islanders. A grim visage and the tone of a prosecutor added to Popillius' fearsome image. His colleague C. Decimius put on a milder front but advised punishment of guilty leaders who had acted against the interests of Rome.[2] The Rhodians scrambled to fend off retaliation. They hunted down former leaders whose behavior could be construed as anti-Roman, engaging in hasty prosecutions, expulsions, and executions.[3] It was to no effect in deflecting Roman determination.

Delegates from Rhodes ran into a storm of hostility in Rome in the spring of 167. The praetor, M'. Iuventius Thalna, even proposed a formal motion for declaration of war on Rhodes, a move that stunned and terrified the delegates. How much of this was mere saber-rattling and how much a serious intent to mobilize is impossible to say. Thalna bypassed the senate and went straight to the people, perhaps an indication that the *curia* felt no enthusiasm for the proposal. Tribunes emerged to veto it, and Thalna himself was silenced by being dragged from the rostra. The controversy sparked debate in the senate, a debate which included Cato's famed *Pro Rhodiensibus*. Who, in fact, genuinely desired and expected a war on Rhodes? Cato castigated the advocates of war as men of the highest influence who sought to plunder the wealth and resources of the island. That may be rhetoric. According to Livy, the principal opponents of Rhodes in the senate were the consuls, praetors, and legates who had served against Perseus. Their attitudes could well reflect annoyance with inadequate Rhodian zeal or support for their campaigns. But those men had no reason to count on reappointment in a new war, and thus could hardly expect to realize material profits from it. Advocates of the proposal perhaps relied more on the threat of war than on the waging of it—an enforcement of *deditio* and a lesson in humility.[4] It

2. Livy, 45.10.4–11: *vir* (Popillius) *asper ingenio augebat atrocitatem eorum quae dicerentur voltu truci et accusatoria voce*; Dio, 20.68.1.

3. Polyb. 30.31.14, 30.31.20; Livy, 45.10.12–15; Dio, 20.68.1; cf. Polyb. 30.7.9–30.9.19.

4. Thalna's proposal and the events that flowed from it: Polyb. 30.4; Livy, 45.20.4–45.25.4; Diod. 31.5. Fragments of Cato's speech derive from Gellius, 6.3; collected in Malcovati, *ORF*[3], 62–67. New edition, translation, and commentary by Calboli, *M. Porci Catonis Oratio Pro Rhodiensibus*, 247–330. The speech, written up and inserted in Cato's *Origines*, also receives mention by Livy, 45.25.2, and Appian, *Lib.* 65. That advocates of war intended a full-scale contest is assumed by almost all scholars. Doubted, however, by Niese, *Geschichte* III : 192; cf. Gruen, *CQ* 25 (1975): 77. Calboli, *op. cit.*, 120, defends the seriousness of the proposal once more—but admits that its authors may have expected to take over the island without fighting. Calboli's lengthy ar-

certainly had that effect. The representatives from Rhodes fell into a panic, all but prostrated themselves before friends in Rome, begged, implored, and wept in order to ward off disaster. The war motion aborted. Cato and others had marshalled weighty objections to the proposal. It was no longer necessary anyway. The official senatorial response was brusque and cold: the Rhodians can consider themselves fortunate in escaping the treatment they deserved; they would not be declared enemies, but they had forfeited the status of allies.[5]

The harshness did not arise primarily, if at all, from anger at Rhodian misbehavior and disloyalty. There was no "disloyalty"; and the subsequent charges resolve themselves into pretext and posture.[6] Rome had determined to make a display of her power and to administer a lesson to states which had grown too great since Apamea. The Republic had learned her own lesson from the Third Macedonian War and intended to remove the likelihood of a similar test in the future. Rhodes, which had reached a height of power in the post-Apamea period, presented a logical target for emasculation.

Roman displeasure had immediate repercussions. Cities under the thumb of Rhodes seized the occasion to break free. The Caunians raised revolt, troops from Mylasa took cities in Euromus, Alabanda and Cibyra swiftly sent forces to back the rebels, Stratonicea shook off the Rhodian yoke. The island's holdings on the mainland disintegrated in short order. Rome accelerated the process by announcing

---

gument about Rome's economic motivations is indecisive: *op. cit.*, 120–224, *passim*; cf. Kienast, *Cato der Zensor*, 124. Cato's assertions about Romans seeking to pillage the island for their own profit: Gellius, 6.3.7: *quorum opibus diripendis possidendisque non pauci ex summatibus viris intenti infensique erant*; 6.3.52. The Livian account gives a different impression; 45.25.2: *infestissimi Rhodiis erant, qui consules praetoresve aut legati gesserant in Macedonia bellum*. The view that this was a contest between a hard-line senatorial faction and one of a more generous character—as Briscoe, *Historia* 18 (1969): 62–63; cf. Scullard, *Roman Politics*, 216–217—has little to recommend it. See above pp. 245–246. There is no evidence, for example, to link Thalna with Q. Marcius Philippus. To be sure, Philippus was among the consuls who had fought Perseus. But so was P. Crassus. And Crassus was no friend of Iuventius Thalna: Livy, 43.4.5. For Schmitt, *Rom und Rhodos*, 153–154, Thalna's unconventional procedure in taking his bill directly to the senate roused the opposition of Cato and others. But nothing in the fragments of Cato's speech makes specific allusion to that issue; see Astin, *Cato the Censor*, 279–280, n. 27.

5. Polyb. 30.4.9: εἰ μὴ δι᾽ ὀλίγους ἀνθρώπους τοὺς αὐτῶν φίλους, καὶ μάλιστα δι᾽ αὐτούς, ἤδεισαν καλῶς καὶ δικαίως ὡς δέον ἦν αὐτοῖς χρήσασθαι; Livy, 45.25.4: *Rhodiis responsum ita redditum est ut nec hostes fierent nec socii permanerent*. The distress and humbling of the envoys: Polyb. 30.4.3–5; Livy, 45.20.8–10; Diod. 31.5. Polybius was critical of the speech delivered by Astymedes, one of the Rhodian representatives; 30.4.10–17. The speech may or may not have resembled the version transmitted by Livy, 45.22–24. How far Cato's speech was instrumental in turning aside sentiment for war remains uncertain. Astin, *Cato the Censor*, 273–274, has doubts.

6. See above pp. 565–566; and Gruen, *CQ* 25 (1975): 77–80.

the liberation of all parts of Lycia and Caria that had been awarded the Rhodians at Apamea. After Rhodes had suppressed the uprisings in Caunus, Stratonicea, and Euromus, her countermeasures were undone by senatorial declarations of freedom. The *patres* could with some legitimacy step in to emancipate Lycia and Caria, which Roman victories had secured for Rhodes in the first place. Liberation of sites like Caunus and Stratonicea, however, sites obtained by the Rhodians from Ptolemaic and Seleucid rulers, represents a more obnoxious and less defensible interference.[7] Worse still, the island of Delos became a free port on senatorial directive and was placed under the authority of Athens. Rhodes lost some handsome revenues when stripped of Lycia and Caria, and suffered additional decline in income when Caunus and Stratonicea gained their freedom. The heaviest blow fell after Delos' new status deprived Rhodes of the lucrative harbor dues that had been instrumental in her prosperity.[8] Panic set in and fear of worse to come. Three Rhodian delegations came to the senate in 167 and 166 to ask for formal treaty of alliance, an abrupt reversal of long-standing policy. The island had always shunned binding compacts in the past, in order to play various powers off against one another. This time, however, survival of the state dictated a humbling process. A *foedus* would at least give signal to others that Rhodes was no longer to be victimized. The *patres* put off that request for some years, leaving Rhodes dangling and increasingly insecure, until ca. 164, when they consented to enter into alliance. By then the island had sunk to second-class status, the treaty a mere gesture that halted her slide into oblivion.[9]

The example was not lost on the smaller states of the Aegean and Asia Minor. Others sought and got treaties with Rome, perhaps in the wake of Pydna or in the years that followed: Cibyra and Hera-

---

7. Polyb. 30.5.11–16, 30.21.3–5, 30.31.4–6; Livy, 45.25.4–6, 45.25.11–13; cf. 44.15.1.

8. Loss of revenue from Lycia and Caria: Polyb. 30.31.4; from Caunus and Stratonicea: Polyb. 30.31.6–7. The making of Delos into a free port and its consequences for Rhodes: Polyb. 30.20.1–7, 30.31.9–12. On Polybius' puzzling language in 30.31.12, see Schmitt, *Rom und Rhodos*, 161–163; Calboli, *M. Porci Catonis Oratio Pro Rhodiensibus*, 118–119, n. 19; Walbank, *Commentary* III:459–460. In general, Schmitt, *op. cit.*, 156–167.

9. For sources and discussion, see above pp. 39–42. Schmitt, *Rom und Rhodos*, 163–165, goes too far in interpreting Polyb. 30.31.10 and 30.31.16—passages from a Rhodian speech—to mean that the island had been compelled by Rome to suspend its own constitution; cf. Walbank, *Commentary* III:459. When the *patres* at last yielded and agreed to a *foedus*, they employed a familiar charade: agreement was preceded by a favorable report from Ti. Gracchus; Polyb. 30.31.19–20. That they, in fact, needed the reassurance of such a report is absurd. Gracchus announced that Rhodes had executed all her miscreants—an event already known to the Romans three years earlier! Polyb. 30.31.14; Livy, 45.10.12–15, 45.24.5–6.

clea Pontica. Adulations for the conqueror proliferated, as did the cult of Roma. Gifts, protestations of loyalty, and handsome tokens to appease the western power came from places like Alabanda and Lampsacus, from Caunus and Stratonicea, from Lycia, from Delos and Melos, from Teos and Aphrodisias. The showering of blandishments do not signify a Roman takeover. Treaties were no more than a formality, unintended for implementation; cultic offerings and lavish presents came on the initiative of the eastern cities hoping to escape Rome's wrath or to claim her favor for their own ends.[10] But the Republic's stern posture after the fall of Perseus intimidated the communities of the East and engendered those outbursts of sycophancy.

A coolness entered also into relations between Rome and the king of Pergamum. The *patres* ceased to show favor to the king. He had helped bring them into the war, but they were not eager to have him reap all its benefits. Whatever Eumenes' behavior in the conflict itself, Rome would now make it more difficult for him to employ her name and her authority to advance his influence in Anatolia.

If Polybius is to be believed, Roman senators went further still: deliberate embarrassment for Eumenes, and conscious encouragement of his rivals and enemies. The Galatians grasped the occasion when Pergamene troops were engaged in the Third Macedonian War to attack Eumenes' territory. Setbacks induced the king to send his brother Attalus to Rome with a request for the Republic's intervention ca. spring, 167. Senators lavished attention upon Attalus—but not with Eumenes' welfare in mind. In Polybius' account, they endeavored to turn brother against brother, promising territory in Asia Minor to Attalus and even the possession of Aenus and Maronea in Thrace. Attalus in the end, so goes the tale, held to familial loyalty and declined to intrigue. The *patres*, abashed and annoyed, liberated the Thracian cities to keep them out of Pergamene clutches and sent a token embassy which brought no relief to Eumenes in his Galatian war.[11] Worse was yet to come. Prusias II of Bithynia arrived in Rome during the winter of 167/6, bowing and scraping before the senate, clad in the garb of a freedman, playing up to the *patres* with fawning servility. The scene outraged Polybius, the more so as Prusias got warm welcome and kind treatment. By contrast, Eumenes, on his way to Italy to make personal appeal for aid against the Gauls, got only humiliation. The senate would not give him audience, having hastily concocted a measure to ban kings from the *curia*. While Prusias, a neutral at the outset of the war and a token supporter afterwards, was

10. See discussions above, pp. 46–49, 186–187.
11. Polyb. 29.22, 30.1–3; Livy, 45.13.12, 45.19.1–45.20.3, 45.34.10–14; Diod. 31.12–13.

entertained in style and came away with costly gifts, Eumenes, a primary protagonist and active participant, reached the shores of Italy and was abruptly rebuffed, turned tail and sailed back without the courtesy of a hearing. The ignominy of that episode deflated Eumenes' prestige at home and further emboldened the Galatians. The king, now thrust back on his own resources, rallied nobly and crushed Gallic resistance—only then to have Rome, in 166, declared the Galatians free and autonomous! The humbling of Eumenes seemed complete and decisive.[12]

Polybius' analysis dominates modern reconstructions: Rome consciously undermined Pergamene power, encouraged the Galatians, and weakened Eumenes in the face of neighbors and rivals, thus to make him more dependent upon the Republic.[13] That Rome turned a cold shoulder to the king is plain enough. Rejection and disapproval would administer the same object lesson delivered to Rhodes. Rome had grown suspicious of power concentrations in the East and would not promote the interests of states which had attained too much authority since Apamea. But how far was she prepared to go? How tightly drawn were the reins applied to Pergamum? In short, had Rome produced a blueprint to hold in check the principalities of Asia Minor and to manipulate their fate?

Polybius perhaps detects a more elaborate design than was there. The tale of Rome's attempted enticement of Attalus and his last-minute reversion to loyalty hardly warrants the confidence that al-

12. Prusias' trip to Rome and his reception: Polyb. 30.18; Livy, 45.44.4–21; Diod. 31.15; Zon. 9.24. Eumenes' arrival in Italy and his rebuff: Polyb. 30.19; Livy, Per. 46; Justin, 38.6.4; cf. Polyb. 29.6.2–4. Evidence on the course of the Galatian war is too fragmentary to allow any secure reconstruction. The initial attack on Pergamene territory came, it appears, in 168, prompting Attalus' mission: Polyb. 29.22; Diod. 31.12. Anecdotal information in Polyaean. 4.8.1 and Diod. 31.13 indicates Gallic successes, probably in the initial phases of the war. Eumenes' recruitment of mercenaries and defeat of the Gauls finds mention in Diod. 31.14: πᾶν τὸ τῶν Γαλατῶν ἔθνος ὑποχείριον ἐποιήσατο; see also IvPergamon, 165. Honors heaped on Eumenes by the Sardians at Delphi perhaps celebrate the victory: OGIS, 305. Also the gratitude expressed to him by the Ionian Federation: OGIS, 763 = Welles, RC, no. 52. See Holleaux, Etudes II:153–178. Cf. OGIS, 751 = Welles, no. 54: relief of reparations imposed by Pergamum upon the city of Amlada for its actions in the Gallic war. For Rome's announcement of autonomy for the Galatians, see Polyb. 30.28.

13. Polyb. 30.19.12–13: προφανὲς ἦν ὅτι διὰ τὸν σκυβαλισμὸν τοῦτον οἱ μὲν τοῦ βασιλέως σύμμαχοι ταπεινωθήσονται πάντες, οἱ δὲ Γαλάται διπλασίως ἐπιρρωσθήσονται πρὸς τὸν πόλεμον. διὸ πάντῃ πάντως βουλόμενοι ταπεινοῦν αὐτὸν ἐπὶ ταύτην κατηνέχθησαν τὴν γνώμην. Moderns generally do not question the analysis; see, e.g., Hansen, Attalids, 122–124; Badian, Foreign Clientelae, 103–105; Briscoe, Historia 18 (1969): 54; Liebmann-Frankfort, La frontière orientale, 99–100, 103–105; Errington, Dawn of Empire, 243–245; Hopp, Untersuchungen, 51–52.

most all scholars have placed in it.[14] Distinguished (unnamed) *nobiles*, according to Polybius, took Attalus aside and dangled before him the prospect of a separate kingdom of his own, detached from the holdings of his brother.[15] The prince was tempted, even eager, but dissuaded by the sage advice of Eumenes' doctor who reminded him that the whole kingdom would soon be his anyway.[16] A most implausible scenario. Would Eumenes entrust his brother with a delicate mission if he already suspected his disloyalty and had to send along a personal physician to keep Attalus honest by reminding him of what he already knew?[17] The sequel is even harder to credit. Senators allegedly expected Attalus to announce the division of the kingdom, agreed to turn over to him the cities of Aenus and Maronea, but, when he failed to play along, withdrew their promise and testily liberated the Thracian towns.[18] Can one believe that *principes* in the *curia* outlined Attalus' speech and, when he delivered a different one, reversed themselves in a fit of pique, snatching Aenus and Maronea from his grasp? If the towns had been kept from Pergamene control while Perseus was alive, would the senate even consider handing them over to an Attalid after collapse of the Macedonian monarchy? The *patres* were bound to frown upon Pergamene expansion to the west. A healthy dose of skepticism needs to be applied. Attalus' handsome reception, followed by the snubbing of Eumenes, perhaps gave rise to the speculation about promoting brother against brother. If there ever was plan to carve up the kingdom (a most dubious scheme), it never got started and was never mentioned again. The senate had devised no new political geography for Asia Minor.

The Prusias-Eumenes episode, far from suggesting carefully wrought guidelines for setting Anatolia in order, indicates just the reverse. Prusias' abject sycophancy sickened Polybius. The king had good cause for apprehension, as brother-in-law of Perseus and a man whose support for Rome had been tardy and minimal. No wonder he outdid all in toadyism and self-abasement. Polybius' indignation

14. See the works cited above, n. 13. Hansen, *Attalids*, 121–122, expresses doubts about the story; endorsed now by Walbank, *Commentary* III: 416.

15. Polyb. 30.1.4–10: ἔνιοι τῶν ἐπιφανῶν ἀνδρῶν . . . ἐνίους τῶν ἀξιολόγων ἀνδρῶν. Livy softens the impact of this story. He has Attalus conceive the scheme of winning Roman favor to gain advantages over Eumenes and characterizes the Romans who cooperated with him simply as *non boni auctores*: 45.19.4–7.

16. Polyb. 30.2; Livy, 45.19.7–45.20.1.

17. Polybius has to make Eumenes divine the future in sending his doctor as watchdog; 30.2.1: ὀττευσάμενος ὁ βασιλεὺς τὸ μέλλον ἐπιπέμπει Στρατίον τὸν ἰατρόν.

18. Polyb. 30.3.3–7. The about-face by the senate is deftly omitted by Livy, 45.20.2–3, for it did not shine a pleasant light on Rome.

knows no bounds here: the senate indulged Prusias with kindness precisely because he was altogether contemptible! The historian abandons all semblance of objectivity.[19] Roman writers had a different version, perhaps no more objective. The servility of Prusias is omitted in their accounts. The king simply came to congratulate Rome on her victory, asked for renewal of their *societas*, requested some territory, and entrusted his son Nicomedes to the senate's care. He got a warm reception and send-off.[20] The softened tale may be a response to Polybius' cynical narrative, so unflattering to the *patres*. To what degree, however, did Rome in fact indulge Prusias at the expense of Pergamene interests? Polybius gives no details. The Livian account provides a revealing one: the senate granted Prusias all requests except that for an increase of territory. The king had hoped for some land seized two decades earlier from Antiochus but unassigned and now occupied by Galatians. Senators had not anticipated that petition and did not yield to it. They professed ignorance as to the status of the land. An embassy would go to determine ownership rights and, it was suggested, Prusias should be prepared for disappointment.[21] The matter gets no further mention in our sources. The *patres* were hardly building up Prusias as counterweight to Eumenes. If anything, the Bithynian's visit caught them unawares. They had not worked out a plan to partition Asia Minor.

News of Eumenes' imminent arrival caused even greater consternation. As Polybius' discussion shows, the senate was utterly unprepared for it. Senators wished to give no encouragement to Eumenes, but at the same time could not face the embarrassment of publicly disavowing a man on whom they had heaped such honor in the past. Hence they hit upon the idea of prohibiting all royal visits.[22] The decision responded to *ad hoc* circumstance, not a considered policy. Prusias' own visit may have called it forth, as much as Eumenes' announced arrival. The *patres* had had enough of royal importunings. The blandishments of Prusias must have made some of them uncomfortable; Eumenes' presence could only increase the discomfort. Rome's snub of the Pergamene stemmed from last-minute improvisation rather than a drive for emasculation.

19. Polyb. 30.18; see 30.18.7: φανεὶς δὲ τελέως εὐκαταφρόνητος ἀπόκρισιν ἔλαβε δι᾽ αὐτὸ τοῦτο φιλάνθρωπον. Diod. 31.15 inadvertently or deliberately misreads this to mean that the senate gave Prusias a rude response.

20. Livy, 45.44.4–17. Livy knows Polybius' version as well, but appears to prefer that of the annalists: 45.44.18–21.

21. Livy, 45.44.9–12.

22. Polyb. 30.19.1–6; Livy, *Per.* 46.

It is equally difficult to find considered policy in Rome's treatment of the Galatian question. Polybius certainly had no evidence for one. He did not know even what instructions the senate gave to its legates sent to the area on Attalus' appeal. The Greek historian had to guess on the basis of what the embassy actually did.[23] Moderns claim to know, without hesitation and almost without exception, that the legates went to encourage Galatian aggression against Eumenes.[24] The assertion is groundless. Polybius' extant text gives nothing on the mission itself, but Livy drew on him and tells enough: the legates were commissioned to put an end to the war between Pergamenes and Galatians.[25] Such commissions, as we have seen, were entirely conventional. The historian's explicit statement can stand. The legates endeavored to dissuade Solovettius, leader of the Gauls, from his assaults on Pergamene territory. They got nowhere—an all too common result of Roman mediating efforts in the East. The mediators did not care enough to press the point.[26]

Eumenes, as noted above, went on to subdue the Gauls himself, earning plaudits and prestige. The dispute came up again before the Roman senate in 166, presumably brought by the Galatians who hoped to turn military defeat into diplomatic victory. A single Polybian fragment gives the senatorial decision: the Galatians are to enjoy autonomy. Another effort to checkmate Eumenes and to rob him of the fruits of victory? So it is usually taken. Yet one may recall that it was the Galatians, not Pergamum, who had frustrated Roman peace efforts the previous year. It was the Galatians too who had set events in motion originally by violating the territory of Pergamum. The senate's pronouncement, in the formulation of Polybius, seems directed more against Galatia than against Eumenes. It asserted that the Galatians can have "autonomy" but only so long as they stay inside their own realm and do not cross the borders in arms.[27] Pergamene projects were not undone by that declaration, as the sequel shows. Eumenes

---

23. Polyb. 30.3.7–8: οἷς ποίας μὲν ἔδωκαν ἐντολὰς εἰπεῖν οὐ ῥᾴδιον, στοχάζεσθαι δ᾽ ἐκ τῶν μετὰ ταῦτα συμβάντων οὐ δυσχερές.

24. E.g., Hansen, *Attalids*, 122; Badian, *Foreign Clientelae*, 104; McShane, *Foreign Policy*, 183; Will, *Histoire politique* II:246; Errington, *Dawn of Empire*, 244–245; Hopp, *Untersuchungen*, 52; Walbank, *Commentary* III:416, 441.

25. Livy, 45.34.10: *legati qui cum Attalo ad finiendum bellum inter Gallos et regem Eumenem missi erant.*

26. Livy, 45.34.11–14: *legatorum Romanorum verba . . . apud Gallos nullius momenti fuisse.* Rightly, Briscoe, *Historia* 18 (1969): 54: "they did not try very hard."

27. Polyb. 30.28: συνεχώρησαν τὴν αὐτονομίαν μένουσιν ἐν ταῖς ἰδίαις κατοικίαις καὶ μὴ στρατευομένοις ἐκτὸς τῶν ἰδίων ὅρων. Galatia's original aggression: Polyb. 29.22.4. Her frustration of Roman envoys: Livy, 45.34.11–14.

made further encroachments into Galatia.[28] Of systematic Roman policy to cripple the Attalids there is no sign.[29]

The dust of Pydna had settled by the mid-160s. Rome had administered her lesson to Rhodes, stripping the island of most of its mainland possessions and ruining its economic prosperity. She had slighted Eumenes, effectively denying him support against his foes and withdrawing any sanction for his aggrandizement. She had hosted Prusias but obstructed his plans for territorial acquisition. She advocated autonomy for Galatians but insisted that they keep to their place. Senatorial declarations showed some sternness and vigor. How long did that last? By 164 Rome had accepted the Rhodians into alliance. And her embassies to Asia Minor had begun to show that same indecisiveness and half-hearted character familiar from the era prior to the Third Macedonian War. Yet another Roman retreat into indifference was underway.

## Recovery and Revival

Rhodes would not again be a major power. But her alliance with Rome halted the slide in prestige and boosted confidence. Advertisement of the revived association allowed her to reassert some authority in her own domains. To that end came erection of a colossal statue to the Roman people and, perhaps about this time, inauguration of festivals for the goddess Roma.[30] The Rhodians hastily moved to capitalize, requesting sanction from Rome ca. 163 for control over Calynda and for restoration of Rhodian property in Lycia and Caria. The senate by now had ceased to care. Calynda rebelled against Caunian overlordship and delivered herself to the protection of Rhodes. Rome endorsed developments after the fact.[31]

The Rhodians had to rely on their own resources, neither helped nor hampered by Rome. A decline in revenues eroded their naval power. War against Cretans in the mid-150s stretched Rhodian capability to its utmost. The island's envoys sought succor first in Achaea, then in Rome. Sympathy but no support came from the

28. Polyb. 30.30.2.

29. Note the coinage of the realm, the *cistophori* instituted by Eumenes, an exclusive currency of the Pergamenes, designed to underscore their independence; H. Seyrig, *RevNum* 5 (1963): 22–31; Kleiner and Noe, *The Early Cistophoric Coinage*, 10–18.

30. Polyb. 31.4.4; *IG*, XII, 1, 46; XII, 1, 730 = *Syll.*³ 724; cf. Schmitt, *Rom und Rhodos*, 175–176, n. 1; Mellor, *ΘΕΑ ΡΩΜΗ*, 34–35.

31. Polyb. 31.4–5. It would be a reasonable presumption that Rhodians recovered their property in Lycia and Caria as well.

Achaeans; the Roman senate sent its usual embassy with instructions to reconcile the combatants. The outcome does not stand on record. In light of parallel episodes one may surmise that the diplomatic intervention accomplished little. The war evidently fizzled out to an inglorious conclusion.[32] Rhodes' military fortunes had sunk to a low ebb, her once proud navy now a shell of its former self and her citizens, according to Polybius, in a state of disarray.[33]

Diplomacy, however, could substitute for war. The Rhodians retained the diplomatic skills that for so long had permitted them to maneuver among larger powers and to play an independent role in the Aegean. Information is too scanty to follow Rhodian history in the mid- and later second century. Surviving hints suggest that Rhodes returned to her old games with some success. The city of Ceramus entered into a Rhodian alliance some time in this period. Priene requested one too, for protection against her foes in Asia Minor. Rhodes' stock evidently rose. She reached accommodation with Pergamum as well. Eumenes supplied large amounts of grain to the island, and had promised construction of a marble temple. More was still coming, due after the death of Eumenes. Rhodes maintained the good relations, supplying ships for Attalus II's campaign against Bithynia. Gifts in the form of grain arrived also from Demetrius of Syria. The island recreated a network of connections. As Diodorus observes, Rhodes was especially adept at employing flattery and cajolery which induced princes to compete for her favors.[34] Economic recovery came too—not perhaps to the pre-167 level, but commercial contacts revived or continued, and the Rhodians enjoyed a modicum of prosperity.[35] Rome kept her distance. The harshness that had followed Pydna softened to apathy. Rhodes had lost the military and economic predominance she once enjoyed in the Aegean, but resumed the diplomatic machinations that had characterized her heyday and that now gave her place again on the international scene.

Roman withdrawal from the affairs of Asia Minor stands out more starkly still. Polybian analysis has clouded understanding here.

32. Polyb. 33.13.2, 33.15.3–33.16.8; Diod. 31.45; Trogus, *Prol.* 35. See *Syll.*³ 570; Segré, *RivFilol* 11 (1933): 379–392—honorary decrees for a certain Pamphilidas for service in a Cretan war, perhaps this one.

33. Polyb. 33.17; Diod. 31.38, 31.43; cf. Polyb. 33.4.

34. Rhodian alliance with Ceramus: Michel, *Recueil*, no. 458, lines 13–18; see Robert, *Villes d'Asie Mineure*, 60–61; Fraser-Bean, *Rhodian Peraea*, 110–111; Schmitt, *Rom und Rhodos*, 176–177. The request of Priene: Polyb. 33.6.7. Cooperation with Pergamum: Polyb. 31.31, 33.13.1–2; Diod. 31.36. On gifts from Demetrius and Rhodian general policy, see Diod. 31.36.

35. Strabo, 14.2.5 (C 652–653); T. Hackens, *BCH* 89 (1965): 518–532; Ferrary, in Nicolet, *Rome et la conquête*, 786.

The Greek historian, writing after 146 and exposing, as he thought, the underside of Roman policy, dwells on a recurrent theme: senatorial suspicion of and hostility to Eumenes II. That interpretation, as we have seen, led him to oversimplify and perhaps to misconstrue Roman-Pergamene interchanges in the immediate wake of Pydna. It goes back further, to his embrace of dubious tales regarding Eumenes' intrigues with Perseus during the Third Macedonian War. A dark coloration pervades Polybius' discussion. It has also seduced some moderns into adopting comparable explanations: that criticism of Eumenes was spread by Roman agents in Anatolia, thereby to keep pressure on the Pergamene and provide pretext for increasing Roman control.[36] Yet the historian's own narrative undermines his interpretation.

The Galatians had a right to complain. Pergamene intervention or intrigue inside the Galatian sphere persisted. Prusias II stood to gain as well from raising objections to alleged Attalid encroachments. The Bithynian prince took encouragement from his generous treatment by Rome in 167. During the next several years he organized a series of diplomatic campaigns designed to goad Rome into action against Eumenes. In 165 a Bithynian legation charged that Eumenes had appropriated territory from that kingdom and continued to harass Galatia by promoting his own partisans there, in violation of senatorial decrees. Other Asian cities too had spokesmen in Rome, probably prompted by Prusias, and hinted at sinister collaboration between Eumenes and Antiochus IV of Syria.[37] A year later, Prusias stitched together another set of grievances and rounded up another group of complainants, from Galatia, the city of Selge, and various Asian communities.[38] The Bithynian was not easily discouraged. He tried the same maneuver in 160/59, shipping envoys from his own realm, from Galatia, and elsewhere to deliver the same shopworn complaints.[39]

With what results? The senate supplied courtesies and embassies, as usual. It accomplished (and intended to accomplish) nothing tangible. The ever congenial Ti. Gracchus returned from a visit to the royal courts in 165 and gave Eumenes a clear endorsement. The *patres* mouthed mere platitudes about confirming Galatian autonomy.[40] The

---

36. The Polybian reiteration of Roman hostility to Eumenes: Polyb. 30.19.12–13, 30.30.5, 31.1.6, 31.6.6, 32.1.7; Diod. 31.7.2. Cf. Liebmann-Frankfort, *La frontière orientale*, 105: "Dans tout cela transparaît l'attitude soupçonneuse de Rome à l'égard du roi de Pergame"; Errington, *Dawn of Empire*, 245: "Prusias was also an immensely useful agent for Rome, since he immediately began to accuse Eumenes . . . just the sort of thing the Senate wanted to hear . . . . the continuing disfavour with which Rome viewed Eumenes."

37. Polyb. 30.30.2–4; Livy, *Per.* 46.    38. Polyb. 31.1.3; cf. Diod. 31.7.2.
39. Polyb. 31.32.1, 32.1.5–6.    40. Polyb. 30.30.6–7.

next year Eumenes' own brothers, Attalus and Athenaeus, came to dispute Prusias' allegations, made a convincing case, and drew from the senate an open dismissal of those allegations, as well as a vote of honors for themselves.[41] The legation headed by C. Sulpicius Gallus followed, setting up shop in Sardis and soliciting complaints against Eumenes for a period of ten days. Gallus took pride in his quarrel with the Pergamene king, according to Polybius—and was mentally unstable on top of it.[42] The analysis will not stand up. Gallus' brief sojourn was just that. The time limit of ten days would provide a show of good faith, get all the accusations over with in a short compass, and leave no opportunity for serious investigation of them. None was ever acted upon, to our knowledge, nor was any action intended. The fact is confirmed four years later when Prusias, still undaunted, tried again to regale the *patres* with indictments of Eumenes' behavior. Results were the same as before. The senate lavished kindnesses upon Eumenes' brother Attalus and rejected Prusias' charges in short order.[43]

The narrative of events tells an unambiguous tale. Polybius reports it faithfully but strains to explain it away. So, he suggests that Ti. Gracchus was enticed into friendliness by flattering receptions at royal courts. And he balances every senatorial action on behalf of Pergamum with insinuations about unspoken mistrust of the king.[44] The repetition becomes a worn refrain, Polybius' means of salvaging a theory increasingly at variance with the facts. His embarrassment surfaces when registering the senate's conspicuous graciousness toward Attalus and dismissal of Prusias' bill of grievances. Polybius does his best to explain this away also: the more alienated the *patres* were from Eumenes, the more favor they showed to Attalus.[45] That, of course, is nonsense. The two brothers maintained a united policy throughout. Polybius conveniently forgets his own discussion of an earlier encounter when the Roman senate found that Attalus could not be manipulated against his family.[46] The historian's reconstruction falls afoul of his own information.

41. Polyb. 31.1.2–5: οὐ μόνον ἀποτρεψάμενοι τὰς ἐπιφερομένας αἰτίας, ἀλλὰ καὶ τιμηθέντες ἐπανῆλθον εἰς τὴν Ἀσίαν; Diod. 31.7.2.

42. Polyb. 31.1.6–8, 31.6.1–5. That Gallus was arrogant and a hothead may well be true; cf. Paus. 7.11.2–3.

43. Polyb. 31.32.1, 32.1.5–6: οὐ μόνον ἀπέλυσε τῶν διαβολῶν τὸν Ἄτταλον, ἀλλὰ καὶ προσαυξήσασα τοῖς φιλανθρώποις ἐξαπέστειλε.

44. On Ti. Gracchus, Polyb. 30.30.7–8. Suspicions of Eumenes, see above n. 36.

45. Polyb. 32.1.7: καθ' ὅσον γὰρ ἀπηλλοτρίωτο τοῦ βασιλέως καὶ διεφέρετο πρὸς τὸν Εὐμένη, κατὰ τοσοῦτον ἐφιλοποιεῖτο καὶ συνηῦξε τὸν Ἄτταλον.

46. Polyb. 30.3.6–7. On harmony among the brothers, see Polyb. 32.8.6–7; Strabo, 14.1.24 (C 641); OGIS, 303–304, 325.

Prusias and the Galatians needed no prodding from Rome to level charges against Pergamum. The prodding indeed was theirs. Some of the charges also had substance. Accusation of meddling in the affairs of Galatia at least had foundation in fact. Correspondence between the Pergamene royal family and Attis, priest of the temple estate at Pessinus, establishes it well enough. The letters are worded with circumspection and the most sensitive matters left for personal encounter. But traces of intrigue remain, military collaboration is alluded to, and the target unquestionably was Galatian territory.[47] All the more significant then is Roman restraint. The *patres* honored Prusias but let Eumenes have his way.

The conclusion gains greater authority by a glance at Roman dealings with the kingdom of Cappadocia. Ariarathes IV owed a heavy debt of gratitude to Eumenes, who had interceded for him after the Antiochene war, winning Roman forgiveness and favor. The king was succeeded by his son Ariarathes V in 163, brother-in-law of Eumenes and a man who maintained close relations with the Attalid house. Not coincidentally, he suffered military incursions by the Galatians, the foes also of Eumenes II.[48] The Galatians attempted against Ariarathes the same maneuver they had employed against Eumenes. When military attacks failed, they endeavored to discredit the Cappadocian by incriminating him before the Roman senate.[49] Ariarathes had more than one reason for soliciting Roman benevolence. His hold on the throne was recent and shaky. Pretenders lay in wait, other sons (real, adopted, or feigned) of Ariarathes IV, in particular Orophernes who would soon challenge for legitimacy.[50] The new monarch naturally played up to Rome, rivaling even Prusias in obsequious cajolery. An amateur philosopher and student of the Academy, he

47. *OGIS*, 315 = Welles, *RC*, nos. 55–60.

48. On relations between the Pergamene and Cappadocian royal families, see above p. 550. Galatian attacks on Ariarathes V's realm: Polyb. 31.8.1–2; cf. 31.15.10.

49. Polyb. 31.8.2: ἐπειδὴ γὰρ οὐκ ἠδυνήθησαν οἱ Τρόκμοι δι᾽ αὑτῶν ἀποτεμέσθαι τῆς Καππαδοκίας οὐδέν . . . καταφυγόντες ἐπὶ Ῥωμαίους διαβάλλειν ἐπειρῶντο τὸν Ἀριαράθην.

50. Diod. 31.19.7; Zon. 9.24. One of the supposed sons, not mentioned again, had been placed under the tutelage of the Roman senate in 172: Livy, 42.19.3–5. Hopp, *Untersuchungen*, 64–65, suggests that he is the future Ariarathes V himself—which is at variance with Diod. 31.19.7, unless one were to postulate two separate members of the royal family sent for nurture to Rome. Whether Ariarathes V was, in fact, the rightful heir cannot be ascertained with any degree of confidence. Note the reference to Ariarathes IV, his wife, and τέκνα in a recently published document: Pugliese Carratelli and Segré, *PP* 27 (1972): 182–185. If correctly dated to the period 182–179, it suggests that the elder sons were officially recognized as legitimate. The story of supposed sons sent out of the country to clear a path for Ariarathes V may owe something to sources favorable to the new king—or perhaps to Ariarathes himself. See now L. Doria, *PP* 33 (1978): 104–129, with bibliography.

showed little philosophical restraint upon accession to the throne. Only security counted. Ariarathes hastily dispatched envoys to renew *amicitia*, pledging good will and pro-Roman zeal, and evinced great joy at obtaining a positive response.[51] Roman representatives who visited Cappadocia were received with enthusiasm. Ariarathes promised full compliance with any decision and offered armed escort for further travels.[52] The king acted with great circumspection, staying his hand from foreign ventures that might cause offense.[53] He declined a marriage alliance dangled by Demetrius of Syria, and announced proudly to the Romans that he had done so on their account.[54] In 160 he spared no expense in tangible demonstration of good will, presenting a crown composed of ten thousand gold pieces.[55]

Rome quickly relieved Ariarathes of anxiety. Ti. Gracchus had brought home yet another optimistic assessment in 164, giving the senate grounds for prompt reaffirmation of the *amicitia* and gracious diplomatic courtesies.[56] Two separate Roman delegations stopped in Cappadocia during the next year, made some noises about Ariarathes' quarrel with the Galatians, but took no action, only acknowledged the king's kindness and characterized him as among the true friends of Rome.[57] Galatian complaints against Ariarathes, as against Eumenes, went unheard. Ti. Gracchus looked into them once again, among many other things, on a later trip ca. 161. He returned with additional praise for the Cappadocian, and authenticated his trustworthiness, the occasion for Rome's acceptance of the costly crown.[58] The Galatians did not get satisfaction. Rome's handsome treatment of Ariarathes, relative and ally of Eumenes, belies the notion of a policy to emasculate the Pergamenes.[59]

51. Polyb. 31.3.1–5, 31.7.1; Diod. 31.19.8. On the intellectual interests of Ariarathes, see Diod. 31.19.7–8; Diog. Laert. 4.65; *Syll.*³ 666. Cf. Mattingly, *Historia* 20 (1971): 29–32; Hopp, *Untersuchungen*, 62–65.

52. Polyb. 31.8, 31.32.3: διότι πᾶν ποιήσειν ἕτοιμός ἐστι Ῥωμαίοις τὸ παραγγελλόμενον.

53. As in declining the proposal of Artaxias of Armenia for a partitioning of Sophene: Polyb. 31.16.1–2; Diod. 31.22.

54. Diod. 31.28: ἔτι δὲ τὴν δι᾿ ἐκείνους γενομένην ἀπόρρησιν τοῦ γάμου καὶ φιλίας πρὸς Δημήτριον; cf. Justin, 35.1.2. The passage by no means proves that Rome had urged Ariarathes to reject the marriage, as is asserted again by Hopp, *Untersuchungen*, 39, and Liebmann-Frankfort, *Le Monde grec: Hommages à Claire Préaux* (1975), 418–419.

55. Polyb. 31.32.3, 32.1.1; Diod. 31.28.

56. Polyb. 31.3.3–5.

57. Polyb. 31.2.13, 31.8.

58. Polyb. 31.15.10, 31.32.3, 31.33.1, 32.1.2–3; Diod. 31.28.

59. No evidence whatever supports the view of Liebmann-Frankfort, *Le Monde grec: Hommages à Claire Préaux* (1975), 418–419, that Ariarathes catered to Rome by breaking with Eumenes.

The reputation of Eumenes II stood high in the last years of his reign. Polybius, true to his thesis, offers an explanation: the more harshly he was treated by Rome, the more sympathy he engendered from Greeks.[60] Yet Greek tributes to the Pergamene ruler in the epigraphic documents (however conventional) show respect, adulation, and gratitude, anything but commiseration. Polybius, in more sober moments, recognizes the truth. Eumenes' benefactions won him friends, allies, and supporters. Even Rhodes had come into his debt: states and individuals were beholden to him, the greatest of Hellenistic patrons.[61] Pergamene fortunes flourished with the compliance of, not in defiance of, Rome.

## The Successes of Attalus II

Attalus II, brother and successor of Eumenes, had first-hand acquaintance with Rome and the Romans. He had served with Roman generals in war and had hobnobbed with Roman senators in peacetime. The new monarch knew the Republic's leaders and understood its diplomacy. Attalus' reign reincarnated the glories of Pergamum's past. The guiding hand of Rome disappears from sight. That Attalus could ever have been regarded as a Roman agent or a puppet on Rome's string is mystifying. In fact, his tenure best exemplifies the latitude accorded by the Republic's indifference to Anatolia. Pergamum meddled, intruded, and generally threw her weight around in the affairs of Asia Minor and elsewhere, in grand old Hellenistic style, confident about the limits of Rome's interest and the measure of her own authority.[62]

Attalid involvement in Cappadocia illuminates the political atmosphere clearly enough. Ariarathes V, despite an *amicitia* with Rome and conspicuous mutual expressions of good will, lost his kingdom when expelled by the forces of Demetrius I of Syria. Demetrius championed instead the claims of Oropherves, now newly installed on the Cappadocian throne. The upheaval fell in Eumenes' last year,

60. Polyb. 31.6.6: καθ' ὅσον ἐδόκουν οἱ Ῥωμαῖοι βαρύτερον τῷ Εὐμένει προσφέρεσθαι, κατὰ τοσοῦτο συνέβαινε τοὺς Ἕλληνας προσοικειοῦσθαι.

61. Polyb. 32.8.3–5: πλείστας μὲν τῶν καθ' αὑτὸν βασιλέων πόλεις Ἑλληνίδας εὐεργέτησε, πλείστους δὲ κατ' ἰδίαν ἀνθρώπους ἐσωματοποίησε. For epigraphic honors, see above pp. 197–198. Pergamene subsidization of Rhodes: Polyb. 31.1.1; Diod. 31.36. Eumenes' death came, it seems, in 158; G. Petzl, ZPE 30 (1978): 263, no. 12.

62. Recent works continue to see Attalus as cowed by Rome and as servant of her interests; e.g., Liebmann-Frankfort, *La frontière orientale*, 105–108; Errington, *Dawn of Empire*, 246–247; Hopp, *Untersuchungen*, 59–85. Notable exceptions are McShane, *Foreign Policy*, 186–192, with earlier literature, and Sherwin-White, *JRS* 67 (1977): 62–66.

a challenge to the influence of Pergamum in Anatolia.[63] Rome was of no help. Ariarathes went there in 158, an exile now instead of a king, his charges refuted by representatives of Orophernes more through royal demeanor than through argument. The *patres* confined themselves to a suggestion that the two claimants share Cappadocia, but they would offer no assistance to that end. Ariarathes fell back upon his house's longstanding association with Pergamum. It was Attalus II who supplied the force to effect Ariarathes' restoration in 157 or 156 and drove Orophernes to a refuge at the Seleucid court. If there had been any senatorial pronouncement on dividing the Cappadocian realm, Attalus blithely ignored it. The Pergamene had served notice of the character of his rule. His would be the dominant voice in Anatolia.[64]

Attalus, in fact, had more extensive plans: overt interference in the Syrian succession. Rivalry with Demetrius over indirect control in Cappadocia led the Pergamene king to harbor designs on the Seleucid throne itself. A plot was hatched to cultivate the claims of an obscure but handsome young man who bore resemblance to the line of Antiochus IV. Attalus subsidized and publicized the pretender, setting him up in Cilicia, whence messages of his availability for royal office further undermined the already shaky regime of Demetrius I.[65] As usual, representations were made in Rome. The pretender Alexander Balas laid his claims before the senate in 153, accompanied and

63. Polyb. 3.5.2; Diod. 31.32, 31.32a; Livy, *Per.* 47; Appian, *Syr.* 47; Zon. 9.24; Justin, 35.1.1–2; cf. Trogus, *Prol.* 34.

64. Polyb. 32.12: Ἄτταλος ὁ ἀδελφὸς Εὐμένους παραλαβὼν τὴν ἐξουσίαν πρῶτον ἐξήνεγκε δεῖγμα τῆς αὑτοῦ προαιρέσεως καὶ πράξεως τὴν Ἀριαράθου καταγωγὴν ἐπὶ τὴν βασιλείαν; also Polyb. 3.5.2; Zon. 9.24. Livy, *Per.* 47, wrongly makes Rome responsible for Ariarathes' restoration. The confrontation of Ariarathes and Orophernes' legates in Rome: Polyb. 32.10.1–8. The results: Diod. 31.32.b; Appian, *Syr.* 47; Zon. 9.24. Orophernes' own misdemeanors contributed to his downfall: Polyb. 32.11.1, 32.11.8–10; Diod. 31.32, 31.34. Cf. Gruen, *Chiron* 6 (1976): 89–90. Attalus further backed Ariarathes about two years later in a raid on Priene to force that city to disgorge a monetary deposit left by Orophernes. Priene looked for succor first to Rhodes, then to Rome. It was not forthcoming. The senate sent a letter of some kind to the two monarchs; its fragmentary condition prevents reconstruction: *OGIS*, 351 = Sherk, *RDGE*, no. 6. A courtesy to the Prienians, no doubt. But as Polybius, who gives the background to these events, notes, Rome did not act on the Prienian request: Polyb. 33.6.1–8. Priene eventually restored the deposit to Orophernes but fell victim to the raids of Ariarathes: Polyb. 33.6.9; Diod. 31.32. Chronology is uncertain. Hopp, *Untersuchungen*, 65–68, dates the events to 153/2 rather than the usual ca. 155, a plausible enough placement. But his assertion that the Roman letter forbade Attalus and Ariarathes from molesting Priene receives no tangible support from the extant fragments of that document.

65. Diod. 31.32a—who attributes the scheme to Eumenes, probably wrongly; cf. Niese, *Geschichte* III:259–260, n. 6. In any case, it manifests itself in the reign of Attalus.

supported by Heraclides, another bitter foe of Demetrius. And, as usual, the *patres* gave polite reception and an encouraging resolution: Alexander had their permission to seek recovery of his ancestral kingdom and he could count on their backing.[66] That backing, of course, did not include physical force. Alexander would have to round up his own armies. But the moral suasion of a Roman pronouncement carried some weight—if properly exploited. Attalus II, whose dynasty had well-developed skills in such exploitation, utilized them to good effect again. He had not himself accompanied Alexander Balas to Rome, but chose the occasion to send his nephew, the future Attalus III, who cultivated his father's acquaintances and connections in senatorial circles, obtaining a conspicuous welcome. The prince, in the tradition of his forefathers, advertised that reception on his voyage home and collected the adulation of Greek cities as he passed through.[67] Alexander, no doubt with the counsel and aid of the Pergamene monarchy, recruited mercenary forces for the assault on Syria. His headquarters were at Ephesus, within the sphere of Attalid influence.[68] Three years later Demetrius was toppled from his throne. Alexander Balas had gained the support of a consortium of Hellenistic kings, all of them eager to remove the tottering Demetrius. Ptolemy Philometor stood in the foreground, his object to extend Ptolemaic influence in Syria. Attalus II, however, who had engineered the scheme from its outset, played the principal role. He and his ally Ariarathes provided many of the resources with which Alexander Balas rode to victory in 150.[69] Power struggles of the most conventional Hellenistic variety occupy the stage here. It might as well have been the middle of the third century B.C. Rome's part in it extended only so far as eastern monarchs and pretenders employed her name in their causes. Attalus had made the largest strides, his protégés now sitting on the thrones of both Cappadocia and Syria. Pergamene authority commanded international respect.

It is noteworthy that the only Roman diplomatic interventions in Asia Minor during the 150s actually furthered the cause of the Attalids. The actions arose out of renewed conflict between Pergamum

66. Polyb. 33.15.1–2, 33.18.6–13. On Heracleides, see further Diod. 31.27a; Appian, *Syr.* 45, 47. Polybius once again disparages senatorial attitudes, regarding the *patres* as embracing the worse cause through deception. The historian has his own axes to grind; cf. Gruen, *Chiron* 6 (1976): 91–93.

67. Polyb. 33.18.1–4.

68. Polyb. 33.18.14.

69. Attalus receives specific mention in Strabo, 13.4.2 (C 624); Justin, 35.1.6–11; Eusebius, *Chron.* I, 255, Schoene. Other evidence on the fall of Demetrius and triumph of Alexander Balas: Polyb. 3.5.3; 1 Macc. 10:1–58; Jos. *Ant.* 13.35–61, 13.80–83; Appian, *Syr.* 67; Diod. 32.9c; Livy, *Per.* 52.

and Bithynia from 156 to 154. No fewer than five Roman embassies moved to and from Anatolia during that short time. And in the end it was Attalus who had his way. Invasion of Pergamene territory by Prusias II in 156 set in motion the chain of events. Delegates of both contending kings exchanged accusations in Rome. The senators, so says Polybius, were inclined to distrust Attalus' complaints, judging them a mask for his own intended aggressions against Bithynia.[70] As often, the historian's surmise carries less authority than objective reporting. Whatever the *patres* may or may not have been inclined to believe, the fact is that they sent off two separate embassies in short order to look into conflict between the kings, one of which returned in the company of Attalus' brother and verified the Pergamene charges.[71] The additional intelligence prompted still another Roman embassy, this one with explicit instructions to prevent Prusias from waging war on Attalus.[72]

The circumstances and consequences bear notice on several fronts. They shed important light both on the policies of Hellenistic princes and on the attitudes of Rome. Attalus had succeeded in generating a series of senatorial delegations (there were still two more to come) who would take his part and incline the Republic's diplomacy in his direction. That development not only underscores the shrewdness of Attalid policy, long adept at advertising and manipulating connections in Rome, but it gives the lie to assumptions that the senate sought to clip Pergamum's wings. More striking still are the actions of Prusias. The same man who little more than a decade before had groveled at the feet of the *patres*, designating himself a "freedman" at the service of the "savior gods," now defied them in startling fashion. Roman envoys delegated to prohibit Prusias' aggression met with scorn and recalcitrance. The Bithynian indeed stepped up his assaults, drove Attalus and even the envoys to seek rescue inside the walls of Pergamum, and proceeded to destroy or pillage sacred shrines in the temple precinct outside the city.[73] There can be but one

70. Polyb. 32.16.2–4. The mission of Attalus' envoy Andronicus may be referred to in *OGIS*, 323, lines 15–23.

71. Polyb. 32.16.1–5, 33.1.1. The frustratingly fragmentary character of the Polybian information makes it impossible to reconstruct the sequence of Roman embassies with any certainty. The mission of L. Apuleius and C. Petronius left in response to news that tended to confirm Attalus' charges: Polyb. 32.16.5. A separate confirmation, however, came from P. Lentulus who returned from Pergamum in the company of Attalus' brother Athenaeus; for his report prompted the dispatch of yet a third delegation: Polyb. 32.16.1, 33.1.1–2. Willingness to make a positive response to Attalus, however, seems clear—despite Polybian remarks about Rome's distrust.

72. Polyb. 33.1.2: ἐντολὰς δοῦσα κωλύειν τὸν Προυσίαν Ἀττάλῳ πολεμεῖν.

73. Polyb. 32.15, 33.7.1–2; Appian, *Mithr.* 3; Diod. 31.35. See Robert, *Études*

explanation for Prusias' extraordinary contempt for Rome's advice. He did not take seriously the prospect of her intervention. Memories of Pydna were fading. A decade of inaction and indifference spawned a new set of expectations. Prusias anticipated a free hand against Pergamum.

Hellenic calculations reflect the experience of the past decade. And these episodes illuminate the Roman side as well. Despite protest, pronouncement, and command, senatorial policy kept its own restraints and inhibited the actions of its own representatives. The sequel makes that clear enough. Mistreatment of Roman envoys should have raised a storm of protest from the *patres*. Instead, the embassies multiplied. When the previous ambassadors brought word of Prusias' transgressions, an irate senate appointed nothing less than a ten-man commission with orders to terminate the war and compel Prusias to submit to arbitration on his felonies.[74] Does this signify that Rome at last meant business and would coerce truculent Hellenic rulers into submission? Prusias evidently did not think so. He conceded on a few points but resisted on most. The king, in effect, called Rome's bluff and expected to get away with it.[75] The Roman commission indignantly broke off formal relations and declared the friendship and alliance with Prusias at an end. Only then did the king suddenly realize that he might have gone too far. He swiftly trailed the legates as they headed for Attalus, hoping to make amends, but got nowhere.[76] How sharp a turn, in fact, does this represent in Roman policy? The commissioners advised Attalus to build up his defenses, to secure his cities and villages, but to avoid opening hostilities. They then divided efforts, some returning home to announce Prusias' uncooperativeness, some making the rounds in Ionia and the Hellespont to encourage defection from Prusias and support for Attalus.[77] The limitations on Roman involvement here come to the surface. A sequence of the Republic's embassies had been ignored, abused, or toyed with. There would, however, be no militant response, only a severance of diplomatic relations. Burden would be shifted onto Greek communities to provide a united (though defensive) front to overawe Prusias and

---

*Anatoliennes*, 111–118; Habicht, *Hermes* 84 (1956): 101–110, on the chronology and ordering of the Polybian fragments. In general, Habicht, *RE* XXIII.1, "Prusias II," 1115–1120; and cf. now Walbank, *Commentary* III: 536–542.

74. Polyb. 33.7.1–4: ἐντολὰς αὐτοῖς δοῦσα διαλῦσαι τὸν πόλεμον καὶ τὸν Προυσίαν ἀναγκάσαι δίκας ὑποσχεῖν Ἀττάλῳ τῶν κατὰ πόλεμον ἀδικημάτων.

75. Polyb. 33.12.4: ὁ δὲ Προυσίας ἔνια μὲν τῶν προσταττομένων προσεδέχετο, τοῖς δὲ πλείστοις ἀντέλεγε.

76. Polyb. 33.12.5–6.

77. Polyb. 33.12.7–9.

keep him in his place. Rome plainly hoped for a peaceful settlement—
and one in which the Hellenes would be their own policemen. The
posture does not differ much from past behavior.

Attalus paid as little heed to Roman counsel as did Prusias. His
aim had been to instigate a show of Roman support, thereby to gain
the upper hand over his rival. The show of support once achieved, he
proceeded to take military action, in disregard of the Republic's advice. A huge fleet of eighty vessels was assembled from various allies
which then assaulted Hellespontine communities tied to Bithynia.
Attalus had the command not only of Pergamene land forces but of
infantry and cavalry supplied by his *philoi* Ariarathes V of Cappadocia
and Mithridates IV of Pontus. Those forces, it appears, had penetrated into Bithynian territory.[78] Rome in the meanwhile sent still another embassy, this time to insist upon terminating the war. A treaty
followed in 154, in which Attalus had all the best of it. Prusias consented to surrender ships, pay a hefty indemnity, and make reparations to cities he had violated. The territorial divisions between
Pergamum and Bithynia would revert to a *status quo ante*.[79] Roman
delegates, the fifth embassy to Asia Minor in the space of three years,
had helped at last to bring peace negotiations to fruition, though only
after a succession of false starts and abortive attempts. But it was not
they alone who brought about the result. Attalus' forces and the
coalition of his allies, capitalizing upon Roman pronouncements but
relying upon their own resources, had played their part in coercing
Prusias into compliance.

Attalus' gains continued and his prestige swelled. The wretched
Prusias soon lost hold of his own realm. Polybius has nothing but
contempt for him. The man who once prostrated himself before the
senate, then blustered mightily only to capitulate, now gave way to
sensual pleasures, lacking in capacity to make war or keep peace, a
prince devoid of culture. Such, at least, is the Polybian portrait. Prusias became increasingly intolerable to his own countrymen, and popular favor eventually fastened upon his son Nicomedes.[80] Just when
this happened is unclear and unimportant. Prusias commissioned
Nicomedes to undertake an extended visit to Rome in the late 150s.
Our sources excogitate the logical motive: the king hoped to get
his son out of the way, thus to clear the route for other heirs. That

78. Polyb. 33.12.1, 33.13.1–3. Occupation of Bithynian territory seems implied
by Polyb. 33.13.9.

79. Polyb. 33.13.4–10; Appian, *Mithr.* 3; cf. *OGIS*, 327, line 4.

80. Polyb. 36.15; Appian, *Mithr.* 4; Diod. 32.19; Zon. 9.28. On the Polybian portrait, cf. Welwei, *Könige und Königtum*, 114–116. On Prusias II, see especially Habicht,
*RE* XXIII.1 "Prusias II,' 1120–1124.

explanation is plausible but incomplete. Prusias intended to take political profit from the Roman connections that Nicomedes might summon, just as Philip V had done with Demetrius a generation before. Nicomedes was instructed to argue for a remission of the indemnity owed to Pergamum.[81] Attalus sprang into action. His representatives hastened to Rome, where their arguments prevailed. There would be no remission of the monies due. And they did more. Attalid envoys catered to Nicomedes, encouraging a rebellion against the king. Suspicion had already arisen between father and son, aggravated by failure to halt the indemnity payments, a prolonged economic hardship on the Bithynian realm. Attalus had chosen the right moment to strike. Pergamene subsidies and soldiers gave Nicomedes the courage to announce a claim on his father's realm.[82]

The reign of Prusias II rapidly disintegrated. He tried braggadocio on Attalus, to no avail. An appeal to Rome in 149 got the usual senatorial embassy—or rather less than the usual, an incompetent trio, mocked by Cato, a mission doomed to failure and ridicule. Their selection, so it is reported, came from a praetor sympathetic to Attalus. Once again Pergamene expansion could proceed unhindered by the western power. The king, in any case, awaited no Roman embassy. He marched troops into Bithynia and roused Prusias' subjects into insurrection. A request for peace talks by the Roman envoys was deftly sidestepped. Bithynian spokesmen had been coached to state that they found Prusias intolerable and to produce a list of charges against him. The Romans returned home without accomplishment. Their presence had only contributed to a charade which gave Attalus a free hand. Pergamene armies drove Prusias off his throne, set up his assassination, and carried Nicomedes to the kingship. Attalus had choreographed it all. The Romans, swift to acknowledge the status quo, immediately gave Nicomedes formal recognition.[83]

81. Appian, *Mithr.* 4; cf. Zon. 9.28. On Philip and Demetrius, see above p. 402. Cf. Vitucci, *Il regno di Bitinia*, 82–84. The motive of seeking to get rid of Nicomedes is given also by Justin, 34.4.1. Nicomedes' associations in Rome very likely stemmed from an earlier stay there, beginning in 167: Livy, 45.44.4, 45.44.9, 45.44.13.

82. Appian, *Mithr.* 4–6; Strabo, 13.4.2 (C 624). Cato's speech, *de rege Attalo et vectigalibus Asiae*, probably took place at the hearing on remission of Prusias' indemnity: Malcovati, *ORF*, no. 190. The elaborate tale about plot and counterplot in Appian, *Mithr.* 4–6, may or may not be true; cf. also Zon. 9.28; Justin, 34.4.1. It does not much matter.

83. The principal evidence is in Appian, *Mithr.* 6–7. The Roman embassy and Cato's mockery also in Polyb. 36.14.1–5; Diod. 32.20; Livy, *Per.* 50; Plut. *Cato*, 9. The fall of Prusias also in Polyb. 36.15.7; Diod. 32.21; Strabo, 13.4.2 (C 624); Livy, *Per.* 50; Justin, 34.4.2–5; Zon. 9.28. Attalus' victory is commemorated in *OGIS*, 327; cf. also *OGIS*, 299, with C. P. Jones, *Chiron* 4 (1974): 186–189. Zonaras, 9.28, suggests Rome's irrita-

The Pergamene ruler now had protégés on the thrones of Syria, Cappadocia, and Bithynia. His stature as preeminent power in Anatolia went unchallenged. Diplomacy, intrigue, and force secured him that position, the contests and their outcome determined in traditional Hellenistic fashion, not a design drawn up in Italy. The energy and aggressiveness of Attalus evidently continued through the last decade of his reign. That much is discernible even from the wretched fragments of our extant testimony. They show expansion into Thrace in 145, at the expense of the Thracian chieftain Diegylis who paid for his earlier support of Prusias.[84] Attalus consolidated his realm with urban foundations and collected honors from various areas in Hellas.[85]

The long reign had seen an almost unbroken string of successes. Not least of the reasons was Attalus' skillful advertisement of his connections with Rome. Roman influence in Asia Minor operated usually through indirect mobilization by the Pergamene king. We have come upon the phenomenon again and again. It receives exemplary illustration in Attalus' own dedication after the victory over Prusias in 149. Rome had had no hand in it, her envoys asking for peace and withdrawing without effect. Yet Attalus' dedication announces that Prusias was punished for violating a treaty sanctioned by Rome.[86] Shrewder still was his invocation of the Republic when he declined a request from Attis of Pessinus to wage war, presumably against the Galatians. Attalus resorted to a letter. He had himself been willing to help, so the letter stated, but his counselors gradually dissuaded him by pointing out the risks of Roman displeasure. The king had mastered the art of manipulation. He could utilize the name of Rome either to mask intervention or to justify inaction.[87] To Roman military

---

tion, stifled by her unwillingness to take up arms in Anatolia· ταῦτα ἠνίασο μὸν τοὺς Ῥωμαίους, οὐ μὴν καὶ εἰς πόλεμον ἐξηρέθισε. Liebmann-Frankfort, La frontière orientale, 93–94, infers, without any justification, that the Romans insisted upon Pergamene withdrawal from Bithynia.

84. Strabo, 13.4.2 (C 624); Trog. Prol. 36; Diod. 33.14–15; see OGIS, 330: οἱ ἐκ Παραλείας στρατιῶται οἱ διαβάντες ἐν τῶι ιέ ἔτει εἰς τοὺς κατὰ Χερρόνησον καὶ Θράικην τόπους εὐχήν.

85. On consolidation of the kingdom, see Hopp, Untersuchungen, 102–106. Attalus' honors, see above pp. 197–198.

86. OGIS, 327, line 4: παραβάντα τὰς διὰ Ῥωμαίων γε[νομένας συνθήκας].

87. OGIS, 315 = Welles, RC, no. 61. The letter includes an assertion that Attalus would henceforth make regular reports to Rome; lines 20–22: ἔκρινον οὖν εἰς μὲν τ[ὴ]ν Ῥώμην ἀεὶ πέμπειν τοὺς συνεχῶς ἀναγγελοῦν[τας] τ[ὰ δισ]τ[α]ζόμενα. The document has therefore almost always been taken as demonstration of Attalid subservience to Rome; e.g., Magie, RRAM I:27; Hansen, Attalids, 132; Liebmann-Frankfort, La frontière orientale, 105–108; Hopp, Untersuchungen, 68–70. McShane, Foreign Policy, 186–187, is uncomfortable with that analysis but has none other to offer and simply plays down the significance of the evidence. Sherwin-White, JRS 67 (1977): 64, takes the letter to

ventures he gave token support, some ships for Metellus Macedonicus' campaign against Andriscus in 148 and a contingent of troops to assist Mummius in quelling the Achaean war in 146.[88] It was a profitable investment. The cooperation cost him little, while it lent weight to his claims of association with the Republic. At Attalus' invitation perhaps, Scipio Aemilianus made Pergamum one of the stops on his lengthy tour of the East ca. 140.[89] The king had successfully carried on a worthy tradition that stretched back for two generations. At the end of the third century Attalus I had enlisted Roman aid to the advantage of Pergamum in the power struggles of the Hellenistic East. More than sixty years later, that pattern of behavior still prevailed.


## The Bequest of Pergamum and Its Consequences

The succeeding reign, that of Attalus III, last of the Pergamene line, twisted the pattern in intriguing fashion. A quite surprising development on the surface, but, on reflection, a logical outcome of past experience. Attalus composed a will which bequeathed his kingdom to Rome.[90]

Why did it happen and what did it mean? Attalus III was an eccentric, or perhaps worse. He reigned for but a short time (138–133

---

prove the *absence* of Roman supervision—on the grounds that Attalus had not considered any Roman reaction until his advisers brought it up. Sherwin-White, however, bypasses the sentence quoted above and never raises the possibility that the letter may mean more (or less) than appears on the surface of the stone.

88. The campaign against Andriscus: Strabo, 13.4.2 (C 624); Zon. 9.28; against Achaea: Paus. 7.16.1; cf. the anecdote in Pliny, *NH*, 7.39.12, 35.8.24.

89. Lucian, *Macrob.* 12.

90. The fact is attested in numerous sources, including an indirect reference in a contemporary document: *OGIS*, 338, lines 5–7: δεῖ δὲ ἐπικυρωθῆναι τὴν διαθή[κην] ὑπὸ Ῥωμαίων. The evidence is cited and much of it quoted by G. Cardinali, *Saggi di storia antica a G. Beloch* (Rome, 1910), 274–276. Its authenticity is questioned only in the letter of Mithridates composed by Sallust, *Hist.* 4.61.8, Maur., an obviously tendentious statement. Liebmann-Frankfort, *RIDA* 13 (1966): 75–77, 80–83, finds a difference in terminology among the sources: the earlier and more accurate ones speak of "leaving," "giving," or "bestowing" the kingdom, the later ones have Attalus make Rome his heir. The imperial authors imported an idea from Roman law, whereas Attalus looked upon Rome as a successor or an heir. So also F. Carrata Thomes, *La rivolta di Aristonico e le origini della provincia romana d'Asia* (Turin, 1968), 32–35; Hopp, *Untersuchungen*, 126–127. The distinction is rather a fine one. And Liebmann-Frankfort's division into earlier and later sources involves considerable chronological overlap; e.g. Strabo, 13.4.2 (C 624) is placed among the late sources, Appian, *BC*, 1.111 among the early! And the Livian *Periochae* qualify under both headings; *Per.* 58: *heredem autem populum Romanum reliquerat Attalus; Per.* 59: (Asia) *testamento Attali regis legata populo Romano.* The matter need not be pursued.

B.C.) and died young, in his mid-thirties, his personality and achievements an enduring puzzle. Public documents throw a favorable light upon him, especially his cultic benefactions, and disclose even a military success over unnamed foes.[91] Yet he earned an evil reputation too, reflected in the literary sources. Morbid suspicion and paranoia set in, we are told, after the deaths of his mother and fiancée. Attalus took grim vengeance on friends and relatives, then shunned the public eye, retreated to seclusion, and let the governance of his realm slip away. He preferred to dabble in pharmacology and medicinal plants—which malicious rumor naturally characterized as preparation of poisonous substances to be distributed as gifts to his intended victims.[92] The truth eludes inquiry. Public documents present only the official posture. Literary evidence, exaggerated for narrative effect, is no more reliable on the other side. The question of whether Attalus was a scientific resercher or a mad poisoner lies outside our purview. Relations with Rome remained cordial. Attalus had been introduced to the senate as a boy in 152, obtaining a warm reception. The news preceded his return and won him the cheers of Greek communities on his route. Young Attalus had come to know the influence that accrued from association, real or alleged, with the Republic. Nearly two decades later he sent expensive gifts to Scipio Aemilianus as congratulatory tokens for his victory at Numantia.[93] None of this, however, can have prepared contemporaries for what followed, the bequest of the Attalid kingdom itself. Whether madman or sane, persecutor or persecuted, Attalus' action demands explanation.

Explanations have not been wanting. The scholarly literature boasts an ever increasing number of them. Irrational rancor on the part of Attalus against his own subjects has been suggested, a desire to bring them under the heel of Rome. Or, conversely, he expected Rome to take up the role of protector of the Greeks in Asia. Others postulate a prearrangement: Attalus had concerted plans in advance with the Romans, who looked forward to the annexation of Asia. The king recognized his incompetence in holding together a strife-ridden realm and decided to turn the task over to Rome. An alternative hypothesis has the Pergamene upper classes concoct the scheme in the

---

91. Attalus III had been carefully groomed for his task; cf. *ÖstJahrb* 47 (1964–65): 2–5. For some of his benefactions, see *OGIS*, 331 = Welles, *RC*, no. 66–67; *OGIS*, 333 = Welles, *RC*, no. 68; no. 69. The military triumph: *OGIS*, 332, lines 23–24.

92. See, especially, Diod. 34·5.3; Justin, 36.4.1–5; cf. also Strabo, 14.1.39 (C 647), with J. Fontenrose, *TAPA* 91 (1960): 83–99. Other sources and discussion in Cardinali, *Saggi di storia antica a G. Beloch* (Rome, 1910), 269–274; Hopp, *Untersuchungen*, 107–120.

93. Attalus' visit to Rome as a boy: Polyb. 33.18.1–4; his gifts to Aemilianus: Cic. *Pro Deiot.* 19; cf. Schol. Ambros. 272, Stangl.

hope that Rome would uphold their authority against a revolutionary tide in the land. Or (the most prevalent view) Attalus merely put the finishing touch on a process long in development and nearly complete, i.e. the encroaching dominion of Rome over the affairs of Asia.[94]

The conjectures proliferate but fail to provide satisfaction. That Attalus had it in for his subjects and expected Rome to wreak his vengeance lacks all plausibility. His testament, in fact, insisted on freedom for the city of Pergamum and its territory.[95] The insertion of that phrase implies not only that Attalus wished to secure Pergamenes from a subject status but also that he lacked confidence in Rome's restraint. Of prior collaboration on framing the will our evidence breathes no hint, and the likelihood is remote. Roman leaders indeed were quite unprepared for the legacy, which immediately became an issue in the political controversies of Ti. Gracchus' tribunate.[96] The idea that the Pergamene upper classes looked to Rome as a prop for their social system lacks any basis in the evidence. The decree of the Pergamene *demos*, passed shortly after Attalus III's death, alludes with respect and gratitude to the king's testament and looks ahead to Roman ratification, while at the same time extending the franchise to certain groups in the area and elevating the civic status of others. This is not the manifesto of an elite class clinging to its privileges.[97] Nor does any advantage accrue from the notion that Attalus' deed simply gave *de iure* recognition to the sovereignty that Rome had already exercised *de facto*. The exposition above should put that view out of court. Rome shrank from such sovereignty, and the Attalid kings knew of none.

A different solution is available, offered long ago, subsequently discredited, and recently revived. Attalus III faced a dynastic chal-

94. Irrational rancor: Mommsen, *Römische Geschichte*, II[9], 53. Rome as protector of Asian Greeks: McShane, *Foreign Policy*, 194. A combined plan by Rome and Attalus: J. Vogt, *Ancient Slavery and the Ideal of Man* (Cambridge, Mass., 1975), 96. The king turned to Rome as a power to impose order in Asia: Magie, *RRAM* I: 31–32; V. Vavrinek, *La révolte d'Aristonicos* (Prague, 1957), 20. A move on behalf of the Pergamene upper classes: J. C. Dumont, *Eirene* 5 (1966): 189–190; Carrata Thomes, *La rivolta di Aristonico*, 30–31. A formal acknowledgement of Rome's *de facto* ascendancy in Anatolia and the Aegean: Mommsen, *op. cit.*, 53; Cardinali, *Saggi di storia antica a G. Beloch* (Rome, 1910), 278–280; Hansen, *Attalids*, 148–149. The view of Z. Rubinsohn, *Rend-IstLomb* 107 (1973): 550–556, that senior members of the royal administration drew up the will after Attalus' death and that Rome plotted against Attalus, is unintelligible.

95. *OGIS*, 338, lines 5–6: ἀπολέλοιπεν τὴ[ν πατρί]δα ἡμῶν ἐλευθέραν, προσορίσας αὐτῆι καὶ πολε[ιτικὴν] χώραν ἣν ἔκριν[εν]. Cf. Livy, *Per.* 59: *Aristonicus . . . Asiam occupavit, cum testamento Attali regis legata populo Romano libera esse deberet.*

96. Cf. Plut. *Ti. Gr.* 14; Livy, *Per.* 58.

97. *OGIS*, 338, lines 5–25.

lenge, real or anticipated. His hold on the throne and on the hearts of his subjects was far from secure.[98] A rival waited in the wings, Aristonicus, a bastard son of Eumenes II, or so he claimed. Our sources take the claim seriously, for the most part, and Attalus, a man given to unreasoned suspicions, would have had more than enough cause to suspect this potential foe.[99] Whether Aristonicus burst into open revolt while Attalus III was still alive remains an open question, insoluble and unnecessary to solve. What matters is not so much the precise timing of the revolt as Attalus' perception of the threat. The timing is close on any reckoning. Attalus died probably in the spring of 133.[100] A series of *cistophori* bearing the legend BA EY and almost certainly attributable to Aristonicus, who claimed to be son of Eumenes II and evidently took the name Eumenes III, runs over a four-year period. Aristonicus' fall came in 130; hence his usurpation of the kingly title dates to 133, and possibly rather early in that year.[101]

98. Diod. 34-5.3: μισηθεὶς οὐ μόνον ὑπὸ τῶν ἀρχομένων ἀλλὰ καὶ τῶν πλησιοχώρων πάντας τοὺς ὑποτεταγμένους ἐποίησε μετεώρους πρὸς καινοτομίαν. Cf. Justin, 36.4.1–3. The portrait may well be overdrawn, but surely not without some basis.

99. Aristonicus' claim to be son of Eumenes is accepted without question by a number of the authors; e.g. Justin, 36.4.6; Livy, *Per.* 59; Eutrop. 4.20; cf. 4.18. Only Velleius denies it: 2.4.1. Strabo, 14.1.38 (C 646), withholds judgment; cf. Plut. *Flam.* 21.6. On Attalus' paranoia: Diod. 34-5.3.

100. Word of his death and the terms of the will reached Rome between the passage of Ti. Gracchus' land bill and the tribune's death, thus evidently early summer, 133: Plut. *Ti. Gr.* 13.1, 14.1; Livy, *Per.* 58; Orosius, 5.8.4; *Vir. Ill.* 64.5. After passage of the land law voters returned to the fields: Appian, *BC*, 1.13. Tribunician elections were approaching and θέρος δ᾽ ἦν ἤδη: Appian, *BC*, 1.14. J. Carcopino, *Autour des Gracques* (2nd ed., Paris, 1967), 32–38, pointed to the notice of Justin, 36.4.5, that Attalus died of sunstroke, dated that event to late July, but had to throw out the entire ancient tradition on the connection between the will and the Gracchan land measure. His theory has been refuted many times; see bibliography in Hopp, *Untersuchungen*, 129, n. 36. Sherwin-White, *JRS* 67 (1977): 68, n. 40, puts Attalus' death in September, 134, thus allowing both for the sunstroke and for use of the will by Ti. Gracchus. But this demands an inexplicably long delay before news of the will reached Rome. The king may not have died of sunstroke anyway: Strabo, 13.4.2 (C 624).

101. On the *cistophori*, see E. S. G. Robinson, *NC* 14 (1954): 1–8; Kleiner-Noe, *The Early Cistophoric Coinage*, 103–106; cf. Appian, *Mithr.* 62: Ἀριστονίκῳ καθ᾽ ἡμῶν τέτταρσιν ἔτεσι συνεμαχεῖτε; *BC*, 1.17; Vell. Pat. 2.4.1. For the fall of Aristonicus in 130, see below p. 602. Another *cistophorus*, from Synnada in Phrygia, carries the legend BA ΣΥ AP; *Sylloge Nummorum Graecorum Deutschland*, Sammlung von Aulock (Berlin, 1957–1968), no. 6670; Kleiner-Noe, *The Early Cistophoric Coinage*, 81, plate XXX, nos. 4 and 5. This is often taken to mean that Aristonicus first claimed royal prerogatives under his original name, only later taking the appellation Eumenes—and that thus the revolt may predate Attalus' demise. So, most recently, Hopp, *Untersuchungen*, 122–125. But the coin cannot sustain that hypothesis; see Kienast, *Historia* 26 (1977): 250–252; Mørkholm, *ANSMN* 24 (1979): 52–54. The highly speculative reconstruction of J. P. Adams, *Historia* 29 (1980): 302–311, is unconvincing—based in part on a misdating of *IGRR*, IV, 292.

Attalus, not the most stable of characters, could therefore see the challenge coming, perhaps saw it already arrive. Framing of the will which awarded his kingdom to Rome under those circumstances had an obvious precedent: the testament of Ptolemy Euergetes in 155, a document plainly contrived to give its author the upper hand over his brother Philometor. Attalus employed the device either in hopes of winning Roman protection or of depriving Aristonicus in advance of any potential profits from an insurrection.[102] It was but a small step beyond the policy of his predecessors. While the earlier Attalids had invoked Roman help in struggles against foreign foes, Attalus III invoked it to checkmate a domestic rival. Pergamene intrigue, rather than Roman aggrandizement, persists down to the very bequest of the kingdom.

Attalus was right to anticipate trouble. The swiftness with which rebellion erupted is clear from the steps taken by the government after the death of Attalus and before acceptance of the will by Rome. Full citizenship was awarded to *paroikoi*, i.e. resident aliens, to soldiers settled in the city and the land, and to other free men dwelling in the area, garrison troops or auxiliary forces, together with their wives and children. In addition, the status of *paroikoi* was offered to children of freedmen and to royal slaves, with the exception of those purchased in the previous two reigns, those acquired through confiscation of property, and public slaves. An emergency was at hand, as the document recording these measures explicitly states.[103] Its thrust does not derive from an act of generosity or any ideological liberalism. The projected beneficiaries are soldiers and military colo-

102. The hypothesis that Attalus' motive was to halt the insurrection of Aristonicus dates back to M. P. Foucart, *MémAcadInscr* 37 (1904): 297–339. It was rejected and largely ignored on grounds that there was no sign of Aristonicus' uprising before the death of Attalus; see especially Cardinali, *Saggi di storia antica a G. Beloch* (Rome, 1910), 278–279; Vavrinek, *La révolte d'Aristonicos*, 18. But a challenge to the throne could readily have been anticipated even without open rebellion. The political character of Attalus' will, with the object of undermining Aristonicus' aspirations, is recognized by Liebmann-Frankfort, *RIDA* 13 (1966): 83–85; and, most recently, Sherwin-White, *JRS* 67 (1977): 66–67; Hopp, *Untersuchungen*, 121–126. Ferrary in Nicolet, *Rome et la conquête*, 2:774, oddly sees Attalus' move directed against a party of nobles in Pergamum. For the will of Ptolemy Euergetes, see *SEG*, IX, 7.

103. *OGIS*, 338, line 8: ἕνεκα τῆς κοινῆς ἀσ[φ]αλείας. Grants of franchise and elevated status in lines 12–26. Among the numerous discussions of this inscription, see Vavrinek, *La révolte d'Aristonicos*, 18–20; Dumont, *Eirene* 5 (1966): 190–193; Vogt, *Ancient Slavery*, 93–97; Carrata Thomes, *La rivolta di Aristonico*, 35–41; Hopp, *Untersuchungen*, 131–134; C. Delplace, *Athenaeum* 66 (1978): 21–28. Little plausibility attaches to the theory of Rubinsohn, *RendIstLomb* 107 (1973): 566–567, that liberation of the slaves had as its purpose the freeing of the royal bureaucracy for fear of its fate in the event of Roman annexation.

nists, descendants of freedmen and slaves in the prime of life, men encouraged by such awards to fight for the regime. The emergency which called forth such measures can hardly be any other than the drive of Aristonicus to seize the throne and the realm.

The character and aims of the insurrection continue to generate debate without cease, a matter of but marginal importance for our purposes. To what degree Aristonicus represented the aspirations of the downtrodden and championed a rising of slaves will never be fully determinable. Evidence is too thin to draw such conclusions. The emancipation of certain groups of slaves in the Pergamene decree noted above establishes only the government's need for manpower, not an attempt to outbid Aristonicus for the support of servile elements. The pretender did indeed recruit slaves, but (according to what little testimony we have) at a later stage of the conflict, after suffering a severe naval defeat and withdrawing into the interior of Anatolia. So, it was an afterthought, not a matter of ideology.[104] Nor should one see social ideology in the fact that Aristonicus designated his have-not followers as "Heliopolitans," a name attested but once in the sources on this rebellion and without elaboration. It may signify no more than a propaganda effort to suggest protection by the Sun god for Aristonicus' cause.[105] It is best to focus on what is known. Aristonicus claimed royal blood and aspired to the crown of Pergamum. Beyond that it would be unsafe to tread.[106]

104. Strabo, 14.1.38 (C 646): ἡττηθεὶς ναυμαχίᾳ περὶ τὴν Κυμαίαν ὑπὸ Ἐφεσίων, εἰς δὲ τὴν μεσόγαιαν ἀνιὼν ἤθροισε διὰ ταχέων πλῆθος ἀπόρων τε ἀνθρώπων καὶ δούλων ἐπ᾽ ἐλευθερίᾳ κατακεκλημένων. The same seems to be implied by Diod. 34/35.2.26.

105. Strabo, 14.1.38 (C 646), is the only evidence, and he makes nothing of it. One will hardly find ideological significance in the fact that Blossius of Cumae fled to Aristonicus after the death of Ti. Gracchus and the reaction against his followers: Cic. De Amic. 37; Plut. Ti. Gr. 8.4–5, 20.3–4; Val. Max. 4.7.1. The sources give no hint of such significance; cf. Rubinsohn, RendIstLomb 107 (1973): 567–568. The conception of Aristonicus as a socialist reformer or the champion of slave emancipation has had its advocates; e.g. Vogt, Ancient Slavery, 93–102; Vavrinek, La révolte d'Aristonicos, 28–43. The most vigorous retort in Carrata Thomes, La rivolta di Aristonico, 55–60. A valuable Forschungsbericht on the subject may be found in Vavrinek, Eirene 13 (1975): 109–129. Cf. Ferrary in Nicolet, Rome et la conquête, 2:776–777. Since then, Hopp, Untersuchungen, 135–147, has taken a strong line against the view of Aristonicus as social reformer. By contrast, Delplace, Athenaeum 66 (1978): 33–53, revives that view, at least as part of Aristonicus' appeal. The résumé of Stoic egalitarian ideas, however, does not help, for there is no evidence of their influence on Aristonicus. And Delplace's argument from the coins of Aristonicus, that the representation of Apollo signalled a promise of liberty to the poor and oppressed, is far-fetched.

106. Dumont, Eirene 5 (1966): 192–195, goes so far as to argue that Aristonicus' principal support came from upper-class elements in Pergamum, a view endorsed, in modified form, by Will, Histoire politique II:356; Carrata Thomes, La rivolta di Aristonico,

Reactions to Aristonicus' thrust for power varied and his fortunes fluctuated. The details do not lend themselves to secure reconstruction. Support emerged, it can be readily surmised, from diverse elements, not bound by social class, who would fight for continuation of the Attalid monarchy. The tradition of rule by that royal clan had well over a century's history.[107] Resistance arose from communities who feared the wrath of Rome and from princes who hoped to draw off tangible gains from upheaval in the Pergamene realm.[108] Aristonicus' initial campaigns on the western shores of Asia Minor featured a mixture of successes and frustrations. He established a stronghold at Leucae, won the support of Phocaea, and reduced Myndus, Colophon, and Samos to submission.[109] Then came setbacks. Aristonicus failed to take Smyrna, and he suffered a damaging naval defeat near Cyme at the hands of the Ephesians. The campaign thus turned inland; the coastal regions were temporarily lost, but new gains offset them. Aristonicus took Thyateira, Apollonis, Stratonicea. It was the time that he offered liberty to slaves and swelled his ranks. The recovery, however, soon roused more formidable opposition. Threatened cities sent contingents against him, and then a consortium of Anato-

---

49–54; and Delplace, *Athenaeum* 66 (1978): 36. The surmise rests on a provision in the Pergamene decree of 133 which disenfranchises and confiscates the property of those who abandoned the city or the land, or intended to do so: *OGIS*, 338, lines 26–31: ὅσοι δ[ὲ] τῶν κατοικούντων ἢ ὅσαι ἐγλελοίπασιν ὑπὸ τὸν καιρὸν τῆς (τελευτῆς) τοῦ βασιλέως ἢ ἐγλίπωσιν τὴν πόλιν ἢ τὴν χώραν, εἶναι αὐτοὺς κα[ὶ] αὐτὰς ἀτίμους τε καὶ τὰ ἑκατέρων ὑπάρχοντα τῆς πόλεως. But that clause need not mean that persons of property had joined the movement of Aristonicus in any numbers. The pronouncement may be more a warning than a sign of widespread defection among land owners. And some of those who had abandoned their property might have done so under threat from Aristonicus rather than in sympathy for him. On Aristonicus' claims as a legitimate Hellenistic monarch, see now F. Collins III; *Ancient World* 3 (1980): 83–87; *ibid.*, 4 (1981): 39–43—though he assumes, without evidence, that the pretender engaged in "anti-Roman" resistance.

107. Florus, 1.35.4: *Aristonicus, regii sanguinis ferox iuvenis, urbis regibus parere consuetas partim facile sollicitat.*

108. Justin, 36.4.7: *civitates, quae metu Romanorum tradere se eidem nolebant;* Appian, *Mithr.* 62. The statements are wrongly stigmatized as fiction by Magie, *RRAM* II:1036, n. 7. T. W. Africa, *Int. Review of Social History* 6 (1961): 110–124, recognizes the nationalistic sentiments that backed Aristonicus' movement. But his characterization of Aristonicus as a national opponent of Roman expansion is misdirected. What Roman expansion had there been?

109. Leucae: Strabo, 14.1.38 (C 646). Phocaea: Justin, 37.1.1. Myndus, Colophon, and Samos: Florus, 1.35.4; cf. Justin, 36.4.7. The idea that Aristonicus actually held Pergamum for a time can be discarded. It rests on the interpretation of *IGRR*, IV, 292, lines 11–13, which reports the elimination of certain elements from the city by Mithridates, supposedly Mithridates V, one of the opponents of Aristonicus; cf. Justin, 37.1.2; Eutrop. 4.20.1; Oros. 5.10.2. But the inscription has been redated recently and definitively to the time of Mithridates VI: Jones, *Chiron* 4 (1974): 190–205.

lian princes mobilized forces to check him: Nicomedes of Bithynia, Mithridates V of Pontus, Ariarathes V of Cappadocia, and Pylaemenes of Paphlagonia. They would have no hesitation in carving up the territory of Pergamum.[110]

A remarkable fact springs to the fore. All these events transpired before Rome had made so much as a single move.[111] The fact deserves to be emphasized. Roman slowness to act in eastern matters is, of course, quite characteristic. We have seen it again and again. This time the Romans had a particularly good reason for being at a loss: they had never before had a kingdom bestowed upon them.

The news of Attalus' will had reached Rome around the early summer of 133—at a time when the struggle over Ti. Gracchus' land bill was reaching fever pitch.[112] Circumstances ruled out any measured debate on the significance and implications of the bequest. Ti. Gracchus grasped the opportunity for his own ends. He sponsored a bill before the assembly to divert proceeds from Attalus' gift to facilitate implementation of the agrarian bill. The tribune obviously looked first to the cash that might accrue from the royal estates. As for the cities included in the will, Tiberius insisted that the senate had no authority to consider them; he would himself propose a resolution to

110. Aristonicus' failure at Smyrna: Aristeides, *Orat.* 19.11. The defeat at Cyme, the movement inland, the appeal to servile elements, and the taking of Thyateira, Apollonis, and "other fortresses" all may be found in Strabo, 14.1.38 (C 646). Among those other places is Stratonicea, one of the sites, along with Thyateira and Apollonis, of Aristonicus' cistophoric coinage. The mobilization of the various princes: Strabo, 14.1.38 (C 646); Justin, 37.1.2; Eutrop. 4.20.1; Oros. 5.10.2.

111. That sequence is given explicitly by Strabo, 14.1.38 (C 646)—which there is no good reason to question. Magie, *RRAM* I:151, II:1037–1038, nn. 10–11, dates the battle of Cyme after the arrival of Crassus and Roman forces in 131, thus reversing Strabo's order. The argument depends on Aristonicus' holding of Leucae when Crassus arrived, whereas Strabo has him abandon it after the battle of Cyme: not a compelling argument. Aristonicus could have regained it in the meantime; cf. B. Schleussmer, *Chiron* 6 (1976): 102, n. 29; Hopp, *Untersuchungen*, 145, n. 116.

112. Conventional wisdom has it that a *clientela* connection between the Attalids and the house of the Gracchi gave Tiberius immediate access to the information and an opportunity to preempt any senatorial action; e.g., Badian, *Foreign Clientelae*, 173–174; *ANRW*, I:1 (1972), 712–713; Bernstein, *Ti. Gracchus*, 39, 207. The one relevant text, however, by no means demands that conclusion; Plut. *Ti. Gr.* 14.2: Q. Pompeius, Tiberius' neighbor, sought to discredit the tribune by claiming that he had seen the Pergamene envoy present him with a diadem and purple robe. That is all; the rest is inference. The notion of a familial patronage stems from the fact that Ti. Gracchus the elder had once returned from a mission with a favorable report on Pergamum: Polyb. 30.30.7–8. But, as we have seen, Gracchus brought home favorable reports on every principality he visited, Eumenes' kingdom being but a brief stopover. Evidence on the visits elsewhere in Broughton, *MRR* I:438. The Gracchi did not become patrons of all the East on the basis of that journey!

the people. As is plain, the entire episode is enmeshed in the political battle between Gracchus and his opponents. The question of endorsing the will had simply not yet arisen, let alone that of annexing the kingdom. Gracchus jumped the gun and laid claim to the legacy for the *populus Romanus*, even playing fast and loose with the terms of the gift.[113] This was politics, not foreign policy.

The assassination of Ti. Gracchus in midsummer 133 and the shock waves it produced swept over the Roman scene. In addition, the lengthy Spanish wars had just come to an end, with the settlement still awaited, and in Sicily a slave rebellion raged. Affairs in Asia could hardly have held much attention. Word of Aristonicus' armed insurrection presumably arrived in Rome sometime in the second half of the year 133. Months elapsed, however, before any action was taken, a long period during which Aristonicus contended with Greek communities and then Anatolian princes, a series of battles that convulsed western Asia Minor and even stirred a slave uprising.[114] The senate merely dispatched a five-man embassy to Asia, no earlier, it seems, than the year 132. Bequest or no bequest, Rome had ignored the eastern situation for quite some time, and even then refrained from a vigorous response.[115]

113. Attalus had left Pergamum autonomous; OGIS, 338, line 5—and perhaps the other Greek cities of his kingdom as well; cf. Livy, *Per.* 59, quoted above, n. 95. Gracchus, however, asserted that the fate of the cities in Attalus' realm rested with the Roman people: Plut. *Ti. Gr.* 14.2. His proposal to use the cash from Pergamum for his agrarian schemes: Plut. *Ti. Gr.* 14.1; Livy, *Per.* 58; Oros. 5.8.4; *Vir. Ill.* 64.5. This implies that the king had bequeathed personal possessions, as indicated also by Florus, 1.35.2–3; Seneca, *Contr.* II, *ad fin.*; Justin, 36.4.9. Badian, *Roman Imperialism*, 21–22, interprets Gracchus' move as an effort to force acceptance of the bequest over objections by a senate reluctant to annex Pergamum. The theory is rejected by Harris, *War and Imperialism*, 147–149, who sees no senatorial reluctance. The issue is a false one. Circumstances in Rome had not yet reached the point of debate over annexation.

114. See above pp. 598–599.

115. The information derives from Strabo, 14.1.38 (C 646), whose truncated narrative gives the series of battles, the arrival of Roman legates, and then the armed intervention by P. Crassus: ἔπειτα πρέσβεις Ῥωμαίων πέντε ἦκον, καὶ μετὰ ταῦτα στρατιὰ καὶ ὕπατος Πόπλιος Κράσσος. This last came in 131. It seems unlikely that the embassy arrived any earlier than 132. P. Scipio Nasica, the slayer of Ti. Gracchus, was sent on a mission to Asia by the senate, supposedly to defuse public hostility, and perished there: Plut. *Ti. Gr.* 21.2–3; Val. Max. 5.3.2e; Pliny, *NH*, 7.120; *Vir. Ill.* 64.9; cf. Cic. *Pro Flacco*, 75; *De Rep.* 1.6; *ILS*, 8886 = *IGRR*, IV, 1681. A separate legation would be implausible. Nasica was doubtless a member of the five-man group, as commonly assumed. If Plut. *Ti. Gr.* 20.3–4 be right, then Nasica was still in Rome in early 132, so could not have set out before then. But he may not belong in that story; see Cic. *De Amicit.* 37; Val. Max. 4.7.1 The year 132, it might be objected, seems too late, for reaction had set in against the Gracchi by that time; hence there would be no need to appease public opinion by shipping off Nasica. But Nasica may well have been reckoned an embarrassment, whatever the political climate. And the alleged motive for sending him sounds suspiciously *post factum* anyway.

What was the business of the five-man commission? Strabo, our one source on the matter, leaves it unsaid. Hypotheses have been substituted. The commission, so some scholars suggest, departed before Aristonicus' uprising was known and hence expected a smooth takeover of the inheritance. On a different view, they came as legates with extraordinary powers, including the right to take up arms against Aristonicus. Or else they left to accompany a new Roman governor and to help organize the kingdom of Pergamum into a province.[116] A fundamental *petitio principii* underlies all these reconstructions, i.e. the assumption that Rome had already determined to annex the realm of the Attalids. The evidence does not suggest it, and the circumstances argue against it. The senate, confronted suddenly with the unique situation of an overseas territorial bequest, had no precedents on which to act and little time in which to deliberate. The revolt of Aristonicus must have been known in Rome well before the end of the year 133, and thus before the dispatch of the envoys. A summons from abroad very likely called them forth. Their purpose can be divined from numerous earlier parallels: to check on reports and investigate the situation, to help bring hostilities to an end, or to encourage allies to fight for the better cause. Successful diplomacy could obviate the need for armed intervention by Rome. Peaceful negotiation, if possible; otherwise, let Hellenic states carry the burden of warfare. It was an old story.[117]

Procrastination and delay still characterized Roman behavior with regard to Asian affairs. Despite Attalus' will, the Republic continued to refrain from direct involvement, in hopes that the Greeks could somehow work out matters for themselves. But matters got out of hand. The situation had taken on a new aspect, for the bulwark of stability in Asia Minor, the Attalid dynasty, was no more. Its demise left a troublesome vacuum. Aristonicus proved more formidable than anticipated. A servile rising had supervened to augment the dangers. No less worrisome, it might be inferred, was the consortium of Asiatic princes, from Bithynia, Pontus, Cappadocia, and Paphlagonia,

116. Departure before news of Aristonicus' revolt: Cardinali, *Saggi di storia antica a G. Beloch* (Rome, 1910) 296–297; Magie, *RRAM* I: 148, II, 1033, n. 1. Legates with military powers: Vogt, *Ancient Slavery*, 98–100; Rubinsohn, *RendIstLomb* 107 (1973): 560. Commissioners to organize a new province: Schleussner, *Chiron* 6 (1976): 104–111; accepted in modified form by Hopp, *Untersuchungen*, 141–142.

117. Military preparations and expectations are often ascribed to these legates by association with the στρατηγοί mentioned in *OGIS*, 435 = Sherk, *RDGE*, no. 11, line 7. But the association is unwarranted; see below pp. 603–605. The soundest description of the envoys' purpose is Vavrinek's, *La révolte d'Aristonicos*, 33: "Ladite commission fut chargée d'examiner, tout d'abord, la situation, de prendre des mesures nécessaires et d'établir, avec l'aide des alliés romains, à savoir des villes grecques et des rois vassaux, l'ordre."

who would be prepared to parcel out the realm of the Attalids for themselves. Their future rivalries were already predictable, and the effects could be far-reaching: a stimulus to the ambitions of Thracian barbarians, a menace to the Hellespont, and repercussions even in Macedonia.[118]

Rome finally determined to check the falling of the dominoes. A consular army under P. Crassus Mucianus set out in 131, about two years after the death of Attalus III. Its departure too had been delayed by a political battle over the command. The Republic had been in no hurry to mount this expedition.[119] News of the decision, however, stirred action in Asia Minor. Various cities hastened to show their enthusiasm for the Roman cause, lest they be caught on the wrong side, cities like Cyzicus, Sestus, Byzantium, Halicarnassus, and possibly Pergamum herself.[120] The Anatolian princes who had previously taken up arms against Aristonicus now showed active cooperation with the Roman forces.[121] Rome's dilatoriness nonetheless bore a price. Crassus Mucianus, legal scholar, pontifex maximus, and friend of the Gracchi, who had intrigued for the command (avarice was his motive, says a hostile source) paid with his life. Roman troops suffered defeat in early 130, Crassus was captured, and hastened his own death to avoid further disgrace. His head was conveyed to Aristonicus—not the last Crassus whose head would become the sport of an eastern potentate.[122] Patience snapped in Rome. The *patres* would brook no further embarrassment. They hurried a new army to Asia, under the consul of 130, M. Perperna. Results were more propitious this time. The intensified effort crushed Aristonicus' forces and made a captive of the pretender who eventually perished in a Roman prison.[123] Even that was not quite the end. A typical contention for *gloria* ensued. M' Aquillius was assigned Asia for 129 and raced to the front, hoping to rob Perperna of the distinction of bringing Aristoni-

118. Not a far-fetched scenario. The Cyzicenes, when their city was besieged, probably by Thracians, sent for aid to M. Cosconius, Roman commander in Macedonia, who was conducting operations against the Scordisci in 135: *IGRR*, IV, 134, lines 7–10; Livy, *Per.* 56. Cf. Magie, *RRAM* II:1038, n. 13; Vavrinek, *La révolte d'Aristonicos*, 32. Aristonicus had substantial numbers of Thracians in his retinue: Val. Max. 3.2.12. And notice also the Thracian threat to Sestus at about this time: *OGIS*, 339, lines 16–17.

119. The political controversy: Cic. *Phil.* 11.18; Livy, *Per.* 59. Other sources on Crassus' command in Broughton, *MRR* I:500.

120. Cyzicus: *IGRR*, IV, 134, lines 11–22; Sestus; *OGIS*, 339, lines 16–22; Byzantium: Tac. *Ann.* 12.62; Halicarnassus: *JOAI* 11 (1908): 69–70; Pergamum: *Syll.*³ 694, lines 11–20. Other Asian cities too later claimed to have been loyal and active against Aristonicus: Tac. *Ann.* 4.55.

121. Eutrop. 4.20.1; Oros. 5.10.2; Justin, 37.1.2.

122. Sources in Broughton, *MRR* I:503.

123. Sources in Broughton, *MRR* I:502.

cus back in chains. The capture, however, had already taken place, and Perperna's own death in Pergamum prevented an ugly scene between the Roman generals.[124] Aquillius still had some pacification to carry out. Fighting continued in Mysia and Caria. Some cities that had declared for Aristonicus were coerced into submission by poisoning their wells. Aquillius wanted his triumph.[125] The struggle had been a remarkably tough one. Its duration and its violence testify to the strength of feeling for the Attalid monarchy, the stubborn resistance in the realm to the ambitions of dynasts from Bithynia, Pontus, Cappadocia, and Paphlagonia, and the commitment to old traditions.[126] Like the rising of Andriscus in Macedonia and the Achaeans in the Peloponnese, Aristonicus' movement did not direct itself against Rome but fell afoul of her.

Only after the defeat of Aristonicus did the senate turn attention with some seriousness to a lasting settlement for western Asia Minor. The war-torn area needed a substantial injection of stability. The end of the Attalid line, the ambitions of Anatolian princes, the specter of Thracian barbarians and servile revolt, and, not least, exasperation in Rome at the costs in time and lives (including the lives of two consuls) all combined to demand a closer surveillance by the Republic. Rome would now take up the legacy of Attalus, divert some of the wealth of Asia, and accept responsibility for the security of the region, as she had done in Macedonia nearly two decades before. What form would the new settlement take and how large a role did Rome expect to play?

A decree of the senate delivered instructions to strategoi bound for Asia: they are to leave undisturbed all official acts and measures of the Pergamene kings down to the day before Attalus III's death.[127] The document carries significant implications. Scholars have, almost without exception, dated it to the later months of 133, have seen it as ratification of the inheritance recently announced, and have employed it as proof that Rome determined upon the provincialization of Asia almost immediately. None of those inferences, however, is

---

124. Justin, 36.4.9–11; cf. Strabo, 14.1.38 (C 646); Vell. Pat. 2.4.1; Val. Max. 3.4.5; Florus, 1.35.6; Eutrop. 4.20.

125. Florus, 1.35.7. A decree from Bargylia sheds light on some of Aquillius' operations: Holleaux, *Études* II:179–198; Robert, *Études Anatoliennes*, 463–465. And another from Maconia in Lydia on Aquillius' legate Q. Caepio: Herrmann, *Denkschr. Akad. Wien*, 80 (1962): 5–8. Discussions of the campaigns by Hansen, *Attalids*, 155–159; Vavrinek, *La révolte d'Aristonicos*, 43–51; Magie, *RRAM* I:147–154.

126. Observe that the Attalid cult was still honored in Pergamum a half-century later: *IGRR*, IV, 292, lines 40–41. For the date, see Jones, *Chiron* 4 (1974): 190–205.

127. *OGIS*, 435 = Sherk, *RDGE*, no. 11; cf. T. Drew-Bear, *Historia* 21 (1972): 75–79.

verifiable. The enactment makes no explicit allusion to Attalus' will; it refers broadly to the measures taken by Pergamene kings with regard to their subjects over an indefinite period of time.[128] Absence of any notice of Aristonicus' insurrection provides an additional clue. That Rome was unaware of it in the later months of 133 is quite unlikely. The *senatus consultum* makes better sense after Aristonicus had been crushed and a new settlement was in prospect. Mention of *strategoi* for Asia in the plural suggests present and future Roman command- ers in the East, a prospect hardly in focus as early as 133, in the midst of the Gracchan upheaval. The fact that the decree sanctions all At- talid enactments until the death of the last king in 133 by no means necessitates a date in that year. The provision simply abolishes by im- plication any measures or decisions taken in the royal name by Aris- tonicus.[129] Rome had neither the opportunity nor the inclination to confront a long-term settlement in Asia before the elimination of Aris- tonicus. The *senatus consultum* belongs most naturally in 129.[130]

Set in that year, the document provides a window on Roman at- titudes. The *patres* accepted the responsibility of policing the former kingdom of Pergamum. Commanders with *imperium* would represent the Republic in Asia Minor. That much is authorized, or rather as- sumed, in the decree. But the senatorial instructions tell us more still. The *strategoi* are to respect and uphold all the ordinances and regula-

128. *OGIS*, 435 = Sherk, *RDGE*, no. 11, lines 13–15: [ὅπω]ς ὅσα βασιλεὺς Ἄτταλος οἵ τε λο[ιποὶ βασιλεῖς] διώρθωσαν ἐζημίωσαν ἢ [ἀφῆκαν ἐδωρήσαντο]. The restorations are reasonably secure, on the basis of lines 8–10.

129. A close parallel occurs in the *senatus consultum* of a few years later which sanctions all the official acts of Mithridates V down to the day of his death: *OGIS*, 436 = Sherk, *RDGE*, no. 13. The parallel is closer still if the decree dates to 116, as often ar- gued, for Mithridates died in 120. But the year 119 is equally possible: Sherk, *loc. cit.*; Drew-Bear, *Historia* 21 (1972): 79–85.

130. The case for 129 was made long ago, with some good and some bad argu- ments, by Magie, *RRAM* II: 1033–1034, n. 1. His view is regularly rejected—but never refuted. E.g., Vavrinek, *La révolte d'Aristonicos*, 22, n. 56; Hansen, *Attalids*, 150; Lieb- mann-Frankfort, *La frontière orientale*, 139, n. 2; Schleussner, *Chiron* 6 (1976): 107; Hopp, *Untersuchungen*, 138, n. 80; Harris, *War and Imperialism*, 148–149, n. 4. See also Brough- ton, *MRR* I: 496–497; Sherk, *RDGE*, pp. 60–62; Delplace, *Athenaeum* 66 (1978): 30–31. Only one other advocate of a late date: Sherwin-White, *JRS* 67 (1977): 68—who here, however, tends to assert rather than argue. That the decree came in the later months of the year is clear from lines 4–5: πρὸ ἡμ[ερῶν . . . .]εμβρίων. But the consular year is not given and the praetorship of the presiding officer, C. Popillius, is unknown. At the very least, the near-unanimity on 133 needs rethinking. Vogt, *Ancient Slavery*, 99–101, identifies the στρατηγοί in the decree with the five-man legation recorded by Strabo, 14.1.38 (C 646). That is certainly wrong. The five legates were πρέσβεις. And contem- porary documents distinguish quite unambiguously between the two terms; see, espe- cially, *OGIS*, 339, lines 22–23: πρός τε τοὺς στρατηγοὺς τοὺς ἀποστελλομένους ὑπὸ Ῥωμαίων εἰς τὴν Ἀσίαν καὶ τοὺς πεμπομένους πρεσβευτάς.

tions of the Attalid kings.[131] The stress on continuity with the Pergamene past stands out unmistakably. Romans had not come to install a new system but to preserve ties with previous traditions. The claim can hardly be fraudulent, whatever it may mean in practice. Endorsement of Attalid enactments should include at least that measure of the last king which gave freedom to Pergamum and the territory belonging to the city.[132] The fact is confirmed by a formal treaty of alliance entered into by Rome and evidently Pergamum shortly thereafter.[133] If Pergamum herself, seat of the former kingdom, were treated as free and autonomous, would Rome have reduced other cities to a state of subjection? No source declares it or implies it.[134]

The "provincialization of Asia" spooks about repeatedly in modern works. Wherein lies the evidence? M'. Aquillius stamped out the last embers of Aristonicus' uprising and was then joined by the customary commission of *decem legati* from Rome.[135] Such commissions, armed with guidelines drawn up in the senate, regularly assisted victorious commanders in arranging postwar settlements. Their activities by no means entailed provincialization. Aquillius stayed for three years in Asia, an unusually long time. We have few details and nothing to suggest the mulcting of territory for Rome. Aquillius, in fact, presided over the distribution of land to princes and dynasts who had joined forces against Aristonicus. Greater Phrygia went to Mithridates V of Pontus, Lycaonia to the sons of the recently fallen Ariarathes V of Cappadocia.[136] The legacy of Attalus did not translate itself into major territorial acquisitions for Rome—if any.[137] Aquillius spent

131. *OGIS*, 435 = Sherk, *RDGE*, no. 11, lines 6–10: τίνες ἐντολ[αὶ ἔσονται τοῖς εἰς Ἀ]σίαν πορευομένοις στρατηγοῖς ὅ[σα ἐν Ἀσίαι ἔω]ς τῆς Ἀττάλου τελευτῆς ὑπὸ τῶν [βασιλέων δι]ωρθώθη ἐδωρήθη ἀφέθη ἐζημιώ[θη ὅπως ταῦτα ἦι κύ]ρια. The restorations are based largely on lines 13–19.

132. *OGIS*, 338, lines 5–6.

133. *Syll.*[3] 694. Specific reference to the war against Aristonicus gives the approximate date: lines 15–16. The city involved here is very probably Pergamum; see Robert, *Études Anatoliennes*, 49; cf. Jos. *Ant.* 14.247–255.

134. One city only was marked out for destruction, Phocaea, for she had taken up arms against Rome not only on behalf of Aristonicus but in the previous Antiochene war as well. And even she was spared, upon the intercession of Massilia: Justin, 37.1.1.

135. Strabo, 14.1.38 (C 646). But Strabo's statement, that Aquillius fixed the form of the province that endured to his own (Strabo's) day, is oversimplified and misleading. There were frequent changes and important ones in the meanwhile, including the financial bill of C. Gracchus and the reorganization after the Mithridatic wars. The statement is too broad to be helpful: διέταξε τὴν ἐπαρχίαν εἰς τὸ νῦν ἔτι συμμένον τῆς πολιτείας σχῆμα.

136. Justin, 37.1.2, 38.5.3. Report had it even that Aquillius was bribed by Mithridates for these territorial benefactions: Appian, *Mithr.* 12, 57; cf. *BC*, 1.22; Gellius, 11.10.

137. Among modern efforts to determine the boundaries of the "province," see

his time constructing, repairing, or extending the network of roads in western Asia Minor, as amply attested by the milestones that bear his name.[138] They would facilitate ready movement of men and materials. Aquillius concentrated on the security of the area rather than on the installation of Roman suzerainty. Grateful Pergamum instituted a cult in honor of the Roman proconsul. Aquillius returned home to celebrate a triumph in late 126.[139]

The foregoing constitutes the sum of our knowledge on the activities of Aquillius and the *decem legati*. The prevailing assumption that Asia began pouring her wealth into Roman coffers in 129 as a tribute-paying member of the empire rests largely on guesswork.[140] No specifics survive on Aquillius' settlement. One piece of evidence, however, points in a very different direction. Appian puts into the mouth of M. Antony a speech to the Greeks of Asia Minor stating that Rome had canceled their tribute after the legacy of Attalus and released them from financial burdens until demagogic agitators (presumably C. Gracchus) reimposed them.[141] The source is late, the story in a late context, and the speech perhaps tendentious. Yet no obvious motive for invention suggests itself. And what is there to set against it?[142]

One item alone has bedeviled understanding. A *senatus consultum*, partially preserved in two fragmentary copies, announces decision on a dispute brought before the *patres* regarding the borders of Pergamene land subject to the operations of Roman *publicani*.[143] The accepted date is 129 B.C. and, if that date be right, it has unsettling consequences. Tax farmers had already set up shop in the former

Magie, *RRAM* I:154–155, with corresponding notes; Liebmann-Frankfort, *La frontière orientale*, 143–144.

138. *CIL*, I², 2, 646–651; Magie, *RRAM* I:157–158, II:1048–1049, nn. 39–40.

139. The cult of Aquillius: *IGRR*, IV, 292, line 39. His triumph: Broughton, *MRR* I:509.

140. No need to catalogue the roster of scholars who have taken this line. Opinion is now virtually unanimous. Even those like Magie and Badian who have challenged the *communis opinio* on several points assent to this proposition: Magie, *RRAM* I:155–156, II:1046–1047, n. 36; Badian, *Roman Imperialism*, 47–49. Sherwin-White, *JRS* 67 (1977): 69, skirts the issue.

141. Appian, *BC*, 5.4: οὓς γὰρ ἐτελεῖτε φόρους Ἀττάλῳ, μεθήκαμεν ὑμῖν, μέχρι δημοκόπων ἀνδρῶν καὶ παρ' ἡμῖν γενομένων ἐδέησε φόρων.

142. Velleius, 2.38.5, in a summary of Roman conquests and creation of provinces, asserts that *Asiam . . . M. Perpenna capto Aristonico fecit tributariam.* That is inaccurate on any reckoning, since the settlement in Asia was Aquillius' settlement and not Perperna's. And the letter of Mithridates, composed by Sallust, has an obvious axe to grind: Sallust, *Hist.* 4.69.9, Maur. Its bald statement, *Asia ab ipsis* (the Romans) *obsessa est*, provides no hard information.

143. The two copies are from Adramyttium (*IGRR* IV, 262) and from Smyrna (Passerini, *Athenaeum* 15 [1937]: 252–283). Best text in Sherk, *RDGE*, no. 12. See especially lines 5, 15, 22.

realm of the Attalids, hence evidently had been awarded a contract by the censors of 131, and had now crept to the boundaries of Pergamum itself. Rome, in short, wasted no time in seizing upon the revenues of Asia.[144] Yet the paradoxical consequences that this scenario demands strain the imagination. Not only must we discard the text of Appian, a relatively minor sacrifice; more difficult, we must posit a censorial *locatio* at a time when Aristonicus' revolt had reached a peak, the establishment of Roman tax-farming companies in Asia after the Republic's forces had been whipped and a Roman consul killed, and the extension of the *publicani's* activities to the point of generating arbitration on territorial authority even before Aquillius went to fight the remaining battles of the war. And finally we need to juggle and reinterpret the otherwise consistent evidence that C. Gracchus introduced *censoria locatio* and organized arrangements for the *publicani* in Asia in 123.[145] There must be a simpler solution.

It lies ready to hand. The date of the *senatus consultum* is anything but secure. A consul Aquillius gets named, evidently the chief magistrate in office. That allows for two possibilities: 129 B.C. or 101 B.C. Nothing in the document points decisively to the earlier date. Economy and logic demand the later. It requires no explaining away of embarrassing evidence or erecting of implausible constructions.[146]

The story falls into place. M'. Aquillius wiped out the last vestiges of Aristonicus' movement in 129, then stayed as proconsul with the *decem legati* to assure pacification of the area and arrange a

144. This is the dominant view, with little dissent; see bibliography in Sherk, *RDGE*, p. 63; especially Passerini, *Athenaeum* 15 (1937): 252–283; G. Tibiletti, *JRS* 47 (1957): 136–138; more recently, Badian, *Publicans and Sinners*, 59–60, 63.

145. Cic. *Verr.* 2.3.12: *censoria locatio constituta est, ut Asiae lege Sempronia;* Schol. Bob. 157, Stangl: *nomine publicanorum ut cum iis ratio putaretur lege Sempronia;* Fronto, *Ep. ad Verum,* 2.1.17: *Gracchus locabat Asiam;* Appian, *BC,* 5.4, quoted above, n. 141. *Publicani* might, of course, have moved into Asia without official sanction by the state and without benefit of a *censoria locatio,* as was the case elsewhere and later in the East: Diod. 36.3.1; Cic. *De Leg. Agrar.* 2.50. This could explain the lines of Lucilius, 671–2, Marx, perhaps written as early as 131 and implying at least the prospect of *publicani* in Asia. On this, see W. J. Raschke, *JRS* 69 (1979): 79–83.

146. The consul [. . .]ύλλιος appears in Sherk, *RDGE,* no. 12, line 17, which, in this period, can only be a M'. Aquillius. Elsewhere, line 9 gives [. . .]νιος ὕπατος. Usually restored as [καὶ Μάνιος Ἀκύλλιος Γαῖος Σεμπρώ]νιος, i.e. the consuls of 129. The men referred to, however, need not be the chief magistrates of the year of the inscription—rather those in office when the original dispositions on the Pergamene boundaries were made. The argument for 101 was made succinctly by Magie, *RRAM* II: 1055–1056, n. 25; without endorsement until H. B. Mattingly, *AJP* 93 (1972): 412–423, who usefully suggests the names of Cn. Domitius Ahenobarbus and C. Fannius, the consuls of 122 B.C., for line 9—the year after the passage of C. Gracchus' measure. And see his plausible identifications for several of the individuals on the praetor's *consilium* listed in lines 23–47.

postwar settlement. The arrangements involved a division of territorial spoils to Rome's allies in Pontus and Cappadocia and establishment or strengthening of the great highways to protect western Anatolia. The senate envisioned dispatch of commanders to Asia for the future to police the district when necessary. We cannot be sure that this was intended to be put on a regular basis. Terms like "annexation" and "provincialization" may be premature even now. The decision for a permanent commitment need not yet have come. Of financial exactions nothing is heard. The Attalid treasury and royal estates, willed to Rome, might have served to defray the costs of war and support any subsequent military operation. Installment of a taxation system, however, awaited the tribunate of C. Gracchus. As his brother had endeavored to appropriate the Attalid legacy for his own reform plans in 133, so Gaius conceived a scheme whereby to increase markedly the revenues of the Roman people while, at the same time, playing to the financial interests of the *publicani*.[147] In both cases politics, or perhaps political ideology, called forth the actions, but not foreign policy. When the *lex Sempronia* authorized state contracts for the farming of Asian taxes, more than six years had passed since the capture of Aristonicus, nearly a decade since the bequest of Attalus III. Rome had not leaped to the legacy. Internal difficulties meant hesitation, Asian turmoil forced delay, and, in the end, domestic circumstances rather than imperialist expansionism put the resources of the East at the disposal of the Republic.[148]

147. On the Gracchan law, see sources cited above, n. 145. Gaius' open concern for the increase of state revenues appears quite clearly in a fragment of his speech against a certain *lex Aufeia*: Gellius, 11.10 = Malcovati, *ORF*, no. 48, fr. 44: *ego ipse, qui aput vos verba facio, ut vectigalia vestra augeatis*. Just what the *lex Aufeia* provided for cannot be discerned. It is often reckoned as the measure for ratification of Aquillius' Asian settlement; e.g., Badian, *Foreign Clientelae*, 183–184; Gruen, *Roman Politics and the Criminal Courts, 149–78 B.C.* (Cambridge, Mass., 1968), 77. Nothing in the fragment can be interpreted to that effect. The bill addressed a dispute between Nicomedes and Mithridates, the latter of whom would benefit from its passage. Gaius argued against it and took his stand on the need to augment state revenues. That suggests an effort on Gaius' part to reserve for Roman taxation land otherwise earmarked for Mithridates. Only a few years later, after the death of Mithridates V, Rome did, in fact, remove Greater Phrygia from the Pontic kingdom and put it under her own control: Justin, 38.5.3; Appian, *Mithr.* 11, 15, 56, 57; cf. *OGIS*, 436 = Sherk, *RDGE*, no. 13.

148. The so-called "provincial era" of Asia does not stand against this. The date, as beginning an era, is attested only by the coins of Ephesus—and hence may refer to the liberation of that city rather than to any act of provincialization; so K. J. Rigsby, *Phoenix* 33 (1979): 39–47; Adams, *Historia* 29 (1980): 311–314. Observe that the Attalid *cistophori* continued to be the principal currency in the former Pergamene realm even after Rome had established her suzerainty: Kleiner, *ANSMN* 18 (1972): 17–32.

**V**

Establishment of Roman suzerainty in Hellenic Asia Minor and the Aegean came very late in this story and with no sign of premeditation. Patterns of relationship instituted toward the end of the third century held tenaciously over the decades. Greek cities and principalities coaxed Rome into intervening on their behalf, claimed special association with the Republic, or took advantage of Roman victories. Pergamene rulers showed themselves especially adept at this maneuvering, others imitated with mixed success. The Rhodians, a little more attached to both the appearance and the fact of independence, trod a finer line but made it pay off in dominion and prestige. So long as the Roman colossus encroached but briefly, and otherwise slumbered, enterprising Greek states could draw the benefits.

The Third Macedonian War and the harsh aftermath of Pydna proved to be less a turning point than an interruption. Rome bullied her erstwhile allies for a time, then reverted to earlier neglect. The tide of Roman involvement ebbed and flowed, rather than swamped the East. Even Rhodes, despite severe setbacks suffered after Pydna, was able to recover esteem and regain standing among Hellenic states as the western tide receded. In Asia Minor the results of Pydna encouraged a scramble among dynasts to enlist the Republic's services for territorial claims and aggrandizing moves against one another. Roman behavior, however, relapsed, for the most part, into listlessness and diplomatic tokenism. Neither the calculated subservience of Prusias nor the anxious deference of Ariarathes secured tangible benefits from the senate. The converse was equally true. Coolness toward Eumenes, such as it was, did not diminish Pergamene prestige or check Pergamene authority.

Hellenic contests of an old and familiar sort resurfaced in the 150s and 140s. Attalus II, drawing on the experience of his predecessors, held the advantage. By capitalizing upon favorable pronouncements from Rome and ignoring inconvenient ones, he bent other principalities to his will. Attalid candidates were soon sitting on the thrones of Cappadocia, Syria, and Bithynia. There was no sign of a Roman takeover and no hint that any such was even contemplated in Italy.

It took an odd and unanticipated combination of circumstances to produce that result. The will of Attalus III started the chain of events—not in concert with Rome but as device to undermine the aspirations of Aristonicus. Attalus' death set loose other forces: a drive to retain the monarchy, a slave uprising, and the mobilization of Anatolian princes from Pontus, Bithynia, and Cappadocia. Reaction in Rome, however, was typically slow to develop. The legacy of Attalus had immediate impact on Rome's domestic politics, but little effect on the sluggishness of her foreign policy. Inadequate diplomacy, then ineffective force expanded the conflict and dragged on hostilities for four years. In the end, the *patres* saw the need for a more direct role in overseeing the security of the area. Even then they shrank from expropriating its revenues. Domestic politics again forced that issue a few years later, thus setting the stage for the provincial administration that characterized the late Republic. Roman imperialism in the most tangible sense made its appearance in this area more than three-quarters of a century after the initial diplomatic contacts. And, far from showing a gradual process of encroachment over the decades, it took hold with suddenness. A singular set of conditions in the East and an unprecedented political upheaval at home turned Asia into a dependency of Rome.

# Chapter 17

# Rome and the Seleucid Kingdom

The kingdom of the Seleucids was in existence for over a century before any significant contact was made with Rome. Its founder, Seleucus I, had laid claim (however briefly and abortively) to all the lands and peoples conquered by Alexander the Great. That heritage—or rather aspiration—was never lost sight of by subsequent monarchs of the realm. Realities intruded, to be sure. Eastern provinces broke away from Seleucid overlordship, conflicts with the Ptolemies strained resources, upheavals in Anatolia came largely at the expense of Seleucid influence, and dynastic strife weakened control at the center. Territory of the Seleucids shrank and their influence waned. But imperial ambitions continued to motivate the monarchs. In the last quarter of the third century the spectacular exploits of Antiochus III revived the spirits and prestige of the Seleucid house. It obtained new power in Asia Minor, gained suzerainty in Coele Syria and Palestine, and even recovered influence in Iranian lands through Antiochus' celebrated *anabasis*.

Seleucid authority extended to a length and breadth well exceeding that of the other successor kingdoms in the third century. Centrifugal tendencies might make that authority nominal in certain areas and at certain periods, but a proud legacy drove on rulers and leaders of the realm. Dynastic symbols, vigorous colonization, and the shrewd deployment of propaganda maintained Seleucid vitality in the lands of the Near East.[1] External ambitions embroiled the

1. The internal affairs of the Seleucid state are outside our scope. See, among recent works, Musti, *StudClassOrient* 15 (1966): 61–197; Orth, *Königlicher Machtanspruch, passim*; H. Kreissig, *Wirtschaft und Gesellschaft in Seleukidenreich* (Berlin, 1978), *passim*; G. M. Cohen, *The Seleucid Colonies* (Wiesbaden, 1978), *passim*.

Seleucids repeatedly and periodically with the Attalids and other powers in Anatolia, with the Ptolemies in the Levant, with rebellious and rival dynasts in the east. The ambitions, however, persisted, and the most far-flung aims were brought near to realization by Antiochus the Great. Intricate diplomacy involving both the cultivation of image and the selective use of force dated back to Seleucus I and marked the history of his successors throughout. The aspirations of the Seleucids and the means of furthering them existed well before they crossed the path of Rome—and continued afterward. Rome's might eventually, of course, set insurmountable limits to those aspirations. But she did not come to reverse the entire course of Seleucid history.

## The Aims and Achievements of Antiochus the Great

When did the two powers first take notice of one another? The earliest alleged contact came in the third quarter of the third century, an episode that rests on late authority and provokes suspicion. The emperor Claudius, an assiduous researcher into antiquity, discovered a letter in Greek in which senate and people authorized an *amicitia* and *societas* for Seleucus, on condition that he cancel in perpetuity any tribute owed by the people of Ilium, *consanguinei* of the Romans.[2] No means exist to verify the authenticity of the document. And many have rejected it as outright falsification.[3] That conclusion is understandable, but unnecessary. The Seleucus in question may most appropriately be identified with Seleucus II (247–226 B.C.). Setbacks suffered in the Third Syrian War and in the war against Antiochus Hierax (ca. 246–237 B.C.) provide a suitable context for Seleucus to cast about for friends and allies. Rome's victory over Carthage must certainly have captured the attention of the Hellenic world. A Seleucid embassy to the western power should not cause surprise. And the legend of Rome's Trojan origins was well known by this time. The senate may have made allusion to it in a response to the mission, whether or not Seleucus was in a position to enforce the demand.[4]

The consequences of this interview, if ever it took place, were rather less than earth-shaking. Claudius' citation of the letter gave only the Roman response. We are not informed even that an *amicitia*

2. Suet. *Claud.* 25.3; see above pp. 64–65.
3. So, most prominently, Holleaux, *Rome, la Grèce*, 47–58; and again in a recent discussion with bibliography, E. Weber, *WS* 85 (1972): 217–218; cf. also Cimma, *Reges socii et amici*, 69–70.
4. Cf. now Rizzo, *Studi Ellenistico-Romani*, 83–88; Orth, *Königlicher Machtanspruch*, 72–73.

was accepted, let alone that it had any practical effect. At most, the two powers held a cordial diplomatic exchange which, in retrospect, could be seen as the origin of amicable relations. At the time, neither one had any remote claim or interest in the sphere of the other.[5]

Antiochus III created an altogether new situation at the end of the third century. The young monarch's energy and aggressiveness threw the eastern world into turmoil. Seleucid fortunes revived in dramatic fashion. The battle of Raphia in 217 only temporarily checked Antiochus' ambitions in Coele Syria and Phoenicia. The long-range aim of humbling the Ptolemies, which had motivated most of his predecessors on the throne, continued to drive him on. In the meantime, Antiochus discharged equally formidable tasks. A successful war against his cousin Achaeus between 216 and 213 restored Seleucid authority to the inland regions of Anatolia and incorporated Pamphylia on the coast. During the next seven or eight years the great king traversed the upper satrapies, making the needed show of force and diplomacy which resurrected Syrian hegemony in Armenia, Parthia, Bactria, and Gandhara, a remarkable achievement. Remarkable though it was, however, Antiochus intended it only as a beginning. He was back in Asia Minor by ca. 204, pushing Seleucid influence to the coastal regions. Ptolemies and Attalids both lost ground to the military power and diplomatic arts of Antiochus the Great. As Polybius observes with admiration, the king had not only made the upper satraps subject to his rule, but added the maritime cities and dynasts on the other side of the Taurus, bringing security to his kingdom and striking fear in his dependents through courage and diligence.[6]

Antiochus' imperialist appetite was insatiable. He now cast his gaze once again upon the lands of Coele Syria and Phoenicia, bones

5. Little faith can be placed in the notice of Eutropius, 3.1, who has Roman legates go to Ptolemy after the First Punic War and promise assistance against the assault of "Antiochus." Quite apart from an error in the name (Seleucus II was the reigning monarch, not any "Antiochus"), it is nearly unthinkable that Rome would offer military assistance and entangle herself in an eastern Mediterranean conflict when she had just emerged from more than two decades of a Carthaginian war. Cf. H. Heinen, *ANRW* I: 1 (1972), 638–639, with bibliography. The report may be embellishment upon a simple fact: a Roman embassy to Ptolemy expressing gratitude for his refusal to side with Carthage; cf. Appian, *Sic.* 1.

6. Polyb. 11.34.14: οὐ μόνον τοὺς ἄνω σατράπας ὑπηκόους ἐποιήσατο τῆς ἰδίας ἀρχῆς, ἀλλὰ καὶ τὰς ἐπιθαλαττίους πόλεις καὶ τοὺς ἐπὶ τάδε τοῦ Ταύρου δυνάστας, καὶ συλλήβδην ἠσφαλίσατο τὴν βασιλείαν, καταπληξάμενος τῇ τόλμῃ καὶ φιλοπονίᾳ πάντας τοὺς ὑποταττομένους. Sources, literature, and a brief summary of these events in Will, *Histoire politique* II: 36–59, 96–98. On Antiochus' encroachment upon the Attalid sphere, see above p. 532. A general assessment of his policy in Schmitt, *Untersuchungen*, 85–107.

of contention between Ptolemies and Seleucids through four Syrian wars in the previous three-quarters of a century. The appropriate time arrived opportunely. Ptolemy IV Philopator died in 204/3 or 203/2, leaving a five-year old boy as successor, surrounded by some devious manipulators who vied for authority.[7] The new government had reason to fear the aggressions of Antiochus III. They resorted swiftly to diplomacy. An envoy went to Antiochus asking him to hold to their friendship and not violate the agreement entered into after Raphia. A second ambassador headed for the Macedonian court to arrange for a marriage alliance with the house of Philip V. And a third had orders to go to Rome, with a lengthy stay in Greece on the way.[8] No concrete results, so far as our evidence goes, emerged from these efforts. Antiochus would not be deflected from his purpose. He was now engaged in some clandestine negotiations of his own: a private agreement with Philip V which would facilitate the aggrandizement of both powers at the expense of Egypt. The nature of the pact and its terms—if indeed any were explicitly spelled out—remain obscure. Rumors and conjecture bedeviled reconstruction from the start, engendering conflicts in testimony among our confused sources.[9] Precision is impossible to attain, but precision itself may be irrelevant in this case. The purposes of the partners are clear enough. Philip geared his mobilization for a major Macedonian push to the east, into the Aegean, the Propontis, and western Asia Minor. The push had already begun and now accelerated. An agreement with Antiochus that would allow Philip a free hand in Ionia and Caria naturally suited the Macedonian's plans.[10] The Syrian monarch was willing to tolerate Macedonian expansion in the area, for he was in pursuit of larger game: revenge for Raphia,

7. The date of Philopator's death is a notorious, and perhaps insoluble, problem, which needs no solution here. See the extended discussion by Schmitt, *Untersuchungen*, 189–237, with bibliography; cf. Walbank, *Commentary* II:435–437; K. Abel, *Hermes* 95 (1967): 72–90.

8. Polyb. 15.25.13.

9. Evidence on the agreement in Polyb. 3.2.8, 15.20.2, 16.1.8; cf. 16.10.1, 16.24.6; Appian, *Mac.* 4; Livy, 31.14.5; Justin, 30.2.8; Porphyry, *FGH*, 260 F 44; John of Antioch, fr. 13. It is unnecessarily extreme, however, to reject the pact as fabrication; see above pp. 387–388.

10. On Philip's eastward aggressions in the last years of the third century, see above p. 384. That there was some understanding, whether detailed or not, with regard to operations in Asia Minor, seems clear from Philip's negotiations with Zeuxis, chief representative of Antiochus in the region: Polyb. 16.1.8: κατὰ τὰς συνθήκας; 16.24.6—hardly a private arrangement with the satrap, as proposed by Errington, *Athenaeum* 49 (1971): 341–342, 349–354. Ptolemaic holdings were surely reckoned as fair game under this agreement, as the sources state with unanimity. That Philip only began his assault on Ptolemaic towns in Thrace in 200 does not affect the conclusion. He evidently did take the Ptolemaic garrison at Samos by force in 202 or 201; Habicht, *AthMitt* 72 (1957): 233–241.

Seleucid suzerainty in Coele Syria, Palestine, and Phoenicia, and reduction of Egypt to a second-class power. The ancestral aims of the
Seleucids predominated.

It was a marriage of convenience, not destined to last and probably not intended to do so. The partners linked themselves only in lim-
itless greed and aggression.[11] Little active assistance came from the
Seleucid for Philip's operations in Asia Minor.[12] And Philip did not
hesitate to extend his power into Caria where Antiochus had been de-
veloping a sphere of interest.[13] The aggrandizers soon betrayed one
another.[14] There is every likelihood that Antiochus expected Philip to
become bogged down in struggles with Pergamum and Rhodes. The
Seleucid could achieve his principal objective against Egypt—and
later reclaim his position in Anatolia.[15]

The war on Egypt took first place, the culmination of Antiochus'
long-gestating scheme. The king commenced this Fifth Syrian War
probably in 202, gaining notable successes the next three years. His
victory at Panion and the capture of Sidon in 200 or 199 collapsed
Ptolemaic resistance in Phoenicia and established the foundation for
unchallenged Seleucid hegemony in Coele Syria.[16] Antiochus the
Great had succeeded in reviving, indeed eclipsing the glories of his
ancestors.

What was there in all of this to interest or concern Rome? The
Egyptian regime, after the death of Ptolemy Philopator, sent an envoy
to Rome with instructions to delay his journey for some time in
Greece. The mission is reported in a context of measures taken to protect against the anticipated aggression of Antiochus III. Whether the
envoy ever reached Rome and what message he carried we simply
do not know.[17] Word of the clandestine pact between Antiochus and

---

11. Polyb. 3.2.8: κακοπραγμονεῖν; 15.20.4: τῆς ὑπερβαλλούσης πλεονεξίας.

12. Note the grudging cooperation of Zeuxis: Polyb. 16.1.8–9, 16.24.5–6.

13. Observe Philip's ravaging of Alabanda (Polyb. 16.24.8), a city with ties to
Antiochus (OGIS, 234).

14. Polyb. 15.20.6: αὐτῶν παρασπονδούντων μὲν ἀλλήλους.

15. Cf. the analysis of Schmitt, Untersuchungen, 243–250, 256–261—who, however, unnecessarily insists on the initiative of Philip. For Walbank, Commentary II:
471–473, the initiative belongs to Antiochus. Polybius remains the best guide: the
kings urged on one another: 15.20.2: παρακαλέσαντες ἀλλήλους.

16. The Fifth Syrian War is notoriously ill-documented. For a reconstruction of
the chief events and chronology, see Holleaux, Études III:317–335; cf. Walbank, Commentary II:523–525, 546–547.

17. Polyb. 15.25.13. Alexandrian envoys reported the pact of Philip and Antiochus to Rome and pleaded for protection of the young king, according to Justin,
30.2.8. It is unsafe, however, to identify this embassy with the mission recorded by
Polybius, as does Holleaux, Rome, la Grèce, 72, n. 2; see Schmitt, Untersuchungen, 258,
n. 2; Heinen, ANRW I:1 (1972), 644. It is especially unsafe to bring in Appian, Syr. 2,
which refers to a later time.

Philip did eventually reach Rome, conveyed either by Rhodians or by Alexandrians, according to sources of less than unimpeachable reliability.[18] Even if true, however, the impact on Rome was minimal. It certainly cannot explain Roman entrance into the Second Macedonian War.[19] As for taking notice of Antiochus III, the senate made one move only in 200. The ambassadors who were sent to Greece to raise up support against Philip V had as part of their task a commission to reconcile the rulers of Egypt and Syria.[20] Those instructions make perfectly good sense. The Republic sought to reassure itself that a conflagration in the Near East would not spread to the Aegean world and thus complicate immeasurably the efforts to roll back the gains of Philip V.[21] It is uncertain even that any direct encounter with Antiochus took place—and inconceivable that the Seleucid would retreat from his goals on the advice of a Roman legation. The fact that fighting confined itself to Phoenicia and Coele Syria, without any immediate danger to Egypt itself, would have sufficed for reassurance. Rome was soon engulfed in war with Macedonia. The activities of Antiochus Megas barely touched the margins of her concern.

The Great King completed the subjugation of Coele Syria in 198.[22] Military victory had come earlier; Antiochus now eradicated the last vestiges of Ptolemaic political influence in the cities of the region. It was a triumph of marked proportions for the Seleucid kingdom, a fulfillment of the king's longstanding goal. But the drive for aggrandizement would not let him rest with that accomplishment.

The ancestral holdings of Antiochus' line encompassed a considerable portion of Asia Minor. And he had given notice of his own prestige in the region ca. 204–203.[23] The death of Ptolemy Philopator and the temptations of Coele Syria diverted his energies for the next several years. Antiochus' arrangement with Philip V allowed the Macedonian to make substantial gains in coastal Anatolia. Seleucid withdrawal, however, was temporary and intended to be so. The Sec-

18. Appian, *Mac.* 4: Rhodians; Justin, 30.2.8: Alexandrians.

19. See above pp. 387–388.

20. Polyb. 16.27.5: ἀπέπλευσαν ὡς Ἀντίοχον καὶ Πτολεμαῖον ἐπὶ τὰς διαλύσεις.

21. The simple truth as given by Polybius is distorted by Appian and Justin into a Roman ultimatum to Antiochus and Philip that they keep their hands off Egypt: Justin, 30.3.3, 31.1.2; Appian, *Mac.* 4. According to Livy, 31.2.3–4, the embassy was sent to Egypt to thank Ptolemy for his aid in the Hannibalic war and to ask for his continued good will in the event of war with Philip: Livy, 31.2.3–4. As principal object of the mission that is, of course, absurd—though the envoys' instructions may well have contained such diplomatic niceties.

22. Livy, 33.19.8.

23. As at Teos: Herrmann, *Anatolia* 9 (1965): 29–159, with the relevant documents at 34–42. And at Alabanda: *OGIS*, 234.

ond Macedonian War offered irresistible opportunities, not only by occupying Philip but by drawing off the resources of Attalus. Antiochus would not waste the opportunity. In 198 while he established political control in Coele Syria, his forces also made inroads into the territory of the Attalids, now denuded of protection because of Pergamene collaboration in the war on Macedonia. Just where the Syrian armies went and what the invasion accomplished cannot be known. The sequel has greater importance, for it affords a glimpse into Roman-Seleucid formal relations at this point. Attalus had sent word of his plight to the senate and urged that a Roman army be posted to Asia or that his own troops be permitted to return in order to check the Seleucid advance. The *patres'* reply referred to Antiochus as *socius et amicus* of the Roman people, rejected taking action against him, but offered to send envoys who would ask the king to refrain from attack on Pergamene dominions.[24] The outcome was amicable. Antiochus withdrew his army from the limits of Attalus' kingdom upon the request of the envoys, and subsequently sent a delegation to Rome which enjoyed a warm reception and honorific decrees.[25]

Antiochus, to be sure, had no intention of staying his hand in Anatolia forever. The *amicitia* with Rome, however, might have valuable diplomatic benefits, and it would be foolish to court a break. The Republic had spoken up on behalf of an ally, but had no direct interest in Asia Minor. Antiochus still had plenty of room to maneuver. The *amicitia* could be employed to his advantage.[26]

The king simply shifted his route in the following year. He mobilized vast naval and land forces, readied in the spring of 197, to make assault on Ptolemaic possessions along the southern coast of Anatolia from Cilicia to Caria.[27] A number of successes followed, as towns and garrisons surrendered themselves to the Seleucid armada. They were checked only at Coracesium, where envoys of Rhodes declared that their state would block any further advance. The confrontation provides useful insight into Hellenic manipulation of Roman power. Both sides invoked Rome's name as shield, threat, or pretext. The Rhodians interposed themselves, so they claimed, to

24. The evidence is contained only in Livy, 32.8.9–16. Its authenticity, however, should stand. On the controversy and the scholarly literature, see above pp. 538–539.

25. Livy, 32.27.1, 33.20.8–9; cf. 33.34.2–3, with Holleaux, *Études* V:160–163. Schmitt's conjecture, *Untersuchungen*, 273–276, that Attalus and Antiochus framed some compromise agreement that divided up territory, is unnecessary.

26. Establishment of the *amicitia* whose existence is attested for 198 may go back to the time of Seleucus II, if the letter found by Claudius is genuine; Suet. *Claud.* 25.3. Or else it stems from interchange in 200; Polyb. 16.27.5; see above p. 616. Cimma, *Reges socii et amici*, 71–73, wrongly concludes that they framed a treaty of *amicitia*.

27. Livy, 33.19.8–11.

prevent Antiochus from linking himself to Philip in the war on Rome. Antiochus had the appropriate retort: he was himself an *amicus* of Rome, he would do nothing to jeopardize that relationship, and he could point to honors bestowed on his legates in a recent visit to the Roman senate. The encounter ended abruptly and amicably. News of Cynoscephalae robbed the Rhodians of their pretext; and Antiochus preferred a pacific arrangement that would allow him to make gains elsewhere in Asia Minor without the opposition of Rhodes.[28] Roman might served as a convenient screen for Hellenic states to further their own aims. The western power had evinced no direct interest in Anatolia and, so long as that attitude prevailed, Antiochus cultivated his connection and profited from it.

Cynoscephalae gave increased impetus to the Seleucid's plans. Philip's defeat meant that Macedonian holdings in Asia Minor, like Ptolemaic holdings, were vulnerable. Antiochus took immediate advantage. He seems to have reached an accord of some sort with Rhodes which allowed the island to pose as patron of Ptolemaic cities while Antiochus could extend his influence into Lycia, Aeolia, Ionia, and even Caria.[29] The fragmentary character of our evidence prevents a full detailing of Seleucid gains during 197. But they were substantial. A late source registers cities in Cilicia, Pamphylia, and Lycia that fell to Antiochus.[30] In Caria, largely a region of Rhodian influence, the king's authority was recognized at Iasus and perhaps elsewhere.[31] Acquisitions in Ionia and Aeolia need to be conjectured, for the most part, from their later status. By the winter of 197/6, however, An-

28. The narrative is to be found in Livy, 33.19.9–33.20.7; cf. Polyb. 18.41a.1; Porphyry, *FGH*, 260 F 46. It is most unlikely that Antiochus ever had any intention of coming to Philip's aid. He had more to gain—or so it must have appeared at this juncture—from Philip's defeat. It was Macedonia, not Rome, whose ambitions reached to the Seleucid sphere of influence in Asia Minor. The fact that Antiochus appealed to his *amicitia* with Rome in response to Rhodes indicates that the Rhodians had brought Roman interests into the discussion; this was not simply Livy's addition to the Polybian text; *contra*: Rawlings, *AJAH* 1 (1976): 25, n. 45. The skepticism of Passerini, *Athenaeum* 10 (1932): 116–121, about this entire narrative, is extreme and unjustifiable.

29. Antiochus' interest in an accord is attested by Livy, 33.20.7: *legatos se Rhodum missurum respondit iisque mandaturum ut renovarent vetusta iura cum ea civitate sua maiorumque suorum*. Rhodian patronage of Ptolemaic cities: Livy, 33.20.11–12. An informal arrangement of some kind between the two states is a reasonable inference, though not explicitly attested. It is unnecessary to believe in an official pact. See discussion and bibliography above pp. 540–541.

30. Porphyry, *FGH*, 260 F 46: *eo enim tempore captae sunt Aphrodisias et Soloe et Zephyrion et Mallos et Anemurium et Selenus et Coracesium et Corycus et Andriace et Limyra et Patra et Xanthus*. The Cilician cities are confirmed by Livy, 33.20.4. On Xanthus, see also *OGIS*, 746. One can add Arycanda in Lycia: Agatharchides, *FGH*, 86 F 16.

31. Iasus: *OGIS*, 237; *Annuario*, 29–30 (1967–68): 2.I and II, pp. 445–448; cf. Livy, 37.17.3. Elsewhere in Caria: Schmitt, *Untersuchungen*, 280–281.

tiochus had established his control at Ephesus, a prime objective, and now impinged upon territory within the orbit of the Pergamene throne. The death of Attalus I in 197 stimulated Seleucid ambitions, as the death of Ptolemy IV had done six or seven years earlier.[32]

Antiochus Megas now made no secret of his goals: all the cities of Asia were to be brought under Seleucid dominion and to acknowledge the suzerainty of old.[33] In late 197 or early 196 he turned to the subjugation of Aeolia, the Troad, and the Hellespont. Abydus had already come into his power, the Macedonian garrison evidently expelled or surrendered. Antiochus then laid Smyrna and Lampsacus under assault, with the expectation that other Aeolian and Hellespontine cities would follow them into subservience. They could then expect to attain their "freedom"—when it was clear that such a privilege came at the king's behest.[34] The defeat of Macedonia, the death of Attalus, and the compliance of Rhodes all played into the hands of Antiochus the Great and promoted the resurgence of Seleucid domination.

Smyrna and Lampsacus resisted siege and blandishments. But Antiochus would not be deterred from further advance. In the spring of 196 he ordered troops across the Hellespont to the Chersonesus. Sestus and other towns of the region surrendered themselves. Antiochus proceeded to occupy Lysimacheia, and then to ravage the adjoining areas of Thrace. The king proclaimed "liberty" for Lysimacheia, as he customarily did for cities that came into his power. The claims on Europe made nearly a century before by Seleucus I were now revived by the greatest of his descendants.[35]

---

32. Antiochus was able to winter at Ephesus in 197/6; Livy, 33.38.1. He may have had Rhodian assistance in the taking of the city; Frontinus, *Strat.* 3.9.10; Rawlings, *AJAH* 1 (1976): 13–14. Porphyry, *FGH*, 260 F 46, mentions Ephesus immediately after Xanthus, perhaps an indication that Antiochus bypassed conquests in southern Ionia. The desirability of Ephesus is stressed by Polyb. 18.41a.2. On the cities north of Ephesus, the evidence is assembled by Schmitt, *Untersuchungen*, 282–283. The death of Attalus: Livy, 33.21.1. On the campaign of 197, see also Walbank, *Commentary* II:610–611, 614–615; Mastrocinque, *PP* 31 (1976): 307–318.

33. Livy, 33.38.1: *Antiochus rex . . . omnes Asiae civitates in antiquam imperii formulam redigere est conatus*; cf. Polyb. 18.41a.2.

34. Livy, 33.38.2–6: *haud difficulter videbat iugum accepturas . . . ab rege impetratam eos libertatem*. Control of Abydus is attested at 33.28.4, 33.28.8. The attacks on Smyrna and Lampsacus are generally placed in late 197, prior to Antiochus' entrance into winter quarters: Schmitt, *Untersuchungen*, 289–295; Walbank, *Commentary* II:620; Briscoe, *Commentary*, 320–321. But they may have awaited the beginning of the spring campaigning season; Mastrocinque, *PP* 31 (1976): 318–321.

35. Polyb. 18.49.1–2; Livy, 33.38.4–14; Appian, *Syr.* 1. Antiochus' arrangements with Lysimacheia have now come to light in a recently discovered document; *ZPE* 17 (1975): 101–102 = *IvIlion*, no. 45.

## The Origins of Conflict with Rome

The Roman reaction needs scrutiny. Antiochus' spectacular gains could endanger the balance of the East. Yet they had passed unhindered by action or protest from Rome. It is worth inquiring just when the Seleucid advance became a matter of concern to the Republic.

Two or three weeks after Cynoscephalae, probably in late June, 197, Flamininus, Philip, and the Greek allies gathered to discuss peace terms. According to Polybius, Flamininus was in a hurry to make peace, having learned that Antiochus had set out from Syria with his army and had prepared an expedition against Europe.[36] The notice has gone unquestioned, a surprising scholarly lapse.[37] Yet in the weeks after Cynoscephalae Antiochus had gotten no further than Cilicia, his targets were Ptolemaic cities on the southern coast of Asia Minor, and his progress was temporarily halted by Rhodes.[38] Even if a report of Antiochus' movements had reached Flamininus by this time, they could hardly be regarded as a thrust toward Europe—or an authentic reason for hastening peace with Philip. Polybius has anticipated events and imputed motives.

The major gains of Antiochus came in 197 and early 196. Rome, far from feeling threatened, did not even seem aware of them. In the spring of 196 Roman legates brought a *senatus consultum* to Greece, announcing the terms on which a peace treaty would be based. They included a withdrawal of Macedonian garrisons from Euromus, Pedasa, Bargylia, Iasus, Abydus, Thasos, Myrina, and Perinthus. Of those cities, Iasus and Abydus were certainly already in Antiochus' hands and some of the others may have been.[39] It will not do to surmise that this liberation of Asian cities served as a warning to Antiochus. The senatorial decree directed itself explicitly at Philip, and the cities named therein coincided almost exactly with those from which

36. Polyb. 18.39.3: ἐπυνθάνετο τὸν Ἀντίοχον ἀπὸ Συρίας «ἀν»ῆχθαι μετὰ δυνά-μεως ποιούμενον τὴν ὁρμὴν ἐπὶ τὴν Εὐρώπην; Livy, 33.13.15: *Antiochum bellum tran-situmque in Europam moliri constabat*; cf. Polyb. 18.43.2; Livy, 33.27.6. On the chronology, see Mastrocinque, *PP* 31 (1976): 315–316.

37. As, e.g., Badian, *Studies*, 116–117, who has Flamininus already hatching a diplomatic scheme to employ against Antiochus. The assertions in Polybius and Livy are passed by without comment by Walbank, *Commentary* II:601, and Briscoe, *Commentary*, 275.

38. News of Cynoscephalae reached Antiochus at Coracesium: Livy, 33.20.10. Mastrocinque, *PP* 31 (1976): 316, has the chronology right, but does not doubt that Flamininus was influenced by fear of Antiochus' advance—word of which, for Mastrocinque, must have been conveyed by Rhodians.

39. Polyb. 18.44.4; Livy, 33.30.3. See above pp. 541–542.

Rhodes had demanded evacuation of Macedonian garrisons for more than a year.[40] The Romans had simply not kept in touch with the movements of Antiochus the Great.[41]

By the time of the Isthmian declaration in the summer of 196 word of Antiochus' advance had surely spread to Greece. The cities of Smyrna and Lampsacus at least, still under siege by Seleucid forces, applied for rescue to the Romans or would soon do so.[42] Antiochus knew the risks and had taken precautions. Envoys from the Syrian court arrived in Corinth in time for the Isthmian games, to seek an interview with Flamininus and the *decem legati*. The king obviously wished to reassure Rome and to reaffirm their *amicitia*. His quarrel was not with the Republic. But the Romans, who had just made a grandiloquent pronouncement of liberty for all Greeks, could hardly exempt the Greeks of Asia from that proclamation. Their directives to Antiochus followed from the Isthmian declaration: he was to stay away from the autonomous cities of Asia, to make war on none of them, to evacuate his forces from those places that he had captured from Ptolemy and Philip, and to refrain from crossing over to Europe with an army.[43] The posture is less one of belligerence than of maintaining public consistency. The *decem legati* had neither instructions nor intention to declare an ultimatum. Indeed, they made certain to

---

40. Polyb. 18.2.3–4. That the *s.c.*, or this portion thereof, was designed as a warning to Antiochus was needlessly postulated by Holleaux, *Études* IV: 309, n. 2; followed, e.g., by Walbank, *Commentary* II: 611. Rightly questioned by Briscoe, *Commentary*, 305–306; Mastrocinque, *PP* 31 (1976): 315–316. In the more extreme formulation of Desideri, *StudClassOrient* 19–20 (1970–71): 499–500, Rome is here creating an anti-Seleucid politico-military bloc.

41. That fact also casts doubt on Polybius' assertion that the senate left open the matter of the Three Fetters out of concern regarding Antiochus' obvious desire to meddle in the affairs of Europe: Polyb. 18.45.10–11; Livy, 33.31.5–6, 33.31.10. Such a desire was not yet "obvious" to the Romans. Polybius' interpretation has intervened here.

42. The time of this appeal cannot be pinned down. It does not appear in the extant text of Polybius (though a fragment of a Lampsacene speech has indirect relevance: Polyb. 18.49.1), and Livy omits it. The representatives of Lampsacus and Smyrna went to Flamininus in Greece, according to Appian, *Syr.* 2, to the senate, according to Diod. 29.7. The mission of Hegesias on behalf of Lampsacus, despite common assumption, must have been a separate and earlier one. Its purpose was to gain inclusion of Lampsacus among the signatories to the peace with Philip. No mention is made of Antiochus in the document which praises Hegesias, nor any suggestion that the city is under siege. Inclusion in the peace treaty would afford future protection: *Syll.*[3] 591, lines 32–34. Flamininus and the *decem legati* sent letters to the "kings" (lines 75–76)— who may be Eumenes and Prusias, for all we know; in any case, the missives were not directed to Antiochus alone.

43. Polyb. 18.47.1–2; Livy, 33.34.2–4. Antiochus had evidently not yet crossed— or, at least, Rome did not know of his crossing.

keep negotiations open by appointing some of their members to meet personally with the king.[44] This was not a step toward war.

The meeting with Antiochus took place at Lysimacheia in the early fall of 196. The senate had sent a special envoy, L. Cornelius, for the purpose, and with a special mission: to effect reconciliation between Antiochus and Ptolemy![45] The motive seems astonishing at first glance. The Fifth Syrian War was long since over. And surely Seleucid aggrandizement in Asia Minor, the Hellespont, and Thrace should take first place on the agenda. Yet the items are not incompatible, and the aim of Cornelius' mission may be the best indicator of Roman attitude. The senate's delegation to Alexandria in 200 had had the same commission. It accomplished little or nothing, and Rome had subsequently been absorbed in the Macedonian war. Renewed appeal came to the *patres* from the court of Ptolemy V when the king had been stripped of possessions in Cilicia.[46] Ptolemy had suffered further losses in the interim, notably cities in Lycia, and Ephesus in Ionia. And if Antiochus was now moving into areas of Thrace vacated by Philip, he would threaten ancestral Ptolemaic possessions. In short, it was entirely congruent for L. Cornelius to seek a rapprochement beween Antiochus and Ptolemy while demanding that the Seleucid withdraw from Europe and evacuate places that he had seized from Philip and Ptolemy. Cornelius was joined at Lysimacheia by three members of the *decem legati*, but he served as spokesman. The demands duplicated those made at Corinth, with the addition that the king must remove his army from Thrace (it had not been there, to Rome's knowledge, at the time of the Corinth meeting).[47] They can now been seen in a clearer light. The *patres* endeavored to keep faith with Ptolemy, to reconcile two warring *amici*, and to maintain consistency with their own proclamation of freedom at the Isthmian games. They did not regard Antiochus as a menace to their interests, let alone seek to provoke a confrontation.[48]

44. Polyb. 18.47.3. The item is omitted in Livy's account, which gives a harsher tone to the encounter than is to be found in Polybius'; cf. Passerini, *Athenaeum* 10 (1932): 121–122. Nothing warrants the statement that the Romans "were indeed thoroughly frightened"; Badian, *Studies*, 117.

45. Polyb. 18.49.3: ἐπὶ τὰς διαλύσεις ἐξαπεσταλμένοι τὰς Ἀντιόχου καὶ Πτολεμαίου; Livy, 33.39.1; Appian, *Syr.* 2.

46. The appeal is registered explicitly by Appian, *Syr.* 2. Holleaux, *Rome, la Grèce*, 50, n. 3, unjustifiably seeks to amalgamate this with a Ptolemaic embassy to Rome in 203/2: Polyb. 15.25.14.

47. Polyb. 18.50.1–9; Livy, 33.39.2–7; Appian, *Syr.* 3; Diod. 28.12.

48. On the matter of consistency, see, especially, Polyb. 18.50.6: γελοῖον γὰρ εἶναι τὰ Ῥωμαίων ἆθλα τοῦ γεγονότος αὐτοῖς πολέμου πρὸς Φίλιππον Ἀντίοχον ἐπελθόντα παραλαμβάνειν. Cornelius' point, that the crossing to Europe could only be

The king, in fact, had a suitable retort on every score. He wondered what justification the Romans had in questioning his control of Asian towns when he had never involved himself with the affairs of Italy—an overt disclaimer of anti-Roman intentions. His expedition to Europe had full legitimacy, an ancestral sanction, for the Chersonese and the cities of Thrace had belonged to the Seleucid house long before Ptolemaic and Antigonid usurpation. The rebuilding of Lysimacheia would provide a residence for his son, not a menace to Rome. As for the autonomous cities of Asia, Antiochus insisted quite properly that, if they were to obtain freedom, it should come as his gift, not on Roman instruction. And, on the quarrel with Ptolemy, a major item on the Roman list, the king brilliantly turned the tables: he announced that reconciliation had already come, to be followed shortly by marriage alliance. Rome had no *locus standi* in the matter.[49]

The senate's legates had nearly run out of grievances. They now called upon envoys from Smyrna and Lampsacus who began to deliver a harangue against the king. Antiochus, however, cut them short: he was prepared to submit all complaints to an impartial arbiter, namely the island of Rhodes.[50] No one could grumble about that solution, a standard Hellenic solution, least of all Rome, the *amicus* of the Rhodians. The conference soon came to an abrupt halt, when a false rumor of Ptolemy's death scattered the participants.[51]

On the face of it, Lysimacheia represents a dazzling diplomatic triumph for Antiochus the Great. And so it was, in terms of sanctioning his gains and giving public expression to the legitimacy of Seleucid aspirations in Asia Minor and Thrace. More to the point, however, Rome had no grounds for discontent. Antiochus had disclaimed any designs on Roman interests, had affirmed his commitment to liberating Asian cities, and had announced his good relations with the Republic's own *amici* Ptolemy and Rhodes. The Great King went further still, sending ambassadors to Flamininus to give reassurance that he would do nothing to strain the relationship between the two powers.[52] Conflict had been averted and now seemed remote. The senate had achieved its principal end.

Antiochus Megas stood firm on his claims to the Seleucid

interpreted as prelude to an attack on Rome, is rhetorical—even if one assumes that Polybius has reproduced it accurately: Polyb. 18.50.8–9; cf. Livy, 33.39.7; Appian, *Syr.* 3; Diod. 28.12. It goes too far to reckon this embassy as dictating to Antiochus the extent of Rome's sphere of interest in Asia, as Dahlheim, *Struktur und Entwicklung*, 97–98.

49. Polyb. 18.51.1–10; Livy, 33.40.1–6; Appian, *Syr.* 3; Diod. 28.12.

50. Polyb. 18.52.1–4.

51. Livy, 33.41.1–4; cf. Polyb. 18.52.5; Appian, *Syr.* 4.

52. Livy, 33.41.5: *qui ad fidem faciendam nihil novaturum regem de societate agerent.*

heritage and on his privileges as a Hellenistic monarch. At the same time he had every reason to maintain and enhance cordial relations with Rome. The king's envoys conversed with Flamininus at Corinth in the spring of 195 and evidently raised the possibility of expanding their *amicitia* into a full-fledged alliance. The proconsul disclaimed authority to act on the matter and referred Antiochus' legates to the senate.[53] Whether they proceeded to Rome is unknown and unimportant. The senate shied away from formal alliances with eastern principalities at this time anyway. But Antiochus had reaffirmed his good will toward the Republic and had expressed his desire to make their association a permanent one.[54]

The king had practical motives for seeking the security of a formal alliance. He soon embarked on new expansionism and preferred to avoid the nuisance of victimized states appealing to Rome. Antiochus' movements in 195 and 194 cannot be charted in any detail because of gaps in the evidence. We do know, however, that he mounted a major land and naval expedition into Europe, i.e. Thrace, in 195.[55] During that campaigning season and probably the next as well, Antiochus had made substantial military and diplomatic gains. Much of the Thracian area came under his sway as the king "liberated" Greek towns from barbaric rule, including Aenus and Maronea. He courted the allegiance of Byzantium, thus to gain access to the Black Sea. And he made considerable headway in Asia Minor as well. Seleucid bounty drew the Galatians into cooperation, and a network of marriage alliances aimed at solidifying the position in Anatolia: with Ptolemy, Ariarathes, and even Eumenes.[56] The king practiced standard Hellenistic politics—though with unusual vigor and success.

Those years of Seleucid advance passed without Roman protest or action. The Republic had issued extensive demands to Antiochus at Corinth and Lysimacheia in 196. The king, however, had pursued his own course. Far from evacuating Europe or the cities once held by Ptolemy or Philip, he had progressively added to his dominions.

53. Livy, 34.25.2: *legatis de societate agentibus*.

54. Holleaux, *Études* V:165, argued plausibly that the embassy did not go to Rome.

55. Livy, 33.44.6–7, 34.33.12, 34.43.4. The king's headquarters were at Ephesus, where he could keep pressure on the Pergamene realm, in addition to planning operations in Thrace: Livy, 33.49.6–7; cf. 35.13.4; Appian *Syr.* 6.

56. Eumenes alone declined to be drawn into the Seleucid orbit. See above pp. 544–545. The timing of these events is uncertain. Appian, *Syr.* 5–6, supplies the principal evidence and his compressed account cannot be employed for chronological precision. The military events seem to fall in 195 and 194, though the marriage alliance may have come two or three years later. A similar compression in Zon. 9.18. See O. Leuze, *Hermes* 58 (1923): 205–213. The capture of Aenus and Maronea probably came during these years; Livy, 37.60.7.

Rome had backed off. Why? Surely not because her representatives had been out-debated by Antiochus at Lysimacheia. That could only spur rather than curb Roman indignation. To be sure, there were those who did regard the Seleucid advance as a threat to Rome's security—or professed to do so. The *decem legati* returned to Rome in 195 with tales of Antiochus' splendid army and enormous fleet.[57] Rumors circulated that Hannibal was in correspondence with Antiochus and men pondered the awesome prospect of a war against the Seleucid monarchy abetted by Carthage and her ex-general.[58] Other reports hinted that Nabis of Sparta might count on the backing of Antiochus—reports which the tyrant did nothing to discourage.[59] P. Villius, as *legatus* in 195, verified the accounts of extensive naval and land forces which Antiochus had brought into Thrace.[60] At the beginning of 194, Scipio Africanus, newly elected consul, seized the occasion to argue for the allotment of Macedonia as a consular province, on grounds that Antiochus had invaded Europe, summoned by Aetolia and goaded by Hannibal.[61] Some or all of these notices can be dismissed as fabricated rumor, self-interested exaggeration, or *post eventum* concoction. The essential fact remains: the Roman state showed no official concern for the aggrandizements of Antiochus the Great. The alarming reports of the *decem legati* lost their force when word arrived that the king had returned to Syria.[62] Hannibal fled to the Seleucid court probably in the summer of 195, but provoked not so much as a note of protest from Rome.[63] The alleged link between Nabis and Antiochus was nothing more than scare tactics, and, more probably, later invention.[64] Scipio, of course, hoped to exploit the circumstances and obtain an eastern command for himself. How much support he had we cannot know. The important fact is that the senate decided against assignment of Macedonia as a province in 194, and, indeed, ordered the evacuation of all Roman forces from Greece.[65]

57. Livy, 33.44.6–9; cf. 33.43.6.   58. Livy, 33.45.5–6.
59. Livy, 33.43.6, 34.37.5.   60. Livy, 34.33.12.
61. Livy, 34.43.4–5.   62. Livy, 33.45.1–2.
63. Livy, 33.49.1–8; Appian, *Syr.* 4.
64. Note the absence of any reference to Antiochus in Livy, 34.41.5–7.
65. Livy, 34.43.7–8. It is futile to hypothesize political parties organized around differences of foreign policy here, as in McDonald's contrast between Scipio's "Hellenistic" approach and Flamininus' "Hellenic" policy; *JRS* (1938): 153–164; endorsed by Scullard, *Roman Politics*, 116–117; rightly criticized by Badian, *Foreign Clientelae*, 81–82; cf. Cassola, *Labeo* 6 (1960): 116–118; Desideri, *StudClassOrient* 19–20 (1970–71): 515–537. Nor does it advance matters to divide senatorial opinion into those who subordinated diplomacy to strategy and those who did the reverse; Badian, *Studies*, 122–123. The reconstruction of Schlag, *Regnum in Senatu*, 115–139, who sees a "war party" headed by Sulpicius Galba and opposed by Scipio Africanus and his followers, is entirely fanciful.

The decision expresses majority senatorial opinion unambiguously: Seleucid advances in Asia and Thrace did not represent a threat to Italian interests. That attitude confirms the conclusion arrived at earlier. The conference at Lysimacheia satisfied rather than distressed the Romans. They had made the logical extension of their propaganda, and had kept faith with their *amici*. Antiochus' justifications proved sufficient for the Republic which wanted no pretext for renewed warfare in the East.

The king quite properly took the signal as giving him a free hand in Asia Minor and Thrace. So far as we know, there was not a single Roman mission to Antiochus during the years of 195 and 194 when Seleucid power grew and territory multiplied.[66] In the winter of 194/3, however, Antiochus felt the need to dispatch envoys to Rome. Diplomacy resumed as the king's representatives assured senators that his actions did not violate their interests. Our sources fail to give the occasion for this resumption of talks. Reasonable surmise can fill the gap. Delegates from all over Greece and a large part of Asia had crowded into Rome, including appointees of various kings.[67] There can be little doubt that the ruler of Pergamum had a hand in generating grievances against Antiochus the Great. Seleucid inroads into Ionia, Aeolia, and the Troad had badly eroded Pergamene authority. Eumenes II had to exert diplomatic pressure where he could for survival of his realm and influence, particularly among cities under threat or siege by Antiochus, like Lampsacus, Smyrna, and Alexandreia Troas. The representatives of Asian cities and principalities who filed into Rome in winter 194/3 unquestionably included those who came at Eumenes' prompting to express alarm at Seleucid encroachment.[68] Antiochus' revival of talks is no mystery. He needed to neutralize complaints and dispel Roman concern, thereby removing obstacles to expansionism.

The Seleucid envoys urged upon Rome the same proposal mooted in early 195: that there be a *foedus sociale* between the two powers.[69] Such a pact would advertise harmony and a permanent relationship, thus to discourage Greek opposition and further complaints to Rome. The *patres*, however, were now under the pressure of

66. Conjectures about Roman envoys to Antiochus on the basis of Livy, 34.33.12 and 34.59.8, were effectively refuted by Holleaux, *Études* V:166–175; see also Leuze, *Hermes* 58 (1923): 214–220. Walbank, *Commentary* II:621, leaves the matter open.

67. Livy, 34.57.2–4; Appian, *Syr.* 6. They were there, in part, to bring testimony on the new settlement of Greece. The explanation of Diodorus, 28.15.1, that Rome sought to win Greek support for a war on Antiochus is plainly anticipatory.

68. See sources and discussion above pp. 544–545.

69. Livy, 34.57.6–11: *cum, qui numquam hostes fuerint, ad amicitiam sociali foedere inter se iungendam coeant*; Appian, *Syr.* 6; Diod. 28.15.2.

numerous Hellenic embassies, seeking some recourse or at least a gesture on their behalf. Rome's sensitivity to her public image demanded a step in that direction—yet one that would not lead to armed conflict. As negotiations were likely to be long and complex, the senate directed Flamininus and the *decem legati* to deal with the matter in a private parley and to act in accordance with the dignity and interest of Rome.[70] The situation called for delicate diplomacy.

Antiochus' envoys were cordial but firm. They expressed their desire for a treaty, on the basis of mutual respect and equality. The king continued to insist on his rightful claims to ancestral territories in Asia and Europe.[71] His stated position essentially duplicated the one presented at Lysimacheia. Flamininus, with an eye to Greek public opinion, needed to show a sterner Roman posture, while avoiding a path toward war. The Roman spokesman hit upon a promising formula. He offered two options to Antiochus: he must stay out of Europe altogether, in which case the Romans would not interfere with the cities of Asia, or, should he fail to adhere to those limits, they would come to the aid of their Asian *amici* and liberate them as they had liberated Greece from Philip.[72] The proposal gave Rome a stronger stance than before, a means to assuage Hellenic doubts. At Lysimacheia the demands made on Antiochus had been much the same, but no threats were issued in the event of noncompliance. And indeed noncompliance had brought no retaliation. This time Flamininus indicated that a breakdown of negotiations might prompt active intervention. The suggestion served to hearten Hellenic *amici*. At the same time, however, Flamininus offered the king a way out of the impasse. Retreat from Europe would satisfy many complainants and demonstrate Rome's persuasiveness, while Antiochus could rest assured of no Roman meddling in his Asian ventures.[73] The Seleucid envoys, however, held back from compliance, for they lacked instructions to authorize a withdrawal from Europe.[74] The private conclave broke up.

70. Livy, 34.57.4–5: *cum Antiocho quia longior disceptatio erat . . . T. Quinctio mandatum ut . . . regis verba audiret responderetque iis, quae ex dignitate atque utilitate populi Romani responderi possent*; Diod. 28.15.1. The procedure suggests that the *patres* did not wish to occupy an inordinate amount of their own time on this issue.

71. Livy, 34.57.6–11; Diod. 28.15.2; Appian, *Syr.* 6.

72. Livy, 34.58.1–3, 34.58.10–12; Diod. 28.15.3.

73. Cf. Diod. 28.15.3: μηδὲν πολυπραγμονεῖν Ῥωμαίους τῶν κατὰ τὴν Ἀσίαν. This ought not to be regarded as a concession or a retreat on Rome's part, let alone a betrayal of Greek liberty, as Passerini, *Athenaeum* 10 (1932): 333. She had never offered to liberate the Asian Greek cities by force in the past. Rather, she had insisted on acknowledgment of their liberty. Nothing in her present proposal contradicted that insistence, even if Antiochus should evacuate Europe; cf. Livy, 34.58.8–9. Declarations of ἐλευθερία by Antiochus for Asian Greeks would suffice to meet the demand.

74. Livy, 34.58.4–7, 34.59.1–3; Diod. 28.15.4.

Flamininus now hastened to announce its outcome to the assembled Greeks, a public show of Roman *fides*: if Antiochus did not depart from Europe, the Republic would defend the freedom of Asian Greeks.[75] The pronouncement was hailed with applause by the Greek envoys who were present.[76] And no wonder. A retreat from Europe would be a major concession by Antiochus, perhaps a sign of further withdrawal to come. And if he did not comply with the demand, Rome had indicated her willingness to stymie the king in Asia. Seleucid gains could now be rolled back.

Rome had acknowledged Hellenic opinion and served her public image. But the intention was not to signal a break with Antiochus or accelerate the movement toward war. The Seleucid envoys were taken aback by Flamininus' maneuverings, unprepared with appropriate responses. They could hardly acquiesce in yielding up their king's European conquests, nor, on the other hand, did they wish to precipitate a conflict. They made the only request possible: a plea for time which would allow Antiochus to ponder the proposals; concession or compromise could be expected.[77] The *patres* were happy enough to comply. They had made their point and had no more desire than Antiochus to enter into an armed contest. Diplomacy would continue, as the senate appointed three delegates to meet with the king.[78] Antiochus did not, of course, get his treaty of alliance; that would be an unpardonable affront to those Hellenes who had suffered from his aggrandizement and were in Rome to complain of it. The interchange, however, ended in amicable, rather than stormy, fashion. That fact is underscored by an event not reported in the literary tradition, ob-

---

75. Livy, 34.59.4–5; Diod. 28.15.4. Badian, *Studies*, 126–127, argues that the terms offered in the private colloquy differed from those announced in public: Flamininus could only insist on evacuation of both European and Asian cities in his speech to the Greeks. The idea seems supported by Appian, *Syr.* 6: ἐὰν Ἀντίοχος αὐτονόμους τοὺς Ἕλληνας ἐᾷ τοὺς ἐν Ἀσίᾳ καὶ τῆς Εὐρώπης ἀπέχηται, Ῥωμαίοις αὐτὸν ἔσεσθαι φίλον, ἂν ἐθέλῃ. But Appian's condensed account knows no distinction between private and public meetings and would seem, in fact, as it stands, to apply to the former! Both Livy and Diodorus give the same conditions to the private negotiations as to the public pronouncement; Livy, 34.58.1–3, 34.58.12, 34.59.5; Diod. 28.15.3–4. Their presentations plainly derive from Polybius, and it is unnecessary either to impute an error to him or to assume that his meaning was misunderstood; cf. Balsdon, *Phoenix* 21 (1967): 187–189; Bredehorn, *Senatsakten*, 263–265; Desideri, *StudClassOrient* 19–20 (1970–71): 507–508; cf. Briscoe, *Latomus* 31 (1972): 34–36.

76. Diod. 28.15.4.

77. Livy, 34.59.6–7: *cogitaturum, cum renuntiatae condiciones essent, et impetraturum aliquid aut pacis causa concessurum.*

78. Livy, 34.59.8.

sessed as it is by circumstances which anticipate the coming war. One of Antiochus' envoys at the parley, Menippus, also asked Roman approval for the *asylia* of Teos. The senate readily assented and furthermore recorded on stone its high regard for Menippus, the representative of the king.[79] They merely observed formalities, so it might be said. Perhaps: nonetheless, those formalities express continued *amicitia*.

The Roman embassy to Antiochus in the spring of 193 first stopped at Pergamum. It was important to reassure Eumenes that the senate continued to take account of his interests. Eumenes immediately grasped the occasion to deliver frightening tales about Antiochus' aggressive aims and to urge the envoys to war.[80] The Pergamene had more to gain from such a conflict than did Rome.[81] The encounter with Antiochus came some time during the summer at Apamea. In Livy's report, the exchange largely repeated that of a few months before in Rome between Flamininus and the Seleucid envoys. This would be the expected initial sparring. Matters got no further, however, for news announcing the death of Antiochus' son called a halt to proceedings.[82] When the conference resumed, it did so at Ephesus and without Antiochus. His minister Minnio represented the king's interests. Debating points were rehearsed by both sides, as usual. A wrangle over whether Rome's suzerainty over Greek cities in Italy was analogous to Seleucid dominion over Asian Greeks occupied the participants for a time, but did not constitute serious bargaining.[83] Antiochus did have some serious proposals, however, concessions indeed, which could move the talks in a positive direction. He offered to respect the autonomy of Rhodes, Cyzicus, and Byzantium, in fact of all Asian Greeks, with the exception of those in Aeolia and Ionia, where he would not yield up traditional claims, in return

---

79. *Syll.*³ 601 = Sherk, *RDGE*, no. 34. The interpretation of Errington, *ZPE* 39 (1980): 279–284, implying cynical subterfuge on Antiochus' part and an assertion of claims on Asia by Rome is unconvincing.

80. Livy, 35.13.6–10.

81. P. Villius, one of the Roman envoys, made a side trip to Ephesus where he met with Hannibal and expressed Rome's pacific intentions. The purpose, so we are told, was to bring Hannibal into suspicion with Antiochus; Livy, 35.14.1–4, 35.19.1; Appian, *Syr.* 9; Polyb. 3.11.2. If true, this is another indication of Rome's eagerness to avoid conflict—by isolating the militant Hannibal. The tale of Hannibal's interview with Scipio Africanus is unquestionably apocryphal: Livy, 35.14.5–12; Appian, *Syr.* 10–11; Zon. 9.18; Plut. *Flam.* 21; Holleaux, *Études* V: 184–207; Leuze, *Hermes* 58 (1923): 247–268.

82. Livy, 35.15.1–2.

83. Livy, 35.16.1–13.

for a treaty with Rome.[84] The Seleucid posture was thus consistently conciliatory. Antiochus wanted a treaty, not war. To that end he would grant concessions, though not to the point of dismantling all his external possessions. On the face of it, this would seem a reasonable compromise. But the Roman envoys were caught in a dilemma. Pressure from Eumenes played a part, and representatives of various Greek cities in Asia, prodded and prompted by Eumenes, were in Ephesus to sound the alarm against Antiochus.[85] The legates might otherwise have arranged a *modus vivendi* with the king, but Hellenic opinion (at least as represented by Eumenes and his dependents) had not been mollified, and Roman policy still resisted treaties of alliance. The dilemma meant that talks ended inconclusively. The legates, not hostile or belligerent, but simply at a loss in dealing with conflicting pressures, went home without accomplishment.[86]

The king of Syria had deliberately and conscientiously shunned any bellicose acts that might embroil him in conflict with Rome. His designs had focused on entrenching Seleucid hegemony in various regions of Asia Minor and Thrace, designs which continued unchanged. In early 193 Antiochus personally led his entire land army in an assault on the troublesome mountaineers of Pisidia.[87] The breakdown of talks with the Roman envoys must have been a disappointment, but did not cause the king to veer from his course. There were doubtless militants among his counselors, men from Syria and Greece, in addition to Hannibal, men resentful or scornful of Roman pronouncements, who prodded Antiochus into a more belligerent posture. The unwillingness of Rome's legates to consider a compromise must have strengthened the hand of those advisers. Yet Antiochus showed no interest in moving against the Republic.[88] His troops had engaged the Pisidians in southern Asia Minor, as well as continuing their assault on the key coastal cities of northwestern Asia Minor,

84. The notice occurs in Appian, *Syr.* 12. Rightly accepted as plausible by, e.g., Leuze, *Hermes* 58 (1923): 242, n. 2; Badian, *Studies*, 138, n. 78. See the discussion by Desideri, *StudClassOrient* 19–20 (1970–71): 508–510. Appian has Antiochus himself offer the proposals, but he places the meeting at Ephesus, not Apamea, and almost certainly refers to the negotiating session with Minnio.

85. Livy, 35.17.1–2.

86. Livy, 35.17.2: *itaque nec remissa ulla re nec impetrata, aeque ac venerant, omnium incerti legati Romam redierunt.*

87. Livy, 35.13.5, 35.14.1; Appian, *Syr.* 9, 12. Unfortunately, no account of the campaign and its results has been preserved.

88. Livy gives a lengthy and one-sided account of the king's council, as members vied with one another to denounce Rome and urge mobilization: Livy, 35.17.3–35.19.7. Its authenticity as a whole, however, may be questioned. And the concluding statement that the council opted for war is refuted altogether by the king's subsequent actions; cf. Badian, *Studies*, 129.

Smyrna, Lampsacus, and Alexandreia Troas.[89] And in early 192 the king mounted still another expedition into Thrace.[90] Antiochus proceeded unremittingly with the consolidation of Seleucid gains in areas already staked out. This was not a buildup for confrontation with Rome.

Pressures began to mount in 193. The absence of a permanent accord with Rome was troubling, for it left open the path for Antiochus' enemies to goad the Republic against him. His own advisers (or some of them) pushed for more decisive actions. And now the Aetolian League sought alliance with the king to elevate its own prestige and to issue a challenge to Rome—or rather to build a coalition that would discourage any Roman intervention in Greece.[91] The initial Aetolian envoy Dicaearchus, brother of the *strategos*, apparently aroused no response from Antiochus.[92] A second embassy followed, in late 193 or early 192, headed by Thoas, the *strategos* himself, and got better results. Thoas returned in spring, 192, with an emissary of the king in tow. Antiochus was prepared at least to deliver a message of good will and support. Allies in Greece would enhance his status and increase his influence. Antiochus took the opportunity to reverse the propaganda that Roman *legati* had employed against him in 196 and 193. His minister Minnio addressed the Aetolian assembly, outlined the vast wealth and resources of the king, and proclaimed that Antiochus would be a genuine champion of Greek liberty, by contrast with Roman dominion.[93] The stance neither declared nor intended war. An invitation to exercise patronage in Greece was simply too

89. Polyb. 21.13.3; Diod. 29.7; Livy, 35.42.2. Alexandreia Troas is not mentioned as a target before 192. But she may well have been under attack a year or more earlier: Livy, 34.57.2, 34.59.4; see Walbank, *Commentary* III:106, with bibliography.

90. The report that he had crossed the Hellespont came to Rome via Attalus, brother of the Pergamene king, in early 192: Livy, 35.23.10. And Livy records a similar message delivered by the Aetolian Alexamenus to Nabis at about the same time: 35.35.7. Those who delivered the news, of course, had axes to grind, exaggerating the forces of the king and wrongly imputing to him the design of marching on Greece. But an expedition into Thrace to shore up his position there, a continuation of his policy of the previous several years, is entirely plausible. So, rightly, Leuze, *Hermes* 58 (1923): 244, n.2, against Holleaux, *Études* V:194, n. 1.

91. Livy, 35.12.15–18; see above p. 457. The king's envoy Hegesianax is honored in a catalogue of Delphic *proxenoi* under the year 193: *Syll.*[3] 585, n. 18. But this should not be taken as official Seleucid diplomatic contact with the Aetolian League, as Badian, *Studies*, 127; Musti, *StudClassOrient* 15 (1966): 172. Hegesianax appears in the inscription as an individual, not a royal emissary. Nor is any mention made of his ambassadorial colleague Menippus.

92. Livy, 35.13.1.

93. Livy, 35.32.2–4, 35.32.8–11: *neque omnia sub nutum dicionemque Romanam perventura . . . Aetolis sociis Antiochus quamvis inclinatas Graeciae res restituere in pristinam dignitatem.*

tempting to resist. Since Rome did not accede to an alliance, the king short-circuited Hellenic complaints by becoming guarantor of Hellenic *eleutheria* himself. The Aetolians accordingly passed a decree requesting Antiochus to be liberator of Greece and arbitrator of quarrels between Rome and Aetolia. The Seleucid monarch's prestige escalated while his posture remained pacific.[94]

Far from planning war on Rome, the king pressed ahead with unfinished business. His forces redoubled efforts to take the recalcitrant cities of Smyrna, Lampsacus, and Alexandreia Troas, which held out against his blandishments and power.[95] Additional Seleucid resources were being mobilized for a different venture altogether. Antiochus had authorized naval support for Hannibal's scheme to return to Africa and stir up trouble there—though in the end he drew back even from the limited assistance he had offered. The object may have been a diversionary tactic, thus to distract Rome's attention while the king planned a triumphant tour in Greece.[96]

In the autumn of 192, at last, Antiochus made the crossing to Greece, leading ships and troops to Demetrias, a city that had now attached itself to Aetolia and a place where Aetolians could assure the king of a warm reception. The event in retrospect was seen as the opening salvo in the Roman-Syrian war.[97] But that misunderstands both the intent of Antiochus and the impact of his arrival. The Syrian forces he brought with him could not have held even an unresisting Greece, and a war on Rome would be unthinkable.[98] Antiochus had come to make a demonstration, not to wage a war. This was a show of solidarity with Aetolia and an acceptance of his role as champion of Hellenic freedom. On that basis he received rousing welcome in Thessaly.[99]

94. Livy, 35.33.8; cf. 35.45.3. See above p. 459, and cf. the perceptive analyses of Holleaux, *Études* V: 394–395, and Badian, *Studies*, 131.

95. Livy, 35.42.2: *neque ab tergo relinquere traiciens ipse in Europam volebat.*

96. In Livy's narrative, the Aetolian Thoas talked Antiochus out of the scheme: Livy, 35.42.3–35.43.1; cf. 34.60.5. This sheds some interesting light on Aetolian policy. As their leaders knew, nothing could so readily stir Rome into action as a conflagration promoted by Hannibal. According to Nepos, *Hann.* 8.1, Hannibal actually did reach Cyrene in hopes of arousing Carthage.

97. So Polyb. 3.7.3: ἀρχὴν δὲ τοῦ πολέμου τὸν Ἀντιόχου κατάπλουν εἰς Δημη-τριάδα; Livy, 36.3.12.

98. Livy, 35.42.4–5, 35.43.2–6: *vix ad Graeciam nudam occupandam satis copiarum, nedum ad sustinendum Romanum bellum*; 35.44.3, 35.49.9–11; Appian, *Syr.* 12; Zon. 9.19.

99. Livy, 35.43.7–35.45.1. The notion of Antiochus as popular with the lower classes and opposed by Roman-backed oligarchic parties is emphasized by moderns, with little support in the evidence; cf., e.g., Musti, *StudClassOrient* 35 (1966): 163–177; Deininger, *Widerstand*, 66–96; largely based on Livy, 35.34.3; Plut. *Flam.* 15.1. See the proper skepticism of Mendels, *RivStorAnt* 8 (1978): 27–38.

Differences of opinion surfaced in Aetolia, between hard-liners and more moderate voices, as to how best to exploit the Syrian connection. The militants succeeded so far as to have the assembly name Antiochus general and head of the League. The purpose of that gesture, however, was to strengthen the king's hand in any negotiating or arbitration with Rome and to give him greater authority in the counsels of Hellas.[100] Aetolian zeal was pushing matters closer to the brink. Yet the propaganda of Antiochus, as he approached various Greek states, concentrated upon the benefits he could bring in peace and the vast wealth and power he could muster in the event of war. The king reproduced tactics that Rome had employed in the preliminaries to her contest with Philip: to proclaim his advocacy of Greek interests and to gather broad-based support among Hellenes. A show of unity and combined purpose might, in fact, discourage war.[101] Antiochus was led on by the dream of eclipsing his Seleucid forebears as protector of Greeks in Europe and Asia.

The Roman Republic had shown no more eagerness to engage in armed confrontation than had Antiochus. Rumors flew about in early 192 that the king intended to use Aetolia only as a stopover, thence to ship his fleet to Sicily. Report after report insisted that war was imminent, and Italy under direct threat. Even Livy, however, acknowledges that the stories were insubstantial, conveyed anonymously, containing numerous inventions mingled with fact.[102] The source of some of these rumors at least can be easily guessed at: the agents of Eumenes of Pergamum. Livy confirms that Attalus fanned the flames of his brother's anti-Antiochene propaganda during his visit to Rome at this time.[103] But hysteria did not sweep through the Roman senate. The *patres* had more reliable sources of information. Their envoys who had interviewed Antiochus and his ministers at Apamea and Ephesus returned to throw cold water upon hearsay accounts. They affirmed that no cause existed for war and that nothing impended from Antiochus.[104] Official decisions reflect the impact of those communications. The senate allotted Italy as province for both consuls, a clear sign that it did not expect and would not provoke an

---

100. Livy, 35.45.2–9; Appian, *Syr.* 12. See the fuller analysis above pp. 460–462.

101. Livy, 35.46–50, 36.6.3–4. See above p. 462.

102. Livy, 35.23.2–3: *rumores temere sine ullis auctoribus orti multa falsa veris miscebant;* 35.23.8, 35.24.1. The rumors do not by any means establish an Antiochus "psychosis" among the Romans; as Will, *ANRW* I:1 (1972), 603, n. 7. Similarly, Passerini, *Athenaeum* 10 (1932): 340.

103. Livy, 35.23.10: *addidit alimenta rumoribus adventus Attali.*

104. Livy, 35.22.1–3: *cum nihil quod satis maturam causam belli haberet . . . quando nihil ab Antiocho instaret.*

armed clash in the East.[105] Precautions were taken, to be sure. Among other things, they might quiet rumors and comfort allies. The senate instructed the consuls to be prepared in the event that circumstances called upon one of them to lead an army outside of Italy. Directions went to one praetor to bring naval forces to Greece in defense of allies and to another to mobilize armed support from southern Italy for possible operations in the East. And a subsequent order authorized the latter to take troops from Brundisium to Apollonia.[106] The object of these maneuvers, however, was to throw a scare into Nabis of Sparta, not to prepare for conflict with Antiochus.[107] A single diplomatic mission, headed by Flamininus, also went to Greece.[108] Further conferences with Antiochus would be pointless. The two powers guarded their reputations and competed for Hellenic opinion.

The competition rapidly escalated. Flamininus' embassy made its way through various Greek states, countering anti-Roman propaganda spread by Aetolians. His arguments failed to sway the disgruntled citizens of Demetrias, and Achaean national pride interfered with his efforts to order events in the Peloponnese.[109] The arrival of Antiochus with armed forces, however inadequate, injected a serious new element into the contest for popularity and loyalty. The king was no longer a remote Asian ruler, but an active ally of Aetolia. Amynander of Athamania expressed willingness to cooperate with him, Boeotia inclined in his direction, and he had sympathizers in Athens. A Seleucid spokesman tempted even Achaea toward a position of neutrality, calling forth an impassioned speech by Flamininus to hold the Confederacy in line.[110] Tension now approached the breaking point. The Achaeans sent garrisons to Chalcis and Athens to keep those cities out of Seleucid hands. Eumenes had personally brought a Pergamene contingent, made contact with Flamininus, and doubtless intensified his propaganda campaign against Antiochus.[111] As the year drew to a close, talk in Rome of a possible war became heated, and the *patres* began to take steps toward that eventuality. Italy was to be assigned to just one consul, the other *provincia* to be held in abeyance, thus leaving available the option of designating it as a *bellum Antiochum*.[112] A minor incident now would suffice to touch off a conflagration. It was not long in coming. Antiochus hastened to install a force in Chalcis, hoping to anticipate Achaea and Eumenes in

105. Livy, 35.20.1–2.
106. Livy, 35.20.3, 35.20.10–13, 35.22.2, 35.23.4–5, 35.24.7.
107. Livy, 35.20.13, 35.22.1–2, 35.37.3.
108. Livy, 35.23.5.          109. Sources and discussion, above pp. 458, 464–467.
110. Livy, 35.47.2–35.50.5, 36.6.1–5.          111. Livy, 35.39.1–2, 35.50.2–4.
112. Livy, 35.41.1–4.

the process. A detachment of Roman soldiers, sent to Greece originally in order to support the Achaeans against Nabis, now endeavored to add strength to the Pergamene and Achaean garrisons in
Chalcis. They were caught unawares at Delium by Seleucid forces,
most of them were cut down and some captured. The fact that Delium was a sanctuary added sacrilege to the deed. Rome could now
declare war, with the gods on her side. The incident itself was obviously unplanned and unexpected. But it supplied the *casus belli*.[113]
The formal declaration came at the beginning of the consular year
191.[114]

The rehearsal of events brings important conclusions into focus.
The two protagonists neither desired nor planned for armed conflict
with one another. Antiochus the Great had set his aim on recovery of
Seleucid dominions throughout the Near East. His entire career was
absorbed in that ambitious resolve, punctuated by remarkable successes and only temporary setbacks. The triumphal *anabasis* in Iran
and beyond, followed by the conquest of Coele Syria, stimulated the
king to implement his designs on Asia Minor, the Hellespont, and
Thrace. Italy and the Far West were not on the agenda and there is no
reason to believe that they ever would have been. Antiochus was persistent and sincere in seeking a permanent accord with Rome—which
could only ease his path by discouraging Hellenes from appeal to the
Republic as protector. He showed eagerness for alliance and offered
compromise to avoid friction, though he would not yield on his privileges as a Hellenistic ruler or surrender the claims of his Seleucid heritage. The Romans in turn made demands consonant with the Isthmian declaration and responsive to the requests of allies and friends,
but took no steps to halt the Syrian advance. Indeed they withdrew
all troops from Hellas in 194, satisfied that their interests were unaffected by Antiochus' pursuit of his purposes. The two powers had
more to gain from a *modus vivendi* than from a direct confrontation.

It is equally clear, however, that the war did not spring with sudden surprise just from the killing of Roman soldiers at Delium. A
background of propaganda and competition set Antiochus and Rome
on the course to conflict. The Republic had embraced Hellenic sloganeering in the war against Philip and proclaimed it for all the world
at the Isthmian games. "Freedom" and "autonomy" had the appropriate high-sounding ring, familiar and welcome to Greeks. Logic demanded that it be extended to Asian Greeks as well, lest the gesture

113. Livy, 35.50.7–35.51.5; Diod. 29.1; Appian, *Syr.* 15. Antiochus, so we are
told, when he discovered Roman captives at Chalcis, ordered them all released: Zon.
9.19—a plausible enough tale.
114. Livy, 36.1.1–6, 36.2.1–2.

be exposed as patent sham. But Antiochus and his predecessors on the Seleucid throne had been employing the terminology for generations. *Eleutheria* was his to bestow on Asian Greeks, not the preserve of a western usurper. The rival sloganeering caused friction, though not irremediable friction. When other states endeavored to exploit it to their own advantage, as was conventional in the Hellenistic world, they hastened the onset of strife. Cities like Lampsacus and Smyrna called upon Rome to live up to her pronouncements, Eumenes pressed for a halt to Seleucid violations of independent communities, and Aetolia summoned Antiochus to liberate Hellas from the false liberator Rome.[115] The king, who had made no headway with Rome in seeking a permanent accord, now relished the prospect of replacing her as guarantor of Greek freedom. The mottoes and catchwords came with increasing frequency as the lesser powers manipulated them and the stakes rose in 193 and 192. Pride and commitments soon left little room for backing away. In the end, Rome and Antiochus were driven to war by the logic of their own propaganda.[116]

## The War and Its Implications

The course of the war itself need not here be detailed.[117] Only the effects matter: a rapid disintegration of Seleucid dominions in the West.

Antiochus gained some initial successes in the late autumn and the winter of 192/1. His forces took Chalcis, and all of Euboea followed shortly thereafter. Boeotia came into alliance. And the king earned some military victories in Thessaly.[118] He refurbished and reinforced his image as philhellene. As he had made conspicuous sacrifice to Athena at Ilium before embarking from Asia, so now he offered

115. On the "autonomy" propaganda repeated by both sides during these years, see the sources and discussion above pp. 148–151. A good collection of the evidence on this and other elements of the propaganda war in Mastrocinque, *AttiIstVeneto* 36 (1977–78): 1–17.

116. Best treatment of this subject is still Badian, *Studies*, 112–139. Bickermann, *Hermes* 67 (1932): 66–76, recognized that neither Rome nor Antiochus desired the war, but he ascribed its outbreak to mutual fear, especially Rome's dread of powerful neighbors. This purportedly defensive motive is rejected by Harris, *War and Imperialism*, 219–223, who, however, offers nothing as substitute.

117. The events can be followed in standard accounts; e.g. Niese, *Geschichte* II: 695–707, 717–762; E. R. Bevan, *The House of Seleucus*, (London, 1902), 72–114; Holleaux, *Études* V: 397–426; De Sanctis, *Storia dei Romani* IV: 1.137–161, 168–204; Will, *Histoire politique* II: 173–187.

118. Chalcis and Euboea: Livy, 35.51.6–10; Appian, *Syr.* 15; Boeotia: Polyb. 20.7.3–5; Livy, 36.6.1–5; Thessaly: Livy, 36.9.9–36.10.2.

sacrifice to Apollo at Delphi, a deliberate advertisement of his role as patron and protector of Greeks.[119] Part of the winter was spent at Chalcis, where Antiochus married a young Chalcidian girl and celebrated the occasion with a public festival. The event later gave rise to exaggerated tales of debauchery and idleness leading to demoralization of the army and ultimate defeat. The embroidery can be dismissed. More interesting is the fact of the marriage and Antiochus' renaming of his bride as "Euboea." His previous marriage had been to a daughter of the Pontic royal house, and other marriage ties were established or offered to the rulers of Egypt, Pergamum, and Cappadocia. The political implications of these links are plain enough as demonstrations of Seleucid influence in Asia Minor and the Near East. His new wedding had parallel intentions. Antiochus' bride was "Euboea," a signal that he was no longer just an Asian monarch, but was putting down roots in mainland Greece.[120]

Success of the propaganda depended on success in the field. When the reverses came, Antiochus' support in Hellas melted away rapidly. Roman troops, now linked with Philip of Macedonia, halted Seleucid advances in Thessaly and the tide of war turned. The Aetolians did not show the same zeal in mobilization as they had in propagandizing, and produced only a minimal force. Antiochus became disgruntled with his own allies. At Thermopylae in the summer of 191, he suffered a decisive defeat.[121] The cities and states of Greece had chosen sides out of need for security, not through loyalty or ideology. The outcome of Thermopylae settled matters for almost all of them.[122] Antiochus hastily turned his back on Greece. Aetolia would continue the fight for her own purposes. But the king headed for Ephesus, his dreams of a Seleucid hegemony in Hellas now shattered.

Antiochus' Asian empire was still intact. For a moment he may have expected or hoped that Rome would settle for a *status quo ante bellum*. The Republic's forces had never yet crossed to Asia.[123] An arrangement might still be worked out under which each power would go its own way, competitors but not contestants, as had been the case through most of the 190s. If the king entertained such ideas, however, he had to abandon them swiftly. Rome might make compromises

---

119. Ilium: Livy, 35.43.3; Delphi: Livy, 36.11.6.

120. Evidence on the wedding is all hostile to Antiochus: Polyb. 20.8.1–5; Livy, 36.11.1–4; 36.17.7; Appian, *Syr.* 16; Diod. 29.2; Plut. *Flam.* 16.1–2; *Phil.* 17.1; Zon. 9.19. On Antiochus' marriage ties generally, see J. Seibert, *Historische Beiträge zu den dynastischen Verbindungen in hellenistischer Zeit* (Wiesbaden, 1967), 60–68.

121. Livy, 36.10.10–14, 36.13–19; Appian, *Syr.* 16–20, *et al.*

122. See above pp. 475–479.

123. Livy, 36.41.1.

and show generosity after the war, but she would see the fight through to its finish. Combined Roman and Pergamene fleets defeated the king's forces off the coast of Asia Minor in late summer or autumn, 191.[124] It was a harbinger of things to come. L. Scipio took command in 190, with his more illustrious brother as legate and adviser. Antiochus called up troops everywhere in his dominions, from the upper satrapies to Galatia. Unlike the situation in Greece, Seleucid rule still held demonstrable authority in the East. The long reign and exploits of Antiochus had not come for naught.[125] But he was overmatched by the skill and might of his adversaries. The Rhodian fleet had joined the fray, now in collaboration with the navies of Pergamum and Rome. When news arrived that the Roman consular army had reached the Hellespont and was on the point of crossing to Asia, Antiochus for the first time showed willingness to negotiate a settlement. Eumenes, however, interposed decisive objections: Pergamum was still under attack, and no agreement could be authorized in the absence of the consul anyway.[126] The outcome would have to be decided by force.

Decision drew near in the summer of 190. The Romans made their appeal to Hellenic sentiment, as Antiochus had done. The praetor C. Livius Salinator led Roman ships to the Hellespont in preparation for Scipio's army and made certain to preside over a sacrifice to Athena in Ilium. And when the consul crossed to Asia, he too performed this sacrifice among his initial acts, a publicizing of Rome's Trojan origins, thus going the Seleucid one better.[127] Antiochus made a last effort to employ propaganda as means of rallying support. His letter to Prusias of Bithynia alleged that Rome was bent on deposing all monarchs. But a counter-missive from the Scipios reassured Prusias and kept him out of a Seleucid alliance.[128] Rome had topped each move in the propaganda war. No avenues were left for Antiochus but to take the field. The navies of Rome and Rhodes then delivered a crushing blow to the Seleucid fleet at Myonessus.[129] The Hellespont was now entirely in Roman hands and the war at sea decided. Antiochus withdrew his garrison from Lysimacheia, thus effectively surrendering his claims on Thrace.[130] The end was in sight.

Rome's consular army crossed the Hellespont and reached Asi-

---

124. Livy, 36.43–45; Appian, *Syr.* 22.
125. Livy, 37.8.4; Appian, *Syr.* 21.
126. Polyb. 21.10.1–11; Livy, 37.18.10–37.19.6.
127. Salinator: Livy, 37.9.7; Scipio: Livy, 37.37.2–3; cf. Justin, 31.8.1–4.
128. Polyb. 21.11.1–13; Livy, 37.25.4–14; Appian, *Syr.* 23.
129. Livy, 37.26–30; Appian, *Syr.* 27.
130. Livy, 37.31.1–3; Appian, *Syr.* 28; Diod. 29.5.

atic shores in autumn, 190. Antiochus was now ready to offer generous terms: Rome could have the cities that contested his rule,
Lampsacus, Smyrna, and Alexandreia Troas, as well as any other in
Aeolia and Ionia that had cooperated with her in the war. Of Europe
the king took no further notice; it was Rome's. And he would pay half
the expenses that the war had imposed. A private parley followed
with Scipio Africanus. Antiochus' representative had instructions to
offer a handsome bribe if Scipio should help him obtain the terms requested. Nothing came of the negotiations, public or private. Antiochus had proposed a settlement on conditions roughly similar to
those demanded by Rome at Lysimacheia six years earlier. But that
was before Roman forces had entered Asia and demonstrated military
superiority. The response to Antiochus gave him no quarter: he
would pay all the war's expenses, yield up all claims to Anatolia, and
withdraw beyond the Taurus. The severity of those demands exceeded anything the king could consider. Antiochus gathered his
army and steeled himself for a final contest.[131] The battle of Magnesia,
fought probably in December, 190, administered the decisive defeat.
The forces of Rome and Pergamum, strengthened by volunteers from
Macedonia and Achaea, smashed the Seleucid army. Antiochus and
his family abandoned the field and headed for Apamea. The cities of
Asia Minor rushed to surrender themselves to Roman *fides*. The Scipios now occupied Sardis.[132]

It remained only to establish the terms of settlement. Scipio repeated with elaboration the demands made prior to the battle: withdrawal beyond the Taurus, a heavy indemnity with down payment
and twelve annual installments to cover war costs, additional cash
and grain owed to Eumenes, delivery of certain prominent enemies of
Rome, including Hannibal and Thoas, and surrender of twenty hostages. Antiochus' delegates had no recourse but to obey. The matter
would now go to Rome for ratification.[133] The substance of those
terms found acceptance by senate and people in the summer of 189.[134]
The *decem legati* were dispatched to hammer out details in conjunction
with Cn. Manlius Vulso, successor of L. Scipio as consular commander in Asia.[135] Manlius' campaign against the Galatians intervened, then further Roman military successes, and a hailing of the

---

131. Polyb. 21.13–15; Livy, 37.34–36; Appian, *Syr.* 29; Diod. 29.7–8; Justin,
31.7.4–9.

132. Livy, 37.38.1–37.45.3; Appian, *Syr.* 30–36.

133. Polyb. 21.17.1–9; Livy, 37.45.13–20; Appian, *Syr.* 38; Diod. 29.10.

134. Polyb. 21.24.2: εὐδόκησαν ταῖς γεγονημέναις ὁμολογίαις πρὸς τοὺς περὶ τὸν
Σκιπίωνα κατὰ τὴν Ἀσίαν; Livy, 37.55.2–3; Appian, *Syr.* 39.

135. Polyb. 21.24.5–9; Livy, 37.55.4.

commander for relieving the Asian Greeks of the barbaric menace.[136] It was not until spring, 188 that the final peace terms were agreed upon at Apamea. And they differed little, except for detailing of specifics, from the concessions demanded by Scipio two years before. The Romans knew what they wanted from this contest.

The Peace of Apamea has already received treatment here in a number of connections. It is time to draw the threads together.[137]

In its fundamentals this was a peace treaty imposed by the victor upon the vanquished. A number of clauses spoke directly to that fact, undisguised and acknowledged, meting out penalties to the loser. Most substantial, of course, was the war indemnity. It had long been Roman policy to require defeated foes to reimburse her for all expenses incurred—and then some. A severe imposition and a long-term payment plan would underscore the enduring superiority of the victor. The resources of Antiochus' kingdom allowed an unusually stiff assessment: 12,000 talents over a period of a dozen years, in addition to 3,000 already paid and 540,000 *modii* of grain.[138] The king would also have to discharge a handsome debt to Eumenes, spread through five yearly installments, thereby giving the Pergamene ruler conspicuous and continuing prestige in Asia Minor.[139] Antiochus made comparable commitments to Rhodes under the treaty. He would respect the property rights of Rhodians within his dominions, repay debts owed, and guarantee exemption from customs duties.[140] Rome's principal allies thus got explicit benefits. Antiochus would further fulfill the customary obligations of the vanquished: the return of war prisoners and fugitive slaves, the delivery of hostages, and (a less regular feature) the surrender of specified troublemakers.[141] All of this spoke to Roman martial pride. The conqueror claimed due rights and privileges.

Other clauses held greater significance, with long-range ends in view. The treaty of Apamea specified the elimination of any future Seleucid threat to Asia Minor and the West. Rome had resolved that the imbroglio which had provoked her entrance into Asian conflict would not be repeated. Arms limitations exemplified that resolve. Antiochus had to turn over all his elephants in Apamea and to retain no oth-

136. Polyb. 21.41.1–2; Livy, 38.37.2–4.
137. We are concerned now with relations between Rome and the Seleucid kingdom. For the benefits awarded to Eumenes and Rhodes and the implications of the settlement for Asia Minor, see above pp. 547–550.
138. Polyb. 21.43.19; cf. 21.17.5, 21.41.8; Livy, 38.38.13.
139. Polyb. 21.43.20–21; Livy, 38.38.14.
140. Polyb. 21.43.16–17; Livy, 38.38.11–12.
141. Polyb. 21.43.10–11, 21.43.22; Livy, 38.38.7, 38.38.15, 38.38.18.

ers.[142] Sharp restrictions were placed on the naval armaments of the king.[143] Antiochus was furthermore barred from recruiting in the West: he could acquire no soldiers from the Attalid kingdom, had to release those drawn from cities taken by the Romans, and was forbidden to hire mercenaries from lands under Rome's authority.[144] The pact imposed additional and more serious restrictions upon Seleucid military activities in the West. Most of Asia Minor was, in effect, declared off limits. Antiochus had to evacuate all cities, lands, villages, and fortresses on the western side of the Taurus mountain range up to the Tanais river.[145] Those boundaries were to be rigid. The treaty obliged Antiochus to remove garrisons and soldiers even from cities that he had entrusted to others, and forbade him to accept subsequent defections.[146] His ships were prohibited from sailing beyond the line of the Calycadnus, except to bear tribute, envoys, or hostages.[147]

142. Polyb. 21.43.12; Livy, 38.38.8.

143. Polyb. 21.43.13; Livy, 38.38.8; Appian, *Syr.* 39. Corruptions in both the Polybian and Livian texts forbid certainty on the specifics; see the discussion of McDonald and Walbank, *JRS* 59 (1969): 30–39; cf. Walbank, *Commentary* III:159–160.

144. Polyb. 21.43.7–8, 21.43.15; Livy, 38.38.6–7, 38.38.10; Appian, *Syr.* 39. A parallel obligation to restore men from the Seleucid kingdom did not hold for Rome—though individuals could return if they wished: Polyb. 21.43.9; Livy, 38.38.7. The ἐκ τῆς ὑπὸ 'Ρωμαίους ταττομένης probably refers to Italy. *Contra*: Will, *ANRW* I:1 (1972), 610–611.

145. The geographic limits appear in Livy's account which supplies a lacuna in the Polybian text; Polyb. 21.43.6. ἐκχωρείτω δὲ πόλεων καὶ χώρας . . . ; Livy, 38.38.4: *excedito urbibus agris vicis castellis cis Taurum montem usque ad Tanaim amnem et ea valle Tauri usque ad iuga qua in Lycaoniam vergit.* A long debate rages over identification of the "river Tanais," otherwise unknown. Emendation to *ad Halym* instead of *ad Tanaim* has been the most popular solution, on the basis of Strabo, 6.4.2 (C 287) and Appian, *Mithr.* 6. See Holleaux, *Études* V:208–243, with earlier bibliography; recently reargued by Liebmann-Frankfort, *La frontière orientale*, 48–64. The manuscript tradition, however, is strong, and emendation not easily defensible. The suggestion of McDonald, *JRS* 57 (1967): 1–8, that the "Tanais" is the upper course of the Calycadnus, has won considerable support; e.g. Will, *ANRW* I:1 (1972), 608, n. 18; Walbank, *Commentary* III:157–158; Ferrary, in Nicolet, *Rome et la conquête* 2:746–747. But the Calycadnus receives explicit mention elsewhere in the treaty: Polyb. 21.43.14; Livy, 38.38.9. It would, at the least, be misleading to refer to the upper and lower reaches of the same river by two different names in the same document without some acknowledgment. Further, if the upper Calycadnus were designated as a boundary, it is hard to see how there could have been any question as to whether Pamphylia was forbidden territory to Antiochus: Polyb. 21.46.11; Livy, 38.39.17. The matter should be left open. Holleaux, *Études* V: 213–216, took Polybius' ἐκχωρεῖν to mean not simply "evacuate" but "to renounce all claim to." That applies a much wider meaning than the context permits. Reference to Antiochus' removal of nothing from this area except the arms borne by his own soldiers shows that "evacuation" is meant here: 21.43.6. Livy correctly translates: *excedito.*

146. Polyb. 21.43.18; Livy, 38.38.12.

147. Polyb. 21.43.14; Livy, 38.38.9; Appian, *Syr.* 39.

And a key clause made explicit the ban on military adventurism in the West: it denied Antiochus the right to make war on the islands or anywhere in Europe.[148]

These two categories of provisions, interspersed in the document, expressed the superiority of the victor and the consequences of defeat. They imposed penalties and obligations on the one hand and set boundaries to future ambitions on the other. Yet the peace of Apamea wore a different visage as well. Rome embraced features of Hellenistic diplomacy and entered a concert of Hellenistic powers. Antiochus the Great was allowed due recognition in the pact, still ruler of the Seleucid kingdom and an independent force on the international scene. The treaty, in fact, instituted a *philia* for all time between the king and the Republic, in proper Hellenic form.[149] The signatories made mutual commitments: neither would give aid or passage to the enemies of the other. This was no military alliance, offensive or defensive; but the reciprocal commitment gave voice to a Hellenistic *entente* designed to have enduring force.[150] The treaty cut off the western reach of Seleucid imperialism, but did not infringe the integrity of the kingdom itself. Antiochus had full freedom to defend his holdings against attack even from those cities and people against whom he was precluded from waging offensive war—though he could not add them to his dominions.[151] Disputes and grievances arising out of these quarrels would go to arbitration, the conventional Greek remedy.[152] The document closes on a formal note of equality: any additions or subtractions to the agreement require common consent of the parties.[153]

The meaning of this pact needs to be understood without hindsight or distortion. To most interpreters it has represented the establishment of Roman hegemony in Asia: the inequality inherent in the document advertised Rome's superiority, Seleucid military capacity was crippled, the benefits to friends and allies created a Roman protectorate, the territorial limits imposed by the peace produced a kind

---

148. Polyb. 21.43.4: μὴ πολεμῆσαι δὲ ᾿Αντίοχον τοῖς ἐπὶ ταῖς νήσοις μηδὲ τοῖς κατὰ τὴν Εὐρώπην; Livy, 38.38.3.

149. Polyb. 21.43.1: φιλίαν ὑπάρχειν ᾿Αντιόχῳ καὶ ῾Ρωμαίοις εἰς ἅπαντα τὸν χρόνον; Livy, 38.38.2; cf. Appian, *Syr.* 38; Diod. 31.8.1. The conditional clause, ποιοῦντι τὰ κατὰ τὰς συνθήκας, had precedents in earlier treaties; cf. Walbank, *Commentary* III:156. It is erroneous to take the clause as a contrivance on Rome's part, whereby she could scrap the treaty and provoke war through declaring Antiochus' noncompliance; as Polacek, *Listy Filologické* 92 (1969): 12; Liebmann-Frankfort, *La frontière orientale*, 67.

150. Polyb. 21.43.2–3; Livy, 38.38.2–3.

151. Polyb. 21.43.24–25; Livy, 38.38.16.

152. Polyb. 21.43.26; a confused version in Livy, 38.38.17.

153. Polyb. 21.43.27; imprecisely rendered by Livy, 38.38.18.

of frontier zone which defined Roman interests and influence.[154] A different emphasis will allow for a more balanced assessment. The treaty exacted reparations for the war and required surrender of captives, hostages, and war criminals. Those provisions, however, characterized a postwar settlement; they did not define relations between the protagonists. Other clauses set boundaries to Seleucid westward expansion: holdings in Asia Minor were to be abandoned, ventures into the Aegean and Europe prohibited. The stipulations did not produce a Roman hegemony; rather they achieved augmented power for Eumenes and Rhodes, the new sentinels of security in Anatolia. Measures of that sort aimed to recreate the stability in western Asia Minor, the Aegean, and Thrace that had been upset by the aggrandizements of Antiochus the Great. The restriction on armaments would further foster a sense of security in the region. In this context, the *amicitia* "for all time" fits appropriately. It proclaimed harmony and an equilibrium among the powers. An enduring peace would allow Rome to tend to matters nearer home and of more immediate interest—namely Liguria, Gaul, and Spain. The purpose was not to emasculate the Seleucid kingdom.[155] Antiochus had free rein to consolidate and entrench his control in the center of his empire, in the upper satrapies, and in Coele Syria; indeed nothing prevented an expedition against Egypt, should the opportunity arise. The strain on the treasury wrought by indemnity payments would, of course, postpone any expensive crusades. But the kingdom was wealthy and recovery foreseeable. The ban on elephants, the reduction of the navy, and the restraints placed on recruitment aimed to erase concerns about Seleucid expansion in the West. If a rebuilding of forces directed itself to movement elsewhere, Rome was unlikely to raise objections.[156] Antiochus sat securely on his throne. His Seleucid realm, diminished but far from demolished, remained a dominant force in the East. He had paid the price of war with Rome. But the arrangements at Apamea made him an associate in the enterprise to maintain Mediterranean concord.

154. The inequality of the pact is stressed by Polacek, *RIDA* 18 (1971): 602–613, who fails to distinguish between provisions which impose short-term penalties and those which establish long-term conditions of amity. The crippling of Seleucid power: De Sanctis, *Storia dei Romani* IV:1.201; a Roman protectorate: Dahlheim, *Struktur und Entwicklung*, 266–267; Will, *ANRW* I:1 (1972), 615–616; the frontier zone: Liebmann-Frankfort, *La frontière orientale*, 41–48.

155. So, rightly, Holleaux, *Études* V:425–426.

156. Paltiel, *Antichthon* 13 (1979): 30–35, recognizes that Antiochus III's successors took liberties with some of the provisions of the treaty, but wrongly concludes that they were binding only upon the king who signed it.

## The Aftermath of Apamea

Antiochus the Great perished in the year after Apamea. Financial troubles engendered by exactions under the treaty prompted an expedition to Elymais, where the king's attempt to confiscate the temple treasury ended in his death.[157] His son and successor, Seleucus IV, inherited a kingdom under the cloud of military defeat and economic difficulty. His reign of a dozen years (187–175) has left little mark on history. Seleucus acquired a reputation for excessive caution, weakness, and inactivity.[158] Did the Seleucid realm then sink into decline, truncated and enfeebled, its fate to be that of a second-class power?

The repute of Seleucus IV is undeserved. Under the circumstances, caution in internal and external policy was inevitable. Silver seems to have been in short supply, doubtless a consequence of the indemnity.[159] Seleucus also, it appears, fell slightly behind in his annual payments.[160] The loss of Asia Minor must have had repercussions elsewhere in the dominions of the monarchy. An independence movement surfaced in Armenia where two native dynasts, appointees of Antiochus III, shook off allegiance to the crown and divided the land between them.[161] Antiochus' last and fatal expedition to Elymais may have had political, as well as economic, motivation: the need to shore up Seleucid control in the region. No clear evidence survives on the upper satrapies, although it would not be rash to conclude that the hold of the Syrian monarchy was shaky indeed.[162] Yet the heartland of the empire remained intact: Cilicia, Syria, Coele Syria, the Fertile Crescent, Media, and Susiana. Seleucus IV still had an extensive realm to administer. More to the point, however, he had not abandoned the goal of leadership within the community of Hellenic nations, a goal cherished by his activist forebears. It is a mistake to assume that Rome had foreclosed the possibility of such ambition.

Since so little information remains on the reign of Seleucus IV, the few surviving items take on greater meaning. They disclose a king very different from Seleucus' image as timid and idle. And they shed light also on the relationship between Rome and the Syrian kingdom as it evolved out of Apamea. In 187, near the beginning of his reign,

157. Diod. 28.3, 29.15; Justin, 32.2.1–2. On the date, July, 187, see Sachs and Wiseman, *Iraq* 16 (1954): 207.

158. Polyb. fr. 96: εὐλάβειαν καὶ ἀπραγίαν; Appian, *Syr.* 66: ἀπράκτως ἅμα καὶ ἀσθενῶς; Porphyry, *FGH*, 260 F 48.

159. H. Seyrig, *Syria* 35 (1958): 194–196; Boehringer, *Zur Chronologie*, 96.

160. Cf. Livy, 42.6.6–7; 2 Macc. 8:10.

161. Strabo, 11.14.5 (C 528); 11.14.15 (C 531); cf. Appian, *Syr.* 45, 66.

162. Cf. Mørkholm, *Antiochus IV*, 28–29.

Seleucus dispatched envoys to the Achaean Confederacy, seeking renewal of *philia* and offering a gift of ten long ships. Achaeans had fought on the side of Rome and Pergamum in the previous war, even engaging Seleucus directly as he led a contingent for his father. The new king now sought to relegate that antagonism to oblivion. Achaea declined the ships but renewed the "friendship."[163] The gift itself, even if a gesture, carries significance: the Syrian monarchy was still a naval power.[164] Further, we may be sure that Seleucus' agents did not stop in Achaea alone. An inscription of 186 happens to reveal an exchange of ambassadors between Athens and the Syrian court.[165] Diplomatic relations resumed and were advertised. The mission or missions served to show that neither Thermopylae nor Magnesia had terminated Seleucid influence in Hellas.

The influence extended beyond mainland Greece. Seleucus gave the name Demetrius to his first-born in 186, a name hitherto closely associated with the Antigonid dynasty and not previously found among the Seleucids. The choice was deliberate, a sign that the king angled for a revival of relations between the Macedonian and Syrian royal houses that had so frequently held during the third century. With Macedonia, as with Achaea, Seleucus was binding up old ties that had been severed in the Antiochene war. The overture found welcome. Within a decade, Seleucus' daughter became the bride of Perseus, the new ruler of Macedonia. Rhodian ships ferried the wedding party to Perseus, a scene that dramatized the recovery of Seleucid international esteem.[166] Hindsight wrongly fixes this event as an anti-Roman coalition.[167] In fact, it was a dynastic marriage of the traditional sort, a shifting of alliance in the familiar game of Hellenistic diplomacy. Insofar as the coalition had a target, it was Eumenes II of Pergamum, not Rome. The Republic was unperturbed. Seleucus, far from idle or passive, had taken the initiative toward this union.[168]

---

163. Polyb. 22.7.4, 22.10.13. Diodorus, 29.17, wrongly says that the ships were accepted. On the date, see Errington, *Philopoemen*, 257–263.

164. The figure of ten ships corresponds to the limit fixed by the terms of Apamea: Polyb. 21.43.13; Livy, 38.38.8. But Seleucus was surely not stripping his kingdom of its last ship.

165. W. K. Pritchett and B. D. Merritt, *The Chronology of Hellenistic Athens* (Cambridge, Mass., 1940), 117–118.

166. Polyb. 25.4.7–10; cf. Livy, 42.12.3–4; Appian, *Mac.* 11.2. J. Helliesen, in Dell, *Ancient Macedonian Studies in Honor of Charles F. Edson* (1981): 224–228, suggests that Seleucus may have married an Antigonid princess.

167. Cf., e.g., Meloni, *Perseo*, 122–125; Mørkholm, *Antiochus IV*, 34–35; Seibert, *Historische Beiträge*, 43; Will, *Histoire politique* II:255. See above p. 404.

168. Cf. Livy, 42.12.3: *Seleuci filiam duxisse eum* [*sc.* Perseus], *non petentem, sed petitum ultro.*

Alliance with Macedonia and cooperation with Rhodes not only elevated his stature but undermined the ascendancy of the Pergamene. Seleucus had even contemplated an expedition across the Taurus. Pharnaces of Pontus made a tempting offer of 500 talents in the late 180s for Seleucid troops in his war on Eumenes. Seleucus went so far as to mobilize his forces, but reconsidered the project and abandoned it. A direct violation of the Apamea pact would run too large a risk.[169] The fact that he consented to the project in the first place and nearly went through with it is of the greatest interest. Seleucus IV found considerable room to operate in the dozen years after Apamea. Rome might take umbrage at flagrant violations, but she did not intend the treaty to reduce Syria to impotence. Seleucus began the process of putting his realm back into the center of Hellenistic politics—and generated no Roman protest.

Seleucus was assassinated in September, 175, the victim of a palace conspiracy. The assassin Heliodorus, minister to the king, stepped in as spokesman for Seleucus' son, still a small boy and now proclaimed ruler.[170] The long-range plan, however, did not come to fruition. Seleucus' younger brother, Antiochus IV Epiphanes, had spent about a decade in Rome, the prize hostage among those surrendered by his father after the war.[171] Some time before 178/7 a hostage exchange released Antiochus: his nephew Demetrius, son of Seleucus IV, had come to replace him. Seleucus had shipped Demetrius there as a gesture of good will, a sign of continued harmony between the Republic and the Seleucids. Antiochus was in Athens when word arrived of Seleucus' murder.[172] The prince soon received powerful support for his own claims. Eumenes II ordered Pergamene armed forces

169. Diod. 29.24: ἔννοιαν δὲ λαβὼν τῶν πρὸς Ῥωμαίους τῷ πατρὶ γενομένων συνθηκῶν, καθ᾽ ἃς οὐκ ἐξῆν . . . On the five hundred talents, see Polyb. fr. 96. There is nothing in Diodorus' text to show that *Rome* called Seleucus to his senses, as is assumed by Liebmann-Frankfort, *La frontière orientale*, 77–78. Flamininus' embassy to Prusias in 183 was to include a visit with Seleucus, for reasons unspecified: Polyb. 23.5.1; probably little more than a courtesy call. It is, in any case, too early to be taken in connection with Seleucus' near participation in the war between Pharnaces and Eumenes; Walbank, *Commentary* III:221.

170. Appian, *Syr.* 45.

171. Appian, *Syr.* 39.

172. Appian, *Syr.* 45. On relations between Antiochus and Demetrius, not necessarily hostile, see Paltiel, *Antichthon* 13 (1979): 42–47. It is often surmised that Rome issued the directive to substitute Demetrius for Antiochus, for she had grown suspicious of Seleucus; e.g., Bevan, *House of Seleucus*, 124; Mørkholm, *Antiochus IV*, 36; Will, *ANRW* I:1 (1972), 617. Nothing in the evidence implies Roman initiative, and Polybius indicates the reverse; 31.2.2: δοθῆναι γὰρ ὑπὸ Σελεύκου τοῦ πατρὸς τῆς ἐκείνου πίστεως ἕνεκεν. The hypothesis is now nearly excluded by a new discovery showing that Antiochus IV was in Athens by 178/7, thus not readily manipulatable by Rome; *Hesperia* 51 (1982): 61–62.

to escort Antiochus to the Syrian border and to intimidate his enemies. Heliodorus vanished from the scene and Antiochus IV took the throne.[173] Scholars have conceived an even more elaborate plot: the assassination of Seleucus, elimination of Heliodorus, and installation of Antiochus were all orchestrated by Rome.[174] The reconstruction is fanciful and unnecessary. Eumenes found the opportunity tailor-made for his interests. Establishment of Antiochus on the Seleucid throne, a man beholden to Pergamum, would end the tension between the two realms and give Eumenes the upper hand. It was standard Hellenistic maneuvering.

The new king and his policies have received extensive treatment elsewhere.[175] What needs stress here simply is the continuity in attitude and aims from the regime of Seleucus IV to that of Antiochus Epiphanes. The shift in political alignment from opposition to cooperation with the Attalids was ephemeral and secondary. The drive for consolidation of the realm and restoration of Seleucid international prestige remained central. In this regard Antiochus IV did not represent a new departure but built on the work of his predecessor. Seleucus had begun the process of forging diplomatic links in mainland Greece and establishing alliances with Hellenistic monarchs. The known examples of Achaea, Athens, Macedonia, and Pontus probably constituted only a fraction of Seleucus' endeavors; scantiness of evidence conceals the rest. Antiochus moved along the same paths more speedily and more successfully.

Success in wooing the cities of Greece proper, the islands, the Hellespont, and western Asia Minor can be read in the documents: dedications and benefactions by Antiochus, decrees in his honor or in honor of his ministers, embassies to his court, memorials to his deeds.[176] The king was assiduous in courting favor and spreading his fame. The gifts and awards indicate a resurgence of prosperity in the realm, a fact further borne out by the increased volume of coinage evident after the first few years of the reign.[177]

173. *OGIS*, 248; Appian, *Syr.* 45. On the boy-king Antiochus, his circumstances, and his fate, see especially Mørkholm, *ANSMN* 11 (1964): 63–76; *Antiochus IV*, 44–50; bibliography on this much discussed subject in Walbank, *Commentary* III:284–285.

174. So, e.g., A. Bouché-Leclercq, *Histoire des Seleucides* (Paris, 1913–14) I:241; Will, *Histoire politique* II:255–256; *ANRW* I:1 (1972), 617–618; Bruzzi, *I sistemi informativi*, 238–240; cf. Walbank, *Commentary* III:285.

175. Most notably in Mørkholm, *Antiochus IV, passim*. Add also the recent special studies of Bunge, *Historia* 23 (1974): 57–85; *Historia* 24 (1975): 164–188.

176. See above pp. 189–190. One will consult with profit the collection and discussion of material by Mørkholm, *Antiochus IV*, 51–63; cf. Walbank, *Commentary* III: 287–288. Note the remark of Polybius, 26.1.10: ἐν δὲ ταῖς πρὸς τὰς πόλεις θυσίαις καὶ ταῖς πρὸς τοὺς θεοὺς τιμαῖς πάντας ὑπερέβαλλε τοὺς βεβασιλευκότας.

177. Boehringer, *Zur Chronologie*, 86.

Antiochus, like his predecessor, felt relatively unencumbered by Roman power. Polite diplomatic exchanges maintained cordiality. The pact of Apamea did not prevent him from framing alliances abroad or strengthening control within his dominions. The ties to Eumenes and through him to the house of Cappadocia gave Antiochus a diplomatic foothold in Asia Minor. And he could soon turn attention to a still more coveted prize: the land of the Nile.

Most of the shadows cast by Apamea had now been dispelled. Antiochus had a free hand to entrench personal control of his kingdom. A year and a half passed on the throne before he even sent an embassy to Rome.[178] At that point, however, a sense of some urgency seems to have attended the mission. Antiochus' minister Apollonius appeared before the *patres* with apologies for delinquency in remitting the annual indemnity payments: he had now brought a lump sum to cover arrears and settle the debt, as well as a generous gift of gold vases, 500 pounds in weight. Apollonius conveyed his master's greetings and warm wishes, with reminiscences of the kind treatment and benefits he had received during his years in Rome, treated more as king than as hostage. Antiochus now sought formal renewal of his *amicitia* with the Republic, presenting himself as a loyal ally of Rome ready to perform her every command.[179]

What occasioned that presentation by the Seleucid ruler? It can hardly be dismissed as routine. Antiochus had sent no previous embassy to Rome. Indeed this is the first recorded Seleucid delegation to the senate since the peace of Apamea, itself a notable and noteworthy fact.[180] Payment of overdue indemnity does not suffice as explanation. And the conventional *amicitiam renovare* could have come at any time. Antiochus' expensive gifts and expansive protestations of loyalty suggest something more. The idea that he came to show solidarity with Rome in anticipation of a war with Perseus carries little weight. Rome was not yet considering such a move in early 173.[181] The embassy arises out of a Near Eastern context, not a Roman one. An ancient Hellenistic rivalry, it can be argued, lies behind this turn of events: the contest of Seleucid and Ptolemy for the coveted lands of Coele Syria.

178. There had been a Roman mission to Syria in 174: Livy, 42.6.12. Its purpose is unrecorded and uncertain. Livy's account suggests a warm reception at the court. In all probability, this embassy may have had a variety of duties abroad, Syria not being its only destination, but the object merely of a courtesy call.

179. Livy, 42.6.6–9: *petere regem ut, quae cum patre suo societas atque amicitia fuisset, ea secum renovaretur, imperaretque sibi populus Romanus, quae bono fidelique socio regi essent imperanda.*

180. Some envoys may, of course, have accompanied Demetrius to Rome when he came as a hostage in exchange for Antiochus.

181. See above pp. 406–408. The idea is advocated by Mørkholm, *Antiochus IV*, 64–65.

The rulers of Egypt had not ceased to cast longing eyes upon those lands since their conquest nearly a generation before by Antiochus the Great. Report has it that Ptolemy V intended a recapture of the region during his reign in the 180s. Nothing came of it; but the ambition is plausible and the report credible.[182] Antiochus Epiphanes had reason to be concerned for his dominions upon accession to the throne in a shaky and uncertain situation. His sister Cleopatra had ruled in Egypt, the widow of Ptolemy V, until her death in 176. The palace ministers Eulaeus and Lenaeus took over as regents for the young Ptolemy Philometor and soon began to revive Egyptian claims on Coele Syria as a Ptolemaic legacy.[183] Antiochus took his precautions, preparing for the eventuality of conflict. The king appeared at the penteteric games for Hercules in Tyre probably in 174, thus showing himself in the disputed area and calling forth demonstrations of loyalty from various cities and peoples—like the "Antiochenes in Jerusalem."[184] At this time or not much later Antiochus sent his representative Apollonius to attend a festival in honor of young Ptolemy Philometor. Formal relations evidently still held between the powers. But Apollonius reported hostility to Antiochus in the Egyptian court. The king swiftly took measures to provide for the security of his realm: he made personal trips to Joppa and Jerusalem and he encamped an army in Phoenicia. Precise dating of these events is unattainable, although they fall somewhere within 174 or 173.[185]

In light of such circumstances, the Seleucid mission to Rome in early 173 becomes intelligible and meaningful. It is hardly coincidence that the head of that mission, Apollonius, is the very man who had served Antiochus as governor of Coele Syria and Phoenicia and who witnessed the hostility to him on the visit to Egypt.[186] A prospective clash between Egypt and Syria lurks here in the background. The evidence fits together, and the connection, rarely considered in modern works, is almost inevitable. Antiochus Epiphanes, who had seen no

182. Diod. 29.29; Porphyry, *FGH*, 260, F48.

183. They alleged that Antiochus III had pledged it to Ptolemy V upon his marriage to the Seleucid king's daughter Cleopatra: Polyb. 28.20.9; Appian, *Syr.* 5; Jos. *Ant.* 12.154; Porphyry, *FGH*, 260 F 47.

184. 2 Macc. 4:18–20. On the chronology, see the arguments of Bunge, *Historia* 23 (1974): 63–66.

185. 2 Macc. 4:21–22. The events precede the deposition of Jason from the high priesthood in Jerusalem, which came in 173/2: 2 Macc. 4:7, 4.23. The πρωτοκλίσια or πρωτοκλήσια of Ptolemy, attended by Apollonius, is unhappily neither datable nor identifiable with accuracy. Bunge, *Historia* 23 (1974): 70–72, offers the tempting solution that it celebrated the first anniversary of Philometor's coronation, thus placing it in spring, 174. A more cautious assessment by Habicht, *2. Makkabäerbuch*, 219; Walbank, *Commentary* III:323–324.

186. On Apollonius as governor of Coele Syria and Phoenicia, see 2 Macc. 3:5, 4:4; cf. Abel, *Les livres des Maccabées*, 317–318.

prior need to lavish gifts on Rome, to promise her his fidelity, or to seek public renewal of his *amicitia*, found compelling reasons in 173. Friction with Egypt had resumed, and the king needed assurance of Rome's good will—or, at least, a public expression thereof, which could be used to intimidate his Egyptian foes. The senate, innocent of interest and information on quarrels between Syria and Egypt, received Antiochus' tribute and gifts most graciously, renewed the *amicitia*, and made generous provision for the delegation.[187]

Our sources divide on the ascription of responsibility for the Sixth Syrian War. The ministers of young Ptolemy VI, the much maligned Eulaeus and Lenaeus, bear the brunt of blame in the tradition. A eunuch and a Syrian slave respectively, they were obvious candidates for depiction as the evil influence on the boy-king and the perpetrators of a war from whose consequences they received their just deserts.[188] Other evidence fixes blame upon Antiochus. Jewish sources charge him with having in mind an invasion of Egypt from the time he had established his rule: since minors sat on the Lagid throne, Antiochus could not resist the temptation to seize it for himself.[189] And the charge does not depend on Jewish sources alone.[190] The affix-

---

187. Livy, 42.6.10–12. The connection is made by Otto, *AbhMünch* 11 (1934): 32–33. But his reconstruction depends, in part, on an erroneous dating of the πρωτο-κλίσια of Ptolemy Philometor to his official marriage in 175/4: *op. cit.*, 13–19. In fact, the marriage took place prior to the accession of Antiochus IV; A. F. Shore and H. S. Smith, *JEA* 45 (1959): 52–60. And Otto wrongly brings Livy, 42.29.6 into the reckoning; *op. cit.*, 33, n. 3—that passage says nothing about Antiochus' promises to Rome regarding Egypt. It is true indeed that no evidence exists for Apollonius' even mentioning the Egyptian issue in Rome, a fact stressed by Mørkholm, *Antiochus IV*, 65, and Walbank, *Commentary* III:324. Antiochus' purpose, however, was not to raise the alarm over Egyptian aggression. There had been none as yet. The king wanted merely a public show of solidarity with Rome, thus to deter Egyptian aggression—or, perhaps, to smooth a path for his own. That we cannot know for certain whether Apollonius' trip to Egypt preceded or followed the mission to Rome is similarly true. But the former provides so logical a background for the latter that the hypothesis of its precedence in time has considerable force. Bunge's chronology, *Historia* 23 (1974): 70–72, allows easily for that sequence, though he never makes the connection and omits discussion of Apollonius' Roman mission.

188. See, especially, Diod. 30.15–16, which evidently stems from Polybius; cf. Polyb. 28.20.5, 28.21.1–5; Livy, 42.29.7; Diod. 30.2; Porphyry, *FGH*, 260, F49. The depiction is largely accepted by Otto, *AbhMünch* 11 (1934): 24–27; Swain, *CP* 39 (1944): 75. But see Mørkholm, *ClMed* 22 (1961): 32–43.

189. 1 Macc. 1:16: καὶ ἡτοιμάσθη ἡ βασιλεία ἐνώπιον Ἀντιόχου καὶ ὑπέλαβεν βασιλεῦσαι γῆς Αἰγύπτου, ὅπως βασιλεύσῃ ἐπὶ τὰς δύο βασιλείας; Jos. *Ant.* 12.242.

190. Cf. Justin, 34.2.7; Appian, *Syr.* 66; Zon. 9.25; and, especially, Livy, 42.29.5: *Antiochus imminebat quidem Aegypti regno, et pueritiam regis et inertiam tutorum spernens.* Mørkholm, *Antiochus IV*, 68, n. 16, summarily dismisses the testimony against Antiochus as "worthless"—but fails to cite either Appian or Livy in this connection. For Will, *Histoire politique* II:265–266, this is the *Roman* tradition, misled by hindsight after the war, an explanation which can hardly account for Justin.

ing of responsibility, however, misses the point. Coele Syria and Phoenicia, as prizes of conquest, were rarely far from the thoughts of either Lagid or Seleucid. The ministers of Ptolemy Philometor staked their claim upon the supposed promises of Antiochus III, grandfather of the royal youth. That propaganda, coming as it did at the time of upheaval and a change of rulers in the Seleucid house, was enough to alarm Antiochus and to provoke a military buildup. Under such circumstances, it matters little who struck the first blow. The old Hellenistic quarrel set events in motion—and it provoked a flurry of diplomatic dealings with Rome.

The senate had treated Antiochus' delegates with courtesy and generosity in 173. And why not? They had settled the overdue indemnity, brought gifts besides, and asked nothing but a formalistic renewal of *amicitia*. The *patres* were happy enough to oblige. At about the same time they dispatched envoys to the East, among whose tasks was renewing *amicitia* with Egypt.[191] Rome maintained an even-handed attitude. It must have satisfied Antiochus, and possibly the rulers of Egypt as well. Neither party would welcome active Roman interference. A show of Rome's favor, however, might help to deter or intimidate the foe.

Restraint held for nearly four years. The reasons escape secure conjecture. The ministers in Egypt perhaps awaited the majority of Ptolemy VI; and Antiochus awaited the time when the ambiguity of a joint rule with his nephew, son of Seleucus IV, could be resolved and his own rule would be uncontested. Both of these events occurred in 170/69.[192] Evidence fails us almost altogether for the intervening years. Roman legates who moved about the Greek world in the autumn of 172 to test sentiments in the event of war with Perseus naturally found welcome reception at the courts of both Antioch and Alexandria.[193] In early 171 representatives from both courts were in Rome

191. Livy, 42.6.4.

192. The *anecleteria* of Ptolemy VI: Polyb. 28.12.8–10—probably winter 170/69; Otto, *AbhMünch* 11 (1934): 44–45. This would presumably have strengthened the hand of Eulaeus and Lenaeus, regents for the young king. Less likely is the suggestion of Swain, *CP* 39 (1944): 80–81, that this move was manipulated by an opposition group in Egypt. The event occurred at a time not far distant from declaration of a joint-rule of Ptolemy VI, his sister-wife, and his younger brother; E. G. Turner, *BRL* 31 (1948): 148–161; J. D. Ray, *The Archive of Hor* (London, 1976), 125. The purpose surely was to give strength and legitimacy to the regime. A good summary of the chronological problems and scholarly views in Walbank, *Commentary* III: 322–323. The joint rule is attested in a new document: P. Aupert, *BCH* 106 (1982): 263–277—though this probably belongs to 168–164, rather than to 170. Antiochus Epiphanes' execution of the young boy who had served as figurehead co-ruler came in August, 170; Sachs and Wiseman, *Iraq* 16 (1954): 208; see the cogent discussion by Mørkholm, *Antiochus IV*, 42–49.

193. Livy, 42.26.7–8; Appian, *Mac.* 11.4.

pledging active and vigorous support for the Macedonian war.[194] In the event, neither one provided assistance of any substance, being embroiled in their own conflict. Protestations of good will toward the Republic, however, afforded important publicity.[195] Open hostilities between Egypt and Syria, interestingly enough, still lay in the future. Common assumption explains the timing of the outbreak in terms of the Roman-Macedonian war: with the western power occupied, the Near Eastern states could feel free to engage one another.[196] In fact, war raged between Rome and Perseus for nearly two years before the outbreak of hostilities in Egypt. There can be no direct connection. Internal circumstances, not Rome's situation, triggered events in the Near East: the new confidence of the Ptolemaic regime and the unchallenged control in Syria by Antiochus Epiphanes.

An Egyptian attack opened the war in late 170 or early 169. Whether it should be described as aggressive or preemptive makes little difference. Antiochus was ready, more than ready. The first battles, in fact, took place on Egyptian soil. The Seleucid king knew what was coming. He had prepared both his war machine and his propaganda engine. He warned of Ptolemaic mobilization in advance, then evidently waited for Egypt to make the first strike—thereby to launch his own with greater justification.[197] Antiochus' forces had all the better of it, smashing the armies of Egypt at Mt. Casius and then taking Pelusium. In the course of the campaign, young Ptolemy Philometor headed for Samothrace, on advice of the regents Eulaeus and Lenaeus. The latter themselves soon vanish from the scene. The route to Alexandria lay open to Antiochus Epiphanes in the spring of 169. His successes had been swift and convincing.[198]

Antiochus' aims are no mystery: to extend Seleucid suzerainty

194. Livy, 42.29.6–7.

195. Antiochus twice received overtures from Perseus, but held himself aloof from that alliance: Livy, 42.26.8; Polyb. 27.7.15.

196. Livy, 42.29.5–6, ascribes such motivation to Antiochus; accepted by Otto, AbhMünch 11 (1934): 43–44.

197. The first battles took place in Egypt: Porphyry, FGH, 260 F 49; cf. Diod. 30.14, 30.16. Antiochus' envoys had earlier informed Rome about Ptolemy's preparations for attack, in the autumn of 170: Polyb. 27.19; cf. 28.1.7. This put the Seleucid in a better propaganda position. War had broken out by early 169, according to Polyb. 28.1.1. Yet the fact, if it is a fact, was unknown in Achaea in spring, 169: Polyb. 28.12.8–9. So the initial attack may have come in the spring; Walbank, Commentary III: 321–324, with bibliography.

198. Antiochus' opening victory: Porphyry, FGH, 260 F 49; Diod. 30.14, 30.16; the flight of Philometor: Polyb. 28.21.1–5; Diod. 30.17; cf. 1 Macc. 1:18; the capture of Pelusium: Polyb. 28.18; Diod. 30.18. The convoluted chronological problems need not be examined here; see, especially, Otto, AbhMünch 11 (1934): 40–49; Bickermann, ChronEg 27 (1952): 396–403; Mørkholm, Antiochus IV, 73–77; Will, Histoire politique II: 266–268; Walbank, Commentary III: 27, 352, 356–357.

from Coele Syria to Egypt itself. What form the suzerainty took is a secondary matter, unnecessary to resolve here. Antiochus gave cordial hearing to a number of Hellenic missions, from Athens, Achaea, and elsewhere who sought to mediate on behalf of Philometor, now back in Alexandria under the tutelage of a new group of advisers. The Seleucid monarch played his role of philhellene to the hilt, but insisted on ancestral rights to Coele Syria and continued on his march to Alexandria. An arrangement was entered into between Antiochus and the young Egyptian ruler, an arrangement whose precise nature is unknown but whose general import is clear enough: Ptolemy Philometor officially sat on the throne, but Antiochus adopted the posture of his protector and patron. Seleucid overlordship now extended through much of Egypt. Antiochus Epiphanes neared an accomplishment that had eluded even his great ancestor Antiochus Megas. He courted Hellenic opinion by presenting himself as defender of the Ptolemaic dynasty rather than its oppressor, while in fact making the Ptolemaic ruler his personal dependent.[199]

Epiphanes' plans, on the brink of fruition, soon met frustration. The Alexandrians rejected a puppet king and elevated Philometor's younger brother Euergetes and his sister Cleopatra to a joint rulership. The turn of affairs compelled Antiochus to move against Alexandria in force, though he could still parade the plausible pretext of backing the legitimate monarch's claim against the usurpers. The expedition, however, ran into stiff opposition. The Alexandrians stubbornly resisted siege, unmoved by Seleucid propaganda. Antiochus gave up and returned to Syria in late 169.[200] The reasons for

199. Antiochus' cordial dealings with Greek embassies are recorded by Polyb. 28.19–20. Philometor had returned from Samothrace, or perhaps never reached there: Polyb. 28.19.1. The arrangement between Antiochus and Philometor is alluded to but not detailed by Polyb. 28.23.4: πρὸς δὲ τοῦτον καὶ διαλελύσθαι πάλαι καὶ φίλους ὑπάρχειν; cf. Suda, s.v. Ἡρακλείδης Ὀξυρυγχίτης. On Antiochus' control of much of the country, see Polyb. 28.19.1, 28.20.1. Polybius subsequently accuses Antiochus of neglecting his arrangement with Ptolemy: 29.26.1; cf. 30.26.9. In Diodorus' formulation Antiochus deceived Ptolemy and endeavored to destroy him: Diod. 30.18.2. Otto, Abh-Münch 11 (1934): 51–57, takes these passages in conjunction with a fragment of Porphyry, FGH, 260 F 49, who indicates that Antiochus took the Egyptian throne himself and made the land subject to him; cf. also Fraser, Ptolemaic Alexandria II: 211–212. This is hard to square with the rest of our evidence which consistently has the Seleucid king setting up Philometor as a figurehead: Polyb. 28.23.4; Diod. 31.1; Livy, 44.19.8, 45.11.1, 45.11.8. The papyrological testimony, referring to the regnal years of Philometor, stands in support; T. C. Skeat, JEA 47 (1961): 107–112. See the cogent arguments of Mørkholm, Antiochus IV, 80–84; cf. Will, Histoire politique II: 268–269; Walbank, Commentary III: 357–358.

200. The elevation of Euergetes and Cleopatra: Polyb. 29.23.4; Livy, 44.19.6–8; the assault by Antiochus: Livy, 44.19.7–9; Jos. Ant. 12.243; Diod. 31.1; the cessation of the siege and withdrawal: Polyb. 28.22.1; Livy, 45.11.1; Porphyry, FGH, 260 F 49; 1 Macc. 1:20.

withdrawal are unrecorded, though it is not difficult to surmise that internal difficulties in Syria or Palestine drew him off.[201] What needs stress is the fact that withdrawal was temporary and intended to be so. Antiochus abandoned neither military nor propaganda claims on Egypt. A Seleucid garrison remained in Pelusium.[202] To Rhodian envoys who came to effect mediation, the king emphasized his relationship as friend and protector of Philometor.[203] And he sent messages to that effect, as well as cash gifts, to numerous Greek cities.[204] Antiochus Epiphanes continued to cultivate the image of philhellene, now extended as patron of Egypt and its rightful ruler. The propaganda could provide justification for a renewed invasion of the land.

The Egyptian opposition to Antiochus, lacking military resources, struck at his propaganda. A reconciliation between the brothers Ptolemy took effect during the winter of 169/8, thus snatching away Antiochus' pretext and restoring Lagid authority. Joint rule surfaced once again under a Ptolemaic banner.[205] Plausible motive having been removed, Antiochus resorted to naked force. The Seleucid king preferred indirect suzerainty and a puppet ruler. Failing that, he would strip off the mask rather than surrender imperialist ambitions. Antiochus mobilized forces in the spring of 168 and undertook operations on land and sea. Cyprus fell to his navy, and the army marched unopposed into Egypt. A request for terms by the Ptolemaic government met with a severe response: Antiochus insisted upon the annexation of all of Cyprus, of Pelusium, and of the surrounding region. This would mean a permanent Seleucid occupying force in key cities, and a decisive subordination of Egypt. The regime had to reject those conditions. But their power to resist was inadequate. Antiochus Epiphanes took Memphis, became lord of Upper Egypt, and headed straight for Alexandria. Seleucid authority was on the point of its most dramatic expansion.[206]

201. As is suggested by Otto, *AbhMünch* 11 (1934): 65–67, although he erroneously specifies the revolt of Jason, the Jewish High Priest, as provoking the return; 2 Macc. 5:5–11. That revolt is explicitly associated with Antiochus' second invasion of Egypt; 2 Macc. 5:1. Other disturbances elsewhere in the realm may hold the explanation. There is neither evidence nor plausibility for Swain's view that Antiochus returned to mount an invasion of the eastern satrapies; *CP* 39 (1944): 84.

202. Livy, 45.11.4–5: *Pelusi validum relictum erat praesidium; apparebat claustra Aegypti teneri, ut, cum vellet, rursus exercitum induceret.*

203. Polyb. 28.23.1–5.

204. Polyb. 28.22.3; Livy, 45.11.8.

205. Polyb. 29.23.4; Livy, 45.11.2–7. The fact is affirmed in recently published demotic texts: Ray, *Archive of Hor*, 126, with reference to the texts.

206. Livy, 45.11.8–45.12.2. Whether Antiochus actually had himself crowned as king in Memphis is not altogether certain: Porphyry, *FGH*, 260 F 49A; *PTeb*, 698; cf. Fraser, *Ptolemaic Alexandria* II:211, n. 213; Ray, *Archive of Hor*, 127.

In this lengthy battle of words and deeds, marked by Antiochus' unswerving commitment to Seleucid imperialism, where had Rome stood? The king's envoys were in Rome in winter 170/69 to alert the *patres* to an imminent and unjustified Ptolemaic invasion of Coele Syria.[207] The object was not to solicit Roman aid which Antiochus neither needed nor wanted. The move had public relations value. It announced the justice of Antiochus' cause in advance, an announcement that very likely also traveled to various Greek states. Ptolemy's representatives made their way to the senate as well, in part to cast a wary eye on the dealings between Rome and Antiochus' envoys.[208] The senate acted in customary and innocuous fashion: they renewed *amicitia* with Egypt, and asked the consul, Q. Marcius Philippus, to write to Ptolemy as he saw fit on the matter.[209] Antiochus' mission had accomplished its purpose: Ptolemy had been labelled as aggressor in advance and Rome would take no steps to halt Antiochus' "self-defense."

By the time hostilities began between Syria and Egypt, Rome had already been at war with Perseus for nearly two years—without notable success. She could hardly divert serious attention to the affairs of the Near East. Antiochus IV had raised a large army and fleet, even included elephants in his forces, all apparent violations of the peace of Apamea, yet all without complaint from Rome.[210] He could expect to be free of interference. The *patres*, in fact, pursued a consistent policy with regard to the Sixth Syrian War: they encouraged a reconciliation among the warring parties, but without exerting themselves unduly.

Philippus, intent upon the Macedonian war, did nothing until the summer of 169; then his one act was to advise the Rhodians to mediate between Egypt and Syria.[211] At some time during that same year the senate itself sent out a delegation headed by T. Numisius to bring a peaceful resolution to the conflict.[212] In the winter of 169/8, when appeals came to Achaea from the newly reconciled brothers Ptolemy, a message of Philippus arrived urging the League to

207. Polyb. 27.19, 28.1.1–6; Diod. 30.2.

208. Polyb. 28.1.1, 28.1.7–8.

209. Polyb. 28.1.8–9: Κοίντῳ Μαρκίῳ δώσει τὴν ἐπιτροπὴν γράψαι περὶ τούτων πρὸς Πτολεμαῖον, ὡς αὐτῷ δοκεῖ συμφέρειν ἐκ τῆς ἰδίας πίστεως.

210. Cf. 1 Macc. 1:17; Livy, 45.11.9; Polyb. 30.25.3–11. Polyaenus, 4.21, preserves a tale that Antiochus actually supplied elephants for Rome's war against Macedonia; cf. Paltiel, *Antichthon* 13 (1979): 33.

211. Polyb. 28.17.4–15; on the difficulties in this passage, see discussion and bibliography in Gruen, *CQ* 25 (1975): 72–74; Walbank, *Commentary* III:350–352.

212. Polyb. 29.25.3. The time of Numisius' mission cannot be fixed, except that it evidently preceded the winter of 169/8: Polyb. 29.23.1.

refrain from military intervention and to promote concord among the kings.[213]

The Roman attitude is intelligible enough. It parallels closely the stance taken at the outset of the Second Macedonian War when a senatorial embassy endeavored to promote peace between Antiochus III and the Egyptian regime.[214] Conflagration in the East could spread to areas of more direct concern. Rome hoped to avoid a wider war that would encumber or fragment her efforts against Perseus. The Macedonian king had earlier wooed the affections of Antiochus Epiphanes. He repeated the overtures in 172. Perseus then sent another legation in 171, which was intercepted by Rhodians. In winter 169/8 still further Macedonian importunings reached Antiochus, claiming that Rome proposed to topple all kings, and asking for Seleucid assistance as ally or mediator.[215] Rome had good reason to seek an end to the Syrian war, and thus reduce the risk of a larger and more complex conflict.

The peacemaking efforts, however, proved futile. Antiochus had fixed his targets and would not veer from them. He had confidence in the effectiveness of both his armed might and his propaganda. Rhodian arbiters, on Philippus' suggestion, met with Antiochus in Egypt shortly after he had given up the siege of Alexandria, probably in late summer, 169. The king had an unanswerable response to their proposal for reconciliation: he was already reconciled to Philometor and would support his rightful claims on the throne.[216] The mission of T. Numisius encountered similar frustration. He returned to Rome without accomplishment.[217] As for the Achaean efforts to mediate in the winter of 169/8, nothing further is heard of the three-man delegation sent by the League and no likelihood exists that they achieved anything.[218] Antiochus was unquestionably polite but firm with each mediating embassy. He made a point of dispatching envoys and cash to Rome, after his temporary withdrawal from Alexandria, while also sending monetary gifts to various Greek communities.[219] His image as friend of Rome and benefactor of Greeks served

213. Polyb. 29.25.2: παρεκάλει τοὺς Ἀχαιοὺς ἀκολουθοῦντας τῇ Ῥωμαίων προαιρέσει πειρᾶσθαι διαλύειν τοὺς βασιλεῖς.

214. Polyb. 16.27.5; see above p. 616.

215. 172: Livy, 42.26.7–8; 171: Polyb. 27.7.15; 169/8: Polyb. 29.4.8–10; Livy, 44.24.1–7.

216. Polyb. 28.17.15, 28.23.1–5.

217. Polyb. 29.25.4: ἀδυνατήσαντες τοῦ διαλύειν ἀνακεχωρήκεισαν εἰς τὴν Ῥώμην ἄπρακτοι τελείως.

218. Polyb. 29.25.6.

219. Polyb. 28.22.1–3.

the same purpose: to buttress his role as patron of the Egyptian royal house. On that ambition Rome had not made an impact.

The Ptolemies, of course, sought succor from Rome. Envoys of Ptolemy Euergetes and his sister Cleopatra appeared before the senate as bedraggled and unkempt suppliants, garbed thus to dramatize the sorry plight of their masters. Unless Rome were to call Antiochus to a halt, so they lamented, Ptolemy and Cleopatra would soon arrive as pitiable pleaders, deprived of their legacy. In the narrative of Livy, the *patres* were moved by these entreaties and sent off a legation under C. Popillius Laenas to insist upon a conclusion of the war.[220] Here the chronology is important and revealing. The Ptolemaic ambassadors came at a time when Antiochus had gained substantial victories in Egypt, was conducting the siege of Alexandria, and was on the point, it seemed, of taking it. That places the circumstances in late summer, 169, prior to Antiochus' withdrawal from Egypt and, of course, prior to the alliance of the two brothers. Yet the hearing in the *curia* came at the beginning of the consular year, March 15, 168—or January by the Julian calendar.[221] A gap of perhaps four months or more stretched between the dispatch of Egyptian representatives, at a time of crisis for their state, and their actual audience before the Roman senate. It is difficult to avoid the conclusion that the *patres* deliberately postponed the hearing, unwilling to reject the suppliants but equally unwilling to engage in the affairs of the Near East.[222] A delay

220. Livy, 44.19.6–14.

221. Livy, 44.19.1.

222. Otto, *AbhMünch* 11 (1934): 60–63, sought to get around the problem by discrediting Livy's account. For Otto, the delegation sent by Euergetes and Cleopatra came to Rome in late summer, 169, and prompted the dispatch of T. Numisius' mission: Polyb. 29.25.3. A subsequent delegation, after the change of regime, was sent by the newly reconciled Ptolemy brothers and it was this appeal which produced the embassy of Popillius Laenas ca. January, 168, as indicated by Justin, 34.2.8–34.3.1. The reconstruction is adopted by, e.g., Will, *Histoire politique* II:273; *ANRW* I:1 (1972), 620; Heinen, *ANRW* I:1 (1972), 656–657. An alternative theory retains the Livian chronology for an Egyptian appeal from Euergetes in January, 168, but postulates a second, later appeal from both brothers which explains Popillius' appointment; so Mørkholm, *Antiochus IV*, 88–91; considered but not adopted by Briscoe, *JRS* 54 (1964): 71–72. It is, however, unnecessary and unwise to rewrite Livy's text. A Polybian fragment shows that the Greek historian's version is being followed by Livy. Polybius has the senate dispatch Popillius at a time when it heard that Antiochus had gained control of Egypt and nearly of Alexandria; Polyb. 29.2.1–2: ἡ σύγκλητος πυνθανομένη τὸν Ἀντίοχον τῆς μὲν Αἰγύπτου κύριον γεγονέναι, τῆς δ' Ἀλεξανδρείας παρ' ὀλίγον. That passage surely corresponds to Livy, 44.19.9: *obsidione ipsam Alexandream terrebat, nec procul abesse quin potiretur regno opulentissimo videbatur*; so, rightly, Walbank, *Commentary* III:363. Thus, it was the appeal of Euergetes and Cleopatra which induced the senate to create the Popillius commission, at a time when the withdrawal of Antiochus from Alexandria

might allow Egyptian affairs to sort themselves out, thus permitting Rome to avoid entanglement.

In fact, the delay was longer still. Popillius Laenas did not complete his mission until July, 168, half a year after his appointment. The embassy moved from Rome to Chalcis and thence to Delos, where they remained until news of Pydna arrived. Popillius then paused at Rhodes to browbeat the Rhodians, before his legation reached Alexandria just in time to check Antiochus at the suburb of Eleusis.[223] During the course of these months the Egyptian situation had indeed changed markedly. Antiochus' withdrawal, followed by reconciliation and coalition of the brothers, held out promise of a peaceful arrangement. Philippus encouraged that result by urging the Achaeans to arbitrate rather than to assist the Ptolemies in war. When Antiochus resumed hostilities in the spring, however, the temporary hope of concord was dashed again. Popillius doubtless received word of all these developments while his mission delayed in Greece. It was part of his charge precisely to wait and watch upon events.[224] Two events in particular triggered Popillius' decision finally to head for Egypt: Antiochus' march on Alexandria and the battle of Pydna. That those episodes coincided was itself a coincidence. The combination determined Rome's belated move.[225]

The "day of Eleusis" lives in infamy. C. Popillius Laenas brusquely confronted the king of Syria in that village on the outskirts of Alexandria and delivered the *senatus consultum*. Antiochus asked time for consultation with his advisers. The Roman legate gave him

---

and the coalition of the brothers was not yet known in Rome. Whether a subsequent appeal came after the change of regime, as in Justin's account, is unclear. Walbank, *loc. cit.*, rejects it outright (a view at variance with what he says later: 396). But a mission parallel to one which the brothers did send to Achaea in winter 169/8 cannot be ruled out: Polyb. 29.23.1–5. It would be irrelevant, however, for the appointment of Popillius Laenas. Swain, *CP* 39 (1944): 90–91, correctly holds to the text of Polybius and Livy, but offers a very tight chronology and arbitrarily dates the Egyptian mission to December, 169, thus eliminating any significant delay. But Antiochus' withdrawal from Alexandria came most probably in late summer, 169; Walbank, *Commentary* III:358–359. Mørkholm, *Antiochus IV*, 88, acknowledges the delay and the most plausible reason for it: Roman procrastination. Walbank, *Commentary* III:361–363 gives the best discussion of the chronological tangle.

223. Livy, 44.20.1, 44.29.1–5, 45.10.2–15, 45.12.1–3.

224. Polyb. 29.2.3: καθόλου θεασομένους τὴν τῶν πραγμάτων διάθεσιν ποία τις ἐστίν. Swain, *CP* 39 (1944): 93, oddly assumes that Popillius' legation lost its purpose when the Egyptian political situation changed, and that Popillius was henceforth on his own, with no further instructions from Rome.

225. Livy, 45.10.2–3: C. *Popillius . . . postquam debellatum in Macedonia . . . audivit . . . ad susceptam legationem peragendam navigare Aegyptum pergit, ut prius occurrere Antiocho posset quam ad Alexandreae moenia accederet.*

none. Popillius drew a circle around the monarch and demanded a reply before he stepped out of it. Humble acquiescence followed. Seleucid troops were removed from Egypt, and Popillius shortly thereafter cleared Antiochus' fleet out of Cyprus as well. The Sixth Syrian War was over, on Roman orders.[226] The occasion has been taken as the keystone of Rome's farsighted and masterful diplomatic scheme and as the entrenchment of Roman control over the affairs of the East.[227] In light of the previous discussion and in the larger context of Roman diplomacy, this assessment needs revision and reformulation. The *senatus consultum* which framed the terms of Popillius' appointment specified his goal: to bring the war in Egypt to an end.[228] That assignment marked no change in Roman attitude or policy. It pursued the same line as Numisius' embassy and as Philippus' counsel to the Rhodians and Achaeans. Mediation, reconciliation, and concord continued to be the aim. Only this time the Romans did not wish to suffer further frustration and embarrassment. The instructions to Popillius evidently directed him to stall in Greece until Egyptian circumstances rectified themselves, or the kingdom appeared in danger of collapse, or a victory in the Macedonian war allowed Rome to insist on a settlement without fear of failure. As it happened, the latter two contingencies arose almost simultaneously, lending both urgency and force to Popillius' completion of his mission. The mission itself simply carried out previous Roman policy rather than signaled a departure from it. A swift conclusion to the Syrian war was as important to Rome after Pydna as before. While conflict with Perseus raged, the Republic needed to prevent a broader conflagration that might divide her energies or raise a larger coalition against her. After it was over, she needed to demonstrate that peace held throughout the eastern Mediterranean and that a settlement would have lasting effect. Those aims set Popillius' actions in the proper light. The blunt talk and severe demeanor may be due largely to the personality of the man.[229] Once Antiochus agreed to withdraw and end the war, however, cordiality resumed. There were warm handshakes all around and an amicable parting.[230] The king's envoys later delivered greetings

226. The famous confrontation finds repeated mention in the sources; see, especially, Polyb. 29.27.1–10; Livy, 45.12.3–8; Diod. 31.2; Appian, *Syr.* 66; Justin, 34.3.1–4; Cic. *Phil.* 8.23; Vell. Pat. 1.10.1; Val. Max. 6.4.3; Porphyry, *FGH*, 260 F 50; Pliny, *NH*, 34.24; Plut. *Mor.* 202F. Reference to Antiochus' withdrawal has now been discovered in Egyptian evidence; see Ray, *Archive of Hor*, 127–128.

227. So, e.g., Otto, *AbhMünch* 11 (1934): 81; Will, *Histoire politique* II:273.

228. Polyb. 29.2.3: τόν τε πόλεμον λύσοντας; Livy, 44.19.13: *ad finiendum inter reges bellum*; cf. Justin, 34.3.1.

229. Cf. Livy, 45.10.8: *vir asper ingenio*; 45.12.5: *asperitate animi*.

230. Polyb. 29.27.6; Diod. 31.2.2; Livy, 45.12.6.

and congratulations in Rome, expressing pleasure in a peaceful outcome and receiving agreeable response in turn.[231] Rome had insisted
upon evacuation of Egypt, thus to terminate hostilities and advertise
harmony. Both Ptolemies and Seleucids would remain *amici* of the Republic, as before.

## The Resurgence

The "day of Eleusis" must be kept in perspective. Rome had asserted herself to assure the integrity of Egypt and the stability of the
region. The aftermath of the Third Macedonian War, as we have seen
in numerous contexts, induced Rome to make a sharp display of her
authority, thus to dramatize the anticipated permanence of the postwar settlement. But she did not render the Seleucid kingdom impotent, take over direction of its foreign policy, or reduce it to the status
of Roman dependency. The years immediately following the war, the
final years of Antiochus IV, demonstrate this with full clarity.

The king staged elaborate festivities at Daphne, a suburb of
Antioch, in 166. He paraded the armed forces of Syria in impressive
numbers and finery, a vast military array that included infantry, cavalry, chariots, and the supposedly banned elephants. The purposes of
such ostentation can hardly be in doubt. Antiochus was making a
public statement that the Seleucid incursion into Egypt had brought
victory, not failure. His whole pageant was modeled on Aemilius
Paullus' triumph and designed to parallel it. Withdrawal from Egypt
notwithstanding, the successes counted and were to be commemorated. Egyptian spoils financed the festival itself. The military parade
showed to all the increased strength of the realm, quite possibly lay-
ing the groundwork for an intended eastward campaign. Antiochus
had rebounded and appeared the stronger for it. A Babylonian document duly terms him "savior of Asia."[232] Rome found nothing disturbing in all this. An embassy of Ti. Gracchus visited the king and pronounced itself satisfied. If there were suspicions and anxieties in
Rome, they were not serious enough to prompt any public action.[233]
The Seleucid kingdom remained an independent force in the East.

231. Livy, 45.13.2–3, 45.13.6.

232. The festival at Daphne: Polyb. 30.25–26; Diod. 31.16; most recent discussion
by Bunge, *Chiron* 6 (1976): 53–71; Walbank, *Commentary* III:448–453. The Babylonian
inscription: *OGIS*, 253; improved text by Zambelli, *RivFilol* 88 (1960): 374–380; cf.
Bunge, *op. cit.*, 58–64. Note also Diodorus' description of Antiochus as greater in
strength than any of his contemporary monarchs; Diod. 31.17a.

233. Polyb. 30.27.2–4, 30.30.7–8; Diod. 31.17; cf. Gruen, *Chiron* 6 (1976): 77.

Antiochus Epiphanes encountered no further interference from Rome in the remaining years of his reign, absorbed as they were in grappling with Jewish resistance and in resuming Seleucid imperialism to the east. Religious controversy in Palestine and the Maccabaean revolt have, of course, received endless discussion and are not to the point in this study.[234] One might observe, however, that the public relations advantages obtained by the spectacular show at Daphne may also help to explain Antiochus' surprising oppression of the Jews, a policy quite out of character with traditional Seleucid attitudes. Despite victories and spoils, Epiphanes had returned from Egypt without conquest or annexation. The prestige of the dynasty required a display of armed might, as at Daphne. Victimization of the Jews served the same purpose.[235] A single Roman embassy receives mention in connection with the bitter struggle of Jew and Greek in the time of Epiphanes. The envoys offered to deliver Jewish proposals to Antioch, but only if they were formulated immediately and did not delay the embassy which had other matters to discuss.[236] Plainly, Rome remained indifferent to the internal upheavals of the Seleucid dominions.

The same holds for Epiphanes' efforts to consolidate the eastern portions of his realm. The king spent much of the last two years of his life endeavoring to shore up Seleucid authority in Armenia, Persia, Media, and Elymais. He may even have engaged Syrian forces against the Parthians. Death came prematurely to Antiochus in the autumn of 164, after he had attempted to seize the temple treasures of Elymais, presumably to finance further campaigns.[237] The king had free

234. An important bibliography in Schürer, *History of the Jewish People*, 137–166; see further M. Hengel, *Judaism and Hellenism* (2nd ed., London, 1974) I:267–309; T. Fischer, *Seleukiden und Makkabäer*, 55–132; and the general bibliography on the Jews in the Hellenistic era in Nicolet, *Rome et la conquête*, 2:528–539.

235. That motive is, in fact, ascribed to Antiochus by our one contemporary source, Daniel, 11.30, who regards the king's persecution of Jews as a reaction to his rebuff by the Romans in Egypt. This is not inconsistent with the statement in 2 Macc. 5:11–12 that the king assaulted the Jews because they had rebelled while he was in Egypt—although that was more pretext than motive. Less plausible is the explanation of 1 Macc. 1:41–42 that Antiochus sought to bring all the peoples of his realm under a uniform set of customs and laws. Internal struggles among the Jewish leadership, of course, played a large role in these developments; see Hengel, *Judaism and Hellenism* I:267–309; Bringmann, *Antike und Abendland* 20 (1980): 176–190; Fischer, *Seleukiden und Makkabäer*, 13–53. Few will follow the hypothesis of Goldstein, *I Maccabees*, 125–140, that Antiochus' persecution of the Jews was modeled on Roman hostility to philosophers and foreign rites, in particular the suppression of the Bacchic cult.

236. 2 Macc. 11:34–38. A fuller discussion below, Appendix II.

237. The sources for these campaigns are fragmentary and quite inadequate to provide a detailed grasp of events. A sensible discussion by Mørkholm, *Antiochus IV*,

rein to restore and expand Seleucid imperial holdings in the East. Outside of Egypt, the effects of Eleusis were indiscernible.

Antiochus Epiphanes received mixed judgments from ancient writers. He generated respect for his energy and magnanimity, hatred for his oppression of the Jews, puzzlement and even contempt for his eccentricities. This was no ordinary man. Antiochus took pleasure in mocking convention and violating proprieties. Various tales had the king slipping away from court, circulating among tradesmen and artisans, drinking with common citizens and aliens, bursting in on banquets to lead the entertainment, bathing in the public baths, and playing practical jokes upon fellow bathers! Wags derided his epithet, converting "Epiphanes" into "Epimanes" ("madman").[238] To what extent these stories stem from gossip or hostile invention cannot be known.[239] But unconventional behavior of some sort there must have been to give rise to them. In this context one should understand Antiochus' imitation of certain Roman practices: doffing his royal garb to walk about the agora in a whitened toga soliciting votes like a Roman candidate for the aedileship or tribunate, and sitting upon a curule chair dispensing justice like a Roman praetor.[240] Is this flattery of Rome or deliberate currying of Roman favor?[241] That puts too rational a construction on his behavior. Romans could hardly be impressed or gratified by a Hellenic king parading about in a toga and mimicking Roman institutions. The actions were playful rather than serious, gentle mockery rather than serious imitation. The king did not employ Rome as mentor or model.

Antiochus was born to be a Hellenistic monarch and took up that station with relish. Seleucid traditions, not Roman practices, provide the context for his actions. His eccentricities may themselves

---

166–180, with references. The Parthian war is noted only in an obscure allusion by Tac. *Hist.* 5.8. On the death of Antiochus, see, most recently, Walbank, *Commentary* III: 473–474.

238. Principal evidence in Polyb. 26.1. Derivative from his account is Diod. 29.32. Somewhat different information in Livy, 41.20.1–4. See also the stories of bizarre behavior during the festival at Daphne: Polyb. 30.26.4–8; Diod. 31.16.2–3.

239. Welwei, *Könige und Königtum*, 68–76, stresses the objectivity of Polybius' assessment; Mørkholm, *Antiochus IV*, 181–188, impugns his testimony.

240. Polyb. 26.1a.2, 26.1.5–6; Diod. 29.32; Livy, 41.20.1.

241. So, De Sanctis, *Storia dei Romani* IV : 3.102–103; Bunge, *Historia* 23 (1974): 67. Goldstein, *I Maccabees*, 104–125, goes further and sees Antiochus' years in Rome as shaping most of the policies and attitudes of his reign, especially Roman practices in the extension of citizenship. For Mørkholm, *Antiochus IV*, 40, the king introduced Roman institutions in order to promote public spirit in Antioch! One would not, of course, deny that Antiochus did make some use of the experience gained in Rome. Note the soldiers armed in Roman fashion, the gladiatorial shows, and the adaptation of a Roman triumphal procession: Polyb. 30.25.3, 30.25.6, 30.26.1; Livy, 41.20.9–13.

have been contrived to endear him to the populace of Antioch. More important, however, was a vigorous foreign policy that put the Seleucid kingdom back in the center of Eastern international affairs. Alliance with Pergamum afforded power and prestige. Generosity to communities all over the Hellenic world made Antiochus the most conspicuous of patrons. The invasions of Egypt revived ancient glories, bolstered the treasury, and nearly made the Ptolemaic crown a gift of the Seleucids. Antiochus' dealings with the Romans were shrewd and calculated. His embassies to Rome sought expressions of good will to strengthen his own hand, intimidate foes, and supply justifications for his own actions. The timing of Pydna wrecked his Egyptian plans, for Rome felt it necessary to halt conflict among her *amici* and exert authority for an enduring peace in the eastern Mediterranean. But the king simply returned to other projects incumbent upon the heir of Seleucus Nicator and Antiochus Megas: suppression of rebellion among subject peoples and expansion of Seleucid dominions to the east.

The reign of Antiochus IV set a pattern for Roman-Seleucid relations for the next generation. Rome had intervened only to insist on concord in the immediate aftermath of the Third Macedonian War. Otherwise her victory would be hollow and her settlement fragile. That point having been made, however, Roman power receded. Antiochus was at liberty to frame alliances with other Hellenic states, to build up military resources, to patronize Greeks, to struggle with Jews, and to penetrate into Iran—all the while retaining an *amicitia* with Rome. Antiochus proved himself a monarch worthy of the royal dignity.[242]

## The Decline

The following generation produced variations on these themes. A detailed examination would be superfluous. It can be found elsewhere.[243] A few highlights will suffice to show that Roman involvement in the affairs of the Syrian kingdom remained sporadic, erratic, and largely ineffectual.

The brief reign of the boy-king Antiochus V began and ended in turmoil. His cousin Demetrius, son of the former king Seleucus IV, was still in Rome as a hostage. Demetrius now pressed a claim for

242. Polyb. 28.18: τοῦ τῆς βασιλείας προσχήματος ἄξιος; cf. Diod. 30.18, 31.17a: ἰσχύων κατ᾽ ἐκείνους τοὺς χρόνους ὡς οὐδεὶς τῶν ἄλλων βασιλέων; Appian, *Syr.* 45: Συρίας καὶ τῶν περὶ αὐτὴν ἐθνῶν ἐγκρατῶς ἦρχε.

243. See Gruen, *Chiron* 6 (1976): 73–95, with bibliography cited there.

release, in order to take up his rightful legacy in Antioch. The *patres*, however, continued to hold him in custody—probably to avoid contributing to any further instability in the region. They gave due recognition to the legitimacy of Antiochus V.[244] A Roman embassy under Cn. Octavius toured the East in 163, with a commission to look in on Macedonia, Galatia, Cappadocia, and Egypt, as well as Syria. Octavius carried out his task with brutal scrupulousness, hamstringing the elephants and burning the ships of the Seleucid kingdom that violated the terms of Apamea. The act came with stunning suddenness—and defies explanation. What needs stress is that Octavius' outburst is an aberration, rather than representative of Roman policy. The senate had ignored Seleucid military buildup in the past and would do so in the future. Octavius perhaps took his instructions more literally than his senatorial colleagues had intended. The outcome of this episode, in any case, provides the most striking testimony to Roman attitude. Octavius was slain by enraged citizens of Laodicea. But the senate never made a move to avenge its own legate, even when his assassin offered himself in person.[245] Rome turned her back on the affair.

Demetrius tried once more to obtain senatorial permission for a return to Syria and was once more rebuffed. He then took matters into his own hands. The prince made a clandestine escape from Italy in 162, aided by various Greek friends, including an envoy of Ptolemy Philometor and the historian Polybius. The Ptolemaic regime had an interest in deposing the progeny of Antiochus IV from the Seleucid throne. A link with Egypt and a break with Pergamum would alter the course of Seleucid foreign policy—in a manner familiar to the traditional shifts in diplomacy among Hellenistic powers. The Roman senate expressed displeasure with Demetrius' flight but did not pursue him. The vagaries of Seleucid politics could be left to run their own course. Demetrius soon installed himself in Antioch, eliminated Antiochus V and his minister Lysias, and was hailed as Demetrius I of Syria. A Roman embassy under Ti. Gracchus found nothing of which to complain, and the new king gained recognition for his hold on the

---

244. Polyb. 31.2.1–6; Appian, *Syr.* 45–46; Zon. 9.25; Gran. Licin. 10 Flem. Polybius offers a cynical motive for this, as he does for so many of Rome's actions in these years: Polyb. 31.2.7; Appian, *Syr.* 45; Zon. 9.25; cf. Cic. *Phil.* 9.4. But the government of Antiochus V, guided by his chief minister Lysias, seemed to give the best opportunity for stability; Gruen, *Chiron* 6 (1976): 80–81.

245. Polyb. 31.2.9–14, 31.11.1–3, 32.2.4–32.3.13; Appian, *Syr.* 46–47; Zon. 9.25; Cic. *Phil.* 9.4; Pliny, *NH,* 34.24; Obseq. 15. Notice that elephants turn up again in the Syrian forces in 161; 2 Macc. 14:12, 15:20.

crown.[246] Demetrius, like his predecessors, fostered good relations with the western power. It was, of course, in his interests to publicize the *amicitia* and to assure Rome's acquiescence or, at least, indifference to his own designs. Demetrius' legate in 159 carried gifts to the senate and brought back the message that he could expect kindnesses from Rome so long as the conduct of his reign proved acceptable.[247]

That message was vague and noncommittal rather than intimidating. In fact, Demetrius pressed ahead with a vigorous foreign policy that paid little heed to what might or might not be acceptable to Rome. This had been true from the start. The new king, as yet insecure on his throne, faced defection and rebellion immediately. A renegade satrap Timarchus, who controlled Media and possibly Babylonia and who made common cause with Artaxias of Armenia, even obtained some kind of Roman recognition in a senatorial decree. Demetrius, however, did not hesitate to crush that rebellion ca. 161 when it spilled over into Mesopotamia and threatened to cross the Euphrates.[248] He also played the customary game of dynastic marriage to gain alliance with neighboring powers. Demetrius' seizure of the throne at the expense of Antiochus IV's progeny severed relations with the Pergamene royal house. Hence, he sought his allies elsewhere in Asia Minor. A marriage between Pharnaces of Pontus and Nysa, daughter of Antiochus, was arranged at the outset of Demetrius' reign.[249] The Seleucid monarch further offered his sister to young Ariarathes V of Cappadocia, in hopes of detaching him from his Pergamene alliance. In this instance, however, the overtures were rebuffed. Ariarathes, his own crown insecure, preferred to hold to the connection with Pergamum and to claim to Rome's envoys that he

246. For the escape of Demetrius, see Polyb. 31.11–15; cf. R. Laqueur, *Hermes* 65 (1930): 129–166; more recent bibliography in Walbank, *Commentary* III:478. The hypothesis that the Scipios assisted in Demetrius' flight is no more than that, though embraced again by Doria, *PP* 33 (1978): 126; cf. Walbank, *loc. cit.* Demetrius' seizure of the throne: 1 Macc. 7:1–4; 2 Macc. 14:1–2; Jos. *Ant.* 12.389; Appian, *Syr.* 47; Zon. 9.25; Livy, *Per.* 46; Justin, 34.3.8–9; cf. Polyb. 33.19. The embassy of Gracchus and the recognition of Demetrius as king: Polyb. 31.15.9–10, 31.15.13, 31.33.1–3; cf. Diod. 31.28. Whether the senate itself accorded formal recognition is not quite clear. Polybius implies it: 31.33.4, 32.3.3. Moderns doubt it; Walbank, *Commentary* III:517, with references; cf. Doria, *PP* 33 (1978): 127.

247. Polyb. 32.3.13; Diod. 31.30.

248. Diod. 31.27a; Appian, *Syr.* 47; cf. Trogus, *Prol.* 34. Timarchus' coinage represented him as "Great King"; see A. R. Bellinger, *ANSMN* 1 (1945): 37–44; G. Le Rider, *Suse sous les Séleucides et les Parthes* (Paris, 1965), 332–334. A rebellion by Ptolemy of Commagene may have come at about this same time. It was checked by Ariarathes of Cappadocia, and the region probably reverted to Seleucid rule: Diod. 31.19a.

249. *OGIS*, 771 = Dürrbach, *Choix*, no. 73 = *IdeDélos*, 1497 (160/59 B.C.).

rejected the alliance on her account.[250] The senate awarded full recognition to Ariarathes' kingship, ignoring the challenge of his real or supposed brother Orophernes. Demetrius, in turn, ignored the Roman posture, backed Orophernes against Ariarathes, and pushed Seleucid influence into Anatolia by placing his client on the Cappadocian throne. Further representations in Rome by all sides in 158/7 produced only compromise resolutions and inaction. Orophernes was eventually driven out again by the forces of Attalus II, gaining refuge with Demetrius, whom he served as a useful instrument.[251] The power politics of the Hellenistic world governed these struggles. Asia Minor was once again a stage for the rival ambitions of Pergamene and Seleucid kings. Demetrius strained at no Roman leash. His marriage compacts, diplomatic interventions, and military actions followed the paths of his ancestors.

Nor did Rome exercise a check on Demetrius' activities elsewhere in his dominions. The king's struggles with recalcitrant Jews drove the latter to seek and obtain an alliance with the Republic in 161. The pact may have boosted Jewish morale, but it evoked no concrete assistance. Rome stood by, indeed was not even called upon, as Demetrius defeated the rebels and brought Judaea to heel once again.[252]

The idea that Rome intrigued to undermine Demetrius' position and weaken the Seleucid kingdom is well off the mark.[253] Demetrius' own weaknesses did him in. His inaccessibility, stern measures, and gruff personality, perhaps aggravated by a drinking problem, made the king increasingly unpopular among his own citizenry. Uprisings in Antioch itself rocked the throne.[254] Further, he alienated Ptolemy Philometor by yet another foreign adventure, a fruitless attempt to take Cyprus in 155/4 by bribing the Ptolemaic governor of the island.[255]

Hellenistic powers coalesced to remove Demetrius: a combined effort of Pergamum, Cappadocia, and Egypt. Attalus II took the lead, just as his brother had done in the installation of Antiochus IV two decades before. The Pergamene prince found a pretender, propped him up as Alexander Balas, supposed son of Antiochus Epiphanes,

250. Diod. 31.28; cf. Justin, 35.1.2. It does not follow that Rome actually pressured him to decline. See above pp. 582–583.

251. References and discussion, above pp. 584–585. See Gruen, *Chiron* 6 (1976): 88–90; cf. Walbank, *Commentary* III:529–531.

252. On all this, see above pp. 242–246.

253. This is still the prevailing view; see bibliography in Gruen, *Chiron* 6 (1976): 73, n. 3.

254. Justin, 35.1.3–5, 36.1.1; Diod. 31.32a, 31.40a; Jos. *Ant.* 13.35–36, 13.111. The drinking problem: Polyb. 31.13.8, 33.19.

255. Polyb. 33.5. On the chronology, Walbank, *Commentary* III:546–547.

and advanced his claims on the throne occupied by Demetrius I. A personal appeal went to the Roman senate, which gave Balas an endorsement in 153/2. The *patres* held no brief for Demetrius, whose tottering regime and restive subject populace only added to the instability of the East. But Balas and his backers would have to do their own recruiting and their own fighting. Rome contributed neither manpower nor resources. The consortium of monarchs provided the means. Demetrius fell at last in 150, more than two years after the Roman pronouncement for his foe. The kings accomplished that task by and for themselves.[256]

Alexander Balas was essentially a figurehead—and an ineffectual one at that. Ptolemy Philometor stood as power behind the throne. He married Alexander to his daughter Cleopatra, a wedding celebrated, symbolically enough, in Ptolemais.[257] The affairs of Syria took second place to the interests of Philometor and the private predilections of Alexander Balas. Internal strife erupted, the Jewish nation attained near autonomy, and even the satrapies of Media and Susiana broke away. Balas acquired a reputation for apathy and total poverty of character.[258] Challenge was not long in coming. Demetrius, son of Demetrius I, led the reaction against his father's ouster, gathered mercenaries in 147, and rallied support for his cause. The issue was decided, however, not by Seleucid rivals but by Ptolemy VI. The Egyptian ruler advanced an army into Palestine, ostensibly in support of Balas, only to alter his resolve, transfer his daughter from Balas to Demetrius, and oust his erstwhile son-in-law in favor of his new one. The most conspicuous change came through the installation of Ptolemaic garrisons in the cities of Palestine.[259] Ptolemy Philometor had now turned the tables on the Seleucids, having accomplished the reverse of what Antiochus IV had nearly achieved. Ptolemy had become master of Coele Syria, and Antioch itself was at his disposal, as Alexandria had almost been at Antiochus'. The crowns of both Egypt and Syria were Ptolemy's for the asking. He seems even to have accepted some such title. But the formal rule would be by proxy:

256. Attalus' patronage of Alexander Balas: Diod. 31.32a; Justin, 35.1.6–8; the appeal to Rome and its result: Polyb. 33.15.1–2; 33.18; the coalition of kings: Polyb. 3.5.3; Justin, 35.1.6–11; Appian, *Syr.* 67; Strabo, 13.4.2 (C 624); cf. 1 Macc. 10:51–58; Jos. *Ant.* 13.80–83; Diod. 32.9c; Livy, *Per.* 52; discussion in Gruen, *Chiron* 6 (1976): 91–93.

257. 1 Macc. 10:51–58; Jos. *Ant.* 13.80–83.

258. Diod. 32.9c: τῆς ψυχῆς παντελῆ ἀδυναμίαν; cf. Diod. 33.3; Livy, *Per.* 50. For a summary of the reign, see Bevan, *House of Seleucus* II:212–222; Bouché-Leclercq, *Histoire des Séleucides* I:338–346; H. Volkmann, *Klio* 19 (1925): 405–412.

259. 1 Macc. 10–11; Jos. *Ant.* 13.86–115; Diod. 32.9c; Appian, *Syr.* 67; Livy, *Per.* 52; Justin, 35.2.1–4.

Ptolemy installed Demetrius II as his vassal king at Antioch.[260] Philometor, once the intended puppet of Antiochus IV, now had his own creature on the throne of Syria.

The elaborate design suddenly unraveled. Battle wounds felled Ptolemy VI in 145, shortly after the head of Alexander Balas had been brought to him.[261] Demetrius II had lost his overlord, but also his protector. The gradual erosion of Seleucid authority that had occurred during the reigns of Antiochus V, Demetrius I, and Alexander Balas, could no longer be reversed. The receding of Ptolemaic suzerainty meant only that the Syrian kingdom surrendered itself to internal strife and civil war.

It pays few dividends to rehearse the dismal history of the Seleucids in the succeeding decades. The Hellenistic powers had effectively reduced the kingdom to second-class status—and then left it to devour itself. Demetrius II was challenged almost immediately by another pretender, one Diodotus, who took the name Tryphon and professed to be acting on behalf of Antiochus VI, infant son of Alexander Balas. The tide of war flowed back and forth for the next several years, as Tryphon and Demetrius II struggled for the dwindling portion of what remained under Seleucid suzerainty. The Hasmonean dynasts of Judaea often held the balance of power as they deftly manipulated the warring factions for the advancement of their own nation. Disintegration continued, to the advantage not only of the Jews but of Parthia, which gradually absorbed the upper satrapies. As the most dramatic instance of the shift in power, Demetrius II, defeated in battle, became the captive of the Parthian "king of kings" in 140/39, who displayed his humiliated prisoner to those regions that had once acknowledged Seleucid authority. Tryphon fared no better. After his murder of the boy Antiochus VI ca. 139, so as to take full power, he rapidly lost ground to Demetrius II's brother Antiochus VII Sidetes and committed suicide, probably in 138. Antiochus VII himself made a bid to revive old Seleucid glories. Initial successes against the Parthians emboldened him to take on the title of "Great King." It proved both premature and anachronistic. Antiochus' Parthian expedition ended in disaster, the king himself defeated and killed in 129.

260. 1 Macc. 11:13 actually has Ptolemy wearing the crowns of both "Egypt and Asia." Polybius, 39.7.1, calls him "king of Syria"; cf. L. Santi Amantini, *RIL* 108 (1974): 511–526; Walbank, *Commentary* III:737–738. For Josephus, *Ant.* 13.114–115, he declined the dual monarchy out of modesty and caution, with an eye to the Romans—but he accepted responsibility for overseeing the actions of Demetrius II; cf. Goldstein, *I Maccabees*, 426–428. See also the dedication by Demetrius for Ptolemy; *SEG*, VI, 809 = XIII, 585. And see below pp. 709–711.

261. 1 Macc. 11:14–19; Jos. *Ant.* 13.116–119; Livy, *Per.* 52; cf. Diod. 32.9d–10.1; Justin, 35.2.3–4; Appian, *Syr.* 67.

The Jewish state broke away to independence. And the eastern provinces were lost forever. The downward slide of the Seleucids could no longer be halted.[262]

The tale is an unedifying one and need not be carried further. Hellenistic states like Pergamum, Egypt, and Cappadocia hastened the decline of Syria, the Jews undermined it from within, the Parthians stripped it of external holdings, and dynastic civil strife drained it of vitality. The idea that Rome worked behind the scenes to cripple the Seleucids is manifestly absurd. What need would there be and what advantage would accrue? Rome in fact barely receives notice in our sources on events in this sector of the world. Her agreement with the Jews was periodically renewed, always on Jewish initiative and never with any expectation of material assistance.[263] Tryphon, in a desperate move as his position deteriorated, sent a fabulously expensive gold statue to Rome, hoping for recognition and support. The senate responded with contempt: they took the statue but inscribed it with the name of Antiochus VI, the puppet king whom Tryphon had assassinated.[264] Roman opinion obviously treated Seleucid affairs with undisguised disdain. No positive action on the senate's part stands on record for these years. The eastern tour of Scipio Aemilianus and his ambassadorial colleagues in 140/39 stopped in Syria among many other places. Its accomplishment, if any, does not receive notice in the evidence. Most of our sources give the purpose as merely investigatory: the envoys were to look in on the kingdoms and peoples of the East. That Scipio brought any Roman influence to bear on the affairs of Syria is unattested.[265] The vagaries of Hellenistic politics and the

262. The evidence on these years is scanty and fragmented, with connected narratives available only in the Jewish sources and with regard to Jewish-Seleucid relations. For modern discussions, with references to the texts, see, in general, Bevan, *House of Seleucus* II:223–246; Bouché-Leclercq, *Histoire des Séleucides* I:347–384; De Sanctis, *Storia dei Romani* IV.3:190–206; Will, *Histoire politique* II:340–349; Schürer, *A History of the Jewish People*, 189–207. On Tryphon, see T. Fischer, *Chiron* 2 (1972): 201–213; on Parthia, Le Rider, *Suse*, 361–380; on Antiochus VII's Parthian war, Fischer, *Untersuchungen zum Partherkrieg Antiochos' VII im Rahmen der Seleukidengeschichte* (Diss. Munich, 1970).

263. See sources and discussion in Appendix III.

264. Diod. 33.28a.

265. Strabo, 14.5.2 (C 669): ἐπισκεψόμενον τὰ ἔθνη καὶ τὰς πόλεις; Justin, 38.8.8: *ad inspicienda sociorum regna veniebant*; Plut. *Mor.* 200E; *Vir. Ill.* 58.7. Other references in Broughton, *MRR* I:418. A fragment of Polybius does suggest a more significant mission: to settle the kingdoms of the world and make sure they were in proper hands; fr. 76 = Athenaeus, 6.273A: ἐπὶ τὸ καταστήσασθαι τὰς κατὰ τὴν οἰκουμένην βασιλείας, ἵνα τοῖς προσήκουσιν ἐγχειρισθῶσιν; cf. Diod. 33.28b.4. It has often been conjectured that one of Scipio's acts was to effect Roman recognition for the claims of Antiochus VII Sidetes; De Sanctis, *Storia dei Romani* IV.3:202–203; Niese, *Geschichte* II:292, n. 4; Astin, *Scipio Aemilianus*, 127, 138–139; and, most elaborately argued by Liebmann-Frankfort,

internecine struggles among would-be rulers brought about the demise of the Seleucids. To the Romans, they were not worth bothering about.

## V

The battle of Magnesia and the "day of Eleusis" too often serve as landmarks to define the relations between Rome and the Seleucid monarchy. In fact, throughout almost the whole of the third and second centuries the two powers held one another at a distance. Relations were formal, friendly, and remote. The Antiochene war of 191–188 was a solitary outburst, the check of Epiphanes at Eleusis an episode dictated by singular circumstances. One will not thereby minimize the effects of those events. But the long-range view provides a better perspective.

An *amicitia* existed between the Republic and the kingdom by the end of the third century. That arrangement carried implications of cordiality, but little more. Their areas of interest did not overlap, and the two states had hardly ever come into contact. The aggressions of Antiochus the Great in Asia Minor and Coele Syria did nothing to disturb the *amicitia*. Antiochus was recovering ancient Seleucid holdings, at least by his reckoning. Hellenistic history, not confrontation with Rome, molded the king's expansionism. Tensions arose only after the Isthmian declaration of 196. Rome felt obliged to carry her freedom pronouncements outside the perimeters of mainland Greece, thus treading on sensitive toes in the East. The Seleucids had a much longer record of championing liberty among the Greek cities of Asia. Diplomatic disputes and touchy negotiations proceeded intermittently. Neither side sought or desired conflict. Antiochus' further aggrandizements went without Roman protest. But both parties strove to gain the advantage in Greek opinion. The propaganda war proved poisonous. Complicated as it was by fears and ambitions on the part of other Hellenic states like Pergamum and Aetolia, the rivalry itself intensified until it pushed the two powers over the brink.

Victory belonged to Rome, and the settlement was hers to impose. That settlement placed certain confines on the export of Se-

---

*La frontière orientale*, 128–133. Antiochus did later send gifts to Scipio when he campaigned in Spain in 134: Livy, *Per.* 57. That may suggest that the two became acquainted during Scipio's voyage to the East—but hardly that Scipio helped determine the accession to the Syrian throne. T. Rajak, *GRBS* 22 (1981): 65–81, has Rome express support first for Sidetes, then for the Jews. Her argument that Roman diplomatic intervention caused Sidetes to give up the siege of Jerusalem in 135/4 is intriguing but altogether speculative.

leucid influence and the extent of Seleucid power. The principal object of the postwar arrangements, however, was to publicize concord, not to humiliate Antiochus III. The "friendship for all time" would signal stability in the East, a stability in which the Seleucids would participate both by restraint and by vigilance. The reigns of Seleucus IV and Antiochus IV show that Apamea had left considerable latitude for Seleucid international activity in the traditional manner: alliances with other Hellenistic powers, the extension of favors to Greek communities, the build-up of military resources, consolidation of the realm, expansion to the east, and even armed conflict with Egypt. The *amicitia* between Rome and Syria reverted essentially to the situation prior to the war of 191–188. So long as Seleucid imperialism directed itself away from the West, Rome remained indifferent. The Sixth Syrian War arose out of an ancient Hellenistic quarrel. Antiochus Epiphanes fell afoul of Rome only because his climactic assault on Alexandria proved ill-timed. Pydna gave the Republic both means and occasion to deliver stern pronouncements and call a halt to unsettling expansionism.

The "day of Eleusis" deserves notoriety more for its immediate drama than for its lasting effect. Egypt was now foreclosed to Seleucid ambition. In other regards, however, behavior in both Rome and Syria followed a familiar course. Antiochus IV and his successors involved themselves in diplomatic intrigue, the regathering of allies, the coercion of subject peoples, the endeavor to hold on to eastern possessions. Rome turned her attention elsewhere, her pronouncements noncommittal, her endorsements merely *pro forma*. A decline in Seleucid fortunes set in rapidly from the middle of the second century, but not as Rome's doing. Rival Hellenic powers outmatched the Syrian kingdom, a succession of ineffective rulers reduced its authority, Jewish rebellion and Parthian resurgence strained its resources, and dynastic strife tore the fabric of the state.

Results had come full circle. Seleucid power and prestige had reached a peak under Antiochus the Great, stimulated by Hellenistic traditions and ancestral aspirations. War with Rome administered a setback to expansion but did not erase ambition. The same traditions and aspirations that had made the Seleucids mighty proved to be their undoing: the competitive struggles of the Hellenistic world.

# Chapter 18

# Rome and Ptolemaic Egypt

The empire of the Ptolemies had its heyday in the third century B.C. Centered in the opulent land of Egypt, it extended its tentacles through important stretches of the Levant and the eastern Mediterranean. The celebrated reigns of Ptolemy II and Ptolemy III represented the height of Lagid prestige and power. Theocritus' paean to the second Ptolemy hailed his rulership over Syria and Phoenicia, Arabia, Libya, and Ethiopia, Caria, Lycia, Pamphylia, and Cilicia, and the Cycladic isles.[1] A century later Polybius gave similar appraisal to the international authority of the second and third Ptolemies: they overawed the rulers of Syria, they were lords of Coele Syria and Cyprus, they held sway over Asian principalities and islands, they controlled the whole coastline from Pamphylia to the Hellespont and Lysimacheia, and, through holdings on the Thracian littoral, they wielded influence in Thrace and Macedonia. Their special zeal manifested itself in the exercise of overseas power.[2] Polybius observed a decline under Ptolemy IV in the late third century, a neglect of foreign affairs, an indifference to the external authority of his realm. But that verdict is simplistic and misleading: Ptolemy IV, through diplomacy and policy, expanded Egypt's network of foreign connections and maintained a key position on the international scene.[3] Decline in Ptolemaic overseas status came in the second century. Greater powers eclipsed the prestige of that ancient land. The network of associations would then serve more often

1. Theocritus, 17.86–92.
2. Polyb. 5.34.5–9: τὴν σπουδὴν εἰκότως μεγάλην ἐποιοῦντο περὶ τῶν ἔξω πραγ-μάτων; cf. Robert, BCH 106 (1952): 327–329.
3. Polybius' judgment in 5.34.3–4, 5.34.10. But see the thorough reassessment of Ptolemy IV's external policy by Huss, Untersuchungen, passim.

for protection than for advancement. Through it, however, the Ptolemies might still hope to regain some of their earlier luster. As with other Hellenistic kingdoms, the burden of the past inspired recurrent efforts to emulate it.

The evolution of Roman-Egyptian relations exemplifies the pattern. The connection dates back to an early period of Ptolemaic history, a time when the kingdom vigorously pursued a course of extending ties to states and peoples in various parts of the Mediterranean. Competition for ascendancy among the Hellenistic powers dictated the policy. Cordial relations subsisted through the following generations, though contacts were few. Rome and Egypt directed their attention to separate sectors of the world and maintained a distant mutual respect. As Ptolemaic influence waned in the second century and external struggles became compounded by internal strife, rivalry for the throne occasionally induced claimants to seek Roman backing and to manipulate Roman opinion against one another. But the grandeur of old remained a compelling memory. The imperial ambitions of the early Ptolemies resurfaced long after the glory days had passed. Competition for control of the realm and appetite for territorial expansion persisted even in the mid-second century. Appeals to Rome as arbiter or ally remained sporadic and rare. And when they occurred, they stemmed from Hellenistic circumstances rather than from western meddlesomeness.

## The Third-Century Association

Diplomatic contact between Rome and Egypt had its origin early in the reign of Ptolemy II Philadelphus. An embassy from the king came to Rome in 273 bearing presents and friendship. The *patres* sent a return delegation, headed by the distinguished ex-consul Q. Fabius Maximus Gurges. Ptolemy provided a warm welcome and bestowed lavish gifts—which the envoys generously offered to the *aerarium*, thus gaining repute for abstinence.[4] That anecdote derives from negotiations of some import: they resulted in an enduring *amicitia*.[5]

The sources supply neither clear motives nor circumstances for the arrangement. They agree, however, on one matter: Ptolemy initiated the contact, his embassy was the first sent, his envoys sought and obtained the *amicitia*.[6] The timing can hardly be irrelevant. Rome

4. Dio, fr. 41 = Zon. 8.6.11; Dion. Hal. 20.14.1–2; Val. Max. 4.3.9; Justin, 18.2.9.
5. Appian, *Sic.* 1; Eutrop. 2.15; cf. Dio, fr. 41 = Zon. 8.6.11; Livy, *Per.* 14. See the discussion, with references to modern views, above pp. 62–63.
6. Eutrop. 2.15; Dio, fr. 41 = Zon. 8.6.11.

had recently driven Pyrrhus from Italian shores; the flamboyant Epirote prince retreated to contend for control of Macedonia and to stir up the affairs of Greece. News of Roman success obviously penetrated the Hellenic East. The thwarting of Pyrrhus made a deep impression. Ptolemy II's mission was prompted, so Dio reports, by Pyrrhus' defeat and Rome's growing power.[7] The king's intention receives no explicit statement and we can omit elaborate conjectures.[8] A change in the balance of forces in Hellas seemed imminent with the return of Pyrrhus to his homeland and his invasion of Macedonia in 274. At or about this time Philadelphus faced the defection of Cyrenaica under his half-brother Magas and an assault by Antiochus I upon Coele Syria, the so-called "First Syrian War."[9] The ruler of Egypt, understandably enough, looked about for diplomatic ties that might extend his overseas network and shore up his international standing.

The advantage to Rome in this relationship is more difficult to ferret out. Eminent names graced the diplomatic mission: Q. Fabius Maximus Gurges, consul 292 and 276, N. Fabius Pictor, consul 266, and Q. Ogulnius Gallus, consul 269. Yet no obvious political or military purpose serves to explain the move. Rome lacked connections and interests in the eastern Mediterranean.[10] Did commercial benefits promote the interchange? A long roster of scholars has embraced some form of that proposition: Rome entered into an economic relationship with the Ptolemies, access was assured to the ports of each power, perhaps even Egyptian metal sought as the material for Rome's new silver coinage, and commercial regulations established by mutual agreement.[11] The whole hypothetical structure, however, is ramshackle. Chief exhibit for the case consists of two parallel coin issues, one a pre-denarius didrachm issue from Rome, the other a Ptolemaic series struck in honor of Philadelphus' sister-wife Arsinoe, each with nearly identical control marks. Some association seems un-

7. Dio, fr. 41 = Zon. 8.6.11: τόν τε Πύρρον κακῶς ἀπηλλαχότα καὶ τοὺς Ῥωμαίους αὐξανομένους ἔμαθε.

8. For various hypotheses, see the works cited above p. 63, n. 48.

9. On these events, see the summary in Will, *Histoire politique* I: 125–130. Precise chronology and details remain quite uncertain.

10. Harris, *War and Imperialism*, 183–184, suggests a mutual concern about Carthage. But Rome and Carthage had recently collaborated in the Pyrrhic war, and no sign of friction between them had yet surfaced. As for Egypt, a φιλία held between her and Carthage: Appian, *Sic.* 1.

11. So, e.g., Colin, *Rome et la Grèce*, 32–33; A. Bouché-Leclercq, *Histoire des Lagides* (Paris, 1903–1907) I: 175, 319; M. I. Rostovtzeff, *The Social and Economic History of the Hellenistic World* (Oxford, 1941), I: 394–397; Neatby, *TAPA* 81 (1950): 89–98; Will, *Histoire politique* I: 174–175; Cassola, *I gruppi politici*, 45–46; Fraser, *Ptolemaic Alexandria* I: 154–155.

deniable.[12] Yet the notion of an actual "commercial agreement" has little to recommend it. No discernible precedents offer themselves.[13] The coinage issues were probably confined to a short span of time, not, as was once believed, a fifty-year sequence stemming from a long-term arrangement between the states.[14] Nor is there any good reason to connect these issues with the exchange of embassies in 273. The Arsinoe coins can hardly have been minted until after institution of Arsinoe's sole cult in 271/0. They may, in fact, belong a quarter-century later. And any adaptations in the West would require a gap of more years still.[15] The argument for commercial clauses in a Roman-Egyptian treaty collapses. It is easier to postulate the intermediacy of southern Italian Greek cities in explaining Roman imitation of Ptolemaic coinage than to invent an economic pact between Philadelphus and the senate. *Amicitia* could do without such mercantile arrangements.

The eminence of Rome's delegation to Alexandria in 273 need not carry political implications. The Ptolemaic mission, elegant and expensive, had flattered Roman self-esteem. Representatives from that wealthy and distant kingdom recognized Rome's achievement and courted her favor. The senate responded in kind, with full diplomatic courtesies: an embassy of distinguished aristocrats to affirm *amicitia*. Nothing in this signifies a concrete commitment or undertaking. From the vantage point of Rome, who was just recently rid of Pyrrhus and was still engaged in a war on Tarentum, the affairs of Egypt held only remote interest.[16]

The record, defective and skimpy, reveals little contact between

12. The connection was first noted by J. Svoronos, *Die Münzen der Ptolemäer* (Athens, 1908), 4:83–85, 142–145; see further H. Mattingly, *JRS* 35 (1945): 68–69; *NC* 6 (1946): 63–67; R. Thomsen, *Early Roman Coinage* (Copenhagen, 1957–1961) III:127–136, 166–167; E. Huzar, *CJ* 61 (1966): 337–346; R. E. Mitchell, *NC* 6 (1966): 69–70; Fraser, *Ptolemaic Alexandria* II:268–269, n. 185; Crawford, *RRC* I:39–40.

13. One will hardly imagine anything like the Roman-Carthaginian treaties with their explicit limitations on each party's trading activities in the other's sphere: Polyb. 3.22–24.

14. That idea was successfully demolished by Thomsen, *Early Roman Coinage* III:133–134.

15. Crawford, *RRC* I:39–40, places the Roman issues at the time of the First Punic War. More recently, H. B. Mattingly, *NC* 17 (1977): 201–202, suggests a date late in the reign of Philadelphus or even the early years of Euergetes.

16. That isolated Romans served in the mercenary armies of the Ptolemies does not, of course, signal state involvement or concern. Observe Δίννος Ῥωμαῖος τῶν Αὐτομέδοντος in an Alexandrian loan contract of 252/1 B.C.: *PLond* 2243. And Λεύκιος Γαίου Ῥωμαῖος, φρουραρχῶν, an officer of Philopator at Itanus: *IC*, III, 4, 18. Other Romans registered in third-century Egypt are given in Fraser, *Ptolemaic Alexandria* II:169–170, n. 347.

the two powers through the remaining three decades of Philadelphus' reign and the next forty years that spanned the rules of Ptolemy III Euergetes and Ptolemy IV Philopator. It is obvious that each
state stood barely even at the margins of the other's foreign policy.
Roman *amicitia* was not called upon in the Chremonidean war nor in
the second, third, and fourth Syrian wars against the Seleucids. The
military expansionism of Euergetes and the far-flung diplomacy of
Philopator proceeded without Roman assistance. The *amicitia* was la-
tent and inert.

Not that it was meaningless. In the course of the First Punic War
Carthaginian envoys requested a loan of two thousand talents from
the treasury in Alexandria. Philadelphus acknowledged the *philia*
with Carthage but turned aside the request: Rome too was a "friend"
and the dual relationship demanded neutrality.[17] Egypt stayed out of
the conflict. At its conclusion, so Eutropius reports, the Romans, now
successful and renowned, offered to bring aid to Ptolemy III Euergetes in his struggle against the Syrian monarchy. Euergetes declined
the offer with thanks: the contest against Syria was already over.[18]
That notice, in the form preserved by Eutropius, is altogether incredible. The Romans, fresh from an exhausting and expensive war of over
two decades against Carthage, would hardly commit forces to the Levant in order to bolster Egyptian claims on Coele Syria.[19] The tale,
however, must be more than sheer invention. Ptolemy Philadelphus
died in 246, succeeded by Euergetes. Five years later, Rome at last
brought the protracted Punic war to an end. A period of respite and
rebuilding was at hand. It would be appropriate for the Republic to
express gratitude for Ptolemaic neutrality during the war, to greet the
new ruler of Egypt, and to reaffirm the continuity of good relations.[20]
Association between the states endured, distant but amicable.

The same cordiality without commitment prevailed in the reign
of Ptolemy IV Philopator. Victory at Raphia in 217 elevated the king's
international stature. His cultivation of foreign contacts kept Alexandria as an active center of Hellenistic diplomacy, while he avoided
excessive meddlesomeness in areas outside his control.

17. Appian, *Sic.* 1: τῷ δ' ἦν ἔς τε 'Ρωμαίους καὶ Καρχηδονίους φιλία. The doubts
of Dahlheim, *Struktur und Entwicklung*, 145, regarding the authenticity of this passage
have no basis.

18. Eutrop. 3.1.

19. The story is generally rejected, though a few scholars have embraced it; see
the list in Dahlheim, *Struktur und Entwicklung*, 145, n. 53.

20. An offer of military force—if such there was—would be no more than a
token gesture and perhaps a public demonstration that Rome's energy had not been
spent by the Punic War. For a balanced view of the story in Eutropius, see Heinen,
*ANRW* I.1 (1972), 638–639.

A benign neutrality characterized Ptolemaic policy in the Second Punic War. The Capuan exile Decius Magius, captured and deported by Hannibal, escaped to find refuge at the court of Ptolemy in 216.[21] The following year saw a change in regime in Syracuse, and an anti-Roman shift. The new ruler Hieronymus sent his brothers to Alexandria, evidently to gain Egyptian support and tilt the balance against Rome. What became of that mission is unknown. Certainly Ptolemy took no action against Rome. But his court was open to Syracusan exiles—as to Capuan. The connection between Alexandria and Syracuse held despite conflagration in the West.[22] More important, the Romans counted on continuation of their friendly accord. A senatorial delegation brought handsome gifts to Ptolemy and his queen in 210, providing reminder and reconfirmation of the *amicitia*.[23] That embassy was very likely occasioned by serious grain shortages resulting from Hannibal's devastations in Italy. As Polybius observes, Roman envoys requested a supply of grain from Egypt, the one land at present untroubled by war.[24] Philopator seems to have accommodated all applicants—without engaging his kingdom on any side of the conflict.

The Ptolemaic course steered toward peace. When Roman arms were drawn to the East after Philip's pact with Hannibal, the emissaries of Ptolemy, together with representatives of other neutral states, offered themselves three times as intermediaries between the warring powers.[25] These efforts carried no anti-Roman overtones.[26] Philopator simply emulated a policy pursued by his grandfather Ptolemy II who had attempted to reconcile Rome and Carthage in the First Punic War.[27] Moreover, Philopator's own diplomacy had played a

---

21. Livy, 23.10.3–13; cf. 22.53.5.

22. Hieronymus' dispatch of his brothers: Polyb. 7.2.2. Philopator provided refuge to the Syracusan Zoippus, uncle of Hieronymus, who, however, claimed to have broken with the regime: Livy, 24.26.1, 24.26.4, 24.26.6. The episode is too obscure for confident conjecture; cf. the discussions of Holleaux, *Rome, la Grèce*, 74, n. 2; Heinen, *ANRW* I:1 (1972), 639; Huss, *Untersuchungen*, 173–175.

23. Livy, 27.4.10: *ad commemorandam renovandamque amicitiam missi*.

24. Polyb. 9.11a. It seems easiest to identify this mission with the renewal of *amicitia* recorded by Livy; so Holleaux, *Rome, la Grèce*, 66–68, who, however, needlessly questions the value of Livy's information; cf. Huss, *Untersuchungen*, 165–167. Polybius does not explicitly give Ptolemy's response. But it can hardly be doubted that the king proved obliging. See Livy, 31.2.3–4. Heinen's misgivings, *ANRW* I:1 (1972), 640, are unjustified.

25. Livy, 27.30.4, 27.30.10, 27.30.12, 28.7.13–14; Polyb. 11.4.1; Appian, *Mac.* 3. The precise chronology of these missions, between 210 and 207, remains disputed. See, especially, Schmitt, *Rom und Rhodos*, 193–211; Huss, *Untersuchungen*, 110–113.

26. See Manni, *RivFilol* 27 (1949): 92–94, as against Holleaux, *Rome, la Grèce*, 73–75.

27. Appian, *Sic.* 1.

role in bringing the Social War in Greece to a pacific conclusion in 217.[28] Both economics and politics prompted the stance of mediator between warring parties. Conflict among the major powers raised havoc with Mediterranean commerce. And a successful diplomacy of peace in Hellas could win Philopator points among the Greeks. It might also establish a relationship with Macedonia, a valuable asset should there be friction with the Seleucids. The interests of Egypt held paramount place. Ptolemy Philopator instituted or expanded contacts with a range of states, a policy that included Rome at its periphery. The king maintained his Roman connection for present convenience and future advantage.

## Strains and Setbacks

Ptolemy Philopator perished under mysterious circumstances in 204/3 or 203/2. A court cabal held the reins of power as Philopator's young son Ptolemy V Epiphanes took up his inheritance. The kingdom faced a precarious situation. Antiochus III of Syria readied himself for new aggrandizement. Philip V now trained his sights upon the eastern Mediterranean. With a young boy nominally on the throne and intrigues rampant in the court, Egypt appeared especially vulnerable.

The regime dispatched three embassies as precaution and anticipation. One went to Antiochus, requesting that he not violate the friendship concluded with Philopator, a second to Philip V in expectation of a marriage alliance, and a third headed for the Roman senate—although a stay in Greece postponed its mission.[29] The combination aimed to deter Antiochus from aggression against Egyptian holdings. Ptolemaic envoys courted Philip with that explicit purpose. And the government also set about hiring mercenaries in Greece in preparation for possible hostilities against Antiochus.[30] The embassy to Rome must have had a similar goal: to report the accession of young Ptolemy and to seek some indication of Roman favor in the event of a Syrian invasion. Polybius does not, in fact, record the ar-

28. Polyb. 5.100.9–10.

29. Polyb. 15.25.13–15.

30. Polyb. 15.25.13: παρακαλέσοντα [Philip] βοηθεῖν, ἐὰν ὁλοσχερέστερον αὐτοὺς Ἀντίοχος ἐπιβάληται παρασπονδεῖν; 15.25.16–17: ἀποχρῆσθαι τοῖς ξενολογηθεῖσιν εἰς τὸν πρὸς Ἀντίοχον πόλεμον. The prospective marriage into the Macedonian ruling house, probably between young Ptolemy and a daughter of Philip, followed a policy of Philopator who had brought Egypt into closer rapport with the Antigonids; cf. Huss, *Untersuchungen*, 127–129.

rival of the delegation in Rome. The envoy spent time in Greece look-ing up friends and relations.[31] His object no doubt was to find backing for the Ptolemaic cause in Hellas. The diplomacy of the court endeav-ored to gather sympathy and support wherever possible, in hopes of intimidating Antiochus. Rome was but one of the stops on this tour. The effort shows an expectation of continued amity—though not nec-essarily of active aid.[32]

Antiochus was undeterred. The diplomacy of Egypt proved in-effective. Philip of Macedon arrived at an understanding with the Se-leucid ruler, and neither Rome nor the states of Hellas made any rep-resentations on behalf of the Ptolemies. The Fifth Syrian War, from ca. 202 to 199, saw Antiochus strip Egypt of Phoenicia and Coele Syria, while Philip seized Samos and annexed Ptolemaic holdings in Thrace.[33] The external possessions of Egypt contracted sharply and the kingdom's fortunes sank to a low ebb. Civil strife in the court brought new leadership and further instability.[34]

Under such circumstances, it might seem logical to expect addi-tional appeals to Rome. Yet the evidence is thin and questionable. Only Justin registers an Alexandrian embassy to Italy, whose mem-bers pleaded for aid and protection, and cited the pact between Anti-ochus and Philip. The notice receives no corroboration; other testi-mony has word of this pact brought to Rome by the Rhodians.[35] Nothing in Livy's narrative betrays any hint of urgent Egyptian sup-plication. To the contrary: Livy has envoys from Alexandria come to Rome in 200 to report that Athens had asked for Ptolemaic aid against Philip. The kingdom was willing to provide it, so claimed the envoys, though only if Rome preferred not to take up arms herself. The senate gave gracious response and announced that Rome would assume the burden: Ptolemy's services could be spared.[36] Some have cast doubt upon the episode. Yet an Athenian application to Egypt is indepen-dently attested. And, since the regime's hands were full with the Syrian war, it may have seemed an appropriate solution to pass the

31. Polyb. 15.25.14: συμμίξῃ τοῖς ἐκεῖ φίλοις καὶ συγγενέσιν.

32. Cf. the discussion of Holleaux, *Rome, la Grèce*, 70–73; Winkler, *Rom und Aegypten*, 12–13; Manni, *RivFilol* 27 (1949): 95–97; Heinen, *ANRW* I:1 (1972), 642–644; Huss, *Untersuchungen*, 170–171.

33. For references and bibliography, see above pp. 615–616.

34. Polyb. 15.26–33, 16.21–22; Justin, 30.2.1–7.

35. Justin, 30.2.8: *legatos Alexandrini ad Romanos misere, orantes ut tutelam pupilli susciperent tuerenturque regnum Aegypti, quod iam Philippum et Antiochum facta inter se pac-tione divisisse dicebant.* The other version, omitting Egyptian envoys, in Appian, *Mac.* 4.2.

36. Livy, 31.9.1–5.

request on to Rome.[37] The delegates had reaffirmed *amicitia* between the states but had not humbled Egyptian pride.

The Roman senate, intent upon the activities of Philip V in 200, restrained any response toward affairs in the Near East. Its three-man delegation to Hellas in 200 had as commission, according to Livy, a statement of gratitude to Egypt for loyalty during the Hannibalic war and a request that the loyalty be maintained in the event of conflict with Philip.[38] That can hardly have been the embassy's sole or primary purpose, as Polybius' account shows quite conclusively. But it is entirely plausible that a polite representation at Alexandria was among the duties delegated to the envoys.[39] With regard to the Syrian war, the ambassadors had instructions only to seek a reconciliation between Antiochus and Ptolemy—a secondary matter to be attended to rather late in their travels through the Hellenic world.[40] A peaceful settlement of that struggle would be welcome, in view of the impending conflagration with Macedon. But Rome would not take the part of Egypt nor give offense to Antiochus. Even the effort at reconciliation seems perfunctory, and came to naught.[41] The Roman bonds with Egypt were still slack.

The idea that Rome had undertaken any formal or informal *tutela* of the Egyptian kingdom at this time is manifestly false. That notion stems from confused, unreliable, and conflicting sources. Justin's narrative has Ptolemy Philopator before his death entrust to the Romans the care and supervision of his infant son—a duty then bestowed by the senate specifically upon M. Aemilius Lepidus, one of the ambassadors to the East in 200. For Justin, Rome proceeded

---

37. That Athens sought Egyptian assistance against Philip is confirmed by Pausanias, 1.36.5. Doubts expressed, e.g., by Niese, *Geschichte* II:580, n. 3; Holleaux, *Rome, la Grèce*, 64, n. 4; Winkler, *Rom und Aegypten*, 19–20. Certainly the particulars in the exchange as given by Livy are subject to question. But the episode need not be jettisoned. A balanced assessment in De Sanctis, *Storia dei Romani* IV:1.21–22, n. 56; Manni, *RivFilol* 27 (1949): 103, n. 1.

38. Livy, 31.2.3–4.

39. See above p. 616. The authenticity of this notice is argued by Bredehorn, *Senatsakten*, 126–130.

40. Polyb. 16.27.5. The characterization of this endeavor by Appian and Justin as a demand that Antiochus stay out of Egypt is plain distortion: Appian, *Mac.* 4; Justin, 30.3.3., 31.1.2. See above p. 616; and cf. Winkler, *Rom und Aegypten*, 14–16; Dahlheim, *Struktur und Entwicklung*, 257–258. A comparable demand was, of course, delivered to Philip with regard to Ptolemaic possessions; Polyb. 16.34.3—after he had made his inroads in Thrace.

41. The extant text of Polybius notes only the intention of sailing to meet the monarchs and bring about a settlement: 16.27.5. The envoys next turn up on Rhodes, and they postponed their voyage south because of Philip's siege of Abydus: Polyb. 16.34.2–3. Whether they went at all is uncertain.

to exploit that *tutela* both as pretext for war on Philip and a means whereby to bully Antiochus the Great.[42] Valerius Maximus preserves a variant version, or perhaps a different interpretation of the same version. In his account, an unspecified "Ptolemy" made Rome tutor to his son, and the senate appointed Lepidus to the task late in his career, some time after his second consulship of 175.[43] A reference to this tradition surfaces in passing in Tacitus' *Annals*, only here Lepidus is appointed as tutor to the *children* of Ptolemy.[44] The testimony is skimpy and riddled with discrepancies.

Weighty objections can be raised. That Ptolemy Philopator would resign the care of his son to Rome ca. 204 or 203, when Romans were still engaged in the Hannibalic war, makes little sense and is at sharp variance with the cordial but distant relations that had hitherto prevailed between the two states.[45] M. Lepidus as tutor of the royal claimant in 200 or thereabouts is unthinkable. Lepidus was still a young man, at the beginning of his career, hardly one to be charged with the supervision of a kingdom—a position in any case quite unknown to the Romans.[46] Not a trace of this tradition exists in Polybius or Livy. And more than a mere argument from silence comes into play here. Polybius records the supervision of affairs and guardianship of young Ptolemy Epiphanes assumed by Agathocles and Sosibius upon Philopator's death. Their claims were then challenged by Tlepolemus, who expected a consortium of men to serve as a regency and who later took on the role of guardian himself.[47] No room exists in this sequence for any exercise of *tutela* by Rome. Livy gives both the senatorial commission to Egypt in 200 which was to thank Ptolemy for his loyalty during the Second Punic War and the Egyptian embassy to Rome in that same year which announced Athens' request for military aid.[48] Neither delegation is compatible with the idea that the kingdom had come under Rome's protection or that its boy-king had become a ward of the senate. A *tutela* of Egypt instituted around 200 is out of the question. Egypt would not desire it, and Rome would not consider it.

The tale developed later. Embellishments by the family of the Lepidi perhaps distorted and magnified it. Lepidus may indeed have

42. Justin, 30.2.8, 30.3.1, 30.3.4, 31.1.2.

43. Val. Max. 6.6.1: *bis consulem*.

44. Tac. *Ann.* 2.67.4.

45. Heinen, *ANRW* I:1 (1972), 647–649, attempts to defend this tradition. His arguments, weak and implausible, are disposed of by Huss, *Untersuchungen*, 168–170.

46. The point has been made frequently and properly; e.g. Niese, *Geschichte*, II:637–638, n. 2; Winkler, *Rom und Aegypten*, 17; Otto, *AbhMünch* 11 (1934): 28.

47. Polyb. 15.25.5, 15.25.27–29, 15.31.4, 16.22.2, 16.22.7.

48. Livy, 31.2.3–4, 31.9.1–5.

visited the court of Ptolemy in 200, thus making himself known to the Egyptian leadership. Thirty years later a Ptolemaic embassy to Rome sought and abided by his advice in a delicate situation.[49] Even then, however, their application to Lepidus may stem more from his position as *princeps senatus* than from any special patronage. And the record preserves no further action of his on behalf of the kingdom.[50] That Lepidus took some particular interest in Egypt need not be denied. The fact was remembered by family tradition and commemorated by a late Republican denarius of the future triumvir M. Lepidus. The coin depicts his ancestor as crowning a symbolic representation of Alexandria and identifies him as *tutor reg.*[51] This denotes an association with Egypt and a claim to be her benefactor, as viewed from the perspective of the mid-first century B.C. and through the lenses of family tradition. It cannot be taken as an official *tutela* of the realm. And it has no value as evidence for circumstances at the turn of the third century.[52]

Roman objectives did not include advancing the interests of Egypt. The senate's attention concentrated upon the second war with Philip. Ptolemaic claims went unheard. Far from exercising a *tutela*, Rome largely ignored the Egyptian situation—except to utilize it for propaganda purposes. The contest between Rome and Philip V proved convenient for Antiochus the Great: a time for further aggrandizement in the Near East and Asia Minor. He had annexed Coele Syria by 198 and then pursued his expansionism against Ptolemaic holdings in southern Asia Minor during the following year. Rhodes, for her own purposes, acted as protector of those holdings; Rome showed no interest. Antiochus made headway elsewhere in Asia Minor, including among his conquests the key city of Ephesus, previously a prized possession of the Ptolemies.[53] Emissaries from Alexandria complained in Rome of the depredations of Antiochus.[54] The Republic had in the meantime decisively defeated Philip and terminated the Macedonian war. Egypt, however, received satisfaction neither from the outcome of that conflict nor from representations against Seleucid encroachments. In negotiations with Philip during the course of the

49. Polyb. 28.1.8.

50. Otto's view, *AbhMünch* 11 (1934): 29, that Lepidus served as *tutor* for Ptolemy Eupator in the 150s, is sheer conjecture and decisively refuted by De Sanctis, *Storia dei Romani* IV:3.101–102, n. 49.

51. Crawford, *RRC* I:no. 419.2.

52. F. R. D. Goodyear, *The Annals of Tacitus* (Cambridge, 1981) II:404–405, usefully notes that *tutor reg.* might as easily stand for *tutor regum* as for *tutor regis*, thus indicating a "vaguely honorific designation" rather than any specific task.

53. For references and discussion, see above pp. 617–619.

54. Appian, *Syr.* 2. The mission belongs in 197; Schmitt, *Untersuchungen*, 258, n. 2.

war, Flamininus had demanded that, among other things, the king evacuate all cities taken from Ptolemaic control—evidently those in Thrace—since the death of Ptolemy Philopator.[55] What was to become of those cities went unspecified. The *senatus consultum* on the terms of settlement in 197/6 noticeably omitted any mention of Ptolemaic holdings.[56]

The claims of Egypt provided serviceable propaganda in Rome's diplomatic sparring with Antiochus the Great. After the Isthmus declaration of summer, 196, the *decem legati* asserted to Antiochus' envoys that the Seleucid should withdraw from all cities that had once belonged to Philip or Ptolemy.[57] The matter would be taken up again at a meeting in Lysimacheia in the early autumn of that year. Roman delegates expected to occupy the high moral ground: they had come to reconcile Antiochus and Ptolemy, and they reiterated the condition that Seleucid forces yield up the Ptolemaic towns they had obtained.[58] It was neither expressed nor implied, however, that those towns would revert to Egypt.[59] Young Ptolemy and his advisers had evidently already come to realize how little could be expected from Roman promises and propaganda. An arrangement between the Hellenistic kingdoms had been made in the interim: Antiochus would betroth his daughter to the fourteen-year old Ptolemy V, thus entrenching a *philia*.[60] That announcement cut the diplomatic ground out from under Roman negotiators. The conference came rapidly to a close. A false rumor of the death of Ptolemy provided reason or pretext for termination of the proceedings.[61]

The kingdom of Egypt had elected to come to terms with Antiochus Megas. Rome, it was now clear, could not be counted on for deliverance or benefaction. The external territory of Egypt had shrunk dramatically. She had lost her possessions in Asia Minor and Thrace and in much of the Aegean. Cyprus and Cyrene remained. But they served more as stimulus for dynastic quarrels than as bulwarks of the realm. Internal upheavals continued to wrack the land. Palace cabals brought a succession of regents: Agathocles, Sosibius, Tlepolemus, Aristodemus. The boy Epiphanes could be no more than a figurehead for intrigues. In 197/6 an attempted coup by the

55. Polyb. 18.1.14; Livy, 32.33.4; cf. Holleaux, *Études* IV: 298–335.

56. Polyb. 18.44.3–5; Livy, 33.30.2–4; cf. Briscoe, *Commentary*, 305–306.

57. Polyb. 18.47.1; Livy, 33.34.3.

58. Polyb. 18.49.3, 18.50.5–6; Livy, 33.39.1, 33.39.4; Appian, *Syr.* 2–3; Diod. 28.12; cf. Justin, 31.1.3; see above p. 622.

59. See above pp. 622–626.

60. Polyb. 18.51.10; Livy, 33.40.3; Appian, *Syr.* 3; Diod. 28.12; cf. Schmitt, *Untersuchungen*, 26; Walbank, *Commentary* II:623.

61. Livy, 33.41.1–4; Appian, *Syr.* 4; cf. Polyb. 18.52; Diod. 28.12.

Aetolian general Scopas threw a scare into the regime before it was thwarted.[62] The loss of external holdings and the insecurity at home left Egypt little choice. Under the circumstances, a *modus vivendi* with Syria seemed attractive, even inescapable. The arrangement for a marriage between Epiphanes and Antiochus' daughter Cleopatra came in 196, the wedding itself in 194/3.[63] The betrothal coincided, more or less, with a symbolic representation of the new stability of the realm: the ceremony, premature but emblematic, of Epiphanes' coming of age.[64] Rome had been impervious to Ptolemaic claims. Egypt now threw in her lot with the Seleucids.

The decision did not prove fortunate. As Rome and Antiochus drifted into confrontation, misgivings and anxiety arose in Alexandria. The parley in Rome in 193 that aired points of difference between the senate and Antiochus paid no attention whatever to Egypt.[65] Diplomacy gave way to hostilities in 191. Ptolemy Epiphanes urgently reconsidered his options. The king's ministers arrived in Rome, so Livy reports, bearing a considerable sum of cash and proposing to send troops to Greece in aid of the Roman cause. The senate declined both offers.[66] After the Republic's forces had dealt Antiochus a severe blow at Thermopylae and had driven him out of Greece, Ptolemy's envoys hastened once more to Rome, presented congratulations, and declared the king's readiness to perform whatever tasks the senate should require.[67] Nothing, in fact, was ever asked of him. The *patres* would not put themselves under obligation to Egypt. They gained decisive triumph without aid from that sector. Ptolemy's *volte-face* came too late to obtain any considerations. The *amicitia* had never guaran-

62. Native revolt in this period is signalled by *OGIS*, 90—the Rosetta stone; cf. Polyb. 22.17.1. And see M. Alliot, *RevBelge* 29 (1951): 421–443; *REA* 54 (1952): 18–26; Walbank, *Commentary* III:203–204. The internal affairs of the court in these years are known only darkly through the fragments of Polybius. The relevant sections are 15.25–35, 16.21–22, 18.53–55.

63. For the date of the wedding, see Livy, 35.13.4; Porphyry, *FGH*, 260 F 47. The chronological problems are discussed by Leuze, *Hermes* 58 (1923): 221–229; Schmitt, *Untersuchungen*, 26; Walbank, *Commentary* II:623; Seibert, *Historische Beiträge*, 65–66. The Alexandrians claimed a generation later that Cleopatra's dowry had included Coele-Syria itself: Polyb. 28.20.9. That claim is repeated by Appian, *Syr.* 5; Jos. *Ant.* 12.154; Eusebius, *Chron.* 2.124 Schoene; Porphyry, *FGH*, 260 F 47. But it is almost certainly false. Antiochus had no need to make such a concession. The tradition is refuted by Polyb. 28.1.2–3; see Holleaux, *Études* III:339–340; Will, *Histoire politique* II:163.

64. Polyb. 18.55.3–4.

65. Livy, 34.57–59; Diod. 28.15; Appian, *Syr.* 6.

66. Livy, 36.4.1–4. The authenticity of that notice has been questioned. See the doubts of Niese, *Geschichte* II:696, n. 1; De Sanctis, *Storia dei Romani* IV:1.125, n. 42. But it would not be inappropriate for Ptolemy to make the gesture—nor for Rome to turn it down; cf. Manni, *RivFilol* 27 (1949): 104, n. 1.

67. Livy, 37.3.9–11.

teed tangible benefits from Rome even in happier days. The son-in-law of Antiochus III could hardly expect any now. In the dispensations at the peace of Apamea in 188 there were no awards to the kingdom of Egypt. Seleucid acquisitions in Asia Minor came under the supervision of Pergamum or Rhodes or received the privilege of autonomy. Ancestral claims of the Ptolemies were ignored and obviously irrelevant. More significantly, the peace terms omitted any mention of Coele Syria. Antiochus III, beaten in battle, would nonetheless hold on to his prize possession. Ptolemy Epiphanes came away without advantage or respect. The relationship with Rome, while still formally amicable, was strained. Egypt had become a second-class power, not worthy of attention by the Republic.

## The Implications of the Sixth Syrian War

The snub turned Ptolemaic energies into different directions. Roman withdrawal from affairs of the Near East after Antiochus' defeat heralded a resurgence of Hellenistic diplomatic activity. Egypt determined to restore her internal and external fortunes.

Ptolemy's representatives presented themselves before a meeting of the Achaean League, probably in 188, to revive their military alliance. The assemblage welcomed that proposition and dispatched some of its most eminent leaders to Alexandria for the formalities. As it happened, the envoys, upon return in the following year, ran into a political contest; confusion over which alliance was to be renewed caused embarrassment and postponement. But the alliance was ratified later. The two states had resumed their diplomatic relations.[68] Ptolemy's maneuvers were dictated as much by internal needs as by desire for external prestige. His ambassadors carried wealthy gifts to Achaea, including six thousand bronze shields for peltasts. The king was obviously angling for mercenaries. Another minister of the crown rounded up soldiers in Hellas for use in crushing native rebellion at home. In 185 or thereabouts Epiphanes succeeded in putting down the insurrection in Lower Egypt, with some brutality, and strengthened his control of the land.[69] The international status of the regime seems to have received a boost. Two inscriptions from Lycia, dated to these years, attest to it. Although Ptolemaic authority no longer

---

68. Polyb. 22.3.5–6, 22.7.1–2, 22.9.1–12, 24.6.4.
69. The gifts to Achaea: Polyb. 22.9.3; the gathering of mercenaries: Polyb. 22.17.6; the crushing of rebellion: Polyb. 22.17.1–5. On the rebellion, see Alliot, *REA* 54 (1952): 18–26; P. W. Pestman, *ChronEg* 40 (1965): 157–170; Walbank, *Commentary* III: 203–205.

reached to that region, an official at Xanthus dedicated religious shrines and statues to Ptolemy V and his queen, and a decree of the Lycian Confederacy honored one of the dignitaries of the Ptolemaic court.[70] In 180 the king reconfirmed his association with Achaea by sending a full squadron of ships to supplement his previous gifts of arms and cash. The grateful Achaeans appointed a new embassy to express appreciation and solidarity, but canceled it upon news of Epiphanes' death in that year.[71]

Egypt had traversed her own diplomatic and military path since Apamea. Establishment of internal stability and revival of foreign associations proceeded without Roman notice or concern. No change is discernible after the death of Ptolemy V Epiphanes, when the reins of government were assumed by his widow Cleopatra, nor after her premature death in 176.[72] The sons of Epiphanes were still minors, and effective administration rested with their ministers, notably the eunuch Eulaeus and the Syrian ex-slave Lenaeus.[73] Affairs of the Near East held little interest for Roman policy makers. The *amicitia* between Egypt and Rome remained as it had always been: dormant and ineffectual.

The recovery of self-esteem in Egypt also brought stirrings of the old avarice for territorial aggrandizement. Ptolemy V himself had gazed covetously upon Coele Syria—or so we are told.[74] Whatever the truth of that tale, he took no overt steps to regain the land. Nor did his widow Cleopatra, understandably enough: she was sister of two successive rulers of Syria. With her death, however, the guardians of young Ptolemy VI Philometor apparently conceived plans to precipitate a break with the Seleucids.[75] Word reached Antiochus IV, who occupied the Seleucid throne, that disaffection brewed in Egypt and that he was its target. The king had to take precautions for his safety.[76] Among those precautions was an embassy to Rome in 173 to strengthen ties and reconfirm association with the Republic. The issue of strained relations with Egypt doubtless surfaced in that inter-

---

70. *OGIS*, 91, 99; cf. R. S. Bagnall, *The Administration of the Ptolemaic Possessions Outside Egypt* (Leiden, 1976), 110.

71. Polyb. 24.6.1–7. On the date, see A. Samuel, *Ptolemaic Chronology* (Munich, 1962), 139.

72. Evidence on the date in Samuel, *Ptolemaic Chronology*, 140.

73. Diod. 30.15. The hypothesis of Swain, *CP* 39 (1944): 75, that Eulaeus and Lenaeus represented an "oriental" movement against Greek influence at the court is baseless; see Mørkholm, *ClMed* 22 (1961): 32–43; further bibliography in Walbank, *Commentary* III: 355–356.

74. Diod. 29.29; Porphyry, *FGH*, 260 F 48.

75. Cf. Diod. 30.16.

76. 2 Macc. 4:21.

change.[77] A Roman legation to the East in the same year had as one of its tasks a visit to Alexandria with the purpose of renewing *amicitia*.[78] It was the first senatorial embassy to Egypt in over a quarter-century. The timing suggests a connection with Antiochus' mission. Rome reasserted her friendship with both states. She would not be drawn into conflict by either side. That posture may itself have helped to deter—or at least to defer—hostilities. Roman envoys who went abroad in late 172 to test Hellenic opinion in anticipation of a clash with Perseus found Antiochus and Ptolemy at one on that issue. Both had resisted the blandishments of the Macedonian monarch, and both pledged full support to the Roman cause.[79]

Once warfare broke out between Rome and Perseus, however, the kingdoms of Syria and Egypt turned attention once more to their own borders and to clashing territorial ambitions. Eulaeus and Lenaeus laid the propaganda foundation by maintaining that Coele Syria had been promised as part of Cleopatra's dowry in her marriage to Ptolemy V. The first fruit of that marriage, the future Ptolemy VI, took the designation "Philometor"—a reference to the Syrian connection and perhaps a symbol of the larger Ptolemaic claims. The ministers of the crown carefully nurtured young Philometor to maturity. A joint rule was proclaimed, associating the boy-king with his younger brother Ptolemy VIII Euergetes II and his sister Cleopatra as heads of state, an advertisement of the unity and strength of the realm. In 170/69 Alexandria celebrated Philometor's official coming of age, an event with international implications.[80] The regime had built confidence and resources, the result of a vigorous foreign policy conducted over the past decade and a half to restore Egyptian pride and standing. Antiochus IV in the meantime had executed his figurehead co-monarch and now readied himself for direct confrontation. Neither side seemed reluctant to test its strength in this revival of their ancient enmity. The Sixth Syrian War signals the replay of longstanding Hellenistic rivalries.[81]

The course of the war itself can be briefly summarized. Egyptian initiative opened the fighting, but Antiochus had anticipated the thrust and swiftly gained the upper hand by spring, 169. The capture of Pelusium placed him in a commanding position. Young Philometor had been spirited off toward Samothrace, perhaps to be out of harm's

77. Livy, 42.6.6–12; see above pp. 648–650.
78. Livy, 42.6.4–5.
79. Livy, 42.26.7–8, 42.29.6–7; Appian, *Mac.* 11.4.
80. News of the celebration reached Achaea, who immediately dispatched delegates to reconfirm relations with Egypt: Polyb. 28.12.8–9.
81. A fuller discussion, with references and bibliography, above pp. 650–652.

way. He supplied a principal source of legitimacy for Eulaeus and Lenaeus. The endeavor failed to save the regime. Eulaeus and Lenaeus disappear from the stage of history. When the curtain rises again, new regents are in charge, Comanus and Cineas, and Ptolemy is back in Alexandria. The king's council scrambled to head off Antiochus' march on the city. They forthwith opened negotiations, employing as mediators a host of envoys from various Greek cities who happened to be on delegations to the Lagid court.[82] The very fact of their presence deserves notice. It attests to Ptolemaic diplomatic successes during the previous two decades. Alexandria had once again become a center of international affairs. The negotiations with Antiochus, however, tilted decidedly in the direction of the Seleucid. Philometor was acknowledged as ruler of Egypt, but he would, in fact, be a client of Antiochus.[83]

Complications set in. A nationalist spirit in Egypt, perhaps rekindled in recent decades, spurned the arrangement. The citizenry of Alexandria rose to establish a joint monarchy of Ptolemy Euergetes and Cleopatra, a government that would not be beholden to the foreigner. Antiochus' retaliation proved inadequate, his siege of Alexandria abortive. Philometor reached his own understanding with his siblings in the winter of 169/8, thus reinstituting the triple rulership that had held before Seleucid intervention. These rapid developments disclose a remarkable vitality in the populace of Alexandria and a patriotic fervor that belies the conventional designation of decadence. But Antiochus had superior firepower. The Seleucid did not accept his setback with equanimity. He mounted a major invasion of Ptolemaic territories in the campaigning season of 168. Egyptian resistance failed to halt the onslaught, and it appeared that the kingdom would soon be at the mercy of Antiochus Epiphanes.[84]

The upheavals of the Sixth Syrian War forced the relationship of Rome and Egypt into a new configuration. What had once been polite formalities now turned into urgent appeals. Ceremonial niceties gave way to calls for rescue. On the face of it, the events of this conflict represent a decisive turning point in the association: the transformation of Egypt into a client state of the Republic. So, at least, it is often stated.[85]

---

82. Polyb. 28.19.1–7. On Comanus and Cineas, see Walbank, *Commentary* III: 353–354.

83. Sources and discussion above pp. 652–653.

84. For a fuller treatment, with references, see above pp. 653–654.

85. Observe, for example, the subheadings by Winkler, *Rom und Aegypten*, 25: "Die Aufnahme Aegyptens in die römische Klientel"; and by Manni, *RivFilol* 28 (1950): 229: "L'instaurazione del protettorato romano."

The proposition needs further analysis. At the outset Egypt maintained her traditional posture. The regents of Ptolemy Philometor promised every assistance to Roman envoys who had come in 172/1 to assess attitudes prior to the war with Perseus.[86] That seemed a reasonably safe commitment. Rome was unlikely, in fact, to call upon Egyptian forces. The affirmation of amity duplicated earlier exchanges, and allowed the ministers to proceed with the main item on their agenda: arrangements for an attack on Syria.[87] Unlike Antiochus, who was eager to obtain expressions of favor, the regime in Alexandria did not even send any delegations to Rome.

The first Ptolemaic mission to the senate in two decades came in winter 170/69. And even then it was not Egyptian initiative which prompted the decision. Antiochus had commissioned emissaries to the *patres* with intent to denounce the war preparations of Alexandria. Egypt's rulers elected to send their own representatives, primarily to observe the proceedings and to protect their own interests.[88] The embassy came equipped with other pretexts: they would, in conventional fashion, renew *amicitia* and they would offer themselves as mediators in the Roman war against Perseus. On the latter point they were dissuaded from intervening by the *princeps senatus* M. Lepidus. It seemed too delicate a matter in view of Rome's difficulties in the war. As it turned out, the envoys had little to do. They exchanged formal greetings with the senate—the usual pious platitudes—and went home.[89] The formalities had been observed and nothing had changed. Rome, in fact, had neither reason nor intent to intervene in the Near East while war raged in Greece and Macedonia. The senate terminated proceedings by simply asking the consul Q. Marcius Philippus to write to Ptolemy as seemed to him appropriate.[90] It was a convenient evasion—and, for the Egyptians, perfectly suitable.

The military events, however, did not turn out as expected in Alexandria. Antiochus' victories altered the situation drastically. Events moved with rapidity in 169: the fall of the regents, Philometor's reinstallation as Antiochus' dependent, the Alexandrian upheaval, the elevation of Euergetes and Cleopatra, the Seleucid siege of Alexandria. Rome, fully absorbed in the contest with Perseus, took no direct

---

86. Livy, 42.29.7: *Romanis omnia pollicebantur ad Macedonicum bellum.*

87. Livy, 42.29.7: *tutores et bellum adversus Antiochum parabant.*

88. Polyb. 27.19, 28.1.1–7: μάλιστα δὲ παρατηρεῖν τὰς τῶν περὶ τὸν Μελέαγρον [Antiochus' envoy] ἐντεύξεις; Diod. 30.2.

89. Polyb. 28.1.8: περὶ δὲ τῶν φιλανθρώπων ἀνανεωσάμενοι καὶ λαβόντες ἀποκρίσεις ἀκολούθους τοῖς ἀξιουμένοις ἐπανῆλθον εἰς τὴν Ἀλεξάνδρειαν; cf. Diod. 30.2.

90. Polyb. 28.1.9. The view of Manni, *RivFilol* 28 (1950): 232–236, that the senate concluded a treaty of alliance with Egypt but did not make it public, lacks plausibility. It is endorsed by Briscoe, *Historia* 18 (1969): 50–51, n. 10.

part in any of these developments. She limited herself to the dispatch of two peace missions in hopes of settling the quarrels: one sent by the senate, the other a Rhodian delegation acting upon encouragement by Philippus. Neither accomplished anything.[91] More interesting, however, is the fact that a long time passed before any Egyptian embassy looked to Rome for aid or mediation. The regents Eulaeus and Lenaeus sent none, nor did their successors Comanus and Cineas, although they used numerous Greek intermediaries in reaching an accommodation with Antiochus. Spokesmen for Ptolemy Philometor, in short, evidently did not consider an appeal to Rome. It was only after the Alexandrian upheaval, the proclamation of Euergetes and Cleopatra as co-rulers, and Antiochus' unchecked march on Alexandria, i.e. probably late summer, 169, that Egyptian ambassadors headed for Rome. The reason is clear enough. Circumstances were desperate. The envoys represented the figurehead children, Ptolemy Euergetes and his sister, insecure and vulnerable on their thrones, faced with the hostility of Philometor and with a Syrian army at the gates of Alexandria. The situation demanded an abject appeal. The histrionics of the envoys, who came in shabby disarray and suggested that the monarchs themselves might soon arrive in similar distress to the shame of Rome, appropriately underscored the singular character of the circumstances.[92] In an important sense, therefore, this did not represent a reversal of long-term Ptolemaic policy and the beginnings of dependence on Rome. The appeal came under special conditions by a newly installed and temporary regime fighting for its legitimacy and its existence.

The senate, as we have seen, was in no hurry even to grant this delegation a hearing. The audience came in January of 168, after perhaps four months during which the emissaries cooled their heels. And then, when the *patres* appointed C. Popillius Laenas and his colleagues to bring about a settlement, they gave instructions for further delay: to wait upon developments.[93] The caution was dictated, in part at least, by doubts about the viability of the government in Alexandria. The Romans had no wish to commit themselves to a crumbling structure.

The caution proved justified. Egypt's ruling order underwent still further change as the dual monarchy became a triple monarchy, thus perhaps gaining a broader national consensus but also provok-

91. See above pp. 655–656.
92. Livy, 44.19.6–12: *si cunctentur facere, brevi extorres regno Ptolemaeum et Cleopatram Romam venturos, cum pudore quodam populi Romani, quod nullam opem in ultimo discrimine fortunarum tulissent.*
93. Livy, 44.19.13–14; Polyb. 29.2.3; see above pp. 657–658.

ing an even more serious assault by Seleucid forces. It is uncertain whether this new order made any appeal to Rome at all, even under dire circumstances. Ptolemy VI Philometor once more stood at its center. He had never made application to Rome before, and may have had no will to do so now.[94] The regime instead asked for aid in winter 169/8 from a tested ally of Egypt: the Achaean Confederacy. Resistance to the aggressor would be a Hellenic resistance. The tight bonds between Achaea and Egypt were cited, a longstanding friendship with mutual pledges.[95] There was considerable sympathy in the League's assembly for the Ptolemaic appeal and an eagerness to enlist forces, but the introduction of a letter from Philippus induced the Achaeans to press for a peaceful resolution rather than to escalate the war.[96]

That had been Rome's posture from the start: a preference for settlement in the Near East instead of armed intervention on behalf of one of the combatants. And that was still the posture represented by Popillius Laenas' mission. Laenas had instructions for a deliberate stall until the situation permitted a termination of the war.[97] Antiochus' renewed invasion of Egypt on the one hand and Rome's success at Pydna on the other provided the circumstances for a decisive Roman move. Popillius' sharp intrusion halted the Seleucid advance at Eleusis, thus saving the regime in Alexandria.[98]

The meaning of this intervention, however, needs to be understood in proper context. It had not been Rome's object to save the Ptolemaic regime as such. The legation of Popillius Laenas, in fact, had been prompted by the request of one Ptolemaic government but eventually acted to preserve another. After Pydna Rome's principal

---

94. The only evidence for such a mission at this time comes in Justin, 34.2.7–34.3.1. That passage, however, contains a conflation of events. Justin maintains, among other things, that the embassy from the joint rulers prompted the dispatch of Popillius Laenas' delegation. Hence, this may be no more than a confused account of the appeal actually made by Euergetes and Cleopatra. Cf. Livy, 44.19.13: *moti patres precibus Alexandrinorum extemplo C. Popillium Laenatem . . . miserunt*; and Justin, 34.2.8–34.3.1: *Movere senatum preces fratrum. Mittitur itaque legatus Popilius ad Antiochum.* See above pp. 657–658, n. 222. Philometor did at one point ship grain to the Roman fleet stationed at Chalcis: *OGIS*, 760. Designation of Philometor on the inscription as Πτολεμαίου τοῦ πρεσβυτέρου led Otto to date the event during the joint rule of the brothers in early 168; *AbhMünch* 11 (1934): 70. But there had been an earlier joint rule as well, in 170, to which this act may belong; cf. Mørkholm, *Antiochus IV*, 91, n. 11. In either case, Philometor's gift represents the benefaction of an *amicus*, not a plea for Roman aid.

95. Polyb. 29.23.1–3, 29.23.8, 29.24.4, 29.24.14.

96. Polyb. 29.23–25.

97. Polyb. 29.2.3: τόν τε πόλεμον λύσοντας καὶ καθόλου θεασομένους τὴν τῶν πραγμάτων διάθεσιν ποία τις ἐστίν.

98. Polyb. 29.27.11: καὶ Ῥωμαῖοι μὲν ὅσον οὔπω καταπεπονημένην τὴν Πτολεμαίου βασιλείαν τούτῳ τῷ τρόπῳ διέσωσαν; further sources and analysis above pp. 658–659.

aim in the Near East was to advertise concord and discourage conflict. Her victory, so it could be affirmed, had brought a new stability to that region. The outcome did not entail, either by intent or by implication, an entirely new relationship between Rome and the kingdom of the Lagids. Ptolemy VI Philometor was chief figure in the ruling order and neither he nor his advisers had shown any inclination to seek the protection of Rome. And the senate's persistent recoil from involvement in the region except to promote pacific settlement hardly bespeaks a desire to make of Egypt a vassal state.[99] The exigencies of the situation, rather than any long-range policy toward Egypt, occasioned the "day of Eleusis."

## Rome and Ptolemaic Dynastic Rivalry

The Seleucid menace now removed, Egypt could revert to consolidation of the realm and repair of the political order. The two brothers, Ptolemy VI Philometor and Ptolemy VIII Euergetes II, ruled jointly, a compromise arrangement that had emerged in the turbulence of the Sixth Syrian War. But that arrangement, imposed by circumstances and in the face of foreign intrusion, was precarious from the start. The brothers were persons of very different ilk. Philometor held himself apart from the unsavory practices that had marred the reigns of his predecessors: he eschewed revenge, court cabals, and executions within the household and the government. So, at least, Polybius' laudatory obituary reports: a man gentle and kind, more so than any king who had sat on the throne.[100] Others, however, arrived at a different assessment. As Polybius admits, Philometor provoked contradictory opinions. The king was at his best in times of crisis, evidently resourceful and accomplished. But success relaxed his concentration, enfeebled his will, and led to reversals of fortune.[101] The years of tutelage under palace ministers and the tumultuous time un-

---

99. The repeated assertions by moderns that the "day of Eleusis" converted Egypt as well as Syria into a Roman client needs important modification and qualification. The claim appears, e.g., in Winkler, *Rom und Aegypten*, 37–38: "die Souveränität der Ptolemäer mehr rechtlich als faktisch bestand"; Otto, *AbhMünch* 11 (1934): 88: Ägypten ist damals der Stempel des römischen Vasallen und Schützlings aufgeprägt worden"; Will, *Histoire politique* II:273: "s'il fallait fixer une date à l'établissement d'un 'protectorat' romain sur l'Egypte, cette journée de juillet 168 pourrait être prise en considération"; Heinen, *ANRW* I:1 (1972), 658: "auf dieselbe Stufe wie Makedonien und das Seleukidenreich herabgedrückt worden."

100. Polyb. 39.7.2–6: πρᾷος μὲν γὰρ ἦν καὶ χρηστός, εἰ καί τις ἄλλος τῶν προγεγονότων βασιλέων; cf. Jos. *Ant.* 13.114; and see Ray, *Archive of Hor*, 129–130.

101. Polyb. 28.21.5, 39.7.1, 39.7.7.

der the wing of Antiochus IV may well have fired Philometor, upon maturity, with the determination to be his own man, an attitude already detectable in the Sixth Syrian War and increasingly evident in subsequent years. Philometor's younger brother Euergetes has suffered from a decidedly negative image. Critics fastened upon him the nick-name Physcon, "puffed-up," a reference to his obesity—and perhaps to his fatuousness. By contrast with Philometor, Euergetes appears in the evidence as cruel, vindictive, and incompetent.[102] The accuracy of these portraits is ultimately indeterminable. Friction between the rulers, however, is plain, a repeated vexation that undermined stability. And it was that friction, not any sense of "clientage," that directed Egyptian diplomacy intermittently toward Rome.

Popillius Laenas' dramatic visit to Alexandria in the summer of 168 rid the kingdom of Seleucid pressure. The Roman legate not only turned back the invader from Egypt but also cleared Syrian troops out of Cyprus, thus restoring that island to full Ptolemaic control.[103] Popillius evidently had no instructions on rearranging the internal affairs of Egypt. Tension between the brothers could hardly escape notice. But Popillius confined himself to encouraging their collaboration. The Roman representatives approved, they did not engender, that fragile collaboration.[104] They issued just one official demand: that Polyaratus, a Rhodian leader presently in Alexandria, whose efforts to mediate the Macedonian war had met with Roman disfavor, be shipped to Rome. Ptolemy's reaction bears notice. He exported Polyaratus, but not to Rome. A sense of regard for and obligation to the Rhodian induced Ptolemy to have him conveyed to Rhodes, as Polyaratus himself had requested.[105] The episode, minor and easily overlooked, gives important insight into Egyptian attitude. Even in the direct aftermath of Antiochus' expulsion and Popillius' diplomatic triumph, the Ptolemies did not consider themselves bound in obedience to the summons of a Roman legate.[106] They intended to take charge of the internal affairs of their kingdom. Of course, a Ptolemaic mission swiftly made its way to Rome to express gratitude for the intervention that had freed Alexandria from investment and prevented a Seleucid

---

102. Cf. Athenaeus, 12.549c; Jos. Contra Apionem, 2.50–53; Justin, 38.8.2–15.

103. Polyb. 29.27.7–10; Livy, 45.12.7–8.

104. Polyb. 29.27.9: παρακαλέσαντες τοὺς βασιλεῖς ὁμονοεῖν; Livy, 45.12.7: concordia etiam auctoritate sua inter fratres firmata, inter quos vixdum convenerat pax; cf. 45.13.1.

105. Polyb. 29.27.9, 30.9.2, 30.9.8.

106. At the same time, they did release the Spartan Menalcidas, upon request from Popillius. But this seems to have been a personal favor to the legate rather than response to an official communication and could be done without compromising public position; Polyb. 30.16.2: Γαΐου Ποπιλίου τὴν ὑπὲρ τῆς ἀπολύσεως χάριν αἰτησαμένου παρὰ τῶν βασιλέων.

takeover.[107] That courtesy was the least that could be expected of *amici*. It was a gesture and nothing more. The Ptolemies had discharged their obligations and turned to the domestic scene.

Once attention was diverted away from external matters, however, coordination broke down rapidly. Strains between the brothers lay just below the surface—and soon burst above it. The rebellious courtier Dionysius Petoserapis sought to capitalize by claiming that Philometor plotted his brother's murder. That report, evidently reckoned as plausible, swept the Alexandrians into a fervor and they threatened to storm the palace on behalf of Euergetes, the youth whom they had earlier elevated in defiance of Antiochus IV. Only a hasty public show of concord between the brothers calmed passions. Dionysius Petoserapis, a man with a foot in both Greek and Egyptian camps, then stirred trouble elsewhere. Having fomented rebellion among the Alexandrians, he recruited disgruntled soldiers at Eleusis, and turned to Egyptians in the countryside. Philometor administered a defeat upon his forces at Eleusis: the outcome of the Egyptian rising is unknown.[108] Details elude us; and no narrative of Ptolemaic history in the years between 168 and 164 can be written. But the scattered testimony of the papyri give ample confirmation to unrest and discontent among Egyptians. Dionysius Petoserapis had a fertile field for exploitation. Cracks in the dual leadership weakened its authority and provided the occasion for uprising.[109]

The uprisings in turn provoked a more serious crisis in the leadership. A quarrel between the rulers erupted in 164 and issued in the expulsion of Philometor on the orders of Physcon.[110] The latter had quite possibly utilized his popularity among the Alexandrians to force out Philometor, in the hope of consolidating control against Egyptian disaffection. Philometor, in flight and deprived of his kingdom, reached Italian shores and obtained lodging in Rome. The purpose, of course, was to secure support for his restoration. But the method was peculiar and striking. Philometor conceived a complex scheme whose import has not been appreciated. His cousin, Demetrius of Syria, at

107. Polyb. 30.16.1–2; Livy, 45.13.4–5. The embassy is noted in a recently published demotic text: Ray, *Archive of Hor*, 22, text 3, verso, lines 21–22—the earliest mention of Rome in an Egyptian document.

108. The sequence of events is preserved only in Diod. 31.15a.

109. Among the papyrological indications of Egyptian rebellion, see *PTeb*, 781; *PAmh*, 30; cf. Diod. 31.17b; see Otto, *AbhMünch* 11 (1934): 91–92, n. 3; Rostovtzeff, *SEHHW* II:719–723; Fraser, *Ptolemaic Alexandria* II:212, n. 219.

110. Diod. 31.18.2; Livy, *Per.* 46; Val. Max. 5.1.1f; Trogus, *Prol.* 34; Zon. 9.25; Porphyry, *FGH*, 260 F 2.7. On the date of the expulsion, shortly after October, 164, see U. Wilcken, *Urkunden der Ptolemäerzeit* (Berlin and Leipzig, 1927) I, no. 110; Samuel, *Ptolemaic Chronology*, 142.

that time a hostage in Rome, offered assistance, bringing with him all the elaborate trappings of monarchy to clothe Ptolemy as befitted a king. Ptolemy pointedly declined the offer. He kept Demetrius at a distance; he would have an unpretentious entourage with none of the accouterments of royalty. Indeed, Ptolemy VI Philometor took up residence with a Greek writer or artist in a cramped and cheap dwelling away from the high-rent district of Rome.[111] The facade of poverty was maintained for some time until word reached the senate of Philometor's circumstances. The *patres* hastened to repair the damage. They brought him to the *curia* and apologized profusely for failure to receive him with due ceremony upon his arrival. They claimed ignorance of his condition, expressing embarrassment and insisting that he reassume all the royal finery that suited his rank.[112]

What meaning does this charade convey? The natural assumption is that Ptolemy played upon the *patres'* sympathies, taking on the role of a humble petitioner, deprived of all that was rightfully his, and throwing himself upon the mercy of the great power. To read his behavior in this way, however, is to misplace the accent. Philometor had not previously made application to Rome for rescue or assistance. Nor, it is essential to stress, did he do so now. The king could have appeared in garb of poverty and deprivation before the senate, pleading for aid, much as envoys of his brother and sister had done in 169.[113] Yet that is precisely what he declined to do. Instead, Philometor set himself up in a proletarian abode, quietly and unobtrusively, and waited for the *patres* to come to him! The scheme worked to perfection. The Roman senate was put on the defensive, chagrined about failing to treat Ptolemy as his status demanded, embarrassed about the absence of proper diplomatic courtesies, and actively seeking ways of making it up to him. That, of course, played directly into the king's hands. The episode is misunderstood when taken to exemplify Egypt's acknowledgment of her client status under Roman protection. In fact, "Egypt" made no appeal for protection against foreign foe or domestic rebellion. Rather, it was rivalry at the top that created the situation, and a deposed exile who made his way to Rome. The machinations of Philometor had as objective the enlisting of Rome in *his* quarrel and on *his* terms. The proud monarch was the manipulator rather than the manipulated.

A different question arises, however, with regard to the senate's willingness to cooperate in advancement of Ptolemy's aims. The *patres* made handsome amends for neglecting him in his squalid lodging.

111. Diod. 31.18.1–2; Val. Max. 5.1.1f.
112. Val. Max. 5.1.1f.
113. See above p. 657.

They paid him public tribute, substituted royal robes for his shabby garments, and lavished gifts upon him.[114] All of this satisfied a sense of obligation for diplomatic proprieties. But how far did the senate go in implementing the king's wish for recovery of his crown? Polybius supplies a relevant item. The delegation of Cn. Octavius in 163, commissioned by the senate primarily to take action in Syria, also had a number of other responsibilities to discharge in Macedonia, Galatia, and Cappadocia. Then, after Octavius' departure, the *patres* added another chore by letter: the envoys were to visit Alexandria and attempt a reconciliation of the kings—if possible.[115] That testimony places senatorial action in proper perspective. Rome's response to the prospect of foreign intervention was, as so often, courteous, gracious—and minimal. There was no promise or suggestion of concrete assistance to Ptolemy Philometor. The senate omitted even to appoint a special diplomatic mission but simply assigned the task as an afterthought to Octavius' delegation, which already had a full agenda. And that task was not defined in terms of reimposing Philometor upon his countrymen through force of Roman power and authority, but as "reconciling the kings." The aim was familiar and consistent, coincidental with the objectives expressed by Roman efforts in the Sixth Syrian War: a peaceful compromise and settlement. The senate showed no eagerness to take sides.

Immediately subsequent events are lost to view. When matters come back into focus, by May of 163, a compromise has indeed taken effect: Ptolemy Philometor has returned to Egypt, and the possessions of the realm have been partitioned between the brothers, the elder to govern Egypt and Cyprus, Euergetes to hold Cyrenaica.[116] Philometor obviously got much the better of the arrangement, a sharp reversal of his previous fortunes. How had it been accomplished? Many moderns see the hand of Rome, an intervention on Philometor's behalf to divide and weaken the Egyptian kingdom or simply to exercise indirect suzerainty over it.[117] But the evidence,

114. Val. Max. 5.1.1f.

115. Polyb. 31.2.9–14: μετὰ δέ τινα χρόνον αὐτοῖς ἐπαπεστάλη γράμματα παρὰ τῆς συγκλήτου καὶ τοὺς ἐν Ἀλεξανδρείᾳ βασιλεῖς διαλῦσαι κατὰ δύναμιν.

116. Polyb. 31.10.1–4; Livy, *Per.* 46–47; Diod. 31.17c; Zon. 9.25; Trogus, *Prol.* 34; Porphyry, *FGH*, 260 F 2.7. For the date, see T. C. Skeat, *The Reigns of the Ptolemies* (Munich, 1954), 33–34; Samuel, *Ptolemaic Chronology*, 142–143.

117. The strongest statement of this view is Otto's; he repeatedly sees Rome as seeking to divide Egypt in order to mold the nation to her will; *AbhMünch* 11 (1934): 90–94. Similar conclusions on Rome's responsibility for the settlement in 163 in De Sanctis, *Storia dei Romani* IV:3.91–93; Badian, *Foreign Clientelae*, 109; Walbank, *Commentary* III:474–476. Doubts about the importance of Roman involvement appear in Winkler, *Rom und Aegypten*, 41–43; Manni, *RivFilol* 28 (1950): 238–239; Will, *Histoire politique* II:303; Briscoe, *Historia* 18 (1969): 50; but none has offered a thoroughgoing argument.

when closely examined, will not sustain that hypothesis. Summary statements in lesser sources imply—or rather assume—Roman involvement in effecting the settlement.[118] A natural assumption, in hindsight. The fragments of Polybius and Diodorus point in a different direction. The embassy of Cn. Octavius can hardly have played a part in the settlement, for Octavius was assassinated in Syria. Polybius makes mention of two other Romans who went to Alexandria: Canuleius and a certain "Quintus." They might possibly have been a detachment from Octavius' legation, or else they went separately as escort for Philometor.[119] The Polybian text, however, does not credit them with a role in division of the kingdom. They merely testified later to the magnanimity of Ptolemy VI in awarding his brother a share in the partition at a time when Euergetes might have been eliminated altogether. The passage gives strong indication that Philometor and his supporters effected the compromise, not any Romans.[120] There is stronger indication still. Ptolemy Euergetes sought a revision of the compact in the following year, through appeal to the senate. In arguing for a change, he complained that he had been forced into the agreement against his will, overcome by the compulsion of the occasion.[121] It would hardly be politic or prudent to make such a statement in courting Roman favor if the king referred to a settlement implemented by the Romans themselves. The authors of that settlement must be the Ptolemies, or rather Ptolemy Philometor obtaining compliance from his brother.

The remainder of our evidence confirms that conclusion. The Alexandrians were responsible for recalling Ptolemy VI to Egypt.

---

118. Trogus, Prol. 34: Romani inter fratres regna diviserunt; Livy, Per. 46: Ptolemaeus Aegypti rex, pulsus regno a minore fratre missis ad eum legatis restitutus est; Zon. 9.25: εἶτα συνηλλάγησαν αὖθις ὑπὸ τῶν ʾΡωμαίων ἐφ᾽ ᾧ τὸν μὲν πρεσβύτερον τὴν Αἴγυπτον καὶ τὴν Κύπρον, τὰ δὲ περὶ τὴν Κυρήνην ἔχειν τὸν ἕτερον.

119. Polyb. 31.10.4; cf. Walbank, Commentary III:475.

120. Polyb. 31.10.4: τῶν δὲ περὶ τὸν Κανολήιον καὶ Κόιντον ἀπομαρτυρούντων τοῖς περὶ τὸν Μένυλλον, τοῖς παρὰ τοῦ πρεσβυτέρου παραγεγονόσι πρεσβευταῖς, διότι καὶ τὴν Κυρήνην ὁ νεώτερος καὶ τὸ πνεῦμα δι᾽ αὐτοὺς ἔχοι. The Greek leaves little doubt that δι᾽ αὐτοὺς must refer to Menyllus and the friends of the king, not to the Roman envoys. But ambiguity attaches to a Polybian statement that follows shortly with regard to a later senatorial deliberation; 31.10.6: ἡ σύγκλητος, ἅμα μὲν ὁρῶσα τὸν μερισμὸν . . . γεγονότα τελέως, ἅμα δὲ βουλομένη διελεῖν τὴν βασιλείαν πραγματικῶς, αὐτῶν αἰτίων γενομένων τῆς διαιρέσεως. Who is meant by αὐτῶν αἰτίων γενομένων? Much of the scholarly dispute revolves around this question; see above pp. 115–116, n. 102. Yet it is hard to see a reference to the senate here. That body appears in the singular, as subject of the sentence. A switch to the plural in the genitive absolute indicates others responsible for the previous arrangement, i.e. presumably the Ptolemaic negotiators.

121. Polyb. 31.10.2: φάσκων οὐχ ἑκών, ἀλλὰ κατ᾽ ἀνάγκην τῷ καιρῷ περιληφθεὶς πεποιηκέναι τὸ προστατόμενον.

Physcon's popularity in the city swiftly wore thin. Arbitrary brutality alienated the citizenry. Pressures from that quarter evidently over-turned Ptolemy VIII's sole rule and forced a new arrangement.[122] The compromise—Egypt and Cyprus for Philometor, Cyrene for Phys-con—was worked out by the brothers, with Philometor having the upper hand and advertising his generosity.[123] The king issued am-nesty for crimes committed prior to his recall, thus to underscore the new spirit of harmony.[124] In all this, the hand of Rome is nowhere evi-dent. The western power was content to let the Ptolemies work out matters for themselves.

Concord and cooperation proved to be difficult of achievement. The earlier discord left its scars, and ill-concealed hostility poisoned relations between the brothers. The reduced external holdings of the kingdom made it the more onerous to accept a partition of what re-mained. And Philometor's sojourn in Rome had established a pattern: competition for ascendancy in Egypt could tempt one or more of the competitors to solicit the Republic's help for his cause.

Ptolemy VIII Euergetes wasted little time in exploring this ave-nue. He appeared in person to make his case to the senate probably in late 163. The division, so he claimed, was inequitable and, besides, adopted only by force of necessity. Cyprus should be added to his do-minions, thereby at least partially to redress the balance.[125] The plea encountered opposition. Philometor's representative Menyllus was also in Rome to dispute the claim, asserting that Euergetes should be more than grateful for Cyrene, which had been awarded to him quite beyond any rightful expectations, a view supported by Rome's own legates to Alexandria.[126] Debate in the senate was followed by a vote which showed the majority sympathetic to Physcon's aims. The *patres* appointed two legates, T. Manlius Torquatus and Cn. Cornelius Me-rula, to accompany the king to Cyprus and see to the implementation of this decree.[127]

Does this imply a reversal of form in Rome? How should one construe senatorial motivation? Polybius has an answer, but a sus-

---

122. Arbitrary actions: Polyb. 31.18.14; Diod. 31.17c, 31.20; popular hostility to Physcon: Polyb. 31.10.4; Diod. 31.17c; the recall of Philometor: Diod. 31.17c.

123. Polyb. 31.10.1–2: μετὰ τὸ μερίσαι τοὺς Πτολεμαίους τὴν βασιλείαν; 31.10.5: λάβοι τοὺς ὅρκους παρὰ τἀδελφοῦ καὶ δοίη περὶ τούτου; 39.7.5–6: κατὰ συνθήκας; cf. 31.19.1; Livy, *Per.* 47: *inter Ptolemaeos fratres, qui dissidebant, foedus ictum, ut alter Aegypto, alter Cyrenis regnaret.*

124. Wilcken, *Urkunden* I, no. 111; Will, *Histoire politique* II: 303; Walbank, *Commentary* III: 468.

125. Polyb. 31.10.1–3.

126. Polyb. 31.10.4–5.

127. Polyb. 31.10.6, 31.10.9; Zon. 9.25.

picious one. The historian elects to generalize about Roman attitudes at this time: the *patres* acted in their own interests, as they did elsewhere, to expand their power while exploiting the mistakes of others and appearing to benefit the offenders. In this instance, Polybius surmises, they feared lest Egypt receive a true leader who might conceive too much ambition.[128] The analysis, however, is of a piece with Polybius' generally cynical judgment of Roman behavior in the post-Pydna period, a judgment arrived at through hindsight and quite probably after the unsettling events of 146.[129] Moreover, the historian's outlook here may not be entirely without bias. He holds a high opinion of Ptolemy VI and a correspondingly low one of his rival.[130] And Polybius had strong ties of friendship with Philometor's spokesman Menyllus, even collaborated with him at this very time to smuggle Demetrius of Syria, cousin and supporter of Philometor, out of Rome.[131] His verdict should not command full confidence. Roman fear of Egypt or of a strong Egyptian ruler is hard to credit.[132] The thesis downplays and even overlooks the actual instructions provided by the senate to its legates: they are to reconcile the brothers and to install Euergetes on Cyprus without use of force.[133] There is no significant reversal of form here. Directives to reconcile the kings had become almost conventional language in senatorial decrees on Egypt. A majority of the *patres* were persuaded that Ptolemy Physcon had legitimate claims on more than just the land of Cyrene. But their object, as so often, was to urge an agreeable solution—and they were not prepared to back Physcon with arms.

128. Polyb. 31.10.7–8: καθορῶντες τὸ μέγεθος τῆς ἐν Αἰγύπτῳ δυναστείας καὶ δεδιότες, ἄν ποτε τύχῃ προστάτου, μὴ μεῖζον φρονήσῃ τοῦ καθήκοντος.

129. See above pp. 346–348.

130. Polyb. 28.21.4–5, 31.18.14, 39.7.5–6.

131. Polyb. 31.12.8–13; cf. Diod. 31.18.1. There is nothing to suggest, however, that Menyllus' involvement in the escape of Demetrius helps to explain Rome's tilt in favor of Euergetes against Philometor. If that were true, Philometor would hardly have sent Menyllus again as his representative in the following year: Polyb. 31.20.1; so, rightly, Winkler, *Rom und Aegypten*, 45–46.

132. Otto, *AbhMünch* 11 (1934): 96–97, who embraces this view, points to Philometor's encouragement of the Jewish high priest Onias to erect a temple in Egypt as challenge to the Seleucids who now controlled the temple in Jerusalem: Jos. *Ant.* 12.385–388, 13.62–72, 20.236. But there is no indication that this would give concern to the Seleucid kingdom—let alone to Rome. Otto's further and much more elaborate argument, *op. cit.*, 97–112, that the will of Ptolemy Euergetes, published in 155, was secretly communicated to the Romans in 162 and thus induced them to take his part, is altogether fanciful. The will makes explicit reference to an attempt on Euergetes' life: *SEG*, IX, 7, lines 6–11. That event belongs to 155: Polyb. 33.11.2; see De Sanctis, *Storia dei Romani*, IV:3.95, n. 37.

133. Polyb. 31.10.10: δόντες ἐντολὰς διαλῦσαι τοὺς ἀδελφοὺς καὶ κατασκευάσαι τῷ νεωτέρῳ τὴν Κύπρον χωρὶς πολέμου; cf. 31.17.4.

The sequel substantiates this conclusion. Ptolemy Physcon hastily recruited mercenaries for an assault on Cyprus in summer, 162. Torquatus, however, reminded him that Rome would support only a negotiating process, arranged for the king to wait on the border of Egypt and Cyrene, and promised an attempt to win over Philometor by persuasion.[134] Philometor, who had manipulated the Romans to good effect before, proved equally skillful on this occasion. He dragged out the talks interminably, cajoled the legates with every form of indulgence, and held them in Alexandria until a massive rebellion in Cyrene threatened to topple Physcon.[135] It was masterful diplomacy. The frustrated Physcon, having cooled his heels on the Egyptian border for six weeks, now had to scrap his plans for Cyprus and concentrate resources for holding Cyrene—a project in which he proved none too successful.[136] His brother could then quite happily terminate the negotiations and release Rome's envoys, with the insistence that he would countenance no change in the original arrangements.[137] The king had orchestrated matters with dexterity. The representatives of the senate, far from imposing Rome's will, had been outmaneuvered—and returned home with nothing to show for their efforts.[138]

Ptolemy VI had gauged the limits of Roman interests in the Near East and had pushed to those limits, perhaps even beyond. Although still in his early twenties he had had considerable exposure to high-level diplomacy and already excelled at it. His brother, worsted in negotiations and on the battlefield, continued to chase after a recognition of his rights and a reversal of his fortunes. The beleaguered claimant sent envoys and angry messages to Rome, denouncing Philometor for his avarice and arrogance.[139] The senate gave audience to Euergetes' representatives in winter, 162/1, and also heard Menyllus, once again the spokesman for Philometor. This time, however, the complaints of Euergetes were seconded by Torquatus and Merula, eager to cover their chagrin at diplomatic failure by pressing for a warmer endorsement of the younger king.[140] Under the circumstances, the *patres* had to take a more forceful stand in order to save appearances and neutralize public embarrassment. A decree issued from the *curia* directing Menyllus to leave the city within five days and terminating Rome's "alliance" with the elder Ptolemy—i.e. a sev-

---

134. Polyb. 31.17.1–8.    135. Polyb. 31.18.1–6.
136. Polyb. 31.18.7–16.
137. Polyb. 31.19.1: διασαφῶν τῷ βασιλεῖ διότι πρὸς οὐθὲν τῶν ἀξιουμένων προσελήλυθεν ὁ ἀδελφός, ἀλλά φησι δεῖν μένειν ἐπὶ τοῖς ἐξ ἀρχῆς διομολογουμένοις.
138. Polyb. 31.19.3: τοὺς περὶ Τίτον ἀπράκτους.
139. Polyb. 31.19.2.    140. Polyb. 31.20.1–2.

ering of diplomatic relations.[141] The senate proceeded to send a new embassy which would announce the decision to Physcon in Cyrene.[142] Once that message arrived, Physcon took heart and resumed vigorous recruiting, with intent to invade Cyprus.[143]

What had Rome, in fact, accomplished? Philometor's cunning dalliance had stymied Euergetes and discomfited Roman envoys. The *patres* needed a strong public statement to cover their embarrassment. But it does not appear that they implemented the statement with action. Evidence fails us for the years immediately following Rome's diplomatic break with Philometor and the military preparations of Physcon in early 161. Whether Physcon even mounted an invasion in those years is unknown. Certainly Rome did not provide him with material or manpower. Senatorial reassurance emboldened the king to mobilize, but he would have to gather forces on his own.[144] Subsequent years are a blank. Ptolemy Euergetes either made an attempt on Cyprus which misfired or postponed any thought of invasion because he had inadequate support.[145] The island, in any case, did not fall into

141. Polyb. 31.20.3: καὶ τὴν συμμαχίαν ἀναιρεῖν τὴν πρὸς τὸν πρεσβύτερον; Diod. 31.23. The συμμαχία is often discussed. Manni, *RivFilol* 28 (1950): 233–237, saw it as evidence for a formal treaty between Rome and the two kings during the Sixth Syrian War; so also Briscoe, *Historia* 18 (1969): 50–51, n. 10. Holleaux, *Rome, la Grèce*, 70, n. 3, considered it a special accord framed with Philometor during his first conflict with Physcon. De Sanctis, *Storia dei Romani* IV: 3.95, speaks obscurely of the συμμαχία as renewal of "piu antichi trattati." In fact, hypotheses are unnecessary. The word should obviously not be taken in a technical sense. Polybius very probably refers to the history of amicable relations between Rome and Egypt, the φιλία καὶ συμμαχία to which Euergetes himself could make reference later in his testament; *SEG*, IX, 7, lines 15–16—wrongly regarded by Winkler, *Rom und Aegypten*, 47, as a special relationship between Rome and Euergetes. The senatorial decree of winter, 162/1 simply announced a diplomatic break. Otto, *AbhMünch* 11 (1934): 108, has it right: "Abbruch der diplomatischen Beziehungen"; cf. Winkler, *op. cit.*, 49. The same action was taken with regard to Prusias of Bithynia in 155/4; Polyb. 33.12.5: τήν τε φιλίαν ἀπείπαντο καὶ τὴν συμμαχίαν.

142. Polyb. 31.20.4. Physcon had evidently recovered some of his authority in Cyrene in the meantime. But Otto's view, *AbhMünch* 11 (1934): 111, n. 3, that this came through Roman assistance, is sheer conjecture.

143. Polyb. 31.20.5–6.

144. Cf. the similar encouragement by the senate of Alexander Balas in 153/2, without supply of any material aid; Polyb. 33.18.12–14.

145. Diod. 31.33, seems to place in 158/7 a military clash between the Ptolemies ending in victory by Philometor, who then behaved with magnanimity toward his brother. The same clash is plainly referred to also by Polybius in his obituary of the elder Ptolemy, with specific reference to a war over Cyprus: 39.7.6. But the settlement of this conflict is portrayed as an enduring one and thus must follow the assault on Cyprus by Euergetes in 155/4; Polyb. 33.11. That Euergetes had made an earlier attempt with similar results in 158/7 cannot be ruled out. But it is much easier to believe that Diodorus has misplaced the event and that only a single contest over Cyprus in 155/4 is

his hands. Polybius reports that Demetrius I of Syria endeavored to have Cyprus betrayed to him in the mid-150s by bribing Archias, governor of the territory and evidently an appointee of Philometor. That scheme aborted, and Archias took his own life.[146] Ptolemy Philometor remained master of the island. Physcon's plans had evidently collapsed. Rome's pronouncement on his behalf in 162/1 endeavored to screen the diplomatic ineptitude of her envoys, and to put a bold face on an awkward situation. She did not intend to compound the error by committing forces to Physcon's ambitions.

## The Schemes of Ptolemy Euergetes II

The foregoing analysis helps to explain the seemingly extraordinary event that occurred in 155. Ptolemy Euergetes II, worsted in competition by his elder brother and hitherto unsuccessful in obtaining tangible assistance from Rome, hit upon a new maneuver. The king published his will. As he had no immediate heirs of his own, Physcon directed the terms of that document to the Roman Republic.

A stone unearthed in Cyrene records the king's dispositions.[147] When taken together, they comprise an unusual hodge-podge. Ptolemy looks forward to vengeance upon those who plotted to deprive him of his kingdom and his life.[148] If he should perish before leaving any heirs, he would bequeath his realm to the Romans with whom he had unstintingly maintained friendship and alliance.[149] The king also entrusts to the Romans protection of his holdings, imploring them by the gods and their own reputation to come to the aid of his cities and land if they should be attacked, an assistance invoked in accordance with their mutual agreement.[150] Ptolemy then summons a number of gods as witnesses, including Jupiter Capitolinus, and announces that

historical. See Holleaux, *Études* III:87–88, n. 3; Winkler, *Rom und Aegypten*, 49–50; Otto, *AbhMünch* 11 (1934): 112–113, n. 4; Walbank, *Commentary* III:553. *Contra*: Niese, *Geschichte* III:211.

146. Polyb. 33.5. He is probably the same Archias who had accompanied Philometor to Rome in 164; Diod. 31.18.1; cf. Bagnall, *Administration*, 257.

147. *Editio princeps* by G. Oliverio, *La stele di Tolomeo Neòteros re di Cirene* (Bergamo, 1932). The edition immediately generated a torrent of scholarly publications. A long bibliography in *SEG*, IX, 7, where the inscription can be conveniently consulted. See, more recently, Liebmann-Frankfort, *RIDA* 13 (1966): 73–94. Among the most important contributions, see Wilcken, *SitzBerlin* (1932): 317–336; Bickermann, *Gnomon* 8 (1932): 424–430; W. Schubart, *PhilWoch* 52 (1932): 1077–1084; A. Piganiol, *RevHistDr* (1933): 409–423; Winkler, *Rom und Aegypten*, 50–59; Otto, *AbhMünch* 11 (1934): 97–111; G. I. Luzzatto, *Epigrafia giuridica greca e romana* (Milan, 1942), 145–164.

148. *SEG*, IX, 7, lines 6–11.

149. *SEG*, IX, 7, lines 11–16.          150. *SEG*, IX, 7, lines 17–23.

copies of the testament have been deposited in Rome and in the shrine of Apollo in Cyrene.[151] Such are the contents, in brief. They provoke a number of thorny questions. What is the relationship between the writing of the will and the publication of the stone? Do the terms depend on Roman or Hellenistic legal practices? Do they look to the present or to the future? Is this, in fact, a legal document—or is it a political manifesto?

The extant text plainly does not duplicate the original. It reports that the testament has already been dispatched to Rome and that another copy has been entrusted to Apollo.[152] But it hardly follows that there were major discrepancies between the initial version and the published text, that years passed between the one and the other, or that the real will was kept secret while the inscription served for public consumption.[153] Conjectures of that sort are unfounded and unnecessary. Ptolemy Euergetes had failed more than once to secure substantial aid from Rome. He was still confined to Cyrene, while his brother held the more desirable portions of the realm, Egypt and Cyprus. A dramatic effort now seemed appropriate. In the next year, Euergetes would make official complaint to the senate, charging Philometor with a plot against his life, and giving a public display of his scars to prove it.[154] There can be little doubt that those same accusations find reference on the stele.[155] Euergetes had every reason to publicize the allegations and no motive to conceal them. Indeed, advertisement of the bequest, with its suggestion of close connection to Rome, could only benefit the king: it might discourage Cyrenaean recalcitrants, intimidate Philometor, and even jog the Republic into cooperation.

Interpretation of the document has led scholars to seek precedents in Roman or in Hellenistic law. Ptolemy assigned to the Romans the task of protecting his domains.[156] That clause has been taken as equivalent to the Roman concept of *fideicommissum*, a duty imposed on a legatee to benefit a third party. On this view, Rome was expected

151. *SEG*, IX, 7, lines 5–6, 24–27.

152. *SEG*, IX, 7, lines 5–6: ὧν καὶ τὰ ἀντίγραφα εἰς Ῥώμην ἐξαπέσταλται; lines 26–27: τὸν Ἀρχηγέτην Ἀπόλλωνα, παρ' ὧι καὶ τὰ περὶ τούτων ἀνιέρωται γράμματα.

153. Wilcken, *SitzBerlin* (1932): 322–331, argued that the will was composed in 155 and communicated privately to the Romans, but otherwise kept secret, lest there be unrest in Cyrene; the stone was erected many years later, either by Ptolemy's heir or by the Romans. Otto, *AbhMünch* 11 (1934): 107–111, by contrast, holds to 155 as date for the setting up of the inscription, but places the private communication of the will in 162.

154. Polyb. 33.11.1–3.

155. *SEG*, IX, 7, lines 6–11: τοὺς συστησαμένους ἐπί με τὴν ἀνόσιον ἐπιβουλὴν καὶ προελομένους μὴ μόνον τῆς βασιλείας, ἀλλὰ καὶ τοῦ ζῆν στερῆσαί με.

156. *SEG*, IX, 7, lines 17–18: τοῖς δ' αὐτοῖς παρακατατίθεμαι τὰ πράγματα συντηρεῖν.

to defend Cyrene while Ptolemy invaded Cyprus.[157] The legal parallel, however, does not hold. *Fideicommissum* in Roman law took effect only upon death of the testator.[158] A Greek precedent would seem more promising. Euergetes' chancellery was hardly well versed in Roman legal practise. One can point to the institution of *parakatatheke*, the entrusting of a person or property on deposit, the deposit eventually to be returned or passed on to another protector under specified conditions. And the word is used, at least in verbal form, in the inscription.[159] But once again the parallel is strained and implausible. The king's domain is not awarded to Rome on deposit with stipulations for future return or transfer. The inscription calls only for Roman aid in the event of attack on Ptolemy's holdings.[160] Efforts to discover the appropriate legal categories may miss the real point. They ignore the peculiar and largely unprecedented character of this document.

Is this, strictly speaking, a will or testament at all? The text certainly does contain some language characteristic of such codicils.[161] Ptolemy couched it in a form partially modeled on Hellenistic testamentary dispositions. But that is not the whole story, or indeed a particularly important part of it. The clauses are ill-fitting: a key segment points to the future, i.e. the bequest to follow on Ptolemy's death; others are plainly geared to the present. The stipulation that Rome will inherit the kingdom if Ptolemy dies childless is sandwiched between hope for retaliation against those who plotted against the king and appeal for Roman aid against those who would invade the king's territory—both clauses referring to circumstances within Ptolemy's lifetime.[162] This is far from a typical last testament.

157. So, e.g., Oliverio, *La stele*, 53–55; De Sanctis, *RivFilol* 60 (1932): 67; Schubart, *PhilWoch* 52 (1932): 1081–1083.

158. Wilcken, *SitzBerlin* (1932): 322–323.

159. *SEG*, IX, 7, line 17: παρακατατίθεμαι; see Bickermann, *Gnomon* 8 (1932): 427–429.

160. *SEG*, IX, 7, lines 18–23. It is no better to regard the text as a form of treaty. The φιλία καὶ συμμαχία is already in existence: lines 15–16, 21.

161. The opening phrase, for example, fits that pattern: *SEG*, IX, 7, line 2: τάδε διέθετο. So also the expressed hope for good fortune (lines 6–11), the conditional bequest (lines 11–16), and the citation of witnesses (lines 24–26). See Luzzatto, *Epigrafia giuridica*, 156–157.

162. Wilcken, *SitzBerlin* (1932): 323–325, takes the clause on Roman assistance in the event of attack as dependent on bequest of the kingdom and thus not to take effect until after Ptolemy's death. That thesis, however, is untenable. The δὲ in τοῖς δ᾽αὐτοῖς (*SEG*, IX, 7, line 17) clearly introduces a new thought, and the following phrases cannot be dependent on what precedes, i.e. the conditional bequest. Moreover, the exhortation to Rome to bring aid in accordance with the φιλία καὶ συμμαχία (lines 18–23) makes no sense if the Romans have already become possessors of Ptolemy's realm. See the cogent remarks of Winkler, *Rom und Aegypten*, 53; cf. Otto, *AbhMünch* 11 (1934): 103–104.

Legal modes are secondary. The document has political aims. Ptolemy Physcon, unrelenting in hostility to his brother and in ambition for territorial gain, fastened upon an ingenious device to turn frustration into success. The testamentary form was mere facade. Rome would inherit only if Ptolemy died childless—an unlikely event, as the king was still in his twenties. The rest of the text dwells on cooperation and alliance between Ptolemy and the Republic, vengeance on the king's enemies, and protection of his dominions. If Ptolemy could not enlist Roman forces on his behalf, he could at least give the impression that he was doing so. The public claim of Rome's favor and the warning to his enemies that the Republic's power might be mobilized against them would help to advance the king's aims. If Ptolemy Philometor had, in fact, plotted against his life—or if Physcon genuinely suspected him of so plotting—the prospect of Rome's inheritance could serve as a useful insurance policy. And, since Physcon planned another trip to Rome with additional requests, it was prudent to have a new and striking card to play.[163]

The scheme was clever but ineffectual. It made little or no impact in Rome. The literary sources pass over the testament of Ptolemy Euergetes altogether.[164] Obviously the senate took scant notice of Physcon's offer at the time, and since the will was never implemented (the birth of a son and heir canceled the legacy), it dropped out of the literary tradition.

The young Ptolemy's machinations continued. He pressed his case for Cyprus, with the aim of earning public favor in the East and perhaps even enticing some assistance from Rome. Publication of the will was only a start. In 154 the king appeared in person before the Roman senate, leveling accusations against his brother and making display of scars allegedly sustained at the hands of would-be assassins. Physcon's histrionics played to the *patres'* compassion.[165] A similar maneuver had been attempted on his behalf a decade and a half earlier, during the Sixth Syrian War, and again, with variation, by Philometor when he took up a lowly residence in Rome. The game of soliciting senatorial sympathies proceeded—not perhaps with the expectation of obtaining material aid but in hope of supportive gestures that might cow one's foes and promote military or political gains.

---

163. The political aspect of this move is correctly underscored by Winkler, *Rom und Aegypten*, 52–59, and Otto, *AbhMünch* 11 (1934): 99–110. De Sanctis, *RivFilol* 60 (1932): 67, draws the wrong conclusion: that the episode exemplifies the servility of Hellenistic kings toward Rome.

164. The nearest to it is a vague reference in Festus which indicates a Ptolemaic bequest to Rome prior to that of Ptolemy Apion; *Brev.* 13.2. Other, later testimony, equally vague, derives from this passage; De Sanctis, *RivFilol* 60 (1932): 63.

165. Polyb. 33.11.1–3.

Philometor's agents were in Rome as well, presenting arguments to contradict the charges of Physcon. The senate's reaction, however, did not rest on the cogency of the argumentation. To maintain some consistency in public posture required a pronouncement on Euergetes' behalf—and, in view of earlier failures, a somewhat stronger stance than before. But not one that would commit the Republic to a military involvement in the East. As so often, the senators opted for compromise: a strong gesture and a weak implementation. They rudely dismissed the representatives of Ptolemy Philometor, appointed a five-man commission headed by Cn. Cornelius Merula and L. Minucius Thermus, each with his own warship, to reinstate Euergetes in Cyprus, and wrote to allies in Greece and Asia, encouraging them to bring assistance for Euergetes' recall.[166]

What did this amount to? The situation is familiar: the combination of forceful statement and restrained action repeated a pattern not only with regard to Egypt but, as we have seen, in Greece, Asia Minor, and Syria as well. The five emissaries with five ships may have bolstered Physcon's confidence, but still constituted no more than a demonstration. If there was fighting to be done, Physcon would have to do it himself, assisted perhaps by friendly eastern states. Roman power would be reserved for matters closer to home.[167]

Whatever support Physcon did muster proved to be inadequate. The attempt on Cyprus miscarried once again. Our fragmentary testimony provides no details of the campaign. But it is evident that Physcon's effort came to an ignominious end, he was besieged at Lapethus, reduced to desperate straits, and then fell into the hands of his brother. Ptolemy Philometor elected to exercise clemency, just as he had a decade earlier after a clash between the brothers. He gave Euergetes assurance of personal security, permitted him to retain control of Cyrene, fashioned an economic agreement, and even promised his daughter in marriage.[168] The generous settlement was characteristic of the man—but also appropriate to the circumstances. Philometor

---

166. Polyb. 33.11.4–7: τούτοις μὲν παρήγγειλε κατάγειν Πτολεμαῖον εἰς Κύπρον, τοῖς δὲ κατὰ τὴν Ἑλλάδα καὶ τὴν Ἀσίαν συμμάχοις ἔγραψαν ἐξεῖναι συμπράττειν τῷ Πτολεμαίῳ τὰ κατὰ τὴν κάθοδον.

167. Even if Rome were inclined to lend material aid—a most implausible assumption—the revival of major fighting in Spain around this time would have ruled it out; cf. Appian, Iber. 56; Livy, Per. 47; Obseq. 17.

168. Polyb. 39.7.6: τοσοῦτον ἀπέσχε τοῦ κολάζειν ὡς ἐχθρὸν ὥστε καὶ δωρεὰς προσέθηκε παρὰ τὰς πρότερον ὑπαρχούσας αὐτῷ κατὰ συνθήκας καὶ τὴν θυγατέρα δώσειν ὑπέσχετο; Diod. 31.33: συνεχώρησε δὲ αὐτῷ τὴν ἀσφάλειαν, καὶ συνθήκας ἐποιήσατο καθ' ἃς ἔδει Κυρήνην ἔχοντα τὸν νεώτερον εὐδοκεῖν καὶ σίτου πλῆθος τακτὸν λαμβάνειν κατ' ἐνιαυτόν. These two passages clearly refer to the same events, even though Diodorus has erroneously assigned them to the year 158. See above pp. 701–702,

needed a unified and harmonious realm, for he had his eye on bigger things: the reconquest of Coele Syria. A reconciliation with his brother, enhanced by marriage ties, would neutralize potential friction within the kingdom. And he took notice also of the Romans. They had played no active role in the events, but their public statements on Euergetes' behalf were troublesome, a possible invitation to dissidents. Philometor made certain to advertise widely his amicable accord with Euergetes and to represent his policy as welcome to the Romans.[169] Consolidation of Ptolemaic holdings and a publicizing of friendly relations with other states, including the Roman Republic and the Cretan *koinon*, would pave the way for further expansion. As so often in the Greek East of the second century B.C., advertisement of an association with Rome, whatever its substantive meaning (or lack thereof), sufficed for the purposes of Hellenic rulers and leaders. Both of the Egyptian kings employed that technique, the elder brother with greater sophistication and with greater success. Philometor now held the reins firmly and would soon mature plans to revive the ancient glories of the Ptolemies.

Roman involvement had been minimal and marginal. The outcome perhaps caused misgivings and even recriminations. Some may have felt that the contrast between verbal assurances and practical inaction had become embarrassing. The Republic's expressed wishes had now been twice thwarted by the craft of Ptolemy Philometor. Only a hint survives, however, of senatorial controversy on the matter. M. Cato delivered a blistering speech against Thermus, an oration entitled *De Ptolemaeo minore contra Thermum*.[170] In that context, Thermus must surely be L. Minucius Thermus, one of the envoys sent to assist Euergetes' attempt on Cyprus in 154.[171] Cato's attack may

---

n. 145. Philometor had the assistance of Cretan auxiliaries in that war, as two inscriptions set up in Delos by the auxiliaries reveal; Dürrbach, *Choix*, no. 92 = *IdeDélos*, 1517; *OGIS*, 116 = *IdeDélos*, 1518; cf. Holleaux, *Études*, 77–97. The latter document, a decree honoring Philometor, makes reference to the mildness and magnanimity he demonstrated in making peace; lines 6–8: πάντων ἀνθρώ[πων] ἡμερώτατος ἐποήσατο τήν τε φιλία[ν καὶ] τὴν εἰρήνην, κατὰ πάντα χρησάμενο[ς] τοῖς πράγμασι μεγαλοψύχως.

169. The attitude is reflected in the decree of the Cretan auxiliaries; *OGIS*, 116 = *IdeDélos*, 1518, lines 9–11: προαι[ρούμε]νος ἐν οἷς μάλιστα χαρίζεσθαι καὶ Ῥωμ[αίοι]ς. In this context, Philometor surely had an eye to further recruitment as well. Crete had previously been a source of mercenaries for his brother: Polyb. 31.17.8. Physcon's last testament may also have served as a deterrent to his elimination. And the proposed marriage link would help assure that the kingdom stayed in the family. This is perhaps hinted at, but in rather too strong language, by Diodorus who has Philometor spare Euergetes partly out of fear of the Romans: Diod. 31.33.

170. The few surviving fragments are registered in Cato, *ORF*, F177–181.

171. Otto's suggestion, *AbhMünch* 11 (1934): 118–119, that Thermus was somehow involved in Philometor's marriage proposal to Cornelia is wholly speculative.

represent, in part, a criticism of Thermus' ineptitude and failures during that mission, thus an indirect verdict on the senatorial decision to send him. A fragment of the speech makes reference to "that best and most beneficent king."[172] Hence, the issue of Rome's attitude toward the rival monarchs seems to have surfaced in the accusations against Thermus. But further conjecture would be unwise. Policy differences can hardly have played a large part. The speech lashed Thermus for corruption, greed, and deception. It is not certain that Cato was taking the part of one king as against another, nor even which king is referred to as best and most generous.[173] Hypotheses about senatorial divisions on foreign affairs should be set aside. The *patres* did not devote a significant part of their business to debate on the Ptolemies.

## The Ambitions of Ptolemy Philometor

After 154 Ptolemy Philometor sat secure on his throne. Having reduced his brother to capitulation and conciliation, Philometor proceeded to ignore him. The king took steps to tighten control over his realm. The promised marriage of his daughter to Euergetes never materialized. Philometor had better things in mind for her—a potential instrument in his designs on the Seleucid kingdom.[174] In the meantime, he set up his young son Ptolemy Eupator as co-ruler in 153, a clear signal for the succession: Euergetes was to be left out. Young Eupator became lord of Cyprus, probably also a sign that the island was closed to Euergetes' influence or expectations.[175] The mercurial Euergetes made one more effort to solicit Roman favor, an effort imaginative to the point of farce: he offered himself in marriage to the noble widow Cornelia, daughter of Scipio Africanus and mother of the Gracchi. The grand matron, of course, would have none of it. The endeavor was but the latest in a series of increasingly pathetic attempts

172. Cato, *ORF*, F180: *rege optimo atque beneficissimo.*

173. Since Thermus was sent to assist Euergetes, it is usually assumed that Cato's praise was reserved for Philometor. So, e.g., De Sanctis, *Storia dei Romani* IV:3.100–101; Briscoe, *Historia* 18 (1969): 61–62. A properly cautious discussion by Astin, *Cato the Censor*, 111, 270–271.

174. Otto's hypothesis, that Roman intervention canceled the wedding plans of Euergetes and Cleopatra, has no basis whatever; *AbhMünch* 11 (1934): 118; cf. Seibert, *Historische Beiträge*, 86.

175. *OGIS*, 125–127. See the reconstruction of Otto, *AbhMünch* 11 (1934): 119–123, who, however, implausibly suggests that Rome induced Philometor to appoint Eupator in order to divide and weaken the kingdom. Rome had never exercised such influence on Philometor in the past. Nor did the appointment of his son to Cyprus, in any meaningful sense, divide the kingdom.

by Physcon to ingratiate himself with the leadership of Rome.[176] Ptolemy Philometor now had a firm hold on his dominions. Egypt and Cyprus gave unstinting allegiance.[177] Euergetes was humbled and impotent in Cyrene. Philometor had publicized his good relations with Rome. And the monarchy had strong influence elsewhere, as in Itanus, the Cretan *koinon*, Methana, Thera, Paros, and Delos.[178]

Philometor prepared to ripen his still more ambitious plans. In 150 he participated in a coalition of Hellenistic kings which lifted the pretender Alexander Balas to the throne of Syria, eliminating his predecessor Demetrius I.[179] Attalus of Pergamum had initiated the project, but Ptolemy Philometor proved to be the principal beneficiary. He gave his daughter, once betrothed to Physcon, as bride to Alexander Balas, thereby establishing a Ptolemaic foothold in the dynastic politics of Syria.[180] Philometor, who twenty years earlier had been the protégé of Antiochus IV when the Seleucid aimed at indirect suzerainty of Egypt, now turned that scheme on its head. He would be the patron of a Seleucid client in Antioch.

A crisis in the Syrian realm gave Ptolemy the opportunity for a more vigorous interference in its affairs. Demetrius II, fifteen-year old son of Demetrius I, collected mercenaries in Crete in 147 and invaded Phoenicia to challenge Alexander Balas.[181] Ptolemy hastened to intervene, bringing vast naval and land forces into Palestine. Whatever the outcome of the fighting between rivals for the Syrian crown, Philometor intended to be in a commanding position: he planted garrisons of his own troops at key sites along the invasion route in Seleucid territory.[182] Ostensibly the Egyptian king came in support of his son-in-law. But circumstances suddenly changed—or else were manipulated. Alexander Balas turned on Ptolemy and plotted his assassination. So, at least, Ptolemy alleged. The allegation provided pretext

---

176. Plut. *Ti. Gr.* 1.4. Plutarch refers to him simply as Πτολεμαίου τοῦ βασιλέως. But it is quite inconceivable that Philometor is meant. Such an offer would be entirely out of character, inopportune, and unnecessary. Philometor was already in secure control—and already married. That Physcon hatched the wild scheme at a time when his fortunes had ebbed is entirely plausible.

177. The youth Ptolemy Eupator died prematurely in 150, but this did not affect the loyalty of Cyprus to the crown.

178. Cf. Bagnall, *Administration*, 118–120, 122, 124–130, 135–136, 150–152.

179. Appian, *Syr.* 67; Justin, 35.1.6–9; cf. Polyb. 3.5.3.

180. The author of 1 Macc. 10:51–58 ascribes to Balas the initiative for this marriage alliance; followed by Jos. *Ant.* 13.80–82. But their source evidently did not know of Philometor's earlier sponsorship of Balas in securing the Seleucid throne. It is unlikely that the calculating Philometor was the passive recipient of an idea that stemmed from the youth Alexander Balas.

181. 1 Macc. 10:67–69; Jos. *Ant.* 13.86–87; Justin, 35.2.1–3.

182. 1 Macc. 11:1–8; Jos. *Ant.* 13.103–105.

for an about-face that would bring greater advantage to the ruler of Egypt. Ptolemy broke with Alexander Balas, annulled the marriage by parental fiat, and offered his daughter to Demetrius II. The new alliance, this time with an untested teenager, would put Philometor in effective control.[183]

The armed might of Ptolemy and the unpopularity of Alexander Balas proved decisive. The people of Antioch expelled Balas in 145 and welcomed the ruler of Egypt.[184] Ptolemy Philometor now stood at the brink of a wholesale shift of power in the Near East, the most dramatic inversion since the triumphs of Antiochus the Great more than a half-century before. In what form or manner Ptolemy proposed to govern these dominions cannot be known with precision. Nor does it much matter. He assumed a double diadem at Antioch, according to the author of 1 Maccabees: the crowns of both "Asia and Egypt."[185] In the text of Josephus, Ptolemy was presented with both diadems, but modestly professed contentment with Egypt alone, persuading the Antiochenes to accept Demetrius II as ruler. At the same time, however, he made clear that he would be tutor, guide, and censor of the young Seleucid.[186] Diodorus' version may preserve the facts with greater exactness: Philometor annexed Coele Syria to his domain but left Demetrius in charge of the traditional holdings.[187] The obituary of Philometor in Polybius accords him the title of "king of Syria"—a designation compatible with Diodorus' account, if one regards it as a shorthand expression for Coele Syria or, perhaps with more pregnant

183. The analysis in 1 Macc. 11:1, 11:8–12, regards Ptolemy as harboring a treacherous plan from the start to deprive Balas of his kingdom. A version favorable to the Ptolemaic cause is preserved in Josephus, who presents the assassination attempt by Balas as genuine, thereby justifying Ptolemy's change of front: *Ant.* 13.106–110. Diodorus puts it somewhat differently: Philometor came in aid of his son-in-law, discovered his mental and moral incapacity, and then alleged a plot, thus bringing about the new marriage alliance: 32.9c. Volkmann, *Klio* 19 (1925): 407–410, follows Diodorus' account. Otto, *AbhMünch* 11 (1934): 124–125, adopts the cynical version expressed in 1 Maccabees. One can hardly imagine that Philometor entered Palestine and installed garrisons out of unselfish motives. Yet it is precisely the Egyptian king's ambition for aggrandizement that makes an assassination attempt by Alexander Balas plausible; cf. Santi Amantini, *RIL* 108 (1974): 517–518; Goldstein, *I Maccabees*, 424–425.

184. 1 Macc. 11:13; Jos. *Ant.* 13.111–112; Diod. 32.9c; Livy, *Per.* 52; cf. Appian, *Syr.* 67; Justin, 35.2.2–3—without mention of Ptolemy.

185. 1 Macc. 11:13: περιέθετο δύο διαδήματα περὶ τὴν κεφαλὴν αὐτοῦ, τὸ τῆς Αἰγύπτου καὶ Ἀσίας.

186. Jos. *Ant.* 13.113–115: διδάσκαλός τε ἀγαθὸν αὐτῷ καὶ ἡγεμὼν ἔσεσθαι διωμολογήσατο καὶ φαύλοις ἐγχειροῦντι πράγμασιν οὐκ ἐπιτρέψειν ὑπέσχετο.

187. Diod. 32.9c: τὴν δὲ Κοίλην Συρίαν ἐπιθυμῶν προσκτήσασθαι, συνέθετο πρὸς Δημήτριον κοινοπραγίαν ἰδίᾳ, κυριεύειν Πτολεμαῖον τῆς Συρίας, τὸν δὲ Δημήτριον τῆς πατρῴας βασιλείας.

meaning, as a description of Philometor's real authority.[188] The basic intent cannot be in doubt. Philometor had reestablished Ptolemaic ascendancy in Coele Syria and Palestine, and, through a compliant vassal king in Antioch, could exercise indirect sway over all Seleucid lands.[189]

The remarkable resurgence of Lagid power promised a new political configuration in the Near East. Yet there is barely a whisper in the sources of Roman interest or concern. Only Josephus reports that Ptolemy declined the crown of Asia lest he appear to give offense to the Romans.[190] The text presents no difficulties, even though not explicitly supported elsewhere. Philometor quite probably considered it prudent to give a nod in Rome's direction, if only to discourage any who might bring protest against him to the Republic. The king had done much the same nearly a decade before, when he had compelled Euergetes into surrender, announced an amicable settlement, and suggested that this had the approval of Rome.[191] Having established his own arrangements at that time, he proceeded to ignore both Euergetes and Rome in conducting his affairs and extending his authority. The Republic had fretted publicly before, complained and remonstrated, even severed diplomatic relations, while Philometor, in fact, went ahead to consolidate control and plan aggrandizement. The experience provided confidence that a friendly gesture to Rome would suffice to give him a free hand. A puppet king would rule in Antioch, while Ptolemy VI spread the prestige of the Lagids into the lands of the East.

The plan never came to fruition. Alexander Balas was defeated and slain, his head brought to Ptolemy Philometor as visible symbol of the king's unequivocal victory. But Ptolemy himself had suffered severe injury in the fighting, and within two days of the conquest he succumbed to his wounds.[192] The project itself, however, carries greater significance than the outcome. Ptolemy VI had enjoyed singular success for two decades. He had had every reason to anticipate a continued march to imperial grandeur—without Roman interference.

188. Polyb. 39.7.1: Πτολεμαῖος ὁ τῆς Συρίας βασιλεύς; similarly, Porphyry, FGH, 260 F 2.7; cf. Santi Amantini, RIL 108 (1974): 523–527.

189. The tutelage is indirectly acknowledged by Demetrius in an inscription honoring Philometor after his death: SEG, VI, 809 = XIII, 585.

190. Jos. Ant. 13.114: φείσασθαι τοῦ μὴ δόξαι εἶναι Ῥωμαίοις ἐπίφθονος ἔκρινε.

191. Such is implied in the decree of the Cretan auxiliaries set up at Delos: OGIS, 116 = IdeDelos, 1518, lines 9–11; see above p. 707.

192. 1 Macc. 11:14–19; Jos. Ant. 13.116–119; Livy, Per. 52; cf. Diod. 32.9d–10.1; Justin, 35.2.3–4; Appian, Syr. 67.

## Instability and Indifference

The death of Philometor shattered the dreams of expansionism. He had brought Ptolemaic fortunes to a high-water mark in 145. Thereafter they plunged. Demetrius II (or his advisers) immediately took charge of affairs in Syria. The Egyptian garrisons were removed and Ptolemy's soldiers in Palestine fled to Alexandria, allowing even their elephants to fall into the hands of Demetrius.[193] Ptolemaic authority abroad slipped elsewhere as well. The evidence for military installations and political influence in places like Methana, Crete, Thera, and the Aegean generally vanishes after the reign of Philometor.[194] The dominion of Egypt contracted.

The internal affairs of the realm became increasingly dismal. Details need not concern us. Philometor had taken the precaution of elevating his infant son Neos Philopator to a joint rule in 145. But his aims came to naught in the immediate aftermath of his death. Ptolemy Euergetes II returned from Cyrene to claim the kingdom, married his brother's widow Cleopatra II, the sister of both men, and did away with the child.[195] The grisly opening of Euergetes' sole reign set a tone that prevailed through many of his thirty years on the throne. The king ordered the execution of Cyreneans who had accompanied him to Egypt, conducted systematic persecutions of the Greek populace in Alexandria who had been supporters of Philometor, and eventually in 131 provoked a rebellion among the citizenry, backed by his wife, which drove him to refuge in Cyprus.[196] The resilient Euergetes, however, had rebounded more than once from setbacks. Intrigue and homicide soon allowed him to recover power. The sources relate that Euergetes murdered his own son by Cleopatra II and had the dismembered body delivered to his mother. Intimidation was followed by armed invasion, as Euergetes gradually reduced the countryside and then cowed the Alexandrians into submission by 127. But the machinations grew ever more complex. Cleopatra II turned to her son-in-law Demetrius II of Syria and soon helped to embroil Seleucids and Ptolemies once again in contests to determine the succession in each of the realms. A precise account of events is no longer possible.

193. Jos. *Ant.* 13.20.

194. Cf. De Sanctis, *Storia dei Romani* IV: 3.187–188; Bagnall, *Administration*, 122, 134.

195. Jos. *Contra Apionem*, 2.49–53; Justin, 38.8.2–4; cf. Otto and Bengtson, *Abh-Münch* 17 (1938): 24–30; on the chronology, see Samuel, *Ptolemaic Chronology*, 144–145.

196. Diod. 33.6–6a, 33.12–13; Justin, 38.8.5–6, 38.8.11; Polyb. 34.14.6–7; Livy, *Per.* 59. The documents that allow for dating are summarized by Samuel, *Ptolemaic Chronology*, 145–147.

But reconciliation in Alexandria seems to have come around 124, a joint rule of Ptolemy Euergetes with Cleopatra II and Cleopatra III, daughter of Philometor, both of whom were now officially Euergetes' wives. The reconciliation, together with some reform measures, allowed the regime to enjoy some smoother years toward the end of Ptolemy VIII's reign. But tension in the court must have endured, and bitterness among the Alexandrian populace cannot have lain far beneath the surface.[197]

Turbulence and instability only increased after the death of Physcon in 116. Cleopatra III stepped onto central stage, but the next quarter-century found the monarchy torn by rivalry between her two sons, Ptolemy IX Soter II and Ptolemy X Alexander, with alternate expulsions and reinstatements of the monarchs, the eventual murder of Cleopatra III, and intensified activities by the Alexandrian populace in determining the political fortunes of their rulers.[198] The decline of Ptolemaic prestige abroad and disintegration of unity within paralleled similar experiences in the Seleucid realm.

What hand did Rome have in these depressing developments? The evidence is thin, fragmented, and inadequate. Yet the nearly total absence of reference to Roman involvement for two generations after Ptolemy Philometor's death is unlikely to be mere happenstance. The modern practice of surmising Roman machinations and orchestration behind the scenes is methodologically indefensible.[199]

The struggle for power between Ptolemy Euergetes and Cleopatra II that followed directly upon the death of Philometor in 145 saw a Roman envoy, Thermus, in Alexandria.[200] His presence there has given rise to excessive conjecture. Thermus is customarily identified with L. Minucius Thermus, one of the Roman legates sent in 154 to assist Euergetes in recovering Cyprus. And his mission in 145, so it is argued, had as purpose the installation of Euergetes as ruler of all

197. Principal literary evidence in Diod. 34/35.14, 34/35.20; Justin, 38.8.12–38.9.1, 39.1.1–39.2.6; Jos. *Ant.* 13.267–269; Livy, *Per.* 59; Val. Max. 9.2.ext.5. An exhaustive study of Euergetes' reign by Otto-Bengtson, *AbhMünch* 17 (1938): 23–112. More briefly: Volkmann, *RE* XXIII:2 "Ptolemaios," no. 27, 1725–1736; Will, *Histoire politique* II:356–369.

198. See, especially, Paus. 1.9.1–3; Justin, 39.3.1–2, 39.4.1–39.5.1; Jos. *Ant.* 13.285–287, 13.351; Porphyry, *FGH*, 260 F 2.8–9; Posidonius, *FGH*, 87 F 26 = Edelstein and Kidd, no. 77. Discussion in Otto-Bengtson, *AbhMünch* 17 (1938): 112–193; Volkmann, *RE* XXIII:2 "Ptolemaios," nos. 30 and 31, 1738–1747; Musti, *PP* 15 (1960): 432–446; Will, *Histoire politique* II:369–373, 435–437.

199. The surmises occur repeatedly in Otto-Bengtson, *AbhMünch* 17 (1938): passim; cf. also De Sanctis, *Storia dei Romani* IV:3.185–190.

200. Jos. *Contra Apionem*, 2.50: ὄντος ἐκεῖ Θέρμου τοῦ παρὰ Ῥωμαίων πρεσβευτοῦ καὶ παρόντος.

Egyptian domains. The king's success in that year, therefore, came with the sanction and approval of Rome.[201] The episode has occasioned other speculation as well: that Thermus was in Alexandria to represent Roman objections to the annexation of Coele Syria by Philometor; or that he came to assure the interests of Roman businessmen in the region; or that he hoped to bring about harmony between Euergetes and Neos Philopator.[202] Proliferation of hypotheses, however, brings little profit. It is particularly paradoxical that those who have interpreted Roman policy as directed toward fragmenting Egyptian holdings, thus to weaken the monarchy, here see the senate in support of Physcon's reunification of the dominions under his own control.[203] Our evidence consists of a single statement, in passing, by Josephus that Thermus was in Alexandria as an envoy in the immediate aftermath of Ptolemy Philometor's death. We do not know his commission nor—equally important—whether he accomplished it. If this is indeed L. Minucius Thermus, he had already suffered severe criticism at the hands of Cato and a trial for corruption. Damage to his prestige may have reduced his effectiveness. And, in view of the series of Roman embassies whose accomplishments were minimal or whose advice was ignored, it is altogether irresponsible to credit Thermus with the settlement that established Ptolemy Euergetes in power.

The celebrated diplomatic tour of eastern kingdoms and republics by Scipio Aemilianus and his colleagues ca. 140 included a stopover in Egypt. The visit prompted moralizing tales and edifying anecdotes. Aemilianus exemplified Roman abstinence and discipline, by contrast with the enormously corpulent Physcon, wallowing in degenerate luxury, his transparent garments revealing more than anyone wished to see. The trim Aemilianus led Physcon at a brisk pace, while the king struggled mightily to keep up, a spectacle to his countrymen.[204] Anecdotes apart, did the Scipionic legation interfere in the affairs of Egypt? There is nothing to suggest it. The envoys visited numerous eastern states, inspected the lands, and occasionally arbitrated disputes.[205] In Egypt, however, Physcon's position was undisturbed—however much contempt Scipio may have had for him.

201. Winkler, *Rom und Aegypten*, 58, 65; Otto, *AbhMünch* 11 (1934): 118–119, 131–132; Otto-Bengtson, *AbhMünch* 17 (1938): 26; De Sanctis, *Storia dei Romani* IV: 3.186–187.

202. The possibilities are canvassed by Manni, *RivFilol* 28 (1950): 250–252.

203. See the cogent criticisms of Otto-Bengtson by Manni, *RivFilol* 28 (1950): 249–250.

204. Posidonius, *FGH*, 87 F 6 = Edelstein and Kidd, no. 58; Justin, 38.8.8–10; Plut. *Mor.* 200F; Diod. 33.28b.1–2.

205. Polyb. fr. 76 = Athenaeus, 6.273A; Diod. 33.28b.4; see above pp. 669–670, n. 265.

The legates affected to scorn all the pomp of the court, and spent their time instead examining the strategic situation of Alexandria, the wealth of the land, the size of the population, and the strength of the kingdom generally. Having surveyed the terrain and the people, they pronounced themselves satisfied: Egypt had the potential to wield vast power—if the kingdom should ever happen upon competent rulers.[206] The remark ought not to be confused with a policy statement, suggesting either eventual annexation or the need to keep feeble monarchs on the throne of Egypt.[207] In the context of our testimony, it merely reflects that contrast on which the sources choose to dwell: between Roman pragmatic astuteness and the luxurious impotence of Egypt's leadership. Scipio disdained the king, but did not disturb his rule.

Our meager sources disclose no official action by Rome with regard to Egypt in the final decades of the second century. Some notice may have been taken of the expulsion of Euergetes by Cleopatra and the Alexandrians in 131. The matter perhaps received discussion in a senatorial sitting, but certainly did not provoke intervention.[208] Euergetes' restoration to Alexandria in 127 evidently benefited Roman shippers and merchants in the city. They set up an inscription in Delos to honor one of Euergetes' generals whose capture of Alexandria for the king had been to their advantage.[209] The event, however, does not reflect upon public opinion at Rome, let alone upon public action.

A high-ranking Roman senator, L. Memmius, visited Egypt in 112, as a letter copied on papyrus happens to reveal. The author specifies detailed arrangements for lodging, gifts, and ceremonies to

206. Diod. 33.28b.1–3: διέλαβον μεγίστην ἡγεμονίαν δύνασθαι συσταθῆναι, τυχούσης τῆς βασιλείας ταύτης ἀξίων τῶν ἡγεμόνων.

207. Winkler, *Rom und Aegypten*, 66–73, rightly discredits the notion that Rome contemplated annexation of the land. But his view, that Scipio sought to establish a personal *clientela* relationship with Egypt, has no basis in the evidence. Otto, *Abh-Münch* 11 (1934): 132, argued that the mission's purpose was to assure Rome that the Egyptian king represented no danger to her. Rome, however, did not require an embassy to ascertain that fact. The suggestion by Otto-Bengtson, *AbhMünch* 17 (1938): 38, that the envoys arrived in connection with a threat to Euergetes' rule by the Athamanian Galaestes (Diod. 33.20, 33.22), is pure conjecture.

208. The fact that Livy chose to record the events in Egypt at about this time suggests that they got some hearing in the senate: Livy, *Per.* 59.

209. OGIS, 135 = Dürrbach, *Choix*, no. 105 = *IdeDélos*, 1526: «Ῥ»ωμαίων οἱ εὐεργετηθέντες ναύκληροι καὶ ἔμποροι ἐν τῆι γενομένηι καταλήμψει Ἀλεξανδρείας ὑπὸ βασιλέως Πτολεμαίου θεοῦ Εὐεργέτου Λόχον Καλλιμήδου. These Romans were probably resident at Alexandria; Fraser, *Ptolemaic Alexandria* I:122; II:217, n. 242; not at Delos, as Otto-Bengtson, *AbhMünch* 17 (1938): 101–103. Note also the dedication of a Delian statue by two Romans to another intimate of Euergetes: OGIS, 133 = Dürrbach, *Choix*, no. 106 = *IdeDélos*, 1527.

assure the comforts and pleasure of Memmius' trip.[210] Scholars have frequently supposed a diplomatic mission: Memmius came with instructions, even secret instructions, to investigate conditions in Egypt and report on any dangers to Rome from rivalry between the sons of Cleopatra III.[211] The speculation is excessive and without basis. The papyrus identifies Memmius as a distinguished senator but nowhere calls him an ambassador. Nor is there the slightest hint of diplomatic duties or official functions. Memmius took a sightseeing trip.[212] The Egyptian officialdom, of course, made certain of gracious receptions and proper treatment. Anything less for a Roman of senatorial rank would be discourteous and offensive. But it is quite superfluous to hypothesize hidden orders and a clandestine spying operation.

The *patres* had neither need nor desire to meddle in the affairs of Egypt. Dynastic divisions wracked the court throughout the second half of the second century—and beyond. Rivals for the throne in this intense—and often murderous—contest would grasp for what support they could get. Hence, it is the more noteworthy that efforts to solicit Roman intervention seem largely to have ceased in this period. The realization had taken hold that such intervention, if it came at all, would be perfunctory and ineffective. Only one maneuver still held some promise. Ptolemy Euergetes II had established the precedent: to will one's dominions to Rome. This might provide personal security, improve political prospects, and possibly even draw the western power into the internecine struggles of the Lagids. Ptolemy Apion, bastard son of Euergetes, ruled Cyrene and bequeathed the land to Rome in 96. Then in the following decade the kingdom of Egypt itself was bestowed upon the Romans by last testament. That the senate itself planned or determined these legacies is unattested and unlikely. In fact, Rome did not even take up the inheritance of Cyrene for twenty years after the death of Ptolemy Apion and probably longer than that. The bequest of Egypt in 88 or 80 engendered controversy in Rome, but politics and war prevented implementation, and the kingdom was not annexed for another half-century.[213] Roman indifference to that land and its troubles had a very long history indeed.

210. *PTeb.* I, 33.

211. See, especially, Otto-Bengtson, *AbhMünch* 17 (1938): 159–160; E. Olshausen, *Rom und Ägypten von 116 bis 51 v. Chr.* (Diss. Erlangen, 1963), 6–11.

212. *PTeb.* I, 33, lines 5–6: τὸν ἐκ τῆς πόλεως ἀνάπλουν ἕως τοῦ Ἀρσινοίτου νομοῦ ἐπὶ θεωρίαν ποιούμενος; cf. line 14: πρὸς τὴν τοῦ λαβυρίνθου θέαν.

213. For discussion of Apion and Cyrene, with references, see Luzzatto, *Epigrafia giuridica*, 165–189; Will, *Histoire politique* II: 372–373; Oost, *CP* 58 (1963): 11–25; Badian, *Roman Imperialism*, 29–30, 35–37; Harris, *War and Imperialism*, 154–155. On the bequest of Egypt and its consequences, see Luzzatto, *op. cit.*, 197–221; Will, *op. cit.*, II: 436–437; Olshausen, *Rom und Ägypten*, 22–37. Badian has made a strong case for dating the will

**V**

An *amicitia* between Rome and the Ptolemaic monarchy came into force in 273 B.C. For nearly two centuries thereafter the loose connection remained essentially unaltered. Conventional analysis traces a different pattern, a downward curve: from a relationship of parity to one of clientage and dependency. That linear interpretation, however, is misleading. In fact, the association remained distant, sporadic— and usually insignificant. The histories of these two states during the long period under scrutiny impinged remarkably little upon one another. Contests for power within the Lagid dynasty did generate a movement toward Rome and, for a time, pulled the affairs of the nations into closer contact. But that development was confined largely to the years of Ptolemy Euergetes II and depended upon the peculiar vagaries of that individual's personality and ambitions. For the most part, the connection was thin and scarcely felt.

The *amicitia* began in the reign of Ptolemy II Philadelphus and on the initiative of that monarch. It fit as part of his larger network of affiliations in both the eastern and western Mediterranean. But the diplomatic recognition involved no commitments or obligations. Egypt remained neutral in both Punic wars and in the First Macedonian War, supplying grain upon request on one occasion, otherwise involved only to offer mediation between Rome and Carthage and again between Rome and Philip. Ptolemaic political and economic interests determined those diplomatic moves, rather than any demands or expectations arising out of *amicitia* with Rome. The concerns of the two powers rarely met in the third century.

Ptolemaic political fortunes slipped after the end of that century. Overseas dependencies broke away or fell under the control of enemies, Egypt suffered losses at the hands of Antiochus III, and then her young king was brought into marriage alliance with the Seleucid, only to encounter severe embarrassment when Rome made war on Antiochus and subdued him. Roman spokesmen found it useful to include Ptolemaic claims in their propaganda against Philip and Antiochus, but Egypt gained nothing from the Republic's victories over those two monarchs. Rome refrained from interference in the Fifth Syrian War and essentially ignored the Ptolemaic kingdom in her own Syrian war.

---

to 88 rather than 80, thus making it a bequest of Ptolemy Alexander I instead of Ptolemy Alexander II: *RhMus* 110 (1967): 178–192; *Roman Imperialism*, 31, 73–74; accepted by Harris, *op. cit.*, 155–158; doubted by J.-M. Bertrand, in Nicolet, *Rome et la conquête*, 2:832.

Egyptian ambitions revived in the 180s and 170s. Ptolemy Epiphanes and the consortium that ruled after him strengthened control at home and built alliances abroad. Self-confidence inspired aggrandizement and provoked the Sixth Syrian War. Rome had taken no notice; nor had the regime in Egypt considered application to the senate. Indeed, the nationalist spirit in Alexandria impelled the populace to take matters into their own hands and to resist the plans of Antiochus IV. It was only a drastic turn in the military fortunes that drove the Egyptians to make appeal to Rome. Representatives of the youth Ptolemy Euergetes II humbled themselves before the senate in 168, an event ostensibly emblematic of a new relationship between the states. Yet Roman attitudes seem fundamentally unchanged. The Republic had done no more than indirectly urge reconciliation during the war. And after Pydna, when she could take direct action, Rome checked Antiochus' advance but only promoted concord between the Seleucids and the Ptolemies.

Rivalry between the brothers Philometor and Euergetes II plagued the Egyptian scene for the next two decades. It also brought intermittent legations to Rome, representing one or the other of the rivals. Philometor came once with a crafty scheme designed to win support but to retain control of the situation. Euergetes tried a host of projects, including outright appeal, a bequest of his kingdom, and even marriage proposals to a Roman matron. The efforts repeatedly miscarried. The king who held Rome at arm's length, evaded her requests, and faced up to her displeasure fared better than his brother who offered full cooperation and a dependent relationship tantamount to clientage. The *patres* were occasionally induced to make pronouncements, but not to take action. Their verbal backing for Euergetes amounted to little of substance. Philometor arranged matters to his own liking, and the *patres* lost interest—if ever they had any. The brothers organized their kingdom as they saw fit.

Philometor avoided a direct affront to Rome. All else, it seems, could be done with impunity. Whether the senate ever formally renewed the diplomatic relations it had renounced in 162/1 is unknown. Philometor's plans, in any case, stayed on course. He brought even the boldest aims into operation: recovery of Coele Syria and, through intrigue and alliance, expansion of Ptolemaic suzerainty to the lands of the Seleucids. Only death halted Ptolemy Philometor, not any objections from Rome.

Leadership disintegrated in the two generations after Philometor's death in 145. Conflict in the court and loss of authority abroad reduced the kingdom to insignificance on the international scene. Rome showed no propensity to intervene, nor did the rulers and claimants to power even trouble to solicit her intervention. One precedent, however, did eventually inspire imitators: the will of Euergetes, on which model were patterned the much later bequests of Cyrene and Egypt in the first century. But Rome, who had ignored the former, neglected for a very long time even to implement the latter. The fortunes of Egypt fluctuated with the strength or weakness of her rulers, the vagaries of her populace, and the contention with rival Hellenic powers. The Roman Republic rarely took account of and even more rarely affected events in the land of the Nile.

# Conclusion

The extension of Roman power into the eastern Mediterranean eventually changed the face of the whole Hellenic world. A natural temptation arises to perceive the process as a relentless march of Roman arms to subdue and subjugate all before them. Closer observation from a vantage point other than Rome's, however, reveals a very different and much more complex picture. The initial stages of expansion need to be understood in their own context, not from the outcome that yielded a world governed and administered from Rome.

The essential foundation for inquiry must be the structures, institutions, and attitudes of the Greeks. That framework gives insight into the vicissitudes and peculiarities, the aberrations and fluctuations that marked Roman-Greek contacts in the third and second centuries B.C. One will not find clear pattern or linear process. The vantage point is crucial. Romans adjusted to and maneuvered within Hellenistic modes of interstate relations; they did not come to impose an Italian system upon the East. And Greeks naturally treated the westerner within their own established terms of reference. The Hellenistic structure provided a basis for the relationship, but also a source for confusion and misapprehension. Romans endeavored to adapt it to their purposes, Greeks to manipulate it for theirs.

The diplomatic practices and expectations followed Hellenic traditions long prevalent in the East. Associations commonly took the form of *philia*, a conveniently elastic arrangement ubiquitous among Hellenes and admirably suitable to the interests of Rome. Formal treaty relationships entailed unwelcome restraints. Romans avoided them for a long time in the East. When they did eventually enter into such relationships, they employed the design of treaties and alliances

familiar to the Greek world. The same holds for the principle of interstate arbitration, a Hellenic means of resolving disputes, initially unknown to the Romans but gradually employed by them as serviceable
to their ends. Conventional sloganeering proved to be similarly serviceable: Roman negotiators and spokesmen eagerly embraced the
Greek mottoes of "freedom and autonomy" with which to characterize and justify their goals. And even the relationship so commonly
associated with Roman practice, the patronage of greater states over
lesser, developed from a Hellenistic background, the benefits and
mutual obligations expected from collaboration between the major
powers and their dependencies. Equally important, the participation
of Rome in these conventions did not transform them into Roman instruments or monopolies. Greek states concluded alliances with one
another, entered into associations of *philia*, conducted interstate arbitration, exploited traditional propagandistic terminology, and engaged in deferential adulation toward powerful princes and principalities even through the late second century B.C.

As the Greeks drew Rome into the matrix of institutions familiar
to themselves, so they also put those institutions to work for their
own ends. Greek initiative repeatedly set events in motion, endeavoring to harness Roman might and authority to Hellenic purposes. So,
cities in Crete, debtors in Aetolia and Thessaly, and factions in Epirus
hoped to engage senatorial arbiters for their disputes; military assistance from Rome was solicited by Pergamum against Macedonia,
by dynasts in Asia Minor against one another, by Spartans against
Achaeans, by contenders for the throne of Egypt against their adversaries. When embassies despaired of armed relief, they might still apply for mediation or diplomatic intervention, or simply profit from
the moral force of a senatorial pronouncement in their favor. Once
Rome took on the Hellenic garb of "liberator," Greeks were swift to
prod her into living up to the role: Achaeans exploited that propaganda line to provoke Roman pressure against Nabis, the Rhodians
reminded Rome of her posture to assure their own protectorate of
"autonomous" cities in Asia, and Lycia pressed the senate to preserve
her "freedom" in the face of Rhodes' authority. The western power
did not convert Greeks into clients. Rather, Greeks put to use a relationship between major and minor states, common in their own experience, by paying homage to the Republic, cultivating its leaders, wor-
shipping Roma, presenting lavish gifts to the senate, and generally
flattering Roman pride in order to mobilize tangible or moral support
for Hellenic goals. Even the depositing of kings' sons in Rome had as
motive the advance of dynastic schemes at home. The efforts to capitalize upon Roman authority stemmed from a wide variety of sources

and locations: cities like Sparta and Lampsacus, princes like Prusias, Ariarathes, and Ptolemy Euergetes, leaders of factions within states like Callicrates of Achaea and Charops of Epirus. Hellenic motivation and manipulation stand forth conspicuously.

The traditional landmarks of Hellenistic history in the later third and second centuries derive from a Rome-centered approach: the three Macedonian wars, the Syrian war, the Aetolian war, the Achaean war—as if each contest simply pitted Rome against an opponent. The terminology obscures some important facts. Internecine Greek quarrels played themselves out in those contests, usually preceding and precipitating Roman involvement, not a mere adjunct thereof. Rome, in fact, had only a minor and accessory role in the "First Macedonian War," entered the second war with Philip after it was well underway, and on other occasions involved herself in conflicts triggered by Hellenic rivalries and engaging Greek states which fought for their own particularist advantages. The antagonisms that divided Achaeans and Spartans, Aetolians and Macedonians, Pergamenes and Bithynians, or Ptolemies and Seleucids, as well as a host of contentions among lesser states, continued to take a central part in provoking the wars and affecting their character.

Even the victories of Roman arms did not remold Greeks, whether allies or opponents, into passive dependencies. The vigorous activity of the Achaean League in pursuing its own political and military goals during the heyday of its leaders Philopoemen and Lycortas—and often in defiance of express wishes conveyed by Rome—provides a valuable illustration. The same combination of maintaining diplomatic correctness with Rome while disregarding her advice and requests may be seen in the complex but independent and largely effective policies of the Rhodian Republic, of the Pergamene rulers Eumenes II and Attalus II, of Antiochus IV and Demetrius I of Syria, of the resourceful Egyptian monarch Ptolemy Philometor. The patterns of Hellenistic politics recurred and endured.

A principal reason for this needs to be underscored. Roman attention to the East was fragmentary, intermittent, and rarely intense—concentrated, short bursts of activity rather than continuous vigilance. The Hannibalic war, of course, was an absorbing preoccupation in the later third century. The decades that followed saw almost uninterrupted engagement against Gallic tribes or Ligurian opponents in northern Italy. Whether these were aggressive or defensive wars is irrelevant. The concerns of Rome for that region took precedence over other foreign affairs. Even when the Republic did engage in eastern conflicts, one consul at least would normally receive Italy, Gaul, or Liguria as his *provincia*. Spain too occupied Roman

energies and military resources for long stretches of time, two decades of warfare from the beginning of the second century and another
two decades when fighting resumed in earnest in the mid-150s. The
East could not command such incessant involvement. Hellenic affairs
were secondary to the protection and control of northern Italy, to the
disciplining and punishment of Boii, Insubres, Ligurians, Celtiberi-
ans, Lusitanians, and Vaccaei. The attitude is reflected in the marked
differences that held between treaty agreements in Italy and those outside the peninsula. The former imposed tight obligations, fixed military commitments, and expected loyalty and collaboration. The latter
were looser in formulation, friendly arrangements rather than formal
pacts or, when modeled on Greek treaties, unrealistic and rarely implemented. Archaic formulas in the pronouncements of censors or
priests regarding the extension of Roman power refer to Italy and justify Rome's dominance therein. But the emotional and juridical attachment to *Italia* gave it a distinct place that compelled public consideration at a level never attained by affairs of the East.

The piecemeal character of Roman attention to the world of the
Greeks did not preclude occasional intervention, violence, and triumph. Scholarship has traditionally dwelled upon the motives for
war, an attempt to discern logical pattern and consistency in the progress of Roman expansion. The attempt, however, may be misguided.
The eastern wars, as already noted, were not simply or primarily of
Rome's making. Hellenic competition and hostilities set them in motion and helped shape their course. As for the motives of Rome, one
will not find systematic design. *Ad hoc* circumstances prompted entrance into the wars, each with its own peculiar nature and objectives.
The importance of holding the loyalty of allies in southern Italy was a
chief priority in Rome's earliest eastern ventures: protection of shipping lanes in the Adriatic and the integrity of Greek cities on the
Straits of Otranto engendered intervention in the Illyrian wars and
the First Macedonian War. Image and reputation played the major
role in inducing the Republic to engage against Philip V and later
against Perseus. Roman behavior in the First Macedonian War had
been the object of harsh criticism among Greeks—both for brutality
and for unreliability. A strong stance against Philip could restore a
more favorable impression. Similarly, the elevated prestige of Perseus, coming as it did to the detriment of Roman repute, irritated senatorial leaders and made them receptive to the complaints of Perseus'
enemies. In the preliminaries to both the Second and Third Macedonian wars, however, the *patres* had good reasons to believe that intimidation through a firm posture and a massing of Hellenic opinion and
resources would bully the kings into compliance, thus achieving their

ends without resort to arms. In other wars still other conditions occasioned Roman involvement. A war of words aggravated relations between Rome and Antiochus III; the propaganda campaign pushed both powers to the brink and over it. The aspirations of Achaea, the esteem of Rome, and the personal ambitions of Flamininus helped maneuver events into the conflict with Nabis. Roman neglect and insensitivity to traditional Macedonian attitudes supplied the conditions which nurtured Andriscus' uprising and led to the subjugation of the land. Ancient Peloponnesian quarrels and the unrelated presence of a Roman army in Macedonia combined to make the Achaean war a concern of Rome's and provoked her to terminate it decisively. A unique sequence of developments eventuated in the annexation of Asia: the bequest of Attalus III, Aristonicus' attempted usurpation, the ambitions of Anatolian dynasts, and political upheaval in Rome. The various interventions do not converge to form a pattern. Individual circumstances and unanticipated events provoked the decisions. The fragmentary quality of Rome's attention to the East is matched by the intermittent and unpredictable occasions of her forceful entrance into it.

By the same token, it is fruitless to postulate a uniform explanation for the imperial expansion of the Republic. Resort to a theory of sheer aggression and militarism is simplistic. The numerous refusals to intervene, the decline of requests and denials of opportunity, the hesitations and delays, the frequent efforts at mediation and reconciliation all belie the theory. The economic advantages of conquest were certainly understood. But they do not account for each decision to move abroad, they were often overridden by other considerations, and emphasis upon them tends to confuse results with motives. Equally inadequate is the hypothesis of a "defensive" mentality, a fear of strong neighbors that impelled Rome to eliminate the external threats to her security. This might help to interpret some attitudes among leaders but it can hardly explain actions against minor states or wars at a considerable distance from the shores of Italy. Nor does it illuminate matters to speak of a "fit of absence of mind." Accident and inadvertence must indeed be given their due. Circumstances which led to individual wars nearly always involved some errors of judgment, miscalculations, and unexpected turn of events. But it is wholly misleading to imagine that Rome stumbled about blindly in the East, ignorant of the consequences of her own decisions, lacking all framework for action, and too shortsighted to recognize the implications of intervention.

Rome's engagement in the East was intermittent, sporadic, and, to the Greeks, often frustrating. But it was not fortuitous. The very spasmodic character of her interest stemmed directly from the system and attitudes of her ruling class.

It is symptomatic that the senate never developed a bloc of "eastern experts," indeed actively discouraged developments that might lead to one. The aristocratic ethos assumed that members of the nobility were highly competent amateurs in all categories of public life. With few exceptions, the commanders of armies and members of diplomatic missions to the East had short stays abroad and did not return. That pattern avoided the political risks of concentrating foreign policy in the hands of area specialists—but also deterred long-range commitments to the regions of the East. Similarly, it discouraged formation of groups within the ruling orders organized on the basis of foreign policy or attachment to Hellenic states. Senatorial debates regarding affairs of the East addressed *ad hoc* issues, and no identifiable individuals or factions held a consistent stance on the role of the Republic abroad. Roman embassies to the East went with great regularity, but their personnel was quite disparate. The combination of frequency and diversity made it easier for the senate as a corporate entity to maintain a distance from the actions and advice of individual legations. The detachment was deliberate and convenient. Assignments to the legates most commonly took the form of "investigation" or inquiry into the situation, a commission deliberately vague and elastic. The repeated embassies gave the impression of concern and interest, while the senate kept its own counsel.

Avoidance of commitment to the East was a logical corollary to dispositions manifest in the governing aristocracy of the Roman Republic. Familiarity with Hellenic language, art, and literature stayed well apart from involvement with Greeks on the level of state policy. The most ardent philhellenes were those most careful not to permit their cultural predilections to affect public action. The reluctance to annex and administer is similarly characteristic of aristocratic outlook in Rome. The business of the nobility was politics and war, not the supervision of administrative details in foreign lands. Hence, Roman forces withdrew after eastern wars, and commissions left the implementation of peace settlements to others; the senate turned the governance of the Macedonian republics over to the Macedonians in 167, and Romans proved slow even to make Greece a province after the Achaean war or to accept the bequest of Attalus III after 133. The *patres* preferred to deliver lessons by crushing opponents and intimidating the survivors rather than staying to assume the role of managers. It is fitting that the very concept of empire, in the sense of an organized unity under Roman control, did not take shape until the first century B.C.

Hellenic institutions and forms of international relations proved most serviceable for Roman objectives. Just as the Greeks utilized those institutions to draw Rome into their affairs, so the Romans employed them to set limits to their involvement. The relationship of *philia* possessed the convenient elasticity that allowed Rome to multiply her connections while minimizing her obligations. The Hellenic practice of interstate arbitration was equally convenient. While Greeks repeatedly called upon the senate to adjudicate their disputes and mediate their quarrels, the *patres* commonly turned to prior Greek rulings, referred cases to Greek tribunals, and endorsed the principle of Greek arbitration in their treaties and settlements. Rome's embrace of Hellenic conventions like the "freedom and autonomy" formula gave her the image of benefactor without contracting any specific responsibilities.

In fact, the Romans had frequent recourse, in their dealings with Greeks, to gestures, symbolic acts, and conventions—a feature inadequately recognized or appreciated. It manifests itself in the treaties adopted with Hellenic states. The specifics of those agreements mattered much less than their implications. So, the compact with Aetolia in 189 enshrined the repentance of that state and proclaimed its future adherence to concord; the Achaean and Syrian treaties signified a new stability among Hellenistic powers; the alliance with Rhodes symbolized her reentry into favor after earlier humiliation; and the agreements with minor cities and states in the later second century were pure formalities, their balanced terms inappropriate to the imbalance in power, but meant only to denote Roman benevolence. The proliferation of amicable interchanges with Hellenic communities created relationships commonly characterized as *philia*, a term which had familiar resonance in the Greek world, intended as a sign of amity rather than a profession of duty. Romans adopted with comparable eagerness the various Hellenic catchwords associated with "liberation." They could thus pose in attractive guise, utilize the propaganda when appropriate, but interpret it in their own interest. The posture both encouraged Greek expectations and permitted Roman detachment. That duality receives illustration in a different way through the philhellenic tendencies of Roman aristocrats whose very admiration for Greek culture obliged them to detach themselves from Greeks and express contempt for their weaknesses. The Romans employed Hellenic institutions to maintain their distance and to keep open their options.

Greeks naturally regarded the Republic in light of their own experience. They looked to Rome as one among a cluster of Hellenistic powers, sought her military aid in their internal fights, encouraged her patronage, and exploited her reputation. The Hellenes drew what seemed obvious conclusions from the decisive victories of Roman legions over Philip and Antiochus in the early years of the second century: that the conqueror would establish hegemony over Hellas. Reactions diverged. Some states nourished bitterness and hostility, others hastened to capitalize by attaching themselves to Rome's interests and claiming her support for their own. Roman behavior seemed for a time to match expectations. The westerners adapted Hellenistic terminology and conventions, professed themselves as liberators and patrons, used the language of *philia*, accepted the principles of interstate arbitration: all of the familiar formulas used by Hellenistic monarchs to realize their hegemonial aspirations. But Romans proved surprisingly reluctant to install direct or indirect rule and became frustratingly resistant to appeals for intervention. The withdrawal seemed to some Greeks a peculiar abdication of responsibility, to others a signal for resumption of former patterns of politics and diplomacy within Hellas. Two decades later, however, the Greek world reeled under the impact of Rome's violent intrusion in the Third Macedonian War. Attitudes shifted once more, the anticipations of Roman dominance revived; but again they encountered retreat and a baffling indifference for another two decades until the explosive events of the mid-140s. It is hardly surprising that Greeks found Roman actions maddeningly difficult to comprehend. Rome had appropriated Hellenic conventions but did not behave accordingly; she persistently raised expectations and just as persistently violated them; she preferred gesture to enforcement, posture to implementation; she seemed deaf to importuning for long stretches of time and then reentered suddenly and briefly with devastating results. Greeks both benefited and suffered from Roman involvement, both solicited and resisted Roman interference, both stimulated Roman pronouncements and balked at their ineffectiveness. They were never able fully to grasp the Republic's indifference to consistency and aversion to commitment.

Rome's aloofness, however, could not endure indefinitely. By the late second century her political and military presence in the East had become permanent. Paradoxically enough, the change in attitude stems in part from the very embrace of Hellenic institutions that Rome had manipulated to preserve her own detachment.

The manipulation itself of those conventions, the repeated use of gestures and formulas familiar to the Greek world had its impact upon the Roman mentality. An increasing number of generals and diplomats received adulation when in Hellas, became knowledgable about Hellenic ways, and made contacts among Greek factions and individuals. The posturing of Rome may have been designed to give her flexibility, but it also gave her an image to protect, a fact of no small importance in prompting intervention against Philip, Nabis, and Perseus. The propaganda of "liberation," when repeated often enough, reduced maneuverability and could draw the Republic into unwanted conflict, as with the Antiochene war. The patronage thrust upon the Romans by Hellenic conventions and expectations could also influence Roman behavior. Representatives of the senate or officers of the forces who received homage in Greece, took pleasure in flattery, and welcomed the requests of potential clients grew in number quite considerably during the course of the second century. Legations from Hellas continued to come with great frequency to the Roman senate—and with greater hopes as they looked to familiar faces and would-be patrons in that body. Even when the appeals were shelved or their implementation ignored, the Greeks might still expect to advertise favorable responses and to exploit Roman prestige to their own purposes. And the *patres* rarely turned back embassies with discourtesy. Quite apart from individual senators who might seek to display magnanimity and extend patronage, the senate as a body was sensitive to image and reputation. It normally opted for token politeness rather than direct action. Collective decision-making in the senate still operated at a level of detachment that permitted the *patres* to judge each situation in its own terms, rather than in conformity with a general "policy." Yet the accumulation of connections, the habit of ambassadorial missions, the repetition of gestures, and the increased familiarity with the Hellenic world induced Roman leaders to accept greater responsibility for the East and ultimately even to adopt the principle of provincialization.

**V**

The world of the eastern Mediterranean had undergone profound change by the end of the second century. Roman authority had extended its giant shadow over the whole region. The process of change, however, had been neither linear nor gradual. A rhythm of intervention and withdrawal characterized it, long stretches of indifference punctuated by short but increasingly ruinous demonstrations of force. Through the course of it Hellenic continuities endured in remarkable and surprising ways. Greek monarchies and republics continued to frame alliances with one another, undertake agreements, rely on mutual exchanges of *philia*, expand a system of interstate arbitration, present themselves as "liberators," show deference or patronage within a network of Hellenic relationships. Roman withdrawal both permitted and encouraged those continuities. The detachment ultimately yielded to a willingness to assume imperial responsibility. But that change took place over a very long period of time—the effect of numerous individual decisions in *ad hoc* situations, not a grand design to control the East.

The foregoing analysis has endeavored to offer an approach quite different from standard treatments of "the age of imperialism." It stresses both Rome's receptiveness to Hellenic principles which she found congenial and the Greeks' ability to take advantage of Roman presence within a system familiar to themselves. Hellas ultimately fell under Roman authority not because the Romans exported their structure to the East, but because Greeks persistently drew the westerner into their own structure—until it was theirs no longer.

## • Appendix I •

# Roman *Foedera* with Greek Cities

Agreements with major eastern powers in 189 and 188 helped to advertise and propagate the stability aimed at by Rome. Similar engagements with lesser states and minor communities in Hellas would not have the same impact. Yet several such engagements are attested by or hypothesized from various sources, some of them placed by scholars in or around 188. What purpose could they serve? In fact, the chronology needs reexamination. The agreements may belong in a wholly different historical context.

An important inscription records the treaty between Rome and the Asian city of Cibyra, dated by most moderns to 188 or shortly thereafter.[1] The beginning of the document is lost, but enough remains to disclose a full-fledged defensive συμμαχία with each party contracting to aid the other if attacked by a hostile power. Copies of the treaty were to be erected and displayed in both states; it was, therefore, a solemn and definitive engagement. How likely is it that Rome entered into such an obligation as early as 188?

Palaeographical and orthographical considerations seem to point to the first half of the second century.[2] They cannot, however, specify a particular date. The year 188, far from a logical conjecture, is a particularly unsuitable time. In the previous year Rome considered Cibyra, a city just east of Caria and north of Lycia, as hostile territory.

---

1. *OGIS*, 762. The date was conjectured by Niese, *Geschichte*, III:61; followed, *inter alia*, by Täubler, *Imperium Romanum*, 454–455; Horn *Foederati*, 70; Accame, *Il Dominio*, 86–87; Sherwin-White, *Roman Citizenship*, 159. Between 188 and 167, according to W. Dittenberger, *OGIS, loc. cit.*; Magie, *Buckler Studies* (1939), 178–179; *RRAM* II: 1122–1123, n. 30.

2. Dittenberger, *OGIS, loc. cit.*

Cn. Manlius, the Roman consul, while leading his forces into central Asia Minor, threatened to sack the city and devastate the surrounding area. A heavy bribe dissuaded him, so we are told, a bribe offered by Moagetes, tyrant of Cibyra, whose self-effacement and hypocritical protestations earned the contempt of Polybius.[3] That Cibyra, of all places, would then receive the signal honor of a formal συμμαχία with Rome surpasses belief. Scholars have fastened on 167 as *terminus ante quem* for the treaty. The arguments carry little weight: when Caunus and Mylasa revolted from Rhodes in 167, Cibyra supported the rebels; and in the same year the Rhodian refugee Polyaratus, demanded by the Romans, sought asylum at Cibyra. The city denied him access and sent him back to Rhodes under instructions from the Roman proconsul.[4] Neither episode even faintly suggests the existence of an alliance. In fact, Polybius explains Cibyra's refusal of Polyaratus as due to fear of danger from Rome.[5] As testimony for date of the treaty this evidence is worthless.

The inscription itself offers some help. The συμμαχία was concluded between the δῆμος of Rome and the δῆμος of Cibyra.[6] It seems a safe assumption that the city was not at that time ruled by a tyrant.[7] We know precious little about the course of Cibyra's history. According to Strabo, a tyranny governed the state continuously until overthrown by the Romans ca. 84.[8] That statement refers to the government of the Tetrapolis, a federation of four cities including Cibyra. The date of its establishment has escaped record, but doubtless fell after the treaty—which was made with Cibyra alone. Prior to that time, the course of the tyranny need not have run so smoothly.[9] A

3. Polyb. 21.34; Livy, 38.14. According to Polybius, Moagetes was received into φιλία by Manlius: 21.34.13—a far cry from an alliance with Rome.

4. On aid to the rebels: Polyb. 30.5.11–15; Livy, 45.25.11–13. On Polyaratus and Cibyra: Polyb. 30.9.13–19. The incidents are regularly cited to show existence of the treaty by 167; see the authors cited above, n. 1. Rightly skeptical is Badian, *Foreign Clientelae*, 295.

5. Polyb. 30.9.16: διὰ τὸ δεδιέναι τὸν ἀπὸ Ῥωμαίων κίνδυνον.

6. *OGIS*, 762, lines 3–4, 6–8.

7. So, rightly, Dittenberger, *ad loc.* That should suffice to rule out a date of 189 or thereabouts when, according to Polybius, it was Moagetes who was accepted into φιλία by the Roman commanders: 21.34.13. The idea that the tyrant's authority had been restricted within Cibyra and hence need not be mentioned in a treaty is a desperate solution; as Täubler, *Imperium Romanum*, 455; Larsen, *CP* 40 (1945): 80; Magie, *RRAM* II:1123. Reynolds, *Aphrodisias and Rome*, 9, suggests that the tyranny was continuous but that public business was officially conducted in the name of the people. But cf. the treaty with Nabis of Sparta in 195; Livy, 34.35.2: *pax cum tyranno*; 34.40.7: *pace dato tyranno*.

8. Strabo, 13.4.17 (C 631).

9. One may note the tyrant of Bubon in the 140s, perhaps also a Moagetes, slain

period of democratic rule temporarily interrupting the tyranny would be the appropriate time. To pinpoint it is impossible. But we can exclude certain significant dates. In 189 Moagetes seems firmly entrenched and, after his bribe, acknowledged by the Romans.[10] Two decades later, in 167, when we hear of Cibyra again, a tyrant once more holds sway, a certain Pancrates.[11] The curtain descends thereafter until the founding of the Tetrapolis, probably some time in the second half of the second century, when the tyranny again controls affairs down to the 80s. A fixed date for the treaty would be mere guesswork and hence pointless. But nothing compels us to put it before 167—and certainly not in 188, the least suitable time.

Another inscription, from the Carian city of Alabanda, shows that her government sent two missions to the Roman senate. The first stressed Alabanda's services to Rome's military operations, seeking to renew friendship and cordiality and to establish a συμμαχία. The second made a plea regarding tribute and received a senatorial resolution affirming immunity. The leader of these legations, honored on the inscription, made yet a third trip to "the king"—for reasons unknown.[12] The decree is generally dated to ca. 188.[13] Did Alabanda secure a Roman alliance at that time?

The proposition admits of serious doubts. In 189 the Roman commander Cn. Manlius Vulso indulged a request from Alabanda to reduce a stronghold and restore it to the city.[14] The sources make no

---

by his brother and later avenged by his sons who instituted a democracy: Diod. 33.5a. The manuscripts give *Molkestes* and *Mokeltes*, usually emended to Moagetes. Cf. also the inscription of Araxa naming a Moagetes as ruler of Bubon, but evidently subject, in some way, to the authority of Cibyra; SEG, XVIII, 570. He may be the same man, as suggested by the inscription's editor; G. E. Bean, *JHS* 68 (1948): 46–56. Or else, the earlier Moagetes, prior to his acquisition of power at Cibyra; cf. J. and L. Robert, *REG* 63 (1950): 185–197; Moretti, *RivFilol* 78 (1950): 326–350; Larsen, *CP* 51 (1956): 151–169.

10. Polyb. 21.34.13; Livy, 38.14.14.

11. Polyb. 30.9.14. Polyaratus expected refuge in Cibyra because the tyrant's sons had been raised in his home.

12. *Editio princeps* in *BCH* 10 (1886): 299–306; republished with expanded historical commentary by Holleaux, *REG* 11 (1898): 258–266. The first mission, lines 11–25; see, especially, lines 12–15: τὴν ὑπάρχουσαν πρὸς Ῥωμαίους οἰκ[είο]τητα καὶ φιλίαν ἀνανεώσασθαι καὶ τὰς χρείας [ἃς] παρέσχηται εἰς τὰ στρατόπεδα αὐτῶν ἐκφαν[εῖς] γενέσθαι πρὸς αὐτοὺς καὶ ποιήσασθαι συμμαχ[ίαν]. The second mission, lines 25–32; it obtained a δόγμα περὶ τῆς ἀφορολογησίας. The embassy to the king, lines 32–34; its purpose, unfortunately, broken off on the stone: πρὸ[ς] τὸ[ν] βασιλέα περὶ τῶν [ ? ].

13. Holleaux, *REG* 11 (1898): 260–266; Bickermann, *REG* 50 (1937): 221, 228, 239; Schmitt, *Rom und Rhodos*, 87–88. An embassy from another Carian city, Apollonia, definitely does belong in 188. But this legation went to the Roman commissioners at Apamea and endeavored to secure favorable treatment in the peace arrangements; it was not seeking an alliance; Robert, *La Carie* (Paris, 1954), II: 303–312.

14. Livy, 38.13.2–4.

other mention of Alabanda in these years. She may indeed have been among the Asian cities which sent representatives to Rome after the battle of Magnesia in the hopes of obtaining senatorial favor. If so, she can hardly have obtained an alliance. The senate gave only a brief and vague response, referring all disputed claims to the *decem legati*, appointed to effect a settlement.[15] Nor does this situation—with Antiochus already defeated—easily correspond to that recorded in the inscription, which alludes to a time of serious danger and praises the honorant for bringing safety and security to the city.[16] The question of the φόρος causes equal difficulty. Alabanda was certainly not a tributary of Rome at this time. The decree of immunity might, of course, have been a mere formality, a declaration of Alabanda's freedom and autonomy.[17] Or else, the city feared lest she, like the rest of Caria, fall under the tight hegemony of Rhodes.[18] All of this, however, is speculation, not proof of a date. And the third mission, to some king, is most troublesome of all. What benefits could Alabanda have expected to acquire from Antiochus after he had been humbled by Rome and had withdrawn beyond the Taurus?[19]

Other dates raise fewer difficulties. In 170, during the Third Macedonian War, Alabanda's envoys to the senate announced that they had established a temple and a festival to Roma and offered lavish gifts to be placed on the Capitol.[20] They intended, no doubt, to contrast their loyalty with the rather lukewarm attitude of Rhodes and to obtain Roman favor.[21] The epigraphically attested embassies may belong here.[22] Or perhaps a much later date—after the Mithridatic wars of the 80s. Heavy exactions were imposed upon eastern cities

15. Polyb. 21.18.1–2, 21.24.4–5.

16. Lines 18–21: πρὸς τὴν τῆς πατρίδος ἀσφά[λειαν] καὶ σωτηρίαν ἀ[ν]ήκουσαν, παρακληθεὶς ὑπὸ τοῦ δή[μου] προθύμως ὑπ[ή]κουσαν οὐθένα κίνδυνον ὑφιδόμεν[ος] καθ᾿ αὑτόν.

17. As in the Roman letter to Teos of 193; *Syll.*³ 601 = Sherk, *RDGE*, no. 34, lines 20–21: ἀφορολόγητον ἀπὸ τοῦ δήμου τοῦ 'Ρωμαίων. Alabanda had earlier had its "democracy and peace" guaranteed by Antiochus; *OGIS*, 234 = *FDelphes*, III, 4, 163, lines 20–22.

18. Cf. Polyb. 21.24.7–8, 21.45.8, 22.5. So, Holleaux, *REG* 11 (1898): 264–265, n.3; Schmitt, *Rom und Rhodos*, 87, n. 1.

19. No other king is possible in 188. Eumenes did not have any claims on Caria. Holleaux, *REG* 11 (1898): 265–266, suggests that the mission sought to recover citizens of Alabanda, prisoners of war, or captured slaves under Antiochus' control—as specified in the peace of Apamea: Polyb. 21.42.8–10. Possible, but far from definitive.

20. Livy, 43.6.5–6.

21. Three years later, when Rhodes had lost Roman favor, Alabanda engaged in open warfare against her: Polyb. 30.5.15; Livy, 45.25.13.

22. Such is cautiously suggested by Magie, *RRAM* II:994–995, n. 32; cf. *idem*, *Buckler Studies* (1939), 174–175. The king would then presumably be Antiochus IV?

to pay the expenses of that war. Many of them, we may be sure, sent representatives to Rome to point out their services and to gain exemption from the financial burden. Stratonicea, a Carian city not far from Alabanda, certainly did so. A letter of Sulla and a senatorial decree of 81 are extant, acknowledging the fidelity of Stratonicea and awarding her numerous privileges.[23] Alabanda might well have put in her claims at about the same time.[24]

A definitive solution is impossible—and it would be futile to attempt one. The dating of Alabanda's embassies, as the above discussion shows, is anything but firm. One important point deserves stress. Even if the legations be placed ca. 188, they by no means demonstrate that the city acquired an alliance with Rome. The inscription states that Alabanda's envoy came to renew $\phi\iota\lambda\iota\alpha$ and to obtain $\sigma\nu\mu$-$\mu\alpha\chi\iota\alpha$. That she achieved the latter aim we simply do not know. The decree offers only a vague formulation: the embassy succeeded in bringing advantages to the city.[25] A far more concrete specification would be expected if Rome actually consented to a *foedus*. She had no motive for doing so, nor is the postulated treaty ever alluded to again in our evidence.[26] The alliance between Rome and Alabanda is a chimera.

Still another pact appears, at first sight, to fall in the aftermath of the Syrian war: a treaty of alliance between Rome and Heraclea Pontica. Reference to it occurs but once, in the fragments of the Greek historian Memnon, writing perhaps in the second century A.D. The treaty receives scant discussion in modern works; generally it is brushed aside or ignored altogether. Yet Memnon's assertion seems clear enough: a compact which bound the two states not only as friends but as allies of one another; and the agreement was described

23. *OGIS*, 441 = Sherk, *RDGE*, no. 18. On the burdensome exactions imposed by Rome elsewhere, see Appian, *BC*, 1.102.

24. The case is argued forcefully by H. Willrich, *Hermes* 34 (1899): 305–311, who rightly calls attention to the Stratonicean decree. Bickermann's objection, *REG* 50 (1937): 239, that Alabanda's mission, if in the 80s, should have gone to Sulla, not to the senate, is invalid. Sulla did compose the letter to Stratonicea, but her privileges were formally awarded by a *senatus consultum*. Of course, the identity of the king is problematical on this theory—as on all others. Willrich suggests that a mission may have been sent to Mithridates in order to recover properties and war captives, on the analogy of the Stratonicean decree: lines 116–119. Willrich's article, it might be noted, even persuaded Holleaux to change his mind; *REG* 12 (1899): 359, n. 1.

25. Lines 21–22: κατώρθωσαν τὰ κατὰ τὴ[ν πρεσ]βείαν συμφερόντως τῆι πατρίδι. Rightly noted by Holleaux, *REG* 11 (1898): 262, and followed by Schmitt, *Rom und Rhodos*, 87, n. 1. Magie, who disputes the date, nonetheless assumes that an alliance was concluded; *RRAM* II:994–995, n. 32.

26. The absence of such a reference in Alabanda's mission to Rome in 170 is striking: Livy, 43.6.5–6.

on bronze tablets set up in both Rome and Heraclea.[27] So definitive a notice must be taken seriously, hardly as an invention by Memnon or his source. How do we date it?

In the extant text, reference to the treaty follows a series of statements regarding Heraclea's communications with Roman generals during the Syrian war: efforts by Heraclea to negotiate a settlement between Rome and Antiochus, friendly letters from the Scipios and others, Antiochus' defeat, and the peace of Apamea.[28] The authenticity of these remarks is not above dispute. Nothing else in our evidence attests peace efforts by Heraclea and messages to the city by Roman commanders. In fact, Heraclea's role in the Syrian war is otherwise altogether unknown.[29] This alone does not authorize us to discard the treaty as fictitious. More serious is the order of the fragments, dependent as they are on the Byzantine excerptor Photius. Immediately after Memnon's notice of an alliance comes a reference to Prusias I's war on Heraclea. But as has long been recognized, that campaign predates the Antiochene war, occurring probably some time in the 190s.[30] The subsequent passage, on the Gallic invasions, refers to yet an earlier time, explicitly inserted as an excursus.[31] A long chronological gap follows; the next item applies to the Social War in Italy, a century later. In fact, the whole treatment of the period of the late third and early second centuries is brief and selective, in sharp contrast to the detailed account of the fourth and third centuries which precedes and of the Mithridatic war which follows. Memnon's chronology of the intervening events is anything but exact.

One may go further. Even if the relevant text be accepted as it stands, it need not imply that a treaty was concluded shortly after the Syrian war. Memnon records the peace of Apamea, then repeated Heraclean embassies to Roman officials in Asia, further expressions

27. Memnon, FGH 3B, 434 F 18.10: καὶ τέλος συνθῆκαι προῆλθον Ῥωμαίοις τε καὶ Ἡρακλεώταις, μὴ φίλους εἶναι μόνον ἀλλὰ καὶ συμμάχους ἀλλήλοις, καθ' ὧν τε καὶ ὑπὲρ ὧν δεηθεῖεν ἑκάτεροι. Magie, Buckler Studies (1939), 178, dismisses the notice simply as "perhaps untrustworthy," followed by Badian, Foreign Clientelae, 295. Elsewhere, however, Magie accepts it—again without discussion; RRAM I:310; II:967, n. 89. M. Janke, Historische Untersuchungen zu Memnon von Herakleia (Würzburg, 1963), 30–31, skims past the treaty and sees no difficulty.

28. Memnon, FGH 3B, 434 F 18.6–9.

29. A letter from a certain "Publius Aemilius" is mentioned by Memnon, FGH 3B, 434, F 18.6. There was no such person: perhaps a mistake for L. Aemilius Regillus, commander of Rome's fleet in the Aegean in 190? On this man, see the sources in Broughton, MRR I:356. Or L. Aemilius Scaurus, an officer under Regillus and posted with ships to the Hellespont? Livy, 37.31.6; cf. Janke, Historische Untersuchungen, 25–27.

30. Memnon, FGH 3B, 434, F 19.1–3; cf. G. Vitucci, Il Regno di Bitinia (Rome, 1953), 51–53; Habicht, RE XXIII:1, "Prusias," no. 1, 1096–1097.

31. Memnon, FGH 3B, 434 F 20.1–3.

of friendship, and finally (τέλος) the alliance.[32] How much time may have elapsed is anybody's guess. The chronological vagueness allows a substantial margin. And the misplacement of surrounding fragments makes for greater uncertainty still. The treaty may well have come much later in the second century.[33] Heraclea did supply two triremes to the Roman cause against Perseus in 171, but nothing implies that this derived from an alliance. Of the other states mentioned in that same connection none is known to have had a συμμαχία and one of them, Rhodes, definitely did not.[34] Additional references to Heraclea in the first half of the second century betray no trace of any formal relationship with Rome.[35] An alliance with a remote Pontic town, at a time when Rome had resigned control of western Asia Minor to Eumenes and Rhodes, is implausible in the extreme.

Scattered epigraphical references record Greek missions to the senate in search of "friendship" or "friendship and alliance." Dating is in most instances insecure or, where definite, much later. The formula φιλία καὶ συμμαχία, in any event, applies broadly, by no means signifying a formal alliance.[36] A Delian embassy to Rome asked for renewal of οἰκειότης καὶ φιλία. The decree honoring the envoy has been placed as early as 193, but this reconstruction is altogether speculative and unfounded.[37] Delos had done nothing to earn Roman favor in the war against Philip; an annalistic tradition even has the island punished by being turned over to Athens in 196.[38] The embassy

32. Memnon, *FGH* 3B, 434, F 18.10. Notice especially the imperfect διεπρεσ-βεύετο—clearly a number of different embassies. P. Desideri, *StudClassOrient* 19–20 (1970–71): 487–537, defends Memnon's account of negotiations prior to the peace at great length, but accepts without discussion conclusion of the treaty shortly after Manlius Vulso's campaign.

33. De Sanctis, *Storia dei Romani*, IV:3. 217, puts it after the Fourth Macedonian War, but without argument. Meloni, *Perseo*, 174, n. 2, states flatly that there was a long gap between the Syrian war and the treaty with Heraclea, but also offers no discussion.

34. Livy, 42.56.6.

35. The city is named as one of the autonomous *adscripti* to a treaty among Asian powers in 179: Polyb. 25.2.13. Moreover, in the 150s a Heraclea was among the victims of Prusias II's campaigns of devastation: Polyb. 33.13.8. If that city is Heraclea Pontica, the event shows that Rome felt no obligation to assist her as late as the 150s. Robert, *Études Anatoliennes* (Paris, 1937), 114–115, in a discussion of Prusias' route, proposes a different Heraclea, an obscure city in Lydia. Questioned by Magie, *RRAM* II:1198, n. 43, who opts for Heraclea Pontica—without noticing the consequences for his own dating of the treaty.

36. Cf. Horn, *Foederati*, 10–12, 72–73.

37. *IG*, XI, 4, 756. See Th. Homolle, *BCH* 8 (1884): 84–88; cf. P. Roussel, *Délos, colonie athénienne* (Paris, 1916), 3, n. 4; Colin, *Rome et la Grèce*, 267.

38. Livy, 33.30.10–11. False, of course: Delos was not put under Athenian control until 167; cf. Holleaux, *Études* V:107–108. But Delos clearly was no *amicus* of Rome at this time.

in any case—whenever it comes—shows that Delos could claim only an *amicitia*, not an alliance. Another decree discloses a mission from Troezen asking for φιλία καὶ συμμαχία. Whether she got it or not is unknown. Letter forms induced the editor to assign the documents to the early second century—again a mere guess and refuted by historical circumstances. Having concluded an alliance with the Achaean League, Rome would hardly frame a separate pact with one of its individual members.[39]

## V

Additional treaties, recorded or attested epigraphically, all fall in the period after the Third Macedonian War, most of them well after.[40]

A new inscription, still to be published with text and commentary, discloses an alliance previously unknown. Rome concluded a pact with Maronea on the Thracian coast.[41] The document is nearly complete, an important find. It signals a φιλία καὶ συμμαχία to hold on land and sea and for all time. The Maroneans promise to prohibit passage through their land and through that of their dependents for those who would make war on Rome and to provide no food, supplies, weapons, or ships to them. The Romans undertake the same commitments.[42] If Rome or her dependents should be attacked by enemies, the people of Maronea will bring assistance—on condition that opportunity allows for it. A parallel clause binds Rome, and on the same condition.[43] In short, a standard defense alliance with the standard escape clause. The closing portions are equally familiar: provision for additions or subtractions to the treaty, subject to agreement by both states and a proclamation that bronze copies are to be displayed at Maronea and on the Capitoline in Rome.[44]

---

39. The mission is recorded in *IG*, IV, 791. The editor compares *IG*, IV, 752, from the early second century. But that is a very different document and the disputes therein recorded are to be arbitrated by Athens; Rome is not considered. Troezen—and the Argolid as a whole—was part of the Achaean Confederacy until 146: Polyb. 38.15.3. If she ever got a treaty, it must have come after that date; cf. Niese, *Geschichte* III: 357, n.5.

40. Athenian cleruchs on Lemnos in a decree ca. 165 gave thanks for their reunification with Athens under Roman auspices. The document, in a damaged portion, heaps praise on the Romans and makes reference to a συμμαχία; *IG*, II², 1224, lines 9–10: τοὺς κοινοὺς εὐεργέτας ἁπάντων ['Ρωμαίους . . . συμ]μαχίαν καὶ καταστὰς πρὸς τοὺς ἀδι[κοῦντας]. There is no reason to believe, however, that this indicates a formal treaty of alliance between Rome and Athens.

41. *BCH* 102 (1978): 724–726 and fig. 176; *ArchDelt* 28 (1973): 464, with a good photograph at pl. 418.

42. Lines 10–30.

43. Lines 30–36: κατὰ [τὸ εὔ]καιρον.

44. Lines 36–43.

What of the date? On the basis of letter forms, the editor placed it tentatively in the second half of the second century. Greater precision may be impossible at this point. The treaty encompasses not only the Maroneans but also those citizens of Aenus who had been declared free by "Lucius" and who evidently enjoyed some civic privileges in Maronea.[45] L. Aemilius Paullus springs immediately to mind as the logical "Lucius," conqueror of Perseus and appropriate "liberator" of people once under Macedonian control.[46] The inference gives 167 as a *terminus post quem* for the alliance. But it can hardly have followed within a short time of the Third Macedonian War. Attalus requested in winter 168/7 that the towns of Aenus and Maronea be turned over to him (or to the Pergamene kingdom), a proposition which, according to Polybius, attracted Roman senators, though in the end they changed their minds and liberated the cities.[47] Aenus and Maronea duly remained outside and independent of the new republics of Macedonia.[48] Nothing in the literary evidence implies or is readily compatible with the idea of a formal alliance in the years immediately after Pydna. Reference to Paullus in the inscription (assuming the identity) certainly does not imply it, but only defines the status of the Aeneans included in the treaty.[49] The phraseology of the document shows some close parallels to that which records the Cibyra alliance, but there are parallels as close or closer to the Roman treaties with Methymna and Astypalaea, which belong to the late second century or later.[50] The tralatician character of the terminology limits its utility for dating purposes. Historical circumstances offer a better guide. They would suggest a date no earlier than the mid-140s,

45. Lines 6–10: [. . . τὸν δῆμον τὸν] Ῥωμαίων καὶ τὸν δῆμον τὸν [Μαρωνίτων . . .] Αἰνίων τοὺς κεκριμένους ὑπὸ Λευκίου ἐλευθέρους καὶ πολιτευομένους με[τ᾽ . . .]των φιλία καὶ συμμαχία.

46. Aenus and Maronea had resisted Roman forces in 170, thus at that time holding to a Macedonian alliance: Livy, 43.7.9–10. Earlier, in the 180s, there had been factional strife in the cities, some leaning to Eumenes, some to Macedonia: Polyb. 22.6.1–2, 22.6.7, 22.11.2; cf. Livy, 39.24.9. L. Paullus, if it is he, presumably granted privileges to the anti-Macedonian groups from Aenus.

47. Polyb. 30.3.3–7; Livy, 45.20.2–3. See above pp. 573–575.

48. Livy, 45.29.6.

49. Cf. the claim of the Narthacians ca. 140 who appeal to Thessalian laws governing their circumstances and established by Flamininus a half-century earlier: *Syll.*[3] 674 = Sherk, *RDGE*, no. 9, lines 48–53, 63–65.

50. Only the closing portion of the Cibyra treaty is extant to provide comparison. *OGIS*, 762, lines 1–16 correspond roughly to lines 33–43 of the Maronea text, though not with exactness of wording or even sequence. The alliance with Methymna offers a fuller parallel. One may compare *Syll.*[3] 693, lines 1–20 with lines 18–41 of the Maronea agreement. A lengthier correspondence still is with the Astypalaean treaty of 105; cf. *IGRR*, IV, 1028 = Sherk, *RDGE*, no. 16B, lines 27–50 with the Maronea pact, lines 10–43. The formulas are not precisely the same, but the substance is nearly identical.

when Rome undertook responsibility for policing the regions of Macedonia and Thrace.[51]

Those circumstances may also explain the pact with distant Callatis on the Black Sea, in what eventually became the province of Moesia Inferior. The alliance came to light a generation ago, in a fragmentary Latin inscription.[52] The damaged character of the stone prevents secure reconstruction. But enough remains to identify a mutual defense alliance, with the customary pledge by each party to come to the aid of the other if attacked.[53] The situation that prompted this agreement eludes discovery. The initial editors put it in 72/1 B.C., the time of M. Lucullus' campaigns in Moesia and contacts with Greek cities on the Black Sea.[54] Lucullus, however, captured and subdued the Hellenic cities, including Callatis; not a propitious time for awarding the favor of an alliance.[55] A more likely occasion, perhaps, was the period 114–107, when Roman consuls and proconsuls first conducted extensive warfare against the Scordisci in Thrace. Callatis quite possibly sought protection and asked for an alliance during those years.[56] If

---

51. See above pp. 435–436. The alliance with Maronea may thus come at a time not far distant from that with Callatis, whose treaty shows close verbal similarity.

52. *ILLRP*, II, no. 516. There was, no doubt, a Greek version also. And the inscription provides for setting up a copy in Rome. The stone was first published by Th. Sauciuc-Saveanu, *Dacia* 3–4 (1927–1932): 456–458. A subsequent edition with commentary by S. Lambrino, *CRAI* (1933), 278–288. Some adventurous restorations by A. Passerini, *Athenaeum* 13 (1935): 57–72—for which there is insufficient room on the stone. A more sober, but still speculative, reconstruction by Dem. St. Marin, *Epigraphica* 10 (1948): 104–114.

53. See the suggested text of St. Marin, *Epigraphica* 10 (1948): 114: *dolo m]alo quo po[plus Romanus socique e]t b[e]llum face[re debento et propria p]equnia adiova[n]to, [sei aliquis faxit, po]plo Romano utei et [Callatinus pro]priod faxit [p]oplo [non aliter ac pop]lus Romanus popl[o faxit Callatin]o.* The additions are, of course, hypothetical, but the character of the treaty is clear.

54. Lambrino, *CRAI* (1933), 278–288. Accepted without argument by Passerini, *Athenaeum* 13 (1935): 71–72, and Accame, *Il Dominio*, 95; restated now by D. M. Pippidi, in *Polis and Imperium*, ed. J. A. S. Evans (Toronto, 1974), 183–200. Sources on Lucullus' campaigns in Broughton, *MRR* II: 118–119.

55. Eutrop. 6.10: *illic Apolloniam evertit, Callatin, Parthenopolin, Tomos, Histrum, Burziaonem cepit*; Appian, *Ill.* 30. Pointed out by St. Marin, *Epigraphica* 10 (1950): 123. But his additional arguments on the "archaic" spelling of some words in the inscription (116–118) are of little value; see Pippidi, *art. cit.*, 186–188. Roman "allies" in Moesia are mentioned during C. Antonius' campaigns in 61: Dio, 38.10.3. But it is not clear that the Greek cities are meant—and, even if they are, this supplies only a *terminus ante quem*.

56. Sources on the warfare in Broughton, *MRR* I: 533, 538, 541, 543, 544, 554. Earlier campaigns are recorded for 135 and 119, but they were praetorian: Broughton, *MRR* I: 489, 526. St. Marin, *Epigraphica* 10 (1950): 125–128, suggests a date not long after the Roman occupation of Macedonia in the 140s, arguing that treaties with Greek states on the Black Sea would have real political and economic advantages. But this gives too much positive force to the alliance—which, like other treaties of this sort, had little substantive weight.

so, it proved to be of small comfort and did not prevent the subjugation of Callatis in 71.

Methymna, on the island of Lesbos, offers another instance. The text of her treaty with Rome survives in its later portions, with lacunae easily filled in. The important clauses are clear: neither state will give aid or passage to enemies of the other; each will come to the assistance of the other in a defensive war—if the situation permits.[57] That last phrase, of course, represents the conventional loophole for inaction. Again the timing and circumstances are unknown: perhaps ca. 129, as is generally thought, about the time when Rome transformed the neighboring mainland into the province of Asia.[58] A decree of the Neoi in Methymna, however, refers to joint military operations with the Romans in Asia and sets them in the context of a συμμαχία.[59] If that alludes to the war against Aristonicus, the treaty may have come in 133 or earlier.[60] But the allusion may, in fact, be to the Mithridatic campaigns, thereby setting the pact in the 90s. The matter should be left open. In any case, an official *foedus* came well after Pydna. Alliance with a minor city in Lesbos again underlines the formalistic character of these arrangements. They were not conceived as serious instruments of policy.

The same holds for the Roman συμμαχία with a city within the former kingdom of the Attalids. A decree found between Elaea and Pitane records the alliance. The city which issued it is unnamed.[61] Here, at least, we have a reasonably firm date: in 129 or shortly thereafter. The stone makes reference to the dangers undertaken and the assistance given to Rome during the revolt of Aristonicus. For that

---

57. *Syll.*[3] 693. Its formulas are discussed, in connection with other treaties, by Täubler, *Imperium Romanum*, 44–62. Note line 12: [ὡς ἂν ἦι] εὔκαιρον.

58. Mommsen, *SBBerlin* (1895): 900–901; followed by most; e.g., Täubler, *Imperium Romanum*, 45; Dittenberger, *Syll.*[3] 693, *ad loc.*; Horn, *Foederati*, 70; Accame, *Il Dominio*, 89.

59. *SEG*, III, 710 = *IG*, XII, Suppl. 31–32, no. 116: διὰ τὴν ὑπάρχουσαν πρὸς αὐτοὺς συμμαχίαν κοινωνοῦντος τοῦ συνεστῶτος αὐτοῖς ἐν τῆι Ἀσίαι πολέμου. The συμμαχία is here distinguished from the εὔνοια καὶ φιλία which Methymna felt for Rome ὑπὸ τῆς [ἀρ]χῆς. Hence, apparently, a reference to the formal alliance—though one cannot rule out the possibility that it signifies simply military cooperation during the Asian war.

60. So Magie, *Buckler Studies* (1939), 179–180; *RRAM* II:967–968, n. 89; cf. Donati, *Epigraphica* 27 (1965): 18–20. But his suggestion of a date before 154 is unfounded. Prusias, after his war against Pergamum and her allies, was asked by Roman mediators to pay reparations to Methymna and three other cities: Polyb. 33.13.8. That in no way implies a Roman alliance with Methymna.

61. *Syll.*[3] 694. Hiller v. Gaertringen, *ad loc.*, leaves the question undecided. For Accame, *Il Dominio*, 80, 89, it is Elaea. Others have opted for Pergamum herself: A. Wilhelm, *JOAI* 17 (1914): 18; Robert, *Études Anatoliennes*, 49, n. 3; Magie, *RRAM*, II, 1045, n. 34.

reason, the city, having maintained her εὔνοια and φιλία toward Rome, now gains reward in the form of a full-fledged alliance, to be inscribed on bronze tablets and duly displayed by both partners.[62] The Pergamene realm had by this time placed itself under Roman authority. Hence, friendship and alliance "for all time" with a city situated inside its borders was, by definition, merely ceremonial.[63] As the inscription announces explicitly, this is a prize for services rendered. In that regard, it supplies a suitable example of agreements in the later second century.[64]

The pattern continues, as revealed by documents uncovered in chance finds. Epidaurus paid homage to an envoy who had gone to Rome in quest of an alliance ca. 112.[65] The Republic consented without difficulty. Epidaurus got authorization to erect a bronze tablet announcing herself as full partner in alliance with Rome.[66] A nearly complete text of the treaty with the insignificant island of Astypalaea in 105 has been preserved. The standard formulas appear: both parties pledge to allow no enemies to pass through their territory; each vows to aid the other in case of attack; and copies of the pact to appear in both Rome and Astypalaea. The phraseology is tralatician. What hostile forces would dream of passing through the territory of Astypalaea?[67] In the same category, quite plainly, is a *foedus* with the Acarnanian town of Thyrreum in 94. Only the prescript remains, but

62. *Syll.*[3] 694, lines 11–31.

63. *Syll.*[3] 694, lines 48–50: εἰς ἄπ[αντα τ]ὸν [χ]ρόνον τὴν πρὸς ['Ρω]μαίους φιλίαν κα[ὶ συμμ]αχίαν.

64. *Syll.*[3] 694, lines 18–23: [ἐξ ὧν ἐ]πιγνοὺς ὁ δῆμος [ὁ 'Ρωμ]αίων τὴν π[ροαίρε]σιν τοῦ ἡμετέρου [δήμου] καὶ ἀποδεξ[άμενος] τὴν εὔνοιαν προσ[δέδεκ]ται τὸν δῆμ[ον] ἡμῶν πρός τε τὴν φ[ιλίαν] καὶ συμμα[χίαν]. The Pergamenes also describe themselves as Roman σύμμαχοι in a decree recorded by Josephus, near the end of the second century: *Ant.* 14.253; see below, Appendix III.

65. *IG*, IV², 1, 63, line 3. In the thirty-fourth year after the new Achaean era, i.e., presumably, since 146: lines 13–14; H. Swoboda, *Hermes* 57 (1922): 518–519.

66. *IG*, IV², 1, 63, lines 5–9. A formal alliance is doubted—unnecessarily—by D. Kienast, *ZSS* 85 (1968): 345, n. 49. Accame, *Il Dominio*, 160, rightly describes the treaty as "solo un atto di benevolenza da parte dei Romani verso Epidauro." But he surprisingly adjudges it unique in this regard. In fact, it is altogether typical.

67. *IGRR*, IV, 1028 = Sherk, *RDGE*, no. 16B. The date is fixed by consular year in the *senatus consultum* appended to the treaty: lines 15–16. The *s.c.* speaks of a "renewal" of the relationship; lines 2–3. If that is taken literally, it should imply that the original treaty came somewhat earlier; so Täubler, *Imperium Romanum*, 124–125. But is is the pact of 105 which is to be inscribed on bronze tablets: lines 6–7, 48–50. The term ἀνανεώσασθαι may signify only recall of earlier friendly relations, now to be affirmed in a formal way; Horn, *Foederati*, 72–73; Accame, *Il Dominio*, 85–86. Other examples of this usage in Daux, *Mélanges Desrousseaux* (1937), 119–122; Robert, *Hellenica* 1 (1940): 96–97, n. 5. The view of Donati, *Epigraphica* 27 (1965): 13–17, that Rome concluded the alliance because of Astypalaea's strategic position is quite unnecessary.

reference to the πίναξ συμμαχίας establishes this as a formal alliance. Its terms doubtless paralleled those found in the Astypalaean treaty.[68]

The survey may conclude with three items stemming from the triumviral period or thereabouts. The Roman practice of forging links with minor communities persists to that late date. A letter of Octavian to Aphrodisias, probably in 39, alludes to an edict, a senatorial decree, a sworn agreement, and a law. The ὅρκιον very probably denotes a treaty of alliance. A *senatus consultum*, included in the dossier with this letter and dating to the triumviral period, affirms Aphrodisias' status as a "friend and ally" of Rome.[69] Since the treaty's text is not extant, we cannot probe further.[70] In these same years came a Roman alliance with the Carian town of Cnidus, revealed in a most fragmentary inscription. That it was a συμμαχία "for all time" seems clear. Otherwise, the only reasonably preserved portion gives the provision for making future changes in the treaty—a common feature in these documents.[71] The missing sections doubtless reproduced closely the standard features of a bilateral pact.[72] Finally, we possess a copy of the formal *foedus* in 25 B.C. with Mytilene, on the island of Lesbos. This text too has suffered mutilation, but extant segments disclose the customary agreement between ostensible equals that repeats

68. *Syll.*[3] 732. The prescript is not a *senatus consultum*, as Täubler thought; *Imperium Romanum*, 364–365. It is, rather, a Thyrrean decree referring to it; Horn, *Foederati*, 78–80; Accame, *Il Dominio*, 89–90. Mention of the consuls of 94 gives the date. The suggestion of Bernhardt, *Imperium und Eleutheria*, 110, that this and other treaties of the period had in view assistance for naval warfare is most implausible.

69. *OGIS*, 453–455; *FIRA*, I, no. 38 = Sherk, *RDGE*, no. 28 = Reynolds, *Aphrodisias and Rome*, 42–43, no. 6. See lines 24–27: ἐπικρίματος καὶ δόγματος καὶ ὁρκίου καὶ νόμου. Cf. Reynolds, *op. cit.*, 57–61, no. 8, lines 32, 91–94; 92–93, no. 9, lines 7–9. On the date, see Reynolds, *JRS* 61 (1971): 285; *Akten des VI Internationalen Kongresses für griechische und lateinische Epigraphik* (Munich, 1973), 116–119 ὅρκιον is used to designate the alliance with Cnidus a few years later. See below n. 71.

70. A single clause is extant: Reynolds, *Aphrodisias and Rome*, 93, no. 9, lines 7–9.

71. Published by J. Matsa, *Ἀθηνᾶ* 11 (1899): 283–284; the text given also in Täubler, *Imperium Romanum*, 450–451. It is headed by the phrase ὅρκιον π[ρ]ὸς Ῥωμαίο[υς]. And see lines 9–10: [. . . Ῥωμα]ίων καὶ δήμου Κνιδί[ων φιλία καὶ] συμμα[χία καὶ εἰρήνη εἰς τὸν ἄπα]ντα χρόνον ἀσφα[λὴς· καὶ βέβαιος] ἔστω [καὶ κατὰ γῆν κατὰ] θάλασσα[ν].

72. Täubler, *Imperium Romanum*, 450–452, wishes to see it as, in part, a "Klientelvertrag" and inserts a phrase binding Cnidus to "preserve the empire and majesty of Rome." But this is wholly a restoration, in no way authorized by the text, and out of tune with all the other epigraphical documents. Properly doubted by Accame, *Il Dominio*, 98–99. The year is not given. Two Romans appear on the inscription, Cn. Domitius M.f. Calvinus, the consul of 40, and a disputable name, possibly Cn. Pompeius Rufus, the suffect consul of 31. Täubler, *op. cit.*, 453–454, suggests a date ca. 29, the time of Octavian's trip to Asia Minor; followed by Accame, *op. cit.*, 98. By contrast, C. Cichorius, *RhM* 76 (1927): 327–329, and Magie, *RRAM* II:1259–1260, n. 5, opt for 45. The question will have to be left unsettled.

a pattern already discerned again and again.[73] Mytilene had once supported Mithridates against Rome and paid for it in 80. She gradually came back into Rome's good graces, through the patronage of Pompey and later through Caesar, and earned the commendation of the senate.[74] Her *foedus*, an award for good behavior, served as capstone of that development. Like other compacts in this period, Mytilene's alliance was an honorary partnership, not a working diplomatic relationship.[75]

73. Most conveniently printed in Sherk, *RDGE*, no. 26d. A *senatus consultum* of 46 or 45 refers to the "renewal" of φιλία and συμμαχία; *Syll.*³ 764 = Sherk, *RDGE*, no. 26b, lines 16–23. This is obviously to be distinguished from the formal treaty, securely dated to 25 by the consulship of M. Silanus; see Horn, *Foederati*, 72–73, and Accame, *Il Dominio*, 90–92, as against Täubler, *Imperium Romanum*, 122–123. Täubler endeavors here also to install a "*maiestas* clause"; *op. cit.*, 64–65; followed by Horn, *op. cit.*, 70–71: ὁ [δῆμ]ο[ς ὁ] Μυτιληναίων ἀρχὴ[ν καὶ δυναστείαν τοῦ δήμου τοῦ 'Ρωμαίων δια]φυλασσέτω. If so, it would be unique in this period and entirely without point. See the alternative restoration in Sherk: ὁ [δῆμ]ο[ς ὁ] Μυτιληναίων ἀρχὴ[ν καὶ ἐπικράτειαν ἣν μέχρι νῦν ἔσχεν] φυλασσέτω; cf. Accame, *op. cit.*, 98–99; V. Arangio-Ruiz, *RivFilol* 20–21 (1942–43): 125–130; Donati, *Epigraphica* 27 (1965): 18–25.

74. Cf. Sherk, *RDGE*, no. 26b, lines 21–22: ἅ τε αὐτοῖς πρότερον ὑπὸ συγκλήτου φιλάνθρωπα συγκεχωρημένα ἦν. On the relations between Mytilene and Rome, see the discussions of Sherk, *GRBS* 4 (1963): 145–153, 217–230.

75. Cf. in this connection the renewals of Rome's treaty with Rhodes in 51 and 48: Cic. *Ad Fam.* 12.15.2; Appian, *BC*, 4.66, 4.68, 4.70; see above pp. 40–41. And Julius Caesar's restoration of the Jewish alliance in 47, confirmed again after his death in 44: Jos. *Ant.* 14.185, 14.196–198, 14.217–222, 14.266–267.

# The First Encounter of Rome and the Jews

The Second Book of Maccabees preserves a letter of Roman envoys to the Jews in 164. It was the first occasion, in our evidence, of contact between the two peoples. The delegates offered assistance in presenting the Jews' case to the Syrian king at Antioch.[1]

Chronological and historical problems abound; and the authority of this item has been impugned.[2] The letter appears amidst a group of documents transmitted by the author of 2 Maccabees and dated to 164, the last year of Antiochus IV's reign—yet placed in a context that follows the death of that monarch. Scholarly disputations on the chronology persist. Whether the message belongs near the end of Antiochus IV's reign or at the beginning of Antiochus V's evades definitive solution. The death of Antiochus IV, it can now be stated confidently, came in the last months of 164.[3] Of the four documents in 2 Maccabees, one, at least, followed the accession of Antiochus V.[4] The other three are dated by the author to 164, in apparent ignorance of the chronological discrepancy. Perhaps they all belong after 164—or, more likely, the author erroneously associated the three items with the letter of Antiochus V and placed them all in his reign.[5]

1. 2 Macc. 11:34–38.

2. Most recent doubts expressed by Mørkholm, *Antiochus IV*, 162–165.

3. A. J. Sachs and D. J. Wiseman, *Iraq* 16 (1954): 202–212. Cf. B. Z. Wacholder in Burstein and Okin, *Panhellenica*, 129–132.

4. 2 Macc. 11:22–26.

5. So R. Laqueur, *HZ* 136 (1927): 231–241, followed by most scholars. The bibliography is large; cf. Will, *Histoire politique* II:279–280, 288; add M. Zambelli, *Miscellanea greca e romana* (Rome, 1965), 213–234; Th. Liebmann-Frankfort, *AntClass* 38 (1969): 102–111; J. G. Bunge, *Untersuchungen zum zweiten Makkabäerbuch* (Bonn, 1971), 386–400; Habicht, *Jüdische Schriften aus hellenistisch-römischer Zeit*, I:3: 2. *Makkabäerbuch* (Gu-

The letter of the Romans makes reference to a communication by Syria's minister Lysias, recorded earlier, agreeing to an amicable settlement with the Maccabean rebels. The Roman legates ask for more details so that they can better present the Jewish case at Antioch.[6] We may be certain that this did not come on Roman initiative. The senate would have had little awareness of—and even less concern for—the struggle of Jewish insurgents in a corner of the Syrian realm. In all probability, representatives of the Jews contacted Rome's envoys, on their way to Antioch, and asked them to support the Jewish cause with Antiochus. The Romans had come on other business.[7] Their letter expressed polite courtesies, a gesture of the envoys rather than an index of senatorial policy. The agreement between Lysias and the Jews had already been made. The Roman delegation simply endorsed it; and (the letter advised) if the Jews wished to make further representations on matters to be raised by Lysias, they had better send someone quickly in order to clarify their position.[8] So, at most,

---

terslöh, 1976), 179–185; and the exhaustive listing of literature by Fischer, *Seleukiden und Makkabäer*, 65–67.

6. 2 Macc. 11:34–38. Lysias' agreement and its background is given in 2 Macc. 11:13–21. This is the first in the series of documents, of which the Roman letter is the fourth. Antiochus V's letter to Lysias is placed second, followed by a letter to the Jews from Antiochus (IV?). Even if the items are authentic, the sequence is certainly wrong. The arrangement is usually reordered by moderns as 1, 4, 3, 2. See the exposition of V. Tcherikover, *Hellenistic Civilization and the Jews* (New York, 1970), 214–219. Cf. Abel's commentary on the text; *Livres de Maccabées*, 425–431; also Dancy, *Commentary on I Maccabees*, 18–19. But the third item, making no reference to the situation in any of the others, may well have come first, hence: 3, 1, 4, 2; so Habicht, *HSCP* 80 (1976), 1–18. Yet another ordering by Fischer, *Seleukiden und Makkabäer*, 64–80. The matter is further complicated by the fact that Lysias' campaign against the Jews which preceded the agreement was followed by another suspiciously similar conflict subsequent to it; cf. 1 Macc. 4:28–35; 2 Macc. 11:1–12; Jos. *Ant.* 12.313–315; and 1 Macc. 6:28–63; 2 Macc. 13:1–26; Jos. *Ant.* 12.366–383. Hence, some have rejected the first campaign as a duplicate; W. Kolbe, *Beiträge zur syrischen und jüdischen Geschichte* (Berlin, 1926), 79–81; Mørkholm, *Antiochus IV*, 152–154. *Contra*: Bickermann, *Der Gott der Makkabäer* (Berlin, 1937), 13–14, n. 7; Goldstein, *I Maccabees*, 268–269. But that does not affect the contents of the documents.

7. The names of the envoys are given by 2 Maccabees as Quintus Memmius and τιτος μανιος ερνιος, persons unidentifiable. The manuscript reading of the second name, however, led Niese, *Hermes*, 35 (1900), 483–484, to suggest Μάνιος Σέργιος and to associate this embassy with one of C. Sulpicius and M'. Sergius, sent to the East in 164: Polyb. 31.1.6–8. His conclusion is highly speculative and hardly warranted by the texts, though accepted without discussion by almost all scholars; so, most recently, Liebmann-Frankfort, *AntClass* 38 (1969): 103; A. Giovannini and H. Müller, *MH* 28 (1971): 170; Walbank, *Commentary* III:464. That mission, in any case, was certainly not dispatched on behalf of the Jews. It had various duties in Greece and Asia, in particular to look into charges against Eumenes II and Antiochus IV: Polyb. 31.1.2–8; cf. 31.6.1–6; Diod. 31.7.2; Paus. 7.11.1–3.

8. 2 Macc. 11:35–37: ὑπὲρ ὧν Λυσίας ὁ συγγενὴς τοῦ βασιλέως συνεχώρησεν

the message conveyed a cordial *ad hoc* response—not an offer to alter arrangements to the advantage of the Jews.[9]

Whether the Romans were here corresponding with the Maccabees or with Hellenizing leaders in Judaea is uncertain. The author of 2 Maccabees certainly thought it was the former. But the address of the letter, τῷ δήμῳ τῶν Ἰουδαίων, does not prove it. And the contents of Lysias' and Antiochus' communications seem to suggest dealings with a party more sympathetic to Syria.[10] In any case, it is most unlikely that the Romans concerned themselves with any such distinctions.

What happened at Antioch, if anything, is simply unknown. The Roman mission—assuming it was genuine—had no tangible issue. Antiochus V's subsequent letter to Lysias, after the Jews reoccupied their temple, awards major concessions, but gives no hint that this was due to Roman intervention.[11] The accords, in any event, broke down almost immediately. Warfare resumed in Judaea and the imbroglio began anew. The negotiations formed but a fleeting and inconsequential episode, preserved in documents whose principal effect has been to plague scholarship.[12]

---

ὑμῖν, καὶ ἡμεῖς συνευδοκοῦμεν ἃ δὲ ἔκρινε προσανενεχθῆναι τῷ βασιλεῖ, πέμψατέ τινα παραχρῆμα ἐπισκεψάμενοι περὶ τούτων, ἵνα ἐκθῶμεν ὡς καθήκει ὑμῖν · ἡμεῖς γὰρ προσάγομεν πρὸς Ἀντιόχειαν · διὸ σπεύσατε καὶ πέμψατέ τινας, ὅπως καὶ ἡμεῖς ἐπιγνῶμεν ὁποίας ἐστὲ γνώμης.

9. Cf. Gruen, *Chiron* 6 (1976): 78. Habicht, *2. Makkabäerbuch*, 260, asserts without argument that the Roman envoys had taken the initiative.

10. 2 Macc. 11:19: ἐὰν μὲν οὖν συντηρήσητε τὴν εἰς τὰ πράγματα εὐνοίαν; 2 Macc. 11:29: ἐνεφάνισεν ἡμῖν Μενέλαος βούλεσθαι κατελθόντας ὑμᾶς γίνεσθαι πρὸς τοῖς ἰδίοις; see Tcherikover, *Hellenistic Civilization and the Jews*, 216–218; *contra*: Liebmann-Frankfort, *AntClass* 38 (1969): 107–110.

11. 2 Macc. 11.27–33; cf. 1 Macc. 6:55–61.

12. If the letters belong in 164, they were followed very shortly by Jewish restoration of the temple in Jerusalem and the attacks by Judas Maccabaeus upon the Idumaeans and Ammonites: 1 Macc. 4:36–5:8; 2 Macc. 10:1–8, 10:14–23; Jos. *Ant.* 12.316–329, 12.353. The agreements are not mentioned in 1 Maccabees and placed after these events by the author of 2 Maccabees, perhaps to disguise the fact that they were violated by Judas. But even if one accepts the sequence in 2 Maccabees, it is clear that fighting—blamed, of course, on the Gentiles—erupted immediately afterwards and the accords were a dead letter: 2 Macc. 12:1ff; cf. 1 Macc. 5:9ff.

· *Appendix* III ·

# Effects of the Roman-Jewish Treaty

The treaty between Rome and the Jews, concluded in 161, gains mention on several subsequent occasions, in terms of renewal or re-affirmation. Jewish sources, however, had special axes to grind. Not all the notices carry conviction. Scrutiny of the evidence may bring some benefit, a better appreciation of the Roman attitude toward that connection.

In 144, we are told, Judas Maccabaeus' brother and successor Jonathan sent envoys to the senate to "renew the friendship and alliance." They obtained a cordial response and letters to various states granting them safe conduct.[1] Perhaps a fabrication and a duplicate of the later mission under Simon? So it has been argued.[2] The timing, however, would not be inappropriate: a year or two after the accession of Demetrius II and after Rome's victory in the Achaean war.[3] Whether or not the legation is historical, the results were obviously negligible. Fighting in Judaea continued, Jonathan himself perished, and the Romans stayed away.[4]

The author of 1 Maccabees then registers another embassy to

1. 1 Macc. 12.1–4, 12.16; Jos. *Ant.* 13.163–165, 13.169.

2. Momigliano, *Prime linee di storia della tradizione maccabaica* (Rome, 1930), 141–159; Giovannini-Müller, *MH* 28 (1971): 164–165, n. 30, 170, n. 53; cf. Abel, *Livres des Maccabées*, 231–232. The authenticity of the renewal goes unquestioned by Goldstein, *I Maccabees*, 445–446.

3. Cf. also Josephus' reference to φιλία with the Romans, concluded at a time when the Jews held Joppa: *Ant.* 14.205. Joppa was captured under Jonathan; 1 Macc. 10:75–76; Jos. *Ant.* 13.91–92. Josephus' ποιούμενοι . . . φιλίαν hardly proves that this was the first such arrangement between Rome and the Jews; as Gauger, *Beiträge*, 253–257.

4. 1 Macc. 12:24–13:30; Jos. *Ant.* 13.174–212.

Rome early in the period of Simon's high-priesthood, ca. 142. Once again there came revival of the treaty, inscribed on bronze tablets, and the gift of a gold shield to confirm the alliance.[5] In this connection, a letter from the Roman consul "Lucius"—perhaps L. Caecilius Metellus, consul 142—to Ptolemy announced renewal of the alliance and requested Ptolemy to refrain from war on the Jews; analogous messages were delivered to numerous other monarchs and cities.[6] That document too has roused much dispute and its genuineness remains in doubt. The author appears to put it ca. 138. Yet the envoy Numenius who brought back these messages is the same man who delivered the gold shield and obtained renewal of the alliance in 142.[7] Better to amalgamate than to assume two separate embassies.[8]

The real difficulty lies in comparison with a senatorial decree recorded by Josephus and issued by a praetor L. Valerius, L.f.[9] The decree shows close resemblances to the letter to Ptolemy and the envoys appear to be the same.[10] Yet Josephus puts it in the ninth year of Hyrcanus II, evidently 47 B.C. A plethora of solutions has been offered, none decisive.[11] One might substitute Hyrcanus I for Hyrcanus II and locate the pact in his ninth year, i.e. 126; or, by emending nine to twenty nine, to bring it down to ca. 106, in conjunction with other dates given in this passage. Alternatively, one fastens on L. Valerius: if he is the consul of 131, his praetorship would fall ca. 134, a plausible time, for it is the beginning of Hyrcanus I's regime. All of these suggestions require divorcing the s.c. in Josephus from the mission recorded in 1 Maccabees. Were there two such nearly identical embassies, one sent by Simon, the other by Hyrcanus I? Resemblances between the two accounts cast doubt on that proposition. Or did the author of 1 Maccabees simply invent his embassy, based on the authentic s.c. which we find in Josephus? That too has been suggested. But, if so, then why did he put it in the time of Simon? The most economic solution is here preferable: to refer both accounts to the same event. Josephus' date can be disassociated from the document he records; it seems, in fact, to belong to the next item in his collection, an

5. 1 Macc. 14:16–18, 14:24. A date before 140 is established by the inscription in Simon's honor; see 1 Macc. 14:40. Framing of an alliance in the time of Simon is mentioned, in passing, by Josephus, *Ant.* 13.227.

6. 1 Macc. 15:15–24.

7. 1 Macc. 14:22, 14:24.

8. On Metellus as the consul "Lucius," see Bickermann, *Gnomon* 6 (1930): 358–359, and, now, Goldstein, *I Maccabees*, 492–494.

9. Jos. *Ant.* 14.145–148.

10. Cf. 1 Macc. 14:22 and Jos. *Ant.* 14.146.

11. Few will now defend Josephus' dating, though it has Mommsen's authority; *Hermes* 9 (1875): 281–291; followed, e.g., by Täubler, *Imperium Romanum*, 164–166.

Athenian decree for Hyrcanus.[12] The year 142 still appears the most plausible.[13]

The contents of the letter to Ptolemy are, to be sure, suspect, as are some of the places to which it was addressed.[14] Whatever one makes of the document, however, this "renewal" had no more tangible consequences than the previous negotiations. Conflicts with Antiochus VII plagued the last years of Simon; the Romans put in no appearance.[15]

Finally, Josephus' collection of decrees includes two further appeals to the treaty. During the high priesthood of Hyrcanus I, 135–104, Jewish legates reminded the senate of their alliance and requested restoration of places taken by Antiochus in contravention of a *senatus consultum*. This last probably refers to the decree of 142 (?), which had been ignored by the Syrian king. The senate gave its usual polite reply: the φιλία and συμμαχία were reaffirmed, the *patres* would deliberate about the complaints when they had time, and the envoys would receive traveling expenses and a safe-conduct home.[16] The date is again a matter of controversy. The presiding praetor was Fannius, M.f. He may well have been C. Fannius, M.f., consul in 122, whose praetorship would have come ca. 125.[17] In any case, no positive action followed. Later in Hyrcanus' years, the Jews had to send another embassy, with similar complaints. This time Rome passed a firmer resolution, demanding Syrian evacuation of territories seized from the Jews. The *s.c.* is included in a decree of Pergamum, evidently one of the states asked to render safe-conduct for the envoys

12. Jos. *Ant.* 14.148–155; so Momigliano, *Giudea Romano* (Bologna, 1934), 30–35.

13. L. Valerius' identity is quite uncertain; he need not be the consul of 131—and we know only one praetor in 142. Bibliography on this question is immense; see the items listed in R. Marcus' Loeb edition of Josephus (Cambridge, Mass., 1943), 775–777; add Abel, *Livres des Maccabées*, 275–276; Dancy, *Commentary on I Maccabees*, 182–183, 189–191; T. Fischer, *Untersuchungen zum Partherkrieg Antiochus VII* (Tübingen, 1970), 97–101; Giovannini-Müller, *MH* 28 (1971): 160–165; Schürer, *History of the Jewish People*, I:194–197; Timpe, *Chiron* 4 (1974): 146–150; Fischer, *ZAlttestWiss* 86 (1974): 90–92; Goldstein, *I Maccabees*, 492–500; Gauger, *Beiträge*, 285–302. Broader doubts about the authenticity of Roman documents found in Josephus have recently been expressed by H. R. Moehring, in J. Neussner, *Christianity, Judaism, and Other Greco-Roman Cults* III (Leiden, 1975), 124–158. On Josephus' handling of documents in general, see Gauger, *Beiträge*, 9–22. A brief survey of recent literature on Rome and the Jews in these years by Fischer, *Gymnasium* 88 (1981): 139–144.

14. Cf. Momigliano, *Giudea Romano*, 33–34; Giovannini-Müller, *MH* 28 (1971): 162; Gauger, *Beiträge*, 297–302.

15. 1 Macc. 15:25–16:10; Jos. *Ant.* 13.223–227.

16. Jos. *Ant.* 13.259–266.

17. So Broughton, *MRR* II:509, n. 2. Giovannini-Müller, *MH* 28 (1971): 158, n. 8, reckon this as impossible, since Antiochus VII's reign ended in 129. But the Jewish complaints about Antiochus' depredations need not have come during his reign itself.

and to help implement Roman wishes.[18] If Josephus is right in identifying the Syrian king against whom the decree is directed as Antiochus, son of Antiochus, this can only be Antiochus IX, 113–96. The measure would thus date to the last years of Hyrcanus, some time before 104.[19] Once again, however, the verbal stance finds no echo in the practical sphere. Enforcement of the resolution is unattested.

The pattern of Roman affirmations on the one hand and lack of implementation on the other has a remarkable regularity. The senate sent *pro forma* messages—and let the recipients work matters out for themselves.

18. Jos. *Ant.* 14.247–255.

19. So Giovannini-Müller, *MH* 28 (1971): 156–158, who also put Fannius' decree down near this time, on the grounds that similar complaints are voiced. Others place both documents in Antiochus VII's reign, arguing that Josephus erred on the name of Antiochus' father; e.g., Schürer, *History of the Jewish People*, 204–206, with bibliography. The possibility of a lengthy interval between the two decrees, however, should not be discounted. Cf. Fischer, *Untersuchungen*, 64–82; Gauger, *Beiträge*, 321–324. Both Antiochus VII and Antiochus IX conducted campaigns against the Jews: Jos. *Ant.* 13.225–227, 13.236–248, 13.274–283. Giovannini-Müller, nevertheless, are surely right that the Fannius decree preceded the *s.c.* contained in the Pergamene document: *op. cit.* 159–160.

# Bibliography

Abel, F. M. *Les livres de Maccabées*. Paris, 1949.

Abel, K. "Der Tod des Ptolemaios IV. Philopator bei Polybios." *Hermes* 95 (1967):72–90.

———. "Die kulturelle Mission des Panaitios." *Antike und Abendland* 17 (1971):119–143.

Accame, S. *Il dominio romano in Grecia dalla guerra acaica ad Augusto*. Rome, 1946.

Adams, J. P. "Aristonikos and the Cistophoroi." *Historia* 29 (1980): 302–314.

Adams, W. L. "Perseus and the Third Macedonian War." In W. L. Adams and E. N. Borza, eds., *Philip II, Alexander the Great, and the Macedonian Tradition*. (1982):237–256.

Africa, T. W. "Aristonicus, Blossius, and the City of the Sun." *International Review of Social History* 6 (1961):110–124.

Albert, S. *Bellum Iustum*. Kallmünz, 1980.

Alföldi, A. *Early Rome and the Latins*. Ann Arbor, 1963.

Allen, R. E. "Attalos I and Aegina." *BSA* 66 (1971):1–12.

Alliot, M. "La Thébaide en lutte contre les rois d'Alexandrie sous Philopator et Épiphane (216–184)." *RevBelg* 29 (1951):421–443.

———. "La fin de la résistance égyptienne dans le sud sous Épiphane." *REA* 54 (1952):18–26.

Andreau, J. "Banque grecque et banque romaine dans le théâtre de Plaute et de Terence." *MEFRA* 80 (1968):461–526.

Arangio-Ruiz, V. "Senatus Consulta Silaniana de Mytilenensibùs." *RivFilol* 20–21 (1942–43):125–130.

Aron, R. *Paix et guerre entre les nations*. Paris, 1962.

754 • BIBLIOGRAPHY

Asheri, D. "Leggi greche sul problema dei debiti." *StudClassOrient* 18 (1969):5–122.

Astin, A. E. "Diodorus and the Date of the Embassy to the East of Scipio Aemilianus." *CP* 54 (1959):221–227.

———. *Scipio Aemilianus.* Oxford, 1967.

———. *Politics and Policies in the Roman Republic.* Belfast, 1968.

———. *Cato the Censor.* Oxford, 1978.

Aupert, P. "Une donation lagide et chypriote à Argos (170–164 av. J.-C.)," *BCH* 106 (1982):263–277.

Aymard, A. "Les stratèges de la confédération achaienne." *REA* 30 (1928):1–62.

———. "A propos d'une assemblée achaienne (l'assemblée d'Argos: début de 188 av. J.-C.)." *Mélanges Glotz* (1932) I:49–73.

———. *Les premiers rapports de Rome et de la confédération achaienne.* Bordeaux and Paris, 1938.

———. "L'organisation de la Macédoine en 167 et la régime représentatif dans le monde grec." *CP* 45 (1950):96–107.

———. *Études d'histoire ancienne.* Paris, 1967.

Badian, E. "The Treaty between Rome and the Achaean League." *JRS* 42 (1952):76–80.

———. "Aetolica." *Latomus* 17 (1958):197–211.

———. *Foreign Clientelae (264–70 B.C.).* Oxford, 1958.

———. *Studies in Greek and Roman History.* New York, 1964.

———. "The Date of Clitarchus." *PACA* 8 (1965):5–11.

——— and R. M. Errington, "A Meeting of the Achaean League (Early 188 B.C.)." *Historia* 14 (1965):13–17.

———. "The Early Historians." In T. A. Dorey, ed., *Latin Historians* (1966):1–38.

———. "The Testament of Ptolemy Alexander." *RhM* 110 (1967):178–192.

———. *Roman Imperialism in the Late Republic.* Oxford, 1968.

———. *Titus Quinctius Flamininus: Philhellenism and Realpolitik.* Cincinnati, 1970.

———. "The Family and Early Career of T. Quinctius Flamininus." *JRS* 61 (1971):102–111.

———. "Review of W. Dahlheim, *Struktur und Entwicklung.*" *RivFilol* 100 (1972):91–99.

———. *Publicans and Sinners.* Ithaca, 1972.

———. "Tiberius Gracchus and the Beginning of the Roman Revolution." *ANRW* I:1 (1972), 668–731.

———. "Ennius and his Friends." *Entretiens Fondation Hardt* 17 (1972):149–208.

———. "An un-serius Fabius." *LCM* 1 (1976):97–98.

———. "Rome, Athens, and Mithridates." *AJAH* 1 (1976):105–128.

Bagnall, R. S. *The Administration of the Ptolemaic Possessions Outside Egypt.* Leiden, 1976.

Balsdon, J. P. V. D. "Some Questions about Historical Writing in the Second Century B.C." *CQ* 47 (1953):158–164.

———. "Rome and Macedon, 205–200 B.C." *JRS* 44 (1954):30–42.

———. "T. Quinctius Flamininus." *Phoenix* 21 (1967):177–190.

———. "L. Cornelius Scipio: A Salvage Operation." *Historia* 21 (1972): 224–234.

———. *Romans and Aliens.* Chapel Hill, 1979.

Balty, J. C. "La statue de bronze de T. Quinctius Flamininus *ad Apollinis in circe.*" *MEFRA* 90 (1978):669–686.

Bandelli, G. "I processi degli Scipioni: le fonti." *Index* 3 (1972):304–342.

———. "Il processo dell' Asiatico." *Index* 4 (1974–5):93–126.

———. "La guerra istrica del 221 a.C. e la spedizione alpina del 220 a.C." *Athenaeum* 69 (1981):3–28.

Bauman, R. A. "*Maiestatem populi romani comiter conservanto.*" *Acta Juridica* (1976):19–36.

Bean, G. E. "Notes and Inscriptions from Lycia." *JHS* 68 (1948): 46–56.

Bellinger, A. R. "The Bronze Coins of Timarchus." *ANSMN* 1 (1945): 37–44.

Bengtson, H. "Das Imperium Romanum in griechischer Sicht." *Gymnasium* 71 (1964):150–166.

———. "Die Inschriften von Labranda und die Politik des Antigonos Doson." *SitzMünch* (1971):1–61.

Bernhardt, R. *Imperium und Eleutheria.* Diss. Hamburg, 1971.

———. "Der Status des 146 v. Chr. unterworfenen Teils Griechenlands bis zur Einrichtung der Provinz Achaia." *Historia* 26 (1977): 62–73.

Bernstein, A. H. *Tiberius Sempronius Gracchus. Tradition and Apostasy.* Ithaca, 1978.

Berthold, R. M. "Lade, Pergamum, and Chios." *Historia* 24 (1975): 150–163.

———. "The Rhodian Appeal to Rome in 201 B.C." *CJ* 71 (1975–76): 97–107.

Berve, H. "Hieron II." *AbhMünch* 47 (1959):1–99.

Besançon, A. *Les adversaires de l'hellénisme á Rome pendant la périod républicaine.* Paris and Lausanne, 1910.

Bevan, E. R. *The House of Seleucus.* 2 vols. London, 1902.

Bickermann, E. "Review of M. S. Ginsburg, *Rome et la Judée.*" *Gnomon* 6 (1930):358–359.

————. "Review of G. Oliverio, *La stele di Tolomeo Neòteros re di Cirene.* *Gnomon* 8 (1932):424–430.

————. "Bellum Antiochum." *Hermes* 67 (1932):47–76.

————. "Rom und Lampsakos." *Philologus* 87 (1932):277–299.

————. "La charte séleucide de Jérusalem." *RevEtudesJuives* 100 (1935): 4–35.

————. "Les préliminaires de la seconde guerre de Macédoine." *RevPhil* 61 (1935):59–81, 161–176.

————. *Der Gott der Makkabäer.* Berlin, 1937.

————. "Notes sur Polybe." *REG* 50 (1937):217–239.

————. "An Oath of Hannibal." *TAPA* 75 (1944):87–102.

————. "Bellum Philippicum: Some Roman and Greek Views concerning the Causes of the Second Macedonian War." *CP* 40 (1945):137–148.

————. "Hannibal's Covenant." *AJP* 73 (1952):1–23.

————. "Sur la chronologie de la sixième guerre de Syrie." *ChrEg* 27 (1952):396–403.

————. "Origines Gentium." *CP* 47 (1952):65–81.

————. "Notes sur Polybe." *REG* 66 (1953):479–506.

Bidez, J. and F. Cumont, *Les mages hellénisés, Zoroaster, Ostanès, et Hystaspe d'après la tradition grecque.* Paris, 1938.

Bivona, L. "Sui rapporti fra Perseo e la repubblica romana." *Kokalos* 2 (1956):50–65.

Bleicken, J. "Review of H. H. Schmitt, *Rom und Rhodos.*" *Gnomon* 31 (1959):440–441.

————. "Review of E. Badian, *Foreign Clientelae.*" *Gnomon* 36 (1964): 176–187.

Bliquez, L. "Gnaeus Octavius and the Echinaioi." *Hesperia* 44 (1975): 431–434.

Boehringer, C. *Zur Chronologie mittelhellenistischer Münzserien, 220–160 v.Chr.* Berlin, 1972.

Bömer, F. "Naevius und Fabius Pictor." *SO* 29 (1952):34–53.

————. "Thematik und Krise der römischen Geschichtsschreibung im 2. Jahrhundert v. Chr." *Historia* 2 (1953–54):189–208.

Bouché-Leclercq, A. *Histoire des Lagides.* 4 vols. Paris, 1903–1907.

————. *Histoire des Séleucides.* 2 vols. Paris, 1913–1914.

Bousquet, J. "Le roi Persée et les romains." *BCH* 105 (1981):407–416.

Bowersock, G. W. *Augustus and the Greek World.* Oxford, 1965.

Bowra, C. M. "Melinno's Hymn to Rome." *JRS* 47 (1957):21–28.

Boyancé, P. "La connaissance du Grec à Rome." *REL* 34 (1956): 111–131.

Braccesi, L. "Roma e Alessandro il Molosso nella tradizione Liviana." *RendIstLomb* 108 (1974):196–202.

———. *Alessandro e i Romani*. Bologna, 1975.

Braunert, H. "Hegemoniale Bestrebungen der hellenistischen Gross-mächte in Politik und Wirtschaft." *Historia* 13 (1964):80–104.

Bredehorn, U. *Senatsakten in der republikanischen Annalistik*. Marburg, 1968.

Bringmann, K. "Weltherrschaft und innere Krise Roms im Spiegel der Geschichtsschreibung des zweiten und ersten Jahrhunderts v. Chr." *Antike und Abendland* 23 (1977):28–49.

———. "Die Verfolgung der jüdischen Religion durch Antiochos IV. Ein Konflikt zwischen Judentum und Hellenismus?" *Antike und Abendland* 26 (1980):176–190.

Brink, C. O. and F. W. Walbank, "The Construction of the Sixth Book of Polybius." *CQ* 4 (1954):97–122.

Briscoe, J. "Q. Marcius Philippus and *Nova Sapientia*." *JRS* 54 (1964): 66–77.

———. "Rome and the Class Struggle in the Greek States, 200–146 B.C." *Past and Present* 36 (1967):3–20.

———. "Eastern Policy and Senatorial Politics, 168–146 B.C." *Historia* 18 (1969):49–70.

———. "Flamininus and Roman Politics, 200–189 B.C." *Latomus* 31 (1972):22–53.

———. *A Commentary on Livy, Books XXXI–XXXIII*. Oxford, 1973.

———. *A Commentary on Livy, Books XXXIV–XXXVII*. Oxford, 1981.

Brizzi, G. *I sistemi informativi dei Romani*. Wiesbaden, 1982.

Broughton, T. R. S. *The Magistrates of the Roman Republic*. 2 vols. New York, 1951–1952.

Brown, T. S. "Clitarchus." *AJP* 71 (1950):134–155.

Brunt, P. A. "The Equites in the Late Republic." In R. Seager, ed., *The Crisis of the Roman Republic* (1969):83–117.

———. *Italian Manpower, 225 B.C.–A.D. 14*. Oxford, 1971.

———. "Laus Imperii." In P. D. A. Garnsey and C. R. Whittaker, eds., *Imperialism in the Ancient World* (1978):159–191.

Bunge, J. G. *Untersuchungen zum zweiten Makkabäerbuch*. Bonn, 1971.

———. "'Theos Epiphanes' in den ersten fünf Regierungsjahren des Antiochus IV Epiphanes." *Historia* 23 (1974):57–85.

———. "'Antiochos Helios.'" *Historia* 24 (1975):164–188.

———. "Die Feiern Antiochos' IV in Daphne im Herbst 166." *Chiron* 6 (1976):53–71.

Burstein, S. M. "The Aftermath of the Peace of Apamea." *AJAH* 5 (1980):1–12.

Cabanes, P. *L'Épire de la mort de Pyrrhos à la conquête romaine (272–167)*. Paris, 1976.

Calabi, I. *Ricerche sui rapporti fra le poleis*. Florence, 1943.

758 • BIBLIOGRAPHY

Calboli, G. *Marci Porci Catonis Oratio Pro Rhodiensibus*. Bologna, 1978.

Calderone, S. Πίστις - *Fides*. Messina, 1964.

———. "Livio e il secondo trattato romano-punico di Polibio." *Miscellanea di studi classici in onore di Eugenio Manni* (1980) II: 363–375.

Candiloro, E. "Politica e cultura in Atene da Pidna alla guerra mitridatica." *StudClassOrient* 14 (1965): 134–176.

Capelle, W. "Griechische Ethik und römischer Imperialismus." *Klio* 25 (1932): 86–113.

Carcopino, J. *Les étapes de l'impérialisme romain*. Paris, 1934.

———. *Autour des Gracques*. 2nd ed. Paris, 1967.

Cardinali, G. "La morte di Attalo III e la rivolta di Aristonico." *Saggi di storia antica a G. Beloch* (1910): 269–320.

———. "Lo Pseudo-Filippo." *RivFilol* 39 (1911): 1–20.

Carrata Thomes, F. *La rivolta di Aristonico e le origini della provincia romana d'Asia*. Turin, 1968.

Cassola, F. "La dedica bilingua di Lindo e la storia del commercio romano." *PP* 15 (1960): 385–393.

———. "La politica di Flaminino e gli Scipioni." *Labeo* 6 (1960): 105–130.

———. *I gruppi politici romani nel III^e secolo A.C.* Trieste, 1962.

———. "Romani e Italici in Oriente." *DialArch* 4–5 (1970–71): 305–322.

Castellani, A. M. "Le relazioni fra Roma e la confederazione Achea da T. Quinzio Flaminino a L. Emilio Paolo." *ContIstFilClass* 1 (1963): 66–136.

Castiglioni, L. "Motivi antiromani nella tradizione storica antica." *RendIstLomb* 61 (1928): 625–639.

Catalano, P. "Appunti sopra il più antico concetto giuridico di Italia." *AttiAccadTorino* 96 (1961–62): 198–228.

Chamoux, F. "Un portrait de Flamininus à Delphes." *BCH* 89 (1965): 214–224.

Charneux, P. "Rome et la confédération achaienne (automne, 170)." *BCH* 81 (1957): 181–202.

Chiranky, G. "Rome and Cotys, Two Problems: I. The Diplomacy of 167 B.C. II. The Date of Sylloge³ 656." *Athenaeum* 60 (1982): 461–486.

Christ, F. *Die römische Weltherrschaft in der antiken Dichtung*. Stuttgart-Berlin, 1938.

Cichorius, C. "Ein Bündnisvertrag zwischen Rom and Knidos." *RhM* 76 (1927): 327–329.

Cimma, M. R. *Reges socii et amici populi romani*. Milan, 1976.

Clavel, M. *Béziers et son territoire dans l'Antiquité*. Paris, 1970.

Clemente, G. *I romani nella Gallia meridionale*. Bologna, 1974.

———. "Esperti ambasciatori del senato e la formazione della politica estera romana tra il III e il II secolo a.C." *Athenaeum* 54 (1976): 319–352.

Coarelli, F. "Architettura e arti figurative in Roma: 150–50 a.C." *Abh-AkadGött* 97.1 (1976): 21–51.

———. "Public Building in Rome between the Second Punic War and Sulla." *PBSR* 32 (1977): 1–23.

Cohen, G. M. *The Seleucid Colonies.* Wiesbaden, 1978.

Colin, G. *Rome et la Grèce de 200 à 146 avant Jésus Christ.* Paris, 1905.

Collart, P. "Les milliaires de la Via Egnatia." *BCH* 100 (1976): 177–200.

Collins, F. "The Macedonians and the Revolt of Aristonicus." *Ancient Society* 3 (1980): 83–87.

———. "Eutropius and the Dynastic Name Eumenes of the Pergamene Pretender Aristonicus." *Ancient World* 4 (1981): 39–43.

Condurachi, E. "Kotys, Rome, et Abdère." *Latomus* 29 (1970): 581–594.

Cordano, F. "Rodii e Italici nel terzo secolo a.C." *Settima Miscellanea Greca e Romana* (1980): 255–270.

Cornell, T. J. "Aeneas and the Twins: The Development of the Roman Foundation Legend." *PCPS* 201 (1975): 1–32.

———. "Aeneas' Arrival in Italy." *LCM* 2 (1977): 77–83.

Cova, P. V. "Livio e la repressione dei Baccanali." *Athenaeum* 52 (1974): 82–109.

Crampa, J. *Labraunda.* Lund, 1969.

Crawford, M. H. *Roman Republican Coinage.* 2 vols. Cambridge, 1974.

———. "Rome and the Greek World: Economic Relationships." *Econ-HistRev* 30 (1977): 42–52.

———. "Greek Intellectuals and the Roman Aristocracy in the First Century B.C." In P. D. A. Garnsey and C. R. Whittaker, eds. *Imperialism in the Ancient World* (1978): 193–207.

———. "Trade and Movement of Coinage across the Adriatic in the Hellenistic Period." In *Essays for H. Sutherland* (1978): 1–11.

Dahlheim, W. *Struktur und Entwicklung des römischen Völkerrechtes im 3 und 2. Jahrhundert v. Chr.* Munich, 1968.

———. *Gewalt und Herrschaft: Das provinziale Herrschaftssystem der römischen Republik.* Berlin, 1977.

Dancy, J. C. *A Commentary on I Maccabees.* Oxford, 1954.

D'Arms, J. H. *Commerce and Social Standing in Ancient Rome.* Cambridge, Mass., 1981.

Daux, G. *Delphes au IIe et au Ier siècle.* Paris, 1936.

———. "Alcibiade, proxène de Lacédémone." In *Mélanges Derrousseaux* (1937): 117–122.

———. "Concours des *Titeia* dans un décret d'Argos." *BCH* 88 (1964): 569–576.

———. "Notes de lecture." *BCH* 89 (1965): 301–306.

——. "Les couronnes du Troyen Cassandros." *BCH* 89 (1965):498–502.

——. "Le milliaire de la Via Egnatia au Musée du Louvre." *Journal des Savants* (1977):145–163.

——. "L'arbitrage IG IX 2, Pages x–xi, 205, 1." *ZPE* 36 (1979):139–144.

Davies, J. K. *Athenian Propertied Families.* Oxford, 1971.

Degrassi, A. "Le dediche di popoli e re asiatici al popolo romano e a Giove Capitolino." *BullCommArchCom* 74 (1951–52):19–47.

Deininger, J. *Der politische Widerstand gegen Rom in Griechenland, 217–86 v. Chr.* Berlin, 1971.

——. "Bemerkungen zur Historizität der Rede des Agelaos, 217 v. Chr. (Polyb. 5, 104)." *Chiron* 3 (1973):103–108.

De Laet, S. J. *Portorium.* Bruges, 1949.

Dell, H. J. "The Origin and Nature of Illyrian Piracy." *Historia* 16 (1967):344–358.

——. "Antigonus and Rome." *CP* 62 (1967):94–103.

——. "Demetrius of Pharus and the Istrian War." *Historia* 19 (1970):30–38.

——. "Macedon and Rome: The Illyrian Question in the Early 2nd Century B.C." *Ancient Macedonia* 2 (1977):305–315.

Delplace, C. "Le contenu social et économique du soulèvement d'Aristonicos: opposition entre riches et pauvres?" *Athenaeum* 66 (1978):20–53.

de Martino, Fr. *Storia della costituzione romana.* 2nd ed. Naples, 1973.

Derow, P. S. "Polybios and the Embassy of Kallikrates." *Essays Presented to C. M. Bowra.* (1970):12–23.

——. "Kleemporos." *Phoenix* 27 (1973):118–134.

——. "The Roman Calendar, 190–168 B.C." *Phoenix* 27 (1973):345–356.

——. "The Roman Calendar, 218–191 B.C." *Phoenix* 30 (1976):265–281.

——. "Polybius, Rome, and the East." *JRS* 69 (1979):1–15.

Desideri, P. "Studi di storiografia eracleota: II. La guerra con Antioco il Grande." *StudClassOrient* 19–20 (1970–71):487–537.

——. "L'interpretazione dell'impero romano in Posidonio." *RendIstLomb* 106 (1972):481–493.

Diehl, E. *Anthologia Lyrica Graeca.* Leipzig, 1925.

——. "Das saeculum, seine Riten und Gebete." *RhM* 83 (1934):255–272, 348–372.

Dinsmoor, W. B. *The Archons of Athens in the Hellenistic Age.* Cambridge, Mass., 1931.

Donati, A. "I romani nell' Egeo: i documenti dell' età repubblicana." *Epigraphica* 27 (1965):3–59.

Dorey, T. A. "Macedonian Troops at the Battle of Zama." *AJP* 78 (1957):185–187.

———. "Contributory Causes of the Second Macedonian War." *AJP* 80 (1959):288–295.

———. "The Alleged Aetolian Embassy to Rome." *CR* 10 (1960):9.

———, S. I. Oost, and E. Badian, "Philip V and Illyria: The Annalistic Point of View." *CP* 55 (1960):180–186.

———. "Scipio Africanus as a Party Leader." *Klio* 39 (1961):191–198.

Doria, L. B. P. "Diodoro e Ariarate V." *PP* 33 (1978):104–129.

Drew-Bear, T. "Three Senatus Consulta Concerning the Province of Asia." *Historia* 21 (1972):75–87.

Drexler, H. "Iustum Bellum." *RhM* 102 (1959):97–140.

Dubuisson, M. "Problèmes du bilinguisme romaine." *LEC* 49 (1981): 27–45.

Dumont, J. C. "A propos d'Aristonicus." *Eirene* 5 (1966):189–196.

Earl, D. C. *The Political Thought of Sallust*. Cambridge, 1961.

Ebel, C. *Transalpine Gaul: The Emergence of a Roman Province*. Leiden, 1976.

Eckstein, A. M. "T. Quinctius Flamininus and the Campaign against Philip in 198 B.C." *Phoenix* 30 (1976):119–142.

———. "*Unicum subsidium populi Romani*: Hiero II and Rome, 263 B.C.–215 B.C." *Chiron* 10 (1980):183–203.

Eddy, S. K. *The King is Dead: Studies in the Near Eastern Resistance to Hellenism, 334–31 B.C.* Lincoln, Nebraska, 1961.

Edelstein, L. and I. G. Kidd, *Posidonius: Vol. I. The Fragments*. Cambridge, 1972.

Edlund, I. "Deinokrates: A Disappointed Greek Client." *Talanta* 8–9 (1977):52–57.

———. "Invisible Bonds: Clients and Patrons through the Eyes of Polybius." *Klio* 59 (1977):129–136.

Edson, C. "Macedonica." *HSCP* 51 (1940):125–136.

———. "A Note on the Macedonian Merides." *CP* 41 (1946):107.

Errington, R. M. *Philopoemen*. Oxford, 1969.

———. *The Dawn of Empire: Rome's Rise to World Power*. London, 1971.

———. "The Alleged Syro-Macedonian Pact and the Origins of the Second Macedonian War." *Athenaeum* 49 (1971):336–354.

———. "Senatus consultum de Coronaeis and the Early Course of the Third Macedonian War." *RivFilol* 102 (1974):79–86.

———. "Rom, Antiochos der Grosse und die Asylie von Teos." *ZPE* 39 (1980):279–284.

Fayer, C. *Il culto della dea Roma*. Pescara, 1976.

Fears, J. R. "Ο ΔΗΜΟΣ Ο ΡΩΜΑΙΩΝ *Genius Populi Romani*." *Mnemosyne* 31 (1978):274–286.

Ferenczy, E. "Zum Problem des *Foedus Cassianum*." *RIDA* 22 (1975): 223–232.

Ferguson, W. S. *Hellenistic Athens*. London, 1911.

Ferrary, J. L. "L'empire de Rome et les hégémonies des cités grecques chez Polybe." *BCH* 100 (1976):283–289.

―――. "Le discours de Philus (Cicéron, *De Re Publica*, III, 8–31) et la philosophie de Carnéade." *REL* 55 (1977):128–156.

Ferrenbach, V. *Die amici populi romani republikanischer Zeit*. Diss. Strasbourg, 1895.

Ferrero, G. *Grandezza e decadenza di Roma* I. Milan, 1907.

Ferro, B. *Le origini della II guerra macedonica*. Palermo, 1960.

Feyel, M. "Paul-Émile et le synedrion Macédonien." *BCH* 70 (1946): 187–198.

―――. "Inscriptions inédites d'Akraiphia." *BCH* 79 (1955):419–422.

Fine, J. V. A. "Macedon, Illyria, and Rome, 220–219 B.C." *JRS* 26 (1936):24–39.

Finley, M. I. *The Ancient Economy*. Berkeley and Los Angeles, 1973.

―――. "Empire in the Greco-Roman World." *Greece and Rome* 25 (1978):1–15.

―――. *Ancient Slavery and Modern Ideology*. New York, 1980.

Fischer, T. *Untersuchungen zum Partherkrieg Antiochus VII*. Tübingen, 1970.

―――. "Zu Tryphon." *Chiron* 2 (1972):201–213.

―――. "Zu den Beziehungen zwischen Rom und den Juden im 2. Jahrhundert v. Chr." *ZAlttestWiss* 86 (1974):90–93.

―――. *Seleukiden und Makkabäer*. Bochum, 1980.

―――. "Rom und die Hasmonäer. Ein Überblick zu den politischen Beziehungen 164–37 v. Chr." *Gymnasium* 88 (1981):139–150.

Flacelière, R. *Les Aetoliens à Delphes*. Paris, 1937.

Flurl, W. *Deditio in Fidem*. Munich, 1969.

Flusser, D. "The Four Empires in the Fourth Sibyl and in the Book of Daniel." *Israel Oriental Studies* 2 (1972):148–175.

Fontenrose, J. "The Crucified Daphidas." *TAPA* 91 (1960):83–99.

Forni, G. "Manlio Curio Dentato, uomo democratico." *Athenaeum* 21 (1953):170–240.

Forrest, W. G. "Review of Thiel, *A History of Roman Sea-Power before the Second Punic War*." *JRS* 46 (1956):169–171.

Forte, B. *Rome and the Romans as the Greeks Saw Them*. Rome, 1972.

Foucart, M. P. "La formation de la province romaine d'Asie." *Mém-AcadInscr* 37.1 (1904):297–339.

Frank, T. "The Diplomacy of Q. Marcius in 169 B.C." *CP* 5 (1910): 358–361.

―――. *Roman Imperialism*. New York, 1914.

———. "Representative Government in the Macedonian Republics." *CP* 9 (1914):49–59.

———. *An Economic Survey of Ancient Rome* I. Baltimore, 1933.

Fraser, P. M. and G. E. Bean, *The Rhodian Peraea*. Oxford, 1954.

Fraser, P. M. *Ptolemaic Alexandria*. 3 vols. Oxford, 1972.

Frei, P. "Späte Zeugnisse für frühen römischen Imperialismus?" *MusHelv* 32 (1975):73–80.

Frier, B. W. *Libri Annales Pontificum Maximorum: The Origins of the Annalistic Tradition*. Rome, 1979.

Fuchs, H. *Der geistige Widerstand gegen Rom in der antiken Welt*. Berlin, 1938.

Fuks, A. "The Bellum Achaicum and its Social Aspect." *JHS* 90 (1970): 78–89.

Furneaux, H. *The Annals of Tacitus*. 2 vols. Oxford, 1896, 1907.

Gabba, E. *Appiani Bellorum Civilium Liber Primus*. Florence, 1967.

———. "Considerazioni sulla tradizione letteraria sulle origini della Repubblica." *Entretiens Fondation Hardt* 13 (1967):133–174.

———. "Storiografia greca e imperialismo romano (III–I sec. a.C.)" *RivStorItal* 86 (1974):625–642.

———. "P. Cornelio Scipione Africano e la leggende." *Athenaeum* 53 (1975):3–17.

———. "Sulla valorizzazione politica della leggenda delle origini troiane di Roma fra III e II secolo a.C." *ContIstFilClass* 4 (1976): 84–101.

———. "Aspetti culturali dell' imperialismo romano." *Athenaeum* 55 (1977):49–74.

———. "Per un' interpretazione politica del *De Officiis* di Cicerone." *RendAccadLinc* 34 (1979):117–142.

———. "Riflessioni antiche e moderne sulle attività commerciali a Roma nei secoli II e I a.C." *MAAR* 36 (1980):91–102.

Gagé, J. *L'Apollon romain*. Paris, 1955.

Galsterer, H. *Herrschaft und Verwaltung im republikanischen Italien*. Munich, 1976.

Garbarino, G. *Roma e la filosofia greca dalle origini alla fine del II secolo a.C.* 2 vols. Turin, 1973.

Garlan, Y. "Décret d'Iasos en l'honneur d'Antiochos III." *ZPE* 13 (1974):197–198.

Gauger, J.-D. *Beiträge zur jüdischen Apologetik*. Köln-Bonn, 1977.

———. "Phlegon von Tralleis, mirab. III." *Chiron* 10 (1980):225–261.

Gauthier, P. *Symbola*. Nancy, 1972.

Gawantka, W. *Isopolitie*. Munich, 1975.

Geer, R. M. "The Scipios and the Father of the Gracchi." *TAPA* 69 (1938):381–388.

Gelzer, M. "Nasicas Widerspruch gegen die Zerstörung Karthagos." *Philologus* 86 (1931): 261–299.

———. "Über die Arbeitsweise des Polybios." *SBHeid* (1956): 3–36.

———. *Kleine Schriften.* 3 vols. Wiesbaden, 1962–1964.

———. *The Roman Nobility.* New York, 1969.

Giovannini, A. "Les origines de la 3ᵉ guerre de Macédoine." *BCH* 93 (1969): 853–861.

———. "Philipp V, Perseus, und die Delphische Amphiktyonie." *Ancient Macedonia* 1 (1970): 147–154.

——— and H. Müller, "Die Beziehungen zwischen Rom und den Juden im 2 Jh. v. Chr." *MusHelv* 28 (1971): 156–171.

———. *Rome et la circulation monétaire en Grèce au IIᵉ siècle avant J.C.* Basel, 1978.

Golan, D. "The Problem of the Roman Presence in the Political Consciousness of the Greeks before 229 B.C." *RivStorAnt* 1 (1971): 93–98.

———. "The Roman Dictate and the Greek ΟΜΙΛΙΑ." *RivStorAnt* 6–7 (1977): 315–327.

Goldstein, J. *I Maccabees.* New York, 1976.

Goodyear, F. R. D. *The Annals of Tacitus* II. Cambridge, 1981.

Gozzoli, S. "Etnografia e politica in Agatarchide." *Athenaeum* 66 (1978): 54–79.

Graetzel, P. *De Pactionum inter Graecos civitates factarum ad bellum pacemque pertinentium appellationibus formulis ratione.* Halle, 1885.

Greco, M. "Lotte politiche alla corte macedone." *Miscellanea di studi classici in onore di Eugenio Manni* (1980) IV: 1157–1171.

Griffith, G. T. "An Early Motive of Roman Imperialism (201 B.C.)." *CHJ* 5 (1935): 1–14.

Grilli, A. "Livio e i Romani in Istria nel 178 av. Chr." *RendIstLomb* 110 (1976): 142–151.

Gruen, E. S. *Roman Politics and the Criminal Courts, 149–78 B.C.* Cambridge, Mass., 1968.

———. "The Supposed Alliance between Rome and Philip V of Macedon." *CSCA* 6 (1973): 123–136.

———. "The Last Years of Philip V." *GRBS* 15 (1974): 221–246.

———. "Rome and Rhodes in the Second Century B.C.: A Historiographical Inquiry." *CQ* 25 (1975): 58–81.

———. "Class Conflict and the Third Macedonian War." *AJAH* 1 (1976): 29–60.

———. "The Origins of the Achaean War." *JHS* 96 (1976): 46–69.

———. "Rome and the Seleucids in the Aftermath of Pydna." *Chiron* 6 (1976): 73–95.

———. "Macedonia and the Settlement of 167 B.C." In W. L. Adams and E. N. Borza, eds., *Philip II, Alexander the Great, and the Macedonian Heritage* (1982):257–267.

———. "Greek Πίστις and Roman *Fides*." *Athenaeum* 60 (1982): 50–68.

Grzybek, E. "Roms Bündnis mit Byzanz (Tac. *Ann.* 12.62)." *MusHelv* 37 (1980):50–59.

Gschnitzer, F. "Die Stellung Karthagos nach dem Frieden von 201 v. Chr." *WS* 79 (1966):276–289.

Guarducci, M. "Gli Scipioni in una nuova iscrizione Cretese ed in altri monumenti dell' epigrafia greca." *RivFilol* 7 (1929):60–85.

———. "Note sul koinon cretese." *RivFilol* 28 (1950):142–154.

Guite, H. "Cicero's Attitude to the Greeks." *Greece and Rome* 31 (1962): 142–159.

Gundel, H. G. "Der Begriff Maiestas im politischen Denken der römischen Republik." *Historia* 12 (1963):283–320.

Haarhoff, T. J. *The Stranger at the Gate*. Oxford, 1948.

Habicht, C. "Über die Kriege zwischen Pergamon und Bithynien." *Hermes* 84 (1956):90–110.

———. "Samische Volksbeschlüsse der hellenistischen Zeit." *AthMitt* 72 (1957):152–274.

———. "Der Stratege Hegemonides." *Historia* 7 (1958):376–378.

———. *Gottmenschentum und griechische Städte*. 2nd ed. Munich, 1970.

———. *Jüdische Schriften aus hellenistisch-römischer Zeit*. I:3: 2. *Makkabäerbuch*. Gutersöh, 1976.

———. "Royal Documents in Maccabees II." *HSCP* 80 (1976):1–18.

———. "Zur Geschichte Athens in der Zeit Mithridates VI." *Chiron* 6 (1976):127–142.

———. *Untersuchungen zur politischen Geschichte Athens im 3. Jahrhundert v. Chr.* Munich, 1979.

———. *Studien zur Geschichte Athens in hellenistischer Zeit*. Göttingen, 1982.

Hackens, T. "Trésor hellénistique trouvé à Délos." *BCH* 89 (1965): 503–566.

Hackl, U. "Poseidonius und das Jahr 146 v. Chr. als Epochendatum in der antiken Historiographie." *Gymnasium* 87 (1980):151–166.

Hamilton, J. R. "Cleitarchus and Aristobulus." *Historia* 10 (1961): 448–458.

Hammond, N. G. L. "The Kingdoms in Illyria circa 400–167 B.C." *BSA* 61 (1966):239–253.

———. "The Opening Campaigns and the Battle of Aoi Stena in the Second Macedonian War." *JRS* 56 (1966):39–54.

———. *Epirus*. Oxford, 1967.

———. "Illyris, Rome, and Macedon in 229–205 B.C." *JRS* 58 (1968): 1–21.

———. *A History of Macedonia*. I. Oxford, 1972.

Hampl, F. "Römische Politik in republikanischer Zeit und das Problem des 'Sittenverfalls.'" *HZ* 88 (1959):497–525.

Hanell, K. "Zur Problematik der älteren römischen Geschichtsschreibung." *Entretiens Fondation Hardt* 4 (1956):147–184.

Hansen, E. V. *The Attalids of Pergamum*. 2nd ed. Ithaca, 1971.

Harmand, L. *Le Patronat sur les collectivités publiques des origines au Bas-Empire*. Paris, 1957.

Harris, W. V. "On War and Greed in the Second Century B.C." *AHR* 76 (1971):1371–1385.

———. *Rome in Etruria and Umbria*. Oxford, 1971.

———. *War and Imperialism in Republican Rome, 327–70 B.C.* Oxford, 1979.

Hartman, L. F. and A. A. DiLella, *The Book of Daniel*. New York, 1978.

Hatzfeld, J. "Les Italiens résident à Délos mentionnés dans les inscriptions du l'île." *BCH* 36 (1912):1–218.

———. *Les trafiquants Italiens dans l'Orient hellénique*. Paris, 1919.

Havelock, C. M. "The Archaistic Athena Promachos in Early Hellenistic Coinage." *AJA* 84 (1980):41–50.

Heidemann, M.-L. *Die Freiheitsparole in der griechisch-römischen Auseinandersetzung (200–188 v. Chr.)*. Diss. Bonn, 1966.

Heinen, H. "Die politischen Beziehungen zwischen Rom und dem Ptolemäerreich von ihren Anfängen bis zum Tag von Eleusis (273–168 v. Chr.)." *ANRW* I. 1 (1972):632–659.

Helliesen, J. M. "Demetrius I Soter: A Seleucid King with an Antigonid Name." In H. Dell, ed., *Ancient Macedonian Studies in Honor of Charles F. Edson* (1981):219–228.

Helly, B. "Politarques, poliarques et politophylaques." *Ancient Macedonia* 2 (1977):531–544.

Hengel, M. *Judaism and Hellenism*. 2nd ed. London, 1974.

Henze, W. *De Civitatibus Liberis*. Berlin, 1892.

Herrmann, P. "Antiochos der Grosse und Teos." *Anatolia* 9 (1965): 29–159.

———. "Die Stadt Temnos in hellenistischer Zeit." *IstMitt* 29 (1979): 239–271.

Heuss, A. *Die völkerrechtlichen Grundlagen der römischen Aussenpolitik in republikanischer Zeit*. Leipzig, 1933.

———. "Abschluss und Beurkundung des griechischen und römischen Staatsvertrages." *Klio* 27 (1934):14–53, 218–257.

———. *Stadt und Herrscher des Hellenismus*. Leipzig, 1937.

———. "Antigonos Monophthalmos und die griechischen Städte." *Hermes* 73 (1938):133–194.

———. "Die Freiheitserklärung von Mylasa in den Inschriften von Labranda." In *Le Monde Grec: Hommages à Claire Préaux* (1975): 404–415.

Hill, H. "Roman Revenues from Greece after 146 B.C." *CP* 41 (1946): 35–42.

Hobson, J. A. *Imperialism: A Study.* 3rd ed. London, 1938.

Hoffman, W. *Rom und die griechische Welt im 4. Jahrhundert.* Leipzig, 1934.

———. "Das Todesjahr des Philopoimen." *Hermes* 73 (1938): 244–248.

———. "Die römische Politik des 2. Jahrhunderts und das Ende Karthagos." *Historia* 9 (1960): 309–344.

Holleaux, M. "Epigraphica." *REG* 11 (1898): 258–266.

———. "Trois décrets de Rhodes." *REG* 12 (1899): 20–37.

———. "Curiae epigraphicae." *REA* 5 (1903): 205–230.

———. "L'alliance de Rome et de l'Achaie." *REG* 34 (1921): 400–422.

———. "Sur un passage de Phlégon de Tralles." *RevPhil* 56 (1930): 305–309.

———. *Rome, la Grèce et les monarchies hellénistiques au III<sup>e</sup> siècle avant J.-C. (273–205).* Paris, 1935.

———. *Études d'épigraphie et d'histoire grecques.* 6 vols. Paris, 1938–1968.

Homolle, Th. "Les Romains à Délos." *BCH* 8 (1884): 75–158.

Hopkins, K. *Conquerors and Slaves (Sociological Studies in Roman History* I). Cambridge, 1978.

Hopp, J. *Untersuchungen zur Geschichte der letzten Attaliden.* Munich, 1977.

Horn, H. *Foederati.* Frankfurt, 1930.

Horsfall, N. "Q. Fabius C. filus Pictor; Some New Evidence." *LCM* 1 (1976): 18.

———. "Some Problems in the Aeneas Legend." *CQ* 29 (1979): 372–390.

Humbert, M. "L'incorporation de Caere dans la civitas Romana." *MEFRA* 84 (1972): 231–268.

Huss, W. "Die zu Ehren Ptolemaios' III und seiner Familie errichtete Statuengruppe von Thermos (*IG* IX, 1, 1², 56)." *ChronEg* 50 (1975): 312–320.

———. *Untersuchungen zur Aussenpolitik Ptolemaios' IV.* Munich, 1976.

Huzar, E. "Egyptian Influences on Roman Coinage in the Third Century B.C." *CJ* 61 (1966): 337–346.

Ilari, V. *Guerra e diritto nel mondo antico. Parte prima: Guerra e diritto nel mondo greco-ellenistico fino al III secolo.* Milan, 1980.

Jahn, J. *Interregnum und Wahldiktatur.* Kallmünz, 1970.

Janke, M. *Historische Untersuchungen zu Memnon von Herakleia.* Würzburg, 1963.

Jocelyn, H. D. "The Poems of Quintus Ennius." *ANRW* I.2 (1972): 987–1026.

————. "The Ruling Class of the Roman Republic and Greek Philosophers." *BRL* 59 (1977): 323–366.

Jones, A. H. M. *The Greek City.* Oxford, 1940.

Jones, C. P. "Diodorus Pasparos and the Nikephoria of Pergamon." *Chiron* 4 (1974): 183–205.

Jucker, H. *Vom Verhältnis der Römer zur bildenden Kunst der Griechen.* Frankfurt, 1950.

Kahrstedt, U. "Zum Ausbruch des dritten römisch-makedonischen Krieges." *Klio* 11 (1911): 415–430.

Kemp. T. *Theories of Imperialism.* London, 1967.

Kienast, D. *Cato der Zensor.* Heidelberg, 1954.

————. "Entstehung und Aufbau des römischen Reiches." *ZSS* 85 (1968): 330–367.

————. "Eine Silbermünze aus der Zeit des Aristonikoskrieges." *Historia* 26 (1977): 250–252.

Klaffenbach, G. "Eine neue Ehrenstatue für T. Quinctius Flamininus." *Chiron* 1 (1971): 167–168.

Kleiner, F. S. "The Dated Cistophori of Ephesus." *ANSMN* 18 (1972): 17–32.

————, and S. P. Noe, *The Early Cistophoric Coinage.* New York, 1977.

————. "Further Reflections on the Early Cistophoric Coinage." *ANSMN* 25 (1980): 45–52.

Klose, P. *Die völkerrechtliche Ordnung der hellenistischen Staatenwelt in der Zeit von 280 bis 168 v. Chr.* Munich, 1972.

Knapp, R. C. *Aspects of the Roman Experience in Iberia.* Vitoria, 1977.

Koebner, R. and H. D. Schmidt, *Imperialism.* Cambridge, 1964.

Koestermann, E. *Tacitus, Annalen* III. Heidelberg, 1967.

————. *C. Sallustius Crispus, Bellum Iugurthinum.* Heidelberg, 1971.

Kolbe, W. *Beiträge zur syrischen und jüdischen Geschichte.* Berlin, 1926.

Koukouli-Chrysanthaki, C. "Politarchs in a New Inscription from Amphipolis." In H. Dell, ed., *Ancient Macedonian Studies in Honor of Charles F. Edson* (1981): 229–241.

Kreissig, H. *Wirtschaft und Gesellschaft in Seleukidenreich.* Berlin, 1978.

Laidlaw, W. A. *A History of Delos.* Oxford, 1933.

Lambrino, S. "Inscription latine de Callatis." *CRAI* (1933): 278–288.

Lanzillotta, E. "Cn. Ottavio e gli Argivi." *Sesta Miscellanea Greca e Romana* (1978): 233–247.

Laqueur, R. "Griechische Urkunden in der jüdisch-hellenistischen Literatur." *HZ* 136 (1927): 231–252.

————. "Die Flucht des Demetrius aus Rom (Ein Beitrag zur Kritik des Polybios)." *Hermes* 65 (1930): 129–166.

Larsen, J. A. O. "Was Greece Free between 196 and 146 B.C.?" *CP* 30 (1935):193–214.

———. "The Peace of Phoenice and the Outbreak of the Second Macedonian War." *CP* 32 (1937):15–31.

———. "Representation and Democracy in Hellenistic Federalism." *CP* 40 (1945):65–97.

———. "*Consilium* in Livy, xlv.18.6–7 and the Macedonian Synedria." *CP* 44 (1949):73–90.

———. "The Araxa Inscription and the Lycian Confederacy." *CP* 51 (1956):151–169.

———. *Greek Federal States.* Oxford, 1968.

Latte, K. *Römische Religionsgeschichte.* Munich, 1960.

———. "Der Historiker L. Calpurnius Frugi." *SBBerlin* (1960):1–16.

Lehmann, G. A. *Untersuchungen zur historischen Glaubwürdigkeit des Polybios.* Münster, 1967.

Lemosse, M. "Réflexion sur la conception romaine de l'arbitrage international." *Gedächtnisschrift für Rudolf Schmidt* (1966):341–348.

Lenin, V. I. *Imperialism, the Highest Stage of Capitalism.* New York, 1939.

Le Rider, G. *Suse sous les Séleucides et les Parthes.* Paris, 1965.

Leuze, O. "Die Feldzüge Antiochos des Grossen nach Kleinasien und Thrakien." *Hermes* 58 (1923):187–229, 241–287.

Lévèque, P. "Lycophronica." *REA* 57 (1955):36–56.

———. *Pyrrhos.* Paris, 1957.

Levi, M. A. "Le cause della guerra romana contro gli Illiri." *PP* 28 (1973):317–325.

Lewis, D. M. "The Chronology of the Athenian New Style Coinage." *NC* 2 (1962):275–300.

Liberanome, M. "Alessandro il Molosso e i Samniti." *AttiAccadTorino* 104 (1970):79–95.

Liebmann-Frankfort, T. "Valeur juridique et signification politique des testaments faits par les rois hellénistiques en faveur des Romains." *RIDA* 13 (1966):73–94.

———. *La frontière orientale dans la politique extérieure de la République romaine.* Brussels, 1969.

———. "Rome et le conflit Judéo-Syrien (164–161 avant notre ère)." *AntCl* 38 (1969):101–120.

———. "Les Étapes de l'intégration de la Cappadoce dans l'empire romain." In *Le Monde Grec: Hommages à Claire Préaux* (1975):416–425.

Lintott, A. W. "Imperial Expansion and Moral Decline in the Roman Republic." *Historia* 21 (1972):626–638.

———. "The Capitoline Dedications to Jupiter and the Roman People." *ZPE* 30 (1978):137–144.

Lippold, A. *Consules. Untersuchungen zur Geschichte des römischen Konsulates von 264 bis 201 v. Chr.* Bonn, 1963.

Luce, T. J. *Livy: The Composition of his History.* Princeton, 1977.

Luzzatto, G. I. *Epigrafia giuridica greca e romana.* Milan, 1942.

Mackay, P. "Macedonian Tetradrachms of 148–147 B.C." *ANSMN* 14 (1968):15–40.

McDonald, A. H. and F. W. Walbank, "The Origins of the Second Macedonian War." *JRS* 27 (1937):180–207.

McDonald, A. H. "Scipio Africanus and Roman Politics in the Second Century B.C." *JRS* 28 (1938):153–164.

———. "Review of G. Klaffenbach, *Der römisch-ätolische Bündnisvertrag vom Jahre 212 v. Chr.*" *JRS* 46 (1956):153–157.

———. "Review of B. Ferro, *Le origini della II guerra macedonica.*" *JRS* 53 (1963):187–191.

———. "The Treaty of Apamea (188 B.C.)." *JRS* 57 (1967):1–8.

———, and F. W. Walbank, "The Treaty of Apamea (188 B.C.): the Naval Clauses." *JRS* 59 (1969):30–39.

McShane, R. B. *The Foreign Policy of the Attalids of Pergamum.* Urbana, 1964.

Magie, D. "The 'Agreement' between Philip V and Antiochus III for the Partition of the Egyptian Empire." *JRS* 29 (1939):32–44.

———. "Rome and the City-States of Western Asia Minor from 200 to 133 B.C." In *Buckler Studies* (1939):161–185.

———. *Roman Rule in Asia Minor.* Princeton, 1950.

Maier, F. G. *Griechische Mauerinschriften.* Heidelberg, 1959.

Manganaro, G. "Una biblioteca storica nel ginnasio di Tauromenion e il P. Oxyr. 1241." *PP* 29 (1974):389–409.

Manni, E. "L'Egitto tolemaico nei suoi rapporti politici con Roma." *RivFilol* 27 (1949):79–106.

———. "L'Egitto tolemaico nei suoi rapporti politici con Roma II: L'instaurazione del protettorato romano." *RivFilol* 28 (1950):229–262.

———. "Sulle più antiche relazioni fra Roma e il mondo ellenistico." *PP* 11 (1956):179–190.

———. "Alessandro il Molosso e la sua spedizione in Italia." *Studi Salentini* 14 (1962):344–352.

Marchetti, P. "La marche du calendrier romain de 203 à 190 (années varr. 551–564)." *AntCl* 42 (1973):473–496.

Maróti, H. "Der Sklavenmarkt auf Delos und die Piraterie." *Helikon* 9–10 (1969–70):24–42.

Marshall, A. J. "Friends of the Roman People." *AJP* 89 (1968):39–55.

———. "The Survival and Development of International Jurisdiction in the Greek World under Roman Rule." *ANRW* II.13 (1980): 626–661.

Martin, V. *La vie internationale dans la Grèce des cités (VI^e–IV^e s. av. J.-C.* Paris, 1940.

Martina, M. "Ennio 'poeta cliens.'" *Quaderni di filologia classica* 2 (1979): 15–74.

———. "I censori del 258 a.C." *Quaderni di storia* 12 (1980):143–170.

———. "Aedes Herculis Musarum." *DialArch* (1981):49–68.

Marx, F. "Animadversiones criticae in Scipionis Aemiliani historiam et C. Gracchi orationem adversus Scipionem." *RhM* 39 (1884): 65–72.

Mastrocinque, A. "Eumene a Roma (172 a.C.) e le fonti del libro macedonico di Appiano." *AttiIstVeneto* 84 (1975–76):25–40.

———. "Osservazioni sull' attività di Antioco III nel 197 e 196 a.C." *PP* 31 (1976):307–322.

———. "L'eleutheria e la città ellenistiche." *AttiIstVeneto* 135 (1976–77):1–23.

———. "Roma e Antioco III. Guerra di propaganda e propaganda per la guerra." *AttiIstVeneto* 136 (1977–78):1–17.

———. *La Carie e la Ionia meridionale in epoca ellenistica.* Rome, 1979.

Matthaei, L. E. "On the Classification of Roman Allies." *CQ* 1 (1907): 182–204.

———. "The Place of Arbitration and Mediation in Ancient Systems of International Ethics." *CQ* 2 (1908):241–264.

Mattingly, H. "The First Age of Roman Coinage." *JRS* 35 (1945): 65–77.

———. "The 'Diana-Victory' Didrachms and the Decadrachms of Arsinoe." *NC* 6 (1946):63–67.

Mattingly, H. B. "Review of M. Thompson, *The Agrinion Hoard.*" *NC* 9 (1969):325–333.

———. "Notes on Some Roman Republican Moneyers." *NC* 9 (1969): 95–105.

———. "Some Problems in Second Century Attic Prosopography." *Historia* 20 (1971):26–46.

———. "The Date of the *Senatus Consultum de agro Pergameno.*" *AJP* 93 (1972):412–423.

———. "Q. Fabius Pictor, Father of Roman History." *LCM* 1 (1976): 3–7.

———. "Coinage and the Roman State." *NC* 17 (1977):199–215.

May, J. M. F. "Macedonia and Illyria (217–167 B.C.)." *JRS* 36 (1946): 48–56.

Mazzarino, S. *Il pensiero storico classico.* Bari, 1968.

Meissner, E. *Lucius Aemilius Paullus Macedonicus und seine Bedeutung für das römische Reich (229–160 v. Chr.)*. Bischberg, 1974.

Mellor, R. *ΘΕΑ ΡΩΜΗ: The Worship of the Goddess Roma in the Greek World*. Göttingen, 1975.

———. "The Dedications on the Capitoline Hill." *Chiron* 8 (1978): 319–330.

———. "The Goddess Roma." *ANRW* II.17 (1981): 950–1030.

Meloni, P. *Perseo e la fine della monarchia macedone*. Rome, 1953.

———. *Il valore storico e le fonti del libro macedonico di Appiano*. Rome, 1955.

Mendels, D. "The Attitude of Antiochus III towards the Class Struggle in Greece (192–191 B.C.)." *RivStorAnt* 8 (1978): 27–38.

———. "Perseus and the Socio-Economic Question in Greece (179–172/1 B.C.). A Study in Roman Propaganda." *Ancient Society* 9 (1978): 55–73.

———. "A Note on the Speeches of Nabis and T. Quinctius Flamininus (195 B.C.)." *Scripta Classica Israelica* 4 (1978): 38–44.

———. "Polybius, Nabis, and Equality." *Athenaeum* 57 (1979): 311–333.

———. "The Five Empires: A Note on a Propagandistic *Topos*." *AJP* 102 (1981): 330–337.

Merkelbach, R. *Griechische Papyri der Hamburger Staats-und Universitäts-Bibliothek*. Hamburg, 1954.

Mesk, J. "Über Phlegons Mirabilia I–III." *Philologus* 80 (1925): 298–311.

Meyer, H. *Cicero und das Reich*. Diss. Köln, 1957.

Michel, J.-H. "Un parallèle romain à une formule Aitolienne d'asylie." In *Le Monde Grec: Hommages à Claire Préaux* (1975): 508–512.

Minns, E. H. *Scythians and Greeks*. Cambridge, 1913.

Mitchell, R. E. "A New Chronology for the Romano-Campanian Coins." *NC* 6 (1966): 65–70.

Moehring, H. R. "The *Acta Pro Judaeis* in the *Antiquities* of Flavius Josephus: A Study in Hellenistic and Modern Apologetic Historiography." In J. Neussner, *Christianity, Judaism, and Other Greco-Roman Cults: Studies for Morton Smith at Sixty* (1975) III: 124–158.

Momigliano, A. *Prime linee di storia della traduzione maccabaica*. Rome, 1930.

———. *Giudea Romana*. Bologna, 1934.

———. "Terra Marique." *JRS* 32 (1942): 53–64.

———. "Review of E. Ciaceri, *Le origini di Roma*." *JRS* 33 (1943): 101–103.

———. "The Locrian Maidens and the Date of Lycophron's *Alexandra*." *CQ* 39 (1945): 49–53.

————. "Atene nel III secolo a.C. e la scoperta di Roma nelle storie di Timeo di Tauromenio." *RivStorItal* 71 (1959):529–556.

————. *Secondo contributo alla storia degli studi classici.* Rome, 1960.

————. "Linee per una valutazione di Fabio Pittore." *RendAccadLinc* 15 (1960):310–320.

————. *Terzo contributo alla storia degli studi classici del mondo antico.* Rome, 1966.

————. "Polibio, Posidonio, e l'imperialismo romano." *AttiAccad-Torino* 107 (1973):693–707.

————. *Alien Wisdom: The Limits of Hellenization.* Cambridge, 1975.

————. "Daniele e la teoria greca della successione degli imperi." *RendAccadLinc* 35 (1980):157–162.

Mommsen, T. "Der Senatsbeschluss bei Josephus, *Ant.* 14.8.5." *Hermes* 9 (1875):281–291.

————. "Mithradates Philopator Philadelphos." *ZeitschrNum* 15 (1887):207–219.

————. *Römisches Staatsrecht.* Leipzig, 1887.

————. "Das Potamon-Denkmal auf Mytilene." *SBBerlin* (1895):887–901.

————. *Römische Geschichte* I. Berlin, 1903.

Moretti, L. "Una nuova iscrizione da Araxa." *RivFilol* 78 (1950):326–350.

————. "Epigraphica 5–6." *RivFilol* 93 (1965):278–283.

————. "Chio e la lupa capitolina." *RivFilol* 108 (1980):33–54.

Morgan, M. G. "Metellus Macedonicus and the Province Macedonia." *Historia* 18 (1969):422–446.

————. "*Imperium sine finibus*: Romans and World Conquest in the First Century B.C." In S. M. Burstein and L. A. Okin, eds., *Panhellenica: Essays in Ancient History and Historiography in Honor of Truesdell S. Brown* (1980):143–154.

Mørkholm, O. "Eulaios and Lennaios." *ClMed* 22 (1961):32–43.

————. "The Accession of Antiochus IV of Syria." *ANSMN* 11 (1964):63–76.

————. *Antiochus IV of Syria.* Gyldendal, 1966.

————. "The Speech of Agelaus at Naupactus, 217 B.C." *ClMed* 28 (1967):240–253.

————. "The Speech of Agelaus Again." *Chiron* 4 (1974):127–132.

————. "Some Reflections on the Early Cistophoric Coinage." *ANSMN* 24 (1979):50–62.

Müller, O. *Antigonos Monophthalmos und 'das Jahr der Könige.'* Bonn, 1973.

Münzer, F. *Römische Adelsparteien und Adelsfamilien.* Stuttgart, 1920.

Musti, D. "I successori di Tolomeo Euergete II." *PP* 15 (1960):432–446.

———. "Sull' idea di συγγένεια in iscrizioni greche." *AnnPisa* 32 (1963):225–239.

———. "Problemi Polibiani (Rassegna di Studi, 1950–1964)." *PP* 20 (1965):380–426.

———. "Lo stato dei Seleucidi." *StudClassOrient* 15 (1966):61–197.

———. "Polibio negli studi dell' ultimo ventennio (1950–1970). *ANRW* I.2 (1972):1114–1181.

———. *Polibio e l'imperialismo romano.* Naples, 1978.

Nachtergael, G. *Les Galates en Grèce et les Sôtéria de Delphes.* Brussels, 1975.

Neatby, L. H. "Roman-Egyptian Relations during the Third Century B.C." *TAPA* 81 (1950):89–98.

Nenci, G. "Le relazioni con Marsiglia nella politica estera romana." *RivStudLig* 24 (1958):24–97.

Nicolet, C. "Polybe et les institutions romaines." *Entretiens Fondation Hardt* 20 (1974):207–265.

———. *Tributum.* Bonn, 1976.

———. *Rome et la conquête du monde méditerranéen.* 2. Paris, 1978.

———. "Économie, société et institutions au IIᵉ siècle av. J.C.: de la lex Claudia à l'ager exceptus." *Annales* 5 (1980):871–894.

Niese, B. *Geschichte der griechischen und makedonischen Staaten seit der Schlacht bei Chaeronea.* 3 vols. Gotha, 1883–1903.

———. "Kritik der beiden Makkabäerbücher nebst Beiträgen zur Geschichte der makkabäischen Erhebung." *Hermes* 35 (1900):268–307, 453–527.

———. "Eine Urkunde aus der Makkabäerzeit." *Orientalische Studien, Theodor Nöldeke* (1906) II:817–824.

Nikiprowetsky, V. *La troisième Sibylle.* Paris, 1970.

Nissen, H. *Kritische Untersuchungen über die Quellen der vierten und fünften Dekade des Livius.* Berlin, 1863.

North, J. A. "Religious Toleration in Republican Rome." *PCPS* 25 (1979):85–103.

———. "The Development of Roman Imperialism." *JRS* 71 (1981):1–9.

Ogilvie, R. M. *A Commentary on Livy Books 1–5.* Oxford, 1965.

Oliverio, G. *La stele di Tolomeo Neòteros re di Cirene.* Bergamo, 1932.

Olshausen, E. *Rom und Ägypten von 116 bis 51 v. Chr.* Diss. Erlangen, 1963.

Oost, S. I. "The Roman Calendar in the Year of Pydna." *CP* 48 (1953):217–230.

———. *Roman Policy in Epirus and Acarnania in the Age of the Roman Conquest of Greece.* Dallas, 1954.

———. "Amynander, Athamania, and Rome." *CP* 52 (1957):1–15.

———. "Philip V and Illyria, 205–200 B.C." *CP* 54 (1959):158–164.

———. "Cyrene, 96–74 B.C." *CP* 58 (1963):11–25.

Orth, W. *Königlicher Machtanspruch und städtische Freiheit.* Munich, 1977.

Osborne, M. J. "Kallias, Phaidros, and the Revolt of Athens in 287 B.C." *ZPE* 35 (1979):181–194.

Otto, W. "Zur Geschichte der Zeit des 6 Ptolemäer." *AbhMünch* 11 (1934):1–147.

———, and H. Bengtson, "Zur Geschichte des Niederganges des Ptolemäerreiches." *AbhMünch* 17 (1938):1–244.

Paltiel, E. "The Treaty of Apamea and the Later Seleucids." *Antichthon* 13 (1979):30–41.

———. "Antiochus IV and Demetrius I of Syria." *Antichthon* 13 (1979): 42–47.

Papazoglou, F. "Notes d'épigraphie et de topographie macédoniennes." *BCH* 87 (1963):517–544.

———. "Les origines et la destinée de l'État illyrien: Illyrii proprie dicti." *Historia* 14 (1965):143–179.

———. "La province de Macédoine." *ANRW* II.7.1 (1979):302–369.

Pape, M. *Griechische Kunstwerke aus Kriegsbeute und ihre öffentliche Aufstellung in Rom.* Hamburg, 1975.

Parke, H. W. and D. E. W. Wormell, *The Delphic Oracle.* Oxford, 1956.

Passerini, A. "Le relazioni di Roma con l'oriente negli anni 201–200 a.C." *Athenaeum* 9 (1931):260–290.

———. "I moventi di Roma nella seconda guerra macedonica." *Athenaeum* 9 (1931):542–562.

———. "La pace con Filippo e le relazioni con Antioco." *Athenaeum* 10 (1932):105–126.

———. "Il testo del *foedus* di Roma con Callatis." *Athenaeum* 13 (1935):57–72.

———. "Nuove e vecchie tracce dell' interdetto *uti possidetis* negli arbitrati pubblici internazionali del II secolo a.C." *Athenaeum* 15 (1937):26–56.

———. "Le iscrizioni dell' agorà di Smirne concernenti la lite tra i publicani e i Pergameni." *Athenaeum* 15 (1937):252–283.

———. "La condizione della città di Elatea dopo la seconda guerra macedonica in una nuova iscrizione." *Athenaeum* 26 (1948): 83–95.

Paterson, J. *"Transalpinae Gentes,* Cicero, *De Re Publica* 3.16." *CQ* 28 (1978):452–458.

Pearson, L. *The Lost Histories of Alexander the Great.* New York, 1960.

Pédech, P. "Polybiana." *REG* 67 (1954):391–395.

———. *La méthode historique de Polybe.* Paris, 1964.

————. "Polybe hipparque de la confédération achéene (170–169 avant J.-C.). *LEC* 37 (1969):252–259.

Perelli, L. "La chiusura delle miniere macedoni dopo Pidna." *RivFilol* 103 (1975):403–412.

————. *Imperialismo, capitalismo e rivoluzione culturale nella prima metà del II<sup>e</sup> secolo a.C.* Turin, 1975.

Peschlow-Bindokat, A. "Heracleia am Latmos." *ArchAnz* (1977): 90–104.

Pestman, P. W. "Harmachis et Anchmachis, deux rois indigènes du temps des Ptolémées." *ChronEg* 40 (1965):157–170.

Petrochilos, N. *Roman Attitudes to the Greeks.* Athens, 1974.

Petzold, K.-E. *Die Eröffnung des zweiten römisch-makedonischen Krieges.* Berlin, 1940.

————. *Studien zur Methode des Polybios und zu ihrer historischen Auswertung.* Munich, 1969.

————. "Rom und Illyrien." *Historia* 20 (1971):199–223.

————. "Die beiden ersten römisch-kartagischen Verträge und das foedus Cassianum." *ANRW* I.1 (1972):364–411.

Philipp, H. and W. Koenigs, "Zu den Basen des L. Mummius in Olympia." *AthMitt* 94 (1979):193–216.

Piccirilli, L. *Gli arbitrati interstatali greci* I. Pisa, 1973.

Piganiol, A. "Observations sur le testament de Ptolémée le Jeune." *RevHistDr* (1933):409–423.

Pighi, G. B. *De ludis saecularibus.* Amsterdam, 1965.

Pippidi, D. M. "Autour de la date du 'Foedus' Rome-Callatis." *Polis and Imperium. Studies in Honour of E. T. Salmon* (1974):183–200.

Piraino, M. T. "Antigono Dosone re di Macedonia." *AttiAccadPalermo* 13 (1952–53):301–371.

————. "La pace di fenice." *RivFilol* 33 (1955):57–73.

Polaček, A. "La paix d'Apamée." *Listy Filologické* 92 (1969):1–18.

————. "Le traité de paix d'Apamée." *RIDA* 18 (1971):591–621.

Pritchett, W. K. and B. D. Merritt, *The Chronology of Hellenistic Athens.* Cambridge, Mass., 1940.

Quass, F. "Zur Verfassung der griechischen Städte im Hellenismus." *Chiron* 9 (1979):37–52.

Raditsa, L. "Bella Macedonica." *ANRW* I.1 (1972):564–589.

Raeder, A. *L'Arbitrage international chez les Hellenes.* Christiania, 1912.

Rajak, T. "Roman Intervention in a Seleucid Siege of Jerusalem?" *GRBS* 22 (1981):65–81.

Raschke, W. "The Chronology of the Early Books of Lucilius." *JRS* 69 (1979):78–89.

Rawley, H. H. *Darius the Mede and the Four World Empires in the Book of Daniel.* Cardiff, 1935.

Rawlings, H. "Antiochus the Great and Rhodes, 197–191 B.C." *AJAH* 1 (1976):2–28.

Rawson, E. "Architecture and Sculpture: The Activities of the Cossutii." *PBSR* 43 (1975):36–47.

Ray, J. D. *The Archive of Hor.* London, 1976.

Reinach, A. J. "Delphes et les Bastarnes." *BCH* 34 (1910):249–330.

Reinach, T. *L'histoire par des monnaies.* Paris, 1902.

Reynolds, J. "Review of R. K. Sherk, *Roman Documents from the Greek East.*" *JRS* 61 (1971):284–286.

———. "Aphrodisias, a Free and Federate City." *Akten des VI Internationalen Kongressen für griechische und lateinische Epigraphik.* (1973): 115–122.

———. *Aphrodisias and Rome.* London, 1982.

Rich, J. W. *Declaring War in the Roman Republic in the Period of Transmarine Expansion.* Brussels, 1976.

Richardson, J. S. "The Spanish Mines and the Development of Provincial Taxation in the Second Century B.C." *JRS* 66 (1976): 139–152.

———. "Polybius' View of the Roman Empire." *PBSR* 47 (1979): 1–11.

Rigsby, K. J. "The Era of the Province of Asia." *Phoenix* 33 (1979): 39–47.

Rizzo, F. P. *Studi Ellenistico-Romani.* Palmero, 1974.

———. "Posidonio nei frammenti Diodorei sulla prima guerra servile di Sicilia." *Studi di storia antica offerti a E. Manni.* (1976):259–293.

Robert, L. *Villes d'Asie Mineure.* Paris, 1935.

———. "Sur un décret d'Abdère." *BCH* 59 (1935):507–513.

———. "Études d'épigraphie grecque." *RevPhil* 10 (1936):113–170.

———. *Études Anatoliennes.* Paris, 1937.

———. *Études épigraphiques et philologiques.* Paris, 1938.

———. "Pergame d'Épire." *Hellenica* 1 (1940):95–105.

———. "Bulletin épigraphique." *REG* 62 (1949):92–162.

———, and J. Robert, "Bulletin épigraphique." *REG* 63 (1950):121–220.

———. *La Carie.* Paris, 1954.

———. "Inscriptions hellénistiques de Dalmatie." *Hellenica* 11–12 (1960):505–541.

———. "Théophane de Mytilène à Constantinople." *CRAI* 59 (1969): 42–64.

———. "Les concours Romaia à Chalcis." *ArchEph* (1969):44–49.

———. "Catalogue agonistique des Romaia de Xanthos." *RA* (1978): 277–290.

———. "Documents d'Asie Mineure." *BCH* 102 (1978):395–543.

———. "Bulletin épigraphique." *REG* 94 (1981):362–485.

————. "Documents d'Asie Mineure." *BCH* 106 (1982): 309–378.

Robinson, E. S. G. "Cistophori in the Name of King Eumenes." *NC* 14 (1954): 1–8.

Roesch, P. *Thespies et la confédération béotienne*. Paris, 1965.

Romiopoulou, C. "Un nouveau milliaire de la via Egnatia." *BCH* 98 (1974): 813–816.

Rostovtzeff, M. I. *The Social and Economic History of the Hellenistic World*. Oxford, 1941.

————. *A Social and Economic History of the Roman Empire*. 2nd ed. Oxford, 1957.

Roussel, D. *Les Siciliens entre les romains et les carthaginois*. Paris, 1970.

Roussel, P. *Délos, colonie athénienne*. Paris, 1916.

————. "Delphes et l'Amphictionie après la guerre d'Aitolie." *BCH* 56 (1932): 1–36.

Rubinsohn, Z. "The Bellum Asiaticum: A Reconsideration." *RendIstLomb* 107 (1973): 546–570.

Ruebel, J. S. "Cato, Ennius, and Sardinia." *LCM* 2 (1977): 155–157.

Ruggiero, E. de. *L'arbitrato pubblico presso i Romani*. Rome, 1893.

Sachs, A. J. and D. J. Wiseman, "A Babylonian King List of the Hellenistic Period." *Iraq* 16 (1954): 202–211.

Sacks, K. "Polybius' Other View of Aetolia." *JHS* 95 (1975): 92–106.

Salmon, E. T. *The Nemesis of Empire*. London, 1974.

Samuel, A. *Ptolemaic Chronology*. Munich, 1962.

Ste. Croix, G. de. *The Class Struggle in the Ancient Greek World*. London, 1981.

Sanctis, G. De. "Il primo testamento regio a favore dei Romani." *RivFilol* 60 (1932): 59–67.

————. *Storia dei Romani* IV.1. Florence, 1969.

————. *Storia dei Romani* IV.3. Florence, 1964.

Sands, P. C. *The Client Princes of the Roman Empire under the Republic*. Cambridge, 1908.

Santi Amantini, L. "Tolomeo VI Filometore re di Siria." *RendIstLomb* 108 (1974): 511–527.

Σαρικακη, Θ. Ῥωμαῖοι Ἄρχοντες τῆς Ἐπαρχίας Μακεδονίας. Thessaloniki, 1971.

Sauciuc, Th. *Andros*. Vienna, 1914.

————. "Callatis, 4ᵉ rapport préliminaire, Fouilles et recherches de l'année 1927." *Dacia* 3–4 (1927–1932): 456–458.

Schachermeyr, F. *Alexander in Babylon*. Vienna, 1970.

Schadewalt, W. "Humanitas Romana." *ANRW* I.4 (1973): 43–62.

Schalit, A. "The Letter of Antiochus III to Zeuxis regarding the Establishment of Jewish Military Colonies in Phrygia and Lydia." *Jewish Quarterly Review* 50 (1959–60): 289–318.

Schenk Graf v. Stauffenberg, A. *König Hieron der Zweite von Syrakus.* Stuttgart, 1933.

Schlag, U. *Regnum in Senatu.* Stuttgart, 1968.

Schlesinger, E. *Die griechische Asylie.* Diss. Giessen, 1933.

Schleussner, B. "Zur Frage der geheimen pergamenisch-makedonischen Kontakte im 3. makedonischen Krieg." *Historia* 22 (1973): 119–123.

———. "Die Gesandschaft P. Scipio Nasicas im Jahr 133/2 v. Chr. und die Provinzialisierung des Königsreichs Pergamum." *Chiron* 6 (1976): 97–112.

———. *Die Legaten der römischen Republik.* Munich, 1978.

Schmitt, H. H. *Rom und Rhodos.* Munich, 1957.

———. *Hellenen, Römer und Barbaren.* Aschaffenburg, 1958.

———. *Untersuchungen zur Geschichte Antiochos' des Grossen und seiner Zeit.* Wiesbaden, 1964.

Schubart, W. "παρακατατίθεσθαι in der hellenistischen Amtssprache." *PhilWoch* 52 (1932): 1077–1084.

Schuler, B. "The Macedonian Politarchs." *CP* 55 (1960): 90–100.

Schumpeter, J. "The Sociology of Imperialism." In B. Hoselite, ed., *Imperialism and Social Classes* (1955): 3–98.

Schürer, E. *The History of the Jewish People in the Age of Jesus Christ (175 B.C.–A.D. 135).* Rev. ed. by G. Vermes and F. Millar. Edinburgh, 1973.

Schwertfeger, T. *Der Achaiische Bund von 146 bis 27 v. Chr.* Munich, 1974.

Scullard, H. H. "Charops and Roman Policy in Epirus." *JRS* 35 (1945): 58–64.

———. "Scipio Aemilianus and Roman Politics." *JRS* 50 (1960): 59–74.

———. *Scipio Africanus: Soldier and Politician.* Ithaca, 1970.

———. *Roman Politics, 220–150 B.C.* 2nd ed. Oxford, 1973.

Seager, R. "The Freedom of the Greeks of Asia from Alexander to Antiochus." *CQ* 31 (1981): 106–112.

Seel, O. *Römische Denker und römischer Staat.* Leipzig and Berlin, 1937.

Seeley, J. *The Expansion of England.* London, 1883.

Segré, M. "ΚΡΗΤΙΚΟΣ ΠΟΛΕΜΟΣ." *RivFilol* 11 (1933): 365–392.

Seibert, J. *Historische Beiträge zu den dynastischen Verbindungen in hellenistischer Zeit.* Wiesbaden, 1967.

———. *Untersuchungen zur Geschichte Ptolemaios I.* Munich, 1969.

Seyrig, H. "Antiquités syriennes no. 67—monnaies contremarquées en Syrie." *Syria* 35 (1958): 187–197.

———. "Monnaies hellénistiques." *RevNum* 5 (1963): 7–64.

Shatzman, I. "The Roman General's Authority over Booty." *Historia* 21 (1972): 177–205.

Shear, T. L., Jr. *Kallias of Sphettos and the Revolt of Athens in 286 B.C.* *Hesperia* Supplement 17 (1978).

Sherk, R. K. "The Text of the s.c. de agro Pergameno." *GRBS* 4 (1963): 145–153, 217–230.

Sherwin-White, A. N. *The Roman Citizenship.* 2nd ed. Oxford, 1973.

———. "Roman Involvement in Anatolia, 167–88 B.C." *JRS* 67 (1977): 62–75.

Shimron, B. *Late Sparta.* Buffalo, 1972.

———. "Polybius in Rome: A Reexamination of the Evidence." *Scripta Classica Israelica* 5 (1979–80): 94–117.

Shore, A. F. and H. S. Smith, "Two Unpublished Demotic Documents from the Asyūt Archive." *JEA* 45 (1959): 52–60.

Simpson, R. H. "Antigonus the One-Eyed and the Greeks." *Historia* 8 (1959): 385–409.

Skeat, T. C. *The Reigns of the Ptolemies.* Munich, 1954.

———. "Notes on Ptolemaic Chronology, II 'The Twelfth Year which is also the First.' The Invasion of Egypt by Antiochus Epiphanes." *JEA* 47 (1961): 107–112.

Smethurst, S. E. "Cicero and Roman Imperial Policy." *TAPA* 84 (1953): 216–226.

Sokolowski, F. *Lois sacreés de l'Asie Mineure.* Paris, 1955.

Sonne, E. *De Arbitris Externis.* Göttingen, 1888.

Sordi, M. *I rapporti romano-ceriti e l'origine della civitas sine suffragio.* Rome, 1960.

Spyridakis, S. *Ptolemaic Itanos and Hellenistic Crete.* Berkeley and Los Angeles, 1970.

———. "Rhodes and Olus." In S. M. Burstein and L. A. Okin, eds., *Panhellenica: Essays in Ancient History and Historiography in Honor of Truesdell S. Brown* (1980): 119–128.

Staerman, E. M. *Die Blütezeit der Sklavenwirtschaft in der römischen Republik.* Wiesbaden, 1969.

Starr, C. G. "Rhodes and Pergamum, 201–200 B.C." *CP* 33 (1938): 63–68.

Steidle, W. *Sallusts historische Monographien.* Wiesbaden, 1958.

Steinwenter, A. *Die Streitbeendigung durch Urteil, Schiedsspruch und Vergleich nach griechischem Recht.* Munich, 1925.

Stier, H. E. *Roms Aufstieg zur Weltmacht und die griechische Welt.* Köln and Opladen, 1952.

St. Martin, D. "Il foedus romano con Callatis." *Epigraphica* 10 (1948): 103–130.

Strasburger, H. "Poseidonius on Problems of the Roman Empire." *JRS* 55 (1965): 40–53.

Suerbaum, W. "Rex ficta locutus est." *Hermes* 92 (1964):85–106.

Sumner, G. V. "Roman Policy in Spain before the Hannibalic War." *HSCP* 72 (1968):205–246.

Sunseri, G. B. "Sul presunto antiromanesimo di Timagene." *Studi di storia antica offerti a E. Manni* (1976):91–101.

Svoronos, J. *Die Münzen der Ptolemäer.* Athens, 1908.

Swain, J. W. "The Theory of the Four Monarchies: Opposition History under the Roman Empire." *CP* 35 (1940):1–21.

———. "Antiochus Epiphanes and Egypt." *CP* 39 (1944):73–94.

Swoboda, H. "Die neuen Urkunden von Epidauros." *Hermes* 57 (1922):518–534.

Taeger, F. *Charisma.* 2 vols. Stuttgart, 1957.

Tarn, W. W. *Alexander the Great.* 2 vols. Cambridge, 1948.

Täubler, E. *Imperium Romanum.* Leipzig, 1913.

Taylor, L. R. "New Light on the History of the Secular Games." *AJP* 55 (1934):101–120.

Tcherikover, V. *Hellenistic Civilization and the Jews.* New York, 1970.

Texier, J.-G. *Nabis.* Paris, 1975.

———. "Un aspect de l'antagonisme de Rome et de Sparte a l'époque hellénistique: l'entrevue de 195 avant J.C. entre Titus Quinctius Flamininus et Nabis." *REA* 78–79 (1976–77):145–154.

Thompson, M. "The Beginning of the Athenian New Style Coinage." *ANSMN* 5 (1952):25–33.

———. *The New Style Silver Coinage of Athens.* New York, 1961.

Thomsen, R. *Early Roman Coinage.* 3 vols. Copenhagen, 1957–1961.

Tibiletti, G. "Il possesso dell' *ager publicus* e le norme *de modo agrorum* sino ai Gracchi." *Athenaeum* 26 (1948):173–236.

———. "Il possesso dell' *ager publicus* e le norme *de modo agrorum* sino ai Gracchi." *Athenaeum* 27 (1949):3–42.

———. "Rome and the *Ager Pergamenus*: The *Acta* of 129 B.C." *JRS* 47 (1957):136–138.

Timpe, D. "Herrschaftsidee und Klientelstaatenpolitik in Sallusts *Bellum Jugurthinum.*" *Hermes* 90 (1962):334–375.

———. "Fabius Pictor und die Anfänge der römischen Historiographie." *ANRW* I.2 (1972):928–969.

———. "Der römische Vertrag mit den Juden von 161 v. Chr." *Chiron* 4 (1974):133–152.

Tod, M. N. *International Arbitration amongst the Greeks.* Oxford, 1913.

———. "The Macedonian Era." *BSA* 23 (1918–19):206–217.

———. "The Macedonian Era II." *BSA* 24 (1919–21):54–67.

———. "The Macedonian Era Reconsidered." *Studies Presented to D. M. Robinson* (1953) II:382–397.

Touloumakos, J. *Der Einfluss Roms auf die Staatsform der griechischen Stadtstaaten des Festlandes und der Inseln im ersten und zweiten Jhdt. v. Chr.* Göttingen, 1967.

———. *Zum Geschichtsbewusstsein der Griechen in der Zeit der römischen Herrschaft.* Göttingen, 1971.

Toynbee, A. J. *Hannibal's Legacy.* 2 vols. Oxford, 1967.

Tränkle, H. *Livius und Polybios.* Basel and Stuttgart, 1977.

Treves, P. "Studi su Antigono Dosone." *Athenaeum* 22 (1934): 381–411.

Trouard, M. A. *Cicero's Attitude towards the Greeks.* Chicago, 1942.

Turner, E. G. "A Ptolemaic Vineyard Lease." *BRL* 31 (1948): 148–161.

Van Effenterre, H. *La Crète et le monde grec de Platon à Polybe.* Paris, 1948.

Van Gelder, H. *Geschichte der alten Rhodier.* The Hague, 1900.

Van Rinsfeld, B. "Cicéron, De Re Publica, III.9.15–16." *Latomus* 40 (1981): 280–291.

Vavrinek, V. *La révolte d'Aristonicos.* Prague, 1957.

———. "Aristonicus of Pergamum: Pretender to the Throne or Leader of a Slave Revolt?" *Eirene* 13 (1975): 109–129.

Verbrugghe, G. F. "Three Notes on Fabius Pictor and his History." *Miscellanea di studi classici in onore di Eugenio Manni* (1980) VI: 2157–2173.

Veyne, P. "Y a-t-il eu un impérialisme romain?" *MEFRA* 87 (1975): 793–855.

Vitucci, G. *Il regno di Bitinia.* Rome, 1953.

Vogt, J. *Ciceros Glaube an Rom.* Stuttgart, 1935.

———. *Orbis.* Freiburg, Basel, Vienna, 1960.

———. *Ancient Slavery and the Ideal of Man.* Cambridge, Mass., 1975.

Volkmann, H. "Demetrios I und Alexander I von Syrien." *Klio* 19 (1925): 373–412.

———. "Griechische Rhetorik oder römische Politik." *Hermes* 82 (1954): 465–476.

———. *Die Massenversklavungen der Einwohner eroberter Städte in helle-nistisch-römischen Zeit.* Mainz, 1961.

von Fritz, K. "Poseidonius als Historiker." *Historiographia Antiqua: Commentationes Lovanienses in honorem W. Peremans septuagenarii editae* (1977): 163–193.

Wacholder, B. Z. "The Date of the Death of Antiochus IV Epiphanes and I Macc. 6:16–17." In S. M. Burstein and L. A. Okin, eds., *Panhellenica: Essays in Ancient History and Historiography in honor of Truesdell S. Brown* (1980): 129–132.

Walbank, F. W. *Philip V of Macedon.* Cambridge, 1940.

———. "A Note on the Embassy of Q. Marcius Philippus, 172 B.C." *JRS* 31 (1941): 82–93.

———. "Roman Declaration of War in the Third and Second Centuries." *CP* 44 (1949):15–19.

———. *A Historical Commentary on Polybius* I. Oxford, 1957; II. Oxford, 1967; III. Oxford, 1979.

———. "Polemic in Polybius." *JRS* 52 (1962):1–12.

———. "Polybius and Rome's Eastern Policy." *JRS* 53 (1963):1–13.

———. "Polybius and the Roman State." *GRBS* 5 (1964):239–260.

———. *Speeches in Greek Historians.* Oxford, 1965.

———. "Political Morality and the Friends of Scipio." *JRS* 55 (1965): 1–16.

———. "The Historians of Greek Sicily." *Kokalos* 14–15 (1968–69): 476–498.

———. *Polybius.* Berkeley and Los Angeles, 1972.

———. "Polybius between Greece and Rome." *Entretiens Fondation Hardt* 20 (1974):3–38.

———. "Polybius' Last Ten Books." *Historiographia Antiqua: Commentationes Lovanienses in honorem W. Peremans septuagenarii editae* (1977):139–162.

———. "The Original Extent of the Via Egnatia." *LCM* 2 (1977): 73–74.

———. "The Causes of the Third Macedonian War: Recent Views." *Ancient Macedonia* 2 (1977):81–94.

———. "Sea Power and the Antigonids." In W. L. Adams and E. N. Borza, eds., *Philip II, Alexander the Great, and the Macedonian Heritage* (1982):213–236.

Walser, G. "Die Ursachen des ersten römisch-illyrischen Krieges." *Historia* 2 (1954):308–318.

Walsh, P. G. "Massinissa." *JRS* 55 (1965):149–160.

Wardman, A. *Rome's Debt to Greece.* London, 1976.

Warrior, V. M. "Livy, Book 42: Structure and Chronology." *AJAH* 6 (1981):1–50.

Wehrli, C. *Antigone et Demetrios.* Geneva, 1968.

Weinstock, S. *Divus Julius.* Oxford, 1971.

Welwei, K.-W. *Könige und Königtum im Urteil des Polybios.* Köln, 1963.

———. "Amynanders ὄνομα τῆς βασιλείας und sein Besuch in Rom." *Historia* 14 (1965):252–256.

Werner, R. *Der Beginn der römischen Republik.* Munich, 1963.

———. "Das Problem des Imperialismus und die römische Ostpolitik im zweiten Jahrhundert v. Chr." *ANRW* I.1 (1972):501–563.

———. "Quellenkritische Bemerkungen zu den Ursachen des Perseuskrieges." *Grazer Beiträge* 6 (1977):149–216.

Westermann, W. L. *The Slave Systems of Greek and Roman Antiquity.* Philadelphia, 1955.

Wilcken, U. *Urkunden der Ptolemäerzeit*. Berlin and Leipzig, 1927.

―――. "Das Testament des Ptolemaios von Kyrene vom Jahre 155 v. Chr." *SBBerl* (1932):317–336.

Wilhelm, A. "Die lokrische Mädcheninschrift." *JOAI* 14 (1911):163–256.

―――. "Urkunden aus Messene." *JOAI* 17 (1914):1–120.

Wilkes, J. J. *Dalmatia*. London, 1969.

Will, E. *Histoire politique du monde hellénistique*. 2 vols. Nancy, 1967.

―――. "Rome et les Séleucides." *ANRW* I.1 (1972):590–632.

Willrich, H. "Alabanda und Rom zur Zeit des ersten Krieges gegen Mithradates." *Hermes* 34 (1899):305–311.

―――. *Urkundenfälschung in der hellenistisch-jüdischen Literatur*. Göttingen, 1924.

Wilson, A. J. N. *Emigration from Italy in the Republican Age of Rome*. Manchester, 1966.

Windisch, H. "Die Orakel des Hystaspes." *VerhandlingenAkadAmsterdam* 28.3 (1929):1–103.

Winkler, H. *Rom und Aegypten im 2. Jahrhundert v. Chr.* Leipzig, 1933.

Wiseman, T. P. "Senators, Commerce, and Empire." *LCM* 1 (1976):21–22.

Witt, N.J. de. "Massilia and Rome." *TAPA* 71 (1940):605–615.

Zambelli, M. "L'ascesa al trono di Antioco IV Epifane di Siria." *RivFilol* 88 (1960):363–389.

―――. "La composizione del secondo libro dei Maccabei e la nuova cronologia di Antioco IV Epifane." *Miscellanea Greca e Romana* (1965):195–299.

Zeller, E. "Über Antisthenes aus Rhodos." *SBBerlin* (1883):1067–1076.

Ziegler, K.-H. "Das Völkerrecht der römischen Republik." *ANRW* I.2 (1972):68–114.

Ziegler, W. *Symbolai und Asylia*. Diss. Bonn, 1975.

Zippel, G. *Die römische Herrschaft in Illyrien bis auf Augustus*. Leipzig, 1877.

# Index of Persons

# Index of Subjects

Acarnania: hostility with Aetolia, 19, 363–364, 439, 444, 476; relations with Rome, 23–24, 64, 439, 476, 506, 511–512; relations with Anactorium, 72; alliance with Illyria, 363–364, 365; in Second Macedonian War, 444; in Antiochene War, 476; in Third Macedonian War, 506, 511–512; loses Leucas, 517

Achaea: relations with Aetolia, 19, 363–365; relations with Pergamum, 22, 34, 467, 483–484, 502, 509–510, 537, 549n, 555; relations with Rhodes, 22, 41–42, 519–520, 536, 578–579; seeks alliance with Rome, 22–23, 443; in Aetolian War, 27, 467; alliance with Rome, 33–38, 184–185; in Antiochene War, 34; conflict with Messenia, 34–35, 468–469, 493–496; in Third Macedonian War, 36–37, 505–506, 507–511; *amicitia* with Rome, 82, 85; relations with Seleucids, 87n, 93, 483, 645; dispute with Athens, 107; conflict with Sparta after 188 B.C., 116, 121–123, 233, 235, 330, 333–334, 481–483, 485–493, 500, 520–521; conflict with Sparta before 188 B.C., 119–121, 151, 333, 445–447, 452–453, 463–468, 471–475; internal politics before 188 B.C., 331–334, 445, 463n, 466–469, 474; defeated by Illyrians, 365; in First Macedonian War, 440,

444; joins Roman side, 442, 445; relations with Macedonia, 444–445, 500–502; aims in Second Macedonian War, 444–447, 448; territorial gains by, 448, 454–455; mediates between Rome and Boeotia, 449; embassies to Rome, 463, 473–474, 482, 493–496, 497–498, 520; tensions with Flamininus, 464–472, 491; conflict with Elis, 469–470; internal politics after 188 B.C., 482–483, 486, 492, 496–502, 507–511, 515–516, 518; relations with Egypt, 483, 500, 510–511, 655–656, 685, 686, 691; relations with Boeotia, 484–485, 522; relations with Crete, 519–520; relations with Thessaly, 520; in war against Rome, 520–523; restructuring of, 523–527, era of, 527. *See also in Index of Persons* Aristaenus; Callicrates; Diophanes; Lycortas; Philopoemen; Polybius

*Adscripti*, 21, 78, 389–390, 441n, 737n

Aenus, 401, 402

Aetolia: alliance with Rome, 17–21, 77, 144, 289, 322, 377–378, 439–440, 441, 530; in First Macedonian War, 18, 77, 377–381, 440; relations with Achaea, 19, 363–365; hostility with Epirus and Acarnania, 19, 363–364, 439, 444, 476; treaties with Greek states, 19–20, 77; in Second Macedonian War, 22; in war against

Rome, 24–25, 400–401; peace treaty with Rome, 26–32, 279, 291, 293, 401, 479; in Achaean War, 31; in Third Macedonian War, 31, 506, 511; in Amphictyonic League, 31–32; civil strife in, 32, 106, 503–504, 515, 519; earliest contact with Rome, 64; *asylia* agreements of, 71; embassy to Rome before Second Macedonian War, 79, 396–397n; *amicitia* with Rome, 82; seeks Roman favor, 164–165; defeated by Illyrians, 363; relations with Macedonia, 404, 503; aims in Second Macedonian War, 442, 444, 447; territorial gains by, 449; criticizes Rome, 452, 453, 454; ambitions in late 190s B.C., 456–462, 465, 466; collaborates with Antiochus III, 458–462, 625, 631–633, 637; attempts to intimidate Rome, 460–462; relations with Pergamum, 530–535

Aetolian War: peace treaty after, 26–32, 279, 291, 293, 401, 479; military appointments in, 209–211, 213, 217–218, 224–225; political repercussions after, 228–229; background of, 456–462, 631–636; effects upon Greek states, 475–479, 636–637

Alabanda, 48, 90, 733–735

Allegiance: acknowledged by Greeks toward Rome, 180, 185–187, 193–197; acknowledged by Greeks toward Greeks, 180–181, 188–191, 519

Alliance, treaties of: *foedus aequum* and *foedus iniquum*, 14–15, 26–27, 40–41; formulaic clauses of, 15, 16, 26–28, 32–33, 35, 40–41, 43–44; Rome and Italian states, 15, 59; bilateral character of, 16, 34–37, 43–44, 48–50, 731, 738, 740–744; Rome and Maronea, 16, 48, 738–740; Rome and Methymna, 16, 49, 741; Rome and Mytilene, 16, 50, 743–744; Rome and Astypalaea, 16, 742; Rome and Callatis, 16, 49, 740–741; Rome and Cibyra, 16, 48, 731–733; for specific purposes, 17–20; Rome and Aetolia in 212 B.C., 17–21, 77, 144, 289, 322, 377–378, 439–440, 441, 530; Rome

and Elis, 20; Rome and Messene, 20; Rome and Sparta, 20, 440; Rome and Athens, 24, 738n; Rome and Aetolia in 189 B.C., 26–32, 479; permanent, 26, 33–35, 39–40, 41–44, 47–51, 731–744; symbolic character of, 29–30, 32–33, 38, 41–42, 45–46, 50–51; Rome and Achaea, 33–38, 184–185; Rome and Rhodes, 39–42, 572, 578; Rome and the Jews, 42–46, 748–751; Rome and Heraclea Pontica, 48, 735–737; Rome and Pergamene city, 49, 605, 741–742; Rome and Epidaurus, 49, 742; Rome and Thyrreum, 49, 742–743; Rome and Aphrodisias, 50, 743; Rome and Cnidus, 50, 743; ratification of, 50–51; Philip V and Hannibal, 60, 375–376, 385; Illyria, Epirus, and Acarnania, 363–364; Philip V and Antiochus III, 387–388, 614–615; Macedonia and Boeotia, 404–405; Pergamum and Aetolia, 530

Ambracia, 310–311

*Amicitia*: Rome and Pergamum, 20, 22, 77–78, 530; Rome and Epirus, 23; Rome and Acarnania, 23–24; Rome and the Seleucid kingdom, 32–33, 64–65, 83–84, 540, 617, 642–643, 648, 650; Rome and Egypt, 47, 62–63, 83–84, 673, 675, 676, 677, 686, 701n; Rome and Alabanda, 48, 733–735; variety of forms of, 55–56, 68, 69–70, 73–76, 88–90; in First Illyrian War, 55–57, 76; Rome and Demetrius of Pharus, 56; elastic in usage, 56, 60–61, 63, 66, 69–70, 73–74, 83; not tantamount to clientship, 57, 76–79, 81–82, 84–85, 86, 90–91; Rome and Italian peoples, 58–59; rarely used in early Roman diplomacy, 58–61; Rome and Alexander of Epirus, 61; as Greek diplomatic concept, 61–63, 68–76, 85–86, 93–94; Rome and Massilia, 65–66; Rome and Messana, 66–67, 77–78; Rome and Hiero, 67–68, 292n; Rome and Rhodes, 68–69n; Egypt and Seleucid kingdom, 73, 623, 683–684; in First Macedonian War, 77–78; Rome and Elis, 77–78; Rome and Sparta, 77–78, 82; in Sec-

# Index of Literary Sources

# Index of Inscriptions and Papyri

## Inscriptions

*no. 563:* 72n91; 102n27
*no. 566:* 149n102
*no. 569:* 533n15
*no. 570:* 41n153; 579n32
*no. 572:* 141n57
*no. 581:* 15n10; 35n118; 532n12
*no. 584:* 181n142; 450n68
*no. 585:* 167n63; 169n73; 541n51;
   631n91
*no. 586:* 537n35
*no. 587:* 179n133
*no. 588:* 21n40; 33n106; 93n228;
   183n157; 540n49; 542n55
*no. 591:* 21n40; 23n56; 65n58; 66n62;
   83n156; 83n158; 147n88; 183n159;
   198n259; 543n56; 621n42
*no. 592:* 167n62
*no. 593:* 172n89; 455n103
*no. 594:* 181n144; 450n68
*no. 595:* 181n145; 544n62
*no. 599:* 98n9; 108n55; 109n59
*no. 601:* 148n100; 173n94; 182n151;
   499n77; 526n222; 629n79; 734n17
*no. 605:* 544n66; 545n71
*no. 606:* 181n141; 467n174
*no. 607:* 168n70
*no. 608:* 168n70
*no. 609:* 152n123; 479n255
*no. 611:* 173n96; 178n125; 179n132,
   479n255
*no. 612:* 152n124; 197n249; 526n222
*no. 613:* 153n133; 185n170
*no. 614:* 109n61
*no. 616:* 167n63
*no. 617:* 168n68
*no. 618:* 151n122; 173n95
*no. 621:* 191n212
*no. 626:* 518n181
*no. 627:* 33n106; 189n200; 554n109
*no. 628:* 189n194
*no. 629:* 189n194; 552n103
*no. 630:* 185n173; 188n192; 552n103;
   553n104
*no. 632:* 190n208
*no. 633:* 15n10; 27n73; 88n190;
   93n229; 110n71; 180n139; 564n157
*no. 634:* 94n236; 122n136; 499n81
*no. 636:* 32n100; 404n34; 503n103;
   517n175
*no. 639:* 189n202; 190n210
*no. 641:* 189n194
*no. 643:* 23n56; 92n224; 129n169;

188n188; 403n30; 406n53; 409n64;
   420n121
*no. 644:* 190n204; 564n156
*no. 645:* 190n204; 564n156
*no. 646:* 89n201; 186n181; 188n191;
   513n161
*no. 649:* 169n74
*no. 650:* 170n78; 269n113
*no. 651:* 189n194
*no. 652A:* 170n80; 267n99; 285n58
*no. 653:* 517n175; 518n177; 519n185
*no. 654:* 518n177; 519n185
*no. 656:* 107n52; 166n56; 198n259
*no. 664:* 106n49; 197n249
*no. 665:* 98n7; 108n54; 196n246
*no. 666:* 583n51
*no. 668:* 109n63; 519n188
*no. 670–672:* 198n253; 519n190
*no. 674:* 47n178; 55n9; 83n155;
   104n38; 107n51; 739n49
*no. 675:* 90n206; 108n54; 109n66;
   196n245; 519n188
*no. 676:* 171n83
*no. 679:* 47n178; 55n9; 86n176;
   108n54
*no. 680:* 171n82
*no. 683:* 108n54
*no. 684:* 155n144; 434n202; 524n211;
   524n216; 525n219
*no. 685:* 94n238; 108n54; 116n106;
   198n258
*no. 686:* 171n86
*no. 688:* 47n178
*no. 692:* 180n136
*no. 693:* 16n14; 44n164; 49n184;
   739n50; 741n57; 741n58
*no. 694:* 49n184; 90n207; 602n120;
   605n133; 741n61; 742n62; 742n63;
   742n64
*no. 702:* 197n247
*no. 704:* 434n202
*no. 705:* 47n178; 434n202
*no. 712:* 110n71
*no. 724:* 187n187; 578n30
*no. 729:* 312n125
*no. 732:* 49n185; 743n68
*no. 742:* 155n145
*no. 747:* 89n202; 90n206; 525n221
*no. 764:* 16n14; 744n73
*no. 826E:* 104n38
*no. 826K:* 185n170
*no. 827:* 104n38

| | |
|---|---|
| Designer: | Sandy Drooker |
| Compositor: | G&S Typesetters, Inc. |
| Printer: | Thomson-Shore, Inc. |
| Binder: | John H. Dekker & Sons |
| Text: | 10/12 Palatino |
| Display: | Palatino & Palatino Italic |